Education at a Glance 2008

OECD INDICATORS

OECD

ORGANISATION FOR ECONOMIC CO-OPERATION AND DEVELOPMENT

The OECD is a unique forum where the governments of 30 democracies work together to address the economic, social and environmental challenges of globalisation. The OECD is also at the forefront of efforts to understand and to help governments respond to new developments and concerns, such as corporate governance, the information economy and the challenges of an ageing population. The Organisation provides a setting where governments can compare policy experiences, seek answers to common problems, identify good practice and work to co-ordinate domestic and international policies.

The OECD member countries are: Australia, Austria, Belgium, Canada, the Czech Republic, Denmark, Finland, France, Germany, Greece, Hungary, Iceland, Ireland, Italy, Japan, Korea, Luxembourg, Mexico, the Netherlands, New Zealand, Norway, Poland, Portugal, the Slovak Republic, Spain, Sweden, Switzerland, Turkey, the United Kingdom and the United States. The Commission of the European Communities takes part in the work of the OECD.

OECD Publishing disseminates widely the results of the Organisation's statistics gathering and research on economic, social and environmental issues, as well as the conventions, guidelines and standards agreed by its members.

This work is published on the responsibility of the Secretary-General of the OECD. The opinions expressed and arguments employed herein do not necessarily reflect the official views of the Organisation or of the governments of its member countries.

Also available in French under the title:
Regards sur l'éducation 2008
LES INDICATEURS DE L'OCDE

FOREWORD

Governments are paying increasing attention to international comparisons as they search for effective policies that enhance individuals' social and economic prospects, provide incentives for greater efficiency in schooling, and help to mobilise resources to meet rising demands. As part of its response, the OECD Directorate for Education devotes a major effort to the development and analysis of the quantitative, internationally comparable indicators that it publishes annually in *Education at a Glance*. These indicators enable educational policy makers and practitioners alike to see their education systems in the light of other countries' performances and, together with OECD's country policy reviews, are designed to support and review the efforts that governments are making towards policy reform.

Education at a Glance addresses the needs of a range of users, from governments seeking to learn policy lessons to academics requiring data for further analysis to the general public wanting to monitor how its nation's schools are progressing in producing world-class students. The publication examines the quality of learning outcomes, the policy levers and contextual factors that shape these outcomes, and the broader private and social returns that accrue to investments in education.

Education at a Glance is the product of a long-standing, collaborative effort between OECD governments, the experts and institutions working within the framework of the OECD's indicators of education systems (INES) programme and the OECD Secretariat. The publication was drafted by the Indicators and Analysis Division of the OECD Directorate for Education, under the responsibility of Andreas Schleicher, in co-operation with Etienne Albiser, Eric Charbonnier, Michael Davidson, Bo Hansson, Corinne Heckmann, Ben Jensen, Karinne Logez, Diana Toledo Figueroa, Sophie Vayssettes and Jean Yip. Administrative support was provided by Cécile Bily and Sandrine Meireles, and editorial support was provided by Elisabeth Villoutreix. The development of the publication was steered by INES National Co-ordinators in member countries and facilitated by the financial and material support of the three countries responsible for co-ordinating the INES Networks – the Netherlands, Sweden and the United States. The members of the various bodies as well as the individual experts who have contributed to this publication and to OECD INES more generally are listed at the end of the book.

While much progress has been accomplished in recent years, member countries and the OECD continue to strengthen the link between policy needs and the best available internationally comparable data. In doing so, various challenges and trade-offs must be faced. First, the indicators need to respond to educational issues that are high on national policy agendas, and where the international comparative perspective can offer important added value to what can be accomplished through national analysis and evaluation. Second, while the indicators need to be as comparable as possible, they also need to be as country-specific as is necessary to allow for historical, systemic and cultural differences between countries. Third, the indicators need to be presented in as straightforward a manner as possible, while remaining sufficiently complex to reflect multi-faceted educational realities. Fourth, there is a general desire to keep the indicator set as small as possible, but it needs to be large enough to be useful to policy makers across countries that face different educational challenges.

The report is published on the responsibility of the Secretary-General of the OECD.

TABLE OF CONTENTS

Name of
the indicator
in the
2007 edition

EDITORIAL

By Barbara Ischinger, Director for Education

Tough choices or tough times - towards sustainable strategies for investing in expanding education systems

OECD governments have high ambitions for their education systems, wanting them to grow both in volume and quality. Yet public budgets face tight constraints, and education remains predominantly a public enterprise. So has education funding been able to meet the extra demands being placed on it, and will it be able to do so in the future?

In volume terms, the decades-old expansion in educational participation and outputs continues – and at a pace that outstrips many past projections. With completion of upper secondary education close to universal in most OECD countries, the greatest recent expansion has come in the tertiary sector. While in 1995, 37% of a cohort went into university-level programmes, it is now 57% on average across OECD countries (Indicator A2). It is always hard to predict the future from past trends. Will the expansion of tertiary education continue at this rapid pace, driven by an ever-rising demand for the highly skilled? Or will it level off and will relative earnings decline? At the beginning of the 20th century, few would have predicted that, among OECD countries, upper secondary education would be largely universal by the end of the century. So it is equally difficult to predict how tertiary qualifications will have evolved by the end of the 21st century.

What is clear is that, for now, the incentives for attaining a tertiary qualification remain strong, both in terms of higher salaries and better employment prospects (Indicators A9 and A10). In addition, the labour market demand for highly qualified workers has grown significantly (Indicator A1).

Meeting the demand while at least maintaining quality is bound to create pressures for current levels of spending to be maintained or increased and to improve the efficiency of spending on education. Recent years have already seen considerable rises in spending levels, both in absolute terms and as a share of public budgets. The total amount of funds allocated to educational institutions across all levels of education rose in all countries over the last decade, and by 19% on average between 2000 and 2005 alone (Indicator B3). By 2005, OECD countries were spending 6.1% of their collective GDP on education at all levels, of which 86% came from public sources and all but 7 of the 28 OECD countries spent at least 5% (Indicator B2). Another visible indication of the efforts made by governments can be found in the fact that from 1995 to 2005, public expenditure on education grew by more than one percentage point as a proportion of all public spending – from 11.9% to 13.2% in 2005. Education spending rose at least as fast as public spending in other sectors in all countries except Canada, France, Hungary, Portugal and Switzerland (Indicator B4).

Alongside the increase in public spending on education, there has also been a search for new sources of funding to accommodate the rapid growth in student numbers (particularly at the tertiary level) and to increase the resources available to educational institutions. Although 86% of spending on education still originates from public sources for all levels of education combined, private spending increased more rapidly than public spending between 1995 and 2005 in nearly three-quarters of the countries examined. In some, the proportion of private funding of tertiary educational institutions is high enough to challenge the view that tertiary education is primarily a state responsibility. In fact, this view is gradually being replaced by the perception that, given the shared public and private returns that education brings, costs and responsibilities for its provision should also be shared between those who directly benefit and society at large (*i.e.* private households and businesses as well as governments), at least at the tertiary level of education (Indicator B3).

While efforts to increase investments in education are clearly visible in this year's indicators, the question remains whether resources kept up with the demographic and structural changes that have occurred during the past decade? Indicators B1 and B2 show that educational expenditure in primary and secondary education rose faster than student numbers in all countries between 1995 and 2005, and even faster than GDP per capita in more that two-thirds of them. Although spending per student at the primary and secondary level rose less rapidly on average between 2000 and 2005 than between 1995 and 2000, it rose by 30% or more in eight OECD and partner countries during the later period (Indicators B1 and B2). As a result, available resources per primary and secondary student have considerably increased over the past decade. Furthermore, in 23 out of 30 OECD countries, the size of the student population aged 5 to 14 years is set to decline over the next ten years (Indicator A11 in *Education at a Glance 2006*), which suggests that resources per primary and secondary student could continue to grow if overall budget envelopes remain stable, releasing resources needed for measures to improve programme quality and student performance.

However, the pattern is different at the tertiary level. Between 1995 and 2005, spending per tertiary student shrank in some cases, as expenditure failed to keep up with expanding student numbers. If tertiary student numbers keep rising and with student mobility into the OECD area adding extra pressures in countries where foreign students do not pay for the full cost of their education, it appears that without additional investments, the tendency towards declining unit expenditure could even accelerate. The continuation of current trends could potentially also widen disparities in funding levels among countries. In 2005, expenditure per tertiary student varied by a factor of 7, from USD 3 421 in the Russian Federation to over USD 20 000 in Switzerland and the United States (Indicator B1).

The challenges to meet additional financial needs are therefore clear, at least for tertiary education. However, it is equally clear that more money alone will not be enough. Investments in education will need to become much more efficient, too. The OECD Economics Department examined this question and estimates that, on average across OECD countries, there is the potential for increasing learning outcomes by 22% while maintaining current levels of resources (Indicator B7 in *Education at a Glance 2007*). This indicates the scale of effort that is needed for education to re-invent itself in ways that other professions have already done and to provide better value for money. Results from PISA have also revealed that the cross-national relationship between the resources invested in education and learning outcomes is moderate at best, suggesting that money is a necessary but not a sufficient prerequisite for high quality learning outcomes.

This year's edition of *Education at a Glance* takes this discussion further by looking into the policy choices that countries make in investing their resources, including trade-offs between the hours that students spend in the classroom, the number of years they spend at school, the number of hours teachers work, class sizes (proxy measure) and teacher salaries. The results show that similar levels of expenditure by countries can mask a variety of contrasting policy choices in upper secondary education. This goes some way towards explaining why there is no simple relationship between how much is spent overall on education and the level of student performance. For example, in Korea and Luxembourg, salary costs per student (as a percentage of GDP per capita, in order to level out significant differences in these countries' national income) are well above the OECD average (15.5% and 15.2%, respectively, compared to 10.9% on average). However, while Korea invests the resources in paying teachers relatively high salaries at the price of relatively large class sizes, in Luxembourg higher than average salary costs per student are almost entirely attributable to very small class sizes (Indicator B7). Countries will need to consider such choices carefully and they will need to improve the knowledge base as to how such choices relate to value for money if the efficiency of educational services is to increase.

The analysis also reveals several other trends. In countries with the lowest per-student salary cost at the upper secondary level (as a percentage of GDP per capita), the main reason is usually comparatively low salary levels as a proportion of GDP per capita. This is true in Iceland, Ireland, Norway, Poland, the Slovak Republic and Sweden. The main exception is Mexico, whose teacher salary costs relative to GDP per capita are well above the OECD average, which have been compensated by large class sizes (Indicator B7).

Again, countries experiencing rises in spending per student need to look carefully at how these are deployed.

At the tertiary level, the financing patterns that have emerged differ from those in primary and secondary education. First of all, the use of private funds is much more common than at the primary and secondary levels. Private funding represents on average 27% of total spending, exceeds the 50% mark in Australia, Japan, the United States and the partner country Israel, and reaches over 75% in Korea and the partner country Chile (Indicator B3). The balance between private and public funding on the one hand, and the ability of countries to provide various forms of public subsidies for tertiary institutions on the other hand, have been two factors that help to explain wide differences in the approaches to the financing of tertiary education. Some countries have found new private sources, some have expanded public funding, while those doing neither increasingly find expansion and quality hard to reconcile.

So far, the Nordic countries have achieved expansion by providing massive public spending on tertiary education, including both support of institutions and support of students and households, as an investment that pays high dividends to individuals and society. Other countries such as Australia, Canada, Japan, Korea, New Zealand, the United Kingdom and the United States have expanded participation in tertiary education by shifting some of the financial burden to students and their families. In many of these countries, tuition fees are set by the institutions (often with a ceiling) and can vary according to students' labour market prospects and expected salary levels upon graduation (Indicator B5). These measures often go hand in hand with financial support to students from less advantaged backgrounds, in the form of loans and/or scholarships, as well as with loans on advantageous terms available to all students. Australia and New Zealand, for example, supplement income contingent loan schemes for tuition fees, which are available to all students, with means tested income support for living expenses and scholarships to assist with general education and accommodation costs that target lower socio-economic background students.

In contrast, many European countries have not increased public investments in their universities to the extent needed to maintain past expenditure per student levels, yet do not allow universities to charge tuition fees. As a result, their institutions' budgetary difficulties are increasing, which may ultimately endanger the quality of the programmes offered. A striking comparison is that average spending per tertiary student in most European countries is now well below half the level in the United States. While choices between greater public investments and a larger share of private money are difficult to make, doing neither in the face of the rising demand for more and better tertiary education seems no longer an option.

In moving their education systems forward, countries need to employ a multipronged approach to ensuring that education is adequately funded. As well as looking at the case for prioritising education in the allocation of public spending, they may need to look at how more private funding can be brought in at the tertiary level, at areas to prioritise for quality improvement within the education system and at ways of deploying resources more efficiently. A challenge here is to achieve this in ways that do not compromise equity. The indicators show that in many countries, students are much more likely to be in tertiary education if their fathers completed tertiary education. This suggests a need for measures encouraging intergenerational progression in terms of educational qualifications. Strengthening public subsidies and achieving a good balance between financial aid in the form of student loans and scholarships can be a way to improve equity in the access to tertiary education. Some analysis suggests that scholarships may be more efficient than loans in encouraging students from disadvantaged socio-economic backgrounds to continue to study, whereas loans may work better for the other socio-economic categories (Indicators A7 and B5).

Beyond the question of resource allocations, improving guidance mechanisms for students to make informed choices between secondary- and tertiary-level programmes could also impact on graduation rates and ease pressures on spending because, on average, some 31% of students do not complete the tertiary studies for which they enrol across the 19 OECD countries for which data are available (Indicator A4).

Indicator A1 also suggests that adapting programmes that yield poor labour market outcomes to the growing needs of human resources in specific sectors is an issue. In OECD countries, the proportion of skilled jobs in the economy is generally larger than the potential supply of individuals holding high-level education and training qualifications matched with those jobs.

Managing the growth and development of educational systems in ways that improve access, enhance quality and boost value for money poses difficult challenges, and countries will need to find ways to address these. The knowledge society is here to stay, requiring capable, highly qualified and innovative citizenry, and rising educational participation suggests that young persons and their families have got that message. While nobody can predict how far the expansion in tertiary education will continue, countries need sustainable financing systems capable of responding to growing student numbers. Not doing so could mean that the knowledge society could be a polarised world, peopled by those who can afford education and those who cannot.

This requires tough choices. An important aim of this year's edition of *Education at a Glance* is to lay out how some of these policy choices are made in different countries. Much more will need to be done to understand how the choices and mixes of policies combine most effectively to promote student learning in the different contexts in which countries operate. International comparisons can be a powerful instrument to facilitate this. They allow education systems to look at themselves through the lenses of policies planned, implemented, and achieved elsewhere in the world. They also show what is possible in education in terms of the quality, equity, and efficiency of educational services, and they can foster better understanding of how different education systems address similar problems. The OECD will pursue the further development of policy-relevant international comparisons vigorously, not just in areas where it is currently feasible, but also in those where a considerable investment still needs to be made in conceptual work. The launch of the OECD Teaching and Learning International Survey (TALIS), which represents a major breakthrough in both conceptual and methodological terms, the further development of the OECD Programme for International Student Assessment (PISA) and its extension through the OECD Programme for the International Assessment of Adult Competencies (PIAAC), as well as initial work on exploring the assessment of higher education learning outcomes (AHELO), will be important steps towards this end.

Barbara Ischinger

INTRODUCTION: THE INDICATORS AND THEIR FRAMEWORK

■ The organising framework

Education at a Glance – OECD Indicators 2008 provides a rich, comparable and up-to-date array of indicators that reflect a consensus among professionals on how to measure the current state of education internationally. The indicators provide information on the human and financial resources invested in education, on how education and learning systems operate and evolve, and on the returns to educational investments. The indicators are organised thematically, and each is accompanied by information on the policy context and the interpretation of the data. The education indicators are presented within an organising framework that:

■ Distinguishes between the actors in education systems: individual learners, instructional settings and learning environments, educational service providers, and the education system as a whole;

■ Groups the indicators according to whether they speak to learning outcomes for individuals or countries, policy levers or circumstances that shape these outcomes, or to antecedents or constraints that set policy choices into context; and

■ Identifies the policy issues to which the indicators relate, with three major categories distinguishing between the quality of educational outcomes and educational provision, issues of equity in educational outcomes and educational opportunities, and the adequacy and effectiveness of resource management.

The following matrix describes the first two dimensions:

		1. Education and learning outputs and outcomes	2. Policy levers and contexts shaping educational outcomes	3. Antecedents or constraints that contextualise policy
I.	Individual participants in education and learning	1.I The quality and distribution of individual educational outcomes	2.I Individual attitudes, engagement, and behaviour	3.I Background characteristics of the individual learners
II.	Instructional settings	1.II The quality of instructional delivery	2.II Pedagogy and learning practices and classroom climate	3.II Student learning conditions and teacher working conditions
III.	Providers of educational services	1.III The output of educational institutions and institutional performance	2.III School environment and organisation	3.III Characteristics of the service providers and their communities
IV.	The education system as a whole	1.IV The overall performance of the education system	2.IV System-wide institutional settings, resource allocations, and policies	3.IV The national educational, social, economic, and demographic contexts

The following sections discuss the matrix dimensions in more detail:

■ Actors in education systems

The OECD indicators of education systems (INES) programme seeks to gauge the performance of national education systems as a whole, rather than to compare individual institutional or other sub-national entities. However, there is increasing recognition that many important features of the development, functioning and impact of education systems can only be assessed through an understanding of learning outcomes and their relationships to inputs and processes at the level of individuals and institutions. To account for this, the indicator framework distinguishes between a macro level, two meso-levels and a micro-level of education systems. These relate to:

- The education system as a whole;
- The educational institutions and providers of educational services;
- The instructional setting and the learning environment within the institutions; and
- The individual participants in education and learning.

To some extent, these levels correspond to the entities from which data are being collected but their importance mainly centres on the fact that many features of the education system play out quite differently at various levels of the system, which needs to be taken into account when interpreting the indicators. For example, at the level of students within a classroom, the relationship between student achievement and class size may be negative if students in small classes benefit from improved contact with teachers. At the class or school level, however, students are often intentionally grouped such that weaker or disadvantaged students are placed in smaller classes so that they receive more individual attention. At the school level, therefore, the observed relationship between class size and student achievement is often positive (suggesting that students in larger classes perform better than students in smaller classes). At higher aggregated levels of education systems, the relationship between student achievement and class size is further confounded, *e.g.* by the socio-economic intake of schools, or by factors relating to the learning culture in different countries. Past analyses, which have relied on macro-level data alone, have therefore sometimes led to misleading conclusions.

■ Outcomes, policy levers and antecedents

The second dimension in the organising framework further groups the indicators at each of the above levels:

- Indicators on observed outputs of education systems, as well as indicators related to the impact of knowledge and skills for individuals, societies and economies, are grouped under the sub-heading *output and outcomes of education and learning;*
- The sub-heading *policy levers and contexts* groups activities seeking information on the policy levers or circumstances which shape the outputs and outcomes at each level; and
- These policy levers and contexts typically have *antecedents* – factors that define or constrain policy. These are represented by the sub-heading *antecedents and constraints*. It should be noted that the antecedents or constraints are usually specific for a given level of the education system and that antecedents at a lower level of the system may well be policy levers at a higher level. For teachers and students in a school, for example, teacher qualifications are a given constraint while, at the level of the education system, professional development of teachers is a key policy lever.

■ Policy issues

Each of the resulting cells in the framework can then be used to address a variety of issues from different policy perspectives. For the purpose of this framework, policy perspectives are grouped into three classes that constitute the third dimension in the organising framework for INES:

- Quality of educational outcomes and educational provision;
- Equality of educational outcomes and equity in educational opportunities; and
- Adequacy, effectiveness and efficiency of resource management.

In addition to the dimensions mentioned above, the time perspective as a fourth dimension in the framework allows dynamic aspects in the development of education systems to be modelled also.

The indicators that are published in *Education at a Glance 2008* fit within this framework, though often they speak to more than one cell.

Most of the indicators in **Chapter A** *The output of educational institutions and the impact of learning* relate to the first column of the matrix describing outputs and outcomes of education. Even so, indicators in **Chapter A** measuring educational attainment for different generations, for instance, not only give a measure of the output of the educational system, but also provide context for current educational policies, helping to shape polices on, for example, lifelong learning.

Chapter B *Financial and human resources invested in education* provides indicators that are either policy levers or antecedents to policy, or sometimes both. For example, expenditure per student is a key policy measure which most directly impacts on the individual learner as it acts as a constraint on the learning environment in schools and student learning conditions in the classroom.

Chapter C *Access to education, participation and progression* provides indicators that are a mixture of outcome indicators, policy levers and context indicators. Entry rates and progression rates are, for instance, outcomes measures to the extent that they indicate the results of policies and practices in the classroom, school and system levels. But they can also provide contexts for establishing policy by identifying areas where policy intervention is necessary to, for instance, address issues of inequity.

Chapter D *The learning environment and organisation of schools* provides indicators on instruction time, teachers' working time and teachers' salaries not only represent policy levers which can be manipulated but also provide contexts for the quality of instruction in instructional settings and for the outcomes of learners at the individual level.

READER'S GUIDE

Coverage of the statistics

Although a lack of data still limits the scope of the indicators in many countries, the coverage extends, in principle, to the entire national education system (within the national territory) regardless of the ownership or sponsorship of the institutions concerned and regardless of education delivery mechanisms. With one exception described below, all types of students and all age groups are meant to be included: children (including students with special needs), adults, nationals, foreigners, as well as students in open distance learning, in special education programmes or in educational programmes organised by ministries other than the Ministry of Education, provided the main aim of the programme is the educational development of the individual. However, vocational and technical training in the workplace, with the exception of combined school and work-based programmes that are explicitly deemed to be parts of the education system, is not included in the basic education expenditure and enrolment data.

Educational activities classified as "adult" or "non-regular" are covered, provided that the activities involve studies or have a subject matter content similar to "regular" education studies or that the underlying programmes lead to potential qualifications similar to corresponding regular educational programmes. Courses for adults that are primarily for general interest, personal enrichment, leisure or recreation are excluded.

Calculation of international means

For many indicators an OECD average is presented and for some an OECD total.

The OECD average is calculated as the unweighted mean of the data values of all OECD countries for which data are available or can be estimated. The OECD average therefore refers to an average of data values at the level of the national systems and can be used to answer the question of how an indicator value for a given country compares with the value for a typical or average country. It does not take into account the absolute size of the education system in each country.

The OECD total is calculated as a weighted mean of the data values of all OECD countries for which data are available or can be estimated. It reflects the value for a given indicator when the OECD area is considered as a whole. This approach is taken for the purpose of comparing, for example, expenditure charts for individual countries with those of the entire OECD area for which valid data are available, with this area considered as a single entity.

Note that both the OECD average and the OECD total can be significantly affected by missing data. Given the relatively small number of countries, no statistical methods are used to compensate for this. In cases where a category is not applicable (code "a") in a country or where the data value is negligible (code "n") for the corresponding calculation, the value zero is imputed for the purpose of calculating OECD averages. In cases where both the numerator and the denominator of a ratio are not applicable (code "a") for a certain country, this country is not included in the OECD average.

For financial tables using 1995 and 2000 data, both the OECD average and OECD total are calculated for countries providing 1995, 2000 and 2005 data. This allows comparison of the OECD average and OECD total over time with no distortion due to the exclusion of certain countries in the different years.

For many indicators an EU19 average is also presented. It is calculated as the unweighted mean of the data values of the 19 OECD countries that are members of the European Union for which data are available or can be estimated. These 19 countries are Austria, Belgium, the Czech Republic, Denmark, Finland, France, Germany, Greece, Hungary, Italy, Ireland, Luxembourg, the Netherlands, Poland, Portugal, the Slovak Republic, Spain, Sweden and the United Kingdom.

Classification of levels of education

The classification of the levels of education is based on the revised International Standard Classification of Education (ISCED-97). The biggest change between the revised ISCED and the former ISCED (ISCED-76) is the introduction of a multi-dimensional classification framework, allowing for the alignment of the educational content of programmes using multiple classification criteria. ISCED is an instrument for compiling statistics on education internationally and distinguishes among six levels of education. The glossary available at *www.oecd.org/edu/eag2008* describes in detail the ISCED levels of education, and Annex 1 shows corresponding typical graduation ages of the main educational programmes by ISCED level.

Symbols for missing data

Six symbols are employed in the tables and charts to denote missing data:

a Data is not applicable because the category does not apply.

c There are too few observations to provide reliable estimates (*i.e.* there are fewer than 3% of students for this cell or too few schools for valid inferences). However, these statistics were included in the calculation of cross-country averages.

m Data is not available.

n Magnitude is either negligible or zero.

w Data has been withdrawn at the request of the country concerned.

x Data included in another category or column of the table (*e.g.* x(2) means that data are included in column 2 of the table).

~ Average is not comparable with other levels of education

Further resources

The website *www.oecd.org/edu/eag2008* provides a rich source of information on the methods employed for the calculation of the indicators, the interpretation of the indicators in the respective national contexts and the data sources involved. The website also provides access to the data underlying the indicators as well as to a comprehensive glossary for technical terms used in this publication.

Any post-production changes to this publication are listed at *www.oecd.org/edu/eag2008*.

The website *www.pisa.oecd.org* provides information on the OECD Programme for International Student Assessment (PISA), on which many of the indicators in this publication draw.

Education at a Glance uses the OECD's StatLinks service. Below each table and chart in *Education at Glance 2008* is a url which leads to a corresponding Excel workbook containing the underlying data for the indicator. These urls are stable and will remain unchanged over time. In addition, readers of the *Education at a Glance* e-book will be able to click directly on these links and the workbook will open in a separate window.

Codes used for territorial entities

These codes are used in certain charts. Country or territorial entity names are used in the text. Note that in the text the Flemish Community of Belgium is referred to as "Belgium (Fl.)" and the French Community of Belgium as "Belgium (Fr.)".

AUS	Australia	ITA	Italy
AUT	Austria	JPN	Japan
BEL	Belgium	KOR	Korea
BFL	Belgium (Flemish Community)	LUX	Luxembourg
BFR	Belgium (French Community)	MEX	Mexico
BRA	Brazil	NLD	Netherlands
CAN	Canada	NZL	New Zealand
CHL	Chile	NOR	Norway
CZE	Czech Republic	POL	Poland
DNK	Denmark	PRT	Portugal
ENG	England	RUS	Russian Federation
EST	Estonia	SCO	Scotland
FIN	Finland	SVK	Slovak Republic
FRA	France	SVN	Slovenia
DEU	Germany	ESP	Spain
GRC	Greece	SWE	Sweden
HUN	Hungary	CHE	Switzerland
ISL	Iceland	TUR	Turkey
IRL	Ireland	UKM	United Kingdom
ISR	Israel	USA	United States

Chapter

THE OUTPUT OF EDUCATIONAL INSTITUTIONS AND THE IMPACT OF LEARNING

TO WHAT LEVEL HAVE ADULTS STUDIED?

This indicator profiles the educational attainment of the adult population, as captured through formal educational qualifications. As such, it provides a proxy for the knowledge and skills available to national economies and societies. To have a better understanding of the demand for education, the distribution of occupations across OECD countries and the matching of tertiary-educated individuals to skilled jobs are also examined in this indicator. Data on attainment by fields of education and by age groups are used to examine the distribution of skills in the population and to furnish a rough measure of skills that have recently entered the labour market and of those that will be leaving the labour market in the coming years.

Key results

Chart A1.1. Proportion of population in skilled jobs and proportion of population with tertiary education (2006)

The chart depicts the proportion of the 25-to-64-year-old working population in skilled jobs and the proportion of the 25-to-64-year-old population with tertiary education (2006).

■ Tertiary attainment (5B, 5A/6)   □ Skilled jobs (ISCO 1-3)

Large proportions of the workforce have moved into skilled jobs in OECD countries. Along with experience gained in working life, education provides a principal source of skills for the labour market. In OECD countries, the proportion of skilled jobs in the economy is generally larger than the potential supply of tertiary educated individuals. For countries in which work-based learning is central to occupational advancement, this difference is large. A broader initial skill base might require additional investment in higher education. In a few countries, tertiary attainment matches or marginally exceeds the proportion of skilled jobs, so that further expansion of higher education will to some extent depend on the growth of skilled jobs in the coming years.

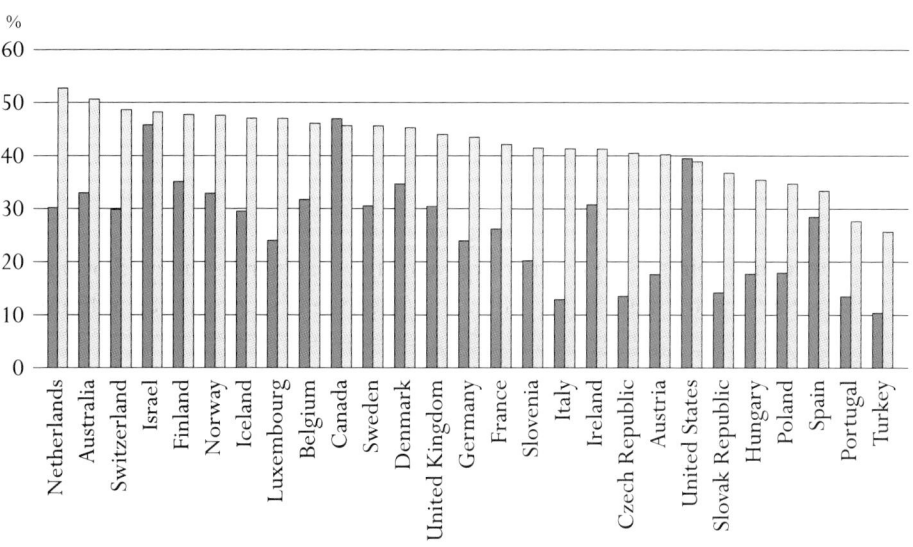

Note: For the United States, ISCO groupings 3 and 9 are not separated and thus distributed among remaining ISCO categories.

Countries are ranked in descending order by the proportion of the population in skilled jobs.

Source: OECD. Table A1.3a and Table A1.6. See Annex 3 for notes (*www.oecd.org/edu/eag2008*).

StatLink ᠁ᛋᣒ http://dx.doi.org/10.1787/401474646362

■ The proportion of individuals who have completed upper secondary education has been growing in almost all OECD countries and has become the norm among the younger cohorts. As of 2006, in 18 OECD countries, the proportion of 25-to-34-year-olds having completed upper secondary education ranged from 80 to 97%.

■ Tertiary attainment levels have also increased substantially, to 33% among 25-to-34-year-olds, on average across OECD countries. This suggests that overall tertiary attainment levels will continue to rise in the coming years. In France, Ireland, Japan and Korea, there is a difference of 25 percentage points or more in tertiary attainment between the oldest and youngest age groups.

■ Social sciences, business and law are the major educational fields in most countries. In OECD countries, they constitute 28% of the overall ISCED 5A and 6 levels of educational attainment in the population. On average, there are 3.6 times as many individuals with degrees in these subjects in the younger cohort than in the older one. In the field of education, this ratio is close to 1 in the OECD countries.

■ Across OECD countries between 1998 and 2006, there was a marked shift from semi-skilled jobs to skilled jobs, with an increase of almost 4 percentage points in skilled occupation and a close to 4 percentage point decline in semi-skilled occupations. At the same time, the proportion of the population working in unskilled occupations remained substantially the same. In most countries, the decline has not been at the very low end of the skill distribution but among semi-skilled jobs.

■ The increase in skilled jobs has been met and exceeded in most OECD countries by increases in the proportion of the population with tertiary attainment. However, in most countries, there are still substantially more skilled jobs than tertiary educated individuals. On average, across OECD countries, 69% of all those with a tertiary type 5B qualification and 85% of those with a tertiary 5A/6 qualification have skilled jobs. However the matching of higher education to skilled jobs varies substantially among countries. Those with a 5A/6 qualification in Denmark, Finland, Luxembourg and the partner country Slovenia do substantially better in finding a skilled job given the labour market conditions for those with tertiary education.

A1

Policy context

A well-educated and well-trained population is essential for the social and economic well-being of countries and individuals. Education plays a key role in providing individuals with the knowledge, skills and competencies needed to participate effectively in society and in the economy. Education also contributes to the expansion of scientific and cultural knowledge. The population's level of educational attainment is a commonly used proxy for the stock of "human capital", that is, the skills available in the population and the labour force. However, comparing different countries' educational attainment levels presupposes that the skills and knowledge imparted at each level of education are similar.

The skill composition of the human capital stock varies substantially among countries depending on the industry structure and the general level of economic development. It is important to understand the mix of skills as well as changes in the skill structure among different age groups in order to gain an idea of the current and future supply of skills in the labour market. One way to track the supply of skills in different areas is to examine replacement ratios in the educational fields of those who recently entered the labour market with those leaving the labour market in the coming years. In gauging the potential effects of these changes in the composition of skills, it is necessary to consider the overall volume of individuals within a certain field, current and future industry composition, and the extent to which lifelong learning provides an alternative for accumulating specific skills.

The International Standard Classification of Occupations (ISCO) provides an opportunity to relate what is produced by the education system to the labour market. In essence, occupational classifications relate to the level of economic development and demand for skills and as such provide a measure of the overall need for education. A key issue for any education system is to supply the labour market with the level and diversity of skills that employers require. The match between educational attainment and occupations can thus be seen as a signal of the overall level and quality of educational investments.

Evidence and explanations

Attainment levels in OECD countries

On average, across OECD countries, fewer than one-third of adults (31%) have undertaken only primary or lower secondary levels of education, 42% of the adult population have completed an upper secondary education and one-quarter (27%) have attained tertiary level qualification (Table A1.1a). However, countries differ widely in the distribution of educational attainment in their population.

In 22 out of 29 OECD countries – as well as in the partner countries Estonia, Israel, the Russian Federation and Slovenia – 60% or more of the population aged 25 to 64 has completed at least upper secondary education (Table A1.2a). Some countries show a different profile, however. For instance, in Mexico, Portugal and Turkey and the partner country Brazil, more than 50% of the population aged 25 to 64 has not completed upper secondary education. Overall, a comparison of the levels of educational attainment in younger and older age groups indicates marked progress with regard to attainment of upper secondary education (Chart A1.2).

A1

Chart A1.2. Population that has attained at least upper secondary education (2006)
Percentage, by age group

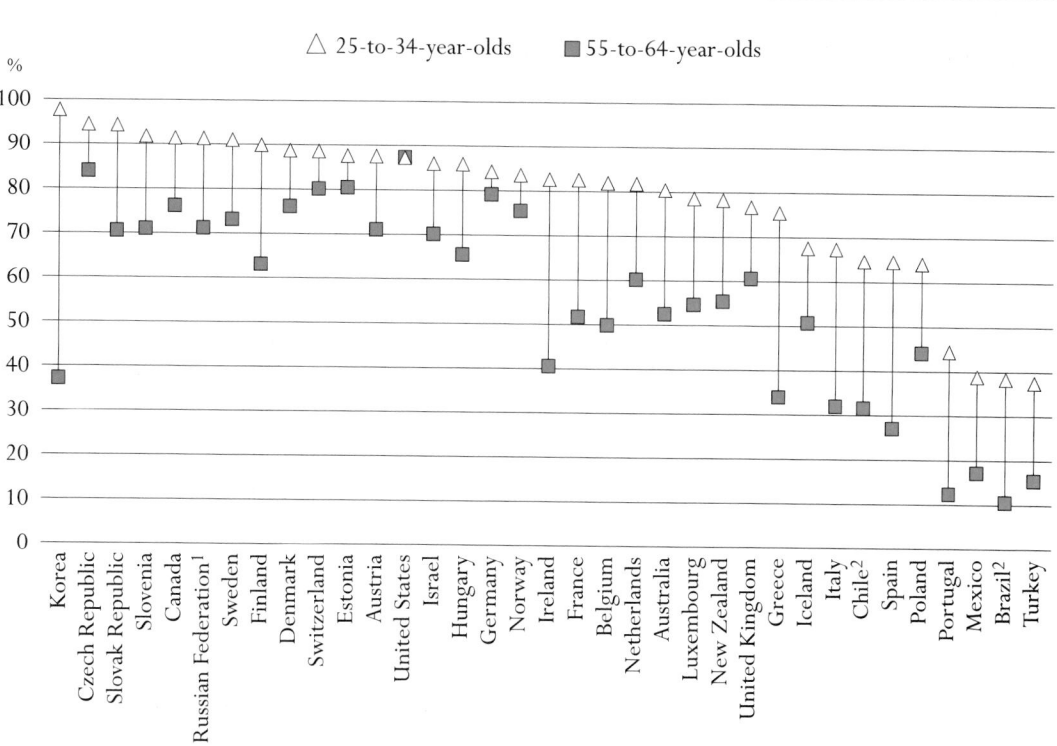

△ 25-to-34-year-olds   ■ 55-to-64-year-olds

1. Year of reference 2002.
2. Year of reference 2004.
Countries are ranked in descending order of the percentage of the 25-to-34-year-olds who have attained at least upper secondary education.
Source: OECD. Table A1.2a. See Annex 3 for notes (*www.oecd.org/edu/eag2008*).
StatLink ⣿⣿⣿ http://dx.doi.org/10.1787/401474646362

On average across OECD countries, the proportion of 25-to-34-year-olds having attained upper secondary education is 23 percentage points higher than that of the 55-to-64-year-olds. This increase has been particularly dramatic in Belgium, France, Greece, Ireland, Italy, Korea, Portugal and Spain, as well as in the partner country Chile, all of which have seen growth of 30 or more percentage points.

In countries whose adult population generally has a high attainment level, differences in attainment among age groups are less pronounced (Table A1.2a). In countries in which more than 80% of 25-to-64-year-olds have at least upper secondary attainment, the difference in the proportion of 25-to-34-year-olds and 55-to-64-year-olds having attained upper secondary level is, on average, 12 percentage points. In Germany and the United States, the proportion of upper secondary attainment is almost the same for all age groups. For countries with more room for increases, the average gain in attainment between these age groups is 28 percentage points, but situations differ. In Norway and Switzerland, the difference in upper secondary attainment between 25-to-34-year-olds and 55-to-64-year-olds is less than 10 percentage points; in Korea it is 60 percentage points.

A1

In almost all countries, 25-to-34-year-olds have higher tertiary attainment levels than the generation about to leave the labour market (55-to-64-year-olds). On average across OECD countries, 33% of the younger cohort has achieved a tertiary education, compared with 19% among the oldest cohort, while the average for the total population of 25-to-64-year-olds is 27%. The expansion of tertiary education differs substantially among countries. In France, Ireland, Japan and Korea, the difference in tertiary attainment between the oldest and youngest age groups is 25 percentage points or more (Table A1.3a).

Chart A1.3. **Population that has attained at least tertiary education (2006)**

Percentage, by age group

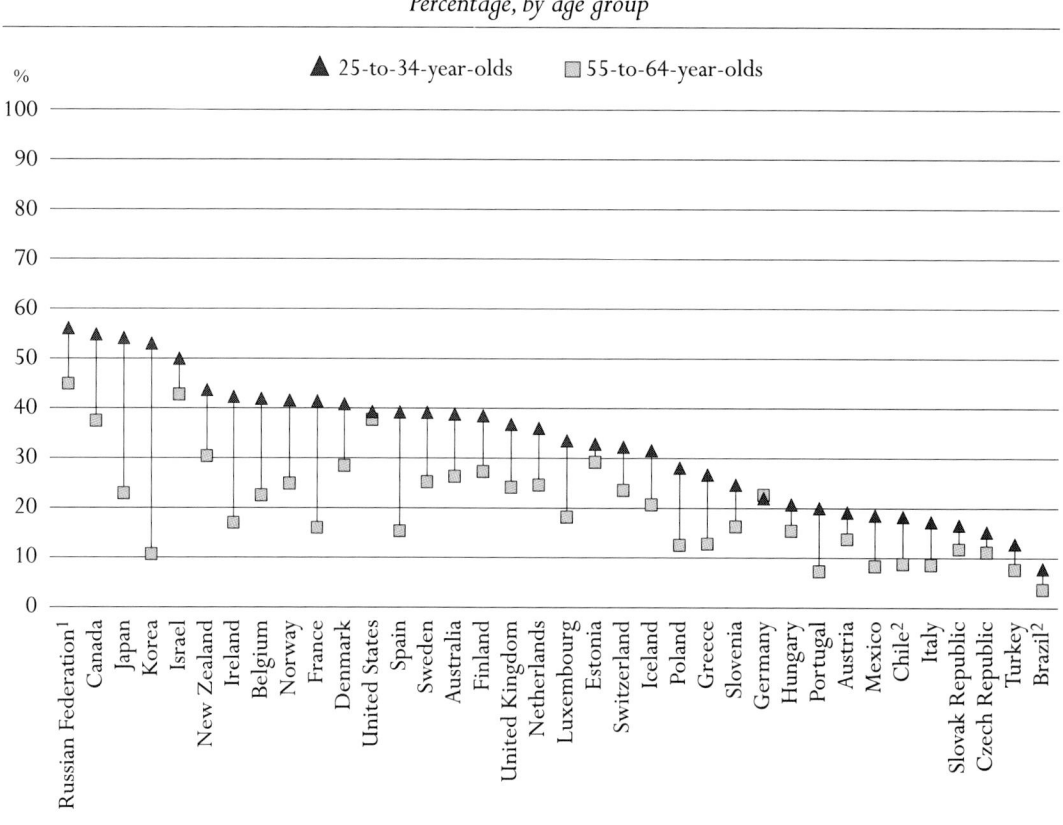

1. Year of reference 2002.
2. Year of reference 2004.
Countries are ranked in descending order of the percentage of the 25-to-34-year-olds who have attained tertiary education.
Source: OECD. Table A1.3a. See Annex 3 for notes (*www.oecd.org/edu/eag2008*).
StatLink http://dx.doi.org/10.1787/401474646362

This rapid expansion has put Japan and Korea in the top group (Chart A1.3). Changes in attainment levels between the youngest and oldest cohorts have been negative in Germany, and expansion has only been a few percentage points in the Czech Republic, the United States and the partner countries Brazil and Estonia, although attainment levels in the total population are still substantially above the OECD average in the United States and Estonia. The highest tertiary attainment levels in the total population are found in Canada and in the partner country the Russian Federation where 47% and 54%, respectively, of the population have a tertiary qualification.

A1

Variation in attainment levels by field of education

As shown above, tertiary attainment levels have risen sharply in many countries, among younger age groups. However, this increase is not spread evenly among different fields of education and has resulted in large shifts among these fields. Table A1.4 shows the distribution of adults at ISCED levels 5A and 6, by field of education. Social sciences, business, and law lead in most countries; however, science is the main field in Ireland, education in Norway, engineering in Finland and the Slovak Republic, and health and welfare in Denmark. Of the population with ISCED 5A and 6 levels of education among the countries included in Table A1.4, 28% are in the field of social sciences, business, and law, 15% in engineering, 14% in education, 13% in health and welfare, 12% in arts and humanities, and 10% in science.

The predominance of social sciences, business, and law is largely due to recent increases in tertiary qualifications in these fields. The ratios in Table A1.5 provide an indication of the shifts by comparing the number of 25-to-34-year-olds with an ISCED level 5A of education and 30-to-39-year-olds with an ISCED level 6 to the number of 55-to-64-year-olds with ISCED levels 5A and 6, for each field. Chart A1.4 shows these generational differences in the fields of social sciences and education.

Chart A1.4. Picture of generational difference in social sciences and in education (2004)

This chart depicts the ratio of 25-to-34-year-olds with an ISCED 5A level of education and 30-to-39-year-olds with an ISCED 6 to 55-to-64-year-olds with an ISCED 5A and 6 in social sciences and in education.

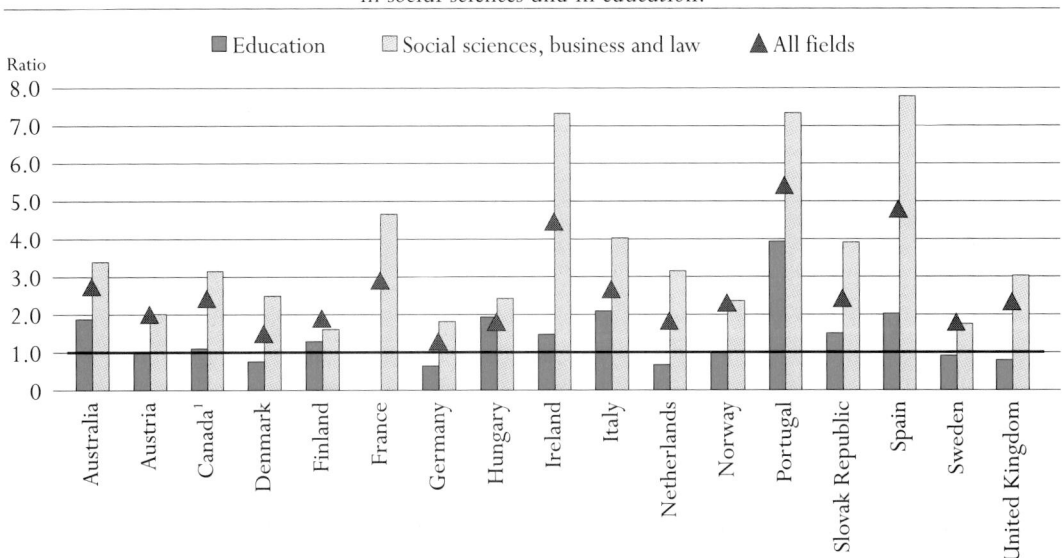

1. Year of reference 2001. Only ISCED 5A level of educationnal attainment.
Source: OECD. Table A1.5. See Annex 3 for notes (*www.oecd.org/edu/eag2008*).
StatLink http://dx.doi.org/10.1787/401474646362

There are three and a half times as many young adults with degrees in social sciences, business and law as in the older age group. This reflects the general increase in attainment levels, but it also reflects the attraction of this field of education. In France, Ireland, Italy, Portugal and Spain, more than four times as many young adults as those in the older age group have degrees in social sciences, business and law. In all countries except Finland, the expansion is above the average increase between the two age groups for all fields of education.

A1

In education as a field of study, a comparison of younger and older age groups shows that supply has, on average, not increased. This largely reflects the relatively stable condition of most countries' education systems. However, in Denmark, Germany, the Netherlands, Sweden and the United Kingdom, the replacement ratio is less than 1, and this may signal a problem for replacing the older generation of teachers when they retire in the coming years.

Table A1.5 also shows large variations among countries in the extent to which younger individuals have chosen science or engineering as compared to the older age group. In these key educational fields, there is also substantial variation within countries, as supply levels in science have risen more than in engineering in all OECD countries except in Finland, Italy and Sweden. In Denmark, Hungary and Norway, some of the increases in science relative to engineering can be explained by the fact that science is a relatively small field in these countries.

Tertiary attainment and skilled jobs

Governments that seek to expand tertiary education have often considered that an advanced knowledge economy needs more high-level skills and thus requires educating a much greater proportion of the workforce beyond the secondary level. As noted in *Education at a Glance 2007*, there seems little or no evidence that the expansion of higher education has led to any negative labour market effects, which suggests that the number of skilled jobs to be filled still outnumbers the supply of tertiary educated. ISCO provides a further opportunity to take a closer look at the match between the education system and the labour market in different countries.

The possibility to accommodate increasing numbers of individuals with tertiary education depends on industry structure and the general level of economic development. The composition of occupational categories in a country captures these factors to some extent, as the distribution of occupations reflects the importance of different sectors and of high-end skills for the economy.

Table A1.6 shows the overall composition of the labour force with regard to occupational skill levels in 2006 and 1998. To facilitate the analysis of tertiary education and skilled jobs, ISCO 1-3 is categorised as skilled occupations, ISCO 4-8 as semi-skilled and ISCO 9 as unskilled. The table shows this classification for the total workforce as well as for the workforce of 25-to-64-year-olds so as to match the tertiary attainment population (25-to-64-year-olds).

On average across OECD countries, the largest occupational group is Technicians and associated professionals (ISCO 3) which has overtaken Craft and related trades workers (ISCO 7) as the main occupational category in the past eight years. Semi-skilled occupations have generally declined in OECD countries, with Clerks (ISCO 4), together with Craft and related trades workers (ISCO 7), showing the biggest drop since 1998. Service workers (ISCO 5) is the only semi-skilled occupation which has seen a relative rise since 1998. Service workers are a key group in Iceland, Norway, Sweden and the United States with more than 20% of the workforce. The number of workers in skilled occupations has generally increased since 1998 and the relative increase in professionals (ISCO 2) and Technicians and associated professionals (ISCO 3) has been around 2 percentage points. The proportion of the workforce at the two ends of the skills distribution – Legislators, senior officials and managers (ISCO 1) and Elementary occupations (ISCO 9) – have been stable over the period.

A1

Chart A1.5. Distribution of skilled, semi-skilled and unskilled occupations in the workforce (2006)

Percentage, sorted by skilled occupations

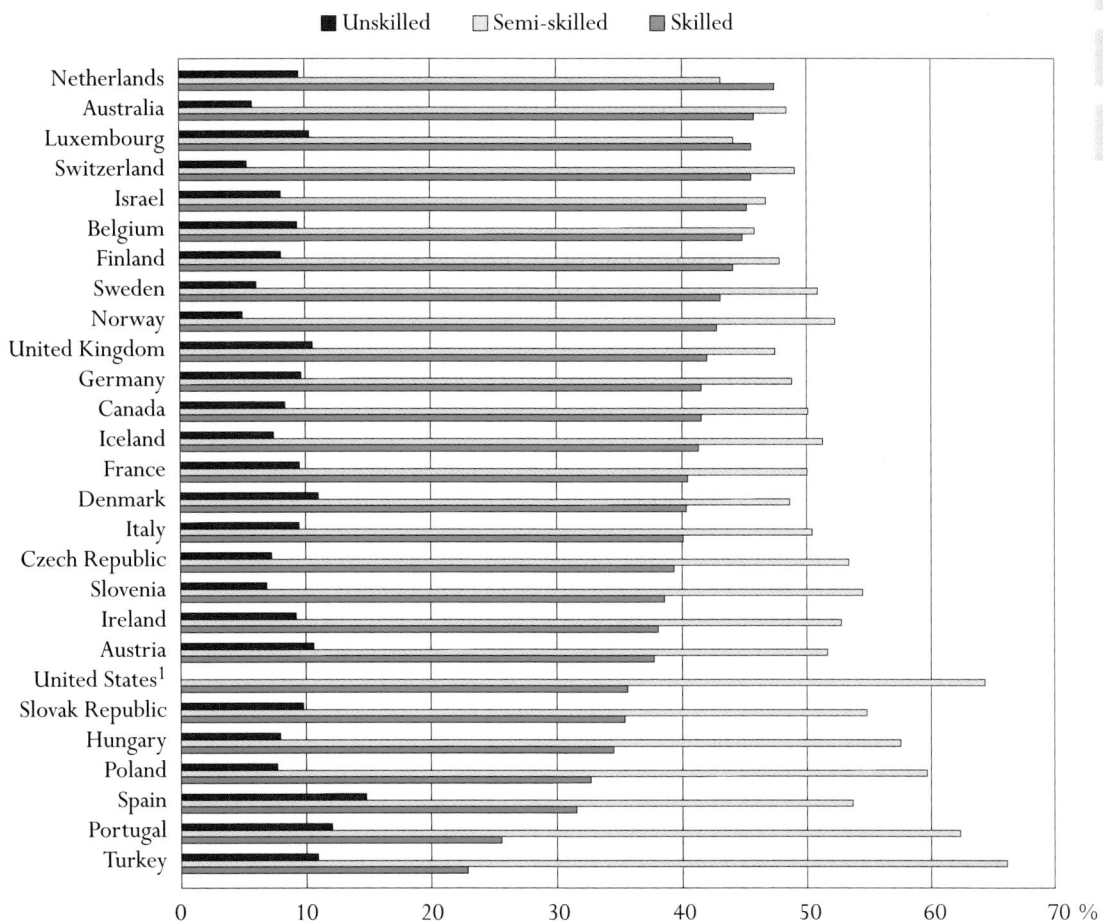

1. ISCO groupings 3 and 9 are not separated and thus distributed among remaining ISCO categories.
Countries are ranked in descending order by skilled occupations.
Source: OECD. Table A1.6. See Annex 3 for notes (*www.oecd.org/edu/eag2008*).
StatLink http://dx.doi.org/10.1787/401474646362

The big shift in OECD countries since 1998 has thus been between skilled and semi-skilled occupations, with almost 4 percentage points more work in skilled occupations and close to 4 percentage points less in semi-skilled occupations. On average, in each of the eight years, 0.5% of the total work force has shifted to skilled occupations. The job squeeze seems thus not to be in the very low end (unskilled occupations) but in mid-range jobs. Among the countries with data for both 1998 and 2006, this translates into the creation of approximately 24 million skilled jobs, of which 16 million outside the United States, 8 million semi-skilled jobs, of which less than a million outside the United States; and approximately 3 million unskilled jobs outside the United States (elementary jobs are not included in the ISCO classification for the United States). Some caution is needed to interpret these figures as a few countries have revised their ISCO classification, but the figures presented in Table A1.6 show that the overall trend towards more skilled jobs in the OECD area is nevertheless evident.

A1

Chart A1.5 shows the distribution of skilled, semi-skilled and unskilled occupations in 2006. The proportion of the workforce in unskilled occupations varies to some degree among countries but typically constitutes less then 10% of all jobs in most countries. The main difference among countries is the proportion of the workforce in skilled and semi-skilled jobs. This further reveals differences in the job market for individuals with tertiary education in OECD countries. In the long run, the high end of the labour market defines the need for such individuals. The proportion of the workforce in skilled professions surpasses the proportion in semi-skilled occupations in the Netherlands and Luxembourg, and, given current growth in skilled occupations among OECD countries, it is only a matter of time before this is also true in Australia, Belgium, Switzerland and the partner country Israel.

The difference between skilled jobs and the proportion with tertiary education, as shown in Chart A1.1, suggests that further expansion of tertiary education may still be an option in most countries. Chart A1.6 therefore relates changes in skilled jobs and changes in tertiary attainment between 1998 and 2006 to the difference in skilled jobs and tertiary educated that still exists in 2006. In relating occupations to educational attainment, it is necessary to recall that the supply of those with tertiary education differs among countries depending on labour market participation and employment rates among different educational groups and that tertiary attainment levels provide information on the potential supply of individuals with tertiary education on the labour market. To narrow down the labour market conditions that face higher educated individuals in different countries, the analysis is restricted to the 25-64-year-old population (as in Chart A1.1).

Shifts in the proportion of the population with tertiary education and the proportion of the population in skilled jobs suggest that tertiary attainment levels have risen relatively faster than skilled occupations in most OECD countries between 1998 and 2006. Notable exceptions are the Czech Republic, Germany and Italy, where the proportion of skilled jobs has outpaced attainment levels in the past eight years, and Austria and Denmark, where the expansion of tertiary attainment has matched that of skilled occupations. In Ireland and the Netherlands, the proportion of the 25-to-64-year-old population in skilled jobs has decreased, which means that relatively more semi-skilled and unskilled jobs have been created during this period (Chart A1.6).

Although the increase in the proportion of the population with tertiary education outpaced the increase in the proportion of the population in skilled jobs in most OECD countries during the past eight years, there still exists a substantial gap in many countries. For countries with large differences in skilled jobs and tertiary attainment levels, the fundamental question is whether higher growth in skilled occupations could be achieved if more individuals with tertiary education were available to the labour market or whether labour market experience and adult learning is sufficient to provide the necessary skills.

Four countries show little difference between the proportion of the population with tertiary attainment and the proportion of the population in skilled jobs. In Canada and the United States, the difference in tertiary attainment and skilled jobs is marginally negative and in Spain and the partner country Israel it is less than 5 percentage points. A close correspondence between tertiary attainment and skilled jobs suggests that individuals with tertiary education will find it more difficult to find skilled jobs at least until the growth in skilled occupations outpaces growth in attainment.

Chart A1.6. Difference between skilled jobs (ISCO 1-3) and proportion of tertiary educated in 2006 and changes in skilled jobs and tertiary attainment between 1998-2006

Percentage, sorted by skilled occupations

A1

☐ Difference between skilled jobs and tertiary educated in the 25-to-64-year-old population (2006)

■ Change in skilled occupations (ISCO 1-3) in the 25-to-64-year-old population between 1998 and 2006

▨ Change in tertiary attainment (ISCED 5/6) in the 25-to-64-year-old population between 1998 and 2006

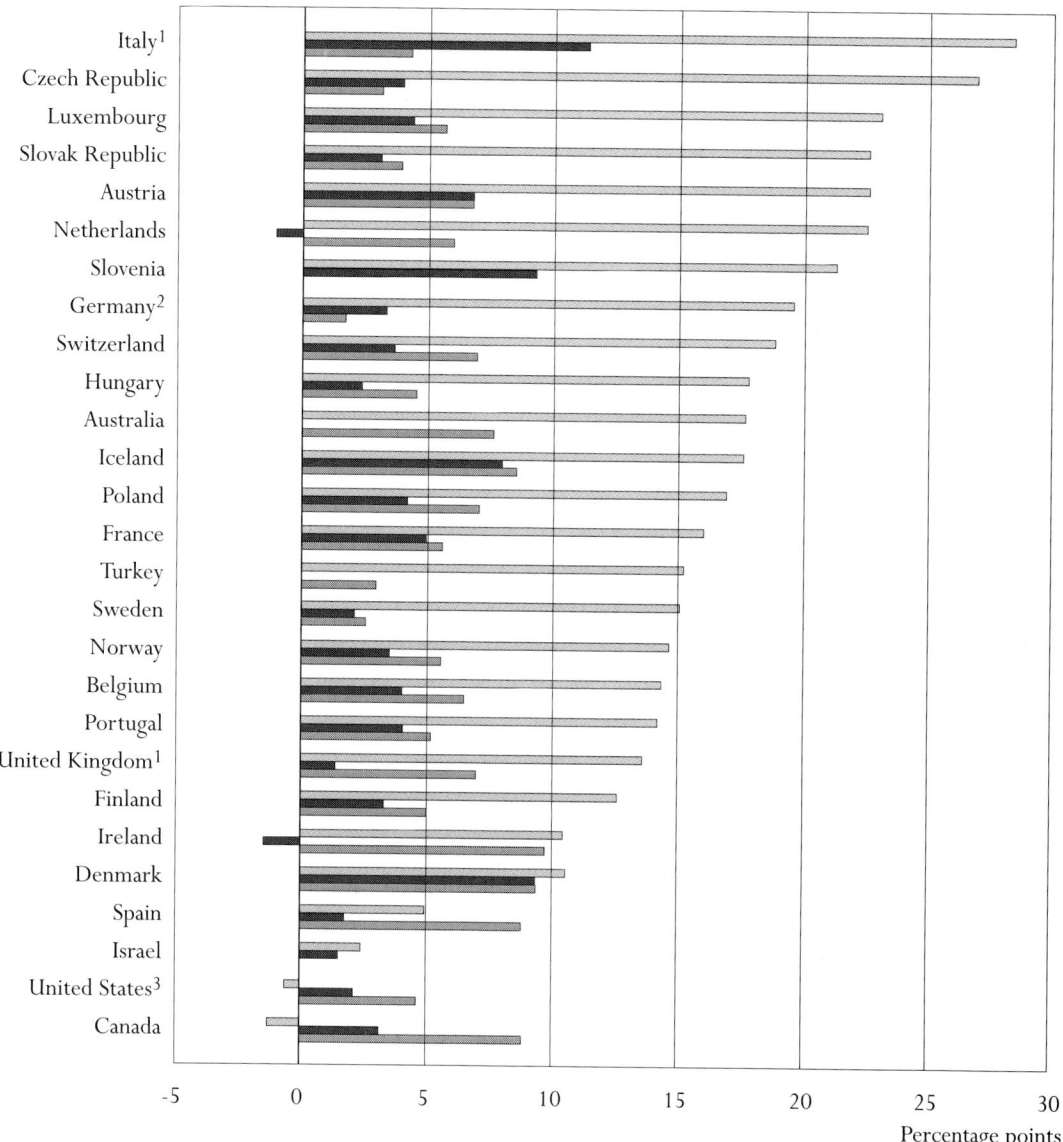

1. Change in survey methodology between 1998 and 2006 influences the comparability.
2. The year of reference is 1999, not 1998.
3. ISCO groupings 3 and 9 are not separated and thus distributed among remaining ISCO categories.
Countries are ranked in descending order of the difference between skilled jobs and tertiary attainment.
Source: OECD. Table A1.3a and Table A1.6. See Annex 3 for notes (*www.oecd.org/edu/eag2008*).
StatLink ⫘⫘ http://dx.doi.org/10.1787/401474646362

A1

Matching tertiary educated individuals to skilled jobs

The match between tertiary educated individuals and jobs is shown in Table A1.7. Among OECD countries the main occupation for those with a tertiary 5B qualification is Technician and associate professionals (ISCO 3) but there are large differences among countries. In the Czech Republic, Denmark, France and Sweden, close to 50% of all tertiary type 5B individuals work in these occupations whereas in Austria, Germany, and Spain close to 20% of those with a tertiary 5B education work in Crafts and related trades (ISCO 7). In the United States, a large proportion of both 5B and 5A/6 educated individuals work in the service sector (ISCO 5).

The main destination for those with a 5A/6 level of qualification is Professionals (ISCO 2) with more than 60% of the working population entering these occupations in Austria, Germany, Luxembourg and Portugal and the partner country Slovenia. On average across OECD countries, 53% are in this category. On average, 14% of those with a 5A/6 level of qualification are also Legislators, senior officials or managers (ISCO 1); in Belgium, the United Kingdom and the United States this figure is above 20%.

Chart A1.7. Relationship between the matching of tertiary education (5A/6) to skilled jobs and the difference between skilled jobs and the proportion of tertiary educated in the economy

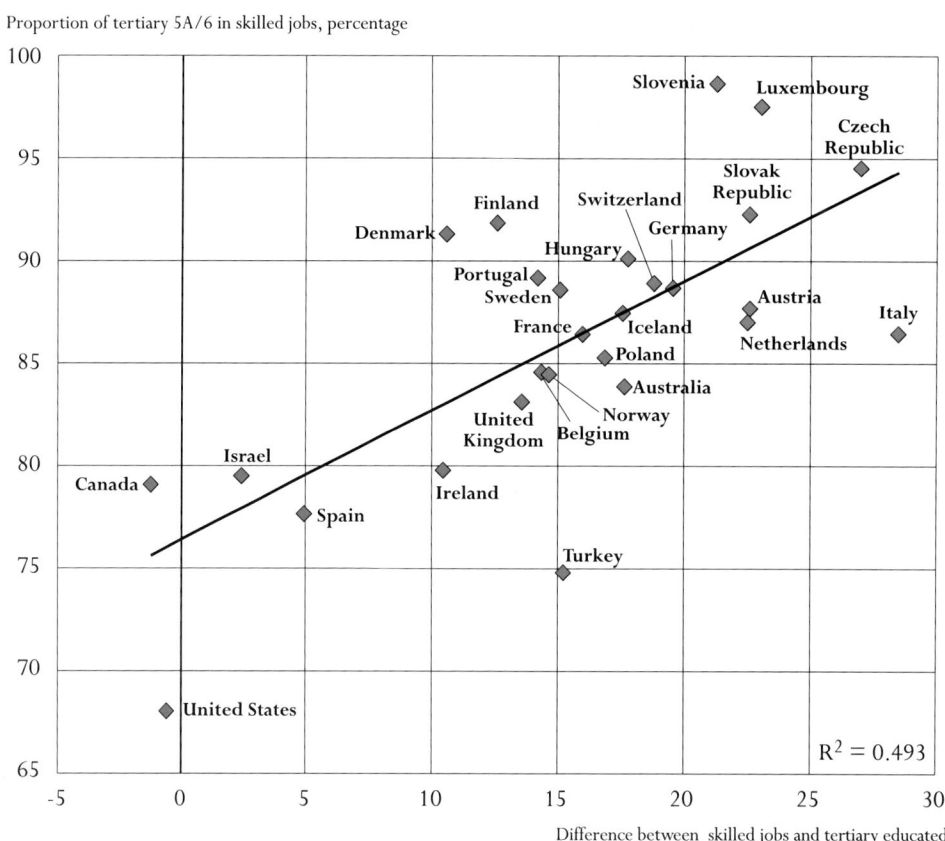

Proportion of tertiary 5A/6 in skilled jobs, percentage

$R^2 = 0.493$

Difference between skilled jobs and tertiary educated in the 25-to-64-year-old population, percentage points

Source: OECD. Tables A1.3a, A1.6 and A1.7. See Annex 3 for notes (*www.oecd.org/edu/eag2008*).
StatLink http://dx.doi.org/10.1787/401474646362

A1

On average, across OECD countries, 69% of those with a tertiary-type 5B qualification and 85% of those with a tertiary 5A/6 level of qualification find skilled jobs. However the match between tertiary education and skilled jobs varies substantially among countries. Much of the variation is driven by supply and demand for skilled jobs in different countries. In other words, the more tertiary educated individuals relative to skilled jobs, the more difficult it is to match individuals with tertiary education to these jobs. Chart A1.7 shows this relationship by relating the difference between skilled jobs and tertiary education (from Chart A1.1) to the match between tertiary 5A/6 educated individuals and skilled jobs.

There is a strong relationship between a large portion of tertiary 5A/6 educated individuals in skilled jobs and the difference between the proportions of skilled jobs and the tertiary educated in the economy. Close to 50% of the matching of individuals with tertiary 5A/6 to skilled jobs is explained by differences in skilled jobs and tertiary education. Using a regression approach is also a way of levelling the playing field when evaluating countries' success in providing skilled jobs to highly educated individuals. Considering differences in supply and demand for skilled jobs, countries above the regression line match those with tertiary education to skilled jobs better and countries below the line do relatively worse in this respect.

By this reasoning Canada and the partner country Israel, which are below the OECD average of 85% of individuals with 5A/6 tertiary education in skilled jobs (Table A1.7), do relatively better than most countries when considering the proportion of tertiary educated individuals relative to skilled jobs in their economies. Given differences in the potential supply of and demand for high-end skills, those with tertiary education in Denmark, Finland, Luxembourg, and in the partner country Slovenia do substantially better in finding a skilled job. The opposite is true for those with a tertiary qualification in Italy, Turkey and the United States, where 8% or more end up outside skilled occupations than labour market conditions would suggest.

The matching of individuals with tertiary education to skilled jobs carries information about the quality of the schooling received and the responsiveness of tertiary education systems to changing demands. However, these figures should be interpreted with caution, because most occupations increasingly require higher skill levels to perform job tasks which are generally not reflected in the current ISCO classification. A better understanding of the differences among countries in these outcomes would require further refinement of the ISCO classification and additional information on fields of education.

Utilisation of human capital is a key issue, but the matching of individuals with tertiary education to skilled jobs is only one indication of the success of higher education systems. Other indicators provide additional and sometimes more crucial information on the outcomes of education systems. Data clearly show that there are substantial rewards associated with attaining tertiary education in all countries, and substantial penalties associated with failing to reach at least upper secondary education. The average earnings premium associated with tertiary education is everywhere more than 15% and in some countries more than 100% (see Indicator A9). Among OECD countries, the average unemployment rate among those with only lower secondary education is 4 percentage points higher than among those whose highest level is upper secondary, and 6 points higher than those with tertiary education (see Indicator A8).

A1

Definitions and methodologies

Data on population and educational attainment are taken from OECD and Eurostat databases, which are compiled from National Labour Force Surveys. See Annex 3 (*www.oecd.org/edu/eag2008*) for national sources.

Attainment profiles are based on the percentage of the population aged 25 to 64 that has completed a specified level of education. The International Standard Classification of Education (ISCED-97) is used to define the levels of education. See Annex 3 (*www.oecd.org/edu/eag2008*) for a description of ISCED-97 education programmes and attainment levels and their mappings for each country.

Successful completion of upper secondary education means the achievement of upper secondary programmes type A, B or C of a similar length; completion of type C programmes (labour market destination) of significantly shorter duration are not classified as upper secondary attainment.

The data for Tables A1.4 and A1.5 originate from a special data collection by the Supply of Skills working group of INES Network B. Data on the distribution by fields of education among the population with tertiary-type 5A/6 levels of education was collected in most cases from the Eurostat labour force survey or national labour force surveys.

The data for Tables A1.6 and A1.7 are provided by the Supply of Skills working group of INES Network B. The information is based on a data collection of ISCO (International Standard Classification of Occupations) and ISCED information from OECD countries. ISCO is the most widely used classification system for organising occupations into groups according to the tasks and duties involved. The ISCO system is maintained by the International Labour Organisation (ILO). The current version, ISCO-88, is being updated for release in 2008.

The ISCO system facilitates international communication about jobs, makes international comparisons possible, and serves as a model for the development of national occupation classification systems. In the ISCO system, an occupation is classified into one of nine major groups, and then further into sub-groups. The analysis in Indicator A1 is at the major group level.

Like other international classification systems, ISCO changes only when major revisions are carried out. This means that ISCO does not fully capture changes in the labour market over time. Occupations evolve, as do their competency requirements. Some types of occupations disappear and others appear, and the nature of these new occupations is sometimes not fully described in ISCO. Accordingly, time series comparisons using the ISCO system should be interpreted with caution, considering the limitations of a static classification system.

Further references

For further information on expansion of tertiary education, see the OECD Education Working Paper, "Effects of Tertiary Expansion: Crowding-out effects and labour market matches for higher education" (on line at: *www.oecd.org/edu/workingpapers*).

The following additional material relevant to this indicator is available on line at:

StatLink ⫶ http://dx.doi.org/10.1787/401474646362

A1

- *Educational attainment: adult population, by gender (2006)*
  Table A1.1b. Males
  Table A1.1c. Females

- *Population that has attained at least upper secondary education, by gender (2006)*
  Table A1.2b. Males
  Table A1.2c. Females

- *Population that has attained tertiary education, by gender (2006)*
  Table A1.3b. Males
  Table A1.3c. Females

- *Table A1.3d. Attainment of tertiary education, by age (1998)*

A1

Table A1.1a.
Educational attainment: adult population (2006)
Distribution of the 25-to-64-year-old population, by highest level of education attained

| | Pre-primary and primary education | Lower secondary education | ISCED 3C (short programme) | Upper secondary education | | Post-secondary non-tertiary education | Tertiary education | | | All levels of education |
				ISCED 3C (long programme)/3B	ISCED 3A		Type B	Type A	Advanced research programmes	
	(1)	(2)	(3)	(4)	(5)	(6)	(7)	(8)	(9)	(10)
OECD countries										
Australia	9	24	a	a	31	3	9	24	x(8)	100
Austria	x(2)	18	2	47	6	10	7	10	x(8)	100
Belgium	15	18	a	9	24	2	18	14	1	100
Canada	5	10	a	x(5)	27	12	23	24	x(8)	100
Czech Republic	n	10	a	42	35	a	x(8)	14	x(8)	100
Denmark	1	16	2	43	4	n	8	27	1	100
Finland	10	10	a	a	44	n	16	18	1	100
France	14	19	a	30	11	n	11	15	1	100
Germany	3	14	a	49	3	7	9	14	1	100
Greece	28	11	3	3	26	8	7	15	n	100
Hungary	2	20	a	30	29	2	n	17	n	100
Iceland	3	27	6	16	10	8	4	25	1	100
Ireland	16	18	n	a	25	11	11	19	n	100
Italy	16	32	1	7	30	1	1	12	n	100
Japan	x(5)	x(5)	x(5)	x(5)	60	a	18	23	x(8)	100
Korea	11	12	a	x(5)	44	a	9	23	x(8)	100
Luxembourg	18	9	8	17	20	5	8	15	2	100
Mexico	48	30	a	7	x(2)	a	1	14	x(8)	100
Netherlands	7	20	x(4)	16	23	3	2	28	1	100
New Zealand	x(2)	22	8	11	9	11	15	23	x(8)	100
Norway	n	21	a	31	12	3	2	30	1	100
Poland	x(2)	14	33	a	31	4	x(8)	18	x(8)	100
Portugal	57	15	x(5)	x(5)	13	1	x(8)	13	1	100
Slovak Republic	1	13	x(4)	35	37	x(5)	1	13	n	100
Spain	23	27	a	8	13	n	9	19	1	100
Sweden	6	10	a	x(5)	47	6	9	22	x(8)	100
Switzerland	3	10	2	46	6	3	10	17	3	100
Turkey	61	10	a	8	10	a	x(8)	10	x(8)	100
United Kingdom	n	14	17	23	16	n	9	21	n	100
United States	5	8	x(5)	x(5)	48	x(5)	5	33	1	100

	Below upper secondary education	Upper secondary level of education	Tertiary level of education
OECD average	31	42	27
EU19 average	31	45	24

	(1)	(2)	(3)	(4)	(5)	(6)	(7)	(8)	(9)	(10)
Partner countries										
Brazil[1]	57	14	x(5)	x(5)	22	a	x(8)	8	x(8)	100
Chile[1]	24	26	x(5)	x(5)	37	a	3	10	x(8)	100
Estonia	1	11	a	5	43	7	11	22	n	100
Israel	4	17	a	x(5)	34	a	15	30	1	100
Russian Federation[2]	3	8	x(4)	16	18	x(4)	33	20	n	100
Slovenia	2	16	a	28	32	a	10	9	2	100

Notes: Due to discrepancies in the data, averages have not been calculated for each column individually.
1. Year of reference 2004.
2. Year of reference 2002.
Source: OECD. See Annex 3 for notes (*www.oecd.org/edu/eag2008*).
Please refer to the Reader's Guide for information concerning the symbols replacing missing data.
StatLink ⫘⫘ http://dx.doi.org/10.1787/401474646362

Table A1.2a.
Population that has attained at least upper secondary education[1] (2006)
Percentage, by age group

	Age group				
	25 to 64	25 to 34	35 to 44	45 to 54	55 to 64
OECD countries					
Australia	67	80	68	63	52
Austria	80	87	84	77	71
Belgium	67	82	74	60	50
Canada	86	91	89	85	76
Czech Republic	90	94	94	89	84
Denmark	82	88	84	78	76
Finland	80	90	87	80	63
France	67	82	72	61	52
Germany	83	84	85	83	79
Greece	59	75	67	53	34
Hungary	78	86	82	77	66
Iceland	63	67	67	64	51
Ireland	66	82	71	58	41
Italy	51	67	55	47	32
Korea	77	97	90	62	37
Luxembourg	66	78	67	60	55
Mexico	32	39	36	28	17
Netherlands	72	81	76	70	60
New Zealand	69	78	72	69	55
Norway	79	83	79	77	75
Poland	53	64	51	49	44
Portugal	28	44	28	20	12
Slovak Republic	87	94	91	86	70
Spain	50	64	55	43	27
Sweden	84	91	90	82	73
Switzerland	85	88	87	84	80
Turkey	28	37	25	22	15
United Kingdom	69	76	70	67	61
United States	88	87	88	89	87
OECD average	*68*	*78*	*72*	*65*	*55*
EU19 average	*69*	*80*	*73*	*65*	*55*
Partner countries					
Brazil[2]	30	38	32	27	11
Chile[2]	50	64	52	44	32
Estonia	88	87	93	92	80
Israel	80	86	82	76	70
Russian Federation[3]	88	91	94	89	71
Slovenia	82	91	85	77	71

1. Excluding ISCED 3C short programmes.
2. Year of reference 2004.
3. Year of reference 2002.
Source: OECD. See Annex 3 for notes (*www.oecd.org/edu/eag2008*).
StatLink ⛁ http://dx.doi.org/10.1787/401474646362

A1

Table A1.3a.
Population that has attained tertiary education (2006)
Percentage of the population that has attained tertiary-type B education or tertiary-type A and advanced research programmes, by age group

		Tertiary-type B education					Tertiary-type A and Advanced research programmes					Total tertiary				
		25 to 64	25 to 34	35 to 44	45 to 54	55 to 64	25 to 64	25 to 34	35 to 44	45 to 54	55 to 64	25 to 64	25 to 34	35 to 44	45 to 54	55 to 64
		(1)	(2)	(3)	(4)	(5)	(6)	(7)	(8)	(9)	(10)	(11)	(12)	(13)	(14)	(15)
OECD countries	Australia	9	10	9	9	8	24	29	24	23	18	33	39	33	32	26
	Austria	7	6	8	9	7	10	13	11	9	7	18	19	19	18	14
	Belgium	18	22	20	15	13	14	19	15	12	10	32	42	35	27	22
	Canada	23	26	25	22	18	24	29	26	21	19	47	55	51	43	37
	Czech Republic	x(11)	x(12)	x(13)	x(14)	x(15)	14	15	15	13	11	14	15	15	13	11
	Denmark	8	9	8	7	7	27	32	28	26	22	35	41	36	33	28
	Finland	16	9	21	18	14	19	29	20	16	13	35	38	41	34	27
	France	11	18	11	8	5	16	24	15	12	11	26	41	27	19	16
	Germany	9	7	10	10	9	15	15	16	15	14	24	22	25	25	23
	Greece	7	9	9	6	3	15	18	18	14	9	22	27	26	20	13
	Hungary	0	1	0	0	0	17	20	17	17	15	18	21	17	17	15
	Iceland	4	3	4	6	3	26	28	30	24	18	30	32	34	29	21
	Ireland	11	14	12	9	6	20	28	20	15	11	31	42	33	24	17
	Italy	1	1	1	0	0	12	17	13	11	8	13	17	14	11	9
	Japan	18	24	21	16	9	23	30	25	24	14	40	54	46	39	23
	Korea	9	20	9	3	1	23	33	28	16	10	33	53	37	19	11
	Luxembourg	8	11	7	5	8	16	23	17	14	11	24	33	24	19	18
	Mexico	1	1	1	1	1	14	17	15	14	8	15	19	16	15	8
	Netherlands	2	2	2	2	2	28	34	28	28	23	30	36	30	30	25
	New Zealand	15	14	15	17	16	23	30	25	21	15	38	44	39	38	30
	Norway	2	2	2	4	2	31	40	32	27	23	33	42	35	30	25
	Poland	x(11)	x(12)	x(13)	x(14)	x(15)	18	28	17	13	13	18	28	17	13	13
	Portugal	x(11)	x(12)	x(13)	x(14)	x(15)	13	20	14	11	7	13	20	14	11	7
	Slovak Republic	1	1	1	1	1	13	16	12	13	11	14	17	13	14	12
	Spain	9	13	10	6	3	20	26	21	17	12	28	39	31	22	15
	Sweden	9	9	9	10	8	22	31	21	19	17	31	39	29	29	25
	Switzerland	10	9	11	11	8	20	23	22	19	15	30	32	33	29	24
	Turkey	x(11)	x(12)	x(13)	x(14)	x(15)	10	13	9	9	8	10	13	9	9	8
	United Kingdom	9	8	9	9	8	22	29	21	20	16	30	37	31	29	24
	United States	5	5	5	5	5	35	35	36	34	33	39	39	41	40	38
	OECD average	*8*	*10*	*9*	*8*	*6*	*19*	*25*	*20*	*17*	*14*	*27*	*33*	*28*	*24*	*19*
	EU19 average	*8*	*9*	*9*	*7*	*6*	*17*	*23*	*18*	*15*	*13*	*24*	*30*	*25*	*21*	*18*
Partner countries	Brazil[1]	x(11)	x(12)	x(13)	x(14)	x(15)	x(11)	x(12)	x(13)	x(14)	x(15)	8	8	9	9	4
	Chile[1]	3	4	3	2	1	10	14	9	9	8	13	18	13	11	9
	Estonia	11	9	12	13	10	22	24	23	22	19	33	33	36	35	29
	Israel	16	15	16	17	16	30	35	28	27	26	46	50	44	44	43
	Russian Federation[2]	33	34	37	34	26	21	21	21	20	19	54	55	58	54	44
	Slovenia	10	9	10	9	10	11	15	11	8	7	20	25	21	17	16

1. Year of reference 2004.
2. Year of reference 2002.
Source: OECD. See Annex 3 for notes (*www.oecd.org/edu/eag2008*).
Please refer to the Reader's Guide for information concerning the symbols replacing missing data.
StatLink ⫘ 🖵 http://dx.doi.org/10.1787/401474646362

Table A1.4.
Fields of education (2004)
Distribution by field of education for the 25-to-64-year-old population with ISCED 5A and 6-level of educational attainment (percentage)

	Education	Arts & humanities	Social sciences, business and law	Science	Engineering	Agriculture	Health and welfare	Services	Other fields	Total
	(1)	(2)	(3)	(4)	(5)	(6)	(7)	(8)	(9)	(10)
Australia	15	11	32	11	10	1	17	2	1	100
Austria	10	15	34	9	15	2	13	2	n	100
Belgium	4	15	30	13	19	2	12	2	3	100
Canada[1,2]	16	12	34	12	11	2	12	2	n	100
Czech Republic	m	m	m	m	m	m	m	m	m	m
Denmark	16	11	19	4	13	1	34	1	n	100
Finland	12	12	22	7	27	4	12	4	n	100
France	9	19	35	15	10	1	7	3	1	100
Germany[3]	22	9	22	8	22	2	12	2	n	100
Greece	m	m	m	m	m	m	m	m	m	m
Hungary	27	5	23	4	21	6	9	5	n	100
Iceland	13	13	32	8	13	c	16	5	n	100
Ireland	12	13	22	23	11	2	10	3	5	100
Italy	4	19	33	12	14	2	15	1	n	100
Japan	m	m	m	m	m	m	m	m	m	m
Korea	m	m	m	m	m	m	m	m	m	m
Luxembourg	2	17	36	12	19	c	10	c	3	100
Mexico	5	17	31	11	13	3	11	7	1	100
Netherlands	20	8	30	6	12	2	17	3	2	100
New Zealand	m	m	m	m	m	m	m	m	m	m
Norway	20	7	18	4	6	1	12	3	29	100
Poland	m	m	m	m	m	m	m	m	m	m
Portugal	16	12	27	13	14	2	12	3	1	100
Slovak Republic	20	6	22	8	26	6	7	4	n	100
Spain	15	11	32	10	12	2	12	4	n	100
Sweden	22	7	24	7	15	1	19	3	1	100
Switzerland	m	m	m	m	m	m	m	m	m	m
Turkey	m	m	m	m	m	m	m	m	m	m
United Kingdom	14	18	28	18	11	1	8	1	n	100
United States[2]	m	m	m	m	m	m	m	m	m	m
OECD average	*14*	*12*	*28*	*10*	*15*	*2*	*13*	*3*	*2*	*100*

Note: Science includes life sciences, mathematics and statistics, computer science and use.
1. Year of reference 2001.
2. Only ISCED 5A level of educational attainment.
3. Distribution for 20-year-olds and above.
Source: OECD, Network B special data collection, Supply of Skills working group.
Please refer to the Reader's Guide for information concerning the symbols replacing missing data.
StatLink ⛭ http://dx.doi.org/10.1787/401474646362

Table A1.5.
Ratio of 25-to-34-year-olds with ISCED 5A and 30-to-39-year-olds with ISCED 6 levels of education
to 55-to-64-year-olds with ISCED 5A and 6 levels of education, by field of education (2004)

	Education	Arts and humanities	Social sciences, business and law	Science	Engineering	Agriculture	Health and welfare	Services	Other fields	All fields combined
	(1)	(2)	(3)	(4)	(5)	(6)	(7)	(8)	(9)	(10)
Australia	1.9	2.2	3.4	3.9	2.3	2.7	1.9	x(10)	2.9	2.6
Austria	1.0	1.8	2.0	4.8	1.8	1.6	1.4	x(10)	0.5	1.9
Belgium	x(10)	3.4	3.9	2.1	2.0	x(10)	2.4	x(10)	2.7	2.6
Canada[1,2]	1.1	2.1	3.2	4.4	2.3	2.1	1.9	5.3	n	2.3
Czech Republic	m	m	m	m	m	m	m	m	m	m
Denmark	0.8	2.3	2.5	3.3	0.8	0.6	1.2	x(10)	n	1.4
Finland	1.3	1.3	1.6	1.6	1.9	1.4	3.9	2.0	n	1.8
France	x(10)	3.0	4.7	3.3	2.4	2.0	1.1	4.9	2.8	2.8
Germany	0.6	1.4	1.8	2.1	0.9	1.0	1.3	1.6	1.1	1.2
Greece	m	m	m	m	m	m	m	m	m	m
Hungary	1.9	2.7	2.4	6.2	0.8	0.9	1.4	1.3	n	1.7
Iceland	x(10)	x(10)	x(10)	x(10)	x(10)	x(10)	x(10)	x(10)	x(10)	2.7
Ireland	1.5	3.4	7.3	6.8	4.2	1.6	3.9	11.5	3.0	4.3
Italy	2.1	1.4	4.0	2.0	3.1	4.4	2.1	3.7	n	2.5
Japan	m	m	m	m	m	m	m	m	m	m
Korea	m	m	m	m	m	m	m	m	m	m
Luxembourg	x(10)	x(10)	x(10)	x(10)	x(10)	x(10)	x(10)	x(10)	x(10)	2.4
Mexico	x(10)	3.9	2.2	3.0	2.4	2.8	1.4	2.9	6.5	2.7
Netherlands	0.7	1.7	3.2	1.8	1.4	1.9	1.7	1.6	5.7	1.7
New Zealand	m	m	m	m	m	m	m	m	m	m
Norway	1.0	0.9	2.4	3.0	0.8	0.7	1.2	x(10)	9.0	2.2
Poland	m	m	m	m	m	m	m	m	m	m
Portugal	3.9	2.7	7.3	10.0	4.3	10.3	4.9	8.5	0.6	5.3
Slovak Republic	1.5	2.8	3.9	2.9	2.0	1.5	2.4	3.5	n	2.3
Spain	2.0	4.0	7.8	8.8	3.5	6.0	3.8	5.2	3.5	4.7
Sweden	0.9	1.9	1.7	4.3	4.7	2.5	1.3	x(10)	1.2	1.7
Switzerland	m	m	m	m	m	m	m	m	m	m
Turkey	m	m	m	m	m	m	m	m	m	m
United Kingdom	0.8	2.5	3.0	2.8	1.9	x(10)	2.8	x(10)	1.6	2.2
United States[2]	m	m	m	m	m	m	m	m	m	m
OECD average	*1.4*	*2.4*	*3.6*	*4.1*	*2.3*	*2.6*	*2.2*	*4.3*	*3.2*	*2.5*

Note: Science includes life sciences, mathematics and statistics, computer science and use.
1. Year of reference 2001.
2. Only ISCED 5A level of educational attainment.
Source: OECD, Network B special data collection, Supply of Skills working group.
StatLink ⫘⫘ http://dx.doi.org/10.1787/401474646362

Table A1.6.
Proportion of the working age population in different occupations (ISCO) (1998, 2006)
Percentage, by ISCO groups

| | | Legislators; senior officials; managers | Professionals | Technicians; associate professionals | Clerks | Service workers | Skilled agricultural and fishery workers | Craft and related trades workers | Plant and machine operators; assemblers | Elementary occupations | All occupations | Total workforce | | | 25-to-64-year-old population | | |
| | | | | | | | | | | | | Skilled occupations | Semi-skilled occupations | Unskilled occupations | Skilled occupations | Semi-skilled occupations | Unskilled occupations |
		ISCO 1	ISCO 2	ISCO 3	ISCO 4	ISCO 5	ISCO 6	ISCO 7	ISCO 8	ISCO 9	Total (1-9)	ISCO 1-3	ISCO 4-8	ISCO 9	ISCO 1-3	ISCO 4-8	ISCO 9
Australia	2006	13	19	14	13	14	2	12	7	6	100	46	48	6	51	44	6
	1998	m	m	m	m	m	m	m	m	m	100	m	m	m	m	m	m
Austria	2006	7	10	21	13	13	5	14	7	11	100	38	52	11	40	49	11
	1998	7	10	14	14	14	6	17	9	9	100	31	60	9	33	57	10
Belgium	2006	12	21	12	15	11	2	10	8	9	100	45	46	9	46	45	9
	1998	11	19	10	16	11	2	13	8	9	100	41	51	9	42	49	9
Canada	2006	9	17	15	14	14	2	10	10	8	100	41	50	8	46	47	7
	1998	10	16	14	14	14	3	10	11	9	100	39	52	9	43	50	8
Czech Republic	2006	7	11	22	7	12	2	18	14	7	100	39	53	7	40	52	7
	1998	7	10	18	8	12	2	21	13	9	100	35	57	9	37	55	9
Denmark	2006	3	15	22	12	17	1	12	8	11	100	40	49	11	45	46	9
	1998	3	13	16	13	16	1	13	9	15	100	32	53	15	36	51	13
Finland	2006	10	17	17	7	16	5	12	8	8	100	44	48	8	48	45	7
	1998	8	17	17	9	12	7	12	10	8	100	42	50	8	44	49	7
France	2006	9	13	18	12	13	4	12	9	10	100	40	50	10	42	48	10
	1998	8	11	17	14	13	5	14	11	8	100	36	56	8	37	55	8
Germany[1]	2006	5	14	22	12	12	2	15	7	10	100	42	49	10	44	47	9
	1998	5	13	20	13	12	1	18	8	10	100	38	52	10	40	50	9
Hungary	2006	8	13	14	9	15	3	18	12	8	100	34	58	8	35	57	8
	1998	6	12	13	9	13	4	23	11	9	100	31	60	9	33	58	9
Iceland	2006	9	17	15	8	20	5	13	6	7	100	41	51	7	47	48	5
	1998	8	12	14	9	18	7	17	7	7	100	34	57	7	39	54	7
Ireland	2006	15	17	6	13	17	1	14	8	9	100	38	53	9	41	50	9
	1998	18	15	5	13	14	1	13	10	10	100	39	52	10	43	48	9
Italy[2]	2006	9	10	22	11	11	2	17	9	9	100	40	50	9	41	49	10
	1998	3	10	15	14	16	4	19	9	9	100	28	62	9	30	61	9
Luxembourg[1]	2006	6	21	18	17	9	2	10	6	10	100	46	44	10	47	43	10
	1998	6	16	19	16	9	3	14	7	10	100	41	49	10	43	47	10
Netherlands[3]	2006	11	19	18	12	14	2	9	6	10	100	47	43	10	53	40	7
	1998	13	17	18	12	13	2	10	6	8	100	48	43	8	54	40	7
Norway	2006	6	12	25	7	24	3	11	7	5	100	43	52	5	48	48	4
	1998	11	9	20	10	20	4	11	8	7	100	40	53	7	44	51	5
Poland	2006	6	15	11	7	12	14	16	10	8	100	33	60	8	35	58	8
	1998	7	10	12	8	10	18	19	9	8	100	28	63	8	31	61	8
Portugal	2006	8	9	9	10	15	10	20	8	12	100	26	62	12	28	60	12
	1998	7	6	8	9	13	11	23	9	13	100	21	66	13	24	63	13

Note: OECD averages are cacluated for countries with data for both years and all ISCO groups.
1. 1999 instead of 1998.
2. Italy: change in survey methodology between 1998 and 2006 affects comparability. United Kingdom: change in national occupation coding frame in 2000 affects comparability for ISCO.
3. 2000 instead of 1998.
4. ISCO groupings 3 and 9 in 2006 are not separated and thus distributed among remaining ISCO categories.
Source: OECD, Network B special data collection, Supply of Skills working group.
StatLink 🖳 http://dx.doi.org/10.1787/401474646362

A1

Table A1.6. *(continued)*
Proportion of the working age population in different occupations (ISCO) (1998, 2006)
Percentage, by ISCO groups

		Legislators; senior officials; managers	Professionals	Technicians; associate professionals	Clerks	Service workers	Skilled agricultural and fishery workers	Craft and related trades workers	Plant and machine operators; assemblers	Elementary occupations	All occupations	Total workforce			25-to-64-year-old population		
												Skilled occupations	Semi-skilled occupations	Unskilled occupations	Skilled occupations	Semi-skilled occupations	Unskilled occupations
		ISCO 1	ISCO 2	ISCO 3	ISCO 4	ISCO 5	ISCO 6	ISCO 7	ISCO 8	ISCO 9	Total (1-9)	ISCO 1-3	ISCO 4-8	ISCO 9	ISCO 1-3	ISCO 4-8	ISCO 9
Slovak Republic	2006	5	11	19	6	14	1	19	15	10	100	35	55	10	37	54	10
	1998	6	10	17	8	13	2	22	14	10	100	32	58	10	34	56	10
Spain	2006	8	12	12	9	15	3	17	9	15	100	32	54	15	33	52	14
	1998	9	12	9	10	14	5	17	11	14	100	29	57	14	32	55	13
Sweden[1]	2006	6	18	19	9	20	1	9	11	6	100	43	51	6	46	49	6
	1998	6	16	20	11	19	1	11	11	7	100	41	52	7	43	50	6
Switzerland	2006	6	18	21	12	14	4	15	5	5	100	46	49	5	49	46	6
	1998	6	16	20	14	14	4	15	5	5	100	42	52	5	45	49	6
Turkey	2006	6	11	6	7	8	9	28	14	11	100	23	66	11	26	64	11
	1998	m	m	m	m	m	m	m	m	m	m	m	m	m	m	m	m
United Kingdom[2]	2006	15	14	13	14	17	1	9	7	11	100	42	47	11	44	50	6
	1998	15	16	9	17	15	1	12	8	8	100	39	53	8	43	50	7
United States[4]	2006	15	21	a	13	28	1	10	12	a	100	36	64	a	39	61	a
	1998	15	15	3	14	26	4	2	17	4	100	33	63	4	37	59	4
OECD average	*2006*	*8.1*	*14.9*	*16.7*	*10.8*	*14.8*	*3.3*	*13.7*	*8.6*	*9.1*	*100*	*39.8*	*51.2*	*9.1*	*42.5*	*49.2*	*8.4*
OECD average	*1998*	*8.2*	*13.0*	*14.7*	*11.8*	*13.8*	*4.3*	*15.7*	*9.3*	*9.2*	*100*	*35.9*	*54.9*	*9.2*	*38.6*	*52.7*	*8.7*
Change 2006-1998		*0.0*	*1.9*	*2.1*	*-1.0*	*0.9*	*-0.9*	*-2.0*	*-0.7*	*-0.2*		*3.9*	*-3.8*	*-0.2*	*3.9*	*-3.6*	*-0.3*
Israel	2006	7	15	23	11	16	1	10	8	8	100	45	47	8	48	44	7
	1998	8	13	22	12	14	2	12	9	8	100	44	48	8	47	46	7
Slovenia	2006	7	15	17	8	12	7	11	16	7	100	39	55	7	41	52	6
	1998	6	10	13	12	12	10	11	21	5	100	29	66	5	32	63	5

Note: OECD averages are caclulated for countries with data for both years and all ISCO groups.
1. 1999 instead of 1998.
2. Italy: change in survey methodology between 1998 and 2006 affects comparability. United Kingdom: change in national occupation coding frame in 2000 affects comparability for ISCO.
3. 2000 instead of 1998.
4. ISCO groupings 3 and 9 in 2006 are not separated and thus distributed among remaining ISCO categories.
Source: OECD, Network B special data collection, Supply of Skills working group.
StatLink ⫘ http://dx.doi.org/10.1787/401474646362

Table A1.7.

Proportion of the working age population in different occupations by destination of tertiary education (2006)

Percentage of tertiary educated (ISCED 5B and 5A/6) in different occupations (ISCO)

		Legislators; senior officials; managers	Professionals	Technicians; associate professionals	Clerks	Service workers	Skilled agricultural and fishery workers	Craft and related trades workers	Plant and machine operators; assemblers	Elementary occupations	All occupations	Skilled occupations	Semi-skilled occupations	Unskilled occupations
		ISCO 1	ISCO 2	ISCO 3	ISCO 4	ISCO 5	ISCO 6	ISCO 7	ISCO 8	ISCO 9	Total (1-9)	ISCO 1-3	ISCO 4-8	ISCO 9
Australia	5B	16	26	23	11	12	2	5	2	2	100	65	33	2
	5A/6	16	56	12	6	5	1	2	1	1	100	84	15	1
Austria	5B	13	25	25	4	5	6	18	2	2	100	62	35	2
	5A/6	12	62	13	5	3	1	1	1	1	100	88	11	1
Belgium	5B	11	45	16	19	4	1	2	1	1	100	72	26	1
	5A/6	22	52	10	11	2	0	1	0	1	100	85	15	1
Canada	5B	9	17	22	17	14	2	8	6	5	100	48	47	5
	5A/6	14	47	17	7	6	1	2	3	2	100	79	19	2
Czech Republic	5B	5	30	50	8	3	0	2	1	1	100	86	13	1
	5A/6	16	54	25	2	2	0	1	1	0	100	95	5	0
Denmark	5B	4	9	48	13	11	2	6	4	4	100	61	35	4
	5A/6	6	49	37	4	3	0	0	1	1	100	91	7	1
Finland	5B	14	15	41	12	8	3	4	2	2	100	70	28	2
	5A/6	19	56	16	3	3	1	1	0	1	100	92	8	1
France	5B	10	12	48	14	7	2	4	2	1	100	70	29	1
	5A/6	16	54	16	6	3	1	1	1	1	100	86	12	1
Germany	5B	8	13	37	7	8	2	18	3	3	100	59	38	3
	5A/6	9	65	14	5	2	0	1	1	2	100	89	10	2
Hungary	5B	11	15	37	18	13	0	2	2	2	100	63	35	2
	5A/6	18	58	15	5	3	1	1	1	0	100	90	10	0
Iceland	5B	12	38	41	5	3	0	1	0	0	100	91	9	0
	5A/6	16	59	12	4	5	1	1	1	1	100	87	11	1
Ireland	5B	16	23	11	16	17	1	9	3	4	100	50	46	4
	5A/6	15	55	9	8	6	0	2	1	2	100	80	18	2
Italy	5B	6	47	27	5	5	0	5	2	3	100	80	17	3
	5A/6	8	51	28	7	3	0	1	1	1	100	86	12	1
Luxembourg	5B	6	67	23	3	1	0	0	0	0	100	95	4	0
	5A/6	11	76	10	1	0	0	0	0	0	100	98	2	0
Netherlands	5B	19	31	31	10	7	0	2	0	0	100	80	20	0
	5A/6	14	55	18	6	4	0	1	1	1	100	87	12	1
Norway	5B	m	m	m	m	m	m	m	m	m	m	m	m	m
	5A/6	10	30	44	3	8	1	2	1	1	100	84	15	1
Poland	5B	m	m	m	m	m	m	m	m	m	m	m	m	m
	5A/6	14	58	13	6	4	1	1	1	0	100	85	14	0
Portugal	5B	10	41	30	9	4	1	3	1	1	100	81	18	1
	5A/6	11	61	18	6	3	0	1	0	1	100	89	10	1
Slovakia	5B	11	25	44	8	5	0	3	3	2	100	79	19	2
	5A/6	16	52	24	3	3	0	1	0	1	100	92	7	1

OECD countries

1. ISCO groupings 3 and 9 in 2006 are not separated and thus distributed among remaining ISCO categories.

Source: OECD, Network B special data collection, Supply of Skills working group.

StatLink ⫘ http://dx.doi.org/10.1787/401474646362

A1

Table A1.7. (continued)

Proportion of the working age population in different occupations by destination of tertiary education (2006)

Percentage of tertiary educated (ISCED 5B and 5A/6) in different occupations (ISCO)

		Legislators; senior officials; managers	Professionals	Technicians; associate professionals	Clerks	Service workers	Skilled agricultural and fishery workers	Craft and related trades workers	Plant and machine operators; assemblers	Elementary occupations	All occupations	Skilled occupations	Semi-skilled occupations	Unskilled occupations
		ISCO 1	ISCO 2	ISCO 3	ISCO 4	ISCO 5	ISCO 6	ISCO 7	ISCO 8	ISCO 9	Total (1-9)	ISCO 1-3	ISCO 4-8	ISCO 9
Spain	5B	7	6	24	16	13	1	19	8	5	100	37	57	5
	5A/6	10	50	18	10	6	0	2	1	3	100	78	20	3
Sweden	5B	7	20	49	6	10	1	2	3	2	100	76	22	2
	5A/6	9	59	21	4	5	0	1	1	1	100	89	10	1
Switzerland	5B	12	29	27	7	7	4	11	2	1	100	68	31	1
	5A/6	12	56	21	4	4	0	2	1	1	100	89	10	1
Turkey	5B	m	m	m	m	m	m	m	m	m	m	m	m	m
	5A/6	15	43	16	12	6	2	3	1	1	100	75	24	1
United Kingdom	5B	20	14	29	11	13	1	6	2	3	100	63	33	3
	5A/6	21	45	18	8	5	0	1	1	1	100	83	16	1
United States[1]	5B	12	26	a	15	24	0	13	11	a	100	38	62	0
	5A/6	25	43	a	9	17	0	3	3	a	100	68	32	0
OECD average	*5B*	*11*	*27*	*32*	*10*	*9*	*1*	*6*	*3*	*2*	*100*	*69*	*29*	*2*
	5A/6	*14*	*53*	*19*	*6*	*5*	*1*	*2*	*1*	*1*	*100*	*85*	*14*	*1*
Israel	5B	7	6	39	11	13	1	11	7	6	100	51	43	6
	5A/6	11	41	28	7	6	0	2	2	2	100	80	18	2
Slovenia	5B	13	49	26	4	3	1	2	1	0	100	88	12	0
	5A/6	21	71	7	1	1	0	0	0	0	100	99	1	0

Partner countries (Israel, Slovenia rows)

1. ISCO groupings 3 and 9 in 2006 are not separated and thus distributed among remaining ISCO categories.

Source: OECD, Network B special data collection, Supply of Skills working group.

StatLink 📊 http://dx.doi.org/10.1787/401474646362

HOW MANY STUDENTS FINISH SECONDARY EDUCATION AND ACCESS TERTIARY EDUCATION?

This indicator shows the current upper secondary graduate output of education systems, *i.e.* the percentage of the typical population of upper secondary school age that follows and successfully completes upper secondary programmes. It also shows the percentage of the youth cohort that will enter different types of tertiary education during their lifetime. Finally, it sheds light on the distribution of new entrants at the tertiary level across fields of study as well as the relative share of females among new entrants.

Key results

Chart A2.1. **Upper secondary graduation rates (1995, 2006)**

The chart shows the number of students completing upper secondary education programmes for the first time in 1995 and 2006, as a percentage of the age group normally completing this level; it gives an indication of how many young adults complete upper secondary education compared to a decade earlier.

■ 2006 ▲ 1995

In the last eleven years, the proportion of students graduating from upper secondary programmes has progressed by seven percentage points on average in OECD countries with comparable data. In 22 of 24 OECD countries and all partner countries with comparable data, the ratio of upper secondary graduates to the population at the typical age of graduation exceeds 70%. In the Czech Republic, Finland, Germany, Greece, Iceland, Japan, Korea and Norway and in the partner countries Israel and Slovenia, graduation rates equal or exceed 90%.

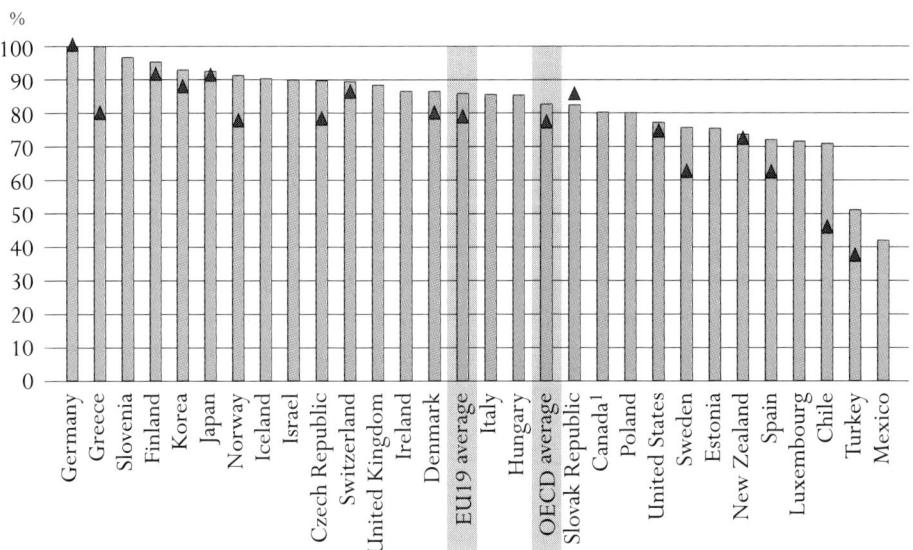

1. Year of reference 2005.
Countries are ranked in descending order of the upper secondary graduation rates in 2006.
Source: OECD. Table A2.2. See Annex 3 for notes (*www.oecd.org/edu/eag2008*).
StatLink ⊞⊒ http://dx.doi.org/10.1787/401482730488

Other highlights of this indicator

- Females are now more likely to complete upper secondary education than males in almost all OECD and partner countries, a reversal of the historical pattern. Today, graduation rates for females are below those for males only in Switzerland and Turkey.

- Most students obtain the upper secondary qualifications that give them access to tertiary-level study (ISCED 5A), although the extent to which students enter higher education varies significantly among countries.

- In some countries, a significant proportion of students broaden their knowledge at the post-secondary non-tertiary level after completing a first upper secondary programme. In the Czech Republic, 20% or more of a typical age cohort completes a post-secondary non-tertiary programme.

- Entry rates in tertiary-type A education increased substantially between 1995 and 2006, by 20 percentage points on average in OECD countries. Between 2000 and 2006, growth exceeded 10 percentage points in 11 of the 25 OECD countries for which data are available. In 2006, in Australia, Finland, Hungary, Iceland, New Zealand, Norway, Poland, the Slovak Republic and Sweden, and the partner country the Russian Federation, it is estimated that 65% and more of young adults will enter tertiary-type A programmes.

- The proportion of students who enter tertiary-type B programmes is generally smaller than for tertiary-type A programmes. In OECD countries for which data are available, 16% of young adults, on average, will enter tertiary-type B programmes, 56% will enter tertiary-type A and 2.8% will enter advanced research programmes.

- In Belgium, and to a lesser extent in the partner country Slovenia, wide access to tertiary-type B programmes counterbalances comparatively low rates of entry into tertiary-type A programmes. New Zealand stands out as a country with entry rates at both levels that are among the highest in OECD countries.

- In almost all countries, the majority of new entrants choose to follow tertiary programmes in the field of social sciences, business, law and services.

- Overall, females represent 54% of new entrants in tertiary education in OECD countries. However, the breakdown by gender varies considerably according to the field of education. Two fields are noteworthy for the strong representation of females, namely health and welfare and humanities, arts and education with 75% and 68%, respectively, of new entrants. The proportion of females choosing science (including life sciences, physical sciences, mathematics, computing, engineering, manufacturing, construction and agriculture) studies ranges from less than 25% in Japan, the Netherlands, Spain and Switzerland and the partner country Chile to more than 35% in Denmark, Iceland, Italy and New Zealand.

A2

Policy context

Rising skill demands in OECD countries have made qualifications at the upper secondary level the minimum credential for successful labour market entry. Upper secondary education serves as the foundation for advanced learning and training opportunities, as well as preparation for direct entry into the labour market. Although many countries allow students to leave the education system at the end of the lower secondary level, in OECD countries those who leave without an upper secondary qualification tend to face severe difficulties when entering the labour market (see Indicators A8 and A9).

High upper secondary graduation rates do not guarantee that an education system has adequately equipped its graduates with the basic skills and knowledge necessary to enter the labour market because they do not capture the quality of educational outcomes. However, graduation rates do give an indication of the extent to which education systems succeed in preparing students to meet the minimum requirements of the labour market.

Entry rate is an estimated probability that a school leaver will enter tertiary education during his/her lifetime. So, entry rate is an indication of the accessibility of tertiary education and the perceived value of attending tertiary programmes. It gives a partial indication of the degree to which a population is acquiring the high-level skills and knowledge valued by the labour market in today's knowledge society. High tertiary entry and participation rates help to ensure the development and maintenance of a highly educated population and labour force.

As students' awareness of the economic and social benefits of tertiary education has increased, so have rates of entry into both tertiary-type A and tertiary-type B programmes. Continued growth in participation, accompanied by a widening diversity in the backgrounds and interests of those aspiring to tertiary studies, will demand new kinds of provision. Tertiary institutions will be challenged not only to meet growing demand through expansion of places offered, but also to adapt programmes, teaching and learning to match the diverse needs of the new generation of students. Moreover, the relative popularity of the various fields of study affects the demand for courses and teaching staff.

Evidence and explanations

Graduation from upper secondary programmes

Graduation from upper secondary education is becoming the norm in most OECD countries. Since 1995, the upper secondary graduation rate has increased by seven percentage points on average among OECD countries with comparable data. The highest growth occurred in Greece, Norway, Sweden and Turkey and in the partner country Chile, while levels in Germany, Japan, New Zealand, the Slovak Republic and the United States have been stable over the last decade. In Mexico and Turkey, the proportion of students graduating at the upper secondary level has progressed strongly since 2000, narrowing the gap between these and other OECD countries (Table A2.2).

In 22 of 24 OECD countries and all partner countries with comparable data, upper secondary graduation rates exceed 70% (Chart A2.1). In the Czech Republic, Finland, Germany, Greece, Iceland, Japan, Korea and Norway and in the partner countries Israel and Slovenia, graduation rates equal or exceed 90%.

The balance of educational attainment between males and females in the adult population differs in most countries. In the past, females did not have sufficient opportunities and/or incentives to reach the same level of education as males. They have generally been overrepresented among those not continuing to upper secondary education and thus underrepresented at higher levels of education. However, these gender differences are most evident in older age groups and have been significantly reduced or reversed among younger age groups (see Indicator A1).

Today, upper secondary graduation rates for females exceed those for males in 22 of 24 OECD countries and in all the partner countries for which total upper secondary graduation rates can be compared by gender (Table A2.1). The exceptions are Switzerland and Turkey, where graduation rates are higher for males. The gap is greatest in Denmark, Iceland, Ireland, New Zealand, Norway and Spain and in the partner countries Estonia and Slovenia, where female graduation rates exceed those of males by more than 10 percentage points.

Although graduation from upper secondary education is becoming the norm, the upper secondary curriculum can vary depending on the type of education or occupation for which it is designed. Most upper secondary programmes in OECD and partner countries are designed primarily to prepare students for tertiary studies; their orientation may be general, pre-vocational or vocational (see Indicator C1).

In 2006, the female graduation rate from general programmes is greater than the corresponding value for males for almost all OECD and partner countries with comparable data. The OECD average graduation rate from general programmes is 53% for females and 41% for males. The higher proportion of females is especially noteworthy in Austria, the Czech Republic, Italy, Norway, Portugal and the Slovak Republic and in the partner countries Estonia and Slovenia, where they outnumber males by three to two. Only in Korea and Turkey do the proportions for both sexes approach equality (Table A2.1)

Females are also more often than in the past graduates of vocational programmes and represent an average of 44% among OECD countries. This pattern can affect the entry rates in tertiary-type B programmes in the following years (Table A2.1).

Transitions following upper secondary education

The vast majority of students who graduate from upper secondary education graduate from programmes designed to provide access to further tertiary education (ISCED 3A and 3B). Programmes to facilitate direct entry into tertiary-type A education are preferred by students in all countries except Austria, Germany and Switzerland and the partner country Slovenia, where both female and male students are more likely to graduate from upper secondary programmes leading to tertiary-type B programmes (Table A2.1).

The graduation rate for ISCED 3C (long programmes) is 20% on average in the OECD countries.

It is interesting, however, to contrast the proportion of students who graduate from programmes designed as preparation for entry into tertiary-type A programmes with the proportion who actually enter these programmes. Chart A2.2 shows this comparison and demonstrates significant variation among countries. For instance, in Belgium, Ireland, Italy,

A2

Japan and Turkey, and in the partner countries Chile, Estonia and Israel, the difference between graduation rates from upper secondary programmes designed for tertiary-type A programmes and the eventual entry rate to such programmes is relatively large (more than 20 percentage points). This suggests that many students who achieve qualifications designed for university level entrance do not in fact take up university studies; however, at least in Belgium and the partner countries Estonia and Israel, such upper secondary programmes also give access to tertiary-type B programmes. In Israel, the difference may be explained by the wide variation in the age of entry to university, which is due in part to the two to three years of military service students undertake before entering higher education.

Chart A2.2. **Access to tertiary-type A education for upper secondary graduates (2006)**

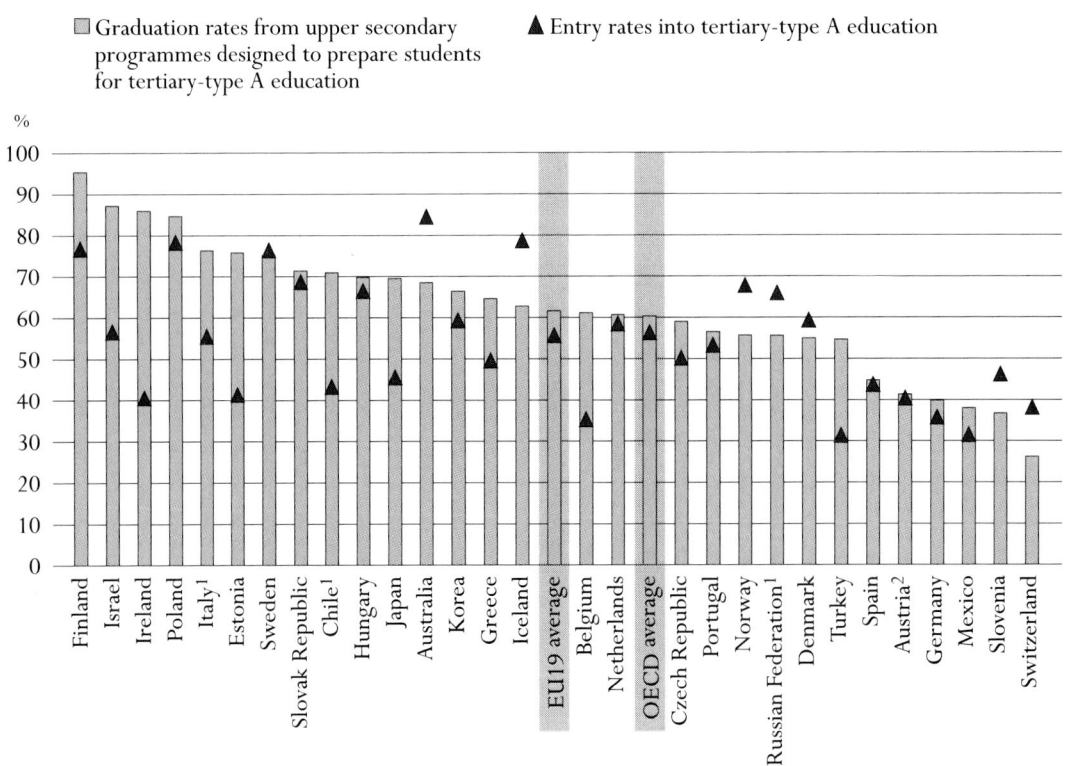

□ Graduation rates from upper secondary programmes designed to prepare students for tertiary-type A education   ▲ Entry rates into tertiary-type A education

1. Entry rate for tertiary-type A programmes is calculated as gross entry rate.
2. Includes ISCED 4A programmes ("Berufsbildende Höhere Schulen").
Countries are ranked in descending order of graduation rates from upper secondary programmes designed to prepare students for tertiary-type A education.
Source: OECD. Tables A2.1 and A2.4. See Annex 3 for notes (*www.oecd.org/edu/eag2008*).
StatLink ⌗⌐ http://dx.doi.org/10.1787/401482730488

In contrast, in Australia, Iceland, Norway and Switzerland and in the partner countries the Russian Federation and Slovenia, the upper secondary graduation rate is markedly lower than tertiary-type A entry rates. In Australia, Norway and Switzerland, this may be due to the high proportion of international/foreign students (see Indicator C3).

Graduation from post-secondary non-tertiary programmes

Post-secondary non-tertiary programmes of various kinds are offered in 26 OECD countries and 4 partner countries. From the point of view of international comparisons, these programmes straddle upper secondary and post-secondary education, but may be considered as either upper secondary or post-secondary programmes in a national context. Although the content of these programmes may not be significantly more advanced than upper secondary programmes, post-secondary non-tertiary programmes serve to broaden the knowledge of participants who have already gained an upper secondary qualification. These students tend to be older than those enrolled at the upper secondary level (Table A2.3).

Typical examples of such programmes are trade and vocational certificates, nursery teacher training in Austria and Switzerland, or vocational training in the dual system for holders of general upper secondary qualifications in Germany. In most countries, post-secondary non-tertiary programmes are vocationally oriented. In the Czech Republic, 20% or more of a typical age cohort complete a post-secondary non-tertiary programme.

In 13 of the 24 OECD countries for which data are available and 1 partner country, most, if not all, post-secondary non-tertiary students graduate from ISCED 4C programmes, which are designed primarily to prepare graduates for direct entry into the labour market. Although the gender difference is not apparent at the level of the OECD average, the proportion of males and females participating in such programmes in each country is very different. In Poland, twice as many females have completed an ISCED 4C programme as males, while the opposite is true in Ireland, where female graduates are seven times less numerous than males (Table A2.3).

Apprenticeships designed for students who have already graduated from an upper secondary programme are also included among post-secondary non-tertiary programmes. However, in 8 out of 24 OECD countries and 2 partner countries, 50% or more of post-secondary non-tertiary graduates have completed programmes designed to provide direct access to either tertiary-type A or B education. In Switzerland, more than two thirds of graduates complete ISCED 4B programmes (Table A2.3).

Overall access to tertiary education

Graduates from upper secondary programmes and those in the workforce who want to upgrade their skills can choose from a wide range of tertiary programmes. The higher the upper secondary graduation rates, the higher the expected entry rates in tertiary education. This indicator examines how students are oriented towards tertiary education and helps to understand the choices made by students at the end of upper secondary education. Furthermore, this orientation is extremely important and will affect dropout rates (see Indicator A4) but also unemployment rates (see Indicator A8) if the programmes proposed are not adjusted to labour market needs.

This indicator distinguishes among different categories of tertiary qualifications: programmes at tertiary-type B level (ISCED 5B); programmes at tertiary-type A level (ISCED 5A); and advanced research programmes at the doctorate level (ISCED 6). Tertiary-type A programmes are largely theory-based and designed to provide qualifications for entry into advanced research programmes and highly skilled professions. Tertiary-type B programmes are classified at the same level of competence as tertiary-type A programmes, but are more occupationally oriented

A2

and lead to direct labour market access. They tend to be of shorter duration than tertiary-type A programmes (typically two to three years) and are generally not designed to lead to university degrees. The institutional location of programmes can give a relatively clear idea of their nature (*e.g.* university or non-university institution of higher education), but these distinctions have become blurred and are therefore not applied in the OECD indicators.

Chart A2.3. **Entry rates into tertiary-type A education (1995, 2000 and 2006)**

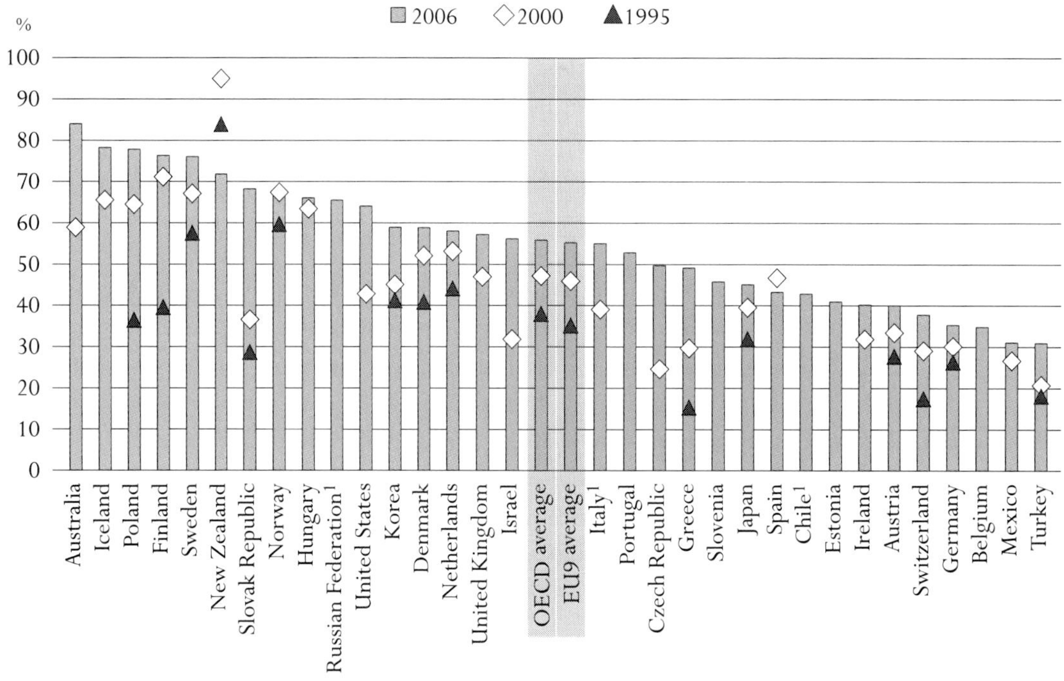

1. Entry rate for tertiary-type A programmes is calculated as gross entry rate in 2006.
Countries are ranked in descending order of entry rates for tertiary-type A education in 2006.
Source: OECD. Table A2.5. See Annex 3 for notes (*www.oecd.org/edu/eag2008*).
StatLink ⬛ᵐˢ⬛ http://dx.doi.org/10.1787/401482730488

It is estimated that 56% of young adults in OECD countries will enter tertiary-type A programmes during their lifetime, assuming that current patterns of entry continue. In Australia, Finland, Hungary, Iceland, New Zealand, Norway, Poland, the Slovak Republic and Sweden, as well as in the partner country the Russian Federation, 65% and more of young adults enter tertiary-type A programmes. The United States has an entry rate of 64%, but both type A and type B programmes are included in the figures for tertiary-type A (Table A2.4).

Although Turkey has had a large increase in the number of students entering tertiary-type A programmes, its entry rate is only 31% and it remains, with Mexico, at the bottom of the scale.

The proportion entering tertiary-type B programmes is generally smaller mainly because these programmes are less developed in most OECD countries. In OECD countries for which data are available, 16% of young adults, on average, enter tertiary-type B programmes. The OECD country average differs somewhat from the EU19 country average (13%). The figures range from 4%

or less in Iceland, Mexico, the Netherlands, Norway, Poland, Portugal and the Slovak Republic to 30% or more in Belgium, Greece and Japan, and in the partner countries Chile, Estonia, the Russian Federation and Slovenia, to more than 45% in Korea and New Zealand. The share of tertiary-type B programmes in the Netherlands is very small but will increase because of a new programme of "associate degrees". Finland no longer has tertiary-type B programmes in their education system (Table A2.4. and Chart A2.4).

In Belgium and to a lesser extent in the partner country Slovenia, broad access to tertiary-type B programmes counterbalances comparatively low entry rates into tertiary-type A programmes, while Iceland, Norway, Poland and Sweden have entry rates well above the OECD average for tertiary-type A programmes and comparatively very low rates for tertiary-type B programmes. New Zealand stands out, with entry rates at both levels that are among the highest in OECD countries.

Chart A2.4. **Entry rates into tertiary-type B education (1995, 2006)**

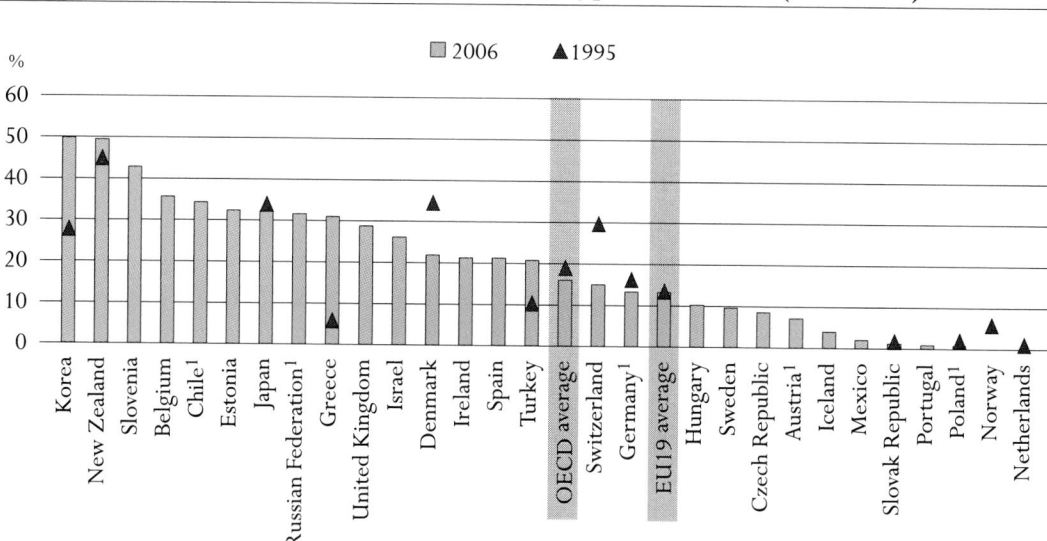

1. Entry rate for tertiary-type B programmes is calculated as gross entry rate in 2006.
Countries are ranked in descending order of entry rates for tertiary-type B education in 2006.
Source: OECD. Table A2.5. See Annex 3 for notes (*www.oecd.org/edu/eag2008*).

StatLink ⚓ http://dx.doi.org/10.1787/401482730488

On average, in all OECD countries with comparable data, 8 percentage points more of today's young adults enter tertiary-type A programmes than in 2000, and more than 20 percentage points more than in 1995. Entry rates in tertiary-type A education increased by more than 15 percentage points between 2000 and 2006 in Australia, the Czech Republic, Greece, Italy and the Slovak Republic and the partner country Israel. New Zealand and Spain are the only OECD countries that show a decrease in entry to tertiary-type A programmes, although in Spain, the decrease is counterbalanced by a significant increase in entry rates to tertiary-type B programmes between 2000 and 2006 (Table A2.5). In New Zealand, the rise and fall in entry rates over the 2000 to 2006 period mirrored the rise and fall in the number of international students over the same period.

A2

Among OECD countries, overall net entry rates to tertiary-type B programmes between 1995 and 2006 have been stable. They decreased slightly, except in Greece, Korea, New Zealand and Turkey, where they increased, and in Poland and the Slovak Republic where they remained stable. The reclassification of tertiary-type B to tertiary-type A programmes in Denmark after 2000 partly explains the changes observed between 1995 and 2006 (Table A2.5 and Charts A2.3 and A2.4).

More than 2.8% of today's young adults in the 20 OECD countries with comparable data will enter advanced research programmes during their lifetime. The figures range from less than 1% in Mexico and Turkey, and in the partner countries Chile and Slovenia, to 4% or more in Austria, Greece, Portugal, Spain and Switzerland (Table A2.4).

Rates of entry into tertiary education should also be considered in light of participation in post-secondary non-tertiary programmes, an important alternative to tertiary education in some OECD countries.

Pathways between tertiary-type A and tertiary-type B programmes

In some countries, tertiary-type A and B programmes are provided by different types of institutions but this is changing. It is increasingly common for universities or other institutions to offer programmes of both types; furthermore, the two levels are gradually growing more similar in terms of curriculum, orientation and learning outcomes.

Graduates from tertiary-type B programmes often have the opportunity to gain admission to tertiary-type A programmes, either in the second or third year of the programme or even to a master's programme. This path is often subject to conditions (special examination, personal or professional past achievements, completion of a "bridging" programme, etc.) depending on the country or programme. Conversely, students that leave tertiary-type A education without having graduated can in some cases be successfully re-oriented towards tertiary-type B programmes (see Indicator A4).

Countries with high entry rates may also be countries that have pathways between the two types of programmes. In Australia and New Zealand, 17 and 14%, respectively, of students who enter a tertiary-type A programme for the first time previously studied at the tertiary-type B level (Table A2.7 on line).

Age of new entrants into tertiary education

The age structure of entrants into tertiary education varies among OECD countries. The typical graduation age for upper secondary education may be different and/or upper secondary graduates may have entered the labour market before enrolling in tertiary education. People entering tertiary-type B programmes may also enter tertiary-type A programmes later in their lives. Adding together tertiary-type A and B entry rates to obtain overall tertiary-level entry rates would therefore result in overcounting.

Traditionally, students enter tertiary-type A programmes immediately after having completed upper secondary education, and this remains true in many OECD countries. For example, in Ireland, Japan, Korea, Mexico, the Netherlands, Poland and Spain and the partner country Slovenia, more than 80% of all first-time entrants into tertiary-type A programmes are under 23 years of age (Table A2.4).

In other OECD and partner countries, the transition to the tertiary level is often delayed, in certain cases by some time spent in the labour force. In these countries, first-time entrants into tertiary-type A programmes are typically older and show a much wider age range at entry. In Denmark, Iceland and Sweden and the partner country Israel, more than half of the students enter this level for the first time at the age of 22 or older (Table A2.4). The proportion of older first-time entrants to tertiary-type A programmes may reflect, among other factors, the flexibility of these programmes and their suitability to students outside the typical age cohort. It may also reflect a view of the value of work experience for higher education studies, which is characteristic of the Nordic countries and common in Australia, the Czech Republic, Hungary, New Zealand and Switzerland, where a sizeable proportion of new entrants is much older than the typical age of entry. It may also reflect some countries' mandatory military service, which would postpone entry into tertiary education. For example, the partner country Israel has mandatory military service from ages 18 to 21 for males and 18 to 20 for females. In Australia, Denmark, Finland, Hungary, Iceland, New Zealand, Norway, Portugal, Sweden and Switzerland, more than 20% of first-time entrants are aged 27 or older.

Entry rate by field of education

In almost all countries, the majority of students choose to follow tertiary programmes in the field of social sciences, business, law and services. This field accounts for over one-third of new entrants except in the Czech Republic, Finland, Germany, Korea, the Slovak Republic, Sweden and the United Kingdom. In Germany and the United Kingdom, the proportion of new entrants is highest in the field of humanities, art and education.

In OECD countries, an average of just over a quarter of all students are new entrants in the science field, which includes life sciences, physical sciences and agriculture, mathematics and computer science, engineering, manufacturing and construction. This proportion ranges from under 20% in Iceland, the Netherlands and Norway to 30% and more in Finland, Germany, Korea, Mexico, the Slovak Republic and Sweden and the partner countries Israel and the Russian Federation (Table A2.6).

The distribution of advanced research programmes by field of education is very different from that observed in tertiary education at a whole. Most students undertake studies in the field of sciences. Only Norway and Portugal have less than 30% of students in these fields, with 21 and 28%, respectively, of new entrants (Table A2.6b on line).

Overall, females represent 54% of the population of new entrants in tertiary education for OECD countries. However, the breakdown by gender varies considerably with the field of education. Women predominate among new entrants in health and welfare and humanities, arts and education where they represent 75 and 68%, respectively, of new entrants. In all countries for which data are available, females far outnumber males in those fields. Although females are in the majority in social sciences, business and law, they are less strongly represented, except in the Czech Republic, Finland, Hungary and the Slovak Republic and in the partner countries Estonia and Slovenia where they account for more than 60% of new entrants.

Sciences (including life sciences, physical sciences, mathematics, computing, engineering, manufacturing, construction and agriculture) attract a smaller proportion of females. The

A2

proportion of females choosing science studies ranges from less than 25% in Japan, the Netherlands and Switzerland and the partner country Chile to more than 35% in Denmark, Iceland, Italy and New Zealand (Chart A2.5). An increase in the proportion of females entering science fields could help alleviate shortages in the labour market in these fields (see Indicator A1).

The situation in the broad field of sciences differs to that in the other fields of education. Over 77% on average of those entering the field of engineering, manufacturing and construction for the first time are males. This proportion exceeds 85% in Ireland, Japan, the Netherlands and Switzerland. The proportion of females in this field, although a minority, is highest in Denmark and Iceland at over 30%. Males also account for 76% of new entrants in mathematics and computer science. The proportion of females in this field exceeds 30% only in Denmark, Finland, Germany, Ireland, Mexico, New Zealand and Turkey. Compared to the other fields included in sciences, females are better represented in life sciences, physical sciences and agriculture where they represent 50% of the new entrants.

Chart A2.5. Proportion of females in new entrants at the tertiary level, by field of education (2006)

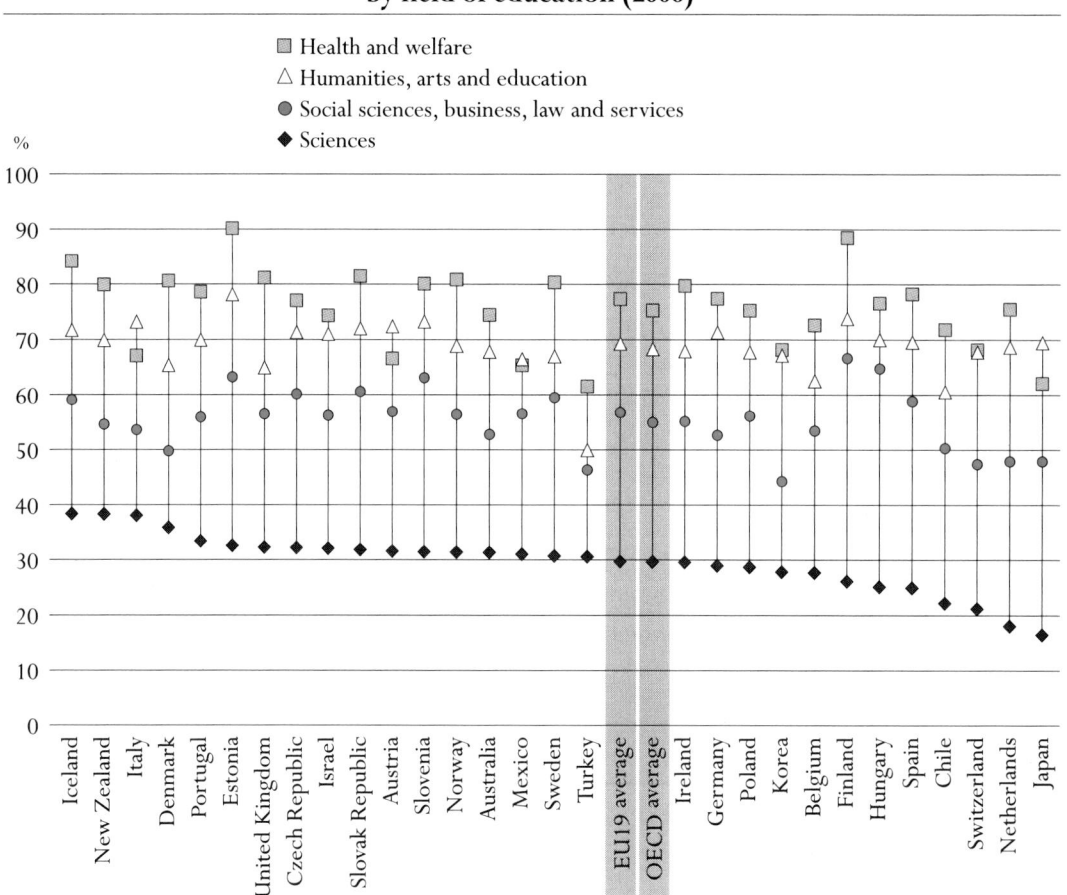

Note: Sciences include life sciences, physical sciences, mathematics, computing, engineering, manufacturing, construction and agriculture.
Countries are ranked in descending order of the proportion of females in sciences.
Source: OECD. Table A2.6. See Annex 3 for notes (*www.oecd.org/edu/eag2008*).
StatLink ⟶ http://dx.doi.org/10.1787/401482730488

Definitions and methodologies

Data refer to the academic year 2005/06 and are based on the UOE data collection on education statistics administered by the OECD in 2007 (for details see Annex 3 at *www.oecd.org/edu/eag2008*).

In Table A2.1, upper secondary graduates are those who successfully complete the final year of upper secondary education, regardless of age. In some countries, successful completion requires a final examination, and in others it does not (see Annex 1).

Upper secondary graduation rates are estimated as the number of students, regardless of age, who graduate for the first time from upper secondary programmes, divided by the population at the age at which students typically graduate from upper secondary education (see Annex 1). The graduation rates take into account students graduating from upper secondary education at the typical (modal) graduation ages, as well as older students (*e.g.* those in "second chance" programmes) or younger students. The unduplicated total count of graduates is calculated by netting out students who graduated from another upper secondary programme in a previous year.

Counts of graduates for ISCED 3A, 3B and 3C programmes are not unduplicated. Therefore, gross graduation rates cannot be added, as some individuals graduate from more than one upper secondary programme and would be counted twice. The same applies for graduation rates by programme orientation, *i.e.* general or vocational. Moreover, the typical graduation ages are not necessarily the same for the different programme types. Pre-vocational and vocational programmes include both school-based programmes and combined school- and work-based programmes that are recognised as part of the education system. Entirely work-based education and training that is not overseen by a formal education authority is not taken into account.

In Table A2.2, data on trends in graduation rates at upper secondary level for the years 1995, 2000, 2001, 2002, 2003 and 2004 are based on a special survey carried out in OECD countries and four of the six partner countries in January 2007.

In Table A2.3, post-secondary non-tertiary graduates are those who successfully complete the final year of post-secondary non-tertiary education, regardless of age. In some countries, successful completion requires a final examination, and in others it does not.

Post-secondary non-tertiary graduation rates are estimated as the number of students, regardless of age, who graduate for the first time from post-secondary non-tertiary programmes, divided by the population at the age at which students typically graduate from these programmes (see Annex 1). The graduation rates take into account students graduating at the typical (modal) graduation ages, as well as older or younger students. The unduplicated total count of graduates is calculated by netting out students who graduated from another post-secondary non-tertiary programme in a previous year.

For some countries, an unduplicated count of post-secondary non-tertiary graduates is unavailable and graduation rates may be overestimated because of graduates who have completed multiple programmes at the same level. Counts of graduates for ISCED 4A, 4B and 4C programmes are not unduplicated. Gross graduation rates cannot be added, as some individuals graduate from more than one post-secondary non-tertiary programme and would thus be counted twice. Moreover, the typical graduation ages are not necessarily the same for the different programme types.

Table A2.4 and Table A2.5 show the sum of net entry rates for all ages. The net entry rate for a specific age is obtained by dividing the number of first-time entrants of that age to each type of tertiary education by the total population in the corresponding age group. The sum of net entry rates is calculated by adding the rates for each year of age. The result represents an estimate of the probability that a young person will enter tertiary education in his/her lifetime assuming current age-specific entry rates continue. Table A2.4 also shows the 20th, 50th and 80th percentiles of the age distribution of first-time entrants, *i.e.* the age below which 20, 50 and 80% of first-time entrants are found.

New (first-time) entrants are students who enrol at the relevant level of education for the first time. Foreign students enrolling for the first time in a post-graduate programme are considered first-time entrants.

Not all OECD countries can distinguish between students entering a tertiary programme for the first time and those transferring between different levels of tertiary education or repeating or re-entering a level after an absence. Thus first-time entry rates for each level of tertiary education cannot be added to form a total tertiary-level entrance rate because it would result in counting entrants twice.

In Table A2.5, data on trends in entry rates for the years 1995, 2000, 2001, 2002, 2003 and 2004 are based on a special survey carried out in OECD countries and four of the six partner countries in January 2007.

In Table A2.6, new entrants to tertiary education are classified by fields of education based on their subject of specialisation. These figures cover new entrants to all tertiary degrees reported in Table A2.4. The 25 fields of education used in the UOE data collection instruments follow the revised ISCED classification by field of education. The same classification by field of education is used for all levels of education.

Further references

The following additional material relevant to this indicator is available on line at:
StatLink ᎒᎒᎓ http://dx.doi.org/10.1787/401482730488

- *Table A2.6a. Percentage of new entrants in tertiary-type A, by field of education (2006)*

- *Table A2.6b. Percentage of new entrants in advanced research programmes, by field of education (2006)*

- *Table A2.6c. Percentage of new entrants in tertiary-type B, by field of education (2006)*

- *Table A2.7. Pathways between tertiary-type A and tertiary-type B programmes (2006)*

Table A2.1.
Upper secondary graduation rates (2006)
Percentage of upper secondary graduates in the population at the typical age of graduation, by programme destination, programme orientation and gender

	Total (unduplicated)			ISCED 3A (designed to prepare for direct entry to tertiary-type A education)		ISCED 3B (designed to prepare for direct entry to tertiary-type B education)		ISCED 3C (long) similar to duration of typical 3A or 3B programmes		ISCED 3C (short) shorter than duration of typical 3A or 3B programmes		General programmes		Pre-vocational/vocational programmes	
	M + F	Males	Females	M + F	Females	M + F	Females	M + F	Females	M + F	Females	M + F	Females	M + F	Females
	(1)	(2)	(3)	(4)	(5)	(6)	(7)	(8)	(9)	(10)	(11)	(12)	(13)	(14)	(15)
Australia	m	m	m	68	74	x(8)	x(9)	41	45	x(8)	x(9)	68	74	41	45
Austria	m	m	m	17	20	50	38	m	m	m	m	17	20	50	38
Belgium	m	m	m	61	67	a	a	20	18	14	17	37	43	58	60
Canada[1]	80	77	84	77	82	a	a	8	7	a	a	77	82	8	7
Czech Republic	90	88	92	59	69	n	n	30	22	a	a	18	23	72	69
Denmark	86	78	96	55	66	a	a	50	56	n	n	55	66	51	56
Finland	95	91	100	95	100	a	a	a	a	a	a	51	61	88	97
France[1]	m	m	m	51	59	14	13	48	47	a	a	51	59	63	60
Germany	103	102	104	40	45	62	59	a	a	1	1	40	45	63	59
Greece	100	96	104	65	73	a	a	36	31	x(8)	x(9)	63	72	35	30
Hungary	85	81	90	70	77	a	a	18	14	x(8)	x(9)	70	77	18	14
Iceland	90	81	100	63	73	1	2	37	30	17	23	66	76	55	54
Ireland	86	81	93	86	92	a	a	5	5	25	37	63	65	53	69
Italy	86	84	88	76	81	2	3	a	a	21	19	31	41	69	62
Japan	93	92	93	70	73	1	n	22	20	x(8)	x(9)	70	73	23	21
Korea	93	92	94	66	67	a	a	27	27	a	a	66	67	27	27
Luxembourg	72	69	74	41	49	9	7	20	17	2	2	28	33	44	41
Mexico	42	38	46	38	42	a	a	4	4	a	a	38	42	4	4
Netherlands	m	m	m	61	67	a	a	18	20	22	18	36	39	66	67
New Zealand	74	63	85	x(1)	x(3)	x(1)	x(3)	x(1)	x(3)	x(1)	x(3)	x(1)	x(3)	x(1)	x(3)
Norway	91	80	103	56	68	a	a	42	40	m	m	56	68	42	40
Poland	80	76	84	85	90	a	a	13	8	a	a	59	70	36	26
Portugal	m	m	m	57	67	x(4)	x(5)	x(4)	x(5)	x(4)	x(5)	40	50	13	13
Slovak Republic	82	80	85	71	77	a	a	20	15	1	1	23	28	69	65
Spain	72	64	80	45	53	a	a	18	19	17	19	45	53	35	38
Sweden	76	73	79	75	79	x(4)	x(5)	n	n	m	m	34	40	42	39
Switzerland	89	90	89	26	28	62	55	10	13	m	m	30	34	69	62
Turkey	51	55	47	55	51	a	a	n	n	m	m	35	35	19	16
United Kingdom	88	85	92	m	m	m	m	m	m	m	m	m	m	m	m
United States	77	75	79	m	m	m	m	m	m	m	m	m	m	m	m
OECD average	*83*	*79*	*87*	*60*	*66*	*8*	*7*	*20*	*18*	*7*	*8*	*47*	*53*	*45*	*44*
EU19 average	*86*	*82*	*90*	*62*	*68*	*9*	*7*	*19*	*17*	*8*	*9*	*42*	*49*	*51*	*50*
Brazil[1]	m	m	m	62	72	8	10	a	a	a	a	62	72	8	10
Chile	71	67	75	71	75	a	a	a	a	a	a	39	43	32	33
Estonia	75	68	83	76	84	a	a	a	a	n	n	58	72	18	12
Israel	90	88	92	87	91	a	a	3	1	a	a	58	63	32	29
Russian Federation	m	m	m	56	x(4)	13	x(6)	20	11	4	2	56	x(12)	36	x(14)
Slovenia	97	89	105	37	45	47	51	n	n	30	26	34	43	79	79

Note: Mismatches between the coverage of the population data and the student/graduate data mean that the participation/graduation rates for those countries that are net exporters of students may be underestimated (for instance Luxembourg) and those countries that are net importers may be overestimated.
1. Year of reference 2005.
Source: OECD. See Annex 3 for notes (*www.oecd.org/edu/eag2008*).
Please refer to the Reader's Guide for information concerning the symbols replacing missing data.
StatLink ᴬᴵˢᴸ http://dx.doi.org/10.1787/401482730488

A2

Table A2.2.
Trends in graduation rates at upper secondary level (1995-2006)
*Percentage of upper secondary graduates (first-time graduation) to the population at the typical age of graduation
(1995, 2000, 2001, 2002, 2003, 2004, 2005, 2006)*

	Typical age in 2006[1]	1995	2000	2001	2002	2003	2004	2005	2006
	(1)	(2)	(3)	(4)	(5)	(6)	(7)	(8)	(9)
Australia	17	m	m	m	m	m	m	m	m
Austria	17-18	m	m	m	m	m	m	m	m
Belgium	18	m	m	m	m	m	m	m	m
Canada	17-18	m	m	m	m	m	m	80	m
Czech Republic	18-19	78	m	84	83	88	87	89	90
Denmark	19	80	90	91	93	87	90	86	86
Finland	19	91	91	85	84	90	95	94	95
France	17-20	m	m	m	m	m	m	m	m
Germany	19-20	101	92	92	94	97	99	100	103
Greece	18	80	54	76	85	96	93	102	100
Hungary	19	m	m	m	m	m	m	84	85
Iceland	20	m	67	67	79	79	84	80	90
Ireland	18-19	m	74	77	78	91	92	91	86
Italy	19	m	78	81	78	m	82	82	86
Japan	18	91	94	93	92	91	91	93	93
Korea	17	88	96	100	99	92	94	93	93
Luxembourg	18-19	m	m	m	69	71	69	76	72
Mexico	18	m	33	34	35	37	39	40	42
Netherlands	17-20	m	m	m	m	m	m	m	m
New Zealand	17-18	72	80	79	77	78	75	72	74
Norway	18-20	77	99	105	97	92	100	93	91
Poland	19-20	m	90	93	91	86	79	86	80
Portugal	17-18	67	52	48	50	59	53	m	m
Slovak Republic	19-20	85	87	72	60	56	83	84	82
Spain	17	62	60	66	66	67	66	72	72
Sweden	19	62	75	71	72	76	78	78	76
Switzerland	18-20	86	88	91	92	89	87	89	89
Turkey	16	37	37	37	37	41	55	48	51
United Kingdom	16	m	m	m	m	m	m	86	88
United States	18	74	74	70	72	75	74	76	77
OECD average		*77*	*76*	*77*	*77*	*78*	*80*	*82*	*83*
OECD average for countries with 1995 and 2006 data		*78*							*85*
EU19 average		*78*	*77*	*78*	*77*	*80*	*82*	*86*	*86*
Brazil	18	m	m	m	m	m	m	m	m
Chile	18	46	63	m	61	64	66	73	71
Estonia	19	m	m	m	m	m	m	m	75
Israel	17	m	m	m	90	89	93	89	90
Russian Federation	17	m	m	m	m	m	m	m	m
Slovenia	18-19	m	m	m	m	m	m	95	97

OECD countries / *Partner countries*

1. The typical age corresponds to the most common age at the end of the last school/academic year of the corresponding level and the programme in which the degree is obtained. It may change slightly over the year.
Source: OECD. See Annex 3 for notes (*www.oecd.org/edu/eag2008*).
Please refer to the Reader's Guide for information concerning the symbols replacing missing data.
StatLink ⟐⟐⟐ http://dx.doi.org/10.1787/401482730488

Table A2.3.
Post-secondary non-tertiary graduation rates (2006)
Percentage of post-secondary non-tertiary graduates in the population at the typical age of graduation, by programme destination and gender

A2

	Total (unduplicated)			ISCED 4A (designed to prepare for direct entry to tertiary-type A education)		ISCED 4B (designed to prepare for direct entry to tertiary-type B education)		ISCED 4C	
	M + F	Males	Females	M + F	Females	M + F	Females	M + F	Females
	(1)	(2)	(3)	(4)	(5)	(6)	(7)	(8)	(9)
OECD countries									
Australia	m	m	m	a	a	a	a	21.7	25.8
Austria	m	m	m	24.8	28.2	3.3	5.6	1.7	2.9
Belgium	m	m	m	7.3	7.2	3.1	3.4	10.0	11.4
Canada[1]	m	m	m	m	m	a	a	4.6	1.0
Czech Republic	22.0	20.7	23.4	21.8	23.3	a	a	0.2	0.1
Denmark	1.1	1.5	0.8	1.1	0.8	a	a	a	a
Finland	3.1	3.2	3.1	a	a	a	a	7.1	7.7
France[1]	m	m	m	0.7	0.9	a	a	0.7	0.8
Germany	14.9	16.1	13.7	11.1	10.4	3.8	3.3	a	a
Greece	13.3	12.0	14.6	a	a	a	a	13.4	14.8
Hungary	18.6	16.4	20.8	a	a	a	a	23.4	26.1
Iceland	8.3	8.4	8.1	n	n	n	n	8.5	8.4
Ireland	11.3	19.6	2.8	a	a	a	a	11.3	2.8
Italy	6.6	5.0	8.2	a	a	a	a	6.6	8.2
Japan	m	m	m	m	m	m	m	m	m
Korea	a	a	a	a	a	a	a	a	a
Luxembourg	2.6	4.2	0.9	a	a	a	a	2.9	1.4
Mexico	a	a	a	a	a	a	a	a	a
Netherlands	m	m	m	a	a	a	a	1.4	1.0
New Zealand	19.4	13.6	25.6	x(1)	x(3)	x(1)	x(3)	x(1)	x(3)
Norway	7.4	8.4	6.3	1.1	0.4	a	a	6.5	6.1
Poland	14.5	11.6	17.6	a	a	a	a	14.5	17.6
Portugal	m	m	m	m	m	m	m	m	m
Slovak Republic	3.1	3.8	2.5	3.1	2.5	a	a	a	a
Spain	a	a	a	a	a	a	a	a	a
Sweden	1.6	1.5	1.7	n	n	n	n	1.6	1.8
Switzerland	14.5	10.0	19.0	5.1	4.6	10.3	15.6	a	a
Turkey	a	a	a	a	a	a	a	a	a
United Kingdom	m	m	m	m	m	m	m	m	m
United States	m	m	m	m	m	m	m	m	m
OECD average	*8.1*	*7.8*	*8.5*	*3.2*	*3.3*	*0.9*	*1.2*	*5.5*	*5.5*
EU19 average	*8.7*	*8.9*	*8.5*	*4.1*	*4.3*	*0.6*	*0.7*	*5.6*	*5.7*
Partner countries									
Brazil	a	a	a	a	a	a	a	a	a
Chile	a	a	a	a	a	a	a	a	a
Estonia	16.1	10.8	21.5	a	a	16.3	21.7	a	a
Israel	m	m	m	m	m	a	a	a	a
Russian Federation	m	m	m	a	a	a	a	5.7	5.6
Slovenia	4.0	3.1	4.9	1.9	2.7	2.1	2.2	n	n

Note: Mismatches between the coverage of the population data and the student/graduate data mean that the participation/graduation rates for those countries that are net exporters of students may be underestimated (for instance, Luxembourg) and those that are net importers may be overestimated.

1. Year of reference 2005.

Source: OECD. See Annex 3 for notes (*www.oecd.org/edu/eag2008*).

Please refer to the Reader's Guide for information concerning the symbols replacing missing data.

StatLink ⫘⊫ http://dx.doi.org/10.1787/401482730488

Table A2.4.
Entry rates to tertiary education and age distribution of new entrants (2006)
Sum of net entry rates for each year of age, by gender and mode of participation

	Tertiary-type B			Tertiary-type A						Advanced research programmes		
	Net entry rates			Net entry rates			Age at:			Net entry rates		
	M+F	Males	Females	M+F	Males	Females	20th percentile[1]	50th percentile[1]	80th percentile[1]	M+F	Males	Females
	(1)	(2)	(3)	(4)	(5)	(6)	(7)	(8)	(9)	(10)	(11)	(12)
Australia	m	m	m	84	74	94	18.7	20.9	27.1	2.9	2.8	3.0
Austria[2]	7	6	8	40	36	44	19.4	20.8	23.7	5.6	5.8	5.5
Belgium	36	34	38	35	32	38	18.4	19.1	23.2	m	m	m
Canada	m	m	m	m	m	m	m	m	m	m	m	m
Czech Republic	9	5	12	50	45	55	19.6	20.5	24.1	3.1	3.5	2.6
Denmark	22	23	21	59	47	71	20.8	22.6	27.9	2.1	2.2	2.0
Finland	a	a	a	76	65	88	19.8	21.6	27.8	m	m	m
France	m	m	m	m	m	m	m	m	m	m	m	m
Germany[2]	13	11	16	35	36	35	19.9	21.2	24.0	m	m	m
Greece	31	29	33	49	38	61	18.2	18.9	25.9	4.6	5.3	3.9
Hungary	10	7	14	66	60	72	19.3	21.0	28.0	1.7	1.8	1.7
Iceland	4	5	3	78	60	97	20.9	23.2	<40	1.4	1.2	1.6
Ireland	21	19	23	40	36	44	18.3	19.1	20.6	m	m	m
Italy[3]	m	m	m	55	47	63	19.2	19.8	23.5	2.2	2.1	2.2
Japan	32	25	40	45	52	38	18.3	18.6	19.2	1.1	1.5	0.6
Korea	50	47	53	59	62	56	18.3	18.8	20.0	2.0	2.5	1.4
Luxembourg	m	m	m	m	m	m	m	m	m	m	m	m
Mexico	2	2	2	31	31	31	18.4	19.5	22.7	0.2	0.2	0.2
Netherlands	n	n	n	58	54	62	18.4	19.7	22.6	m	m	m
New Zealand	49	42	57	72	59	85	18.6	20.8	<40	2.4	2.4	2.3
Norway	n	n	1	67	53	82	18.8	20.1	29.5	2.5	2.7	2.3
Poland[2]	1	n	1	78	72	84	19.5	20.3	22.6	m	m	m
Portugal	1	1	1	53	43	63	18.6	20.1	27.5	7.2	5.9	8.6
Slovak Republic	1	1	2	68	56	80	19.5	20.7	26.5	3.1	3.3	3.0
Spain	21	20	23	43	36	51	18.4	19.0	22.8	4.2	4.0	4.5
Sweden	10	10	10	76	65	87	20.1	22.4	29.6	2.5	2.5	2.4
Switzerland	15	18	12	38	38	38	20.0	21.7	27.4	4.5	5.1	3.8
Turkey	21	23	18	31	34	28	18.5	19.8	23.3	0.7	0.8	0.5
United Kingdom	29	20	38	57	50	65	18.5	19.6	25.4	2.3	2.5	2.1
United States	x(4)	x(5)	x(6)	64	56	72	18.4	19.5	24.9	m	m	m
OECD average	*16*	*14*	*18*	*56*	*50*	*62*				*2.8*	*2.9*	*2.7*
EU19 average	*13*	*12*	*15*	*55*	*48*	*63*				*3.5*	*3.5*	*3.5*
Brazil	m	m	m	m	m	m	m	m	m	m	m	m
Chile[2,3]	34	38	31	43	41	45	m	m	m	0.2	0.2	0.2
Estonia	32	23	41	41	32	50	19.1	19.8	23.2	2.3	2.2	2.5
Israel	26	24	28	56	52	61	21.3	23.7	26.9	2.2	2.1	2.4
Russian Federation[2,3]	32	x(1)	x(1)	65	x(4)	x(4)	m	m	m	1.9	x(10)	x(10)
Slovenia	43	42	44	46	34	58	19.2	19.7	20.8	0.4	0.4	0.3

Note: Mismatches between the coverage of the population data and the student/graduate data mean that the participation/graduation rates for those countries that are net exporters of students may be underestimated (for instance, Luxembourg) and those that are net importers may be overestimated.

1. Respectively 20, 50 and 80% of new entrants are below this age.
2. Entry rate for tertiary-type B programmes calculated as gross entry rate.
3. Entry rate for tertiary-type A programmes calculated as gross entry rate.
Source: OECD. See Annex 3 for notes (*www.oecd.org/edu/eag2008*).
Please refer to the Reader's Guide for information concerning the symbols replacing missing data.
StatLink ᕯᕚᕻ http://dx.doi.org/10.1787/401482730488

Table A2.5.
Trends in entry rates at tertiary level (1995-2006)
Sum of net entry rates for each year of age (1995, 2000, 2001, 2002, 2003, 2004, 2005, 2006)

A2

	Tertiary-type A[1]								Tertiary-type B							
	1995	2000	2001	2002	2003	2004	2005	2006	1995	2000	2001	2002	2003	2004	2005	2006
	(1)	(2)	(3)	(4)	(5)	(6)	(7)	(8)	(9)	(10)	(11)	(12)	(13)	(14)	(15)	(16)
Australia	m	59	65	77	68	70	82	84	m	m	m	m	m	m	m	m
Austria[2]	27	34	34	31	34	37	37	40	m	m	m	m	8	9	9	7
Belgium	m	m	32	33	33	34	33	35	m	m	36	34	33	35	34	36
Canada	m	m	m	m	m	m	m	m	m	m	m	m	m	m	m	m
Czech Republic	m	25	30	30	33	38	41	50	m	9	7	8	9	10	8	9
Denmark	40	52	54	53	57	55	57	59	33	28	30	25	22	21	23	22
Finland	39	71	72	71	73	73	73	76	32	a	a	a	a	a	a	a
France	m	m	m	m	m	m	m	m	m	m	m	m	m	m	m	m
Germany[2]	26	30	32	35	36	37	36	35	15	15	15	16	16	15	14	13
Greece	15	30	30	33	35	35	43	49	5	21	20	21	22	24	m	31
Hungary	m	64	56	62	69	68	68	66	m	1	3	4	7	9	11	10
Iceland	m	66	61	72	83	79	74	78	m	10	10	11	9	8	7	4
Ireland	m	32	39	39	41	44	45	40	m	26	19	18	17	17	14	21
Italy[2,3]	m	39	44	50	54	55	56	55	m	1	1	1	1	1	a	m
Japan	31	40	41	42	43	42	44	45	33	32	31	30	31	32	32	32
Korea	41	45	46	46	47	49	51	59	27	51	52	51	47	47	48	50
Luxembourg	m	m	m	m	m	m	m	m	m	m	m	m	m	m	m	m
Mexico	m	27	27	35	29	30	30	31	m	1	2	2	2	2	2	2
Netherlands	44	53	54	54	52	56	59	58	n	n	n	n	n	n	n	n
New Zealand	83	95	95	101	107	86	79	72	44	52	50	56	58	50	48	49
Norway	59	67	69	75	75	72	76	67	5	5	4	3	1	1	n	n
Poland[2]	36	65	68	71	70	71	76	78	1	1	1	1	1	1	1	1
Portugal	m	m	m	m	m	m	m	53	m	m	m	m	m	m	m	1
Slovak Republic	28	37	40	43	40	47	59	68	1	3	3	3	3	2	2	1
Spain	m	47	47	49	46	44	43	43	m	15	19	19	21	22	22	21
Sweden	57	67	69	75	80	79	76	76	m	7	6	6	7	8	7	10
Switzerland	17	29	33	35	38	38	37	38	29	14	13	14	17	17	16	15
Turkey	18	21	20	23	23	26	27	31	9	9	10	12	24	16	19	21
United Kingdom	m	47	46	48	48	52	51	57	m	29	30	27	30	28	28	29
United States	m	43	42	64	63	63	64	64	m	14	13	x(4)	x(5)	x(6)	x(7)	x(8)
OECD average	*37*	*47*	*48*	*52*	*53*	*53*	*55*	*56*	*18*	*15*	*16*	*16*	*16*	*15*	*15*	*16*
OECD average for countries with 1995, 2000 and 2006 data	*37*	*49*						*57*	*18*	*18*						*18*
EU19 average	*35*	*46*	*47*	*49*	*50*	*52*	*53*	*55*	*12*	*11*	*13*	*12*	*12*	*12*	*11*	*13*
Brazil	m	m	m	m	m	m	m	m	m	m	m	m	m	m	m	m
Chile[2,3]	m	m	32	33	33	34	48	43	m	m	36	34	33	35	37	34
Estonia	m	m	m	m	m	m	55	41	m	m	m	m	m	m	34	32
Israel	m	32	39	39	41	44	55	56	m	26	19	m	17	m	25	26
Russian Federation[2,3]	m	m	m	m	m	m	67	65	m	m	m	m	m	m	33	32
Slovenia	m	m	m	m	m	m	40	46	m	m	m	m	m	m	49	43

1. Entry rate for tertiary-type A programmes includes advanced research programmes for 1995, 2000, 2001, 2002, 2003.
2. Entry rate for tertiary-type B programmes calculated as gross entry rate in 2006.
3. Entry rate for tertiary-type A programmes calculated as gross entry rate in 2006.
Source: OECD. See Annex 3 for notes (*www.oecd.org/edu/eag2008*).
Please refer to the Reader's Guide for information concerning the symbols replacing missing data.
StatLink ⫘⫘ http://dx.doi.org/10.1787/401482730488

A2

Table A2.6.
Percentage of new entrants in tertiary education and proportion of females, by field of education (2006)

	All fields of study	Health and welfare		Life sciences, physical sciences & agriculture		Mathematics and computer science		Humanities, arts and education		Social sciences, business, law and services		Engineering, manufacturing and construction		Not known or unspecified
	% of females	% of new entrants	% of females	% of new entrants	% of females	% of new entrants	% of females	% of new entrants	% of females	% of new entrants	% of females	% of new entrants	% of females	% of new entrants
	(1)	(2)	(3)	(4)	(5)	(6)	(7)	(8)	(9)	(10)	(11)	(12)	(13)	(14)
OECD countries														
Australia	55	15	74	7	52	6	19	22	68	41	53	8	22	n
Austria	53	10	66	8	51	6	22	26	72	35	57	15	24	n
Belgium	53	15	73	7	45	3	11	24	62	38	53	13	23	n
Canada	m	m	m	m	m	m	m	m	m	m	m	m	m	m
Czech Republic	56	11	77	7	58	6	21	18	71	32	60	15	25	10
Denmark	56	23	81	4	46	8	32	18	65	35	50	12	35	n
Finland	56	18	89	5	54	6	32	15	74	29	67	26	19	n
France	m	m	m	m	m	m	m	m	m	m	m	m	m	m
Germany	55	16	77	8	49	7	35	27	71	26	53	15	16	n
Greece	m	m	m	m	m	m	m	m	m	m	m	m	m	m
Hungary	59	8	77	5	46	3	24	20	70	51	65	13	19	n
Iceland	60	10	84	6	59	4	17	31	72	40	59	9	33	n
Ireland	54	13	80	6	58	3	30	25	68	37	55	15	13	1
Italy	55	13	67	9	56	3	26	21	73	40	54	14	29	n
Japan	49	14	62	4	31	x(4)	x(5)	23	69	37	48	16	13	6
Korea	48	12	68	5	46	3	29	27	67	28	44	25	24	n
Luxembourg	m	m	m	m	m	m	m	m	m	m	m	m	m	m
Mexico	50	8	65	6	46	9	35	16	66	41	57	19	24	1
Netherlands	53	19	76	2	45	5	10	22	69	43	48	9	15	1
New Zealand	58	11	80	8	56	8	34	29	70	36	55	6	23	1
Norway	59	17	81	3	57	4	22	25	69	39	56	8	23	4
Poland	53	6	75	6	54	6	15	22	68	47	56	13	23	n
Portugal	58	19	79	6	60	7	23	19	70	35	56	14	27	n
Slovak Republic	57	15	81	7	50	5	18	22	72	32	61	18	28	n
Spain	55	12	78	3	50	6	16	20	70	35	59	17	23	7
Sweden	56	13	80	6	54	6	27	26	67	30	59	18	25	n
Switzerland	47	8	68	7	43	4	16	21	68	43	47	15	13	1
Turkey	44	5	62	7	48	4	34	19	50	51	46	14	20	n
United Kingdom	59	19	81	8	48	6	28	26	65	25	56	8	19	8
United States	55	m	m	m	m	m	m	m	m	m	m	m	m	m
OECD average	*54*	*13*	*75*	*6*	*50*	*5*	*24*	*22*	*68*	*37*	*55*	*14*	*22*	*2*
EU19 average	*55*	*14*	*77*	*6*	*51*	*5*	*23*	*22*	*69*	*36*	*57*	*15*	*23*	*2*
Partner countries														
Brazil	m	m	m	m	m	m	m	m	m	m	m	m	m	m
Chile	48	16	72	5	47	6	15	21	61	36	50	16	16	n
Estonia	61	10	90	6	55	7	28	18	78	47	63	13	25	n
Israel	54	8	74	6	49	3	27	21	71	38	56	21	28	3
Russian Federation	m	6	m	10	m	x(4)	m	13	m	46	m	23	m	2
Slovenia	56	6	80	5	59	4	23	13	73	52	63	20	26	n

Source: OECD. See Annex 3 for notes (www.oecd.org/edu/eag2008).
Please refer to the Reader's Guide for information concerning the symbols replacing missing data.
StatLink ⟨⟩ http://dx.doi.org/10.1787/401482730488

HOW MANY STUDENTS FINISH TERTIARY EDUCATION?

This indicator first shows the current tertiary graduate output of education systems, *i.e.* the percentage of the population in the typical age cohort for tertiary education that successfully completes tertiary programmes, as well as the distribution of tertiary graduates across fields of education. It then describes the evolution of the number of new entrants and graduates at tertiary-type A level over the last eleven years. Finally, it looks at the number of science graduates in relation to employed persons. The indicator also sheds light on the internal efficiency of tertiary educational systems.

Key results

Chart A3.1. **Tertiary-type A graduation rates by gender in 2006 (first-time graduation)**

The chart shows the number of students completing tertiary-type A programmes for the first time in 2006 by gender, as a percentage of the relevant group.

■ Males + Females   ◆ Males   △ Females

Based on current patterns of graduation, on average 37% of an age cohort are estimated to have completed tertiary-type A education in 2006 among the 25 OECD countries with comparable data. Differences between countries are greater when gender is taken into consideration. Significantly more females obtain tertiary-type A qualifications than males, with graduation rates of 45% and 30%, respectively. The gender gap is more than 25 percentage points in Poland and Sweden and 46 percentage points in Iceland.

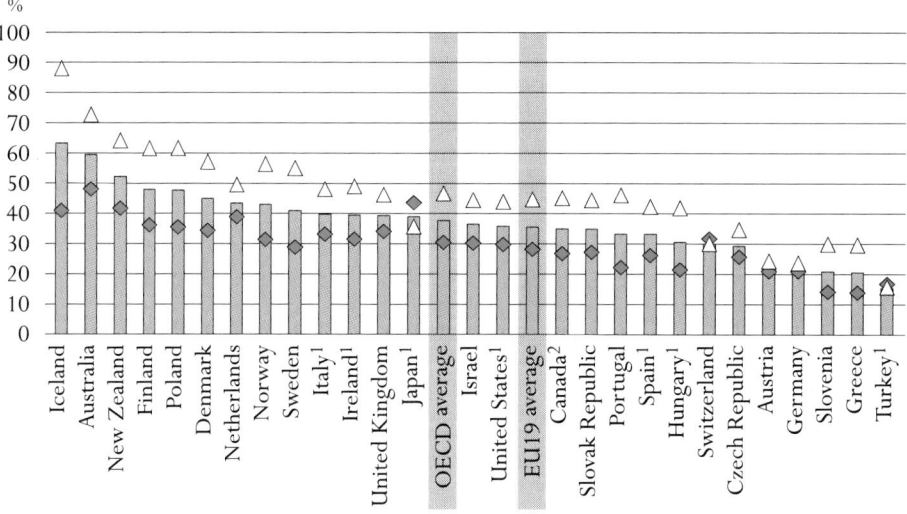

1. Gross graduation rate is calculated for tertiary-type A.
2. Year of reference 2005.
Countries are ranked in descending order of the graduation rates for tertiary-type A education, for both males and females.
Source: OECD. Table A3.1. See Annex 3 for notes (*www.oecd.org/edu/eag2008*).
StatLink ⌨ http://dx.doi.org/10.1787/401523756323

Other highlights of this indicator

- Tertiary-type A graduation rates range from 20% or less in Greece and Turkey to more than 45% in Australia, Finland, Iceland, New Zealand and Poland.

- On average in OECD countries, the tertiary-type A graduation rate has risen by 15 percentage points over the last eleven years. In virtually every country for which comparable data are available, tertiary-type A graduation rates increased between 1995 and 2006, often quite substantially.

- Tertiary-type A graduation rates tend to be higher in countries in which the programmes are mainly of shorter duration.

- The graduation rate is 9% at the tertiary-type B level and 1.4% in programmes leading to advanced research qualifications.

- In 2006, more than half of those at the typical age of graduation completed their first tertiary-type A degree in Australia, Finland, Iceland and New Zealand. For Australia and New Zealand, around one graduate in five previously resided in another country.

- Tertiary-type A graduation rates (first degree) for females equal or exceed those for males in 26 out of 29 OECD countries and in all partner countries.

- On average in OECD countries, more than 70% of the tertiary-type A graduates in the humanities, arts, education or in health and welfare are females, but only around one-quarter of those in mathematics and computer science or in engineering, manufacturing and construction are females.

A3

Policy context

Upper secondary education has become the norm in most countries today. In addition, most students are graduating from upper secondary programmes designed to provide access to tertiary education, which is leading to increased enrolments in tertiary programmes (see Indicator A2). Countries with high graduation rates at the tertiary level are also the ones most likely to be developing or maintaining a highly skilled labour force.

Moreover, specific skills and knowledge of science are of particular interest as they represent an important source of innovation and growth in knowledge-based economies. Differences among countries in the output of tertiary graduates by field of education are likely to be affected by the relative rewards in the labour market for different fields, as well as the degree to which the market drives field selection in a particular country.

Evidence and explanations

Tertiary graduation rates show the rate at which each country's education system produces advanced skills. But tertiary programmes vary widely in structure and scope among countries. Tertiary graduation rates are influenced both by the degree of access to tertiary programmes and by the demand for higher skills in the labour market. They are also affected by the way in which the degree and qualification structures are organised within countries.

Graduation rates at the tertiary level

Tertiary-type A programmes are largely theory-based and are designed to provide qualifications for entry into advanced research programmes and professions with high skill requirements. The organisation of tertiary-type A programmes differs among countries. The institutional framework may be universities or other institutions. The duration of programmes leading to a first tertiary-type A qualification ranges from three years (*e.g.* the bachelor's degree in many colleges in Ireland and the United Kingdom in most fields of education, and the *licence* in France) to five years or more (*e.g.* the *Diplom* in Germany).

In many countries there is a clear distinction between first and second university degrees, (*i.e.* undergraduate and graduate programmes), but this is not always the case. In some systems, degrees that are internationally comparable to a master's degree are obtained through a single programme of long duration. To ensure international comparability, it is therefore necessary to compare degree programmes of similar cumulative duration, as well as completion rates for first degree programmes.

To allow for comparisons that are independent of differences in national degree structures, tertiary-type A degrees are subdivided according to the total theoretical duration of study. Specifically, the OECD classification divides degrees into three groups: medium (three to less than five years), long (five to six years) and very long (more than six years). Degrees obtained from programmes of less than three years' duration are not considered equivalent to the completion of the tertiary-type A level of education and are therefore not included in this indicator. Second degree programmes are classified according to the cumulative duration of the first and second degree programmes. Individuals who already hold a first degree are netted out.

A3

First-time tertiary-type A graduation rates

Based on current patterns of graduation, on average 37% of an age cohort are estimated to have completed tertiary-type A education in 2006 among the 25 OECD countries with comparable data. This figure ranged from 20% or less in Greece and Turkey to more than 45% in Australia, Finland, Iceland, New Zealand and Poland (Table A3.1).

Disparities among countries are greater when gender is taken into consideration. On average in OECD countries, the number of females who obtain tertiary-type A qualifications is significantly higher than the number of males; females' graduation rate is 45% compared to 30% for males. The gender gap is superior to 25 percentage points in Poland and Sweden and equal to 46 percentage points in Iceland. In Austria, Germany, Switzerland and Turkey, the sexes are quite balanced. In Japan significantly more males graduate from tertiary-type A programmes (Table A3.1 and Chart A3.1).

On average in OECD countries, tertiary-type A graduation rates increased by 15 percentage points over the last eleven years. In virtually every country for which comparable data are available, these rates increased between 1995 and 2006, often quite substantially. One of the most significant increases was reported in Italy where the rate doubled to 39% between 2000 and 2006. This was largely due to structural change. The reform of the Italian tertiary system in 2002 allowed university students who had originally enrolled in programmes of longer duration to obtain a degree after three years of study (Table A3.2 and Chart A3.2).

Chart A3.2. Tertiary-type A graduation rates in 1995, 2000 and 2006 (first-time graduation)

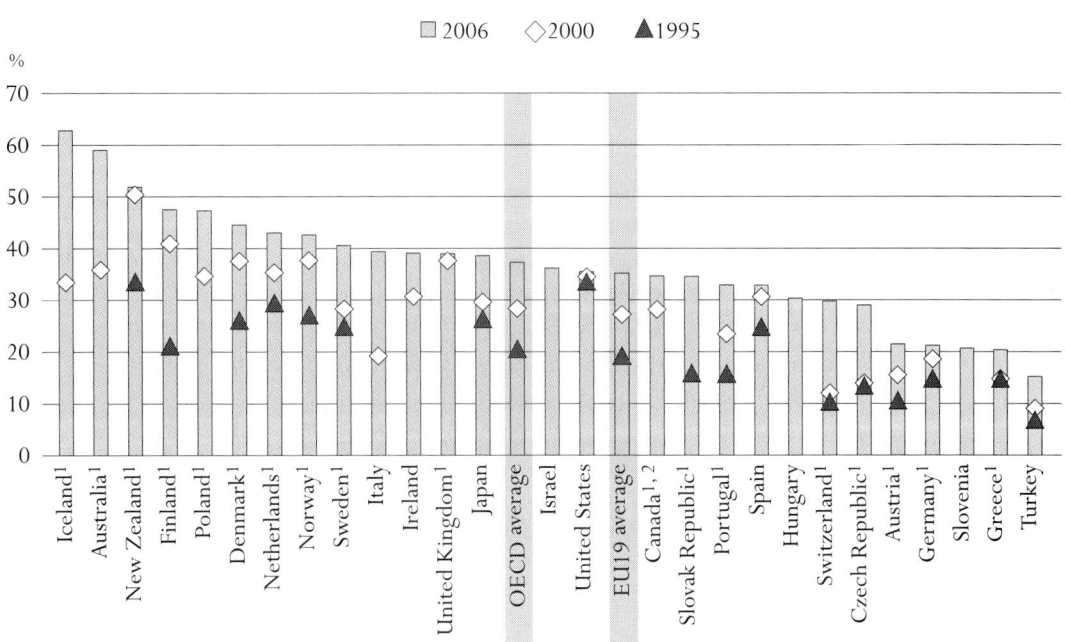

1. Net graduation rate is calculated by summing the graduation rates by single year of age in 2006.
2. Year of reference 2005.
Countries are ranked in descending order of the graduation rates for tertiary-type A education in 2006.
Source: OECD. Table A3.2. See Annex 3 for notes (*www.oecd.org/edu/eag2008*).
StatLink ⟪ᶆₛᶠ⟫ http://dx.doi.org/10.1787/401523756323

A3

From 1995 to 2006, tertiary graduation rates evolved quite differently in OECD and partner countries. In New Zealand and Norway, increases were more marked from 1995 to 2000 than from 2000 to 2006. However, in the Czech Republic, Greece, Japan, Sweden and Switzerland, the increase occurred mainly in the last six years (Table A3.2 and Chart A3.2).

Changes in the number of new entrants and graduates at tertiary-type A level (1995, 2000 and 2006)

Changes in graduation rates need to be linked to changes in entry rates (see Indicator A2). A country's entry rate may increase in a given year for various reasons: the creation of new programmes, restructuring of the tertiary education system, or a rise in the numbers of students attaining upper secondary education and continuing their studies. The country's graduation rate logically rises a few years later if factors such as the dropout rate remain constant (See Indicator A4). The gap between the two indicators corresponds to the duration of the programme that students follow. A comparison of annual variations in numbers of new entrants (1995-2000) and of first-time graduates (2000-2006) is a good proxy for how the education system has evolved in recent years. Annual variations in numbers of new entrants (2000-2006) can help to predict future trends in graduates.

Entry rates increased significantly between 1995 and 2000 and between 2000 and 2006 in almost all OECD and partner countries (see Indicator A2). However patterns differ among countries. For 14 OECD countries with comparable data for both periods, the annual variation in numbers of new entrants evolved faster in the first period in Denmark, Finland, Greece, New Zealand, Poland and Switzerland; figures were relatively stable over both periods in Austria, Germany, Japan, the Netherlands, Norway, Sweden and Turkey; and the rate was higher in the latter period in the Slovak Republic. Many countries undertook reforms in their tertiary education system in the second half of the 1990s to improve access and graduation rates. This has resulted in a rapid evolution in the numbers of new entrants (1995-2000) and subsequently (2000-2006) of numbers of first-time tertiary-type A graduates (Chart A3.3)

In Iceland, Italy and Switzerland, the impressive increase in first-time graduates clearly exceeds the increase in new entrants in both the 1995-2000 and 2000-2006 periods. In Switzerland, for example, the creation in 1997 of the *Fachhochschulen* and their later extension to more institutions and programmes increased the numbers of new entrants (with an annual increase of 11% from 1995 to 2000) and thus from 2001 the number of tertiary-type A first-time graduates, which rose by an annual 19% from 2000 to 2006. However, this increase has corresponded to a decrease in the numbers of tertiary-type B graduates. Since quite a number of tertiary-type B programmes have become *Fachhochschulen* programmes, graduates of such programmes can receive permission to attend second degree programmes at the new *Fachhochschulen*, which means they can also become first-time tertiary-type A graduates. In these countries, the gap between changes in numbers of new entrants and numbers of first-time tertiary-type A graduates will certainly be reduced in the future; the growth in the number of first-time graduates should decrease and, as a consequence better match the change in the number of new entrants.

Denmark, Germany, Japan, the Netherlands, New Zealand, Norway and Spain and the partner country Israel are the countries in which the annual rate of growth in the number of new entrants

Chart A3.3. Average annual growth rate of the number of new entrants and first-time graduates at tertiary-type A level between 1995, 2000 and 2006

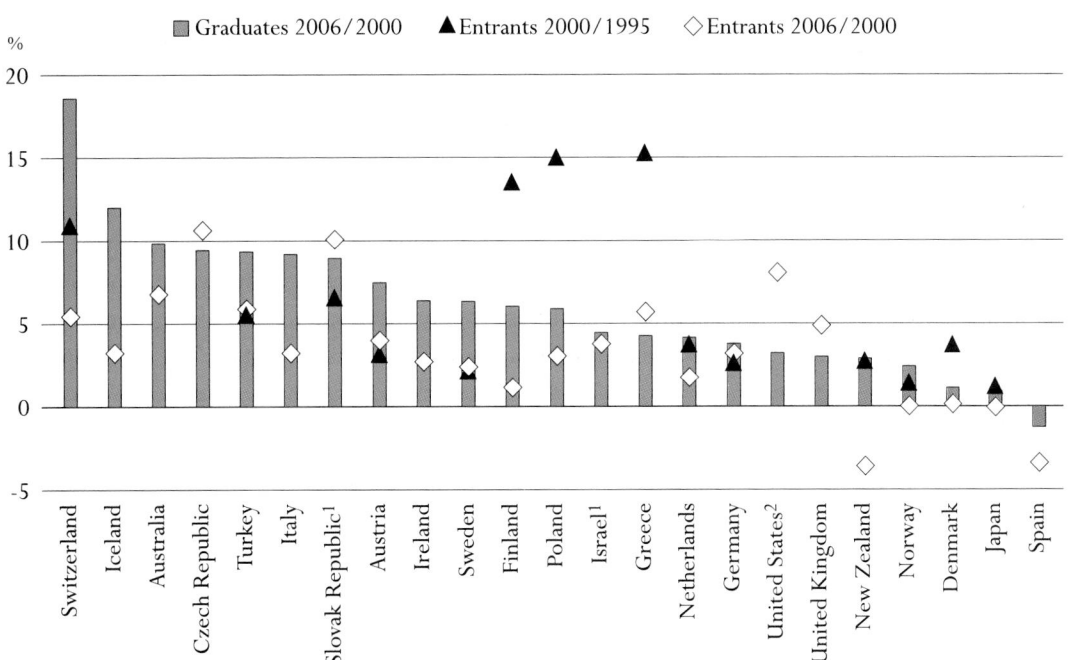

■ Graduates 2006/2000   ▲ Entrants 2000/1995   ◇ Entrants 2006/2000

1. Year of reference 2002 instead of 2000 for graduates.
2. Includes tertiary-type B programmes.
Countries are ranked in descending order of the average annual growth rate of the number of first-time graduates at the tertiary-type A level between 2000 and 2006.
Source: OECD. Table A3.8 on line. See Annex 3 for notes (*www.oecd.org/edu/eag2008*).
StatLink ⟨⟩ http://dx.doi.org/10.1787/401523756323

and first-time graduates is very low (less than 5% or negative). In fact, Spain has seen an absolute decline in the number of graduates and new entrants over the 2000-2006 period, which is offset by a significant increase in graduation and entry rates for tertiary-type B programmes. The situation in Japan is explained by its low birth rate: the number of 22-year-olds – the typical graduation age of bachelors – dropped by more than one third between 1995 and 2006, from 2.1 to 1.5 million.

However some countries with a demographic situation similar to that of Japan continue to improve access to and graduation from the tertiary system. Italy, despite a decrease of 25% in the number of 23-to-25-year-olds between 1995 and 2006, has seen the number of graduates at tertiary-type A level increase every year by 9%.

Tertiary-type A: the shorter the programme, the higher the participation and graduation rates

The duration of tertiary studies tends to be longer in EU countries than in other OECD countries. Two-thirds of all OECD students graduate from programmes with a duration of three to less than five years compared to less than 55 % in EU countries (Table A3.1).

A3

It is evident that, overall, tertiary-type A graduation rates tend to be higher in countries in which programmes are mainly of shorter duration. For example, in Austria, the Czech Republic, Germany and Greece, most students complete programmes of at least five years' duration and tertiary-type A graduation rates are at or below 30%. In the future, with the implementation of the Bologna process (Box A3.1), there may be fewer programmes of long duration in European countries. In contrast, tertiary-type A graduation rates are around 40% or more in Australia, New Zealand, Sweden and the United Kingdom, where programmes of three to less than five years are the norm (more than 90% of graduates follow programmes of three to less than five years). Poland is a notable exception: despite typically long tertiary-type A programmes, its tertiary-type A graduation rate is over 40% (Table A3.1).

First-time tertiary-type B graduation rates

Tertiary-type B programmes are classified at the same competency level as tertiary-type A programmes but are more occupationally oriented and usually lead to direct labour market access. They are typically of shorter duration than type A programmes – usually two to three years – and are generally not intended to lead to university-level degrees. Graduation rates for tertiary-type B programmes average some 9% of an age cohort for the 23 OECD countries with comparable data. In fact, graduation from tertiary-type B programmes is a significant feature of the tertiary system in only a few countries, most notably Ireland, Japan and New Zealand and the partner country Slovenia, where over 20% of the age cohort obtained tertiary-type B qualifications in 2006 (Table A3.1).

Trends in provision of and graduation from tertiary-type B programmes vary even though the OECD average has been stable over the past eleven years. For instance, in Spain, a sharp rise in tertiary-type B graduation rates between 1995 and 2006 is attributable to the development of new advanced level vocational training programmes. In contrast, in Finland these programmes are being phased out and the proportion of the age cohort graduating from them has thus fallen rapidly (Table A3.2).

Advanced research qualification rates

For the 29 OECD countries with comparable data, 1.4% of the population obtained an advanced research qualification (such as a Ph.D.) in 2006. The proportion ranges from 0.1% in the partner country Chile to more than 2% in Finland, Germany, Portugal, Sweden, Switzerland and the United Kingdom (Table A3.1).

Graduation rates: first and second degrees and advanced research qualifications

Graduation rates for first degrees are available for all countries; however, this is not the case for first-time graduation rates, as in some countries, educational data reporting systems do not include enough information to produce the figures on first-time graduates.

In 2006, on average among OECD countries, 37% of an age cohort are estimated to have completed their first degree at tertiary-type A level. The proportion exceeds 50% in Australia, Finland, Iceland and New Zealand. In Australia and New Zealand, around one student in five formerly resided in another country. By contrast, the graduation rate is less than 20% in Belgium, Mexico and Turkey and in the partner country Chile. Belgium and the partner

A3

Box A3.1. **Structure of higher education in Europe – the Bologna process**

The Bologna process had its origins in the Sorbonne Joint Declaration on Harmonisation of the Architecture of the European Higher Education System, signed in 1998 by France, Germany, Italy and the United Kingdom. It was created with the purpose of providing a common framework in tertiary education among these countries at the bachelor, master and doctorate levels. Under the new system on average, the duration of the bachelor's degree is three years, that of the master's degree two years and that of the doctorate three years.

As part of this transformation process, the countries involved have substantially modified the structure of their education system. Some have completed the transformation and others are still in the process of doing so. The extension and scope of this process has gradually increased. It is planned that, by 2010, this common area will be fully operational in 45 countries, mainly in the European area. The reforms allow for easier recognition of diplomas and increased student mobility. They have also gradually entailed related objectives, such as mobility of researchers, a system of common credits (ECTS), the inclusion of joint degrees and European co-operation on quality assurance.

As the Bologna process aims at equivalent education systems in terms of graduation, this will allow for better comparability of data (*e.g.* for first or second degree programmes). In the short term, these reforms also lead to a structural increase in graduation rates. As some countries reduce the length of some of their programmes, students whose first diploma cursus was traditionally longer now graduate in three years. Many countries also propose new study programmes and thus increase their diploma offer at the tertiary level. For example, the large recent increase in the graduation rate in the Czech Republic (Table A3.2) is explained by the implementation of the new structure of the Bologna process and by the expansion of the tertiary system.

However, in some countries, certain fields have not yet shifted to the three cycles and remain as long cycles of five or six years. This is the case, for example, in medical studies, architecture, engineering and theology.

---

country Slovenia are the two countries in which more people obtained their first degree from more occupationally oriented programmes (tertiary-type B) than from the largely theory-based programmes (tertiary-type A). In Korea the rates of graduation from both types of programmes are similar (Table A3.3).

International students' contribution to graduate output

International students make a significant contribution to the tertiary graduate output in a number of countries and these students have a marked impact on estimated graduation rates. In order to compare graduation rates across countries it is important to examine the impact of international students on the graduate output.

A3

In Australia, Germany, Switzerland and the United Kingdom, more than 30% of tertiary-type A second degrees or advanced research degrees are awarded to international students. This pattern implies that the true domestic graduate output is significantly overestimated as a proportion of overall graduation rates. It is most significant for tertiary-type A second degree programmes in Australia and the United Kingdom and for advanced research programmes in Switzerland and the United Kingdom, where international graduates represent more than 35% of the graduate output. The contribution of international students to the graduate output is also significant – although to a lesser extent – in Austria, Canada, Japan, New Zealand and the United States. Among countries for which student mobility data are not available, the contribution of foreign students is significant in Belgium (Table A3.3 and Chart A3.4).

However, the contribution of international students to the tertiary graduate output of Denmark, Finland, Norway and Sweden and the partner countries Estonia and Slovenia is more limited. The same holds for foreign students in the Czech Republic, Hungary, Iceland, Portugal, the Slovak Republic and Turkey (Table A3.3 and Chart A3.4).

Chart A3.4. Proportion of international and foreign graduates in total graduate output, by type of tertiary education (2006)

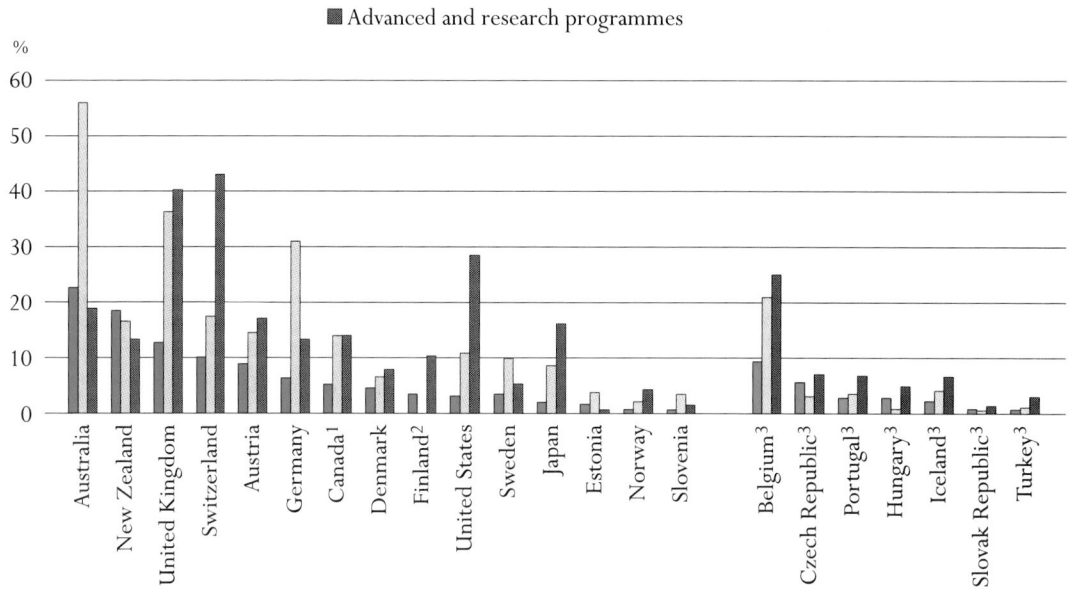

1. Year of reference 2005.
2. First degrees programmes include second degrees.
3. Proportion of foreign graduates in tertiary graduate output. These data are not comparable with data on international graduates and are therefore presented separately.
Countries are ranked in descending order of the proportion of international graduates in tertiary-type A first degree programmes.
Source: OECD. Table A3.3. See Annex 3 for notes (*www.oecd.org/edu/eag2008*).
StatLink 🔗 http://dx.doi.org/10.1787/401523756323

A3

Graduation by field of education

Changing opportunities in the job market, differences in earnings among occupations and sectors, and the admission policies and practices of tertiary education institutions may all affect the fields in which students choose to study. In turn, the relative popularity of various fields of education affects the demand for programmes and teaching staff, as well as the supply of new graduates. The distribution of graduates by field of education is driven by the relative popularity of these fields among students, the relative number of students admitted to these fields in universities and equivalent institutions, and the degree structure of the various disciplines in a particular country.

In 26 of the 28 OECD countries for which data are available and in all partner countries, the fields of social sciences, business, law and services account for the largest concentration of tertiary-type A and advanced research qualifications (Table A3.4a). On average in OECD countries, more than one-third of tertiary-type A graduates obtain a degree in these fields. This ranges from less than 30% in Denmark, Finland, Germany, Korea, and Sweden to more than 45% in Hungary, Mexico, Poland and the United States and in the partner countries the Russian Federation and Slovenia. The field of humanities, arts and education accounts for the largest concentration of tertiary-type A and advanced research qualifications in Germany and the fields of health and welfare in Sweden.

An average of 24% of tertiary-type A and advanced research students receive qualifications in science-related fields (engineering, manufacturing and construction, life sciences, physical sciences and agriculture, mathematics and computing) in OECD countries. The proportion varies between less than 16% in Hungary, Iceland and in the partner country Brazil, to more than 30% in Finland and Korea. Similarly popular on average in OECD countries are the fields of humanities, arts and education, with 25% of tertiary-type A and advanced research student graduates.

For the 27 OECD countries with available data, the share of graduations by field of education at tertiary-type A level (including advanced research qualifications) have changed slightly over the last six years to the benefit of health and welfare and of social sciences, business, law and services. Those two areas represented around one-half of graduates in 2006. Rates in science-related fields (engineering, manufacturing and construction, life sciences, physical sciences and agriculture, mathematics and computing) have decreased overall from 25% in 2000 to 24% in 2006, especially in Ireland, Switzerland and Turkey where the decrease is over five percentage points (Table A3.4a). The effect of this decline may be felt at a moment when there is a risk of shortages in science fields on the labour market (See Indicator A1).

The picture is similar for tertiary-type B education, in which programmes are more occupationally oriented: social sciences, business, law and services have the largest concentration of graduates (39%), followed by humanities, arts and education (24%), and science-related fields (21%) (Table A3.4b on line). The selection of a field of education at this level is heavily dependent on opportunities to study similar subjects. For similar occupations, students may follow a programme at different levels of education, *i.e.* at the post-secondary non-tertiary, tertiary-type A or tertiary-type B level. For example, if nurses in a particular country are trained primarily in tertiary-type B programmes, the proportion of students graduating with qualifications in medical sciences from those programmes will be higher than in countries where they are primarily trained in upper secondary or tertiary-type A programmes.

Gender differences in tertiary graduation (first and second degrees and advanced research qualifications): the higher the level of education, the lower the proportion of females

There are fewer females at the highest levels of education: the proportion of females with a first or second tertiary-type A degree is 58% and 56%, respectively, whereas only 43% of advanced research qualifications are awarded to females. However, the gap between first degrees, second degrees and a Ph.D. decreased between 2000 and 2006 (Table A3.5a and Chart A3.5).

In all OECD countries except France and New Zealand, the proportion of female tertiary-type A graduates (first degree) increased between 2000 and 2006 (Table A3.5a).

Chart A3.5. Percentage of tertiary-type A qualifications awarded to females and breakdown of tertiary graduates by field of education, OECD average (2000, 2006)

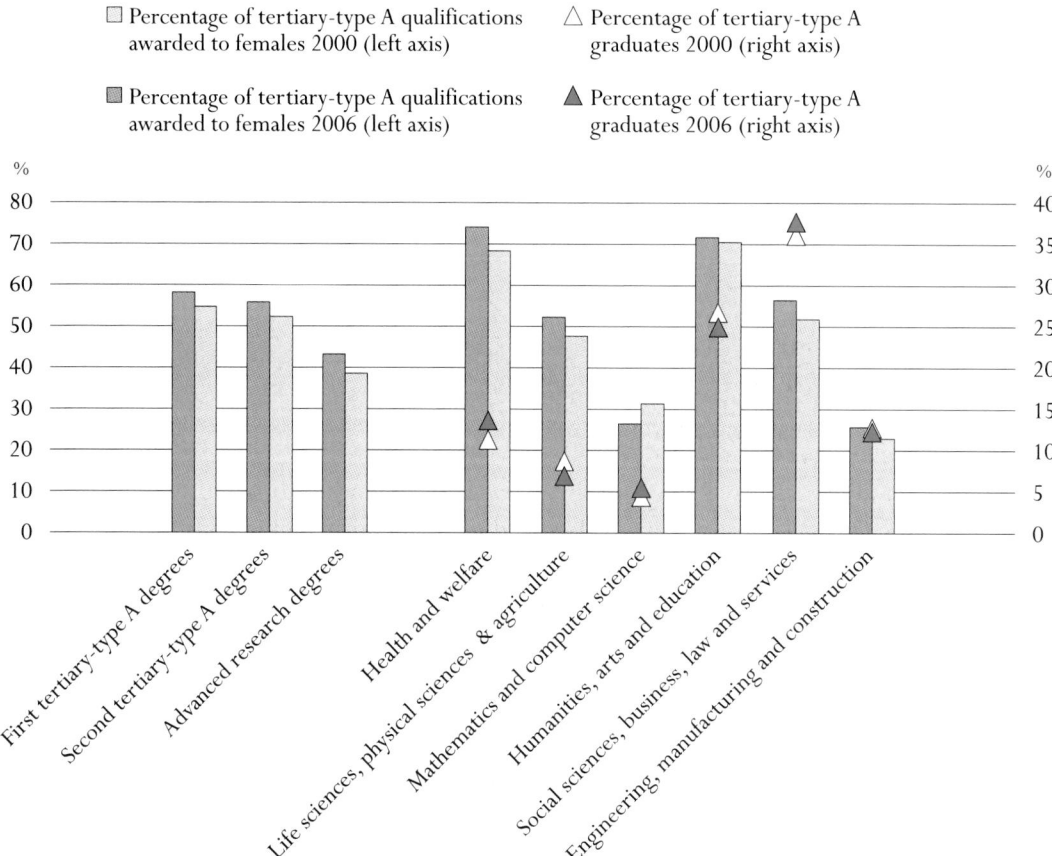

□ Percentage of tertiary-type A qualifications awarded to females 2000 (left axis)

△ Percentage of tertiary-type A graduates 2000 (right axis)

■ Percentage of tertiary-type A qualifications awarded to females 2006 (left axis)

▲ Percentage of tertiary-type A graduates 2006 (right axis)

Source: OECD. Tables A3.4a, A3.5a. See Annex 3 for notes (*www.oecd.org/edu/eag2008*).
StatLink ⟋⟍ http://dx.doi.org/10.1787/401523756323

A3

On average in OECD countries, 58% of all tertiary-type A graduates (first degree) are females. Their tertiary-type A graduation rates equal or exceed those for men in 26 out of 29 OECD countries and in all partner countries. In Iceland and Portugal and in the partner countries Estonia and Slovenia the proportion of females obtaining a tertiary-type A qualification (first degree) is more than 65%, but it is less than 50% in Japan, Korea and Turkey (Table A3.5a).

The proportion of females obtaining a tertiary-type A qualification (second degree) is also greater than the proportion of males, especially in Poland, Portugal and Sweden and in the partner country Estonia, where the proportion equal or exceeds 70%. On average in OECD countries, females obtained 56% of these qualifications in 2006 compared to 52% in 2000 (Table A3.5a).

Males remain more likely than females to obtain advanced research qualifications in OECD countries. Graduation rates from advanced research programmes, *e.g.* Ph.D. programmes, are lower for females than for males in all countries except Iceland, Italy and Portugal and the partner countries Brazil, Estonia and Israel. On average in OECD countries, males still represented 57% of advanced research qualifications (compared to 61% in 2000). In Japan and Korea, around three-quarters of advanced research qualifications are still awarded to males, but the proportion was greater than 80% in 2000 (Table A3.5a).

However, major differences remain between fields of education. In 2006 in humanities, arts, education, and in health and welfare, more than 70% of tertiary-type A graduates on average in OECD countries were female, but only around 25% of mathematics and computer science and of engineering, manufacturing and construction graduates. In 2000, the proportion of females was 68% in health and welfare and 31% in mathematics and computing, an indication that the increase in the proportion of females' graduation has not helped to improve their representation in fields in which they are in minority (Table A3.5a).

Science graduates among those in employment

Examining the number of science (engineering, manufacturing and construction, life sciences, physical sciences and agriculture, mathematics and computing) graduates per 100 000 25-to-34-year-olds in employment provides another way of gauging the recent output of high-level skills from different education systems. The number of science graduates (all tertiary levels) per 100 000 employed persons ranges from below 800 in Hungary to above 2 200 in Australia, Finland, France, Ireland, Korea, New Zealand and the United Kingdom (Table A3.6).

The variation in the number of female science graduates of tertiary-type A education and advanced research programmes per 100 000 25-to-34-year-olds in employment is largely less than for males. The number of female science graduates ranges from less than 500 in Hungary, Japan and the Netherlands to more than 1 500 in Australia, New Zealand and Poland while the number of male science graduates varies from less than 500 in Turkey to over 2 500 in Australia, Finland and the United Kingdom. The OECD average is 985 female science graduates per 100 000 25-to-34-year-olds in employment compared to approximately 1 631 for males (Table A3.6).

This indicator does not, however, provide information on the number of graduates actually employed in scientific fields or, more generally, the number of those using their degree-related skills and knowledge at work.

Chart A3.6. Number of tertiary science graduates per 100 000 employed 25-to-34-year-olds (2006)

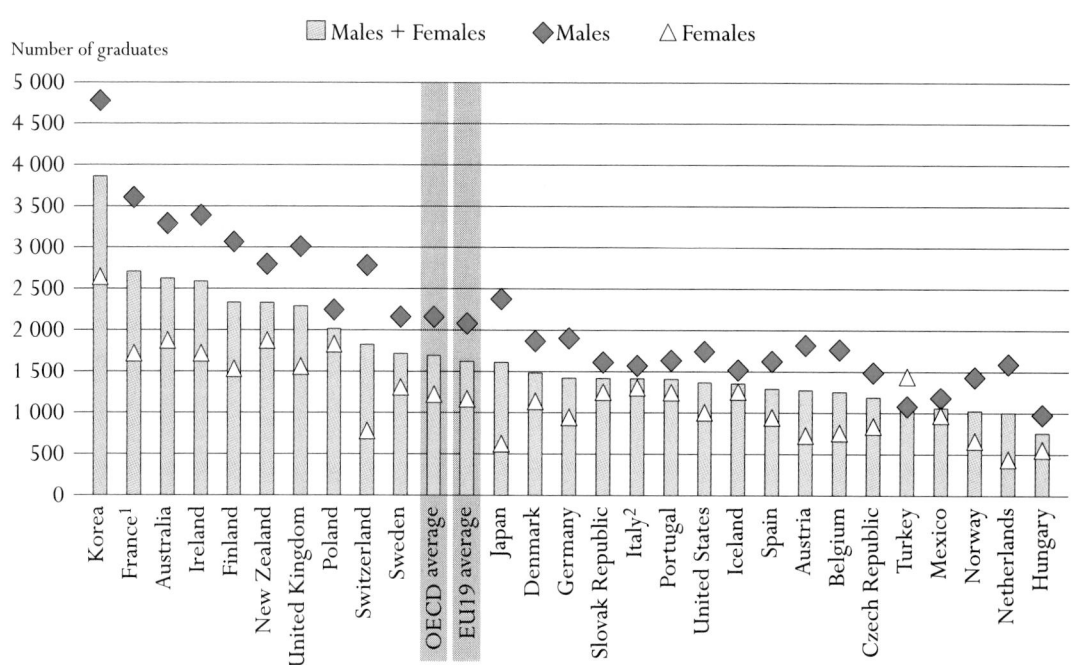

1. Year of reference 2005 for the number of science graduates.
2. Advanced research programmes refer to 2005.
Countries are ranked in descending order of the number of tertiary science graduates in tertiary-type A programmes per 100 000 employed 25-to-34-year-olds.
Source: OECD. Table A3.6. See Annex 3 for notes (*www.oecd.org/edu/eag2008*).
StatLink http://dx.doi.org/10.1787/401523756323

Definitions and methodologies

Data refer to the academic year 2005/06 and are based on the UOE data collection on education statistics administered by the OECD in 2007 (for details see Annex 3 at *www.oecd.org/edu/eag2008*).

Tertiary graduates are those who obtain a tertiary qualification in the specified reference year. This indicator distinguishes among different categories of tertiary qualifications: *i)* tertiary-type B qualifications (ISCED 5B); *ii)* tertiary-type A qualifications (ISCED 5A); and *iii)* advanced research degrees of doctorate standard (ISCED 6). For some countries, data are not available for these categories. In such cases, the OECD has assigned graduates to the most appropriate category (see Annex 3 at *www.oecd.org/edu/eag2008* for a list of programmes included for each country at the tertiary-type A and tertiary-type B levels). Tertiary-type A degrees are also subdivided by their corresponding total theoretical duration of studies, to allow for comparisons that are independent of differences in national degree structures.

In Tables A3.1 and A3.3 (from 2005 onwards), graduation rates for first tertiary programmes (tertiary-type A, tertiary-type B and advanced research programmes) are calculated as net graduation rates (*i.e.* as the sum of age-specific graduation rates). Net graduation rates represent the estimated percentage of the age cohort that will complete tertiary-type A/B education (based on current patterns of graduation). Gross graduation rates are presented for countries that are unable to provide such detailed data. In order to calculate gross graduation rates, countries identify the age at which graduation typically occurs (see Annex 1). The number of graduates, regardless of their age, is divided by the population at the typical graduation age. In many countries, defining a typical age of graduation is difficult, however, because graduates are dispersed over a wide range of ages.

In Table A3.2, data on trends in graduation rates at tertiary level for the years 1995, 2000, 2001, 2002, 2003 and 2004 are based on a special survey carried out in OECD countries and four of the six partner countries in January 2007.

In Tables A3.4a and A3.5a, tertiary graduates who received their qualification in the reference year are classified by fields of education based on their subject of specialisation. These figures cover graduates from all tertiary degrees reported in Table A3.1. The 25 fields of education used in the UOE data collection instruments follow the revised ISCED classification by field of education. The same classification is used for all levels of education.

The labour force data used in Table A3.6 are taken from the OECD Labour Force database, compiled from national labour force surveys and the European Labour Force Survey.

Further references

The following additional material relevant to this indicator is available on line at:
StatLink ⟨◈⟩ http://dx.doi.org/10.1787/401523756323

- *Table A3.4b. Percentage of tertiary-type B graduates, by field of education (2000, 2006)*

- *Table A3.5b. Percentage of tertiary qualifications awarded to females in tertiary-type B programmes, by field of education (2000, 2006)*

- *Table A3.7. Trends in net graduation rates at advanced research qualification rates (1995-2006)*

- *Table A3.8. Average annual growth rate of the number of new entrants and first-time graduates at tertiary-type A level between 1995, 2000 and 2006*

Table A3.1.
Graduation rates in tertiary education (2006)
Sum of graduation rates for single year of age by programme destination and duration

		Tertiary-type B programmes (first-time graduation)			Tertiary-type A programmes (first-time graduation)						Advanced research programmes[2]
					All programmes			Proportion of graduates by duration of programmes (in %)			Ph.D or equivalent
								3 to less than 5 years	5 to 6 years[1]	More than 6 years	
		M+F	Males	Females	M+F	Males	Females	M+F	M+F	M+F	M+F
		(1)	(2)	(3)	(4)	(5)	(6)	(7)	(8)	(9)	(10)
OECD countries	Australia	m	m	m	59.1	47.3	71.2	95	4	n	1.8
	Austria[3]	7.4	7.1	7.8	21.5	20.2	22.8	29	71	n	1.9
	Belgium	m	m	m	m	m	m	m	m	m	1.3
	Canada[5]	m	m	m	34.7	26.1	43.6	m	m	m	0.9
	Czech Republic[3]	5.7	3.2	8.3	29.0	25.0	33.2	43	57	n	1.2
	Denmark	10.0	10.8	9.1	44.6	33.7	55.7	63	37	n	1.2
	Finland	0.1	0.1	n.	47.5	35.5	60.1	59	40	1	2.1
	France[4, 5]	m	m	m	m	m	m	m	m	m	1.2
	Germany[3]	10.8	8.2	13.4	21.2	20.2	22.2	40	60	n	2.3
	Greece	12.2	9.0	15.7	20.4	13.2	28.1	n	100	x(8)	0.9
	Hungary[3, 4]	4.0	2.6	5.6	30.3	20.8	40.4	m	m	m	0.7
	Iceland	4.1	4.0	4.1	62.8	40.2	86.5	87	13	n	0.4
	Ireland[3, 4]	27.1	28.4	25.9	39.1	30.8	47.5	55	45	n	1.3
	Italy[3, 4, 6]	n	n	n	39.4	32.5	46.6	61	39	n	1.2
	Japan[3, 4]	27.9	20.4	35.8	38.6	42.8	34.2	85	15	a	1.0
	Korea	m	m	m	m	m	m	m	m	m	1.0
	Luxembourg	m	m	m	m	m	m	m	m	m	m
	Mexico	m	m	m	m	m	m	m	m	m	0.2
	Netherlands	n	n	n	43.0	38.1	48.1	m	m	m	1.5
	New Zealand	24.3	20.1	28.4	51.9	41.0	62.7	94	6	n	1.1
	Norway	1.1	1.0	1.2	42.6	30.7	55.0	83	11	6	1.3
	Poland	0.1	0.1	0.2	47.3	34.8	60.2	26	74	n	1.0
	Portugal	8.7	6.5	10.9	32.9	21.5	44.7	33	67	n	3.3
	Slovak Republic	1.2	0.7	1.7	34.6	26.5	43.0	23	77	n	1.5
	Spain[4]	14.5	13.0	16.1	32.9	25.5	40.8	45	55	n	1.0
	Sweden	4.9	4.0	5.8	40.6	28.2	53.6	96	4	n	2.2
	Switzerland[3]	9.6	12.1	7.2	29.8	31.0	28.6	62	25	14	3.1
	Turkey[4]	10.8	12.3	9.2	15.2	16.1	14.4	85	13	1	0.2
	United Kingdom[7]	15.0	9.9	20.0	39.0	33.4	44.8	97	3	1	2.2
	United States[3, 4]	9.9	7.3	12.7	35.5	29.1	42.4	55	39	6	1.4
	OECD average	*9.1*	*7.9*	*10.4*	*37.3*	*29.8*	*45.2*	*64*	*34*	*1*	*1.4*
	EU19 average	*7.6*	*6.5*	*8.8*	*35.2*	*27.5*	*43.2*	*54*	*46*	*n*	*1.6*
Partner countries	Brazil[5]	m	m	m	m	m	m	m	m	m	1.4
	Chile	m	m	m	m	m	m	m	m	m	0.1
	Estonia	m	m	m	m	m	m	m	m	m	0.8
	Israel	m	m	m	36.2	29.5	43.0	100	n	n	1.3
	Russian Federation	m	m	m	m	m	m	m	m	m	1.5
	Slovenia	25.9	20.5	31.6	20.7	13.5	28.4	m	m	m	1.3

Notes: Mismatches between the coverage of the population data and the student/graduate data mean that the participation/graduation rates for those countries that are net exporters of students may be underestimated (for instance, Luxembourg) and those that are net importers may be overestimated.

1. Excluding students who subsequently completed a longer programme.
2. Gross graduation rates are calculated for France, Ireland, Italy, Japan, Mexico, the Netherlands, Poland, the United Kingdom and the United States, and the partner countries Chile, Estonia and the Russian Federation.
3. Gross graduation rate is calculated for tertiary-type B.
4. Gross graduation rate is calculated for tertiary-type A.
5. Year of reference 2005.
6. Advanced research programme graduates refer to 2005.
7. The graduation rate for tertiary-type B programmes includes some graduates who have previously graduated at this level and therefore overestimates first-time graduation.

Source: OECD. See Annex 3 for notes (*www.oecd.org/edu/eag2008*).
Please refer to the Reader's Guide for information concerning the symbols replacing missing data.
StatLink http://dx.doi.org/10.1787/401523756323

A3

Table A3.2.
Trends in tertiary graduation rates (1995–2006)
Percentage of tertiary graduates (first-time graduation, tertiary-type A and B) to the population at the typical age of graduation
(1995, 2000, 2001, 2002, 2003, 2004, 2005, 2006)

	Tertiary-type A									Tertiary-type B							
	Typical age in 2006	1995	2000	2001	2002	2003	2004	2005	2006[1]	Typical age in 2006	1995	2000	2001	2002	2003	2004	2005	2006[2]
	(1)	(2)	(3)	(4)	(5)	(6)	(7)	(8)	(9)	(10)	(11)	(12)	(13)	(14)	(15)	(16)	(17)	(18)
OECD countries																		
Australia	20-25	m	36	42	46	50	47	59	59	19-22	m	1	1	m	m	m	m	m
Austria	22-26	10	15	17	18	19	20	20	21	20-21	m	m	m	m	m	7	8	7
Belgium	22-24	m	m	m	m	m	m	m	m	21-22	m	m	m	m	m	m	m	m
Canada	22-25	m	28	m	m	m	m	35	m	21-25	m	m	m	m	m	m	m	m
Czech Republic	23-25	13	14	14	15	17	20	25	29	22-23	6	5	5	4	4	5	6	6
Denmark	24	25	37	39	41	43	44	46	45	23-25	8	10	12	13	14	11	10	10
Finland	25-29	20	41	45	49	48	47	48	48	30-34	34	7	4	2	1	a	a	a
France	20-25	m	m	m	m	m	m	m	m	20-24	m	m	m	m	m	m	m	m
Germany	24-27	14	18	18	18	18	19	20	21	21-23	13	11	11	10	10	10	11	11
Greece	22-24	14	15	16	18	20	24	25	20	22-24	5	6	6	7	9	11	12	12
Hungary	23-24	m	m	m	m	m	29	36	30	21	m	m	m	m	m	3	4	4
Iceland	24-25	m	33	38	41	45	51	56	63	30-34	m	6	8	6	7	5	4	4
Ireland	21-25	m	30	29	32	37	39	38	39	20-21	m	15	20	13	19	20	24	27
Italy	23-25	m	19	21	25	m	36	41	39	22-23	m	n	1	1	m	n	n	n
Japan	22.24	25	29	32	33	34	35	36	39	20	28	29	27	27	26	26	27	28
Korea	21	m	m	m	m	m	m	m	m	19	m	m	m	m	m	m	m	m
Luxembourg	m	m	m	m	m	m	m	m	m	m	m	m	m	m	m	m	m	m
Mexico	23	m	m	m	m	m	m	m	m	20	m	m	m	m	m	m	m	m
Netherlands	21-23	29	35	35	37	38	40	42	43	n	n	n	n	n	n	n	n	n
New Zealand	21-22	33	50	51	46	49	50	51	52	20-23	12	17	17	18	20	21	21	24
Norway	22-25	26	37	40	38	39	45	41	43	21-22	6	6	6	5	5	3	2	1
Poland	23-25	m	34	40	43	44	45	45	47	22	m	m	m	m	n	n	n	n
Portugal	22-24	15	23	28	30	33	32	32	33	21-23	6	8	8	7	7	8	9	9
Slovak Republic	23-24	15	m	m	23	25	28	30	35	21-22	1	2	2	3	2	3	2	1
Spain	20-22	24	30	31	32	32	33	33	33	19	2	8	11	13	16	17	17	15
Sweden	25	24	28	29	32	35	37	38	41	22-23	m	4	4	4	4	4	5	5
Switzerland	24-26	9	12	19	21	22	26	27	30	23-29	13	14	11	11	12	12	8	10
Turkey	22-24	6	9	9	10	11	11	11	15	20-22	m	m	m	m	m	m	m	11
United Kingdom[3]	20-25	m	37	37	37	38	39	39	39	19-24	m	m	12	12	14	16	17	15
United States	22	33	34	33	32	32	33	34	36	20	9	8	8	8	9	9	10	10
OECD average		*20*	*28*	*30*	*31*	*33*	*35*	*36*	*37*		*10*	*8*	*9*	*8*	*9*	*9*	*9*	*9*
OECD average for countries with 1995 and 2006 data		*20*							*34*		*10*							*10*
EU19 average		*18*	*27*	*29*	*30*	*32*	*33*	*35*	*35*		*8*	*6*	*7*	*6*	*8*	*7*	*8*	*8*
Partner countries																		
Brazil	21-24	m	10	10	13	15	m	m	m	21-24	m	m	m	m	m	m	m	m
Chile	24	m	m	m	m	m	m	m	m	20-22	m	m	m	m	m	m	m	m
Estonia	22-24	m	m	m	m	m	m	m	m	22	m	m	m	m	m	m	m	m
Israel	26	m	m	m	29	31	32	35	36	m	m	m	m	m	m	m	m	m
Russian Federation	19-24	m	m	m	m	m	m	m	m	20	m	m	m	m	m	m	m	m
Slovenia	25-26	m	m	m	m	m	m	18	21	23-26	m	m	m	m	m	m	24	26

Note : Up to 2004, graduation rates at the tertiary-type A or B levels were calculated on a gross basis. From 2005 and for countries with available data, graduation rates are calculated as net graduation rates (*i.e.* as the sum of age-specific graduation rates).

1. Net graduation rates are calculated in 2006 for Australia, Austria, the Czech Republic, Denmark, Finland, Germany, Greece, Iceland, the Netherlands, New Zealand, Norway, Poland, Portugal, the Slovak Republic, Sweden, Switzerland and the United Kingdom, and the partner countries Israel and Slovenia.

2. Net graduation rates are calculated in 2006 for Denmark, Finland, Greece, Iceland, New Zealand, Norway, Poland, Portugal, the Slovak Republic, Spain, Sweden, Turkey and the United Kingdom, and the partner country Slovenia.

3. The graduation rate for tertiary-type B programmes includes some graduates who have previously graduated at this level and therefore overestimates first-time graduation.

Source: OECD. See Annex 3 for notes (*www.oecd.org/edu/eag2008*).

Please refer to the Reader's Guide for information concerning the symbols replacing missing data.

StatLink ᵐ⁊ᔕ┗ http://dx.doi.org/10.1787/401523756323

A3

Table A3.3.
Graduation rates at different tertiary levels and proportion of international and foreign graduates in total graduate output (2006)
Calculations based on the number of graduates

	Tertiary-type B programmes (first degree)		Tertiary-type A programmes (first degree)		Tertiary-type A programmes (second degree)		Advanced research programmes	
	Graduation rate	Proportion of international/ foreign graduates in total graduate output	Graduation rate	Proportion of international/ foreign graduates in total graduate output	Graduation rate	Proportion of international/ foreign graduates in total graduate output	Graduation rate	Proportion of international/ foreign graduates in total graduate output
	(1)	(2)	(3)	(4)	(5)	(6)	(7)	(8)
OECD countries								
Australia[1]	16.4	m	59.1	23	17.8	56	1.8	19
Austria[1]	7.4	m	21.5	9	1.1	15	1.9	17
Belgium[3]	30.6	6	19.4	9	10.4	21	1.3	25
Canada[1,4]	m	m	39.3	5.2	7.3	14	0.9	14
Czech Republic[3]	5.7	1	29.8	6	8.5	3	1.2	7
Denmark[1]	11.0	4	45.3	5	13.9	7	1.2	8
Finland[2]	0.1	m	56.8	3	0.8	x(4)	2.1	10
France[4]	24.9	m	34.8	m	m	m	1.2	m
Germany[2]	10.8	m	21.2	6	1.7	31	2.3	13
Greece	13.0	m	22.3	m	4.9	m	0.9	m
Hungary[3]	4.5	1	35.9	3	5.0	1	0.7	5
Iceland[3]	4.2	1	64.5	2	18.8	4	0.4	7
Ireland	27.1	m	39.1	m	16.8	m	1.3	m
Italy[5]	0.1	m	37.6	m	14.5	m	1.2	m
Japan[1]	27.9	3	38.6	2	5.2	9	1.0	16
Korea	34.5	m	35.0	m	3.5	m	1.0	m
Luxembourg	m	m	m	m	m	m	m	m
Mexico	1.3	m	18.4	m	2.6	m	0.2	m
Netherlands	n	n	47.3	m	10.3	m	1.5	m
New Zealand[1]	28.4	21	54.9	18	16.3	17	1.1	13
Norway[1]	1.2	6	44.1	1	10.3	2	1.3	4
Poland	0.8	m	47.3	m	31.0	m	1.0	m
Portugal[3]	8.6	2	32.9	3	1.9	4	3.3	7
Slovak Republic[3]	1.2	m	34.6	1	8.1	1	1.5	1
Spain	14.5	m	30.6	m	m	m	1.0	m
Sweden[1]	5.0	1	41.9	3	3.6	10	2.2	5
Switzerland[2]	21.1	m	27.0	10	8.8	17	3.1	43
Turkey[3]	10.8	n	15.4	1	2.2	1	0.2	3
United Kingdom[1]	15.0	6	39.0	13	23.6	36	2.2	40
United States[1]	9.9	1	35.5	3	15.9	11	1.4	28
OECD average	*12.0*		*36.9*		*9.2*		*1.4*	
EU19 average	*10.0*		*35.4*		*9.2*		*1.6*	
Partner countries								
Brazil[4]	1.2	m	23.1	m	x(4)	m	1.4	m
Chile	9.0	m	15.4	m	3.5	m	0.1	m
Estonia[1]	21.9	n	28.1	2	7.6	4	0.8	1
Israel	m	m	36.2	m	12.0	m	1.3	m
Russian Federation	27.6	m	45.5	m	0.4	m	1.5	m
Slovenia[1]	28.8	1	21.9	1	3.5	3	1.3	2

1. International graduates are defined on the basis of their country of residence.
2. International graduates are defined on the basis of their country of prior education.
3. Foreign graduates are defined on the basis of their country of citizenship. These data are not comparable with data on international graduates and are therefore presented separately in the chart.
4. Year of reference 2005.
5. Advanced research programme graduates refer to 2005.
Source: OECD. See Annex 3 for notes (*www.oecd.org/edu/eag2008*).
Please refer to the Reader's Guide for information concerning the symbols replacing missing data.
StatLink ⬛ᵢₛ⬛ http://dx.doi.org/10.1787/401523756323

Table A3.4a.
Percentage of tertiary-type A and advanced research programmes graduates,
by field of education (2000, 2006)

A3

		Health and welfare		Life sciences, physical sciences & agriculture		Mathematics and computer science		Humanities, arts and education		Social sciences, business, law and services		Engineering, manufacturing and construction		Not known or unspecified	
		2000	2006	2000	2006	2000	2006	2000	2006	2000	2006	2000	2006	2000	2006
		(1)	(2)	(3)	(4)	(5)	(6)	(7)	(8)	(9)	(10)	(11)	(12)	(13)	(14)
OECD countries	Australia	15.0	13.3	8.0	6.2	5.1	8.2	25.2	22.3	38.8	42.8	7.9	7.2	n	n
	Austria	8.1	8.7	9.2	8.7	3.6	9.1	20.4	18.9	41.2	39.9	17.3	14.5	0.2	0.2
	Belgium	13.3	11.7	11.8	10.2	1.6	4.6	22.8	25.6	37.9	36.5	12.5	11.3	n	0.1
	Canada[1]	7.9	10.7	9.3	6.6	4.2	4.5	28.4	26.7	39.6	39.0	8.2	8.2	2.4	4.3
	Czech Republic	12.5	9.4	8.2	7.5	8.3	4.4	20.1	24.3	35.3	34.2	15.5	16.2	a	4.0
	Denmark	5.6	27.7	11.9	4.5	2.8	4.0	25.0	25.6	45.7	28.0	9.0	10.2	n	n
	Finland	19.3	19.2	6.9	5.7	3.3	5.3	20.5	19.9	26.1	29.2	24.0	20.7	n	n
	France[1]	2.9	8.8	13.3	8.8	5.5	5.9	27.3	19.1	39.5	44.8	11.2	12.6	0.3	n
	Germany	m	10.1	m	8.9	m	7.8	m	31.0	m	29.5	m	12.6	m	0.2
	Greece	m	m	m	m	m	m	m	m	m	m	m	m	m	m
	Hungary	7.3	8.8	4.8	4.1	1.1	4.6	31.5	27.7	45.5	48.5	9.8	6.3	a	n
	Iceland	15.3	12.4	7.6	5.8	3.8	2.9	37.8	35.3	28.4	36.9	7.1	6.8	a	n
	Ireland	7.8	14.2	11.8	14.8	9.6	n	29.2	28.6	32.2	34.4	9.3	8.0	0.2	n
	Italy[2]	17.3	14.2	6.9	6.6	3.7	2.1	18.5	22.3	37.6	37.8	16.0	14.9	n	2.1
	Japan	5.2	6.8	7.8	7.9	x(3)	x(4)	24.4	23.2	37.2	38.1	21.3	19.7	4.0	4.4
	Korea	6.6	8.5	9.7	7.5	4.5	5.2	26.5	26.1	25.3	26.7	27.4	26.0	a	n
	Luxembourg	m	m	m	m	m	m	m	m	m	m	m	m	m	m
	Mexico	7.8	9.0	4.2	4.8	6.7	8.2	21.4	18.1	45.9	45.1	14.0	14.3	a	0.4
	Netherlands	21.1	16.5	6.0	3.3	1.7	4.6	23.6	24.2	37.0	42.8	10.6	8.3	n	0.2
	New Zealand	12.9	14.5	12.7	7.9	1.7	5.9	33.9	25.7	30.3	39.9	5.6	5.3	2.8	0.8
	Norway	25.3	25.0	4.0	4.0	3.6	5.5	29.9	26.9	25.4	30.9	6.8	7.6	4.9	0.2
	Poland	1.7	7.9	3.7	5.1	1.4	4.8	20.6	25.2	40.3	48.3	8.0	8.6	24.2	n
	Portugal	10.2	19.7	5.4	6.6	3.3	5.9	30.8	23.4	39.1	32.6	11.2	11.7	n	n
	Slovak Republic	8.5	16.5	6.6	7.7	4.6	4.0	26.5	22.2	38.4	34.4	15.4	15.3	a	n
	Spain	11.9	14.6	8.7	7.1	4.4	5.4	22.8	23.8	39.2	34.6	12.9	14.3	n	0.1
	Sweden	22.8	25.7	5.8	4.8	3.7	3.8	24.5	23.1	22.6	24.6	20.5	18.0	n	n
	Switzerland	11.4	9.7	9.0	9.5	6.9	4.0	21.7	23.3	34.9	40.2	15.7	13.0	0.4	0.4
	Turkey	9.5	5.9	12.4	7.9	3.5	3.3	34.2	34.7	27.0	38.7	13.3	9.4	a	n
	United Kingdom	8.3	12.4	12.0	8.5	5.5	6.8	25.7	27.4	28.8	34.7	9.9	8.8	9.8	1.4
	United States	9.8	9.8	7.9	6.2	3.7	3.9	27.3	28.6	44.6	45.3	6.5	6.2	0.3	n
	OECD average	*11.0*	*13.3*	*8.4*	*6.9*	*4.2*	*5.2*	*26.5*	*24.9*	*35.7*	*37.1*	*12.5*	*11.9*	*1.8*	*0.6*
Partner countries	Brazil[1]	m	13.3	m	4.9	m	3.3	m	32.8	m	40.9	m	4.7	m	n
	Chile	m	13.0	m	6.8	m	3.3	m	26.0	m	35.7	m	15.2	m	n
	Estonia	m	6.1	m	9.3	m	5.7	m	28.3	m	40.9	m	9.7	m	n
	Israel	m	8.5	m	7.4	m	5.0	m	26.8	m	40.6	m	11.7	m	n
	Russian Federation	m	4.3	m	9.8	m	x(4)	m	16.3	m	51.3	m	18.3	m	n
	Slovenia	m	10.6	m	5.8	m	2.5	m	25.4	m	45.5	m	10.2	m	n

1. Year of reference 2005.
2. Advanced research programme graduates refer to 2005.
Source: OECD. See Annex 3 for notes (*www.oecd.org/edu/eag2008*).
Please refer to the Reader's Guide for information concerning the symbols replacing missing data.
StatLink ⫶⫶⫶ http://dx.doi.org/10.1787/401523756323

Table A3.5a.
Percentage of tertiary qualifications awarded to females in tertiary-type A and advanced research programmes, by field of education (2000, 2006)

	All fields of education: first tertiary-type A degree		All fields of education: second tertiary-type A degree		All fields of education: advanced research degree		Health and welfare		Life sciences, physical sciences & agriculture		Mathematics and computer science		Humanities, arts and education		Social sciences, business, law and services		Engineering, manufacturing and construction	
	2000	2006	2000	2006	2000	2006	2000	2006	2000	2006	2000	2006	2000	2006	2000	2006	2000	2006
	(1)	(2)	(3)	(4)	(5)	(6)	(7)	(8)	(9)	(10)	(11)	(12)	(13)	(14)	(15)	(16)	(17)	(18)
OECD countries																		
Australia	57	59	56	46	40	47	76	77	50	55	27	23	70	70	52	54	21	24
Austria	48	53	32	44	36	42	59	65	46	55	15	20	66	70	49	57	18	22
Belgium	50	53	53	60	34	38	59	63	40	51	25	20	65	67	52	57	21	25
Canada[1]	59	62	52	52	39	44	74	82	53	58	28	27	68	70	58	58	23	25
Czech Republic	51	56	53	57	29	36	70	74	45	58	12	20	71	74	54	60	27	21
Denmark	51	63	49	54	38	44	59	81	48	53	28	24	69	68	44	50	26	29
Finland	59	64	59	63	45	48	84	87	51	56	35	37	77	78	65	71	19	22
France[1]	57	55	56	55	41	41	60	56	49	50	31	25	73	73	59	60	24	26
Germany	m	52	m	48	m	41	m	65	m	51	m	34	m	74	m	53	m	22
Greece	m	64	m	53	m	35	m	m	m	m	m	m	m	m	m	m	m	34
Hungary	60	65	36	68	38	44	70	80	42	49	17	20	71	77	51	67	21	29
Iceland	67	69	59	62	50	53	82	90	57	55	22	18	83	80	57	61	25	38
Ireland	55	60	60	60	47	46	75	83	53	49	41	x(10)	69	71	57	57	24	20
Italy[2]	56	58	56	61	53	52	58	65	51	56	54	37	82	79	55	57	28	30
Japan	37	43	23	29	19	27	50	58	30	32	x(9)	x(10)	67	68	26	38	9	11
Korea	47	49	30	40	20	27	50	63	42	46	49	38	70	71	40	45	23	24
Luxembourg	m	m	m	m	m	m	m	m	m	m	m	m	m	m	m	m	m	m
Mexico	52	55	m	50	36	41	61	64	41	46	43	40	65	68	55	59	22	28
Netherlands	54	56	66	59	m	39	76	75	37	48	16	10	71	73	49	52	13	17
New Zealand	64	61	54	62	43	50	79	81	46	55	34	27	73	73	53	57	33	28
Norway	64	64	52	55	33	40	82	83	46	57	15	20	75	69	48	54	27	23
Poland	m	63	68	70	m	50	68	71	64	65	58	29	78	78	64	68	24	32
Portugal	67	67	72	70	52	60	77	80	62	65	56	36	80	78	63	64	35	36
Slovak Republic	52	61	a	56	38	47	69	85	41	51	17	20	71	68	50	60	30	31
Spain	59	60	m	m	44	47	76	78	52	56	34	27	72	74	60	61	27	32
Sweden	60	65	93	76	37	43	79	83	53	58	39	30	75	78	57	62	25	31
Switzerland	42	51	26	39	31	39	54	66	33	43	16	14	62	67	35	44	11	17
Turkey	41	46	39	47	37	40	53	67	44	44	42	39	45	55	39	41	24	25
United Kingdom	54	57	54	56	38	43	71	75	52	50	27	25	67	67	55	56	20	22
United States	57	58	56	59	44	49	75	79	51	54	33	27	68	68	53	55	21	22
OECD average	*55*	*58*	*52*	*56*	*39*	*43*	*68*	*74*	*48*	*52*	*31*	*26*	*70*	*72*	*52*	*56*	*23*	*26*
EU19 average	*56*	*59*	*54*	*60*	*41*	*44*	*69*	*74*	*49*	*54*	*32*	*26*	*72*	*73*	*55*	*60*	*24*	*27*
Partner countries																		
Brazil[1]	m	62	m	m	m	55	m	74	m	53	m	28	m	79	m	56	m	31
Chile	m	56	m	39	m	35	m	68	m	48	m	28	m	69	m	49	m	28
Estonia	m	70	m	73	m	57	m	85	m	67	m	36	m	87	m	70	m	40
Israel	m	59	m	58	m	51	m	77	m	54	m	30	m	76	m	57	m	26
Russian Federation	m	m	m	m	m	m	m	m	m	m	m	m	m	m	m	m	m	m
Slovenia	m	67	m	53	m	50	m	79	m	62	m	15	m	76	m	64	m	30

1. Year of reference 2005.
2. Second tertiary-type A degree graduates partially refer to 2005 and advanced reseach programme graduates refer to 2005.

Source: OECD. See Annex 3 for notes (*www.oecd.org/edu/eag2008*).

Please refer to the Reader's Guide for information concerning the symbols replacing missing data.

StatLink http://dx.doi.org/10.1787/401523756323

Table A3.6.
Science graduates, by gender (2006)
Per 100 000 25-to-34-year-olds in employment

	Tertiary-type B			Tertiary-type A and advanced research programmes			All tertiary education		
	M + F	Males	Females	M + F	Males	Females	M + F	Males	Females
	(1)	(2)	(3)	(4)	(5)	(6)	(7)	(8)	(9)
Australia	444	592	255	2 178	2 656	1 572	2 622	3 248	1 827
Austria	336	534	102	937	1 242	577	1 273	1 776	678
Belgium	413	656	135	839	1 069	576	1 252	1 725	711
Canada[1]	m	m	m	1 119	1 360	847	m	m	m
Czech Republic	74	93	46	1 112	1 353	745	1 186	1 446	791
Denmark	251	267	231	1 234	1 559	859	1 484	1 826	1 090
Finland	n	n	n	2 289	2 971	1 449	2 335	3 026	1 484
France[1]	835	1 264	316	1 871	2 300	1 353	2 706	3 564	1 670
Germany	238	407	34	1 185	1 454	863	1 423	1 861	897
Greece	m	m	m	m	m	m	m	m	m
Hungary	60	78	33	697	855	475	757	934	508
Iceland	47	80	6	1 310	1 398	1 200	1 357	1 478	1 206
Ireland	1 034	1 511	456	1 555	1 837	1 213	2 589	3 348	1 670
Italy[2]	n	n	n	1 416	1 530	1 257	1 416	1 530	1 257
Japan	451	643	176	1 161	1 691	398	1 612	2 334	574
Korea	1 820	2 314	1 103	2 042	2 420	1 493	3 863	4 735	2 596
Luxembourg	m	m	m	m	m	m	m	m	m
Mexico	127	150	89	930	990	836	1 057	1 140	925
Netherlands	n	n	n	1 002	1 548	391	1 002	1 548	391
New Zealand	516	683	318	1 813	2 069	1 509	2 330	2 752	1 827
Norway	11	16	6	1 011	1 375	607	1 022	1 391	613
Poland	a	a	a	2 016	2 203	1 781	2 016	2 203	1 781
Portugal	262	350	161	1 035	1 140	915	1 410	1 594	1 199
Slovak Republic	9	11	5	1 410	1 559	1 196	1 418	1 570	1 201
Spain	445	644	183	844	941	714	1 289	1 585	897
Sweden	151	204	90	1 478	1 800	1 112	1 716	2 118	1 260
Switzerland	716	1 194	145	1 109	1 547	586	1 825	2 741	731
Turkey	558	551	581	564	485	812	1 122	1 037	1 393
United Kingdom	316	439	176	1 974	2 528	1 337	2 290	2 967	1 513
United States	276	406	115	1 093	1 297	841	1 368	1 703	956
OECD average	*361*	*503*	*183*	*1 340*	*1 631*	*985*	*1 694*	*2 118*	*1 172*
EU19 average	*260*	*380*	*116*	*1 366*	*1 672*	*994*	*1 621*	*2 036*	*1 118*
Brazil	m	m	m	m	m	m	m	m	m
Chile	m	m	m	m	m	m	m	m	m
Estonia	m	m	m	m	m	m	m	m	m
Israel	m	m	m	m	m	m	m	m	m
Russian Federation	m	m	m	m	m	m	m	m	m
Slovenia	m	m	m	m	m	m	m	m	m

Note: Science fields include life sciences, physical sciences, mathematics and computing, engineering and engineering trades, manufacturing and processing, architecture and building.
1. Year of reference 2005 for the number of sciences graduates.
2. Advanced research programmes graduates refer to 2005.
Source: OECD. See Annex 3 for notes (*www.oecd.org/edu/eag2008*).
Please refer to the Reader's Guide for information concerning the symbols replacing missing data.
StatLink ⟨⟨⟨ http://dx.doi.org/10.1787/401523756323

HOW MANY STUDENTS COMPLETE AND DROP OUT OF TERTIARY EDUCATION?

Tertiary education covers a wide range of programmes, but serves overall as an indicator of countries' production of advanced skills. A traditional university degree is associated with completion of tertiary-type A courses; tertiary-type B generally refers to shorter and often vocationally oriented courses. This indicator shows current tertiary completion rates in education systems, *i.e.* the percentage of students who follow and successfully complete tertiary programmes. Although "dropping out" is not necessarily an indicator of failure from the perspective of the individual student, high dropout rates may indicate that the education system is not meeting students' needs.

Key results

Chart A4.1. Proportion of students who enter a tertiary programme and leave without at least a first tertiary degree (2005)

The chart shows the proportion of students who enter a tertiary programme and leave without at least a first tertiary degree.

On average in the 19 OECD countries for which data are available, some 31% of tertiary students fail to successfully complete a programme equivalent to this level of education. Completion rates differ widely among OECD countries. In Hungary, Italy, New Zealand and the United States, more than 40% of those who enter tertiary programmes leave without tertiary qualifications (in either a tertiary-type A or a tertiary-type B programme) in contrast to their counterparts in Belgium (Flemish Community), Denmark, France, Germany and Japan and the partner country the Russian Federation where the proportion is less than 24%.

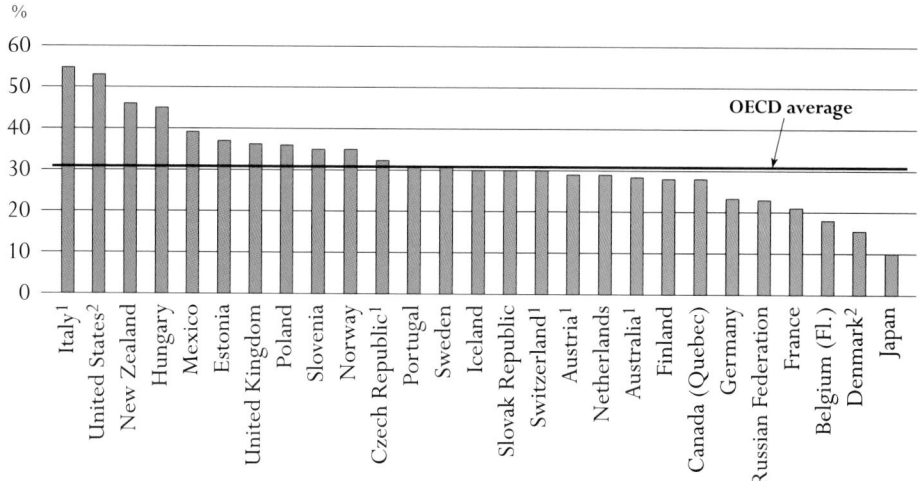

1. Only tertiary-type A programmes.
2. Only full-time students.
Countries are ranked in descending order of the proportion of students who enter into a tertiary programme and leave without at least a first tertiary degree.
Source: OECD. Table A4.1. See Annex 3 for notes (*www.oecd.org/edu/eag2008*).
StatLink ⟦ᴸᴵⁿ⟧ http://dx.doi.org/10.1787/401536355051

- Tertiary-type B completion rates are, at 62%, somewhat lower than those for tertiary-type A, and there is wide country variation. Tertiary-type B completion rates range from above 80% in Belgium (Flemish Community), Denmark and Japan to below 40% in New Zealand, Sweden and the United States.

- Beginning but not completing a tertiary-type A programme does not necessarily represent a failure if students benefit from the time spent in the programme to move successfully to the other tertiary education track. In France and to a lesser extent in Denmark and New Zealand, a significant proportion of students (15% in France and 3% in the two other countries) who do not complete the tertiary-type A programme are successfully re-oriented to a tertiary-type B programme.

- Full-time students have better chances of completing their course than do part-time students. On average in the ten countries for which data are available, 60% of part-time students completed at least a first tertiary-type A degree, while on average 68% of full-time students at this level graduate. The largest differences between full-time and part-time students are observed in Canada (Quebec) and New Zealand where completion rates for full-time students that enter tertiary-type A education are at least 25 percentage points higher than for students with part-time status.

- Non-completion of a degree does not mean that the skills and competencies acquired will be lost and are not valued by the labour market. This is particularly the case in Canada, where one year of study can provide students attractive opportunities for employment on the labour market. This helps explain students' decisions to leave the education system before graduating. In Sweden, students can leave a tertiary-type A programme before completing it, enter the labour market and continue their studies later. They do not lose the benefit of the modules already completed.

- There is no relationship observable between the charging of tuition fees and completion rates. In countries in which tuition fees charged by tertiary-type A educational institutions exceed USD 1 500 (Australia, Canada, the Netherlands, New Zealand, the United Kingdom and the United States), completion rates in tertiary-type A education are significantly lower than the OECD average in New Zealand and the United States but above 70% in the other countries. By contrast, the case of Denmark shows that no tuition fees and a high level of public subsidies available for students can lead to completion rates above the OECD average (81%).

A4

Policy context

Tertiary level dropout and completion rates can be useful indicators of the internal efficiency of tertiary education systems. However, students may leave a tertiary programme for many reasons: they may realise that they have chosen the wrong subject or educational programme; they may fail to meet the standards set by their educational institution, particularly in tertiary systems that provide relatively broad access; or they may find attractive employment before completing their programme. Dropping out is not necessarily an indication of an individual student's failure, but high dropout rates may well indicate that the education system is not meeting the needs of students. Students may find that the educational programmes offered do not meet their expectations or their labour market needs. It may also be that programmes take longer than the number of years for which students can justify being outside the labour market.

Evidence and explanations

Completion rates in tertiary education

Overall tertiary completion rates count as "completing" students who enter a tertiary-type A programme and who graduate with either a tertiary-type A or a type B qualification or those who enter a tertiary-type B programme and who graduate with either a tertiary-type A or a tertiary-type B qualification. On average among the 19 OECD countries for which data are available, some 31% of tertiary students fail to successfully complete a programme equivalent to this level of education. Completion rates differ widely among OECD and partner countries. In Hungary, New Zealand and the United States, more than 40% of those who enter a tertiary programme leave without a tertiary qualification (either tertiary-type A or tertiary-type B) in contrast to their counterparts in Belgium (Flemish Community), Denmark, France, Germany and Japan and the partner country the Russian Federation, where the proportion is less than 24% (Table A4.1 and Chart A4.1).

The difference between the proportion of skilled jobs and the proportion of people with tertiary education (see Indicator A1) suggests that most countries may benefit from further increase in the output of tertiary graduates. Increasing the proportion of students who enter a tertiary programme and leave with a tertiary qualification can help to improve the internal efficiency of tertiary education systems, especially when a small proportion of upper secondary graduates enter tertiary education or when the graduation rate is relatively low compared to the OECD average. In terms of three variables (entry, graduation and completion rates), two countries may have similar graduation rates but significant differences on the two other variables, so that they should adopt different strategies to improve their internal efficiency. For example, Japan and Sweden had similar first-time graduation rates in 2006 (39 and 41%, respectively) but also significant differences in the level of entry and completion rates in tertiary-type A education. Whereas Japan counterbalances below-average entry rates into tertiary-type A programmes (41% in 2001 against 48% on average) with, at 91%, the highest completion rates among OECD and partner countries, Sweden had an entry rate well above the average in 2001 (69%) but a below-average completion rate (69%).

Completion rates in tertiary-type A and tertiary-type B education

On average among the 24 OECD countries for which data are available, some 31% of tertiary-type A students fail to successfully complete the programme they enter. Completion rates differ widely among OECD countries. In Italy, Hungary, New Zealand and the United States, less than 60% of those who enter tertiary-type A programmes go on to successfully complete their programme, in contrast to their counterparts in Denmark, the United Kingdom and the partner country the Russian Federation where the completion rates are around 80% and in Japan where it is 91%. Tertiary-type B completion rates are, at 62% on average, somewhat lower than those for tertiary-type A programmes, and again there is wide country variation. Tertiary-type B completion rates range from above 80% in Belgium (Flemish Community), Denmark and Japan to below 40% in New Zealand, Sweden and the United States (Table A4.1).

Increasing tuition fees to improve completion rates in tertiary-type A education is often debated in OECD countries whose educational institutions charge low tuition fees. In fact, increasing the tuition fees charged by tertiary-type A institutions and exemption from tuition fees for academic merit are measures already used in some OECD countries to try to increase students' incentives to finish their studies quickly. However, it is difficult to see a relationship between completion rates in tertiary-type A programmes and the level of tuition fees charged by tertiary-type A institutions. The countries in which tuition fees charged by tertiary-type A educational institutions exceed USD 1 500 are Australia, Canada, the Netherlands, New Zealand, the United Kingdom and the United States. Completion rates are significantly lower than the OECD average (69%) in New Zealand and the United States but above 70% in the others. By way of contrast, Denmark does not charge tuition fees and provides a high level of public subsidies for students but has completion rates above the OECD average (81%). This is not surprising because all indicators on tertiary education and especially on rates of return show that compared to upper secondary attainment, tertiary-type A educational attainment significantly benefits individuals in terms of earnings and employment. This can create a sufficiently big incentive, independently of the level of tuition fees, for students to finish their studies (see Indicators A9, A10 and B5).

Consequences of non-completion of tertiary-type A programmes

Non-completion and delayed completion may have various consequences. On the one hand, it can be interpreted as an ineffective use of resources as it raises the cost of a tertiary degree and, in systems with limited capacities to enrol students, it may prevent (or delay) some students (with the qualifications to enter tertiary education) from starting their preferred programmes. It may also be detrimental to the quality of teaching and learning (OECD, 2008a). On the other hand, non-completion of a tertiary programme is not always associated with a failure of the education system or time lost and lower benefits for individuals (compared to those who terminate their studies after receiving an upper secondary qualification) for three main reasons.

First of all, beginning a tertiary-type A programme but not graduating is not necessarily linked to failure if students can be successfully re-oriented towards the other track of tertiary education. Thus, in France and to a lesser extent in Denmark and New Zealand, a significant proportion of students (15% in France and 3% in the other two) who have not completed tertiary-type A level are successfully re-oriented to tertiary-type B level. In other words, in France, out of 100 students who start a tertiary-type A programme, 64 will receive at least a first tertiary-type A qualification, 15 will be reoriented to a tertiary-type B programme and only 21 will leave without a tertiary qualification. Re-orientation is more frequent in tertiary-type B education; in Iceland, New Zealand and Sweden 22, 9 and 27%, respectively, of students who do not complete this level are re-oriented to a tertiary-type A programme. Among these countries, only New Zealand has a large proportion of students enrolled in tertiary-type B education (Table A4.1 and Chart A4.2).

A4

Chart A4.2. **Completion rates in tertiary-type A education (2005)**

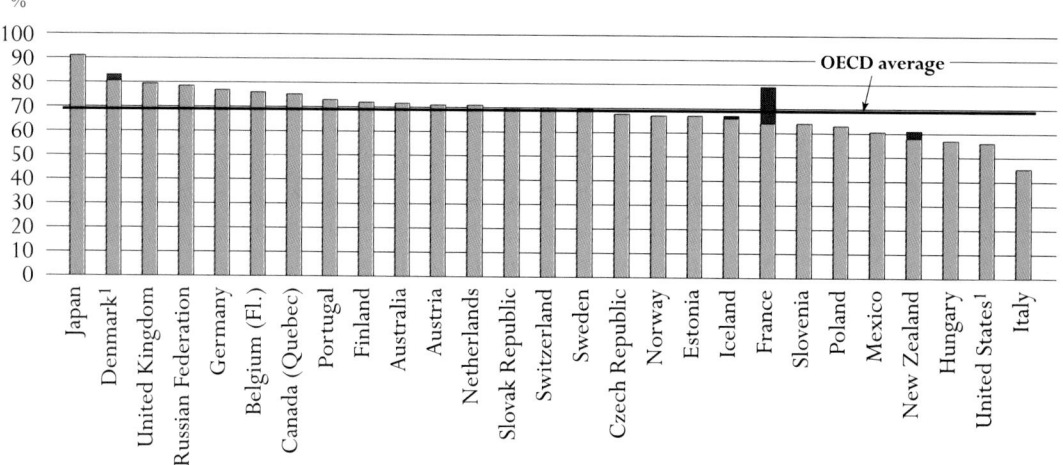

☐ 5A completion rates (at least first 5A programme)

■ Not completed 5A level but re-oriented with success at 5B level

1. Only full-time students.

Countries are ranked in descending order of the tertiary-type A completion rates.

Source: OECD. Table A4.1. See Annex 3 for notes (*www.oecd.org/edu/eag2008*).

StatLink ⟟ॐ http://dx.doi.org/10.1787/401536355051

Second, in some countries not all courses offered in tertiary-type A education are followed to obtain a degree. For instance, an individual might attend courses in a given programme on a part-time basis for professional development, with no intention of completing the associated degree. Some other tertiary students (generally mature students) may also follow courses that are not part of a programme leading to a degree to increase their lifelong learning perspectives. On average for the ten OECD countries for which data are available, students enrolled in part-time studies represent 23% of total enrolment and exceed 40% in Hungary, New Zealand, Poland and the partner economy the Russian Federation. On average, 60% of part-time students who enter a tertiary-type A programme achieve at least a first degree at this level; the average completion rate for full-time students in tertiary-type A education is 68%. The largest differences between full-time and part-time students are observed in Canada (Quebec) and New Zealand, where completion rates for full time students in tertiary-type A education are at least 25 percentage points higher than for students with part-time status (Table A4.2). The large number of part-time students in New Zealand partially explains the high proportion of people leaving without qualifications: part-time students may enrol in a few modules (*e.g.* for vocational upskilling reasons) with no intention of completing all the courses required for the qualification (Table A4.2 and Chart A4.1).

Lastly, in some countries many students successfully complete some parts of a qualification but do not finish the whole programme. Non-completion of a degree does not mean that the acquired skills and competencies are lost and not valued by the labour market in these countries. In Canada, for example, one year of study can provide students attractive opportunities for employment. This may explain why students choose to leave the education system before graduating. In Sweden, students can leave a tertiary-type A programme before completing it, be employed for some time and later decide to continue their studies. They do not lose the benefit of the modules that they successfully completed in the past. In some other countries, students may successfully complete all modules they undertake, yet never enrol in enough modules to complete the qualification. For example, in New Zealand, where part-time study is more common, it is estimated that around one in five students complete all modules they enrol in, yet never enrol in enough modules to complete the qualification.

Thus, the extent to which non-completion of tertiary education is a policy problem will vary between countries and completion rates should be interpreted with caution. It will be interesting to see if changes in the labour market over the next decades in OECD and partner countries will have an effect on the incentives for individuals to complete tertiary studies. If there is further expansion of tertiary education over the next decade (which is a feasible option in most countries), completion of tertiary programmes will be more highly valued on the labour market and the benefit of entering tertiary education without graduating with at least a first degree will be eroded (see Indicator A1).

Definitions and methodologies

Data on completion rates were collected through a special survey undertaken in 2007. The completion rate is calculated as the ratio of the number of students who graduate from an initial degree during the reference year to the number of new entrants in this degree n years before, with n being the number of years of full-time study required to complete the degree. The calculation of the completion rate is defined from a cohort analysis in one-half of the countries listed in Table A4.1 (true cohort method). The estimation for the other countries assumes constant student flows at the tertiary level, owing to the need for consistency between the graduate cohort in the reference year and the entrant cohort n years before (cross-section method). This assumption may be an oversimplification (see Annex 3 at *www.oecd.org/edu/eag2008*).

Dropouts are defined as students who leave the specified level without graduating from a first qualification at that level. The first qualification refers to any degree, regardless of the duration of study, obtained at the end of a programme that does not have a previous degree at the same level as a pre-requisite.

A4

Table A4.1.
Completion rates in tertiary education (2005)
Calculated separately for tertiary-type A and tertiary-type B programmes: Number of graduates from these programmes divided by the number of new entrants to these programmes in the typical year of entrance

		Year used for new entrants		Tertiary education		Tertiary-type A education		Tertiary-type B education	
	Method	5A	5B	Completion rates (at least first 5B or 5A programme)[1]	Leaving without tertiary qualification	5A completion rates (at least first 5A programme)[2]	Not completed 5A level but re-oriented with success at 5B level	5B completion rates (at least first 5B programme)[3]	Not completed 5B level but re-oriented with success at 5A level
Australia	Cross-section	2003-05	m	m	m	72	m	m	m
Austria	Cross-section	2000-03	m	m	m	71	m	m	m
Belgium (Fl.)	Cross-section	1998-2001	2003-04	82	18	76	m	88	m
Canada (Quebec)	True cohort	2000	2000	72	28	75	n	63	n
Czech Republic	Cross-section	m	m	m	m	68	m	m	m
Denmark[4]	True cohort	1995-96	1995-96	85	15	81	3	88	3
Finland	True cohort	1995	1995	72	28	72	a	a	a
France	True cohort	1996-2003	1996-2003	79	21	64	15	78	2
Germany	Cross-section	2001-02	2003-04	77	23	77	n	77	n
Greece	m	m	m	m	m	m	m	m	m
Hungary	Cross-section	2001-04	2004-05	55	45	57	m	44	m
Iceland	True cohort	1996-97	1996-97	70	30	66	1	55	22
Ireland	m	m	m	m	m	m	m	m	m
Italy	True cohort	1998-99	1998-99	m	m	45	m	m	m
Japan	Cross-section	2000 and 2002	2004	90	10	91	m	87	m
Korea	m	m	m	m	m	m	m	m	m
Luxembourg	m	m	m	m	m	m	m	m	m
Mexico	Cross-section	2002-03	2004-05	61	39	61	a	64	a
Netherlands	True cohort	1997-98	1997-98	71	29	71	a	n	n
New Zealand	True cohort	1998	1998	54	46	58	3	30	9
Norway	True cohort	1994-95	1994-95	65	35	67	m	66	m
Poland	Cross-section	2001-04	2003-04	64	36	63	m	71	m
Portugal	Cross-section	2001-06	2004	69	31	73	m	59	m
Slovak Republic	Cross-section	2000-03	2003-04	70	30	70	m	72	m
Spain	m	m	m	m	m	m	m	m	m
Sweden	True cohort	1995-96	1995-96	69	31	69	1	33	27
Switzerland	True cohort	1996-2001	1996-2001	m	m	70	m	m	m
Turkey	m	m	m	m	m	m	m	m	m
United Kingdom	Cross-section	2003-04	2003-04	64	36	79	m	43	m
United States[4]	True cohort	1999	2002	47	53	56	m	33	m
OECD average				69	31	69	~	62	~
Brazil	m	m	m	m	m	m	m	m	m
Chile	m	m	m	m	m	m	m	m	m
Estonia	Cross-section	2003	2003	63	37	67	m	59	m
Israel	m	m	m	m	m	m	m	m	m
Russian Federation	Cross-section	2001-02	2002-03	77	23	79	m	76	m
Slovenia	Cross-section	2001-02	2001-02	65	35	64	m	67	m

Note: The cross-section method refers to the number of graduates in the calendar year 2005 and is calculated according to the traditional OECD approach taking into account different durations. True section method is defined from a cohort analysis and based on Panel data.

1. Completion rates in tertiary education represent the proportion of those who enter a tertiary-type A or a tertiary-type B programme, who go on to graduate from either at least a first tertiary-type A or a first tertiary-type B programme.

2. Completion rates in tertiary-type A education represent the proportion of those who enter a tertiary-type A programme, who go on to graduate from at least a first tertiary-type A programme.

3. Completion rates in tertiary-type B education represent the proportion of those who enter a tertiary-type B programme, who go on to graduate from at least a first tertiary-type B programme.

4. Only full-time students.

Source: OECD. See Annex 3 for notes (www.oecd.org/edu/eag2008).

Please refer to the Reader's Guide for information concerning the symbols replacing missing data.

StatLink 🖼️ http://dx.doi.org/10.1787/401536355051

Table A4.2.

Completion rates in tertiary-type A education by mode of study (2005)

Proportion of those who enter a tertiary-type A programme, who go on to graduate from at least a first tertiary-type A programme, by mode of study

		Method	Year used for new entrants		Porportion of new entrants enrolled in[1]:		5A completion rates (at least first 5A programme)	
			5A	5B	Full-time	Part time	Full-time	Part time
OECD countries	**Canada (Quebec)**	True cohort	2000	2000	91	9	79	38
	Denmark	True cohort	1995-96	1995-96	m	m	81	m
	Hungary	Cross-section	2001-04	2004-05	53	47	60	54
	Italy	True cohort	1998-99	1998-99	100	n	45	n
	Japan	Cross-section	2000 and 2002	2004	97	3	91	85
	Mexico	Cross-section	2002-03	2004-05	100	n	61	n
	Netherlands	True cohort	1997-98	1997-98	90	10	73	57
	New Zealand	True cohort	1998	1998	42	58	73	48
	Norway	True cohort	1994-95	1994-95	85	15	69	57
	Poland	Cross-section	2001-04	2003-04	50	50	66	61
	Slovak Republic	Cross-section	2000-03	2003-04	66	34	64	81
	United States	True cohort	1999	2002	m	m	56	m
	OECD average				***77***	***23***	***68***	***60***
Partner countries	**Estonia**	Cross-section	2003	2003	80	20	70	55
	Russian Federation	Cross-section	2001-02	2002-03	57	43	74	83

1. Based on the data collected in the 2008 OECD survey.

Source: OECD. See Annex 3 for notes (*www.oecd.org/edu/eag2008*).

Please refer to the Reader's Guide for information concerning the symbols replacing missing data.

StatLink http://dx.doi.org/10.1787/401536355051

WHAT CAN 15-YEAR-OLDS DO IN SCIENCE?

This indicator examines the science performance of 15-year-old students, drawing on 2006 data from the OECD's Programme for International Student Assessment (PISA). It describes science proficiency in each country in terms of the percentage of students reaching one of six proficiency levels as well as in terms of the mean scores achieved by students on the overall science scale and on different aspects of science. It also examines the distribution of student scores within countries.

Key results

Chart A5.1. **Distribution of student performance on the PISA science scale (2006)**

The chart summarises the overall performance of 15-year-old students in different countries on the OECD PISA 2006 science scale. The width between the two blue dash symbols indicates the statistical uncertainty of the estimate of the mean performance.

Mean score on the PISA science scale ⟶ ⊙ } 95% confidence interval around the mean score

Finland, with an average of 563 score points, achieved the highest score and was statistically above the average scores of all other countries. Four other high-scoring countries had mean scores of 530 to 534 points: Canada, Japan and New Zealand and the partner country Estonia. Eleven other countries (Australia, Austria, Belgium, the Czech Republic, Germany, Ireland, Korea, the Netherlands, Switzerland and the United Kingdom and the partner country Slovenia) also scored above the OECD average of 500 points. Five countries (Denmark, France, Hungary, Poland and Sweden) performed close to the OECD average, and the remaining 11 OECD countries and 4 partner countries performed below it.

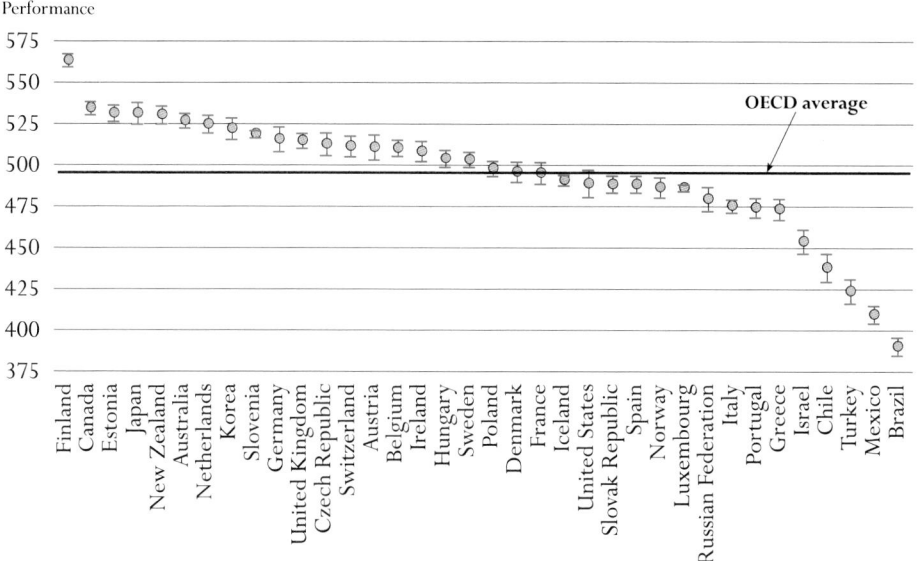

Countries are ranked in descending order of mean score.

Source: OECD. Table A5.1. See Annex 3 for notes (*www.oecd.org/edu/eag2008*).

StatLink ⌖⌗⌗ http://dx.doi.org/10.1787/401573312123

- On average across OECD countries, 1.3% of 15-year-olds reached the highest level of science proficiency (Level 6 of the PISA 2006 science scale). In Finland and New Zealand this figure was at least 3.9%, three times the OECD average. In Australia, Canada, Japan and the United Kingdom, as well as in the partner country Slovenia, between 2 and 3% reached Level 6.

- With the exception of Finland and the partner country Estonia, all countries had at least 10% of students who performed at Level 1 or below. In 15 countries more than 20% of students performed at this level. In Mexico and in the partner country Brazil, a majority of students performed at Level 1 or below.

- Countries demonstrated relative strengths and weaknesses in the specific science competencies measured by PISA (*identifying scientific issues*, *explaining phenomena scientifically* and *using scientific evidence*). Students scored at least 10 points higher in *identifying scientific issues* than in the overall science score in Mexico and Portugal, and at least 10 points lower in the Czech Republic, Hungary, Poland and the Slovak Republic and in the partner countries Estonia and the Russian Federation. Students scored at least 10 points higher in *explaining phenomena scientifically* than in the overall science score in the Czech Republic, Hungary and the Slovak Republic, and at least 10 points lower in France and Korea and in the partner country Israel. Students scored at least 10 points higher in *using scientific evidence* than in the overall science score in France, Japan and Korea and at least 10 points lower in the Czech Republic, Norway and the Slovak Republic, and in the partner country Brazil.

- Males and females performed equally well on the overall science scale in the majority of countries, including 22 of the 30 OECD countries. In two OECD countries and one partner country, females outperformed males, on average, while males outperformed females in six OECD countries and two partner countries. In no OECD country was the gender difference larger than 12 points on the overall science scale. However, similarities in average performance mask certain gender differences. In most countries, females were stronger on average in *identifying scientific issues*, while males were stronger on average in *explaining phenomena scientifically*.

A5

Policy context

For much of the last century, school science and mathematics curricula were dominated by the need to provide the foundations for the professional training of a small number of scientists, engineers and mathematicians. With the growing role of science, mathematics and technology in modern life, however, the objectives of personal fulfilment, employment and full participation in society increasingly require that all adults – not just those aspiring to a scientific career – be scientifically, mathematically and technologically literate. Many situations, problems and issues encountered by individuals in their daily lives require an understanding of science and technology before they can be fully understood or addressed. Individuals need the ability to use science knowledge and apply scientific thought processes not only at the personal level, but at the community, national and global levels as well. An understanding of science and technology is central to a young person's preparedness for life in modern society. It also empowers individuals to participate in the determination of public policy where issues of science and technology affect their lives. This indicator examines the scientific literacy of 15-year-old students and draws on data from the Programme for International Student Assessment (PISA) 2006, in which science was a major focus.

Evidence and explanations

This indicator examines the scientific literacy of 15-year-old students in several ways (see Box A5.1 for a PISA definition of scientific literacy). First, it describes performance in terms of the mean scores achieved by students on the overall science scale and how the means compare among countries and to the OECD average. Then, it describes proficiency in terms of the percentage of students reaching different performance levels on the science scale in each country, highlighting performance at the low and high ends of the distribution. Finally, it shows the countries in which students were relatively stronger and weaker in the three different science competencies as well as gender differences in performance on these competencies.

Mean scores on the overall science scale

One way to summarise student performance and to compare the relative standing of countries in terms of student performance is through the mean scores for students in each country. To the extent that high average performance at age 15 can be considered predictive of a highly skilled future workforce, countries with high average performance will have an important economic and social advantage. This section describes country means on the overall scale.

Chart A5.2 summarises student performance in different countries on the overall science scale, in terms of the mean student score. It indicates which countries performed above, at, or below the OECD average, and it also shows the comparative performance of individual countries with each of the other countries. Only differences that are statistically significant should be taken into account.

Students in Finland scored 563 points on average, compared to the OECD mean of 500. This score was an estimated 29 points above that of any other country, making Finland the highest scoring country in science.

Four other high-scoring countries had mean scores of 530 to 534 points: Canada, Japan and New Zealand and the partner country Estonia. Other countries scoring statistically significantly above the OECD average included Australia, Austria, Belgium, the Czech Republic, Germany, Ireland, Korea, the Netherlands, Switzerland and the United Kingdom and the partner country Slovenia.

Box A5.1. **What is scientific literacy in PISA?**

Scientific literacy is defined as the extent to which an individual:

• Possesses scientific knowledge and uses that knowledge to identify questions, acquire new knowledge, explain scientific phenomena, and draw evidence-based conclusions about science-related issues.

• Understands the characteristic features of science as a form of human knowledge and enquiry.

• Shows awareness of how science and technology shape our material, intellectual and cultural environments.

• Engages in science-related issues and with the ideas of science, as a reflective citizen.

What scales are reported? PISA summarises student performance on an overall science scale that provides a picture of students' accumulated understanding of science at age 15. The results for the overall science scale are completed by a more detailed analysis of performance with scales on the science competencies (identifying scientific issues, explaining phenomena scientifically and using scientific evidence), knowledge domains (knowledge about science and knowledge of science) and content areas ("Physical systems", "Living systems", and "Earth and space systems"). The three competencies were a key organising element of the framework and are reported on individually because of their importance to the practice of science and their connection to key cognitive abilities such as inductive/deductive reasoning, systems-based thinking, critical decision making, transformation of information, construction and communication of arguments and explanations based on data, thinking in terms of models, and use of science.

What do the scale scores mean? The scores on each scale represent degrees of proficiency along each dimension or aspect of science (in this indicator, the overall science scale and the science competency scales are used). For example, a low score on a scale indicates that a student has more limited skills, whereas a high score indicates that a student has more advanced skills in this area.

What are proficiency levels? In an attempt to capture this progression, each of the science scales is divided into six levels based on the type of knowledge and skills students need to demonstrate at a particular level. Students at a particular level are not only likely to demonstrate the knowledge and skills associated with that level but are also likely to demonstrate the proficiencies defined by lower levels. Thus, all students proficient at Level 3 are also proficient at Levels 1 and 2.

Five countries (Denmark, France, Hungary, Poland and Sweden) performed close to the OECD average. The 15 remaining countries (11 OECD countries and 4 partner countries) performed statistically significantly below it. Of the 30 OECD countries, 21 had scores within 25 points of the OECD average of 500. In this closely clustered group of countries, each had a mean score very similar to a number of the others. There is a discontinuity in the mean scores below that of Greece (473): the next highest country, Israel, scored 454 points and only two OECD countries scored below 473 points.

Chart A5.2. Multiple comparisons of mean performance on the PISA science scale (2006)

	Country mean	S.E.	Finland	Canada	Estonia	Japan	New Zealand	Australia	Netherlands	Korea	Slovenia	Germany	United Kingdom	Czech Republic	Switzerland	Austria	Belgium	Ireland	Hungary	Sweden
			563	534	531	531	530	527	525	522	519	516	515	513	512	511	510	508	504	503
			(2.0)	(2.0)	(2.5)	(3.4)	(2.7)	(2.3)	(2.7)	(3.4)	(1.1)	(3.8)	(2.3)	(3.5)	(3.2)	(3.9)	(2.5)	(3.2)	(2.7)	(2.4)
Finland	563	(2.0)	▨	▲	▲	▲	▲	▲	▲	▲	▲	▲	▲	▲	▲	▲	▲	▲	▲	▲
Canada	534	(2.0)	▼	▨	○	○	○	▲	▲	▲	▲	▲	▲	▲	▲	▲	▲	▲	▲	▲
Estonia	531	(2.5)	▼	○	▨	○	○	○	○	▲	▲	▲	▲	▲	▲	▲	▲	▲	▲	▲
Japan	531	(3.4)	▼	○	○	▨	○	○	○	○	▲	▲	▲	▲	▲	▲	▲	▲	▲	▲
New Zealand	530	(2.7)	▼	○	○	○	▨	○	○	○	▲	▲	▲	▲	▲	▲	▲	▲	▲	▲
Australia	527	(2.3)	▼	▼	○	○	○	▨	○	○	▲	▲	▲	▲	▲	▲	▲	▲	▲	▲
Netherlands	525	(2.7)	▼	▼	○	○	○	○	▨	○	▲	▲	▲	▲	▲	▲	▲	▲	▲	▲
Korea	522	(3.4)	▼	▼	▼	○	○	○	○	▨	○	○	○	○	○	▲	▲	▲	▲	▲
Slovenia	519	(1.1)	▼	▼	▼	▼	▼	▼	▼	○	▨	○	○	○	○	▲	○	▲	▲	▲
Germany	516	(3.8)	▼	▼	▼	▼	▼	▼	▼	○	○	▨	○	○	○	○	○	○	▲	▲
United Kingdom	515	(2.3)	▼	▼	▼	▼	▼	▼	▼	○	○	○	▨	○	○	○	○	○	▲	▲
Czech Republic	513	(3.5)	▼	▼	▼	▼	▼	▼	▼	○	○	○	○	▨	○	○	○	○	▲	▲
Switzerland	512	(3.2)	▼	▼	▼	▼	▼	▼	▼	○	○	○	○	○	▨	○	○	○	○	▲
Austria	511	(3.9)	▼	▼	▼	▼	▼	▼	▼	▼	○	○	○	○	○	▨	○	○	○	○
Belgium	510	(2.5)	▼	▼	▼	▼	▼	▼	▼	▼	○	○	○	○	○	○	▨	○	○	▲
Ireland	508	(3.2)	▼	▼	▼	▼	▼	▼	▼	▼	▼	○	○	○	○	○	○	▨	○	○
Hungary	504	(2.7)	▼	▼	▼	▼	▼	▼	▼	▼	▼	▼	▼	▼	○	○	○	○	▨	○
Sweden	503	(2.4)	▼	▼	▼	▼	▼	▼	▼	▼	▼	▼	▼	▼	▼	○	▼	○	○	▨
Poland	498	(2.3)	▼	▼	▼	▼	▼	▼	▼	▼	▼	▼	▼	▼	▼	▼	▼	▼	○	○
Denmark	496	(3.1)	▼	▼	▼	▼	▼	▼	▼	▼	▼	▼	▼	▼	▼	▼	▼	▼	○	○
France	495	(3.4)	▼	▼	▼	▼	▼	▼	▼	▼	▼	▼	▼	▼	▼	▼	▼	▼	▼	▼
Iceland	491	(1.6)	▼	▼	▼	▼	▼	▼	▼	▼	▼	▼	▼	▼	▼	▼	▼	▼	▼	▼
United States	489	(4.2)	▼	▼	▼	▼	▼	▼	▼	▼	▼	▼	▼	▼	▼	▼	▼	▼	▼	▼
Slovak Republic	488	(2.6)	▼	▼	▼	▼	▼	▼	▼	▼	▼	▼	▼	▼	▼	▼	▼	▼	▼	▼
Spain	488	(2.6)	▼	▼	▼	▼	▼	▼	▼	▼	▼	▼	▼	▼	▼	▼	▼	▼	▼	▼
Norway	487	(3.1)	▼	▼	▼	▼	▼	▼	▼	▼	▼	▼	▼	▼	▼	▼	▼	▼	▼	▼
Luxembourg	486	(1.1)	▼	▼	▼	▼	▼	▼	▼	▼	▼	▼	▼	▼	▼	▼	▼	▼	▼	▼
Russian Federation	479	(3.7)	▼	▼	▼	▼	▼	▼	▼	▼	▼	▼	▼	▼	▼	▼	▼	▼	▼	▼
Italy	475	(2.0)	▼	▼	▼	▼	▼	▼	▼	▼	▼	▼	▼	▼	▼	▼	▼	▼	▼	▼
Portugal	474	(3.0)	▼	▼	▼	▼	▼	▼	▼	▼	▼	▼	▼	▼	▼	▼	▼	▼	▼	▼
Greece	473	(3.2)	▼	▼	▼	▼	▼	▼	▼	▼	▼	▼	▼	▼	▼	▼	▼	▼	▼	▼
Israel	454	(3.7)	▼	▼	▼	▼	▼	▼	▼	▼	▼	▼	▼	▼	▼	▼	▼	▼	▼	▼
Chile	438	(4.3)	▼	▼	▼	▼	▼	▼	▼	▼	▼	▼	▼	▼	▼	▼	▼	▼	▼	▼
Turkey	424	(3.8)	▼	▼	▼	▼	▼	▼	▼	▼	▼	▼	▼	▼	▼	▼	▼	▼	▼	▼
Mexico	410	(2.7)	▼	▼	▼	▼	▼	▼	▼	▼	▼	▼	▼	▼	▼	▼	▼	▼	▼	▼
Brazil	390	(2.8)	▼	▼	▼	▼	▼	▼	▼	▼	▼	▼	▼	▼	▼	▼	▼	▼	▼	▼

Legend:

☐ Statistically significantly above the OECD average
▨ Not statistically significantly different from the OECD average
▨ Statistically significantly below the OECD average

▲ Mean performance statistically significantly higher than in comparison country
○ No statistically significant difference from comparison country
▼ Mean performance statistically significantly lower than in comparison country

Source: PISA 2006 Science Competencies for Tomorrow's World, Volume 1, Figure 2.11b.
StatLink ᴍᴤᴸ http://dx.doi.org/10.1787/401573312123

Chart A5.2. (continued) Multiple comparisons
of mean performance on the PISA science scale (2006)

Poland	Denmark	France	Iceland	United States	Slovak Republic	Spain	Norway	Luxembourg	Russian Federation	Italy	Portugal	Greece	Israel	Chile	Turkey	Mexico	Brazil	Country mean / S.E.	Country mean	
498	496	495	491	489	488	488	487	486	479	475	474	473	454	438	424	410	390	S.E.		
(2.3)	(3.1)	(3.4)	(1.6)	(4.2)	(2.6)	(2.6)	(3.1)	(1.1)	(3.7)	(2.0)	(3.0)	(3.2)	(3.7)	(4.3)	(3.8)	(2.7)	(2.8)			
▲	▲	▲	▲	▲	▲	▲	▲	▲	▲	▲	▲	▲	▲	▲	▲	▲	▲	(2.0)	563	Finland
▲	▲	▲	▲	▲	▲	▲	▲	▲	▲	▲	▲	▲	▲	▲	▲	▲	▲	(2.0)	534	Canada
▲	▲	▲	▲	▲	▲	▲	▲	▲	▲	▲	▲	▲	▲	▲	▲	▲	▲	(2.5)	531	Estonia
▲	▲	▲	▲	▲	▲	▲	▲	▲	▲	▲	▲	▲	▲	▲	▲	▲	▲	(3.4)	531	Japan
▲	▲	▲	▲	▲	▲	▲	▲	▲	▲	▲	▲	▲	▲	▲	▲	▲	▲	(2.7)	530	New Zealand
▲	▲	▲	▲	▲	▲	▲	▲	▲	▲	▲	▲	▲	▲	▲	▲	▲	▲	(2.3)	527	Australia
▲	▲	▲	▲	▲	▲	▲	▲	▲	▲	▲	▲	▲	▲	▲	▲	▲	▲	(2.7)	525	Netherlands
▲	▲	▲	▲	▲	▲	▲	▲	▲	▲	▲	▲	▲	▲	▲	▲	▲	▲	(3.4)	522	Korea
▲	▲	▲	▲	▲	▲	▲	▲	▲	▲	▲	▲	▲	▲	▲	▲	▲	▲	(1.1)	519	Slovenia
▲	▲	▲	▲	▲	▲	▲	▲	▲	▲	▲	▲	▲	▲	▲	▲	▲	▲	(3.8)	516	Germany
▲	▲	▲	▲	▲	▲	▲	▲	▲	▲	▲	▲	▲	▲	▲	▲	▲	▲	(2.3)	515	United Kingdom
▲	▲	▲	▲	▲	▲	▲	▲	▲	▲	▲	▲	▲	▲	▲	▲	▲	▲	(3.5)	513	Czech Republic
▲	▲	▲	▲	▲	▲	▲	▲	▲	▲	▲	▲	▲	▲	▲	▲	▲	▲	(3.2)	512	Switzerland
▲	▲	▲	▲	▲	▲	▲	▲	▲	▲	▲	▲	▲	▲	▲	▲	▲	▲	(3.9)	511	Austria
▲	▲	▲	▲	▲	▲	▲	▲	▲	▲	▲	▲	▲	▲	▲	▲	▲	▲	(2.5)	510	Belgium
▲	▲	▲	▲	▲	▲	▲	▲	▲	▲	▲	▲	▲	▲	▲	▲	▲	▲	(3.2)	508	Ireland
○	○	▲	▲	▲	▲	▲	▲	▲	▲	▲	▲	▲	▲	▲	▲	▲	▲	(2.7)	504	Hungary
○	○	▲	▲	▲	▲	▲	▲	▲	▲	▲	▲	▲	▲	▲	▲	▲	▲	(2.4)	503	Sweden
■	○	○	▲	○	▲	▲	▲	▲	▲	▲	▲	▲	▲	▲	▲	▲	▲	(2.3)	498	Poland
○	■	○	○	○	○	○	○	▲	▲	▲	▲	▲	▲	▲	▲	▲	▲	(3.1)	496	Denmark
○	○	■	○	○	○	○	○	○	▲	▲	▲	▲	▲	▲	▲	▲	▲	(3.4)	495	France
▼	○	○	■	○	○	○	○	○	▲	▲	▲	▲	▲	▲	▲	▲	▲	(1.6)	491	Iceland
○	○	○	○	■	○	○	○	○	○	▲	▲	▲	▲	▲	▲	▲	▲	(4.2)	489	United States
▼	○	○	○	○	■	○	○	○	○	▲	▲	▲	▲	▲	▲	▲	▲	(2.6)	488	Slovak Republic
▼	○	○	○	○	○	■	○	○	○	▲	▲	▲	▲	▲	▲	▲	▲	(2.6)	488	Spain
▼	▼	○	○	○	○	○	■	○	○	▲	▲	▲	▲	▲	▲	▲	▲	(3.1)	487	Norway
▼	▼	▼	▼	○	○	○	○	■	○	▲	▲	▲	▲	▲	▲	▲	▲	(1.1)	486	Luxembourg
▼	▼	▼	▼	○	▼	▼	○	○	■	○	○	○	▲	▲	▲	▲	▲	(3.7)	479	Russian Federation
▼	▼	▼	▼	▼	▼	▼	▼	▼	○	■	○	○	▲	▲	▲	▲	▲	(2.0)	475	Italy
▼	▼	▼	▼	▼	▼	▼	▼	▼	○	○	■	○	▲	▲	▲	▲	▲	(3.0)	474	Portugal
▼	▼	▼	▼	▼	▼	▼	▼	▼	○	○	○	■	▲	▲	▲	▲	▲	(3.2)	473	Greece
▼	▼	▼	▼	▼	▼	▼	▼	▼	▼	▼	▼	▼	■	▲	▲	▲	▲	(3.7)	454	Israel
▼	▼	▼	▼	▼	▼	▼	▼	▼	▼	▼	▼	▼	▼	■	▲	▲	▲	(4.3)	438	Chile
▼	▼	▼	▼	▼	▼	▼	▼	▼	▼	▼	▼	▼	▼	▼	■	▲	▲	(3.8)	424	Turkey
▼	▼	▼	▼	▼	▼	▼	▼	▼	▼	▼	▼	▼	▼	▼	▼	■	▲	(2.7)	410	Mexico
▼	▼	▼	▼	▼	▼	▼	▼	▼	▼	▼	▼	▼	▼	▼	▼	▼	■	(2.8)	390	Brazil

Statistically significantly above the OECD average

Not statistically significantly different from the OECD average

Statistically significantly below the OECD average

▲ Mean performance statistically significantly higher than in comparison country

○ No statistically significant difference from comparison country

▼ Mean performance statistically significantly lower than in comparison country

Source: PISA 2006 Science Competencies for Tomorrow's World, Volume 1, Figure 2.11b.
StatLink ⏋⫘▱ http://dx.doi.org/10.1787/401573312123

Proficiency in science

PISA also provides data on students' proficiency in scientific literacy, which is examined at six levels, each representing tasks of increasing complexity (Box A5.2). Chart A5.3 presents an overall profile of students' proficiency on the science scale; the length of the coloured components of the bars shows the percentage of students at each proficiency level. It indicates, for each country, the percentage of students below Level 2, on the left side, and at least at Level 2 on the right side. At Level 2, students start to demonstrate the science competencies that will enable them to participate actively in life situations related to science and technology. In OECD countries, 19.2% of students on average were classified below Level 2, including 5.2% below Level 1, while 1.3% on average reached Level 6 (the highest level), 9.0% reached Level 5 or higher, 29.3% reached Level 4 or higher, 56.7% reached Level 3 or higher, and 80.8% reached Level 2 or higher (Table A5.2).

High levels of proficiency

Examining individual countries' performance by proficiency level shows that in Finland and New Zealand at least 3.9% of students reached Level 6, the highest level on the PISA science scale, three times the OECD average. In Australia, Canada, Japan and the United Kingdom and in the partner country Slovenia, between 2% and 3% reached Level 6.

Including Level 5 brings the level of high performers to 9.0% on average across OECD countries. Over one in five students in Finland (20.9%) and over one in six in New Zealand (17.6%) reached at least Level 5. In, Australia, Canada and Japan the figure was between 14% and 16%. By contrast, two OECD countries and one partner country in the survey had less than 1% of students reaching either Level 5 or Level 6, and six OECD countries and three partner countries had 5% or fewer reaching the two highest levels. It appears that the pool of 15-year-olds who were highly proficient in science is very unevenly distributed across countries.

Medium levels of proficiency

In 12 OECD countries and 2 partner countries, at least one-third of students reached Level 4 and higher on the science scale. In all but five OECD countries and four partner countries, the majority of students reached Level 3 or higher. In all countries, except three OECD countries and three partner countries, three-quarters of students reached at least Level 2.

Low levels of proficiency

The percentage of students at very low proficiency levels is an important indicator of the extent to which young people are being prepared to participate fully in society and in the labour market. At Level 2, students start to demonstrate the science competencies that will enable them to participate actively in life situations related to science and technology. For OECD countries, 19.2% of students on average were classified as below Level 2, including 5.2% below Level 1. In every country except, Finland and the partner country Estonia, 10% or more of students performed at Level 1 or below, and in 11 OECD countries and four partner countries the proportion exceeded 20%. In Mexico and in the partner country Brazil, a majority of students could not complete tasks above Level 1 consistently.

Box A5.2. What can students at each proficiency level do and what scores are associated with the levels?

Level	Lower score limit	Percentage of students able to perform tasks at each level or above (OECD average)	What students can typically do
6	707.9	1.3% of students across the OECD can perform tasks at Level 6 on the science scale	At Level 6, students can consistently identify, explain and apply scientific knowledge and *knowledge about science* in a variety of complex life situations. They can link different information sources and explanations and use evidence from those sources to justify decisions. They clearly and consistently demonstrate advanced scientific thinking and reasoning, and they demonstrate willingness to use their scientific understanding in support of solutions to unfamiliar scientific and technological situations. Students at this level can use scientific knowledge and develop arguments in support of recommendations and decisions that centre on personal, social or global situations.
5	633.3	9.0% of students across the OECD can perform tasks at least at Level 5 on the science scale	At Level 5, students can identify the scientific components of many complex life situations, apply both scientific concepts and *knowledge about science* to these situations, and can compare, select and evaluate appropriate scientific evidence for responding to life situations. Students at this level can use well-developed inquiry abilities, link knowledge appropriately and bring critical insights to situations. They can construct explanations based on evidence and arguments based on their critical analysis.
4	558.7	29.3% of students across the OECD can perform tasks at least at Level 4 on the science scale	At Level 4, students can work effectively with situations and issues that may involve explicit phenomena requiring them to make inferences about the role of science or technology. They can select and integrate explanations from different disciplines of science or technology and link those explanations directly to aspects of life situations. Students at this level can reflect on their actions and they can communicate decisions using scientific knowledge and evidence.
3	484.1	56.7% of students across the OECD can perform tasks at least at Level 3 on the science scale	At Level 3, students can identify clearly described scientific issues in a range of contexts. They can select facts and knowledge to explain phenomena and apply simple models or inquiry strategies. Students at this level can interpret and use scientific concepts from different disciplines and can apply them directly. They can develop short statements using facts and make decisions based on scientific knowledge.
2	409.5	80.8% of students across the OECD can perform tasks at least at Level 2 on the science scale	At Level 2, students have adequate scientific knowledge to provide possible explanations in familiar contexts or draw conclusions based on simple investigations. They are capable of direct reasoning and making literal interpretations of the results of scientific inquiry or technological problem solving.
1	334.9	94.8% of students across the OECD can perform tasks at least at Level 1 on the science scale	At Level 1, students have such a limited scientific knowledge that it can only be applied to a few, familiar situations. They can present scientific explanations that are obvious and that follow explicitly from given evidence.

Chart A5.3. Science proficiency of 15-year-old students (PISA 2006)

Percentage of students at each proficiency level on the science scale

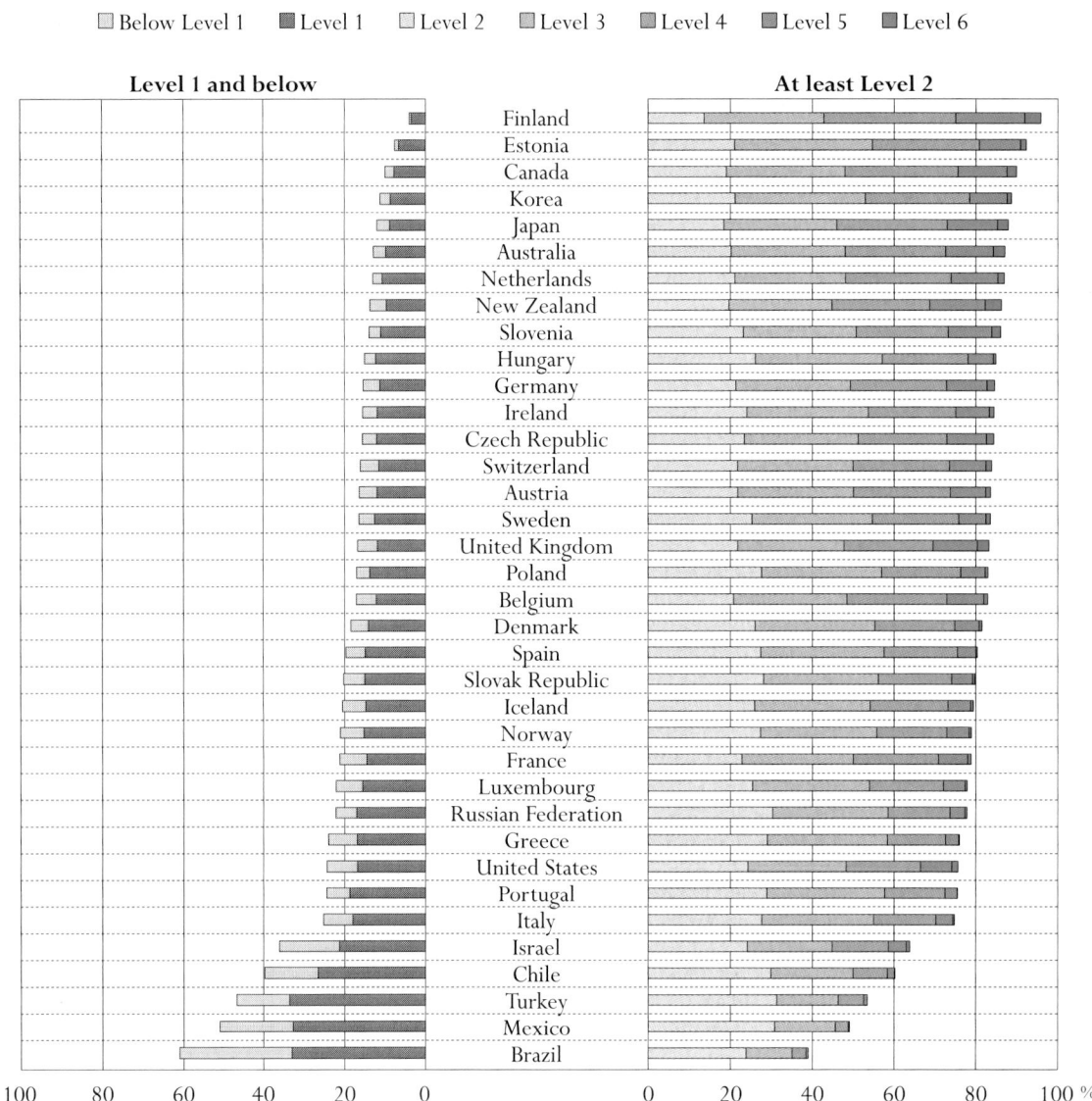

Countries are ranked in descending order of percentage of 15-year-olds at Levels 2, 3, 4, 5 and 6.
Source: OECD. Table A5.2. See Annex 3 for notes (*www.oecd.org/edu/eag2008*).
StatLink 🔗 http://dx.doi.org/10.1787/401573312123

Mean scores on the three science competency scales

One of the strengths of PISA 2006 is that it looks both at students' science competencies and also the science knowledge domains (the latter is not addressed in this indicator). It is important, but not sufficient, for students to understand scientific theories and facts well enough to explain phenomena scientifically. They must also be able to recognise questions that can be addressed scientifically and see how the results can be used, in order to apply their scientific knowledge.

A5

Students' skill profiles on the three science competency scales — *identifying scientific issues*, *using scientific evidence* and *explaining phenomena scientifically* — differed among countries. Understanding students' comparative strengths in different science competencies and knowledge domains can inform policy makers, thus helping them to develop appropriate strategies for achieving scientific literacy. A simplified way of looking at these relative strengths is in terms of a sequence in dealing with science problems: first identifying the problem, then applying knowledge of scientific phenomena, and finally interpreting and using the results. Traditional science teaching often concentrates on *explaining phenomena scientifically*, which requires familiarity with key science knowledge and theories. Yet if students are unable to recognise a science problem and then to interpret findings in ways that are relevant to the real world, they are not fully scientifically literate. A student who has mastered a scientific theory but cannot weigh evidence, for example, will make limited use of science in adult life. This suggest that countries with students who are relatively weak in *identifying scientific issues* or *using scientific evidence* may need to consider how students can acquire wider scientific skills, while those weak in *explaining phenomena scientifically* may need to focus more on mastery of scientific knowledge.

Chart A5.4 presents the performance difference between the overall science scale and each science competency scale. Blue indicates that a country was relatively stronger on that scale than on the overall scale, with the deepest colour indicating the largest difference and thus high relative strength. Grey indicates that a country performed relatively weaker on that scale than on the overall scale, with the deepest colour indicating the greatest weakness and thus high relative weakness.

Countries with similar strengths and weaknesses in science competencies can be separated into different groups.

- In Mexico and Portugal, students were relatively stronger in *identifying scientific issues* than in overall science. But in the Czech Republic, Hungary, Poland and the Slovak Republic and the partner countries Estonia and the Russian Federation, students scored more than 10 points lower in *identifying scientific issues* than in overall science.

- In some countries, students were relatively stronger in *explaining phenomena scientifically* than in other science competencies. Students scored 10 or more points higher in *explaining phenomena scientifically* than in the overall science score in the Czech Republic, Hungary and the Slovak Republic. In some countries, the reverse was true — students were stronger in other science competencies than in *explaining phenomena scientifically*. Students scored 10 or more points higher in overall science than in *explaining phenomena scientifically* in France and Korea and in the partner country Israel.

- In some countries, students showed relative strength in *using scientific evidence*. Students scored 10 or more points higher in *using scientific evidence* than in the overall science score in France, Japan and Korea. In some countries, students showed relative weakness in *using scientific evidence*. Students scored 10 or more points lower in *using scientific evidence* than in the overall science score in the Czech Republic, Norway and the Slovak Republic, and in the partner country Brazil.

In some of these cases, the differences between performances in two different competencies were substantial. For example, in France and Korea, students scored 30 and 27 points, respectively, higher in *using scientific evidence* than in *explaining phenomena scientifically*.

Chart A5.4. Comparison of the performances on the different competency scales in science (PISA 2006)

■ Each scale is 20 or more score points **lower** than the overall science scale
■ Each scale is between 10 and 19.99 score points **lower** than the overall science scale
□ Each scale is between 0 to 9.99 score points **lower** than the overall science scale

■ Each scale is 20 or more score points **higher** than the overall science scale
■ Each scale is between 10 and 19.99 score points **higher** than the overall science scale
□ Each scale is between 0 to 9.99 score points **higher** than the overall science scale

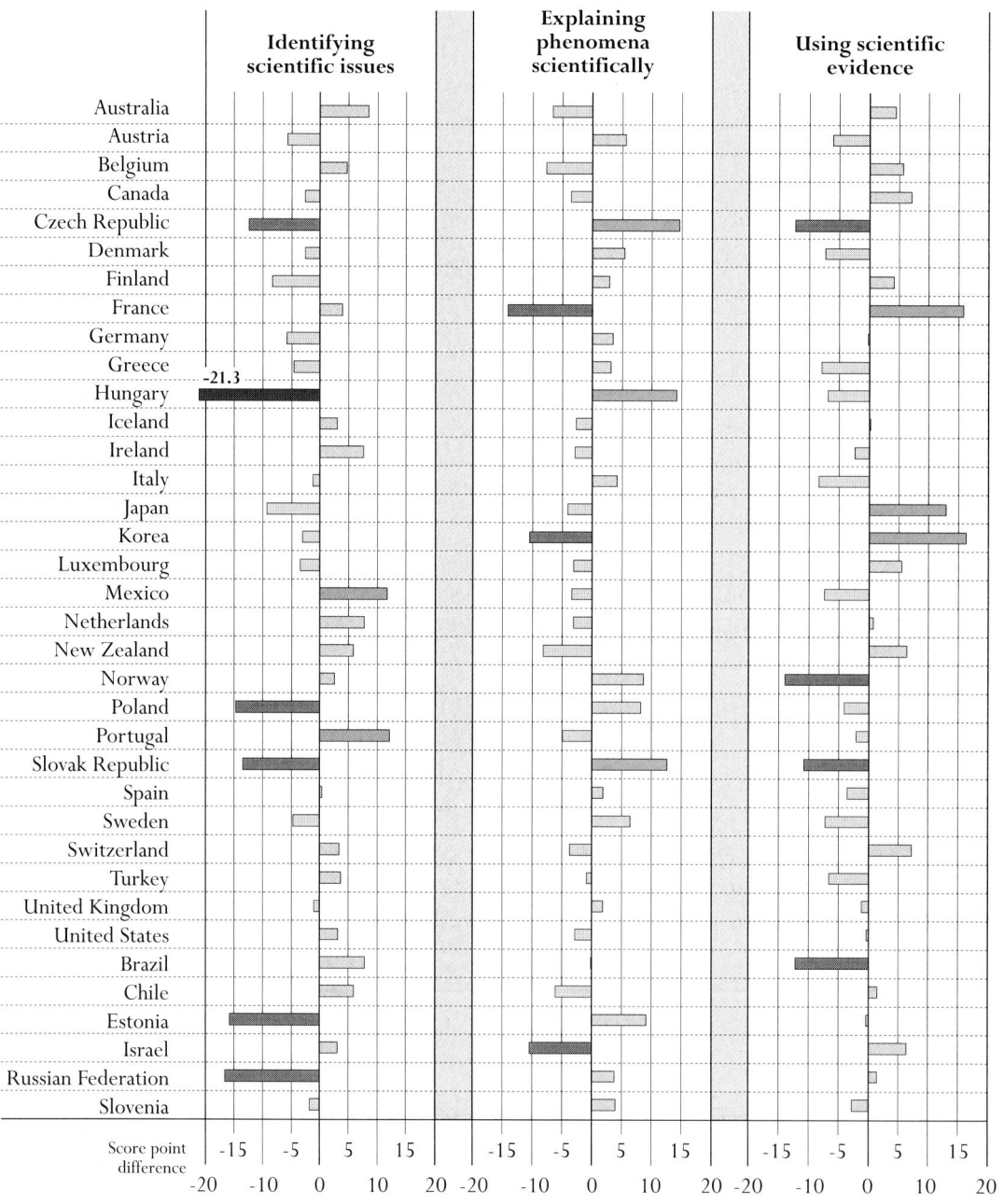

Source: OECD. Table A5.3. See Annex 3 for notes (*www.oecd.org/edu/eag2008*).
StatLink ᵈᵐˢᴸ http://dx.doi.org/10.1787/401573312123

Gender differences

Contrary to reading and mathematics, for which significant gender differences were observed, there was no difference between males and females in average overall science performance in most countries, including 22 of the 30 OECD countries. Only Denmark, Luxembourg, Mexico, the Netherlands, Switzerland and the United Kingdom showed a small advantage for males (between 6 and 10 score points) while Greece and Turkey showed an advantage for females (between 11 and 12 score points). For the remaining OECD countries there are no statistically significant differences. Among the partner countries, Brazil and Chile showed an advantage for males, while Slovenia showed an advantage for females (Table A5.1).

However, similarities in average performance mask certain gender differences: in most countries, females were stronger in *identifying scientific issues*, while males were stronger in *explaining phenomena scientifically* (Chart A5.5, Table A5.3).

• On *identifying scientific issues* females outperformed males by 17 score points, on average for the OECD countries. In a number of countries their advantage was quite large; for example, it was more than 25 points in Finland, Greece, Iceland and Turkey and in the partner country Slovenia.

• On the other hand, on *explaining phenomena scientifically,* males outperformed females by 15 score points, on average. Again, the difference was large in some cases. In the partner country Chile it was 34 score points, and among OECD countries it was 25 score points in Luxembourg, 22 in Hungary and the Slovak Republic, and 21 in the Czech Republic, Denmark, Germany and the United Kingdom.

• In contrast to *identifying scientific issues* and *explaining phenomena scientifically*, there were few significant gender differences in the competency *using scientific evidence*, with only three OECD countries showing females outperforming males and a small overall difference, favouring females, of 3 score points.

When interpreting these gender differences in conjunction with the overall performance of countries on the respective scales, the differences imply that males or females sometimes had very different levels of performance in different areas of science. For example, females' mean score in *identifying scientific issues* in France was above the OECD average at 507 points, but their mean performance in *explaining phenomena scientifically* was much lower at 474 points, equivalent to some of the lowest-performing OECD countries.

The fact that females performed consistently stronger than males in *identifying scientific issues* and weaker in *explaining phenomena scientifically* may suggest a systematic gender difference in the way students relate to science and to the science curriculum. It appears that males may be better on average at mastering scientific knowledge and females better at distinguishing scientific questions in a given situation. While it should be emphasised that in many countries the gender differences were small relative to differences within each gender, overall performance could be raised significantly if the factors behind the gender difference could be identified and tackled.

Chart A5.5. Gender differences in student performance on the PISA science scales (2006)

Note: Statistically significant differences are marked in darker tone.
Countries are ranked in ascending order of difference between boys and girls (B - G) for the overall science scale.
Source: OECD. Tables 5.1 and A5.3. See Annex 3 for notes (*www.oecd.org/edu/eag2008*).
StatLink ⌀⌀⌀ http://dx.doi.org/10.1787/401573312123

A5

Definitions and methodologies

The achievement scores are based on assessments administered as part of the Programme for International Student Assessment (PISA) undertaken by the Organisation for Economic Co-operation and Development (OECD). PISA was administered most recently during the 2006 school year.

The target population studied for this indicator was 15-year-old students. Operationally, this referred to students who were from 15 years and 3 (completed) months to 16 years and 2 (completed) months at the beginning of the testing period and who were enrolled in an educational institution at the secondary level, irrespective of the grade levels or type of institutions in which they were enrolled, and irrespective of whether they participated in school full-time or part-time.

Further references

For further information about PISA 2006, see *PISA 2006: Science Competencies for Tomorrow's World* (OECD, 2007c), and the *PISA 2006 Technical Report* (OECD, 2008b). PISA data are also available on the PISA website: *www.pisa.oecd.org.*

A5

Table A5.1.
Mean score, variation and gender differences in student performance on the PISA science scale (2006)

	All students				Gender differences					
	Mean score		Standard deviation		Boys		Girls		Difference (B - G)	
	Mean	S.E.	S.D.	S.E.	Mean score	S.E.	Mean score	S.E.	Score dif.	S.E.
Australia	527	(2.3)	100	(1.0)	527	(3.2)	527	(2.7)	0	(3.8)
Austria	511	(3.9)	98	(2.4)	515	(4.2)	507	(4.9)	8	(4.9)
Belgium	510	(2.5)	100	(2.0)	511	(3.3)	510	(3.2)	1	(4.1)
Canada	534	(2.0)	94	(1.1)	536	(2.5)	532	(2.1)	4	(2.2)
Czech Republic	513	(3.5)	98	(2.0)	515	(4.2)	510	(4.8)	5	(5.6)
Denmark	496	(3.1)	93	(1.4)	500	(3.6)	491	(3.4)	**9**	(3.2)
Finland	563	(2.0)	86	(1.0)	562	(2.6)	565	(2.4)	-3	(2.9)
France	495	(3.4)	102	(2.1)	497	(4.3)	494	(3.6)	3	(4.0)
Germany	516	(3.8)	100	(2.0)	519	(4.6)	512	(3.8)	7	(3.7)
Greece	473	(3.2)	92	(2.0)	468	(4.5)	479	(3.4)	**-11**	(4.7)
Hungary	504	(2.7)	88	(1.6)	507	(3.3)	501	(3.5)	6	(4.2)
Iceland	491	(1.6)	97	(1.2)	488	(2.6)	494	(2.1)	-6	(3.4)
Ireland	508	(3.2)	94	(1.5)	508	(4.3)	509	(3.3)	0	(4.3)
Italy	475	(2.0)	96	(1.3)	477	(2.8)	474	(2.5)	3	(3.5)
Japan	531	(3.4)	100	(2.0)	533	(4.9)	530	(5.1)	3	(7.4)
Korea	522	(3.4)	90	(2.4)	521	(4.8)	523	(3.9)	-2	(5.5)
Luxembourg	486	(1.1)	97	(0.9)	491	(1.8)	482	(1.8)	**9**	(2.9)
Mexico	410	(2.7)	81	(1.5)	413	(3.2)	406	(2.6)	**7**	(2.2)
Netherlands	525	(2.7)	96	(1.6)	528	(3.2)	521	(3.1)	**7**	(3.0)
New Zealand	530	(2.7)	107	(1.4)	528	(3.9)	532	(3.6)	-4	(5.2)
Norway	487	(3.1)	96	(2.0)	484	(3.8)	489	(3.2)	-4	(3.4)
Poland	498	(2.3)	90	(1.1)	500	(2.7)	496	(2.6)	3	(2.5)
Portugal	474	(3.0)	89	(1.7)	477	(3.7)	472	(3.2)	5	(3.3)
Slovak Republic	488	(2.6)	93	(1.8)	491	(3.9)	485	(3.0)	6	(4.7)
Spain	488	(2.6)	91	(1.0)	491	(2.9)	486	(2.7)	4	(2.4)
Sweden	503	(2.4)	94	(1.4)	504	(2.7)	503	(2.9)	1	(3.0)
Switzerland	512	(3.2)	99	(1.7)	514	(3.3)	509	(3.6)	**6**	(2.7)
Turkey	424	(3.8)	83	(3.2)	418	(4.6)	430	(4.1)	**-12**	(4.1)
United Kingdom	515	(2.3)	107	(1.5)	520	(3.0)	510	(2.8)	**10**	(3.4)
United States	489	(4.2)	106	(1.7)	489	(5.1)	489	(4.0)	1	(3.5)
OECD total	*491*	*(1.2)*	*104*	*(0.6)*	*492*	*(1.4)*	*490*	*(1.3)*	*3*	*(1.3)*
OECD average	*500*	*(0.5)*	*95*	*(0.3)*	*501*	*(0.7)*	*499*	*(0.6)*	*2*	*(0.7)*
Brazil	390	(2.8)	89	(1.9)	395	(3.2)	386	(2.9)	**9**	(2.3)
Chile	438	(4.3)	92	(1.8)	448	(5.4)	426	(4.4)	**22**	(4.8)
Estonia	531	(2.5)	84	(1.1)	530	(3.1)	533	(2.9)	-4	(3.1)
Israel	454	(3.7)	111	(2.0)	456	(5.6)	452	(4.2)	3	(6.5)
Russian Federation	479	(3.7)	90	(1.4)	481	(4.1)	478	(3.7)	3	(2.7)
Slovenia	519	(1.1)	98	(1.0)	515	(2.0)	523	(1.9)	**-8**	(3.2)

Note: Statistically significant values are indicated in bold.
Source: PISA 2006: Science Competencies for Tomorrow's World, Volume 2, Table 2.1c.
StatLink ⟨⟩ http://dx.doi.org/10.1787/401573312123

Table A5.1. *(continued)*
Mean score, variation and gender differences in student performance on the PISA science scale (2006)

A5

		Percentiles										
		5th		10th		25th		75th		90th		95th	
		Score	S.E.	Score	S.E.	Score	S.E.	Score	S.E.	Score	S.E.	Score	S.E.
OECD countries	Australia	358	(3.5)	395	(3.4)	459	(2.6)	598	(2.5)	653	(2.9)	685	(3.4)
	Austria	341	(9.3)	378	(6.2)	443	(5.4)	582	(4.1)	633	(3.6)	663	(4.1)
	Belgium	336	(7.3)	374	(5.4)	442	(3.8)	584	(2.4)	634	(2.3)	660	(2.7)
	Canada	372	(4.7)	410	(3.7)	472	(2.5)	601	(2.2)	651	(2.4)	681	(2.8)
	Czech Republic	350	(6.0)	385	(5.2)	443	(4.6)	583	(3.9)	641	(4.3)	672	(4.7)
	Denmark	341	(5.9)	373	(4.8)	432	(4.3)	562	(2.9)	615	(3.7)	646	(4.3)
	Finland	419	(4.4)	453	(3.3)	506	(2.9)	622	(2.5)	673	(2.9)	700	(3.1)
	France	320	(6.3)	359	(5.5)	424	(5.3)	570	(4.0)	623	(4.0)	653	(3.8)
	Germany	345	(8.1)	381	(7.0)	447	(5.3)	587	(3.6)	642	(3.2)	672	(3.6)
	Greece	317	(7.3)	353	(5.4)	413	(4.4)	537	(3.3)	589	(4.1)	619	(3.8)
	Hungary	358	(4.4)	388	(4.2)	442	(3.5)	566	(3.3)	617	(3.1)	646	(4.2)
	Iceland	328	(4.9)	364	(3.1)	424	(2.6)	560	(2.3)	614	(2.9)	644	(3.4)
	Ireland	351	(5.8)	385	(4.4)	444	(4.6)	575	(3.4)	630	(3.7)	660	(4.9)
	Italy	318	(3.1)	351	(2.8)	409	(3.0)	543	(2.4)	598	(2.6)	630	(2.8)
	Japan	356	(6.1)	396	(6.2)	465	(5.1)	603	(3.1)	654	(3.1)	685	(3.6)
	Korea	367	(8.4)	403	(5.7)	462	(4.1)	586	(3.8)	635	(4.7)	662	(5.9)
	Luxembourg	322	(3.9)	358	(2.8)	419	(2.0)	556	(2.4)	609	(2.8)	640	(2.6)
	Mexico	281	(4.4)	306	(4.2)	354	(3.6)	465	(2.9)	516	(3.0)	544	(3.5)
	Netherlands	362	(5.9)	395	(5.4)	456	(4.7)	596	(2.6)	646	(3.4)	675	(3.6)
	New Zealand	347	(5.2)	389	(4.5)	455	(3.6)	608	(2.9)	667	(3.3)	699	(3.1)
	Norway	328	(7.8)	365	(5.6)	422	(3.9)	553	(3.0)	610	(3.5)	641	(3.4)
	Poland	352	(3.8)	381	(2.9)	434	(2.7)	562	(3.1)	615	(3.3)	645	(3.3)
	Portugal	329	(5.4)	357	(4.8)	411	(4.2)	539	(3.0)	588	(2.9)	617	(3.2)
	Slovak Republic	334	(5.6)	368	(3.7)	426	(3.2)	555	(4.0)	609	(4.1)	638	(3.9)
	Spain	338	(4.1)	370	(3.7)	427	(3.0)	552	(3.1)	604	(3.0)	633	(3.1)
	Sweden	347	(3.8)	381	(4.0)	439	(3.3)	569	(2.8)	622	(2.6)	654	(3.4)
	Switzerland	340	(5.0)	378	(4.9)	445	(3.9)	584	(3.5)	636	(3.8)	665	(4.6)
	Turkey	301	(2.8)	325	(3.2)	366	(2.6)	475	(5.8)	540	(9.7)	575	(9.8)
	United Kingdom	337	(5.4)	376	(4.3)	441	(3.2)	590	(3.1)	652	(2.9)	685	(3.5)
	United States	318	(4.5)	349	(5.9)	412	(5.4)	567	(4.6)	628	(4.3)	662	(4.8)
	OECD total	*321*	*(1.8)*	*354*	*(1.9)*	*416*	*(1.6)*	*567*	*(1.3)*	*626*	*(1.3)*	*659*	*(1.5)*
	OECD average	*340*	*(1.0)*	*375*	*(0.9)*	*434*	*(0.7)*	*568*	*(0.6)*	*622*	*(0.7)*	*652*	*(0.8)*
Partner countries	Brazil	254	(4.5)	281	(3.2)	328	(2.3)	447	(4.5)	510	(5.6)	549	(5.3)
	Chile	295	(4.8)	323	(4.1)	374	(4.0)	501	(5.9)	560	(6.5)	595	(6.1)
	Estonia	392	(4.7)	422	(3.8)	474	(3.2)	589	(3.1)	640	(3.3)	668	(3.7)
	Israel	275	(5.7)	310	(5.2)	374	(4.8)	535	(4.6)	601	(4.5)	636	(5.5)
	Russian Federation	333	(5.6)	364	(5.4)	418	(4.4)	541	(4.2)	596	(3.9)	627	(4.2)
	Slovenia	358	(3.8)	391	(2.8)	449	(2.7)	589	(2.1)	647	(3.3)	680	(3.0)

Source: PISA 2006: Science Competencies for Tomorrow's World, Volume 2, Table 2.1c.
StatLink ⏍⏍⏍ http://dx.doi.org/10.1787/401573312123

A5

Table A5.2.
Percentage of students at each proficiency level on the PISA science scale (2006)

	Below Level 1 (below 334.94 score points)		Level 1 (from 334.94 to 409.54 score points)		Level 2 (from 409.54 to 484.14 score points)		Level 3 (from 484.14 to 558.73 score points)		Level 4 (from 558.73 to 633.33 score points)		Level 5 (from 633.33 to 707.93 score points)		Level 6 (above 707.93 score points)	
	%	S.E.	%	S.E.	%	S.E.	%	S.E.	%	S.E.	%	S.E.	%	S.E.
Australia	3.0	(0.3)	9.8	(0.5)	20.2	(0.6)	27.7	(0.5)	24.6	(0.5)	11.8	(0.5)	2.8	(0.3)
Austria	4.3	(0.9)	12.0	(1.0)	21.8	(1.0)	28.3	(1.0)	23.6	(1.1)	8.8	(0.7)	1.2	(0.2)
Belgium	4.8	(0.7)	12.2	(0.6)	20.8	(0.8)	27.6	(0.8)	24.5	(0.8)	9.1	(0.5)	1.0	(0.2)
Canada	2.2	(0.3)	7.8	(0.5)	19.1	(0.6)	28.8	(0.6)	27.7	(0.6)	12.0	(0.5)	2.4	(0.2)
Czech Republic	3.5	(0.6)	12.1	(0.8)	23.4	(1.2)	27.8	(1.1)	21.7	(0.9)	9.8	(0.9)	1.8	(0.3)
Denmark	4.3	(0.6)	14.1	(0.8)	26.0	(1.1)	29.3	(1.0)	19.5	(0.9)	6.1	(0.7)	0.7	(0.2)
Finland	0.5	(0.1)	3.6	(0.4)	13.6	(0.7)	29.1	(1.1)	32.2	(0.9)	17.0	(0.7)	3.9	(0.3)
France	6.6	(0.7)	14.5	(1.0)	22.8	(1.1)	27.2	(1.1)	20.9	(1.0)	7.2	(0.6)	0.8	(0.2)
Germany	4.1	(0.7)	11.3	(1.0)	21.4	(1.1)	27.9	(1.1)	23.6	(0.9)	10.0	(0.6)	1.8	(0.2)
Greece	7.2	(0.9)	16.9	(0.9)	28.9	(1.2)	29.4	(1.0)	14.2	(0.8)	3.2	(0.3)	0.2	(0.1)
Hungary	2.7	(0.3)	12.3	(0.8)	26.0	(1.2)	31.1	(1.1)	21.0	(0.9)	6.2	(0.6)	0.6	(0.2)
Iceland	5.8	(0.5)	14.7	(0.8)	25.9	(0.7)	28.3	(0.9)	19.0	(0.7)	5.6	(0.5)	0.7	(0.2)
Ireland	3.5	(0.5)	12.0	(0.8)	24.0	(0.9)	29.7	(1.0)	21.4	(0.9)	8.3	(0.6)	1.1	(0.2)
Italy	7.3	(0.5)	18.0	(0.6)	27.6	(0.8)	27.4	(0.6)	15.1	(0.6)	4.2	(0.3)	0.4	(0.1)
Japan	3.2	(0.4)	8.9	(0.7)	18.5	(0.9)	27.5	(0.9)	27.0	(1.1)	12.4	(0.6)	2.6	(0.3)
Korea	2.5	(0.5)	8.7	(0.8)	21.2	(1.0)	31.8	(1.2)	25.5	(0.9)	9.2	(0.8)	1.1	(0.3)
Luxembourg	6.5	(0.4)	15.6	(0.7)	25.4	(0.7)	28.6	(0.9)	18.1	(0.7)	5.4	(0.3)	0.5	(0.1)
Mexico	18.2	(1.2)	32.8	(0.9)	30.8	(1.0)	14.8	(0.7)	3.2	(0.3)	0.3	(0.1)	0.0	a
Netherlands	2.3	(0.4)	10.7	(0.9)	21.1	(1.0)	26.9	(0.9)	25.8	(1.0)	11.5	(0.8)	1.7	(0.2)
New Zealand	4.0	(0.4)	9.7	(0.6)	19.7	(0.8)	25.1	(0.7)	23.9	(0.8)	13.6	(0.7)	4.0	(0.4)
Norway	5.9	(0.8)	15.2	(0.8)	27.3	(0.8)	28.5	(1.0)	17.1	(0.7)	5.5	(0.4)	0.6	(0.1)
Poland	3.2	(0.4)	13.8	(0.6)	27.5	(0.9)	29.4	(1.0)	19.3	(0.8)	6.1	(0.4)	0.7	(0.1)
Portugal	5.8	(0.8)	18.7	(1.0)	28.8	(0.9)	28.8	(1.2)	14.7	(0.9)	3.0	(0.4)	0.1	(0.1)
Slovak Republic	5.2	(0.6)	15.0	(0.9)	28.0	(1.0)	28.1	(1.0)	17.9	(1.0)	5.2	(0.5)	0.6	(0.1)
Spain	4.7	(0.4)	14.9	(0.7)	27.4	(0.8)	30.2	(0.7)	17.9	(0.8)	4.5	(0.4)	0.3	(0.1)
Sweden	3.8	(0.4)	12.6	(0.6)	25.2	(0.9)	29.5	(0.9)	21.1	(0.9)	6.8	(0.5)	1.1	(0.2)
Switzerland	4.5	(0.5)	11.6	(0.6)	21.8	(0.9)	28.2	(0.8)	23.5	(1.1)	9.1	(0.8)	1.4	(0.3)
Turkey	12.9	(0.8)	33.7	(1.3)	31.3	(1.4)	15.1	(1.1)	6.2	(1.2)	0.9	(0.3)	0.0	a
United Kingdom	4.8	(0.5)	11.9	(0.6)	21.8	(0.7)	25.9	(0.7)	21.8	(0.6)	10.9	(0.5)	2.9	(0.3)
United States	7.6	(0.9)	16.8	(0.9)	24.2	(0.9)	24.0	(0.8)	18.3	(1.0)	7.5	(0.6)	1.5	(0.2)
OECD total	6.9	(0.3)	16.3	(0.3)	24.2	(0.4)	25.1	(0.3)	18.7	(0.3)	7.4	(0.2)	1.4	(0.1)
OECD average	5.2	(0.1)	14.1	(0.1)	24.0	(0.2)	27.4	(0.2)	20.3	(0.2)	7.7	(0.1)	1.3	(0.0)
Brazil	27.9	(1.0)	33.1	(1.0)	23.8	(0.9)	11.3	(0.9)	3.4	(0.4)	0.5	(0.2)	0.0	(0.0)
Chile	13.1	(1.1)	26.7	(1.5)	29.9	(1.2)	20.1	(1.4)	8.4	(1.0)	1.8	(0.3)	0.1	(0.1)
Estonia	1.0	(0.2)	6.7	(0.6)	21.0	(0.9)	33.7	(1.0)	26.2	(0.9)	10.1	(0.7)	1.4	(0.3)
Israel	14.9	(1.2)	21.2	(1.0)	24.0	(0.9)	20.8	(1.0)	13.8	(0.8)	4.4	(0.5)	0.8	(0.2)
Russian Federation	5.2	(0.7)	17.0	(1.1)	30.2	(0.9)	28.3	(1.3)	15.1	(1.1)	3.7	(0.5)	0.5	(0.1)
Slovenia	2.8	(0.3)	11.1	(0.7)	23.1	(0.7)	27.6	(1.1)	22.5	(1.1)	10.7	(0.6)	2.2	(0.3)

Source: PISA 2006: Science Competencies for Tomorrow's World, Volume 2, Table 2.1a.
StatLink http://dx.doi.org/10.1787/401573312123

Table A5.3.
Mean score, variation and gender differences in student performance
on the PISA science competency scales (2006)

					Identifying scientific issues scale					
		All students				Gender differences				
		Mean score		Standard deviation		Boys		Girls		Difference (B - G)	
		Mean	S.E.	S.D.	S.E.	Mean score	S.E.	Mean score	S.E.	Score dif.	S.E.
OECD countries	Australia	535	(2.3)	98	(1.2)	525	(3.2)	546	(2.6)	-21	(3.6)
	Austria	505	(3.7)	90	(2.2)	495	(4.2)	516	(4.7)	-22	(4.6)
	Belgium	515	(2.7)	100	(2.3)	508	(3.8)	523	(3.1)	-14	(4.3)
	Canada	532	(2.3)	97	(1.3)	525	(2.7)	539	(2.4)	-14	(2.4)
	Czech Republic	500	(4.2)	99	(3.4)	492	(4.8)	511	(5.3)	-19	(5.7)
	Denmark	493	(3.0)	90	(1.4)	488	(3.5)	499	(3.2)	-11	(3.2)
	Finland	555	(2.3)	84	(1.1)	542	(2.7)	568	(2.6)	-26	(2.8)
	France	499	(3.5)	104	(2.4)	491	(4.6)	507	(3.7)	-16	(4.7)
	Germany	510	(3.8)	98	(2.4)	502	(4.5)	518	(3.9)	-16	(3.4)
	Greece	469	(3.0)	92	(2.1)	453	(4.1)	485	(3.1)	-31	(4.3)
	Hungary	483	(2.6)	81	(1.8)	477	(3.4)	489	(3.3)	-13	(4.1)
	Iceland	494	(1.7)	103	(1.4)	479	(2.9)	509	(2.4)	-30	(4.1)
	Ireland	516	(3.3)	95	(1.7)	508	(4.4)	524	(3.5)	-16	(4.6)
	Italy	474	(2.2)	99	(1.5)	466	(2.9)	483	(2.5)	-17	(3.4)
	Japan	522	(4.0)	106	(2.5)	513	(5.1)	531	(6.6)	-18	(8.5)
	Korea	519	(3.7)	91	(2.4)	508	(4.9)	530	(4.2)	-22	(5.7)
	Luxembourg	483	(1.1)	92	(0.9)	477	(1.7)	489	(1.8)	-11	(2.8)
	Mexico	421	(2.6)	85	(1.6)	418	(2.9)	425	(2.8)	-7	(2.2)
	Netherlands	533	(3.3)	103	(2.9)	527	(3.8)	539	(3.5)	-12	(3.2)
	New Zealand	536	(2.9)	106	(1.6)	525	(3.7)	547	(3.7)	-22	(4.9)
	Norway	489	(3.1)	94	(2.0)	478	(3.9)	501	(3.3)	-24	(3.7)
	Poland	483	(2.5)	84	(1.1)	476	(2.8)	490	(2.7)	-13	(2.5)
	Portugal	486	(3.1)	91	(1.9)	480	(3.6)	493	(3.4)	-13	(3.1)
	Slovak Republic	475	(3.2)	96	(3.6)	465	(4.5)	485	(3.6)	-20	(5.1)
	Spain	489	(2.4)	89	(1.1)	482	(2.7)	496	(2.6)	-15	(2.1)
	Sweden	499	(2.6)	96	(1.4)	491	(2.9)	507	(3.1)	-16	(3.0)
	Switzerland	515	(3.0)	95	(1.4)	510	(3.1)	520	(3.3)	-10	(2.4)
	Turkey	427	(3.4)	79	(2.7)	414	(4.1)	443	(3.6)	-29	(3.8)
	United Kingdom	514	(2.3)	106	(1.5)	510	(2.9)	517	(2.8)	-7	(3.2)
	United States	492	(3.8)	100	(1.7)	484	(4.6)	500	(3.8)	-16	(3.6)
	OECD total	*491*	*(1.1)*	*102*	*(0.6)*	*483*	*(1.3)*	*499*	*(1.2)*	*-16*	*(1.4)*
	OECD average	*499*	*(0.5)*	*95*	*(0.4)*	*490*	*(0.7)*	*508*	*(0.6)*	*-17*	*(0.7)*
Partner countries	Brazil	398	(2.8)	93	(1.9)	394	(3.2)	402	(3.0)	-7	(2.5)
	Chile	444	(4.1)	89	(1.7)	445	(5.0)	443	(4.1)	3	(4.5)
	Estonia	516	(2.6)	77	(1.3)	504	(3.1)	528	(2.6)	-25	(2.8)
	Israel	457	(3.9)	114	(2.0)	451	(5.9)	463	(4.0)	-12	(6.6)
	Russian Federation	463	(4.2)	89	(1.3)	453	(4.6)	472	(4.1)	-20	(2.6)
	Slovenia	517	(1.4)	87	(0.8)	504	(2.0)	530	(2.0)	-27	(2.8)

Note: Statistically significant values are indicated in bold.
Source: PISA 2006: Science Competencies for Tomorrow's World, Volume 2, Tables 2.2c, 2.3c and 2.4c.
StatLink ⟨⟨⟨⟩⟩⟩ http://dx.doi.org/10.1787/401573312123

A5

Table A5.3. *(continued-1)*
**Mean score, variation and gender differences in student performance
on the PISA science competency scales (2006)**

					Explaining phenomena scientifically scale					
		All students				Gender differences				
		Mean score		Standard deviation		Boys		Girls		Difference (B - G)
		Mean	S.E.	S.D.	S.E.	Mean score	S.E.	Mean score	S.E.	Score dif.	S.E.
OECD countries	Australia	520	(2.3)	102	(1.0)	527	(3.1)	513	(2.7)	**13**	(3.6)
	Austria	516	(4.0)	100	(2.1)	526	(4.4)	507	(4.7)	**19**	(4.8)
	Belgium	503	(2.5)	102	(1.9)	510	(3.4)	494	(3.1)	**16**	(4.1)
	Canada	531	(2.1)	100	(1.2)	539	(2.6)	522	(2.3)	**17**	(2.5)
	Czech Republic	527	(3.5)	102	(1.8)	537	(4.3)	516	(4.6)	**21**	(5.7)
	Denmark	501	(3.3)	96	(1.4)	512	(3.8)	491	(3.7)	**21**	(3.4)
	Finland	566	(2.0)	88	(1.1)	571	(2.5)	562	(2.5)	**9**	(3.0)
	France	481	(3.2)	100	(1.8)	489	(4.2)	474	(3.4)	**15**	(4.1)
	Germany	519	(3.7)	103	(2.0)	529	(4.5)	508	(3.7)	**21**	(3.7)
	Greece	476	(3.0)	93	(1.9)	478	(4.3)	475	(3.0)	3	(4.2)
	Hungary	518	(2.6)	94	(1.5)	529	(3.2)	507	(3.6)	**22**	(4.4)
	Iceland	488	(1.5)	92	(1.2)	491	(2.6)	485	(2.1)	6	(3.7)
	Ireland	505	(3.2)	100	(1.6)	510	(4.4)	501	(3.5)	**9**	(4.6)
	Italy	480	(2.0)	100	(1.3)	487	(2.8)	472	(2.5)	**15**	(3.4)
	Japan	527	(3.1)	97	(1.8)	535	(4.6)	519	(4.4)	**16**	(6.6)
	Korea	512	(3.3)	91	(2.3)	517	(4.8)	506	(4.0)	11	(5.7)
	Luxembourg	483	(1.1)	97	(0.9)	495	(1.8)	471	(2.0)	**25**	(3.0)
	Mexico	406	(2.7)	83	(1.6)	415	(3.3)	398	(2.6)	**18**	(2.3)
	Netherlands	522	(2.7)	95	(1.7)	531	(3.1)	512	(3.1)	**18**	(3.0)
	New Zealand	522	(2.8)	111	(1.5)	528	(4.0)	517	(3.6)	**11**	(5.2)
	Norway	495	(3.0)	101	(1.7)	498	(3.9)	492	(3.2)	6	(3.9)
	Poland	506	(2.5)	95	(1.2)	514	(2.9)	498	(2.8)	**17**	(2.7)
	Portugal	469	(2.9)	87	(1.7)	477	(3.6)	462	(3.0)	**16**	(3.2)
	Slovak Republic	501	(2.7)	97	(1.9)	512	(4.0)	490	(3.0)	**22**	(4.7)
	Spain	490	(2.4)	98	(1.0)	499	(2.8)	481	(2.7)	**18**	(2.6)
	Sweden	510	(2.9)	99	(1.8)	516	(3.0)	504	(3.5)	**12**	(3.1)
	Switzerland	508	(3.3)	102	(1.8)	517	(3.4)	498	(3.9)	**18**	(2.8)
	Turkey	423	(4.1)	86	(3.5)	423	(4.7)	423	(4.5)	1	(4.1)
	United Kingdom	517	(2.3)	110	(1.4)	527	(3.0)	506	(2.7)	**21**	(3.5)
	United States	486	(4.3)	110	(1.5)	492	(5.3)	480	(4.0)	**13**	(3.6)
	OECD total	*489*	*(1.2)*	*107*	*(0.6)*	*497*	*(1.4)*	*481*	*(1.3)*	*15*	*(1.2)*
	OECD average	*500*	*(0.5)*	*98*	*(0.3)*	*508*	*(0.7)*	*493*	*(0.6)*	*15*	*(0.7)*
Partner countries	Brazil	390	(2.7)	91	(2.0)	400	(3.0)	382	(2.9)	**19**	(2.4)
	Chile	432	(4.1)	94	(1.8)	448	(5.1)	414	(4.1)	**34**	(4.6)
	Estonia	541	(2.6)	91	(1.3)	544	(3.2)	537	(3.0)	6	(3.3)
	Israel	443	(3.6)	109	(2.0)	451	(5.4)	436	(4.0)	**16**	(6.4)
	Russian Federation	483	(3.4)	90	(1.3)	493	(4.0)	474	(3.4)	**19**	(2.6)
	Slovenia	523	(1.5)	105	(1.1)	528	(2.3)	518	(2.2)	**10**	(3.3)

Note: Statistically significant values are indicated in bold.
Source: PISA 2006: Science Competencies for Tomorrow's World, Volume 2, Tables 2.2c, 2.3c and 2.4c.
StatLink ⟨⟨ http://dx.doi.org/10.1787/401573312123

Table A5.3. *(continued-2)*
Mean score, variation and gender differences in student performance
on the PISA science competency scales (2006)

	Using scientific evidence scale									
	All students				Gender differences					
	Mean score		Standard deviation		Boys		Girls		Difference (B - G)	
	Mean	S.E.	S.D.	S.E.	Mean score	S.E.	Mean score	S.E.	Score dif.	S.E.
Australia	531	(2.4)	107	(1.1)	530	(3.4)	533	(3.0)	-3	(4.2)
Austria	505	(4.7)	116	(3.4)	509	(4.9)	500	(6.2)	9	(6.1)
Belgium	516	(3.0)	113	(2.4)	512	(3.8)	521	(3.8)	-9	(4.7)
Canada	542	(2.2)	99	(1.3)	541	(2.7)	542	(2.3)	-1	(2.3)
Czech Republic	501	(4.1)	113	(2.4)	501	(5.0)	500	(5.4)	1	(6.5)
Denmark	489	(3.6)	107	(1.7)	490	(4.1)	487	(4.0)	3	(3.8)
Finland	567	(2.3)	96	(1.2)	564	(3.0)	571	(2.7)	**-7**	(3.3)
France	511	(3.9)	114	(2.6)	509	(5.0)	513	(4.2)	-4	(4.7)
Germany	515	(4.6)	115	(3.3)	517	(5.6)	513	(4.5)	4	(4.3)
Greece	465	(4.0)	107	(3.2)	456	(5.6)	475	(3.7)	**-20**	(5.4)
Hungary	497	(3.4)	102	(2.1)	497	(4.1)	498	(4.5)	-1	(5.2)
Iceland	491	(1.7)	111	(1.4)	487	(3.1)	495	(2.5)	-7	(4.4)
Ireland	506	(3.4)	102	(1.6)	503	(4.8)	509	(3.5)	-7	(4.8)
Italy	467	(2.3)	111	(1.6)	466	(3.2)	468	(3.1)	-2	(4.2)
Japan	544	(4.2)	116	(2.5)	543	(5.8)	545	(6.4)	-2	(8.9)
Korea	538	(3.7)	102	(2.9)	535	(5.2)	542	(4.5)	-8	(6.4)
Luxembourg	492	(1.1)	113	(1.1)	493	(2.0)	490	(2.2)	3	(3.5)
Mexico	402	(3.1)	94	(1.8)	404	(3.7)	401	(3.0)	3	(2.7)
Netherlands	526	(3.3)	106	(2.0)	527	(3.8)	524	(3.7)	3	(3.5)
New Zealand	537	(3.3)	121	(1.7)	532	(4.4)	541	(4.3)	-10	(5.8)
Norway	473	(3.6)	109	(1.9)	469	(4.2)	476	(3.9)	-7	(3.8)
Poland	494	(2.7)	98	(1.4)	492	(3.0)	495	(3.0)	-3	(2.8)
Portugal	472	(3.6)	103	(1.9)	473	(4.2)	471	(4.0)	2	(3.8)
Slovak Republic	478	(3.3)	108	(2.5)	478	(4.8)	478	(3.6)	0	(5.6)
Spain	485	(3.0)	101	(1.2)	484	(3.4)	485	(3.1)	-1	(2.5)
Sweden	496	(2.6)	106	(1.5)	494	(3.1)	499	(3.2)	-5	(3.4)
Switzerland	519	(3.4)	111	(1.9)	520	(3.6)	517	(3.9)	2	(2.9)
Turkey	417	(4.3)	97	(3.2)	410	(5.2)	426	(4.6)	**-16**	(4.7)
United Kingdom	514	(2.5)	117	(1.7)	517	(3.1)	510	(3.1)	6	(3.8)
United States	489	(5.0)	116	(2.5)	486	(6.1)	491	(4.6)	-5	(4.1)
OECD total	*492*	*(1.5)*	*117*	*(0.9)*	*490*	*(1.7)*	*493*	*(1.6)*	*-2*	*(1.5)*
OECD average	*499*	*(0.6)*	*108*	*(0.4)*	*498*	*(0.8)*	*501*	*(0.7)*	*-3*	*(0.8)*
Brazil	378	(3.6)	105	(2.7)	382	(3.9)	375	(3.8)	**6**	(2.7)
Chile	440	(5.1)	103	(1.9)	447	(6.2)	431	(5.2)	**16**	(5.3)
Estonia	531	(2.7)	93	(1.3)	529	(3.2)	533	(3.0)	-5	(3.3)
Israel	460	(4.7)	133	(2.3)	456	(6.7)	464	(5.4)	-8	(7.6)
Russian Federation	481	(4.2)	102	(1.6)	478	(4.5)	483	(4.4)	-5	(3.1)
Slovenia	516	(1.3)	100	(1.0)	510	(2.3)	522	(2.0)	**-12**	(3.4)

Note: Statistically significant values are indicated in bold.
Source: PISA 2006: Science Competencies for Tomorrow's World, Volume 2, Tables 2.2c, 2.3c and 2.4c.
StatLink ᴍᴧ᎒ᒪ᧟ http://dx.doi.org/10.1787/401573312123

WHAT ARE THE PARENTS' PERCEPTIONS RELATED TO SCHOOL AND SCIENCE LEARNING?

As part of the PISA 2006 assessment, ten OECD countries complemented the perspectives of students and school principals with data collected from the students' parents. These data provide important insights into parents' perceptions of their child's school and instructional quality and how such perceptions relate both to student performance and to the impact which social background has on learning outcomes.

Key results

Chart A6.1. Parents' reports of child's past science reading and student performance on the PISA science scale (2006)

This chart shows the performance difference on the science scale between students whose parents answered "very often or regularly", and those whose parents answered "never or only sometimes", to the question: "Thinking back to when your child was about 10 years old, how often would your child have read books on scientific discoveries?"

☐☐ Difference in score **before** accounting for the socio-economic background of students

■■ Difference in score **after** accounting for the socio-economic background of students

Compared with 15-year-old students who had not, at the age of 10, read books on scientific discoveries, students who had done so performed, on average, 45 score points higher in the PISA 2006 science assessment, more than the equivalent of a school year, and this advantage remained significant, at 35 score points, even after taking into account socio-economic factors (one school year corresponds to an average of 38 score points on the PISA science scale).

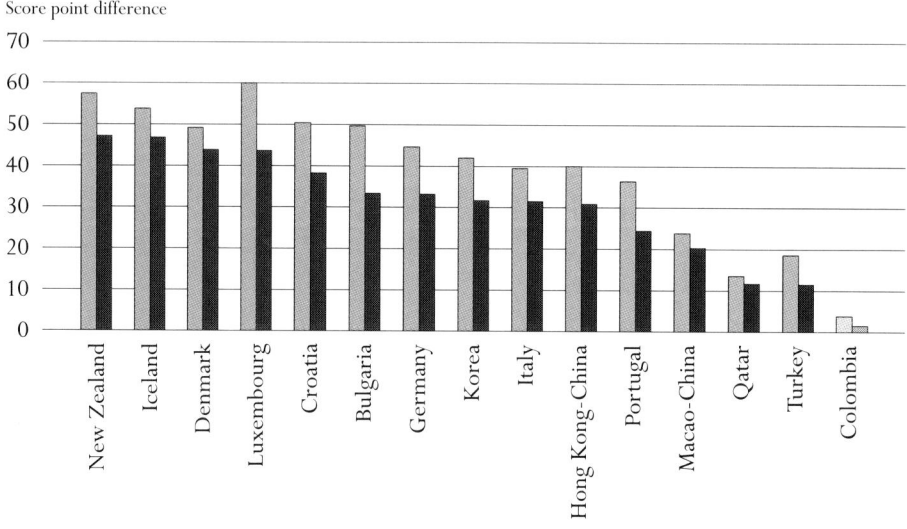

Note: Statistically significant differences are marked in darker tone.

Countries are ranked in descending order of score point difference after accounting for the socio-economic background of students.

Source: OECD PISA 2006, Table A6.1.

StatLink ⌨🖳 http://dx.doi.org/10.1787/401666117553

- Among the 10 OECD countries with available data, on average, 77% of parents "strongly agreed or agreed" that standards of achievement were high in their child's school. Their children scored 20 score points higher on average than students whose parents "disagreed or strongly disagreed" with that statement.

- An average of 79% of parents reported being satisfied with the disciplinary atmosphere in their child's school and 85% felt that the school did a good job of educating students. In both cases, their children had a performance advantage of 12 score points on average.

- On average, 88% of parents "strongly agreed or agreed" that their child's teachers seemed competent and dedicated, but the relationship to student performance was inconsistent across countries, with an average advantage of 7 score points.

- Around 80% of parents reported to be satisfied with the content taught and the instructional methods used in their child's school and 75% considered that their child's progress was carefully monitored. However, in both cases, the difference in students' scores varied markedly among countries for a small overall average advantage of 2 score points.

- Although 73% of parents "strongly agreed or agreed" that the school provided regular and useful information on their child's progress, the relationship of this measure with student performance varied but was largely negative across countries.

A6

Evidence and explanations

Box A6.1. The parent questionnaire

The PISA 2006 parent questionnaire took about ten minutes to complete and one questionnaire was administered per student assessed by PISA. It covered both the parents' socio-economic background and aspects of the following research areas:

- Parental reports related to school and science learning: The students' past science activities, parental perceptions of the value and quality of the student's schooling, parental views on science-related careers and parental general and personal value of science;

- Parental views on the environment: Parental awareness of environmental views and environmental optimism;

- Annual spending on children's education;

- Parental background: Age, occupation (both parents), education (both parents) and household income.

Ten OECD countries, Denmark, Germany, Iceland, Italy, Korea, Luxembourg, New Zealand, Poland, Portugal and Turkey participated in this questionnaire. Also the six following partner countries and economies provided data on this questionnaire: Bulgaria, Colombia, Croatia, Hong Kong-China, Macao-China and Qatar.

Socio-economic background and the role of parents

Parents' responses showed a close relationship between their child's involvement in science-related activities at age 10 and their science performance at age 15. Students whose parents reported that their child had, at the age of 10, read books on scientific discoveries "very often" or "regularly", performed 45 score points higher on the PISA 2006 science assessment (on average across the nine OECD countries that answered this question in the parent questionnaire; Poland did not answer the question) than did students whose parents reported that their children had done this "never" or "only sometimes". This performance advantage was greater than the average performance differences associated with one school year (one school year corresponds to an average of 38 score points on the PISA science scale). The performance advantage was largest in New Zealand, Luxembourg and Iceland where it corresponded to between 54 and 60 score points on the science scale. Even after accounting for the parents' socio-economic level, this performance advantage was still important, with an average difference of 35 score points (Chart A6.1).

Parents in the bottom quarter of the socio-economic distribution were less likely to report that their child had read books on scientific discoveries "very often" or "regularly". In fact, in the top quarter of the socio-economic distribution the percentage was, at 18.3% on average across the nine OECD countries, almost twice that in the bottom quarter (9.6%). It is noteworthy, however, that in most countries the performance advantage of students in the bottom quarter of the socio-economic distribution who had read books on scientific discoveries "very often" or "regularly" at age 10, according to their parents, remained significant, with an average difference of 29 score points. In Denmark, for example, the performance advantage was 64 score points in the most socio-economically disadvantaged quarter and in Iceland, Luxembourg and Germany it was still 35 score points or more (Table A6.1b). One explanation for this observation is that educational activities in childhood can make up for a sizeable part of socio-economic disadvantage.

Similar effects for socio-economically disadvantaged families, while slightly less pronounced, are observed for children who very often or regularly watched TV programmes about science at age 10 or who watched, read or listened to science fiction. On the frequency with which 10-year-olds visited websites about science topics or attended a science club, according to the reports of parents, the relationships are mixed, but the percentages of students engaged in these activities were generally small (*PISA 2006: Science Competencies for Tomorrow's World* [OECD, 2007c]).

Parents' perceptions of school quality

Parents' views of their child's school with regard to high performance aspirations, the disciplinary climate or the competence and dedication of the teachers were also important predictors of student performance.

On average, 77% of parents "strongly agreed or agreed" that standards of achievement were high in their child's school, a figure which ranges from around 71% in Germany and Korea to more than 87% in New Zealand and Poland. Students of parents who "strongly agreed or agreed" that achievement standards were high in their child's school scored, on average across the ten OECD countries, 20 points higher than students whose parents "disagreed or strongly disagreed" with that statement (Chart A6.2a). In Germany and Korea the advantage was 30 score points. Some of this performance difference is accounted for by socio-economic factors, but in Germany, Korea, Luxembourg and Turkey, the performance advantage of students whose parents reported high standards of achievement was more than 23 points in both the top and bottom quarters of the socio-economic distribution (Table A6.2a).

An average of 79% of parents reported being satisfied with the disciplinary atmosphere in their child's school, and their children had a performance advantage of 12 score points on the PISA 2006 science scale on average across the ten OECD countries. This advantage was as high as 21 score points in Germany and 25 score points in New Zealand (Chart A6.2b). However, while the percentage of parents reporting satisfaction with the disciplinary atmosphere in their child's school was, on average, around 80% in both the top and bottom quarters of the socio-economic distribution, the associated performance advantage was about three times larger (at 18 score points) for the top socio-economic group than for the bottom socio-economic group (Table A6.2b).

The picture was similar for parents who reported that their child's school did a good job in educating students. An average performance advantage of 12 score points was observed for students of parents who "strongly agreed or agreed" with this statement. In Denmark, Iceland and New Zealand this performance advantage exceeded 24 score points (Chart A6.2c). On average across the ten OECD countries, around 85% of the 15-year-olds' parents, both at the bottom and the top quarters of the socio-economic distribution, "strongly agreed or agreed" that their child's school did a good job in educating students, but the associated performance advantage was very different among countries in these two quarters. Denmark was the only country where the advantage was observed in both the bottom and top quarters (Table A6.2c).

A6

Chart A6.2. **Parents' view of their child's school and socio-economic background (PISA 2006)**

*Score point differences between students whose parents "strongly agree or agree"
and those whose parents "strongly disagree or disagree" with the following statements:*

■ □ Difference in score **before** accounting for the socio-economic background of students
■ □ Difference in score **after** accounting for the socio-economic background of students

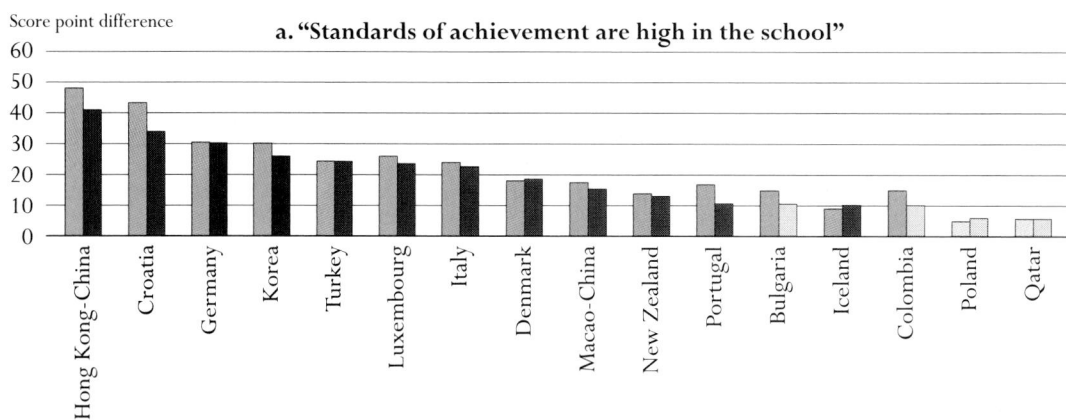

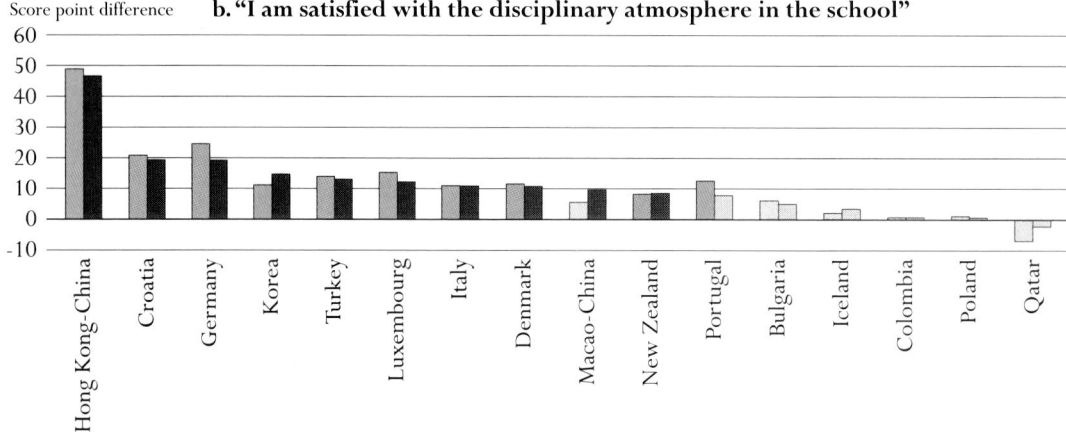

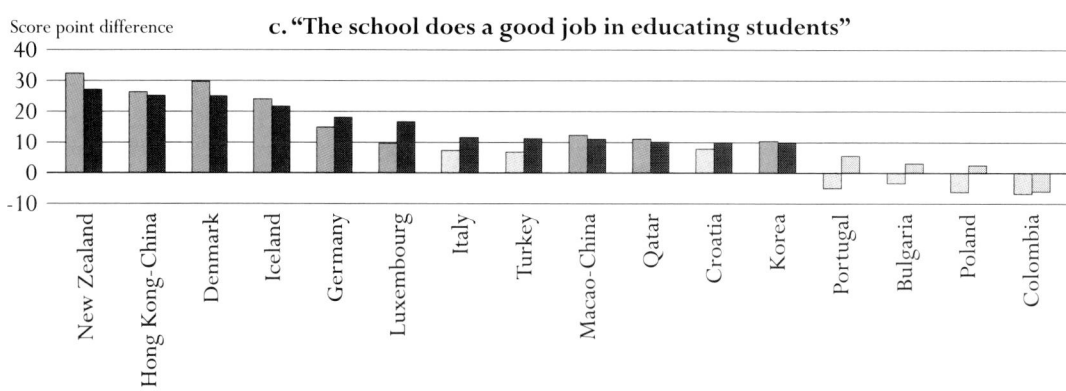

Note: Statistically significant differences are marked in darker tone.

For each chart, countries are ranked in descending order of score point difference after accounting for the socio-economic background of students.

Source: OECD PISA 2006, Tables A6.2a, A6.2b and A6.2c.

StatLink ⊞㎰■ http://dx.doi.org/10.1787/401666117553

A6

On average, 88% of parents "strongly agreed or agreed" that their child's teachers seemed competent and dedicated, ranging from 80% in Germany to more than 90% in Italy, New Zealand, Poland and Portugal. The relationship of this measure with student performance was inconsistent across countries, but was positive on average (7 score points) (Chart A6.3a). Denmark was the only country showing a stable performance advantage (30 score points or more) in both the bottom and the top quarter of the socio-economic distribution. Luxembourg and Turkey showed a performance advantage (23 and 27 score points, respectively) in the bottom quarter, and Portugal did the same in the top quarter (22 score points) (Table A6.3a).

Chart A6.3. **Parents' perceptions of instructional quality (PISA 2006)**

*Performance difference on the science scale between students whose parents "strongly agree or agree",
and those whose parents "strongly disagree or disagree", with the following statements:*

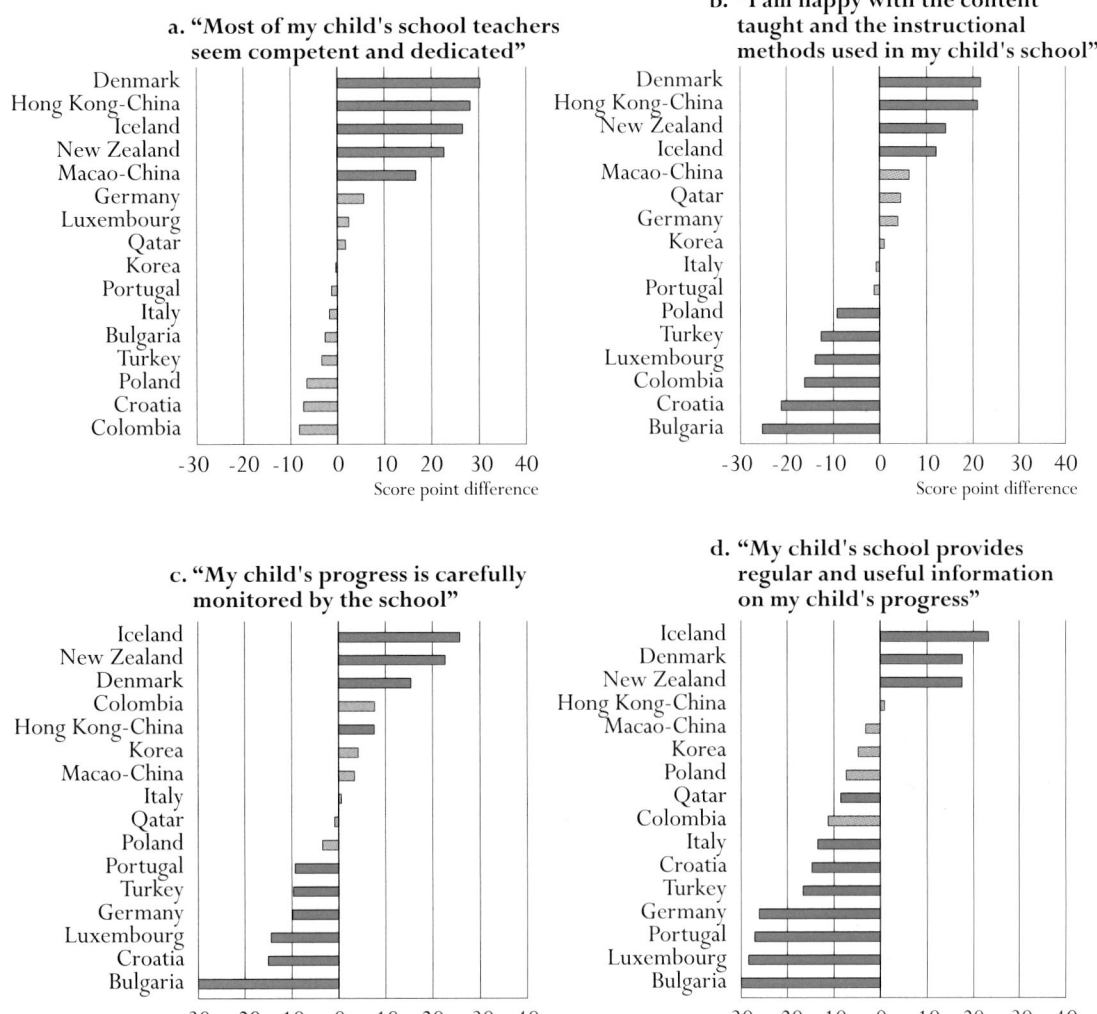

a. "Most of my child's school teachers seem competent and dedicated"

b. "I am happy with the content taught and the instructional methods used in my child's school"

c. "My child's progress is carefully monitored by the school"

d. "My child's school provides regular and useful information on my child's progress"

Note: Statistically significant differences are marked in darker tone.
For each chart, countries are ranked in descending order of score point difference.
Source: OECD PISA 2006, Tables A6.3a, A6.3b, A6.3c and A6.3d.
StatLink ⫘⫘⫘ http://dx.doi.org/10.1787/401666117553

A6

Around 80% of the parents reported being satisfied with the content taught and the instructional methods used in their child's school. The percentage varied among countries from 71 to 87%. The difference in the score of students whose parents "strongly agreed or agreed" compared to other students varied markedly among countries. Some showed an advantage (22 score points for Denmark, 12 for Iceland and 14 for New Zealand) while others showed a disadvantage (-14 score points for Luxembourg, -9 for Poland and -13 for Turkey) (Chart A6.3b). Whereas 83% of parents in the bottom quarter of the socio-economic distribution were happy with the content taught and the instructional methods used in their child's school, the proportion was 76% in the top quarter. In Denmark the performance advantage was 25 score points in the socio-economically most disadvantaged quarter, and 29 in the most advantaged. The performance advantage in the socio-economically most advantaged quarter in Iceland and Portugal was 20 and 22 score points, respectively (Table A6.3b).

While 75% of parents "strongly agreed or agreed" with the statement "My child's progress is carefully monitored", the performance advantage varied, ranging from 26 score points in Iceland to -14 score points in Luxembourg, with an overall average of 2 score points (Chart A6.3c). Also here Denmark had a consistent performance advantage in both the bottom and top quarters of the socio-economic distribution. Iceland showed an advantage of 22 score points in the bottom quarter while New Zealand also had a 22 score point advantage but in the top quarter (Table A6.3c).

On average, 73% of parents "strongly agreed or agreed" that the school provided regular and useful information on their child's progress, but this ranged from less than 50% in Germany to over 90% in Poland. The relationship of this measure with student performance was inconsistent across countries, with an average of -7 score points (Chart A6.3d). In the bottom socio-economic quarter, three countries, Luxembourg, Portugal and Turkey showed a significant negative relationship while in the top socio-economic quarter Denmark and New Zealand had a significant relationship of more than 20 score points (Table A6.3d).

Definitions and methodologies

The achievement scores are based on assessments administered as part of the Programme for International Student Assessment (PISA) undertaken by the Organisation for Economic Co-operation and Development (OECD). PISA was administered most recently during the 2006 school year.

The target population studied for this indicator was 15-year-old students. Operationally, this referred to students who were from 15 years and 3 (completed) months to 16 years and 2 (completed) months at the beginning of the testing period and who were enrolled in an educational institution at the secondary level, irrespective of the grade levels or type of institutions in which they were enrolled, and irrespective of whether they participated in school full-time or part-time.

In examining the results from the PISA parent questionnaire, it should be noted that in some countries non-response was considerable. Countries with a high percentage of missing data in the parent questionnaire are listed in the following together with the proportion of missing data in brackets: Portugal (11%), Italy (14%), Germany (20%), Luxembourg (24%), New Zealand (32%), Iceland (36%) and Qatar (40%).

Further references

For further information about PISA 2006, see *PISA 2006: Science Competencies for Tomorrow's World* (OECD, 2007c), and the *PISA 2006 Technical Report* (OECD, 2008b). PISA data are also available on the PISA website: *www.pisa.oecd.org*.

A6

A6

Table A6.1.
Parents' reports of child's past science reading and student performance on the PISA science scale (2006)

Results based on reports from parents of the students who were assessed and reported proportionate to the number of 15-year-olds enrolled in the school, on the following statement

	"Thinking back to when your child was about 10 years old, how often would your child have read books on scientific discoveries?"									
	Performance on the science scale of students whose parents answered:						Difference in science performance between "very often or regularly" and "never or only sometimes"			
	"Very often or regularly"				"Never or only sometimes"		Before accounting for ESCS[1]		After accounting for ESCS	
	% of students	S.E.	Mean score	S.E.	Mean score	S.E.	Dif. (agree - disagree)	S.E.	Dif. (agree - disagree)	S.E.
OECD countries										
Denmark	9.8	(0.62)	557	(6.1)	508	(3.0)	**49.2**	(6.5)	**43.9**	(6.1)
Germany	12.7	(0.63)	567	(6.0)	522	(3.5)	**44.7**	(5.3)	**33.2**	(5.5)
Iceland	10.7	(0.63)	556	(7.2)	502	(1.8)	**53.7**	(7.5)	**46.8**	(7.4)
Italy	12.5	(0.44)	517	(4.3)	477	(2.0)	**39.6**	(3.7)	**31.5**	(3.1)
Korea	17.8	(0.77)	558	(5.5)	516	(3.1)	**42.0**	(4.7)	**31.6**	(3.6)
Luxembourg	16.7	(0.57)	545	(3.9)	485	(1.4)	**60.0**	(4.1)	**43.7**	(4.1)
New Zealand	12.5	(0.52)	601	(5.7)	544	(2.8)	**57.4**	(6.3)	**47.2**	(5.9)
Poland	m	m	m	m	m	m	m	m	m	m
Portugal	10.8	(0.52)	510	(6.1)	474	(3.0)	**36.4**	(6.2)	**24.3**	(5.6)
Turkey	16.0	(0.63)	440	(6.6)	421	(3.7)	**18.6**	(5.3)	**11.5**	(4.3)
Partner countries/economies										
Bulgaria	11.3	(0.68)	478	(9.22)	429	(5.96)	**49.7**	(7.10)	**33.3**	(5.21)
Colombia	24.9	(0.99)	392	(4.30)	388	(3.45)	3.9	(3.79)	1.6	(4.11)
Croatia	11.3	(0.49)	540	(4.55)	490	(2.51)	**50.4**	(4.30)	**38.3**	(4.10)
Hong Kong-China	9.2	(0.50)	581	(5.45)	541	(2.49)	**40.0**	(5.52)	**30.8**	(5.38)
Macao-China	7.4	(0.41)	533	(5.56)	509	(1.15)	**23.8**	(5.82)	**20.3**	(5.81)
Qatar	15.4	(0.57)	374	(3.87)	360	(1.37)	**13.5**	(4.12)	**11.7**	(4.32)

	"Thinking back to when your child was about 10 years old, how often would your child have read books on scientific discoveries?"													
	Performance on the science scale of students whose parents are in the low quarter of the PISA index of economic, social and cultural status and answered:							Performance on the science scale of students whose parents are in the high quarter of the PISA index of economic, social and cultural status and answered:						
	"Very often or regularly"		"Never or only sometimes"		Difference in score		"Very often or regularly"		"Never or only sometimes"		Difference in score			
	% of students	S.E.	Mean score	S.E.	Mean score	S.E.	Dif.	S.E.	% of students	S.E.	Mean score	S.E.	Mean score	S.E.	Dif.	S.E.
OECD countries														
Denmark	8.4	(1.35)	533	(13.3)	469	(4.7)	**64**	(13.6)	12.1	(1.35)	592	(9.3)	545	(4.6)	**47**	(9.9)
Germany	8.3	(1.06)	503	(17.9)	468	(5.4)	**35**	(16.4)	16.1	(1.03)	609	(6.5)	571	(3.5)	**38**	(6.5)
Iceland	7.2	(1.14)	508	(17.9)	467	(4.2)	**41**	(18.5)	13.4	(1.41)	585	(10.2)	532	(4.1)	**53**	(11.3)
Italy	9.3	(0.67)	461	(7.1)	440	(2.6)	**21**	(7.1)	17.2	(0.82)	551	(7.4)	509	(2.8)	**42**	(6.4)
Korea	11.6	(0.82)	520	(8.3)	491	(4.7)	**29**	(8.5)	27.5	(1.75)	581	(8.8)	551	(4.6)	**30**	(6.8)
Luxembourg	9.0	(1.07)	470	(10.7)	430	(3.1)	**41**	(11.1)	25.2	(1.40)	574	(6.5)	539	(3.6)	**35**	(7.1)
New Zealand	11.4	(1.31)	528	(15.3)	503	(4.7)	25	(15.1)	16.2	(1.21)	644	(9.1)	593	(4.1)	**51**	(9.9)
Poland	m	m	m	m	m	m	m	m	m	m	m	m	m	m	m	m
Portugal	7.3	(0.90)	447	(10.3)	436	(4.3)	11	(11.7)	16.6	(1.10)	554	(6.9)	525	(3.7)	**29**	(7.1)
Turkey	14.0	(1.63)	387	(11.3)	391	(4.6)	-3	(14.4)	20.5	(1.30)	495	(11.3)	468	(7.9)	**27**	(7.2)
Partner countries/economies														
Bulgaria	7.2	(0.89)	390	(15.2)	368	(6.5)	21	(14.9)	17.4	(1.56)	532	(11.7)	497	(7.2)	**34**	(9.6)
Colombia	24.3	(2.28)	357	(6.4)	359	(4.4)	-2	(7.5)	27.7	(1.59)	431	(8.3)	433	(4.4)	-2	(9.3)
Croatia	6.0	(0.80)	480	(13.0)	453	(3.6)	27	(11.9)	17.8	(1.20)	564	(7.4)	528	(3.5)	**36**	(7.6)
Hong Kong-China	5.6	(0.71)	546	(15.1)	514	(3.5)	32	(15.1)	13.8	(1.27)	603	(8.1)	571	(4.8)	**33**	(8.6)
Macao-China	5.1	(0.63)	497	(11.3)	493	(2.7)	3	(11.9)	9.6	(0.98)	538	(11.1)	516	(2.8)	21	(11.7)
Qatar	13.1	(1.11)	337	(6.6)	339	(2.3)	-1	(6.7)	17.9	(1.19)	403	(9.3)	382	(3.6)	21	(10.0)

Note: Statistically significant values are indicated in bold.
1. ESCS: PISA index of economic, social and cultural status.
Source: OECD PISA 2006 database and *PISA 2006: Science Competencies for Tomorrow's World,* Volume 2, Table 4.14.
StatLink ᴍᴎᴸᴸ http://dx.doi.org/10.1787/401666117553

Table A6.2a.
Parents' view of the standards of achievement of their child's school and socio-economic background (PISA 2006)
Results based on reports from parents of the students who were assessed and reported proportionate to the number of 15-year-olds enrolled in the school, on the following statement

A6

	"Standards of achievement are high in the school"								
	Performance on the science scale of students whose parents:					Difference in science performance between "strongly agree or agree" and "disagree or strongly disagree"			
	"Strongly agree or agree"				"Disagree or strongly disagree"		Before accounting for ESCS[1]		After accounting for ESCS	
	% of students	S.E.	Mean score	S.E.	Mean score	S.E.	Dif. (agree - disagree)	S.E.	Dif. (agree - disagree)	S.E.
OECD countries										
Denmark	77.3	(1.33)	517	(2.9)	499	(4.6)	**18.0**	(4.8)	**18.6**	(4.5)
Germany	71.4	(1.06)	537	(3.5)	507	(4.6)	**30.5**	(3.9)	**30.3**	(3.6)
Iceland	72.4	(0.90)	510	(2.2)	501	(3.5)	**9.0**	(4.2)	**10.3**	(3.9)
Italy	80.1	(0.53)	486	(2.2)	462	(3.5)	**24.0**	(3.7)	**22.6**	(3.5)
Korea	71.5	(1.10)	532	(3.7)	502	(4.4)	**30.2**	(5.1)	**26.0**	(4.3)
Luxembourg	76.6	(0.67)	501	(1.7)	475	(3.1)	**26.0**	(3.6)	**23.6**	(3.6)
New Zealand	87.1	(0.75)	553	(2.8)	539	(4.9)	**13.9**	(5.5)	**13.1**	(5.1)
Poland	88.4	(0.67)	502	(2.4)	498	(4.2)	4.9	(4.0)	5.9	(3.8)
Portugal	76.1	(0.91)	482	(3.1)	465	(3.8)	**16.9**	(4.0)	**10.6**	(3.6)
Turkey	72.9	(0.91)	431	(4.6)	407	(3.3)	**24.4**	(4.3)	**24.3**	(3.7)
Partner countries/economies										
Bulgaria	87.2	(0.8)	435	(6.5)	420	(7.3)	**14.9**	(7.3)	10.6	(5.85)
Colombia	86.2	(1.3)	391	(3.4)	376	(5.8)	**15.0**	(5.8)	10.2	(5.29)
Croatia	65.8	(1.0)	510	(2.6)	467	(3.1)	**43.3**	(3.3)	**33.9**	(2.87)
Hong Kong-China	53.8	(1.3)	567	(3.4)	519	(2.7)	**48.0**	(4.0)	**41.0**	(3.52)
Macao-China	73.9	(0.7)	515	(1.3)	498	(2.2)	**17.5**	(2.6)	**15.4**	(2.72)
Qatar	80.2	(0.6)	363	(1.5)	357	(2.7)	5.7	(3.1)	5.7	(3.24)

	"Standards of achievement are high in the school"												
	Performance on the science scale of students whose parents are in the low quarter of the PISA index of economic, social and cultural status and:						Performance on the science scale of students whose parents are in the high quarter of the PISA index of economic, social and cultural status and:						
	"Strongly agree or agree"		"Disagree or strongly disagree"		Difference in score		"Strongly agree or agree"		"Disagree or strongly disagree"		Difference in score		
	% of students	S.E.	Mean score	S.E.	Mean score	S.E.	Dif.	S.E.	% of students	S.E.	Mean score	S.E.	Mean score	S.E.	Dif.	S.E.
OECD countries																
Denmark	78.9	(2.13)	476	(5.1)	464	(9.4)	12	(10.2)	76.2	(2.20)	557	(4.7)	532	(6.7)	**25**	(7.4)
Germany	71.0	(1.57)	480	(5.8)	451	(7.5)	**29**	(6.9)	72.2	(1.65)	587	(3.9)	553	(5.8)	**34**	(6.2)
Iceland	74.8	(1.75)	470	(4.8)	472	(6.7)	-3	(7.8)	71.7	(1.75)	539	(4.2)	538	(7.3)	2	(8.1)
Italy	78.0	(1.11)	447	(2.8)	422	(4.4)	**25**	(4.4)	80.1	(0.88)	520	(3.5)	502	(6.2)	**18**	(6.5)
Korea	68.1	(1.35)	504	(4.5)	476	(5.8)	**28**	(5.3)	76.9	(1.95)	564	(6.5)	542	(5.2)	**23**	(8.5)
Luxembourg	76.3	(1.47)	440	(3.4)	414	(6.3)	**26**	(6.9)	77.8	(1.20)	553	(3.5)	524	(6.5)	**29**	(6.9)
New Zealand	88.4	(1.56)	506	(4.9)	497	(13.5)	10	(13.4)	88.0	(1.20)	603	(4.0)	594	(8.7)	9	(9.3)
Poland	88.7	(1.07)	466	(3.4)	457	(8.0)	9	(8.5)	87.4	(1.06)	549	(3.7)	540	(8.2)	9	(8.7)
Portugal	75.0	(1.33)	436	(4.4)	440	(5.9)	-4	(6.4)	82.5	(1.41)	534	(3.8)	509	(7.2)	**25**	(8.2)
Turkey	72.8	(1.75)	397	(4.3)	373	(4.4)	**24**	(5.8)	72.2	(1.80)	481	(9.7)	456	(7.5)	**26**	(8.7)
Partner countries/economies																
Bulgaria	85.8	(1.66)	370	(6.6)	361	(10.2)	9	(10.0)	87.0	(1.40)	507	(8.0)	480	(10.6)	**27**	(11.6)
Colombia	83.8	(1.86)	360	(4.1)	353	(7.2)	7	(7.8)	89.5	(1.41)	433	(4.0)	425	(10.9)	8	(10.9)
Croatia	55.6	(1.73)	469	(4.6)	438	(4.1)	**30**	(4.9)	76.0	(1.52)	543	(4.0)	507	(4.9)	**36**	(6.3)
Hong Kong-China	43.8	(1.51)	543	(4.0)	493	(4.2)	**50**	(5.1)	65.6	(2.50)	589	(5.5)	549	(5.2)	**40**	(7.3)
Macao-China	68.8	(1.32)	497	(3.3)	484	(4.3)	12	(5.6)	77.5	(1.23)	522	(3.1)	504	(5.4)	**18**	(6.2)
Qatar	80.0	(1.28)	338	(2.7)	344	(5.2)	-6	(6.1)	80.9	(1.35)	390	(3.7)	368	(8.8)	**22**	(9.7)

Note: Statistically significant values are indicated in bold.
1. ESCS: PISA index of economic, social and cultural status.
Source: OECD PISA 2006 database and *PISA 2006: Science Competencies for Tomorrow's World,* Volume 2, Table 4.12 and Table 5.7.
StatLink ⟶ http://dx.doi.org/10.1787/401666117553

A6

Table A6.2b.
Parents' view of the disciplinary atmosphere in their child's school and socio-economic background (PISA 2006)
Results based on reports from parents of the students who were assessed and reported proportionate to the number of 15-year-olds enrolled in the school, on the following statement

	"I am satisfied with the disciplinary atmosphere in the school"								
	Performance on the science scale of students whose parents:					Difference in science performance between "strongly agree or agree" and "disagree or strongly disagree"			
	"Strongly agree or agree"				"Disagree or strongly disagree"		Before accounting for ESCS[1]		After accounting for ESCS	
	% of students	S.E.	Mean score	S.E.	Mean score	S.E.	Dif. (agree - disagree)	S.E.	Dif. (agree - disagree)	S.E.
OECD countries										
Denmark	74.3	(1.32)	516	(3.2)	501	(4.3)	**15.4**	(5.1)	**12.2**	(4.8)
Germany	73.8	(1.08)	534	(3.9)	513	(3.9)	**20.8**	(4.1)	**19.4**	(3.6)
Iceland	76.2	(0.73)	510	(2.2)	498	(4.0)	**12.5**	(4.8)	7.9	(4.7)
Italy	80.9	(0.56)	483	(2.4)	475	(3.3)	**8.2**	(3.7)	**8.5**	(3.5)
Korea	78.4	(0.82)	526	(3.6)	514	(3.9)	**11.5**	(4.1)	**10.7**	(3.5)
Luxembourg	82.9	(0.70)	497	(1.5)	486	(3.9)	**11.1**	(4.2)	**14.8**	(4.1)
New Zealand	82.7	(0.82)	555	(2.7)	531	(4.2)	**24.7**	(4.3)	**19.3**	(4.0)
Poland	79.9	(0.94)	502	(2.4)	500	(3.5)	2.2	(3.3)	3.5	(2.9)
Portugal	80.4	(1.00)	479	(3.2)	473	(3.8)	5.6	(4.2)	**9.7**	(3.8)
Turkey	81.9	(0.74)	426	(4.0)	420	(5.0)	6.2	(4.3)	5.1	(3.8)
Partner countries/economies										
Bulgaria	80.3	(0.9)	432	(6.6)	439	(5.9)	-6.9	(4.94)	-2.2	(4.26)
Colombia	82.7	(1.1)	389	(3.6)	388	(4.2)	0.8	(4.57)	0.8	(4.06)
Croatia	82.2	(0.7)	497	(2.7)	486	(3.6)	**10.9**	(3.66)	**10.9**	(3.46)
Hong Kong-China	88.5	(0.7)	550	(2.4)	501	(5.4)	**48.8**	(5.60)	**46.6**	(5.42)
Macao-China	83.7	(0.6)	513	(1.3)	499	(3.2)	**14.0**	(3.62)	**13.0**	(3.59)
Qatar	79.4	(0.7)	362	(1.4)	361	(3.2)	1.1	(3.62)	0.7	(3.70)

	"I am satisfied with the disciplinary atmosphere in the school"											
	Performance on the science scale of students whose parents are in the low quarter of the PISA index of economic, social and cultural status and:						Performance on the science scale of students whose parents are in the high quarter of the PISA index of economic, social and cultural status and:					
	"Strongly agree or agree"		"Disagree or strongly disagree"		Difference in score		"Strongly agree or agree"		"Disagree or strongly disagree"		Difference in score	
	% of students	S.E.	Mean score	S.E.	Mean score	S.E.	Dif.	S.E.	% of students	S.E.	Mean score	S.E.	Mean score	S.E.	Dif.	S.E.

	% of students	S.E.	Mean score	S.E.	Mean score	S.E.	Dif.	S.E.	% of students	S.E.	Mean score	S.E.	Mean score	S.E.	Dif.	S.E.
OECD countries																
Denmark	71.7	(2.38)	479	(5.2)	461	(8.8)	18	(9.6)	76.4	(2.01)	557	(4.7)	532	(7.6)	**24**	(8.2)
Germany	72.8	(1.46)	474	(6.7)	467	(6.0)	7	(7.4)	75.5	(1.76)	582	(4.0)	565	(6.2)	**17**	(7.1)
Iceland	73.6	(1.76)	471	(5.1)	467	(6.9)	4	(8.9)	81.1	(1.34)	541	(4.2)	531	(8.3)	10	(9.0)
Italy	80.2	(1.02)	443	(2.9)	435	(4.5)	8	(5.0)	80.9	(0.88)	518	(3.8)	509	(6.1)	9	(6.9)
Korea	78.2	(1.44)	498	(4.4)	484	(7.2)	**14**	(6.9)	79.2	(1.75)	562	(6.1)	546	(5.5)	**16**	(7.0)
Luxembourg	85.1	(1.24)	434	(3.3)	426	(7.5)	9	(8.1)	81.7	(1.22)	551	(3.4)	530	(7.1)	**21**	(7.3)
New Zealand	80.4	(1.67)	507	(5.3)	503	(9.9)	4	(10.6)	86.4	(1.19)	606	(4.0)	574	(8.0)	**32**	(9.1)
Poland	80.9	(1.47)	464	(3.4)	469	(6.0)	-6	(6.5)	79.4	(1.33)	552	(3.7)	535	(6.7)	**16**	(7.0)
Portugal	83.4	(1.35)	437	(4.2)	435	(7.4)	2	(7.2)	79.4	(1.26)	535	(4.0)	510	(5.2)	**24**	(6.5)
Turkey	81.3	(1.54)	392	(4.0)	386	(6.0)	6	(7.6)	82.5	(1.27)	477	(8.7)	463	(10.3)	14	(8.4)
Partner countries/economies																
Bulgaria	82.7	(1.70)	366	(6.9)	385	(9.3)	-19	(10.0)	79.2	(1.66)	506	(7.9)	492	(8.5)	14	(7.1)
Colombia	84.6	(1.52)	359	(4.2)	355	(7.6)	4	(8.3)	84.7	(1.57)	434	(4.3)	427	(8.2)	7	(8.9)
Croatia	82.4	(1.21)	456	(4.1)	451	(6.2)	5	(6.6)	82.4	(1.42)	537	(3.8)	521	(7.3)	16	(8.1)
Hong Kong-China	87.8	(1.15)	519	(4.0)	482	(8.0)	**37**	(9.2)	90.0	(1.12)	580	(4.2)	535	(11.5)	**45**	(11.1)
Macao-China	80.1	(1.44)	496	(3.1)	483	(4.6)	**13**	(5.5)	84.7	(1.30)	520	(2.8)	504	(8.2)	16	(8.7)
Qatar	77.9	(1.28)	337	(2.4)	345	(4.9)	-9	(5.2)	80.7	(1.43)	388	(3.7)	376	(9.4)	12	(10.3)

Note: Statistically significant values are indicated in bold.
1. ESCS: PISA index of economic, social and cultural status.
Source: OECD PISA 2006 database and *PISA 2006: Science Competencies for Tomorrow's World,* Volume 2, Table 4.14.
StatLink ⟨⟩ http://dx.doi.org/10.1787/401666117553

Table A6.2c.
Parents' view of the good job in educating students done by their child's school and socio-economic background (PISA 2006)
Results based on reports from parents of the students who were assessed and reported proportionate to the number of 15-year-olds enrolled in the school, on the following statement

		"The school does a good job in educating students"							
		Performance on the science scale of students whose parents:				**Difference in science performance between "strongly agree or agree" and "disagree or strongly disagree"**			
		"Strongly agree or agree"				**"Disagree or strongly disagree"**		**Before accounting for ESCS[1]**		**After accounting for ESCS**	
		% of students	**S.E.**	**Mean score**	**S.E.**	**Mean score**	**S.E.**	**Dif.**	**S.E.**	**Dif.**	**S.E.**
OECD countries	Denmark	78.0	(1.18)	519	(3.1)	489	(4.5)	**29.7**	(5.0)	**25.0**	(4.8)
	Germany	76.2	(0.91)	532	(3.7)	517	(4.4)	**14.9**	(3.9)	**18.1**	(3.7)
	Iceland	82.6	(0.65)	512	(2.0)	488	(5.0)	**24.1**	(5.5)	**21.7**	(5.1)
	Italy	92.1	(0.35)	482	(2.1)	474	(4.3)	7.3	(4.0)	**11.6**	(3.8)
	Korea	79.4	(0.81)	525	(3.6)	515	(4.2)	**10.4**	(4.3)	**9.8**	(3.8)
	Luxembourg	83.5	(0.60)	497	(1.5)	487	(3.7)	**9.7**	(4.0)	**16.7**	(3.6)
	New Zealand	91.2	(0.57)	554	(2.7)	522	(6.3)	**32.3**	(6.8)	**27.1**	(6.4)
	Poland	90.0	(0.55)	501	(2.3)	508	(4.9)	-6.2	(4.4)	2.4	(4.3)
	Portugal	89.1	(0.74)	477	(3.1)	482	(5.3)	-5.0	(5.5)	5.5	(5.1)
	Turkey	85.0	(0.71)	426	(4.0)	419	(5.0)	6.7	(4.5)	**11.2**	(4.2)
Partner countries/economies	Bulgaria	94.3	(0.4)	433	(6.4)	437	(8.6)	-3.4	(8.99)	3.1	(7.82)
	Colombia	95.8	(0.5)	388	(3.4)	395	(6.4)	-6.8	(6.52)	-6.1	(6.03)
	Croatia	91.7	(0.5)	496	(2.6)	488	(4.7)	7.8	(4.40)	**10.0**	(4.18)
	Hong Kong-China	78.8	(0.8)	550	(2.6)	524	(3.5)	**26.3**	(3.68)	**25.1**	(3.37)
	Macao-China	82.0	(0.6)	513	(1.3)	501	(3.3)	**12.3**	(3.85)	**11.0**	(3.80)
	Qatar	84.7	(0.7)	364	(1.5)	353	(3.7)	**11.1**	(4.20)	**10.1**	(4.17)

		"The school does a good job in educating students"												
		Performance on the science scale of students whose parents are in the low quarter of the PISA index of economic, social and cultural status and:							**Performance on the science scale of students whose parents are in the high quarter of the PISA index of economic, social and cultural status and:**					
		"Strongly agree or agree"				**"Disagree or strongly disagree"**		**Difference in score**		**"Strongly agree or agree"**				**"Disagree or strongly disagree"**		**Difference in score**	
		% of students	S.E.	Mean score	S.E.	Mean score	S.E.	Dif.	S.E.	% of students	S.E.	Mean score	S.E.	Mean score	S.E.	Dif.	S.E.
OECD countries	Denmark	73.6	(2.19)	482	(5.5)	447	(8.9)	**35**	(10.3)	80.1	(1.87)	558	(4.4)	524	(8.3)	**34**	(8.5)
	Germany	77.8	(1.51)	474	(6.2)	466	(8.7)	8	(9.8)	75.3	(1.55)	585	(3.7)	559	(5.6)	**26**	(5.9)
	Iceland	82.0	(1.52)	470	(4.8)	468	(8.2)	2	(9.4)	85.3	(1.38)	546	(4.3)	507	(10.4)	**39**	(11.5)
	Italy	93.2	(0.71)	442	(2.7)	436	(6.3)	6	(6.5)	90.9	(0.56)	517	(3.3)	508	(7.6)	9	(7.0)
	Korea	79.8	(1.13)	498	(4.4)	482	(6.8)	**15**	(5.6)	80.2	(1.70)	561	(6.3)	550	(5.7)	11	(8.0)
	Luxembourg	88.5	(1.15)	437	(3.2)	403	(8.0)	**34**	(8.2)	81.4	(1.32)	549	(3.5)	541	(6.9)	8	(7.3)
	New Zealand	89.8	(1.38)	507	(5.1)	493	(12.6)	14	(13.1)	93.0	(1.00)	603	(3.9)	581	(12.3)	22	(12.9)
	Poland	93.6	(0.66)	465	(3.2)	462	(10.8)	3	(10.9)	86.9	(1.04)	549	(3.6)	543	(7.0)	7	(7.0)
	Portugal	92.6	(0.98)	436	(4.1)	444	(10.3)	-8	(10.3)	85.2	(1.32)	532	(3.8)	511	(7.5)	**21**	(7.9)
	Turkey	88.3	(1.08)	392	(3.2)	382	(7.3)	10	(6.5)	82.3	(1.46)	476	(9.0)	463	(8.1)	13	(7.5)
Partner countries/economies	Bulgaria	94.9	(0.88)	368	(6.3)	386	(19.7)	-18	(18.6)	93.4	(1.05)	505	(8.0)	486	(14.6)	19	(16.8)
	Colombia	96.3	(0.91)	357	(3.9)	374	(12.4)	-17	(12.8)	96.5	(0.68)	432	(3.9)	440	(15.3)	-8	(14.9)
	Croatia	92.3	(0.86)	455	(3.9)	452	(8.3)	4	(8.5)	91.2	(0.90)	535	(3.5)	528	(7.6)	7	(7.3)
	Hong Kong-China	77.8	(1.37)	520	(4.1)	494	(6.5)	**26**	(7.9)	79.0	(1.34)	581	(4.7)	554	(6.9)	**27**	(6.5)
	Macao-China	79.1	(1.44)	494	(3.0)	488	(4.9)	6	(5.8)	82.0	(1.44)	520	(2.7)	506	(8.1)	14	(8.6)
	Qatar	84.1	(1.23)	339	(2.5)	336	(6.0)	3	(6.5)	86.8	(1.22)	387	(3.6)	373	(10.9)	14	(11.7)

Note: Statistically significant values are indicated in bold.
1. ESCS: PISA index of economic, social and cultural status.
Source: OECD PISA 2006 database and *PISA 2006: Science Competencies for Tomorrow's World*, Volume 2, Table 4.12 and Table 5.7.
StatLink ⫘ http://dx.doi.org/10.1787/401666117553

A6

Table A6.3a.
Parents' perceptions of competence and dedication of their child's teachers (PISA 2006)
Results based on reports from parents of the students who were assessed and reported proportionate to the number of 15-year-olds enrolled in the school, on the following statement

	"Most of the teachers in the school seem competent and dedicated"							
	Performance on the science scale of students whose parents:							
	"Strongly agree or agree"				"Disagree or strongly disagree"		Difference in science performance between "strongly agree or agree" and "disagree or strongly disagree"	
	% of students	S.E.	Mean score	S.E.	Mean score	S.E.	Dif. (agree - disagree)	S.E.
OECD countries								
Denmark	87.8	(0.69)	516	(2.9)	486	(5.3)	**30.3**	(5.6)
Germany	79.7	(0.68)	530	(3.7)	524	(4.6)	5.7	(4.2)
Iceland	85.9	(0.62)	512	(1.8)	485	(5.1)	**26.6**	(5.1)
Italy	91.2	(0.35)	481	(2.1)	483	(4.4)	-1.7	(4.1)
Korea	83.3	(0.71)	523	(3.6)	523	(3.9)	-0.3	(4.3)
Luxembourg	84.5	(0.67)	496	(1.6)	493	(4.3)	2.5	(4.8)
New Zealand	93.4	(0.41)	553	(2.6)	530	(7.0)	**22.7**	(7.3)
Poland	90.1	(0.55)	500	(2.4)	507	(4.2)	-6.5	(4.0)
Portugal	93.8	(0.44)	477	(2.9)	479	(6.8)	-1.2	(6.7)
Turkey	86.7	(0.62)	424	(3.6)	427	(7.2)	-3.3	(5.5)
Partner countries/economies								
Bulgaria	95.4	(0.44)	433	(6.2)	436	(10.0)	-2.6	(9.2)
Colombia	94.4	(0.55)	388	(3.4)	396	(6.8)	-8.2	(6.8)
Croatia	92.2	(0.41)	495	(2.5)	502	(5.3)	-7.2	(4.9)
Hong Kong-China	89.7	(0.56)	547	(2.5)	519	(4.8)	**28.1**	(4.8)
Macao-China	89.0	(0.53)	513	(1.3)	496	(3.5)	**16.7**	(3.9)
Qatar	86.7	(0.55)	362	(1.3)	360	(3.8)	1.8	(4.1)

	"Most of the teachers in the school seem competent and dedicated"											
	Performance on the science scale of students whose parents are in the low quarter of the PISA index of economic, social and cultural status and:							Performance on the science scale of students whose parents are in the high quarter of the PISA index of economic, social and cultural status and:				
	"Strongly agree or agree"		"Disagree or strongly disagree"		Difference in score			"Strongly agree or agree"		"Disagree or strongly disagree"		Difference in score	
	% of students	S.E.	Mean score	S.E.	Mean score	S.E.	Dif.	S.E.	% of students	S.E.	Mean score	S.E.	Mean score	S.E.	Dif.	S.E.
OECD countries																
Denmark	87.6	(1.40)	478	(5.1)	447	(10.1)	30	(11.1)	88.4	(1.27)	555	(4.4)	518	(10.0)	37	(9.9)
Germany	84.6	(1.13)	474	(5.8)	462	(8.2)	13	(7.8)	78.2	(1.29)	580	(4.3)	567	(5.7)	13	(7.4)
Iceland	84.6	(1.32)	473	(4.4)	457	(9.0)	17	(9.7)	87.5	(1.24)	542	(4.0)	520	(11.9)	23	(12.2)
Italy	92.4	(0.58)	441	(2.7)	441	(8.0)	0	(7.8)	89.2	(0.59)	517	(3.5)	509	(4.9)	7	(5.1)
Korea	84.2	(1.24)	495	(4.8)	495	(7.0)	0	(7.4)	82.6	(1.43)	558	(6.2)	565	(6.3)	-7	(8.0)
Luxembourg	87.7	(1.26)	436	(3.2)	413	(9.8)	23	(10.4)	79.4	(1.21)	548	(3.8)	543	(6.3)	6	(7.3)
New Zealand	92.9	(1.06)	507	(4.8)	489	(18.1)	18	(17.8)	94.6	(0.60)	603	(3.8)	582	(13.9)	21	(14.3)
Poland	93.4	(0.68)	463	(3.3)	475	(10.3)	-12	(10.5)	87.2	(0.98)	549	(3.7)	539	(7.2)	10	(7.7)
Portugal	96.1	(0.79)	436	(4.0)	433	(15.7)	3	(15.4)	91.1	(1.04)	531	(3.8)	509	(8.8)	22	(9.7)
Turkey	89.5	(0.90)	393	(3.7)	366	(7.3)	27	(8.0)	83.3	(1.49)	472	(8.1)	482	(12.8)	-9	(8.8)
Partner countries/economies																
Bulgaria	95.6	(0.68)	369	(6.2)	364	(20.4)	6	(19.4)	95.4	(0.77)	503	(7.7)	495	(14.6)	9	(14.5)
Colombia	94.4	(0.96)	357	(4.1)	374	(11.7)	-17	(13.1)	93.0	(1.13)	432	(4.2)	436	(11.4)	-4	(12.1)
Croatia	92.4	(0.76)	455	(3.8)	462	(9.4)	-8	(9.3)	90.1	(0.89)	534	(3.4)	537	(8.2)	-3	(7.6)
Hong Kong-China	90.1	(1.12)	518	(3.9)	486	(8.5)	**31**	(9.7)	89.0	(1.07)	577	(4.6)	560	(10.3)	17	(9.9)
Macao-China	86.2	(1.04)	494	(2.8)	484	(6.4)	10	(7.2)	90.6	(1.06)	520	(2.9)	499	(7.1)	**20**	(8.0)
Qatar	86.6	(1.15)	338	(2.5)	340	(6.2)	-2	(6.7)	85.3	(1.23)	391	(3.5)	361	(9.4)	30	(9.9)

Note: Statistically significant values are indicated in bold.
Source: OECD PISA 2006 database and *PISA 2006: Science Competencies for Tomorrow's World,* Volume 2, Table 5.7.
StatLink ᴍᴍᴤ http://dx.doi.org/10.1787/401666117553

Table A6.3b.
Parents' perceptions of the content taught and the instructional methods used in their child's school (PISA 2006)
Results based on reports from parents of the students who were assessed and reported proportionate to the number of 15-year-olds enrolled in the school, on the following statement

	"I am happy with the content taught and the instructional methods used in the school"							
	Performance on the science scale of students whose parents:							
	"Strongly agree or agree"				"Disagree or strongly disagree"		Difference in science performance between "strongly agree or agree" and "disagree or strongly disagree"	
	% of students	S.E.	Mean score	S.E.	Mean score	S.E.	Dif. (agree – disagree)	S.E.
OECD countries								
Denmark	77.3	(0.96)	518	(3.0)	496	(4.3)	**21.8**	(4.6)
Germany	71.2	(0.95)	529	(4.0)	525	(3.7)	4.0	(3.7)
Iceland	78.3	(0.82)	510	(2.0)	498	(4.1)	**12.0**	(4.6)
Italy	85.8	(0.54)	481	(2.1)	482	(4.2)	-0.8	(4.0)
Korea	76.8	(0.75)	523	(3.6)	522	(3.7)	1.0	(3.5)
Luxembourg	75.4	(0.77)	491	(1.7)	505	(2.8)	**-13.9**	(3.5)
New Zealand	86.5	(0.63)	553	(2.7)	539	(5.1)	**14.0**	(5.6)
Poland	83.8	(0.66)	500	(2.5)	509	(4.0)	**-9.2**	(4.1)
Portugal	86.6	(0.71)	477	(3.1)	479	(4.5)	-1.3	(4.9)
Turkey	73.4	(0.92)	421	(4.0)	434	(5.1)	**-12.6**	(4.4)
Partner countries/economies								
Bulgaria	90.6	(0.6)	431	(6.3)	456	(7.9)	**-25.3**	(7.3)
Colombia	92.6	(0.5)	387	(3.4)	404	(6.6)	**-16.2**	(6.9)
Croatia	85.0	(0.6)	492	(2.7)	513	(3.7)	**-21.2**	(4.0)
Hong Kong-China	82.1	(0.7)	548	(2.5)	527	(3.7)	**21.1**	(3.5)
Macao-China	84.2	(0.6)	512	(1.3)	505	(2.8)	6.3	(3.3)
Qatar	78.4	(0.7)	363	(1.6)	358	(3.1)	4.6	(3.8)

	"I am happy with the content taught and the instructional methods used in the school"													
	Performance on the science scale of students whose parents are in the low quarter of the PISA index of economic, social and cultural status and:							Performance on the science scale of students whose parents are in the high quarter of the PISA index of economic, social and cultural status and:					
	"Strongly agree or agree"				"Disagree or strongly disagree"		Difference in score		"Strongly agree or agree"				"Disagree or strongly disagree"		Difference in score	
	% of students	S.E.	Mean score	S.E.	Mean score	S.E.	Dif.	S.E.	% of students	S.E.	Mean score	S.E.	Mean score	S.E.	Dif.	S.E.
OECD countries																
Denmark	77.3	(2.05)	480	(5.4)	455	(9.5)	**25**	(11.0)	76.4	(1.92)	558	(4.7)	529	(6.7)	**29**	(7.1)
Germany	74.7	(1.49)	471	(6.3)	473	(7.4)	-2	(7.7)	70.1	(1.49)	581	(4.2)	569	(5.3)	12	(6.4)
Iceland	81.1	(1.55)	470	(4.6)	473	(8.2)	-3	(9.0)	78.4	(1.65)	544	(4.5)	524	(8.0)	**20**	(9.3)
Italy	88.3	(0.69)	442	(2.7)	435	(6.7)	7	(6.7)	82.7	(0.97)	516	(3.5)	513	(6.1)	3	(6.2)
Korea	77.8	(1.03)	494	(4.4)	499	(5.9)	-5	(5.9)	76.4	(1.49)	560	(6.2)	556	(5.4)	5	(6.0)
Luxembourg	84.3	(1.31)	433	(3.4)	436	(8.2)	-3	(9.0)	65.6	(1.51)	549	(4.1)	545	(4.7)	4	(6.0)
New Zealand	88.6	(1.31)	507	(5.2)	504	(14.2)	2	(15.2)	86.8	(1.09)	603	(4.0)	590	(7.6)	13	(8.1)
Poland	89.7	(0.93)	463	(3.5)	459	(8.9)	5	(9.6)	77.6	(1.41)	549	(3.9)	545	(5.7)	5	(6.2)
Portugal	91.1	(0.83)	436	(4.2)	440	(8.5)	-4	(9.1)	82.5	(1.52)	534	(3.7)	512	(6.1)	**22**	(6.7)
Turkey	78.2	(2.07)	390	(5.2)	391	(7.9)	-1	(11.8)	67.1	(1.47)	472	(8.8)	481	(9.3)	-10	(6.1)
Partner countries/economies																
Bulgaria	93.4	(0.89)	368	(6.5)	390	(20.5)	-23	(20.7)	86.5	(1.23)	502	(7.9)	506	(10.5)	-4	(9.5)
Colombia	95.2	(0.88)	358	(3.9)	367	(12.4)	-9	(13.0)	89.5	(1.03)	433	(4.1)	427	(12.2)	7	(12.7)
Croatia	90.4	(0.78)	453	(3.9)	472	(6.3)	**-19**	(6.2)	77.3	(1.52)	531	(3.8)	546	(5.4)	**-15**	(5.7)
Hong Kong-China	83.4	(1.21)	518	(3.7)	494	(7.5)	**25**	(8.0)	79.5	(1.63)	578	(5.2)	565	(7.4)	13	(8.6)
Macao-China	82.0	(1.17)	493	(3.1)	491	(5.8)	3	(7.0)	83.1	(1.08)	518	(3.0)	515	(6.2)	3	(7.0)
Qatar	77.7	(1.28)	340	(2.7)	334	(4.6)	7	(5.3)	80.5	(1.54)	387	(3.7)	380	(9.2)	8	(10.1)

Note: Statistically significant values are indicated in bold.
Source: OECD PISA 2006 database and *PISA 2006: Science Competencies for Tomorrow's World*, Volume 2, Table 5.7.
StatLink ᵐˢᴾ http://dx.doi.org/10.1787/401666117553

A6

Table A6.3c.
Parents' perceptions of the school's monitoring of their child's progress (PISA 2006)
Results based on reports from parents of the students who were assessed and reported proportionate to the number of 15-year-olds enrolled in the school, on the following statement

	"My child's progress is carefully monitored by the school"							
	Performance on the science scale of students whose parents:							
	"Strongly agree or agree"				"Disagree or strongly disagree"		Difference in science performance between "strongly agree or agree" and "disagree or strongly disagree"	
	% of students	S.E.	Mean score	S.E.	Mean score	S.E.	Dif. (agree - disagree)	S.E.
OECD countries								
Denmark	71.6	(1.08)	517	(2.9)	501	(4.1)	**15.4**	(3.8)
Germany	61.4	(1.07)	525	(4.2)	534	(4.0)	**-9.8**	(4.1)
Iceland	81.6	(0.73)	512	(1.9)	487	(4.7)	**25.7**	(5.1)
Italy	84.6	(0.50)	481	(2.1)	481	(3.6)	0.6	(3.2)
Korea	66.1	(1.00)	525	(3.8)	520	(3.4)	4.2	(3.5)
Luxembourg	71.7	(0.68)	491	(1.9)	505	(2.6)	**-14.4**	(3.6)
New Zealand	85.3	(0.70)	554	(2.7)	532	(5.4)	**22.7**	(5.6)
Poland	82.4	(0.75)	501	(2.3)	505	(4.0)	-3.4	(3.7)
Portugal	83.6	(0.65)	476	(3.0)	485	(4.0)	**-9.3**	(3.6)
Turkey	63.8	(1.20)	421	(4.0)	431	(4.6)	**-9.6**	(3.3)
Partner countries/economies								
Bulgaria	83.5	(0.79)	427	(6.2)	465	(7.2)	**-37.8**	(5.7)
Colombia	93.4	(0.53)	390	(3.3)	382	(6.9)	7.7	(6.2)
Croatia	78.0	(0.83)	492	(2.7)	507	(3.4)	**-15.0**	(3.4)
Hong Kong-China	75.3	(0.87)	546	(2.6)	539	(3.8)	**7.7**	(3.8)
Macao-China	83.1	(0.57)	511	(1.2)	508	(3.2)	3.4	(3.6)
Qatar	75.7	(0.63)	362	(1.5)	363	(3.1)	-0.8	(3.8)

	"My child's progress is carefully monitored by the school"															
	Performance on the science scale of students whose parents are in the low quarter of the PISA index of economic, social and cultural status and:								Performance on the science scale of students whose parents are in the high quarter of the PISA index of economic, social and cultural status and:							
	"Strongly agree or agree"				"Disagree or strongly disagree"		Difference in score		"Strongly agree or agree"				"Disagree or strongly disagree"		Difference in score	
	% of students	S.E.	Mean score	S.E.	Mean score	S.E.	Dif.	S.E.	% of students	S.E.	Mean score	S.E.	Mean score	S.E.	Dif.	S.E.
OECD countries																
Denmark	72.7	(2.07)	479	(5.8)	460	(6.9)	**19**	(8.6)	69.5	(1.88)	559	(4.9)	533	(6.7)	**26**	(7.5)
Germany	69.0	(1.82)	469	(6.5)	477	(8.4)	-8	(9.2)	56.7	(1.70)	579	(4.2)	577	(5.2)	2	(6.3)
Iceland	81.5	(1.66)	474	(4.6)	452	(8.2)	**22**	(9.1)	83.0	(1.45)	542	(3.9)	523	(10.2)	18	(10.4)
Italy	85.6	(0.85)	442	(2.6)	436	(6.0)	6	(5.9)	82.8	(0.80)	516	(3.3)	513	(4.8)	3	(4.3)
Korea	65.7	(1.87)	498	(4.9)	489	(5.2)	9	(5.4)	65.9	(1.91)	560	(6.8)	557	(4.7)	3	(6.2)
Luxembourg	80.1	(1.34)	433	(3.6)	436	(7.0)	-3	(8.1)	64.7	(1.70)	548	(4.1)	546	(5.0)	1	(6.5)
New Zealand	85.4	(1.44)	507	(5.2)	501	(12.1)	5	(13.0)	87.6	(1.23)	604	(4.0)	582	(9.4)	**22**	(10.1)
Poland	85.7	(1.05)	464	(3.5)	471	(7.8)	-7	(8.3)	79.6	(1.29)	551	(3.7)	539	(7.3)	11	(7.8)
Portugal	87.9	(1.01)	436	(4.1)	442	(9.6)	-6	(9.6)	78.2	(1.34)	530	(4.1)	526	(5.5)	5	(6.6)
Turkey	66.7	(1.81)	389	(4.3)	393	(4.4)	-4	(5.7)	60.6	(2.23)	472	(9.1)	476	(8.7)	-4	(5.9)
Partner countries/economies																
Bulgaria	89.6	(1.19)	367	(6.4)	389	(11.6)	**-22**	(11.2)	75.3	(1.40)	498	(8.2)	519	(8.1)	**-21**	(6.3)
Colombia	93.5	(1.04)	360	(3.8)	336	(10.6)	**24**	(10.1)	93.4	(0.94)	434	(3.9)	423	(10.1)	11	(9.9)
Croatia	82.6	(1.35)	452	(3.9)	471	(6.6)	**-19**	(6.7)	71.5	(1.59)	531	(3.7)	543	(5.3)	**-12**	(5.2)
Hong Kong-China	75.3	(1.55)	517	(4.5)	508	(5.9)	9	(7.8)	73.9	(1.99)	577	(4.7)	572	(6.4)	5	(5.6)
Macao-China	81.0	(1.10)	493	(3.0)	492	(5.8)	1	(6.8)	81.2	(1.32)	519	(3.0)	513	(6.7)	6	(7.6)
Qatar	75.6	(1.45)	338	(2.6)	340	(5.0)	-2	(5.7)	75.7	(1.59)	389	(3.8)	376	(6.9)	14	(7.7)

Note: Statistically significant values are indicated in bold.

Source: OECD PISA 2006 database and *PISA 2006: Science Competencies for Tomorrow's World,* Volume 2, Table 5.7.

StatLink ⬛️⬛️ http://dx.doi.org/10.1787/401666117553

A6

Table A6.3d.
**Parents' perceptions of the regularity and usefulness of the information provided
by the school on their child's progress (PISA 2006)**
*Results based on reports from parents of the students who were assessed and reported proportionate to the number of 15-year-olds
enrolled in the school, on the following statement*

		"The school provides regular and useful information on my child's progress"						
		Performance on the science scale of students whose parents:						
		"Strongly agree or agree"				"Disagree or strongly disagree"		Difference in science performance between "strongly agree or agree" and "disagree or strongly disagree"	
		% of students	S.E.	Mean score	S.E.	Mean score	S.E.	Dif. (agree - disagree)	S.E.
OECD countries	Denmark	68.4	(1.06)	518	(3.0)	500	(3.8)	**17.5**	(3.9)
	Germany	46.2	(1.08)	515	(4.7)	541	(3.3)	**-26.1**	(4.1)
	Iceland	81.2	(0.73)	512	(2.1)	489	(4.3)	**23.3**	(4.9)
	Italy	83.2	(0.57)	479	(2.1)	492	(3.2)	**-13.5**	(2.7)
	Korea	62.7	(0.90)	521	(4.0)	526	(3.3)	-4.8	(3.5)
	Luxembourg	58.1	(0.88)	483	(2.1)	512	(2.1)	**-28.4**	(3.2)
	New Zealand	82.3	(0.83)	554	(2.7)	537	(5.1)	**17.4**	(5.3)
	Poland	92.7	(0.37)	501	(2.3)	508	(5.2)	-7.4	(4.8)
	Portugal	83.4	(0.80)	473	(3.0)	500	(4.1)	**-27.1**	(4.1)
	Turkey	66.9	(1.09)	419	(4.2)	436	(4.3)	**-16.6**	(3.6)
Partner countries/economies	Bulgaria	84.8	(0.85)	427	(6.1)	472	(9.1)	**-45.1**	(7.6)
	Colombia	92.5	(0.65)	388	(3.3)	400	(6.2)	-11.3	(6.0)
	Croatia	83.8	(0.57)	493	(2.7)	508	(3.9)	**-14.7**	(3.9)
	Hong Kong-China	57.1	(0.96)	545	(3.1)	544	(2.6)	1.0	(3.1)
	Macao-China	75.0	(0.69)	510	(1.4)	513	(2.3)	-3.2	(2.9)
	Qatar	64.7	(0.74)	359	(1.6)	368	(2.7)	**-8.6**	(3.4)

		"The school provides regular and useful information on my child's progress"												
		Performance on the science scale of students whose parents are in the low quarter of the PISA index of economic, social and cultural status and:						**Performance on the science scale of students whose parents are in the high quarter of the PISA index of economic, social and cultural status and:**						
		"Strongly agree or agree"		"Disagree or strongly disagree"		Difference in score		"Strongly agree or agree"		"Disagree or strongly disagree"		Difference in score	
		% of students	S.E.	Mean score	S.E.	Mean score	S.E.	Dif.	S.E.	% of students	S.E.	Mean score	S.E.	Mean score	S.E.	Dif.	S.E.
OECD countries	Denmark	67.0	(2.15)	479	(6.1)	465	(7.1)	15	(9.4)	69.4	(1.83)	558	(4.3)	534	(8.1)	24	(8.3)
	Germany	59.1	(1.74)	467	(6.7)	476	(6.5)	-9	(6.8)	36.2	(1.61)	574	(6.0)	580	(3.6)	-6	(6.4)
	Iceland	80.8	(1.63)	473	(4.7)	459	(7.4)	15	(8.8)	82.3	(1.64)	542	(4.0)	529	(10.4)	13	(10.9)
	Italy	85.1	(1.13)	440	(2.9)	446	(5.2)	-5	(5.7)	80.8	(0.87)	515	(3.2)	518	(5.9)	-3	(5.0)
	Korea	64.0	(1.54)	493	(4.9)	497	(5.3)	-4	(4.9)	61.9	(1.66)	559	(6.9)	559	(5.1)	0	(6.7)
	Luxembourg	68.2	(1.59)	427	(3.9)	447	(4.4)	**-20**	(5.8)	48.1	(1.69)	544	(4.4)	550	(4.1)	-6	(5.5)
	New Zealand	81.9	(1.96)	507	(5.3)	498	(10.2)	10	(11.1)	84.1	(1.39)	605	(4.0)	583	(8.1)	22	(8.7)
	Poland	95.0	(0.78)	465	(3.2)	457	(10.4)	7	(10.6)	90.3	(0.81)	548	(3.7)	545	(9.0)	3	(9.4)
	Portugal	88.8	(1.10)	433	(4.0)	467	(8.5)	**-34**	(8.4)	77.5	(1.82)	528	(3.7)	534	(6.4)	-5	(6.4)
	Turkey	69.3	(2.16)	385	(4.4)	402	(4.8)	**-17**	(6.9)	61.1	(1.95)	473	(9.6)	477	(8.4)	-4	(6.9)
Partner countries/economies	Bulgaria	91.0	(1.10)	366	(6.7)	401	(13.4)	**-36**	(14.2)	76.3	(1.91)	496	(7.2)	527	(10.8)	**-31**	(8.0)
	Colombia	94.3	(0.87)	358	(4.0)	370	(9.8)	-12	(11.0)	91.8	(1.00)	432	(4.1)	439	(9.0)	-7	(9.8)
	Croatia	87.9	(1.03)	454	(3.9)	461	(8.4)	-7	(8.4)	78.3	(1.31)	532	(3.7)	542	(5.6)	-10	(5.7)
	Hong Kong-China	53.5	(1.62)	515	(4.9)	514	(4.2)	2	(5.9)	59.7	(1.93)	574	(5.3)	577	(5.4)	-2	(5.8)
	Macao-China	72.8	(1.53)	491	(3.2)	497	(4.4)	-6	(5.5)	73.1	(1.40)	517	(2.9)	519	(5.4)	-2	(5.9)
	Qatar	65.0	(1.57)	331	(3.0)	353	(4.2)	**-22**	(5.6)	66.0	(1.64)	391	(4.4)	376	(6.3)	14	(8.0)

Note: Statistically significant values are indicated in bold.
Source: OECD PISA 2006 database and *PISA 2006: Science Competencies for Tomorrow's World,* Volume 2, Table 5.7.
StatLink ᗗᏑᏢ http://dx.doi.org/10.1787/401666117553

DOES THEIR PARENTS' SOCIO-ECONOMIC STATUS AFFECT STUDENTS' PARTICIPATION IN HIGHER EDUCATION?

This indicator examines the socio-economic status of students enrolled in higher education, an important gauge of access to higher education for all. Internationally comparable data on the socio-economic status of students in higher education are not widely available. This indicator is a first attempt to illustrate the analytical potential that better data on this issue would offer. It takes a close look at data from ten OECD countries, examining the occupational status (white-collar or blue-collar) of students' fathers and the fathers' educational background, along with data from the OECD Programme for International Student Assessment (PISA) 2000 survey.

Key results

Chart A7.1. Occupational status of students' fathers (2004)

The chart compares the proportion of fathers of higher education students from a blue-collar background with the proportion of all men of the corresponding age group (40-to-60-year-olds), in percentage.

■ Students' fathers (left axis)

▫ Men in the same age group (left axis)

▲ Odds ratio (right axis)

There are large differences among countries in the degree to which students from a blue-collar background participate in higher education. Ireland and Spain stand out as providing the most equitable access to higher education, whereas students from a blue-collar background in Austria, France, Germany and Portugal are about one-half as likely to be in higher education as their proportion in the population would suggest.

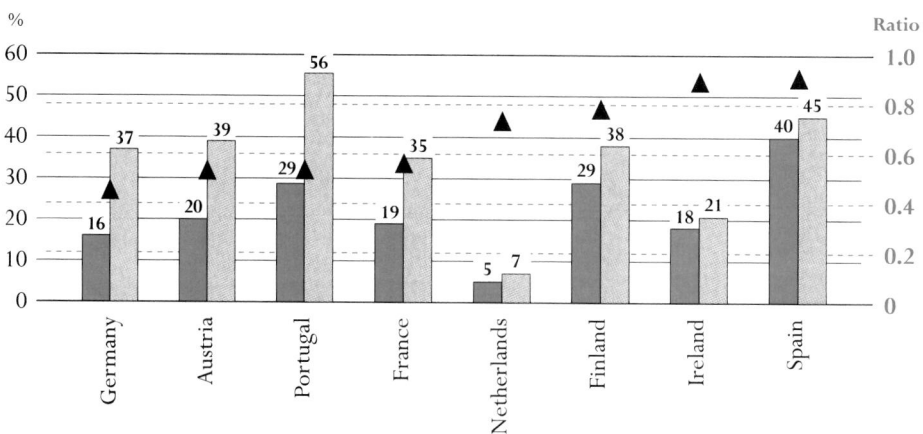

Countries are ranked in ascending order of the odds ratio.
Source: EUROSTUDENT 2005.
StatLink ᗑ⬛ http://dx.doi.org/10.1787/401710587763

Other highlights of this indicator

■ Measuring the socio-economic status of students in higher education by their fathers' educational background reveals large differences among countries. In many countries, students are substantially more likely to be in higher education if their fathers completed higher education. They are more than twice as likely to be in higher education in Austria, France, Germany, Portugal and the United Kingdom than are students whose fathers did not complete higher education. In Ireland and Spain this ratio drops to 1.1 and 1.5, respectively.

■ For the countries providing information on the socio-economic status of students in higher education, inequalities in previous schooling appear to be reflected in the intake of students from less advantaged backgrounds. Countries providing more equitable access to higher education – such as Finland, Ireland and Spain – were also those with the most equal between-school performances in PISA 2000.

A7

Policy context

The pool of available workers with sufficient education and skills will be increasingly important for countries' innovation and future growth. Few countries can afford to rely solely on families that are rich in wealth and/or human capital to provide them. The transfer of low-skill jobs to countries with substantially lower cost structures further suggests that if a large fraction of the workforce has skills levels that are too low to allow them to compete for jobs in the international arena, the result will be an increasing social burden and deepening inequalities.

The socio-economic status of students in higher education can help to show the extent to which countries are making full use of their potential to generate future human capital. A key issue for educational systems is to provide equal opportunities for all individuals, regardless of their socio-economic status. Levelling the playing field between affluent and less affluent students is not simply a matter of equity; it is a way of increasing the recruiting ground for highly skilled jobs and overall labour competitiveness.

Expanding higher education also depends on the quality of the outputs of schools. Findings from the PISA 2000 survey suggest that in most countries, students' performance is linked to their socio-economic status. Intervention at an earlier stage (primary and lower secondary education) therefore appears to be warranted to correct such disadvantages. Successful completion rates of upper secondary education by students with lower socio-economic status is another important threshold that needs to be considered in understanding potentially skewed intake to higher education.

Evidence and explanations

Chart A7.1 above shows substantial differences among countries in the socio-economic composition of the student body in higher education. Note that students in higher education are defined as those attending courses at ISCED levels 5A, 5B and 6. At 40%, Spain has the largest proportion of students whose fathers have blue-collar occupations, followed by Finland and Portugal at 29%. For the remaining five countries covered in this indicator, students whose fathers have blue-collar occupations comprise 20% or less of the student body. The overall intake of students from such backgrounds depends on the proportion of blue-collar jobs within the country. As such, the relation between the two country bars in Chart A7.1 is informative about the student body's socio-economic status. This relation is illustrated by the odds-ratio shown in the chart. With the exception of Ireland and Spain, countries still recruit to higher education proportionally more students whose fathers have white-collar occupations.

The proportion of students in higher education whose fathers completed higher education provides another perspective on the same topic. Chart A7.2a shows the proportion of students' fathers with higher education and the corresponding proportion of men with higher education in the same age group as the students' fathers. Finland, France, the Netherlands and the United Kingdom have the largest intake of students whose fathers hold a higher education degree, whereas Ireland and Italy have the lowest intake from this group. This reflects to some extent attainment levels in different countries, so that to have a better view of the social selectivity in higher education, the attainment level of men in the same age group as students' fathers needs to be taken into account. The ratio of the proportion of students' fathers with higher education to the proportion of men of the corresponding age group with higher education is shown in Chart A7.2b.

Does Their Parents' Socio-Economic Status Affect Students' Participation in Higher Education? – **INDICATOR A7**   CHAPTER A

A7

Chart A7.2a. Educational status of students' fathers (2004)

Proportion of students' fathers with higher education compared with men of corresponding age group as students' fathers with higher education

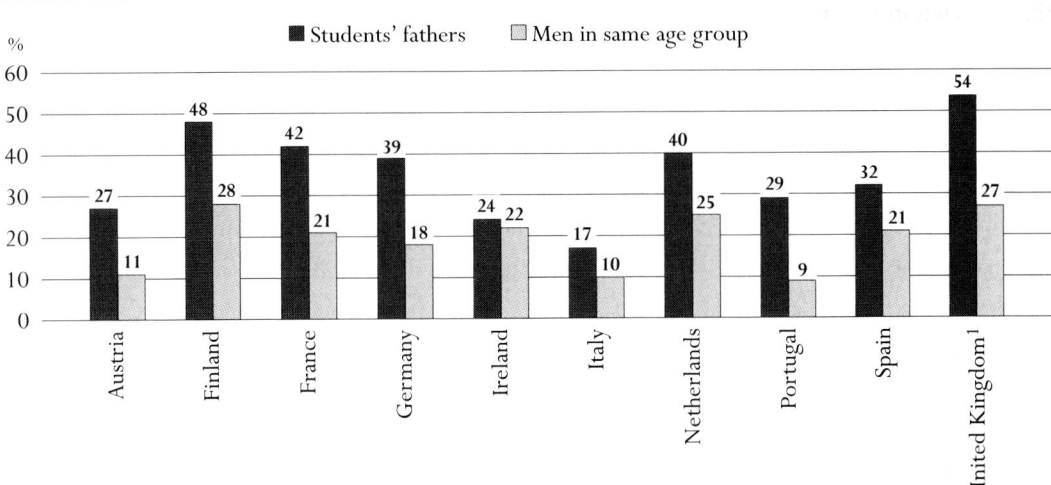

1. England and Wales. Data refer to the parent (male or female) with the highest income.
Source: EUROSTUDENT 2005.
StatLink ⎘ http://dx.doi.org/10.1787/401710587763

Chart A7.2b. Educational status of students' fathers (2004)

Ratio of the proportion of students' fathers with higher education to the proportion of men of the corresponding age group as students' fathers with higher education

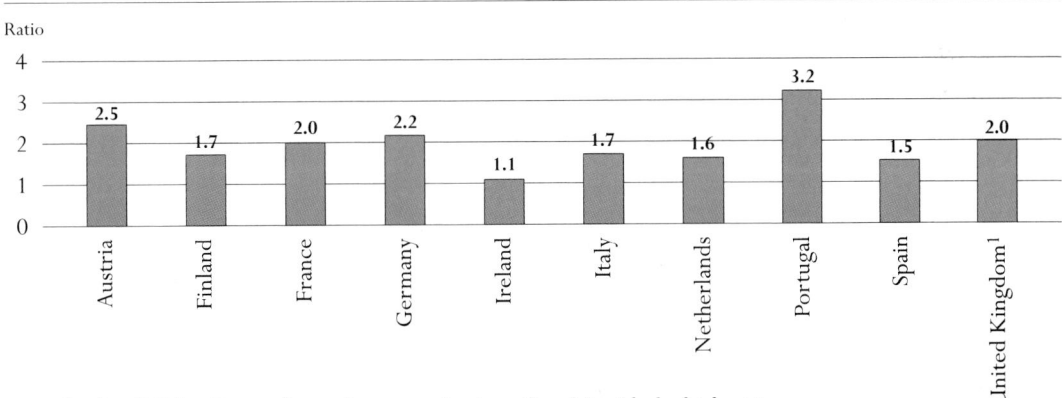

1. England and Wales. Data refer to the parent (male or female) with the highest income.
Source: EUROSTUDENT 2005.
StatLink ⎘ http://dx.doi.org/10.1787/401710587763

For all ten countries, more students are recruited from families in which the father has higher education than is warranted by the percentage of such families in the population. There are also substantial differences among countries on this socio-economic status indicator. The strongest selectivity into higher education is found in Portugal, with a ratio of 3.2. In Austria, France, Germany and the United Kingdom, students are about twice as likely to be in higher education if their fathers hold a university degree as their proportion in the population would suggest. Ireland stands out with a ratio (1.1) almost matching that of the general population.

A7

In most countries, there is a strong socio-economic selection into higher education. Students from homes with a higher education background are overrepresented and students from a blue-collar background are underrepresented (in many cases severely so). Countries vary, however, and in this relatively restricted sample, Ireland and Spain perform substantially better in terms of providing higher education for all, irrespective of the students' background.

Differences between countries in the duration of higher degree programmes, the type of degree students pursue and the existence of non-university institutions all play a role in explaining participation in higher education by students from less advantaged backgrounds. Students from family backgrounds with less education are more often enrolled in non-university institutions, and this may explain, to some extent, differences in the socio-economic status of students, as not all countries provide this type of higher education opportunity. Countries that have expanded tertiary education in recent years will also, by default, have a higher intake of students from less advantaged backgrounds.

Beside these and other factors, there are indications that previous schooling plays an important role in preparing the ground for equal opportunities in higher education. Not surprisingly, inequalities in the performance of students in the PISA survey (15-year-olds) carry forward to higher education. Measures such as the PISA index of economic, social and cultural status (ESCS) of students and variation of PISA scores related to students' fathers' educational background are linked to the intake of students from less affluent backgrounds. The more prominent link, however, appears to be related to inequalities between schools and the extent to which education systems are stratified.

Chart A7.3. Proportion of students in higher education from a blue-collar background (2004) and between-school variance in PISA 2000

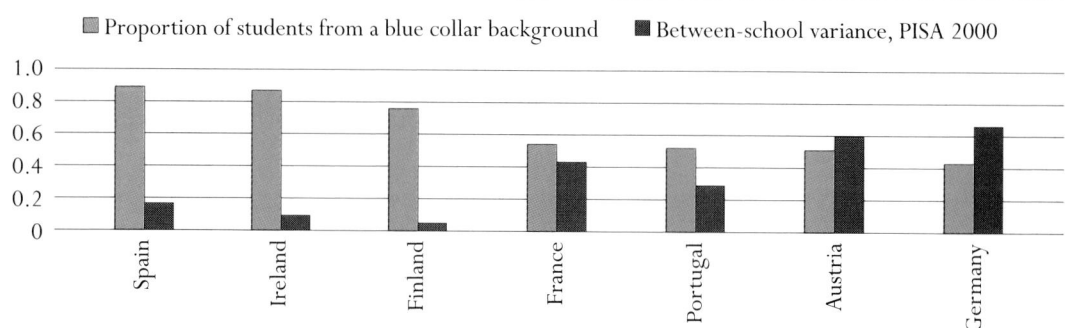

Proportion of students from a blue collar background ■ Between-school variance, PISA 2000

Note: The first bar shows the ratio of students' fathers with a blue-collar background to men of the corresponding age group (40-to-60-year-olds) in blue collar occupations. The second bar shows the between-school variance in mathematics from the PISA 2000 survey.
Countries are ranked in descending order of the proportion of students from a blue-collar background.
Source: OECD PISA 2000 survey, EUROSTUDENT 2005.
StatLink ⟨ﬆﬔ⟩ http://dx.doi.org/10.1787/401710587763

Chart A7.3 shows the relation between the ratio of students from blue-collar backgrounds (from Chart A7.1) and the between-school variance in mathematics performance in PISA 2000. Data from the PISA 2000 survey provide a better match than more recent surveys as some PISA 2000 students have reached university age when surveyed by Eurostudent. For the blue bar, a ratio closer to 1 indicates an intake of students from a blue-collar background in line with the population as a whole. The dark-gray bar shows between-school variance in PISA. The lower the between-school variance, the more equal the school system in terms of

A7

providing similar quality of education irrespective of the schools attended by the students. Ranking countries on equal opportunities in higher education largely resembles the ranking of countries with respect to providing equal education between schools. Among the countries for which data are available on the socio-economic status of students in higher education, it appears that providing a good quality education across all schools is important to have more students from less affluent backgrounds participating in higher education.

At present, there is limited internationally comparable data on the socio-economic status of students in higher education. More information and better country coverage are required for a more thorough understanding of which policies might work and when actions need to be taken to improve the prospect of having more students from disadvantaged backgrounds in higher education. In the present sample, there is a fairly strong link between inequalities between schools in lower secondary education and inequalities in higher education. Better country coverage and data over time would help to understand the main obstacles to a more equitable distribution of students in higher education. The economic motivation for recruiting more students from less affluent homes is in place and better information on student background is essential to know how best this objective can be achieved.

Definitions and methodologies

The participating countries survey their students using the Eurostudent core questionnaire within a specific time frame. In many cases, these questions are integrated into larger national surveys. Most countries have surveyed students attending ISCED 5A and 5B programmes; exceptions are Austria, Germany, Italy and Spain which only surveyed students in ISCED 5A, and Portugal which surveyed students in levels 5A, 5B and 6. The fact that some countries included ISCED levels 5B and 6 whereas other countries did not may distort comparability to some extent. The definition used in Eurostudent for blue-collar background and higher education varies among countries but is harmonised within each country so that ratios will provide consistent estimates. Note also that the corresponding age group for students' fathers with higher education is 40-to-64-year-olds in Italy and that the corresponding age group for students' fathers in blue-collar occupations is defined in Ireland as "fathers of children who are 15 years old or younger".

The number of responses varied between 994 students in Latvia and 25 385 in France, with a response rate of between 30% (Germany) and 100% (Spain, Portugal) depending on survey method used. Most countries used a randomised design (stratified, quota) in sampling the students. However, survey methods varied: a postal questionnaire was used in four countries; an online survey in two countries; telephone interviews in one country; face-to-face interviews in three countries; and classroom questionnaires in two countries.

Further references

This indicator draws on data collected as part of the Eurostudent project (*www.eurostudent.eu*) and published in the *Eurostudent Report 2005: Social and Economic Conditions of Student Life in Europe 2005*, HEIS (HIS) (2005), available on the Eurostudent website.

OECD (2001), *Knowledge and Skills for Life: First Results from PISA 2000,* OECD, Paris.

The following additional material relevant to this indicator is available on line at:
StatLink 🔊📈 http://dx.doi.org/10.1787/401710587763

• *Table A7.1. Occupational and educational status of students' fathers (2004)*

HOW DOES PARTICIPATION IN EDUCATION AFFECT PARTICIPATION IN THE LABOUR MARKET?

This indicator examines the relationships between educational attainment and labour force status, for both males and females, and considers changes over time. It also focuses on employment rates among those nearing retirement age to shed some light on the employment of an ageing population and the links with educational attainment.

Key results

Chart A8.1. **Employment rates of 55-to-64-year-olds (2006)**

This chart shows the percentage of the 55-to-64-year-old population that is employed, by educational attainment.

— ISCED 0/1/2   ■ ISCED 3/4   △ ISCED 5/6

Employment rates generally drop long before the stipulated retirement age in most countries. On average, employment rates among 55-to-64-year-olds are approximately 20 percentage points below those of the total working-age population (25-to-64-year-olds). However, employment rates increase with educational attainment in most countries, and in all countries except Iceland, tertiary attainment provides an employment advantage at an older age. The advantage is particularly large in the Czech Republic, Italy, Luxembourg and the Slovak Republic. As attainment levels rise in most countries, employment rates are likely to follow, with more people working until retirement age and beyond.

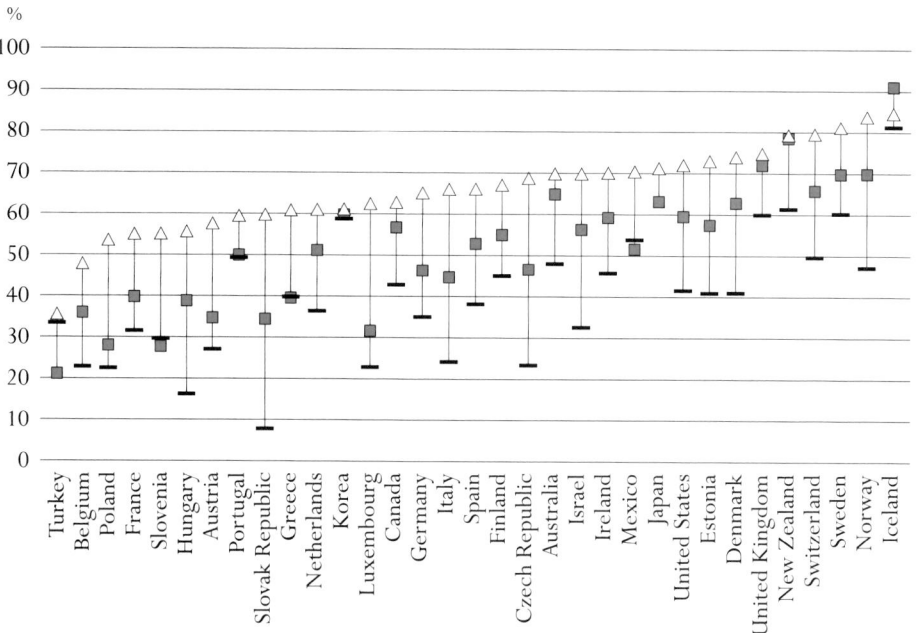

Countries are ranked in ascending order of employment rates in tertiary education.
Source: OECD. Table A8.4. See Annex 3 for notes (*www.oecd.org/edu/eag2008*).
StatLink ⌨ http://dx.doi.org/10.1787/401775543762

■ Employment rates rise with educational attainment. With few exceptions, the employment rate for graduates of tertiary education is markedly higher than the rate for upper secondary graduates. For males, the gap is particularly wide between upper secondary graduates and those without an upper secondary qualification.

■ Those with low educational attainment are both less likely to be labour force participants and more likely to be unemployed. Differences in employment rates between males and females are also wider among less educated groups. The chance of being employed is 23 percentage points higher for males than for females among those without upper secondary qualifications but falls to 10 points for the most highly qualified.

■ Education is an important factor for employment at an older age. On average, 40.2% of 55-to-64-year-olds with below upper secondary education are employed, 52.4% of those with upper secondary and post-secondary non-tertiary education, and 65.9% of those with a tertiary qualification.

■ As employment rises with education, increasing educational attainments will likely alleviate some of the concerns about the costs associated with an ageing population. Countries that seem to be well positioned to benefit from this employment-attainment effect are Finland, Greece, Ireland, Japan, and Spain, where tertiary attainment levels have risen sharply between 45-to-54-year-olds and 55-to-64-year-olds and where employment levels for those with tertiary education are particularly favourable.

Policy content

To further their economic development, OECD countries' economies and labour markets depend upon a stable supply of well-educated workers. As skills levels tend to rise with educational attainment, the costs incurred when those with higher levels of education do not work also rise. As populations in OECD countries age, higher levels of education and longer participation in employment can lower dependency ratios and help to alleviate the burden of financing public pension schemes.

Employment rates normally rise with educational attainment. This is principally due to the larger investment in human capital made by more educated individuals and the need to recoup their investment. However, between country variations in employment rates often reflect cultural differences and, most notably, differences in the labour participation rates among female workers. Similarly, unemployment rates are generally lower for higher-educated individuals, but this is typically because higher educational attainment makes an individual more attractive in the labour market. Unemployment rates therefore include information both on the individual's desire to work and on the individual's attractiveness to potential employers.

In a sense, employment rates are more closely tied to supply while unemployment rates are more closely tied to demand. Time series on both measures thus carry important information for policy makers about the supply, and potential supply, of skills for the labour market and about employers' demand for these skills. Information about supply of and demand for skills is particularly important among the age group approaching retirement age as it can help to indicate potential remedies and policies for prolonging the working life of the adult population.

Evidence and explanations

Employment

Variations among countries in the female employment rate are a primary factor in differences in overall employment rates. The countries with the highest overall rate of employment for 25-to-64-year-olds – Denmark, Iceland, New Zealand, Norway, Sweden, Switzerland and the United Kingdom – also have among the highest female employment rates. The overall employment rate for males aged 25 to 64 ranges from 77% or less in Belgium, Finland, France, Hungary, Poland, the Slovak Republic and Turkey to over 85% in Iceland, Japan, Korea, New Zealand, Mexico and Switzerland (Table A8.1a). In contrast, employment rates among females range from 55% or less in Greece, Italy, Mexico, Poland, Spain and Turkey to above 77% in Iceland and Sweden, an indication of different cultural and social patterns.

Employment rates for graduates of tertiary education are markedly higher – around 9 percentage points on average for OECD countries – than for upper secondary graduates. For 2006, the difference ranges from a few percentage points to 12 percentage points or more in Greece, Poland, the Slovak Republic, Turkey, and the partner countries Israel and Slovenia (Table A8.3a). While there have been some large changes over time in employment rates of educational groups within countries, the OECD averages for lower secondary, upper secondary and tertiary educated adults have been rather stable over the last decade.

The gap in employment rates of males aged 25 to 64 is particularly wide between upper secondary graduates and those who are not. The extreme cases are the Czech Republic, Hungary and the Slovak Republic, where employment rates for males who have achieved an upper secondary education are at least 30 percentage points higher than for males who have not. The gap in employment rates between males with and without an upper secondary education is 7 percentage points or less in Greece, Iceland, Korea, Luxembourg, Mexico and Portugal (Chart A8.2 and Table A8.3b).

Chart A8.2. Employment rates, by educational attainment (2006)

Percentage of the 25-to-64-year-old population that is employed

A8

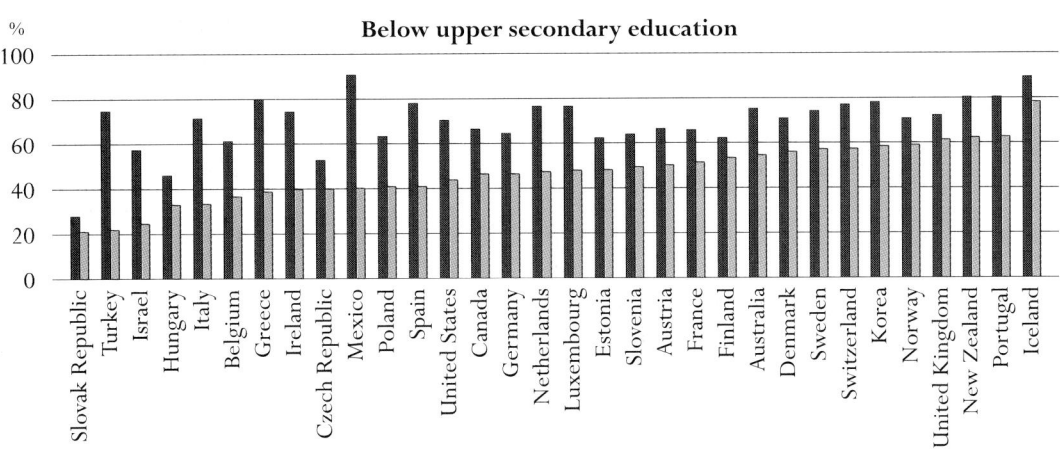

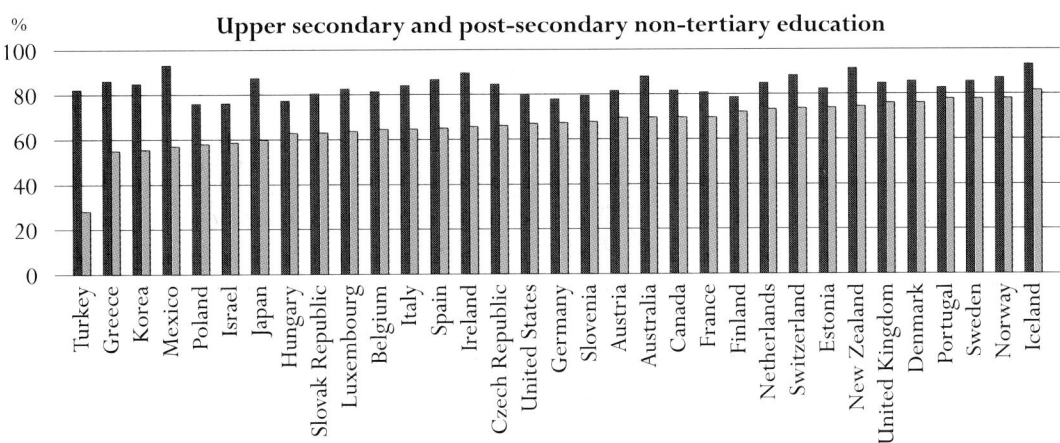

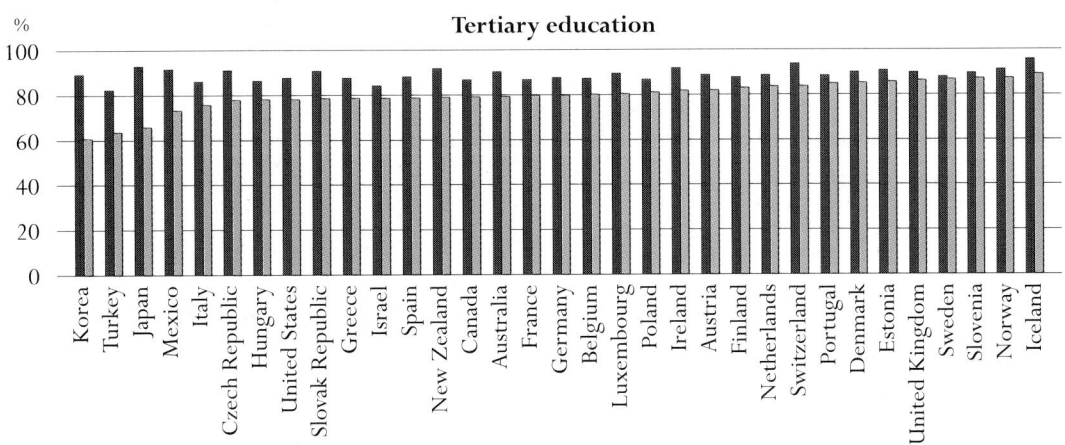

Countries are ranked in ascending order of the employment rate of females.
Source: OECD. Tables A8.3b and A8.3c. See Annex 3 for notes (*www.oecd.org/edu/eag2008*).

StatLink ⌨️ http://dx.doi.org/10.1787/401775543762

A8

In 2006, employment rates for females aged 25 to 64 show substantial differences, not only between those with and without an upper secondary education (15 percentage points or more in 24 out of the 29 OECD countries for which data were available), but also between those with upper secondary and those with tertiary attainment (10 percentage points or more in 18 countries).

Employment rates for females with a lower secondary education are particularly low, averaging 50% for OECD countries overall and less than 30% in Poland, the Slovak Republic, Turkey and the partner countries Chile and Israel. Employment rates for females with tertiary-type A attainment equal or exceed 75% everywhere except Japan, Korea, Mexico and Turkey, but remain below those of males in all countries (Table A8.1a).

On average among OECD countries, the difference between the employment rates of males and females decreases significantly at successively higher levels of educational attainment from 23 percentage points at the below upper secondary level to 10 percentage points at the tertiary level (Tables A8.3b and A8.3c).

Long-term benefits of education

Employment rates of 55-to-64-year-olds are generally lower, by about 20 percentage points, than those of the working age population as a whole (25-to-64-year-olds) (Tables A8.3a and A8.4). For 55-to-64-year-olds with less than upper secondary education, employment rates are 17.9 percentage points lower, for those with upper secondary education, they are 23.1 percentage points lower, and for those with tertiary education, they are 18.4 percentage points lower than those of 25-to-64-year-olds with the corresponding levels of education.

Employment in the older age group has increased in recent years, particularly strongly among those with upper secondary and post-secondary non-tertiary education in OECD countries as a whole and among those with below upper secondary education in the European Union (EU19). Still, there are large differences between the employment rates of different educational groups. The average employment rate for 55-to-64-year-olds in OECD countries is 40.2% for those with below upper secondary education, 52.4% for those with upper secondary and post-secondary non-tertiary education, and 65.9% for those with a tertiary qualification (Table A8.4).

Another way of examining the benefits of higher education in prolonging working life is to compare employment rates of those with upper secondary education and those with tertiary education. They are generally lower for those with upper secondary and post-secondary non-tertiary education than for those with tertiary education in the working-age population (25-to-64-year-olds). In most countries the employment advantage of a tertiary education increases with age (Chart A8.3). Employment rates for upper secondary and post-secondary non-tertiary relative to tertiary education drops for older adults in all but three countries. In Austria, Luxembourg, the Slovak Republic and the partner country Slovenia the disadvantage of having only an upper secondary education at an older age is particularly pronounced. However, in comparing the impact of educational attainment on employment, it is important to consider business cycles. A stronger labour market typically has stronger effects on employment among lower educated individuals.

Chart A8.3. Upper secondary and post-secondary non-tertiary employment rates relative to tertiary employment rates among the 55-to-64-year-old and the 25-to-64-year-old population, 2006

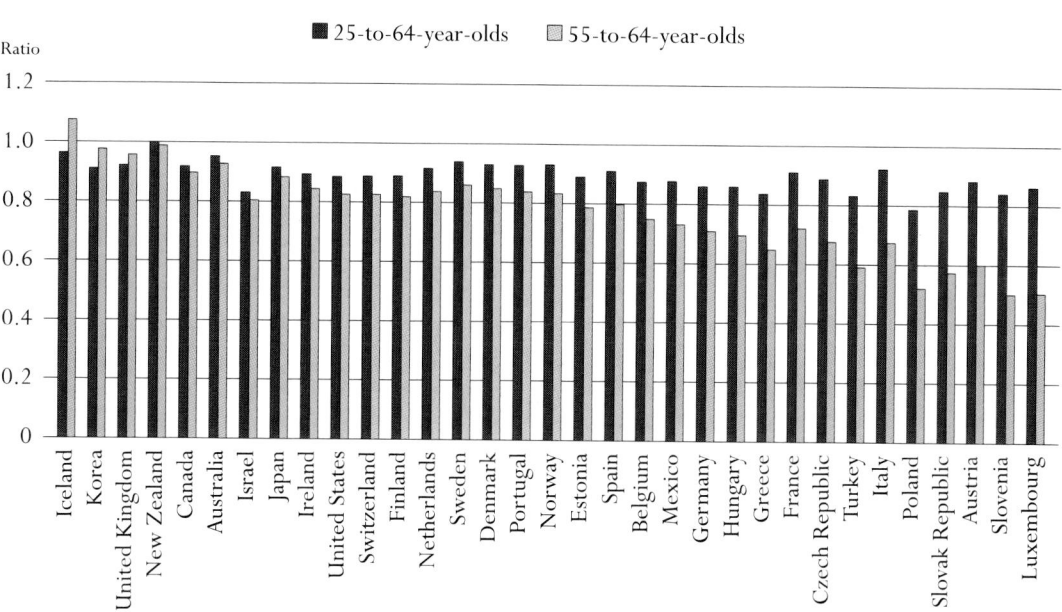

Countries are ranked in ascending order of the difference in relative employment between 25-to-64-year-olds and the older cohort.
Source: OECD. Table A8.4. See Annex 3 for notes (*www.oecd.org/edu/eag2008*).
StatLink ⌨✍ http://dx.doi.org/10.1787/401775543762

Countries in which tertiary education expanded in the 1970s (among 45-to-54-year-olds) and for which there are currently large differences in employment rates between educational attainment levels will likely see increases in overall employment in the coming years. Countries that seem well positioned to benefit from this employment-attainment effect of higher educational attainment are Finland, Greece, Ireland, Japan, and Spain, where tertiary attainment levels have risen sharply between 45-to-54-year-olds and 55-to-64-year-olds (Table A1.3a) and where employment levels for those with tertiary education are particularly favourable. Since almost all countries show higher attainment levels among the 45-to-54-year-olds to 55-to-64-year-olds and as employment rates generally rise with attainment levels, some concerns about the ageing of the population may be somewhat alleviated by increases in educational attainment in recent decades.

Unemployment rates fall with higher educational attainment

The employment prospects of individuals with different levels of educational attainment depend largely on the requirements of labour markets and on the supply of workers with different skills. Unemployment rates therefore provide a signal of the match between what the education system produces and the demand for skills in the labour market. Those with lower educational qualifications are at particular risk of economic marginalisation since they are both less likely to be labour force participants and more likely to be without a job even if they actively seek one.

Among OECD countries, an upper secondary education is typically considered the minimum for a satisfactory competitive position in the labour market. On average, the rate of unemployment among those with an upper secondary education is 4 percentage points lower than among those who have not completed upper secondary education (Table A8.5a). Depending on a country's industry composition and level of economic development, the unemployment risk associated with the lack of an upper secondary level of education varies and is particularly great (10% or more) in the Czech Republic and Germany and especially in the Slovak Republic (34%). Only in Greece, Korea, Mexico and Turkey is the lack of upper secondary education not associated with a higher risk of unemployment; in these countries the unemployment rate is lower for below upper secondary education than for upper secondary and post-secondary non-tertiary education.

On average in OECD countries, male labour force participants aged 25 to 64 and with education below the upper secondary level are more than twice as likely to be unemployed as those who have completed upper secondary education (Table A8.5b on line). The negative association between unemployment rates and educational attainment is similar for females (Table A8.5c on line). Differences in unemployment rates for males and females generally decrease with educational attainment (Chart A8.4). Among females with tertiary education, unemployment rates are above 2 percentage points of those of males only in Greece, Italy, Spain, and Turkey. In 12 OECD countries, unemployment rates for males with less than upper secondary education are higher than those for females.

Between 1997 and 2006, on average among OECD countries, unemployment rates for those with upper secondary and post-secondary non-tertiary education decreased by almost 1.3 percentage points (Table A8.5a). Unemployment rates have improved by 3 percentage points or more in Finland, France, Ireland, Spain and Sweden. Unemployment rates for those with less than upper secondary education have also improved during the period by over 5 percentage points in Finland, Ireland, New Zealand and Spain. However, unemployment rates for those with less than upper secondary education have risen dramatically in the Czech Republic and the Slovak Republic (by more than 10 percentage points) so that the overall improvement in unemployment rates for those with below upper secondary education is modest: they have decreased by 0.5 percentage points across all OECD countries. For those with tertiary education the decrease, in the unemployment rate is 0.6 percentage points.

From 1997 to 2006, the difference in unemployment rates between those with an upper secondary education and those with tertiary education has decreased, from 2.6% to 1.9%. In contrast, the difference between upper secondary and lower secondary unemployment rates increased from 3.4% to 4.2% during this period. The greater difficulty encountered for finding employment with only a lower secondary education suggests that there is relatively little demand for this level of education in most OECD countries.

Although the difference between the unemployment rate for individuals with upper secondary and tertiary education has decreased somewhat in recent years, an upper secondary education makes less difference in the labour market than a tertiary education. The unemployment rate for those with a tertiary education is, except in Denmark, Italy, Mexico, New Zealand, always lower than for those with an upper secondary education (Table A8.5a).

Chart A8.4. **Difference between unemployment rates of females and males, by level of educational attainment (2006)**

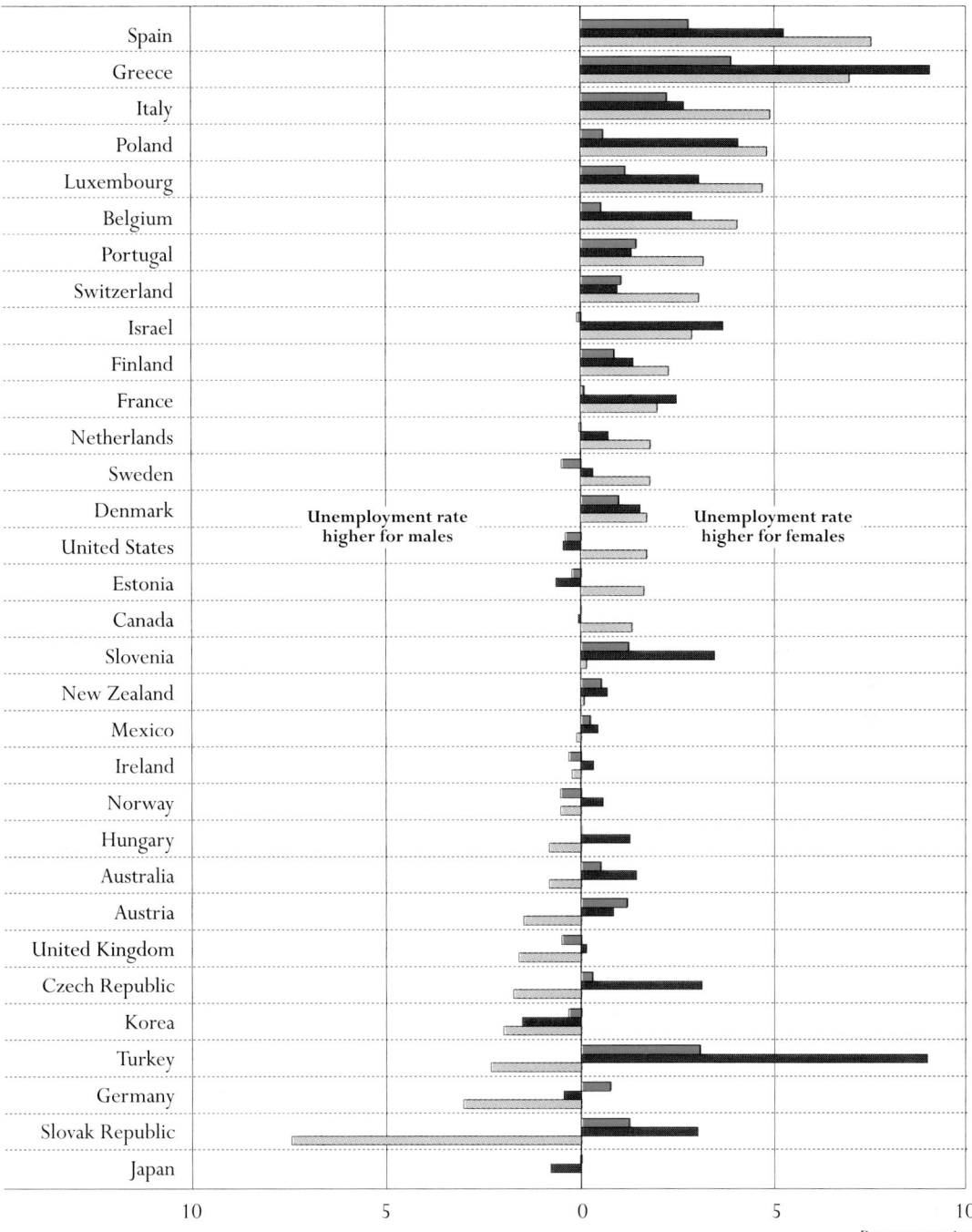

Countries are ranked in descending order of the difference in unemployment rates of females and males who have completed below upper secondary education.

Source: OECD. Tables A8.5b and A8.5c on line. See Annex 3 for notes (*www.oecd.org/edu/eag2008*).

StatLink ᐧᔑᔕᐧ http://dx.doi.org/10.1787/401775543762

A8

Definition and methodologies

Under the auspices of the International Labour Organisation (ILO) and their conferences of labour statisticians, concepts and definitions for measuring labour force participation were established and are now used as a common reference (ILO, 1982). The employment rate refers to the number of persons in employment as a percentage of the population of working age. Unemployment rates refer to unemployed persons as a percentage of the civil labour force.

The unemployed are defined as individuals who are, during the survey reference week, without work, actively seeking employment and currently available to start work. The employed are defined as those who during the survey reference week: *i)* work for pay (employees) or profit (self-employed and unpaid family workers) for at least one hour; or *ii)* have a job but are temporarily not at work (through injury, illness, holiday, strike or lock-out, educational or training leave, maternity or parental leave, etc.).

Further references

The following additional material relevant to this indicator is available on line at:
StatLink ⓂⓈ▰ http://dx.doi.org/10.1787/401775543762

- *Total adult population*
  Table A8.1b. Employment rates and educational attainment (2006)
  Table A8.2b. Unemployment rates and educational attainment (2006)

- *By gender*
  Table A8.3b. Trends in employment rates of males by educational attainment (1997-2006)
  Table A8.3c. Trends in employment rates of females by educational attainment (1997-2006)
  Table A8.5b. Trends in unemployment rates of males by educational attainment (1997-2006)
  Table A8.5c. Trends in unemployment rates of females by educational attainment (1997-2006)

Table A8.1a.
Employment rates and educational attainment, by gender (2006)
Number of 25-to-64-year-olds in employment as a percentage of the population aged 25 to 64, by level of education attained and gender

		Pre-primary and primary education	Lower secondary education	ISCED 3C (short programmes)	Upper secondary education		Post-secondary non-tertiary education	Tertiary education		All levels of education
					ISCED 3C (long programmes)/ 3B	ISCED 3A		Type B	Type A and advanced research programmes	
		(1)	(2)	(3)	(4)	(5)	(6)	(7)	(8)	(9)
Australia	Males	65.1	79.5	a	a	87.7	88.9	89.0	90.7	84.9
	Females	35.5	60.7	a	a	68.4	78.7	75.8	80.9	67.4
Austria	Males	x(2)	65.7	78.3	80.8	78.9	87.6	85.3	91.4	81.0
	Females	x(2)	49.2	61.4	67.2	69.8	78.9	83.6	80.9	66.4
Belgium	Males	47.4	71.0	a	81.6	80.8	87.5	86.8	87.6	76.4
	Females	26.9	45.2	a	60.2	65.5	75.3	79.0	82.5	60.5
Canada	Males	56.0	71.0	a	x(5)	80.8	82.9	86.7	86.7	81.5
	Females	33.0	53.2	a	x(5)	68.7	72.5	78.7	79.6	71.3
Czech Republic	Males	c	54.2	a	82.2	88.2	x(5)	x(8)	91.1	83.4
	Females	c	40.2	a	61.9	69.7	x(5)	x(8)	77.9	64.1
Denmark	Males	54.3	71.4	88.1	86.3	78.6	91.9	89.2	90.3	84.6
	Females	45.8	54.5	70.0	77.3	63.6	c	80.6	86.1	75.3
Finland	Males	52.7	72.5	a	a	78.4	c	83.6	90.4	77.6
	Females	45.8	60.8	a	a	71.9	c	82.5	83.5	73.1
France	Males	52.2	75.4	a	80.6	81.8	x(9)	89.2	85.3	77.7
	Females	40.2	60.0	a	68.6	72.1	x(9)	82.3	77.9	66.2
Germany	Males	54.0	67.4	a	78.0	62.9	84.3	85.9	88.7	78.8
	Females	34.4	48.8	a	66.5	54.4	76.8	78.7	80.4	65.6
Greece	Males	75.6	86.4	86.2	89.7	85.2	86.5	86.9	88.0	83.8
	Females	36.4	44.5	57.5	55.3	51.0	67.9	73.7	80.8	53.4
Hungary	Males	20.0	48.2	a	75.7	79.2	81.5	87.1	86.4	73.0
	Females	6.1	35.2	a	59.2	64.9	67.4	84.4	78.0	58.2
Iceland	Males	92.1	88.9	90.0	94.2	83.3	97.7	95.2	95.7	92.4
	Females	77.2	76.9	85.6	87.8	75.8	84.3	90.3	88.7	82.5
Ireland	Males	62.8	84.8	c	a	88.7	91.2	91.3	92.1	84.5
	Females	30.9	47.5	c	a	64.1	69.3	77.3	84.5	63.0
Italy	Males	51.5	78.6	81.4	84.1	83.8	88.0	85.1	86.2	78.1
	Females	17.1	42.9	53.1	62.0	65.1	71.1	71.8	75.9	51.0
Japan	Males	x(5)	x(5)	x(5)	x(5)	87.3	a	93.0	92.8	89.5
	Females	x(5)	x(5)	x(5)	x(5)	59.8	a	64.6	68.4	62.2
Korea	Males	73.6	81.4	a	x(5)	84.8	a	89.6	89.1	85.3
	Females	57.9	59.0	a	x(5)	55.5	a	61.3	60.5	57.8
Luxembourg	Males	72.7	81.6	81.4	78.9	86.8	81.6	86.2	90.6	82.4
	Females	46.3	44.7	54.5	54.5	68.7	70.3	81.5	79.7	61.4
Mexico	Males	89.5	93.5	a	92.0	x(2)	a	92.1	91.5	91.3
	Females	37.8	49.2	a	59.7	x(2)	a	77.3	72.8	47.4
Netherlands	Males	63.5	81.4	x(4)	81.4	87.5	84.0	85.7	88.9	84.0
	Females	34.9	51.9	x(4)	68.4	76.4	75.5	81.7	83.8	68.2
New Zealand	Males	x(2)	77.4	89.5	90.3	90.5	92.6	91.5	91.9	88.1
	Females	x(2)	57.8	74.4	73.2	75.7	74.9	78.2	79.7	71.8

Source: OECD. See Annex 3 for a description of ISCED-97 levels, ISCED-97 country mappings and national data sources (*www.oecd.org/edu/eag2008*).
Please refer to the Reader's Guide for information concerning the symbols replacing missing data.
StatLink 🔢📊 http://dx.doi.org/10.1787/401775543762

A8

Table A8.1a. *(continued)*
Employment rates and educational attainment, by gender (2006)
Number of 25-to-64-year-olds in employment as a percentage of the population aged 25 to 64, by level of education attained and gender

| | | Pre-primary and primary education | Lower secondary education | ISCED 3C (short programmes) | Upper secondary education | | Post-secondary non-tertiary education | Tertiary education | | All levels of education |
					ISCED 3C (long programmes)/ 3B	ISCED 3A		Type B	Type A and advanced research programmes	
		(1)	(2)	(3)	(4)	(5)	(6)	(7)	(8)	(9)
Norway	Males	c	71.1	a	87.7	84.1	88.1	93.2	90.9	84.6
	Females	c	59.4	a	78.1	76.4	86.6	88.3	87.3	76.6
Poland	Males	x(2)	48.9	68.2	a	75.5	81.4	x(8)	86.8	70.8
	Females	x(2)	29.7	47.4	a	57.0	65.0	x(8)	81.0	55.7
Portugal	Males	78.7	86.3	x(5)	x(5)	82.7	81.7	x(8)	88.5	81.7
	Females	60.0	74.1	x(5)	x(5)	78.1	72.1	x(8)	85.0	68.3
Slovak Republic	Males	c	30.0	x(4)	75.8	86.3	a	86.1	91.0	77.1
	Females	c	21.8	x(4)	56.4	67.5	a	74.8	79.0	57.8
Spain	Males	68.9	85.0	a	89.0	85.3	92.8	88.8	87.8	82.7
	Females	31.7	49.7	a	64.1	65.6	64.6	74.8	80.1	57.0
Sweden	Males	65.5	79.4	a	x(5)	85.4	86.4	85.3	88.8	83.9
	Females	45.7	64.6	a	x(5)	78.1	75.9	84.3	87.9	77.8
Switzerland	Males	73.7	77.3	81.1	88.9	82.7	85.9	94.4	93.3	88.9
	Females	49.4	58.1	67.2	73.5	72.6	79.8	88.2	81.9	72.9
Turkey	Males	73.9	78.4	a	83.4	81.0	a	x(8)	82.4	77.2
	Females	22.2	20.0	a	30.1	26.6	a	x(8)	63.6	26.4
United Kingdom	Males	c	60.2	83.4	83.1	87.0	c	88.2	90.5	82.8
	Females	c	47.8	73.1	73.5	80.0	41.4	84.5	87.1	74.1
United States	Males	72.8	68.9	x(5)	x(5)	79.9	x(5)	84.8	88.1	81.6
	Females	40.0	46.0	x(5)	x(5)	67.0	x(5)	76.1	78.5	68.9
OECD average	***Males***	***64.4***	***73.0***		***84.2***	***82.9***	***87.1***	***88.5***	***89.4***	***82.3***
	Females	***38.9***	***50.1***		***64.9***	***66.6***	***72.4***	***79.0***	***79.8***	***64.1***
EU19 average	***Males***	***58.6***	***69.9***		***84.9***	***82.3***	***86.2***	***86.9***	***88.9***	***80.2***
	Females	***35.9***	***48.1***		***63.9***	***67.6***	***69.4***	***79.7***	***81.7***	***64.1***
Chile[1]	Males	24.4	63.2	x(5)	x(5)	71.8	a	81.1	84.3	74.3
	Females	8.8	26.8	x(5)	x(5)	59.6	a	69.5	80.0	60.8
Estonia	Males	c	64.8	a	69.7	84.1	85.3	88.8	91.6	81.8
	Females	c	49.2	a	61.3	74.1	78.2	81.8	87.9	76.1
Israel	Males	30.8	61.7	a	x(5)	76.0	a	82.7	84.9	75.5
	Females	11.9	28.6	a	x(5)	58.7	a	72.1	82.1	61.9
Slovenia	Males	39.4	68.4	a	77.5	81.3	a	87.3	91.4	78.7
	Females	30.3	51.8	a	65.7	69.2	a	83.4	90.9	68.7

Note: Owing to incomplete data, some averages have not been calculated.
1. Year of reference 2004.
Source: OECD. See Annex 3 for a description of ISCED-97 levels, ISCED-97 country mappings and national data sources (*www.oecd.org/edu/eag2008*).
Please refer to the Reader's Guide for information concerning the symbols replacing missing data.
StatLink ᘖ᠑ http://dx.doi.org/10.1787/401775543762

Table A8.2a.
Unemployment rates and educational attainment, by gender (2006)
Number of 25-to-64-year-olds in unemployment as a percentage of the labour force aged 25 to 64, by level of education attained and gender

| | | Pre-primary and primary education | Lower secondary education | ISCED 3C (short programmes) | Upper secondary education | | Post-secondary non-tertiary education | Tertiary education | | All levels of education |
					ISCED 3C (long programmes)/ 3B	ISCED 3A		Type B	Type A and advanced research programmes	
		(1)	(2)	(3)	(4)	(5)	(6)	(7)	(8)	(9)
Australia	Males	7.8	5.4	a	a	3.3	c	2.0	2.0	3.6
	Females	6.7	4.9	a	a	4.8	4.2	2.8	2.4	4.0
Austria	Males	x(2)	9.1	c	3.4	4.0	2.1	1.9	2.1	3.6
	Females	x(2)	7.8	c	4.4	4.8	2.8	c	4.1	4.6
Belgium	Males	14.9	8.6	a	6.9	5.1	c	3.4	3.5	6.3
	Females	18.8	12.5	a	11.3	7.5	c	3.8	4.5	7.9
Canada	Males	10.2	8.4	a	x(5)	5.7	5.6	4.6	3.7	5.4
	Females	13.2	9.1	a	x(5)	5.6	5.7	4.2	3.9	5.2
Czech Republic	Males	c	23.3	a	5.1	2.6	x(8)	x(8)	2.1	4.8
	Females	c	21.6	a	10.0	5.2	x(8)	x(8)	2.4	8.0
Denmark	Males	c	4.2	c	1.9	c	c	2.7	2.7	2.6
	Females	c	6.7	c	3.5	c	c	4.5	3.5	4.1
Finland	Males	8.9	9.4	a	a	6.4	c	3.7	2.8	5.9
	Females	11.7	11.3	a	a	7.8	c	4.2	3.9	6.6
France	Males	11.3	9.4	a	5.1	6.8	x(9)	4.4	5.5	6.6
	Females	12.2	11.9	a	8.0	7.7	x(9)	4.4	5.7	8.2
Germany	Males	28.5	19.7	a	10.6	9.8	6.6	4.6	4.4	9.9
	Females	25.9	17.2	a	10.4	8.8	5.4	5.6	5.1	10.0
Greece	Males	4.5	5.5	c	c	3.7	7.5	4.7	4.2	4.7
	Females	10.0	15.1	c	25.4	12.6	14.5	10.7	7.2	11.5
Hungary	Males	34.7	14.3	a	6.5	4.1	c	c	2.2	6.2
	Females	51.2	13.5	a	9.1	5.5	5.6	c	2.2	6.9
Iceland	Males	c	c	c	c	c	c	c	c	1.5
	Females	c	c	c	c	c	c	c	c	2.0
Ireland	Males	7.8	4.4	c	a	3.3	2.6	2.8	2.2	3.8
	Females	6.4	5.0	c	a	3.2	3.9	2.7	1.7	3.3
Italy	Males	7.1	4.9	6.4	2.6	3.5	5.8	2.8	3.8	4.3
	Females	11.4	9.8	13.1	5.9	5.9	10.2	6.2	5.9	7.4
Japan	Males	x(5)	x(5)	x(5)	x(5)	4.9	a	3.9	2.7	4.1
	Females	x(5)	x(5)	x(5)	x(5)	4.1	a	3.2	2.5	3.7
Korea	Males	3.6	3.7	a	x(5)	4.0	a	3.8	2.7	3.6
	Females	1.5	1.9	a	x(5)	2.5	a	3.3	2.3	2.3
Luxembourg	Males	c	c	c	3.3	c	c	c	2.4	2.5
	Females	9.4	9.8	c	6.8	5.0	c	c	4.2	5.6
Mexico	Males	2.1	2.6	a	2.3	a	a	1.1	2.9	2.4
	Females	2.0	2.9	a	2.4	a	a	2.0	3.2	2.5
Netherlands	Males	6.8	3.2	x(4)	3.5	3.0	2.6	2.2	2.3	3.1
	Females	9.0	5.0	x(4)	4.4	3.5	3.9	2.8	2.3	3.8
New Zealand	Males	x(2)	3.5	2.0	2.4	1.8	1.7	2.2	2.1	2.3
	Females	x(2)	3.7	2.0	3.5	1.8	c	2.6	2.7	2.8

Source: OECD. See Annex 3 for a description of ISCED-97 levels, ISCED-97 country mappings and national data sources (*www.oecd.org/edu/eag2008*).
Please refer to the Reader's Guide for information concerning the symbols replacing missing data.
StatLink ⟪ᴗᵴᴸ⟫ http://dx.doi.org/10.1787/401775543762

OECD countries

Table A8.2a. *(continued)*

Unemployment rates and educational attainment, by gender (2006)

Number of 25-to-64-year-olds in unemployment as a percentage of the labour force aged 25 to 64, by level of education attained and gender

		Pre-primary and primary education	Lower secondary education	ISCED 3C (short programmes)	Upper secondary education: ISCED 3C (long programmes)/3B	Upper secondary education: ISCED 3A	Post-secondary non-tertiary education	Tertiary education: Type B	Tertiary education: Type A and advanced research programmes	All levels of education
		(1)	(2)	(3)	(4)	(5)	(6)	(7)	(8)	(9)
Norway	Males	c	5.0	a	1.5	c	c	c	2.1	2.7
	Females	c	4.5	a	2.3	c	c	c	1.5	2.5
Poland	Males	x(2)	20.3	13.5	a	8.5	8.7	x(8)	4.7	11.1
	Females	x(2)	23.2	18.3	a	13.1	9.7	x(8)	5.3	12.9
Portugal	Males	6.5	5.3	x(5)	x(5)	6.3	c	x(8)	4.5	6.0
	Females	9.4	9.2	x(5)	x(5)	7.8	c	x(8)	6.0	8.5
Slovak Republic	Males	94.4	45.2	x(4)	11.3	5.5	a	c	2.0	9.9
	Females	91.0	38.7	x(4)	17.0	8.4	a	c	3.3	13.0
Spain	Males	7.3	5.7	c	4.5	4.7	c	4.1	4.1	5.3
	Females	13.7	13.9	c	10.7	9.4	c	8.1	6.5	10.2
Sweden	Males	7.3	6.4	a	x(5)	5.0	4.5	5.2	4.3	5.1
	Females	10.2	7.6	a	x(5)	5.1	6.4	4.1	3.9	5.1
Switzerland	Males	c	6.4	c	2.4	5.8	c	c	2.2	2.7
	Females	13.1	8.2	c	3.7	4.8	c	c	3.6	4.3
Turkey	Males	8.9	8.4	a	6.8	8.0	x(8)	x(8)	5.9	8.2
	Females	5.8	13.3	a	14.7	17.8	x(8)	x(8)	9.0	8.7
United Kingdom	Males	c	8.8	4.8	4.3	3.3	c	3.0	2.3	4.1
	Females	c	6.3	4.1	4.9	2.8	c	1.5	2.1	3.6
United States	Males	5.8	8.8	x(5)	x(5)	4.8	x(5)	4.0	2.6	4.3
	Females	7.9	10.0	x(5)	x(5)	4.3	x(5)	3.2	2.2	3.8
OECD average	***Males***	***14.7***	***9.6***			***5.0***			***3.1***	***4.9***
	Females	***16.2***	***10.9***			***6.5***			***3.9***	***6.1***
EU19 average	***Males***	***18.5***	***11.5***			***5.0***			***3.3***	***5.6***
	Females	***20.8***	***12.9***			***6.9***			***4.2***	***7.4***
Partner countries: **Chile**[1]	Males	5.8	6.9	x(5)	x(5)	6.8	a	12.6	6.0	6.6
	Females	6.1	8.9	x(5)	x(5)	9.2	a	10.7	7.1	8.4
Estonia	Males	c	11.3	a	7.4	5.8	c	5.6	2.4	5.8
	Females	c	13.1	a	c	6.1	c	4.5	2.3	4.8
Israel	Males	21.3	11.1	a	a	7.1	a	5.6	4.1	6.8
	Females	21.1	13.9	a	a	10.8	a	6.0	3.7	7.3
Slovenia	Males	12.7	6.3	a	4.3	4.0	a	2.6	2.0	4.2
	Females	12.7	6.7	a	8.0	7.4	a	4.2	2.9	6.3

Note: Owing to incomplete data, some averages have not been calculated.

1. Year of reference 2004.

Source: OECD. See Annex 3 for a description of ISCED-97 levels, ISCED-97 country mappings and national data sources (*www.oecd.org/edu/eag2008*).

Please refer to the Reader's Guide for information concerning the symbols replacing missing data.

StatLink http://dx.doi.org/10.1787/401775543762

A8

Table A8.3a.
Trends in employment rates by educational attainment (1997-2006)
Number of 25-to-64-year-olds in employment as a percentage of the population aged 25 to 64, by level of educational attainment

		1997	1998	1999	2000	2001	2002	2003	2004	2005	2006
Australia	Below upper secondary	59.5	59.5	59.1	60.8	59.9	60.0	61.0	60.6	62.9	63.5
	Upper secondary and post-secondary non-tertiary	76.1	75.9	76.2	76.7	78.0	77.8	78.7	78.8	79.8	80.4
	Tertiary education	83.4	83.8	82.0	82.9	83.1	83.5	83.2	83.3	84.4	84.4
Austria	Below upper secondary	52.9	52.6	53.3	53.8	53.6	54.7	55.0	52.2	53.3	55.7
	Upper secondary and post-secondary non-tertiary	75.4	75.3	75.6	74.6	74.6	75.3	75.4	73.9	74.3	75.8
	Tertiary education	85.8	86.4	87.0	86.7	86.5	86.0	85.0	82.5	84.5	85.9
Belgium	Below upper secondary	47.5	47.5	49.1	50.5	49.0	48.8	48.9	48.8	49.0	49.0
	Upper secondary and post-secondary non-tertiary	73.4	72.0	74.5	75.1	73.9	73.8	72.8	73.1	74.0	73.2
	Tertiary education	83.9	84.3	85.4	85.3	84.5	83.7	83.6	83.9	84.2	83.6
Canada	Below upper secondary	52.5	53.5	54.4	55.0	54.4	55.3	56.4	57.1	56.4	56.9
	Upper secondary and post-secondary non-tertiary	73.9	74.5	75.4	76.1	75.4	75.9	76.3	76.7	76.3	76.0
	Tertiary education	81.7	82.3	82.4	82.7	81.9	82.0	82.0	82.2	82.2	82.6
Czech Republic	Below upper secondary	51.1	49.5	46.9	46.9	46.7	45.3	46.0	42.3	41.2	43.9
	Upper secondary and post-secondary non-tertiary	79.7	78.2	76.4	75.5	75.7	76.2	75.8	74.8	75.5	75.6
	Tertiary education	89.3	88.7	87.4	86.8	87.8	87.1	86.5	86.4	85.8	85.1
Denmark	Below upper secondary	m	60.9	61.7	62.2	61.5	61.2	62.6	61.7	61.5	62.8
	Upper secondary and post-secondary non-tertiary	m	79.1	80.7	81.0	81.0	80.3	79.8	79.9	79.9	81.3
	Tertiary education	m	87.5	87.9	88.6	87.2	86.0	85.2	85.5	86.4	87.4
Finland	Below upper secondary	54.7	56.2	58.6	57.3	58.2	57.7	58.0	57.1	57.9	58.4
	Upper secondary and post-secondary non-tertiary	72.2	73.1	74.3	74.9	75.5	74.4	73.6	74.4	75.2	75.6
	Tertiary education	82.6	83.2	84.7	84.4	85.1	85.1	85.1	84.2	84.1	85.0
France	Below upper secondary	56.3	56.3	56.4	57.0	57.7	57.8	58.9	59.1	58.6	58.1
	Upper secondary and post-secondary non-tertiary	75.0	75.0	75.1	75.8	76.5	76.7	76.3	75.6	75.6	75.6
	Tertiary education	81.3	81.6	81.8	83.1	83.7	83.3	83.3	82.9	83.0	83.0
Germany	Below upper secondary	45.7	46.1	48.7	50.6	51.8	50.9	50.2	48.6	51.6	53.8
	Upper secondary and post-secondary non-tertiary	68.2	67.9	69.9	70.4	70.5	70.3	69.7	69.5	70.6	72.5
	Tertiary education	82.3	82.2	83.0	83.4	83.4	83.6	83.0	82.7	82.9	84.3
Greece	Below upper secondary	57.4	57.3	57.1	57.9	57.6	58.5	59.7	58.2	59.2	59.5
	Upper secondary and post-secondary non-tertiary	63.3	64.6	64.7	64.7	65.2	65.7	66.8	68.0	69.1	69.7
	Tertiary education	80.2	80.8	81.1	81.4	80.4	81.3	81.9	82.0	82.0	83.3
Hungary	Below upper secondary	36.2	36.2	35.8	35.8	36.6	36.7	37.4	36.9	38.1	38.2
	Upper secondary and post-secondary non-tertiary	70.7	70.9	72.1	72.1	71.9	71.7	71.4	70.9	70.4	70.4
	Tertiary education	81.4	81.0	82.1	82.4	82.6	82.0	82.7	82.9	83.0	81.8
Iceland	Below upper secondary	83.8	85.6	87.2	87.3	87.2	86.4	83.7	81.6	83.0	83.6
	Upper secondary and post-secondary non-tertiary	88.0	88.6	90.5	89.0	89.7	89.4	88.7	87.8	88.2	88.6
	Tertiary education	94.6	94.7	95.1	95.0	94.7	95.4	92.7	92.0	92.0	92.0
Ireland	Below upper secondary	50.3	53.4	54.4	60.7	58.4	56.7	56.6	57.5	58.4	58.7
	Upper secondary and post-secondary non-tertiary	68.7	71.7	74.8	77.0	77.3	76.6	75.6	75.9	76.7	77.3
	Tertiary education	81.9	85.2	87.2	87.2	87.0	86.3	86.1	86.2	86.8	86.5
Italy	Below upper secondary	m	47.8	48.0	48.6	49.4	50.5	50.7	51.7	51.7	52.5
	Upper secondary and post-secondary non-tertiary	m	70.1	70.3	71.2	72.1	72.3	72.4	73.5	73.5	74.4
	Tertiary education	m	80.8	80.7	81.4	81.6	82.2	82.0	81.2	80.4	80.6
Japan	Below upper secondary	69.6	68.8	68.2	67.1	67.5	m	m	m	m	m
	Upper secondary and post-secondary non-tertiary	75.3	75.8	74.2	73.8	74.4	71.9	71.8	72.0	72.3	73.1
	Tertiary education	80.7	79.5	79.2	79.0	79.8	79.1	79.2	79.3	79.4	79.8
Korea	Below upper secondary	71.2	66.1	66.9	68.0	67.8	68.4	66.5	66.4	65.9	66.2
	Upper secondary and post-secondary non-tertiary	71.7	66.5	66.4	68.7	69.3	70.5	69.6	70.1	70.1	70.3
	Tertiary education	80.2	76.1	74.6	75.4	75.7	76.1	76.4	76.7	76.8	77.2
Luxembourg	Below upper secondary	m	m	56.5	58.3	60.0	59.3	60.3	59.1	61.8	60.8
	Upper secondary and post-secondary non-tertiary	m	m	73.9	74.6	74.8	73.6	73.3	72.6	71.7	73.4
	Tertiary education	m	m	85.0	84.3	85.5	85.2	82.3	84.1	84.0	85.2
Mexico	Below upper secondary	61.8	61.3	61.4	60.7	60.5	61.3	60.9	62.2	61.8	62.8
	Upper secondary and post-secondary non-tertiary	70.1	69.1	69.1	70.7	69.8	69.7	69.5	70.3	71.2	73.1
	Tertiary education	83.2	83.2	82.0	82.5	80.9	80.9	81.2	81.4	82.0	83.3

OECD countries

Source: OECD. See Annex 3 for notes (*www.oecd.org/edu/eag2008*).
Please refer to the Reader's Guide for information concerning the symbols replacing missing data.
StatLink ⣿⡿⣴⣪ http://dx.doi.org/10.1787/401775543762

Table A8.3a. *(continued)*

Trends in employment rates by educational attainment (1997-2006)

Number of 25-to-64-year-olds in employment as a percentage of the population aged 25 to 64, by level of educational attainment

			1997	1998	1999	2000	2001	2002	2003	2004	2005	2006
OECD countries	**Netherlands**	Below upper secondary	m	55.3	60.7	57.6	58.8	60.7	59.4	59.4	59.5	60.6
		Upper secondary and post-secondary non-tertiary	m	76.8	79.5	79.4	80.0	79.8	78.8	77.9	77.9	79.1
		Tertiary education	m	85.4	87.2	86.3	86.3	86.5	85.9	85.3	85.6	86.4
	New Zealand	Below upper secondary	63.6	63.0	64.1	65.2	66.4	67.4	67.8	69.3	70.4	70.6
		Upper secondary and post-secondary non-tertiary	80.5	79.4	80.0	80.2	80.4	81.4	81.6	82.9	84.5	84.5
		Tertiary education	82.4	81.6	82.0	82.3	83.8	83.0	82.7	83.4	84.3	84.6
	Norway	Below upper secondary	66.7	67.7	67.1	65.3	63.3	64.2	64.1	62.1	64.3	64.7
		Upper secondary and post-secondary non-tertiary	83.3	83.9	82.9	82.7	82.7	81.5	79.6	78.8	82.4	83.1
		Tertiary education	90.2	90.2	90.2	89.9	89.6	89.5	88.8	89.3	88.8	89.2
	Poland	Below upper secondary	62.4	62.5	59.2	56.1	54.3	51.6	51.5	51.6	52.4	53.6
		Upper secondary and post-secondary non-tertiary	68.8	69.1	72.3	69.2	68.2	66.6	65.1	64.3	64.6	65.6
		Tertiary education	86.7	87.2	86.6	84.5	84.1	83.1	82.6	82.3	82.7	83.5
	Portugal	Below upper secondary	m	71.6	71.9	72.8	73.0	72.8	72.2	71.9	71.5	71.7
		Upper secondary and post-secondary non-tertiary	m	80.0	81.9	83.2	82.6	82.3	81.6	80.3	79.3	80.2
		Tertiary education	m	89.3	90.0	90.7	90.8	88.5	87.3	88.0	87.3	86.4
	Slovak Republic	Below upper secondary	38.9	37.4	33.2	30.9	30.5	28.2	28.5	22.0	21.7	23.5
		Upper secondary and post-secondary non-tertiary	75.9	75.1	72.5	70.6	70.2	70.5	71.2	70.3	70.8	71.9
		Tertiary education	89.8	88.6	87.0	85.6	86.7	86.6	87.1	83.6	84.0	84.9
	Spain	Below upper secondary	48.2	49.5	51.0	53.8	55.1	55.7	56.6	57.6	58.6	59.8
		Upper secondary and post-secondary non-tertiary	66.6	67.5	69.6	72.1	71.8	71.6	72.4	73.2	74.7	75.9
		Tertiary education	75.5	76.3	77.6	79.7	80.7	80.8	81.6	81.9	82.4	83.4
	Sweden	Below upper secondary	67.2	66.4	66.5	68.0	68.8	68.2	67.5	67.0	66.1	66.9
		Upper secondary and post-secondary non-tertiary	78.6	79.3	79.6	81.7	81.9	81.8	81.3	80.7	81.3	81.9
		Tertiary education	85.0	85.5	85.6	86.7	86.9	86.5	85.8	85.4	87.3	87.3
	Switzerland	Below upper secondary	68.5	69.2	69.4	65.5	70.4	69.5	67.6	66.4	66.0	65.3
		Upper secondary and post-secondary non-tertiary	80.1	81.3	81.1	81.9	81.6	81.3	80.8	80.3	80.3	80.1
		Tertiary education	89.1	90.3	90.9	90.9	91.3	90.6	89.7	89.7	90.0	90.2
	Turkey	Below upper secondary	56.9	57.4	55.8	53.1	51.9	50.5	49.1	50.1	49.1	49.0
		Upper secondary and post-secondary non-tertiary	66.8	66.0	63.9	64.0	62.4	61.8	61.1	61.5	63.2	62.7
		Tertiary education	81.7	81.3	79.0	78.5	78.3	76.3	74.9	75.2	76.1	75.5
	United Kingdom	Below upper secondary	64.8	64.8	64.8	65.5	66.0	65.3	66.1	65.9	65.3	66.3
		Upper secondary and post-secondary non-tertiary	79.1	80.2	80.6	81.1	81.3	81.1	81.6	81.2	81.7	80.7
		Tertiary education	87.3	87.3	87.7	87.8	88.3	87.8	88.0	87.6	87.9	88.1
	United States	Below upper secondary	55.2	57.6	57.8	57.8	58.4	57.0	57.8	56.5	57.2	58.0
		Upper secondary and post-secondary non-tertiary	75.7	75.8	76.2	76.7	76.2	74.0	73.3	72.8	72.8	73.3
		Tertiary education	85.4	85.3	84.6	85.0	84.4	83.2	82.2	82.0	82.5	82.7
	OECD average	***Below upper secondary***	*57.7*	*58.0*	*58.2*	*58.3*	*58.5*	*57.9*	*58.0*	*57.3*	*57.7*	*58.4*
		Upper secondary and post-secondary non-tertiary	*74.3*	*74.6*	*75.1*	*75.5*	*75.5*	*75.2*	*74.9*	*74.7*	*75.3*	*75.9*
		Tertiary education	*84.2*	*84.5*	*84.6*	*84.7*	*84.7*	*84.4*	*83.9*	*83.8*	*84.1*	*84.4*
	EU19 average	***Below upper secondary***	*52.4*	*54.0*	*54.4*	*55.0*	*55.1*	*54.8*	*55.1*	*54.1*	*54.6*	*55.5*
		Upper secondary and post-secondary non-tertiary	*72.5*	*73.7*	*74.6*	*75.0*	*75.0*	*74.8*	*74.5*	*74.2*	*74.6*	*75.3*
		Tertiary education	*83.8*	*84.5*	*85.0*	*85.1*	*85.2*	*84.8*	*84.5*	*84.1*	*84.4*	*84.8*
Partner countries	**Estonia**	Below upper secondary	m	m	m	m	m	44.1	49.0	50.9	50.0	56.5
		Upper secondary and post-secondary non-tertiary	m	m	m	m	m	71.9	72.9	72.6	73.6	78.1
		Tertiary education	m	m	m	m	m	81.6	80.3	82.4	84.5	87.7
	Israel	Below upper secondary	m	m	m	m	m	43.5	42.7	40.4	41.2	41.8
		Upper secondary and post-secondary non-tertiary	m	m	m	m	m	66.6	65.9	66.4	66.6	67.5
		Tertiary education	m	m	m	m	m	79.1	79.3	79.2	80.3	81.2
	Slovenia	Below upper secondary	m	m	m	m	m	55.6	54.2	55.9	56.1	55.9
		Upper secondary and post-secondary non-tertiary	m	m	m	m	m	74.0	72.7	74.4	74.6	74.1
		Tertiary education	m	m	m	m	m	86.1	86.1	86.8	87.0	88.2

Source: OECD. See Annex 3 for notes (*www.oecd.org/edu/eag2008*).

Please refer to the Reader's Guide for information concerning the symbols replacing missing data.

StatLink http://dx.doi.org/10.1787/401775543762

Table A8.4.
Trends in employment rates among 55-to-64-year-olds, by educational attainment (1997-2006)
Number of 55-to-64-year-olds in employment as a percentage of the population aged 55 to 64,
by level of educational attainment

		1997	1998	1999	2000	2001	2002	2003	2004	2005	2006	Growth rate 1999/2005
Australia	Below upper secondary	35.6	36.1	35.3	38.6	37.9	39.5	43.3	42.7	45.9	48.0	4.5
	Upper secondary and post-secondary non-tertiary	47.9	51.3	50.5	53.3	55.8	60.3	61.3	62.9	62.3	64.7	3.6
	Tertiary education	63.2	64.1	61.6	64.8	65.6	67.4	67.5	69.0	69.5	69.8	2.0
Austria	Below upper secondary	20.9	20.4	20.6	19.5	18.8	20.2	22.0	19.7	23.5	27.0	2.3
	Upper secondary and post-secondary non-tertiary	31.3	32.0	32.0	28.4	28.6	29.7	30.7	28.8	30.7	34.6	-0.6
	Tertiary education	60.5	59.2	64.3	59.0	56.8	54.3	49.8	47.5	53.7	57.6	-3.0
Belgium	Below upper secondary	15.8	16.4	16.8	19.3	16.8	18.8	20.4	21.4	21.5	22.8	4.1
	Upper secondary and post-secondary non-tertiary	30.4	29.6	32.8	31.1	31.9	32.9	32.8	34.9	38.1	35.8	2.5
	Tertiary education	41.2	41.5	46.4	46.1	45.6	44.1	45.6	47.3	49.3	47.8	1.0
Canada	Below upper secondary	34.6	35.3	36.7	36.7	36.5	37.8	39.9	41.6	40.6	42.8	1.7
	Upper secondary and post-secondary non-tertiary	48.3	49.4	50.2	52.2	51.8	53.5	55.5	56.4	57.1	56.6	2.2
	Tertiary education	56.0	55.1	56.0	57.4	56.8	57.9	61.2	60.9	62.2	62.8	1.8
Czech Republic	Below upper secondary	19.2	17.8	17.4	17.4	16.9	16.6	20.1	18.3	19.6	23.4	2.0
	Upper secondary and post-secondary non-tertiary	42.5	40.5	40.4	39.1	39.6	43.4	45.6	44.7	46.4	46.4	2.4
	Tertiary education	71.2	70.9	70.9	65.6	70.7	70.3	69.2	70.2	69.2	68.7	-0.4
Denmark	Below upper secondary	m	35.4	36.0	41.5	41.3	39.9	44.0	42.1	41.8	41.0	2.5
	Upper secondary and post-secondary non-tertiary	m	53.5	58.6	58.3	60.4	60.2	61.8	61.9	61.0	62.7	0.7
	Tertiary education	m	68.3	71.5	74.5	73.8	72.3	73.3	74.0	72.9	73.9	0.3
Finland	Below upper secondary	29.0	29.6	33.0	32.5	36.6	38.6	41.6	41.4	43.4	45.0	4.7
	Upper secondary and post-secondary non-tertiary	37.9	36.4	39.8	43.4	48.2	45.3	46.9	51.5	53.4	54.9	5.0
	Tertiary education	55.4	56.6	58.5	60.1	62.3	62.9	64.9	65.5	65.6	67.0	1.9
France	Below upper secondary	27.8	26.9	28.3	28.3	30.1	32.4	31.4	31.6	32.2	31.5	2.2
	Upper secondary and post-secondary non-tertiary	37.5	36.6	36.8	36.0	38.3	41.0	38.3	38.5	39.8	39.6	1.3
	Tertiary education	56.5	55.8	55.7	55.3	56.8	59.4	55.1	56.1	55.9	55.0	0.1
Germany	Below upper secondary	25.5	25.1	25.7	25.7	26.6	26.8	27.1	27.4	32.4	35.0	3.9
	Upper secondary and post-secondary non-tertiary	38.1	36.4	37.1	36.7	36.4	37.6	37.7	39.9	43.4	46.2	2.7
	Tertiary education	58.3	58.3	58.4	58.4	58.1	58.9	58.5	59.4	62.7	65.1	1.2
Greece	Below upper secondary	41.7	40.3	39.0	39.8	39.1	39.5	41.2	37.5	39.4	39.8	0.2
	Upper secondary and post-secondary non-tertiary	31.1	28.4	30.8	31.8	29.8	29.8	32.7	35.0	38.2	39.4	3.7
	Tertiary education	49.0	45.6	50.4	51.2	46.8	51.4	53.3	57.3	59.9	60.9	2.9
Hungary	Below upper secondary	12.2	10.7	11.3	12.5	12.7	12.0	13.3	14.0	15.8	16.2	5.7
	Upper secondary and post-secondary non-tertiary	22.9	22.7	26.2	29.3	31.6	35.6	37.7	38.4	39.0	38.7	6.8
	Tertiary education	46.9	43.9	49.5	52.2	53.4	53.5	57.5	60.0	59.9	55.6	3.3
Iceland	Below upper secondary	80.4	83.0	81.4	80.6	83.0	85.8	79.8	77.3	82.1	81.2	0.1
	Upper secondary and post-secondary non-tertiary	86.8	90.8	91.3	89.4	88.1	86.5	86.5	86.0	86.4	90.9	-0.9
	Tertiary education	92.7	94.3	96.6	90.8	89.7	91.7	92.6	90.1	89.1	84.6	-1.3
Ireland	Below upper secondary	35.9	37.3	37.7	40.8	40.7	41.2	42.1	42.7	44.5	45.7	2.8
	Upper secondary and post-secondary non-tertiary	41.3	42.9	47.2	48.7	53.0	53.7	54.1	54.6	56.2	59.1	2.9
	Tertiary education	65.2	65.2	69.4	66.6	66.5	67.6	69.5	68.5	70.3	70.0	0.2
Italy	Below upper secondary	m	23.1	22.6	22.5	21.7	22.8	23.2	23.6	23.6	24.1	0.7
	Upper secondary and post-secondary non-tertiary	m	41.1	40.3	40.6	40.4	41.6	42.4	42.5	43.6	44.5	1.3
	Tertiary education	m	62.3	60.7	58.3	59.4	62.2	63.9	64.6	66.7	66.0	1.6
Japan	Below upper secondary	59.1	59.5	59.7	59.2	59.7	m	m	m	m	m	a
	Upper secondary and post-secondary non-tertiary	62.3	62.7	62.3	61.4	62.2	60.1	60.5	61.7	61.7	63.0	a
	Tertiary education	73.6	72.5	72.7	71.8	69.3	70.4	70.1	70.2	72.2	71.2	-0.1
Korea	Below upper secondary	62.3	58.1	58.8	59.2	59.1	59.4	57.5	58.1	58.2	58.8	-0.2
	Upper secondary and post-secondary non-tertiary	66.6	55.5	53.6	53.4	53.6	57.1	57.0	57.9	59.2	59.7	1.7
	Tertiary education	73.4	71.5	63.8	56.5	63.5	66.1	61.1	62.1	60.9	61.1	-0.8
Luxembourg	Below upper secondary	m	m	16.7	16.3	13.8	17.4	20.2	20.4	21.5	22.8	4.4
	Upper secondary and post-secondary non-tertiary	m	m	31.5	33.0	29.0	29.2	36.1	30.3	29.8	31.5	-0.9
	Tertiary education	m	m	67.2	65.3	65.7	62.0	59.3	61.9	60.1	62.4	-1.8
Mexico	Below upper secondary	53.9	52.1	53.0	50.6	50.0	51.3	51.9	52.9	51.7	53.8	-0.4
	Upper secondary and post-secondary non-tertiary	53.3	46.1	53.8	47.7	50.6	50.0	47.9	50.0	45.7	51.5	-2.7
	Tertiary education	65.1	70.3	72.6	68.7	64.1	65.1	68.6	65.5	68.2	70.4	-1.0

Source: OECD. See Annex 3 for notes (*www.oecd.org/edu/eag2008*).
Please refer to the Reader's Guide for information concerning the symbols replacing missing data.
StatLink ᴬᴵˢᴸ http://dx.doi.org/10.1787/401775543762

A8

Table A8.4. *(continued)*
Trends in employment rates among 55-to-64-year-olds, by educational attainment (1997-2006)
Number of 55-to-64-year-olds in employment as a percentage of the population aged 55 to 64,
by level of educational attainment

		1997	1998	1999	2000	2001	2002	2003	2004	2005	2006	Growth rate 1999/2005
Netherlands	Below upper secondary	m	22.8	27.7	27.7	28.8	32.0	32.7	34.0	34.6	36.4	3.8
	Upper secondary and post-secondary non-tertiary	m	37.3	39.6	43.5	44.7	46.1	47.4	48.0	48.7	51.0	3.5
	Tertiary education	m	52.0	57.0	56.2	55.5	59.5	61.7	60.7	61.9	61.0	1.4
New Zealand	Below upper secondary	44.3	45.7	47.7	48.9	52.2	53.3	55.7	58.1	61.2	61.4	4.2
	Upper secondary and post-secondary non-tertiary	64.2	64.5	64.8	65.0	69.4	72.9	72.2	74.2	75.2	78.4	2.5
	Tertiary education	69.1	68.9	68.2	66.9	70.8	72.3	72.2	76.6	78.4	79.3	2.3
Norway	Below upper secondary	51.6	52.3	51.4	53.1	51.6	53.1	54.4	50.2	48.8	47.1	-0.9
	Upper secondary and post-secondary non-tertiary	69.7	69.6	69.7	68.1	69.1	69.0	69.1	67.4	70.2	69.8	0.1
	Tertiary education	85.9	85.6	86.4	86.2	85.4	86.0	84.8	85.1	84.7	83.8	-0.3
Poland	Below upper secondary	32.2	29.6	28.1	24.9	24.2	22.3	24.0	23.1	23.2	22.4	-3.1
	Upper secondary and post-secondary non-tertiary	29.5	29.2	32.7	28.3	31.1	31.0	29.0	27.1	29.2	27.9	-1.9
	Tertiary education	56.5	59.1	59.2	51.4	53.6	53.6	52.6	53.4	55.4	53.5	-1.1
Portugal	Below upper secondary	m	49.2	49.6	49.8	49.4	50.5	50.6	49.9	49.7	49.3	0.0
	Upper secondary and post-secondary non-tertiary	m	45.6	55.5	50.2	43.5	48.3	48.7	41.4	47.5	49.8	-2.6
	Tertiary education	m	61.9	62.7	69.4	68.5	62.2	61.6	62.2	61.2	59.5	-0.4
Slovak Republic	Below upper secondary	10.6	10.7	8.8	6.7	6.7	6.9	8.8	4.7	5.9	7.8	-6.5
	Upper secondary and post-secondary non-tertiary	27.7	28.8	27.9	27.0	26.8	27.2	27.9	30.9	33.6	34.3	3.2
	Tertiary education	60.1	61.9	59.1	54.0	56.2	51.7	55.0	51.6	54.2	59.7	-1.4
Spain	Below upper secondary	30.7	31.3	31.4	33.1	35.0	35.3	36.4	36.4	37.8	38.1	3.1
	Upper secondary and post-secondary non-tertiary	44.0	49.1	49.2	50.7	48.9	48.6	48.3	47.5	50.7	52.7	0.5
	Tertiary education	62.1	65.1	61.9	63.8	66.9	68.4	67.5	67.8	64.7	66.1	0.7
Sweden	Below upper secondary	55.7	54.9	55.1	56.5	58.5	59.1	59.5	60.5	58.6	60.3	1.0
	Upper secondary and post-secondary non-tertiary	64.7	65.4	66.0	65.9	67.3	68.6	68.7	69.0	69.5	69.6	0.9
	Tertiary education	76.6	76.3	76.4	79.3	80.0	80.9	81.8	81.3	83.1	81.1	1.4
Switzerland	Below upper secondary	53.7	51.8	53.0	47.5	54.3	53.5	52.8	51.0	51.2	49.6	-0.6
	Upper secondary and post-secondary non-tertiary	65.2	65.7	65.2	66.9	68.4	63.8	66.2	65.9	65.4	65.6	0.0
	Tertiary education	77.1	80.7	82.2	77.9	80.7	79.6	79.5	79.4	79.3	79.5	-0.6
Turkey	Below upper secondary	43.1	44.0	41.4	37.7	38.5	37.3	34.5	35.5	33.3	33.4	-3.6
	Upper secondary and post-secondary non-tertiary	24.3	28.3	25.1	19.6	20.0	23.7	20.1	25.5	25.7	21.0	0.4
	Tertiary education	44.6	41.3	42.1	37.4	36.7	38.3	33.9	34.3	35.5	35.5	-2.9
United Kingdom	Below upper secondary	49.0	49.6	49.9	50.6	51.9	53.0	56.6	56.1	55.2	59.9	1.7
	Upper secondary and post-secondary non-tertiary	60.1	61.7	62.9	63.9	64.3	65.3	67.4	68.3	69.6	71.8	1.7
	Tertiary education	65.6	63.8	66.1	65.9	70.3	68.8	71.0	70.9	72.3	74.7	1.5
United States	Below upper secondary	40.5	42.2	40.3	40.4	40.9	40.5	41.8	39.9	39.4	41.5	-0.4
	Upper secondary and post-secondary non-tertiary	58.1	58.1	57.9	57.7	57.9	57.8	58.1	58.0	58.0	59.4	0.0
	Tertiary education	69.8	69.3	70.2	69.7	70.4	70.2	70.3	71.4	72.2	71.9	0.5
OECD average	*Below upper secondary*	*38.6*	*37.6*	*37.1*	*37.3*	*37.8*	*37.8*	*38.9*	*38.3*	*39.2*	*40.2*	*0.9*
	Upper secondary and post-secondary non-tertiary	*47.4*	*46.9*	*47.7*	*47.3*	*48.0*	*49.0*	*49.6*	*50.0*	*51.2*	*52.4*	*1.2*
	Tertiary education	*63.8*	*63.5*	*64.6*	*63.4*	*64.0*	*64.3*	*64.4*	*64.8*	*65.7*	*65.9*	*0.3*
EU19 average	*Below upper secondary*	*29.0*	*29.5*	*29.2*	*29.7*	*30.0*	*30.8*	*32.4*	*31.8*	*32.9*	*34.1*	*2.0*
	Upper secondary and post-secondary non-tertiary	*38.5*	*39.9*	*41.4*	*41.4*	*41.8*	*42.9*	*43.9*	*43.9*	*45.7*	*46.9*	*1.7*
	Tertiary education	*58.9*	*59.3*	*61.3*	*60.7*	*61.4*	*61.3*	*61.6*	*62.1*	*63.1*	*63.5*	*0.5*
Estonia	Below upper secondary	m	m	m	m	m	29.4	34.2	33.4	36.3	40.9	
	Upper secondary and post-secondary non-tertiary	m	m	m	m	m	52.7	52.9	52.0	53.4	57.3	
	Tertiary education	m	m	m	m	m	67.6	65.4	66.9	73.9	72.9	
Israel	Below upper secondary	m	m	m	m	m	31.7	32.7	30.1	31.8	32.5	
	Upper secondary and post-secondary non-tertiary	m	m	m	m	m	54.6	52.5	52.7	52.3	56.2	
	Tertiary education	m	m	m	m	m	62.4	65.4	66.9	67.7	69.8	
Slovenia	Below upper secondary	m	m	m	m	m	21.8	19.9	24.8	26.7	29.6	
	Upper secondary and post-secondary non-tertiary	m	m	m	m	m	21.1	19.5	25.7	26.9	27.6	
	Tertiary education	m	m	m	m	m	45.1	47.8	49.5	50.7	55.1	

Left margin labels: OECD countries (top section), Partner countries (bottom section: Estonia, Israel, Slovenia).

Source: OECD. See Annex 3 for notes (*www.oecd.org/edu/eag2008*).
Please refer to the Reader's Guide for information concerning the symbols replacing missing data.
StatLink ⬛𝖘⬛ http://dx.doi.org/10.1787/401775543762

Table A8.5a.
Trends in unemployment rates by educational attainment (1997-2006)
Number of 25-to-64-year-olds in unemployment as a percentage of the labour force aged 25 to 64, by level of educational attainment

		1997	1998	1999	2000	2001	2002	2003	2004	2005	2006
Australia	Below upper secondary	9.6	9.0	8.4	7.5	7.6	7.5	7.0	6.2	6.3	5.6
	Upper secondary and post-secondary non-tertiary	6.1	5.8	5.1	4.5	4.7	4.3	4.3	3.9	3.4	3.8
	Tertiary education	3.5	3.3	3.4	3.6	3.1	3.3	3.0	2.8	2.5	2.3
Austria	Below upper secondary	6.7	6.9	6.1	6.3	6.4	6.9	7.9	7.8	8.6	7.9
	Upper secondary and post-secondary non-tertiary	3.4	3.6	3.2	3.0	3.0	3.4	3.4	3.8	3.9	3.7
	Tertiary education	2.5	2.0	1.9	1.6	1.5	1.9	2.0	2.9	2.6	2.5
Belgium	Below upper secondary	12.5	13.1	12.0	9.8	8.5	10.3	10.7	11.7	12.4	12.3
	Upper secondary and post-secondary non-tertiary	6.7	7.4	6.6	5.3	5.5	6.0	6.7	6.9	6.9	6.7
	Tertiary education	3.3	3.2	3.1	2.7	2.7	3.5	3.5	3.9	3.7	3.7
Canada	Below upper secondary	12.9	11.9	10.8	10.2	10.5	11.0	10.9	10.2	9.8	9.3
	Upper secondary and post-secondary non-tertiary	8.1	7.5	6.7	5.9	6.3	6.7	6.5	6.2	5.9	5.6
	Tertiary education	5.4	4.7	4.5	4.1	4.7	5.1	5.2	4.8	4.6	4.1
Czech Republic	Below upper secondary	12.1	14.5	18.8	19.3	19.2	18.8	18.3	23.0	24.4	22.3
	Upper secondary and post-secondary non-tertiary	3.4	4.6	6.5	6.7	6.2	5.6	6.0	6.4	6.2	5.5
	Tertiary education	1.2	1.9	2.6	2.5	2.0	1.8	2.0	2.0	2.0	2.2
Denmark	Below upper secondary	m	7.0	7.0	6.9	6.2	6.4	6.7	8.2	6.5	5.5
	Upper secondary and post-secondary non-tertiary	m	4.6	4.1	3.9	3.7	3.7	4.4	4.8	4.0	2.7
	Tertiary education	m	3.3	3.0	3.0	3.6	3.9	4.7	4.4	3.7	3.2
Finland	Below upper secondary	15.6	13.8	13.1	12.1	11.4	12.2	11.1	11.3	10.7	10.1
	Upper secondary and post-secondary non-tertiary	11.9	10.6	9.5	8.9	8.5	8.8	8.7	7.9	7.4	7.0
	Tertiary education	6.5	5.8	4.7	4.7	4.4	4.5	4.2	4.5	4.4	3.7
France	Below upper secondary	15.0	14.9	15.3	13.9	11.9	11.8	10.4	10.6	11.1	11.0
	Upper secondary and post-secondary non-tertiary	9.6	9.6	9.2	7.9	6.9	6.8	6.6	6.7	6.5	6.6
	Tertiary education	7.0	6.6	6.1	5.1	4.8	5.2	5.3	5.7	5.4	5.1
Germany	Below upper secondary	16.7	16.5	15.6	13.7	13.5	15.3	18.0	20.4	20.2	19.9
	Upper secondary and post-secondary non-tertiary	10.1	10.3	8.6	7.8	8.2	9.0	10.2	11.2	11.0	9.9
	Tertiary education	5.7	5.5	4.9	4.0	4.2	4.5	5.2	5.6	5.5	4.8
Greece	Below upper secondary	6.5	7.5	8.4	8.0	7.7	7.4	7.1	8.2	8.2	7.2
	Upper secondary and post-secondary non-tertiary	9.6	10.7	11.4	11.3	10.2	10.1	9.5	10.0	9.3	8.7
	Tertiary education	7.3	6.3	7.8	7.4	6.9	6.7	6.1	7.2	7.0	6.1
Hungary	Below upper secondary	12.6	11.4	11.1	9.9	10.0	10.5	10.6	10.8	12.4	14.8
	Upper secondary and post-secondary non-tertiary	6.9	6.2	5.8	5.3	4.6	4.4	4.8	5.0	6.0	6.1
	Tertiary education	1.7	1.7	1.4	1.3	1.2	1.5	1.4	1.9	2.3	2.2
Iceland	Below upper secondary	4.4	3.2	2.0	2.6	2.6	3.2	3.3	2.5	2.3	2.5
	Upper secondary and post-secondary non-tertiary	2.7	c	c	c	c	c	c	c	c	c
	Tertiary education	c	c	c	c	c	c	c	c	c	c
Ireland	Below upper secondary	14.5	11.6	9.2	5.6	5.2	5.9	6.3	6.1	6.0	5.7
	Upper secondary and post-secondary non-tertiary	6.5	4.5	3.5	2.3	2.4	2.8	2.9	3.0	3.1	3.2
	Tertiary education	4.0	3.0	1.7	1.6	1.8	2.2	2.6	2.2	2.0	2.2
Italy	Below upper secondary	m	10.8	10.6	10.0	9.2	9.0	8.8	8.2	7.8	6.9
	Upper secondary and post-secondary non-tertiary	m	8.1	7.9	7.2	6.6	6.4	6.1	5.4	5.2	4.6
	Tertiary education	m	6.9	6.9	5.9	5.3	5.3	5.3	5.3	5.7	4.8
Japan	Below upper secondary	3.9	4.4	5.6	5.9	5.9	m	m	m	m	m
	Upper secondary and post-secondary non-tertiary	3.4	3.3	4.5	4.6	4.8	5.6	5.7	5.1	4.9	4.6
	Tertiary education	2.3	2.7	3.3	3.4	3.2	3.8	3.7	3.4	3.1	3.0
Korea	Below upper secondary	1.4	6.0	5.4	3.7	3.1	2.2	2.2	2.6	2.9	2.6
	Upper secondary and post-secondary non-tertiary	2.4	6.8	6.4	4.1	3.6	3.0	3.3	3.5	3.8	3.5
	Tertiary education	2.3	4.9	4.7	3.6	3.5	3.2	3.1	2.9	2.9	2.9
Luxembourg	Below upper secondary	m	m	3.4	3.1	1.7	3.8	3.3	5.7	5.1	4.9
	Upper secondary and post-secondary non-tertiary	m	m	1.1	1.4	1.0	1.2	2.6	3.7	3.2	3.8
	Tertiary education	m	m	c	c	c	1.8	4.0	3.2	3.2	2.9
Mexico	Below upper secondary	2.6	2.3	1.5	1.5	1.6	1.7	1.8	2.2	2.3	2.2
	Upper secondary and post-secondary non-tertiary	4.4	3.3	2.5	2.2	2.3	2.3	2.2	3.0	3.1	2.6
	Tertiary education	2.8	3.1	3.5	2.4	2.5	3.0	3.0	3.7	3.7	2.9

Source: OECD. See Annex 3 for notes (*www.oecd.org/edu/eag2008*).
Please refer to the Reader's Guide for information concerning the symbols replacing missing data.
StatLink http://dx.doi.org/10.1787/401775543762

Table A8.5a. *(continued)*

Trends in unemployment rates by educational attainment (1997-2006)

Number of 25-to-64-year-olds in unemployment as a percentage of the labour force aged 25 to 64, by level of educational attainment

			1997	1998	1999	2000	2001	2002	2003	2004	2005	2006
OECD countries	**Netherlands**	Below upper secondary	m	0.9	4.3	3.9	2.9	3.0	4.5	5.5	5.8	4.8
		Upper secondary and post-secondary non-tertiary	m	1.7	2.3	2.3	1.6	2.0	2.8	3.8	4.1	3.5
		Tertiary education	m	c	1.7	1.9	1.2	2.1	2.5	2.8	2.8	2.3
	New Zealand	Below upper secondary	7.3	8.5	7.4	6.4	5.6	4.8	4.2	3.6	3.3	3.1
		Upper secondary and post-secondary non-tertiary	4.3	5.0	4.8	3.8	3.7	3.5	3.3	2.2	2.1	2.2
		Tertiary education	3.5	4.0	3.6	3.3	2.7	3.2	3.0	2.6	2.2	2.4
	Norway	Below upper secondary	4.0	2.9	2.5	2.2	3.4	3.4	3.9	4.0	7.3	4.7
		Upper secondary and post-secondary non-tertiary	3.1	2.4	2.5	2.6	2.7	2.9	3.6	3.8	2.6	2.1
		Tertiary education	1.7	1.5	1.4	1.9	1.7	2.1	2.5	2.4	2.1	1.8
	Poland	Below upper secondary	10.5	9.8	13.9	17.7	20.0	22.4	22.4	22.4	21.4	16.5
		Upper secondary and post-secondary non-tertiary	10.8	10.2	8.6	11.3	12.9	14.3	14.5	14.2	13.7	10.6
		Tertiary education	2.1	2.5	3.1	4.3	5.0	6.3	6.6	6.2	6.2	5.0
	Portugal	Below upper secondary	m	4.4	4.0	3.6	3.6	4.4	5.7	6.4	7.5	7.6
		Upper secondary and post-secondary non-tertiary	m	5.1	4.4	3.5	3.3	4.3	5.1	5.6	6.7	7.1
		Tertiary education	m	2.8	3.0	2.7	2.8	3.9	4.9	4.4	5.4	5.4
	Slovak Republic	Below upper secondary	22.4	24.3	30.3	36.3	38.7	42.3	44.9	47.7	49.2	44.0
		Upper secondary and post-secondary non-tertiary	8.5	8.8	11.9	14.3	14.8	14.2	13.5	14.6	12.7	10.0
		Tertiary education	2.8	3.3	4.0	4.6	4.2	3.6	3.7	4.8	4.4	2.6
	Spain	Below upper secondary	18.9	17.0	14.7	13.7	10.2	11.2	11.3	11.0	9.3	9.0
		Upper secondary and post-secondary non-tertiary	16.8	15.3	12.9	10.9	8.4	9.4	9.5	9.4	7.3	6.9
		Tertiary education	13.7	13.1	11.1	9.5	6.9	7.7	7.7	7.3	6.1	5.5
	Sweden	Below upper secondary	11.9	10.4	9.0	8.0	5.9	5.8	6.1	6.5	8.5	7.3
		Upper secondary and post-secondary non-tertiary	9.4	7.8	6.5	5.3	4.6	4.6	5.2	5.8	6.0	5.1
		Tertiary education	5.2	4.4	3.9	3.0	2.6	3.0	3.9	4.3	4.5	4.2
	Switzerland	Below upper secondary	6.2	5.6	5.0	5.0	3.7	4.2	5.9	6.9	7.2	7.6
		Upper secondary and post-secondary non-tertiary	3.0	2.8	2.3	2.0	1.9	2.3	3.1	3.6	3.6	3.2
		Tertiary education	4.4	2.8	1.7	1.3	1.3	2.2	2.9	2.8	2.7	2.2
	Turkey	Below upper secondary	4.4	4.4	5.3	4.6	6.7	8.5	8.8	8.1	8.7	8.3
		Upper secondary and post-secondary non-tertiary	6.3	6.6	8.2	5.5	7.4	8.7	7.8	10.1	9.2	9.0
		Tertiary education	3.9	4.8	5.1	3.9	4.7	7.5	6.9	8.2	6.9	6.9
	United Kingdom	Below upper secondary	8.6	7.7	7.4	6.7	5.9	6.3	5.4	5.2	4.9	5.7
		Upper secondary and post-secondary non-tertiary	5.6	4.5	4.6	4.2	3.4	3.7	3.5	3.4	2.8	4.0
		Tertiary education	2.9	2.6	2.7	2.1	2.0	2.4	2.4	2.3	2.0	2.2
	United States	Below upper secondary	10.4	8.5	7.7	7.9	8.1	10.2	9.9	10.5	9.0	8.3
		Upper secondary and post-secondary non-tertiary	4.8	4.5	3.7	3.6	3.8	5.7	6.1	5.6	5.1	4.6
		Tertiary education	2.3	2.1	2.1	1.8	2.1	3.0	3.4	3.3	2.6	2.5
	OECD average	***Below upper secondary***	***10.1***	***9.3***	***9.2***	***8.9***	***8.6***	***9.3***	***9.6***	***10.1***	***10.3***	***9.6***
		Upper secondary and post-secondary non-tertiary	***6.7***	***6.5***	***6.0***	***5.6***	***5.4***	***5.7***	***5.9***	***6.2***	***5.8***	***5.4***
		Tertiary education	***4.1***	***4.0***	***3.8***	***3.5***	***3.3***	***3.7***	***4.0***	***4.1***	***3.9***	***3.5***
	EU19 average	***Below upper secondary***	***13.2***	***11.3***	***11.3***	***11.0***	***10.4***	***11.2***	***11.5***	***12.5***	***12.6***	***11.8***
		Upper secondary and post-secondary non-tertiary	***8.5***	***7.4***	***6.8***	***6.5***	***6.1***	***6.4***	***6.6***	***6.9***	***6.6***	***6.1***
		Tertiary education	***4.7***	***4.4***	***4.1***	***3.8***	***3.5***	***3.8***	***4.1***	***4.3***	***4.1***	***3.7***
Partner countries	**Estonia**	Below upper secondary	m	m	m	m	m	19.0	14.8	15.4	13.0	11.7
		Upper secondary and post-secondary non-tertiary	m	m	m	m	m	10.5	9.5	9.5	8.4	5.7
		Tertiary education	m	m	m	m	m	5.8	6.5	5.0	3.8	3.2
	Israel	Below upper secondary	m	m	m	m	m	14.0	15.2	15.6	14.0	12.8
		Upper secondary and post-secondary non-tertiary	m	m	m	m	m	9.8	10.3	10.6	9.5	8.7
		Tertiary education	m	m	m	m	m	6.4	6.4	6.1	5.1	4.5
	Slovenia	Below upper secondary	m	m	m	m	m	8.4	8.7	8.4	8.7	7.0
		Upper secondary and post-secondary non-tertiary	m	m	m	m	m	5.2	5.5	5.3	5.7	5.6
		Tertiary education	m	m	m	m	m	2.3	3.0	2.8	3.0	3.0

Source: OECD. See Annex 3 for notes (*www.oecd.org/edu/eag2008*).

Please refer to the Reader's Guide for information concerning the symbols replacing missing data.

StatLink http://dx.doi.org/10.1787/401775543762

WHAT ARE THE ECONOMIC BENEFITS OF EDUCATION?

This indicator examines the relative earnings of workers with different levels of educational attainment in 25 OECD countries and the partner countries Israel and Slovenia. It also presents data on the distribution of pre-tax earnings at five ISCED levels of educational attainment to help show how returns to education vary within countries among individuals with comparable levels of educational attainment.

Key results

Chart A9.1. Share of 25-to-64-year-olds with lower education and high earnings and vice versa (2006 or latest available year)

This chart shows the proportion of the tertiary-educated population with low earnings and the proportion of the population with education below the upper secondary level and with high earnings (2006 or latest available year).

■ 25-to-64-year-olds with tertiary education and earnings amounting to one half of the country median or less

▨ 25-to-64-year-olds with below upper secondary education and earnings amounting to twice the country median or more

Although education generally leads to substantial earnings advantages, this is not the case for all individuals. The share of individuals with tertiary education who earn substantially less than the median varies among countries; this is typically explained by part-time or part-year work but nevertheless may send the wrong signal from an educational perspective. Females with tertiary education are more disadvantaged than males in terms of realising low earnings; in Austria, Canada and New Zealand, 20% or more of the female population earn less than half the median. While males are less likely to have low earnings, more than 10% earn less than half of the median in Canada, Denmark, Norway and Sweden. This dispersion in educational outcomes provides an indication of the overall investment risk associated with higher education.

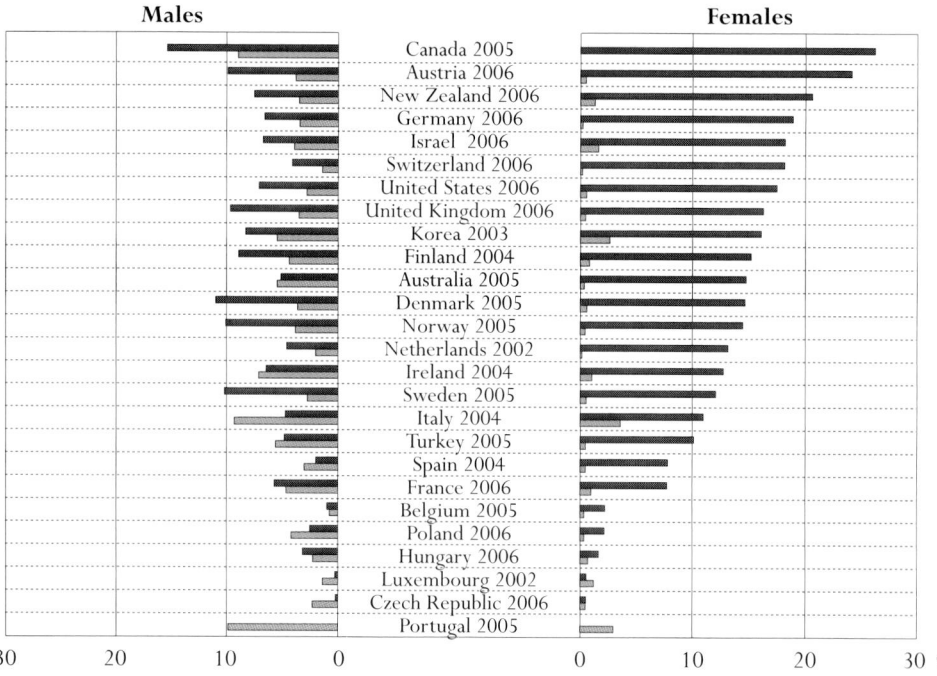

Countries are ranked in descending order of the share of 25-to-64-year-old females with tertiary education and earnings amounting to one half of the country median or less.

Source: OECD. Tables A9.4b and A9.4c on line. See Annex 3 for notes (*www.oecd.org/edu/eag2008*).

StatLink ▤▥ http://dx.doi.org/10.1787/401781614508

Other highlights of this indicator

▪ Earnings increase with each level of education. Those who have attained upper secondary, post-secondary non-tertiary or tertiary education enjoy substantial earnings advantages compared with those of the same gender who have not completed upper secondary education. The earnings premium for those with tertiary education has generally not deteriorated in recent years, and in Germany, Hungary, and Italy it has increased substantially.

▪ The educational earnings advantage increases with age. The difference in relative earnings generally rises for 55-to-64-year-olds with a tertiary education compared to the total population (25-to-64-year-olds). For those with below upper secondary education the earnings disadvantage increases at an older age in all countries but Finland, Germany and New Zealand.

▪ With few exceptions, females earn less than males with similar levels of educational attainment. For all levels of education, average earnings of females between the ages of 30 and 44 range from 51% of those of males in Korea to 89% in Slovenia.

▪ There are significant differences among countries in the dispersion of earnings among individuals with similar levels of educational attainment. The proportion of individuals with tertiary-type A and advanced research programmes in the lowest earnings category (at or below half of the median) varies from 0% in Luxembourg and Portugal to 18% in Canada. Countries also differ in the shares of males and females in the upper and lower categories of earnings.

A9

Policy context

One way in which markets provide incentives for individuals to develop and maintain appropriate skills is through wage differentials, in particular through the higher earnings of persons with higher levels of education. At the same time, education involves costs that must be balanced against these higher earnings. This indicator examines relative earnings associated with different levels of education and the variation in these earnings.

The dispersion in earnings among groups at different levels of educational attainment provides information about the risk associated with investing in education. Relative earnings offer information on what a typical student can, on average, expect to earn after completing a degree or educational programme. The dispersion in earnings provides a more nuanced picture by giving a range of possible outcomes for different educational attainment levels.

The dispersion of earnings is relevant for policies that support attainment of higher levels of education. Evidence suggests that some individuals may receive relatively low returns to investments in education, that is, they earn relatively low wages in spite of relatively high levels of educational attainment. Policy makers may need to consider the characteristics of education programmes that appear to generate low rates of return for some people or the characteristics of individuals in such programmes, such as their gender, time in the labour force, or occupation.

Evidence and explanations

Education and earnings

Earnings differentials according to educational attainment

Earnings differentials are key measures of the financial incentives for an individual to invest in further education. They may also reflect differences in the supply of educational programmes at different levels (or barriers to access to those programmes). The earnings benefit of completing tertiary education can be seen by comparing the average annual earnings of those who graduate from tertiary education with the average annual earnings of upper secondary or post-secondary non-tertiary graduates. The earnings disadvantage from not completing upper secondary education is apparent from a similar comparison of average earnings. Variations among countries in relative earnings (before taxes) reflect a number of factors, including the demand for skills in the labour market, minimum wage legislation, the strength of unions, the coverage of collective bargaining agreements, the supply of workers at various levels of educational attainment, and the relative incidence of part-time and seasonal work.

Chart A9.2 shows a strong positive relationship between educational attainment and average earnings. In all countries, graduates of tertiary education earn more overall than upper secondary and post-secondary non-tertiary graduates. Earnings differentials between those with tertiary education – especially tertiary-type A and advanced research programmes– and those with upper secondary education are generally more pronounced than the differentials between upper secondary and lower secondary or below. This suggests that in many countries, upper secondary (and, with a small number of exceptions, post-secondary non-tertiary) education forms a dividing line beyond which additional education attracts a particularly high premium. As private investment costs beyond upper secondary education typically rise considerably in most countries, a high premium assures an adequate supply of individuals willing to invest time and money in further education.

Chart A9.2. **Relative earnings from employment (2006)**

By level of educational attainment and gender for 25-to-64-year-olds
(upper secondary and post-secondary non-tertiary education = 100) latest available year

■ Below upper secondary education
■ Tertiary-type B education
□ Tertiary-type A and advanced research programmes

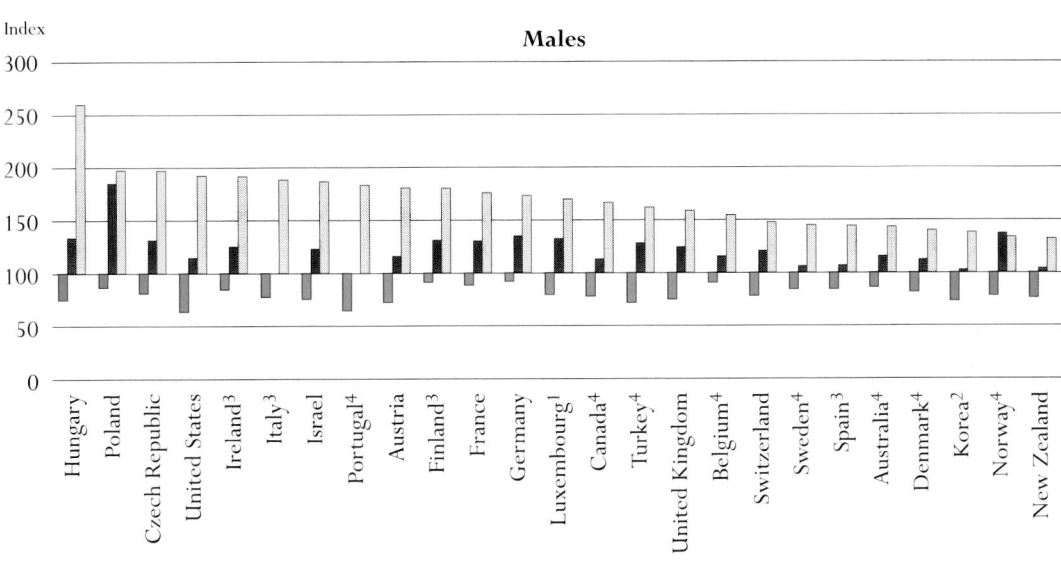

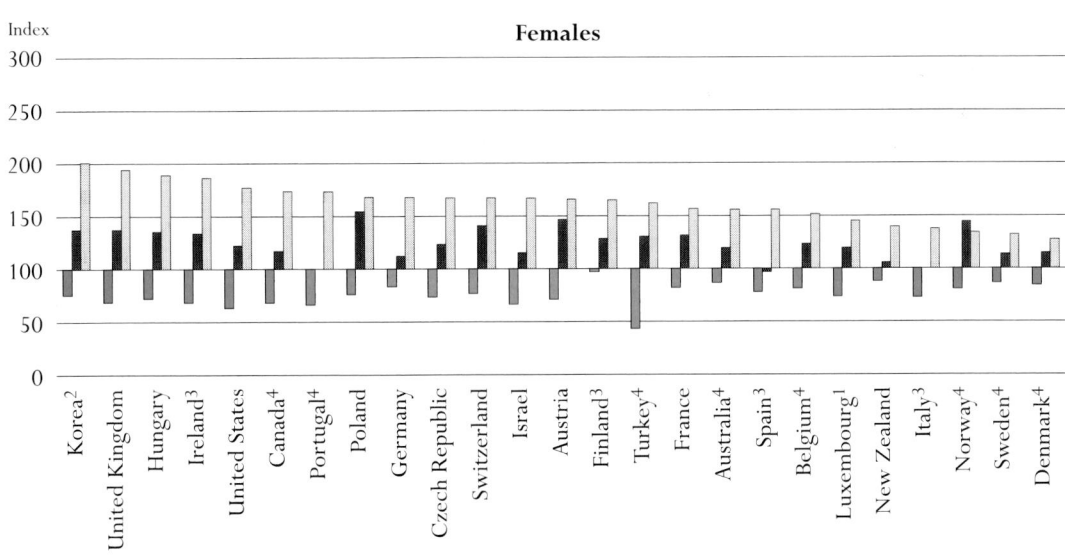

1. Year of reference 2002.
2. Year of reference 2003.
3. Year of reference 2004.
4. Year of reference 2005.

Countries are ranked in descending order of the relative earnings of the population with a tertiary-type A (including advanced research programmes) level of educational attainment.

Source: OECD. Table A9.1a. See Annex 3 for notes (*www.oecd.org/edu/eag2008*).

StatLink ⭐📉 http://dx.doi.org/10.1787/401781614508

Males with a degree from a tertiary-type A or advanced research programme have a substantial earnings premium in the Czech Republic, Hungary and Poland that is close to or more than 100%. In Korea and United Kingdom females have a similar advantage. Females with below secondary education are particularly disadvantaged in Canada, Israel, Turkey, the United Kingdom and the United States, as are males in Portugal and the United States. Table A9.1a shows that the earnings premium for 25-to-64-year-olds with tertiary education, relative to those with upper secondary education, ranges from 15% in New Zealand to 119% in Hungary.

The relative earnings premium for those with tertiary education has been on the rise in most countries over the past ten years, indicating that the demand for more educated individuals still exceeds supply in most countries (Table A9.2a). In Germany, Hungary, Ireland and Italy, the earnings premium has increased substantially during this period. In these countries tertiary attainment levels are low compared to the OECD average, particularly in view of the proportion of the population working in skilled jobs (see Indicator A1).

Some countries have seen a decline in the earnings premium over the past ten years. Spain, but also New Zealand, have seen a marginal decrease in the earnings premiums for those with tertiary education. Whether this is an indication of weakening demand or whether these figures reflect the fact that younger tertiary educated individuals with relatively low starting salaries have entered the labour market, is difficult to know.

Education and earnings at an older age

Table A9.1a also shows how relative earnings vary with age. The difference in relative earnings for those with a tertiary education at age 55 to 64 compared with the total population (25-64-year-olds) is generally larger; on average, the earnings differential increases with 14 index points. These benefits of education are shown in Chart A9.3. While employment opportunities at an older age improve for those with tertiary education in most countries (see Indicator A8), the earnings advantages also increase. In all countries except Australia, Canada, the Netherlands, Turkey and the United Kingdom. Earnings increase for 55-to-64-year-olds is more frequent for those with tertiary education than for those with below upper secondary education.

For those with below upper secondary education the earnings disadvantage increases with age in all countries but Finland, Germany and New Zealand. The increasing earnings disadvantage at an older age for those with below upper secondary education is less marked than the earnings advantage for those with a tertiary education, which indicates that tertiary education is a key to higher earnings at an older age. In most countries, then, tertiary education not only increases the prospect of being employed at an older age but also keeps improving earnings and productivity differentials through to the end of working life.

Education and gender disparity in earnings

For 25-to-64-year-olds, financial rewards from tertiary education benefit females more than males in Australia, Austria, Canada, Korea, the Netherlands, New Zealand, Norway, Spain, Switzerland and the United Kingdom. The reverse is true in the remaining countries, with the exception of Turkey, where – relative to upper secondary education – the earnings of males and females are equally enhanced by tertiary education (Table A9.1a).

Chart A9.3. Difference in relative earnings for the 55-to-64-year-old population and total population (25-to-64-year-olds)

Earnings relative to upper secondary and post-secondary non-tertiary education

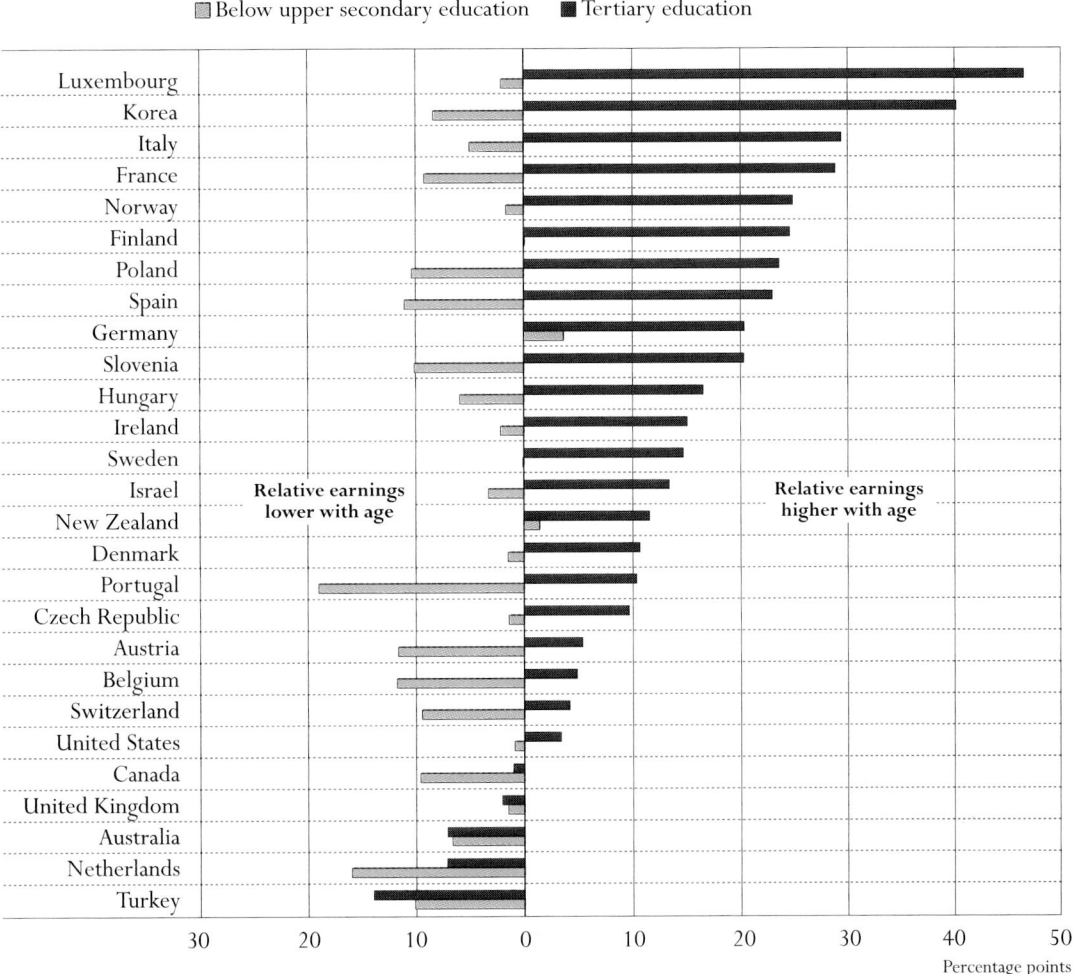

Countries are ranked in descending order of the difference in relative earnings for the 55-to-64-year-old population and total population (25-to-64-year-olds) at the tertiary level of education.
Source: OECD. Table A9.1a. See Annex 3 for notes (*www.oecd.org/edu/eag2008*).
StatLink ᐧᐧ⬛ http://dx.doi.org/10.1787/401781614508

Both males and females with upper secondary, post-secondary non-tertiary or tertiary attainment have substantial earnings advantages (compared with those of the same gender who do not complete upper secondary education), but earnings differentials between males and females with the same educational attainment remain substantial. In all countries, considering all levels of educational attainment, females in the 30-to-44-year-old age group earn less than their male counterparts (Table A9.1b). For all levels of education taken together (*i.e.* dividing total earnings by the total number of income earners, by gender), average earnings of females between the ages of 30 and 44 range from 51% of those of males in Korea to 89% in Slovenia.

This relative differential must be interpreted with caution, however, since in most countries earnings data include part-time work, which is often a major characteristic of female employment and is likely to vary significantly from one country to another. In Luxembourg, Hungary and Poland, where part-time work and part-year earnings are excluded from the calculations, earnings of females between the ages of 30 and 44 reach 84, 86 and 78%, respectively, of those of males.

Chart A9.4. Differences in earnings between females and males (2006 or latest available year)

Average earnings of females as a percentage of average earnings of males (55-to-64 age group), by level of educational attainment

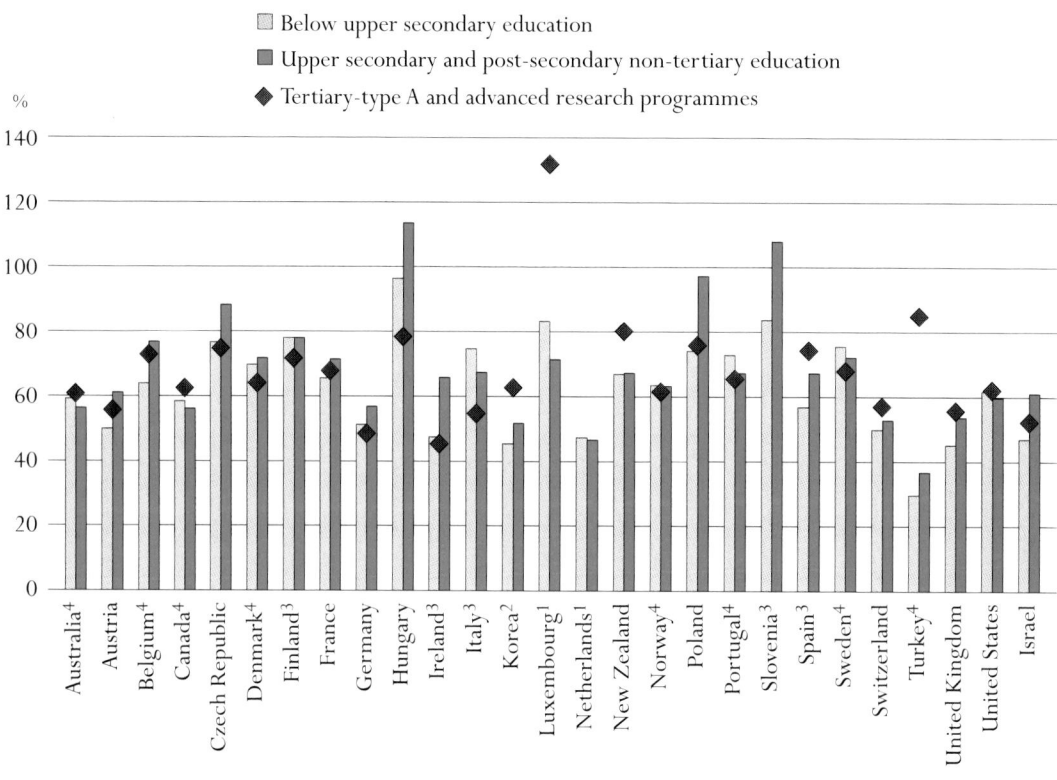

1. Year of reference 2002.
2. Year of reference 2003.
3. Year of reference 2004.
4. Year of reference 2005.
Notes: Data on earnings for individuals in part-time work are excluded for the Czech Republic, Hungary, Luxembourg and Poland, while data on part-year earnings are excluded for Hungary, Luxembourg and Poland.
Source: OECD. Table A9.1b. See Annex 3 for notes (*www.oecd.org/edu/eag2008*).
StatLink ⫘⫘ http://dx.doi.org/10.1787/401781614508

The gap in earnings between males and females presented in Chart A9.4 is due in part to differences in occupations, in the amount of time spent in the labour force, and in the incidence of part-time work. However, among 55-to-64-year-olds, the gap between male and female earnings widens in most countries. Notable exceptions are females with an upper secondary and post-secondary non-tertiary education in Hungary, Poland and Slovenia who earn as much or more than males, and females with a tertiary-type A education or a degree from an advanced research programme in Luxembourg who earn over 30% more than their male colleagues.

While the overall earnings gap between males and females is generally more pronounced for the oldest age cohort, the earnings differentials between males and females in general have narrowed in some countries in recent years (Table A9.3). The most noticeable changes have taken place for females with lower upper secondary education in Hungary, New Zealand and the United States where the earnings gap has closed by more than 10 percentage points over the past decade.

The distribution of earnings within levels of educational attainment

Data on the distribution of levels of earnings among different educational groups can show how tightly earnings are distributed around the country median. Apart from providing information on equity in earnings, they give information about the risks associated with investing in education. As such, the distribution of earnings complements relative earnings by giving information on how these average earnings are distributed within educational groups.

Tables A9.4a, A9.4b and A9.4c show the distributions of earnings among 25-to-64-year-olds for 25 OECD countries and the partner economy Israel among individuals with a given level of educational attainment. Distributions are given for the combined male and female populations, as well as for males and females separately. The five earnings categories range from "At or below one-half of the median" to "More than twice the median". Tables A9.4b and A9.4c (on line) also present the distribution of earnings among males and females relative to the median of the entire adult population with earnings from work.

Indicators based on average earnings do not reveal the range of earnings of individuals with a given level of educational attainment. Chart A9.1 shows that substantial proportions of those with tertiary education, particularly among females, earn half of the country median or less. A large part of the low earnings among the higher educated is typically explained by part-time or part-year work. For countries reporting only full-time and full-year earnings, substantially less of the tertiary educated population has low earnings and the disadvantage for females is eliminated. Whether part-time or part-year work is voluntary or involuntary matters for how to act on these results, but from a societal perspective low earnings or low labour participation both indicate less efficient allocation and utilisation of investments in human capital.

Table A9.4a and Chart A9.5 show that in most countries the share of individuals in the lowest earnings categories falls as the level of educational attainment rises. This result is another way of viewing the well-established positive relationship between earnings and educational attainment. Nonetheless, individuals with higher levels of education are still found in the lower earnings categories in most countries; this suggests that there is a substantial risk associated with investing in tertiary education. The proportion of individuals with the highest educational attainment (tertiary-type A and advanced research programmes) in the lowest earnings category (at or below half of the median) varies from 0% in Luxembourg and Portugal to 18% in Canada.

Across all levels of education, Belgium, the Czech Republic, Luxembourg and Portugal have no or relatively few individuals with earnings either at or below one-half the median. Not surprisingly, a more equal distribution of earnings is generally associated with lower earnings differentials for those with tertiary education but this only explains a portion of a country's earnings inequalities. Factors other than investment in human capital (measured by educational levels) appear to be more important in explaining countries' overall wage structure.

A9

Chart A9.5. Share of 25-to-64-year-olds in earnings categories, by level of educational attainment (2006 or latest year available)

☐ Below upper secondary education

▨ Upper secondary and post-secondary non-tertiary education

■ Tertiary-type A education and advanced research programmes

☐ Tertiary-type B education

▨ All levels of education

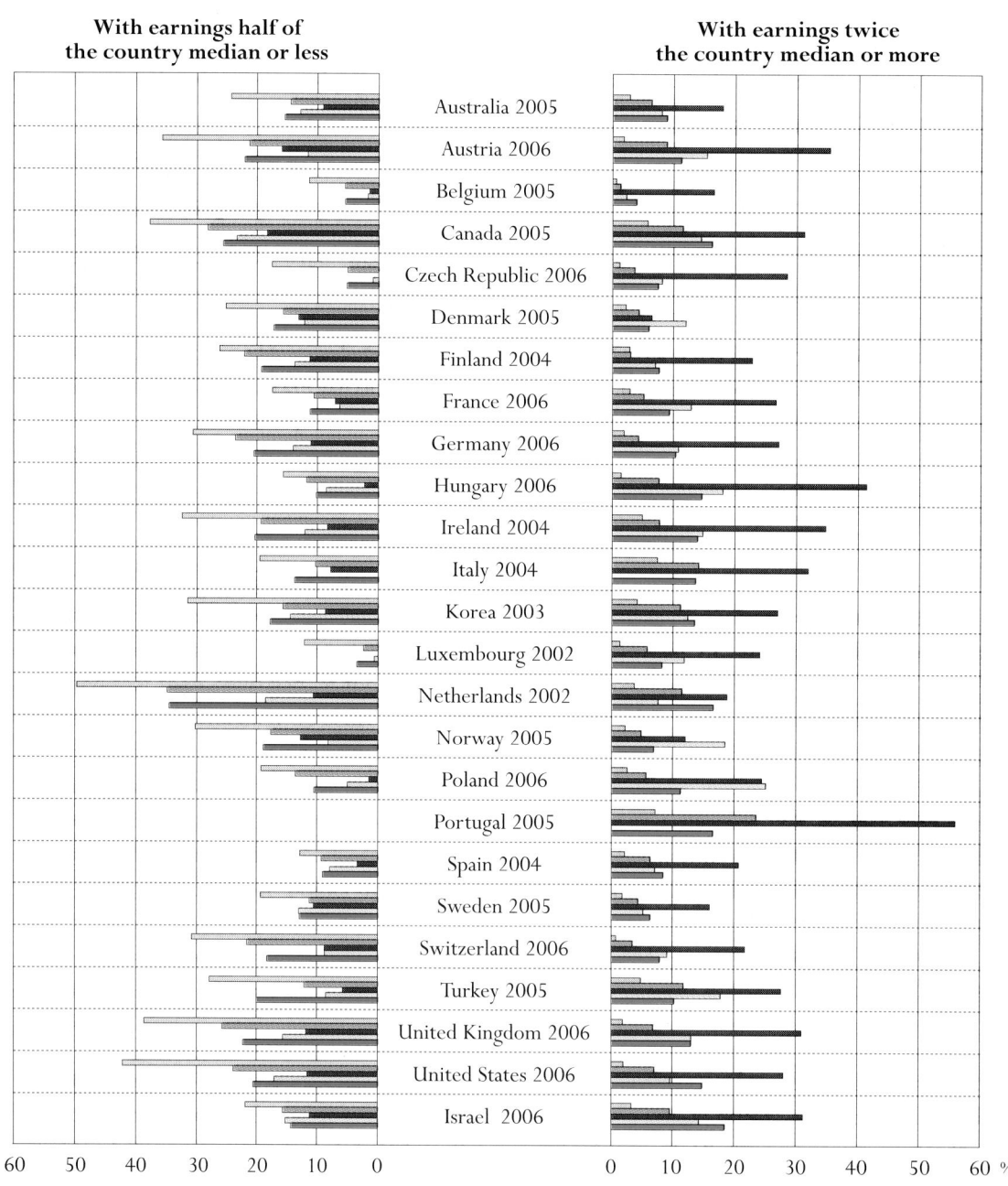

With earnings half of the country median or less

With earnings twice the country median or more

Australia 2005
Austria 2006
Belgium 2005
Canada 2005
Czech Republic 2006
Denmark 2005
Finland 2004
France 2006
Germany 2006
Hungary 2006
Ireland 2004
Italy 2004
Korea 2003
Luxembourg 2002
Netherlands 2002
Norway 2005
Poland 2006
Portugal 2005
Spain 2004
Sweden 2005
Switzerland 2006
Turkey 2005
United Kingdom 2006
United States 2006
Israel 2006

% 60   50   40   30   20   10   0   0   10   20   30   40   50   60 %

Source: OECD. Table A9.4a. See Annex 3 for notes (*www.oecd.org/edu/eag2008*).

StatLink ⌇⌇⌇ http://dx.doi.org/10.1787/401781614508

The interpretation of earnings dispersion data

Factors ranging from differences in institutional arrangements to variations in individual abilities are likely to determine the extent of the dispersion of earnings among individuals of similar educational attainment. At an institutional level, countries in which wage setting is more centralised would tend to have less dispersion, owing to a degree of convergence between occupational status and educational attainment. More broadly, the dispersion of earnings also reflects the fact that educational attainment cannot be fully equated with proficiency and skills. Skills other than those related to educational attainment, as well as experience, are also rewarded in the labour market. Differences in the scale and operation of training systems for adult learners also influence national patterns of dispersion, as do recruitment considerations that are not related to skills, such as gender, race or age discrimination (and consequently the relative effectiveness of national legislative frameworks in countering such problems).

More generally, there are gaps in our understanding of what determines earnings. Research in the United States has shown that for individuals of the same race and sex, over one-half of the variance in earnings is not explained by quantifiable factors such as years of schooling, age, duration of labour market experience, or indeed the schooling, occupation and income of their parents. Some research on the determinants of earnings has highlighted the importance that employers give to so-called non-cognitive skills – such as persistence, reliability and self-discipline – and raises the need for policy-oriented research on the role of education systems, and particularly early childhood education, in developing and signalling such skills.

Definitions and methodologies

Earnings data in Table A9.1a are based on an annual reference period in Austria, Canada, the Czech Republic, Denmark, Finland, Ireland, Italy, Korea, Luxembourg, Norway, Portugal, Spain, Sweden, Turkey and the United States. Earnings are reported weekly in Australia, New Zealand and the United Kingdom, and monthly in Belgium, France, Germany, Hungary, Poland and Switzerland, and the partner country Israel. Data on earnings are before income tax, while earnings for Belgium, Korea and Turkey are net of income tax. Data on earnings for individuals in part-time work are excluded for the Czech Republic, Hungary, Luxembourg and Poland, while data on part-year earnings are excluded for Hungary, Luxembourg and Poland.

The earnings data shown in this indicator differ across countries in a number of ways. The results should therefore be interpreted with caution. In particular, in countries reporting annual earnings, differences in the incidence of seasonal work among individuals with different levels of educational attainment will have an effect on relative earnings that is not reflected in the data for countries reporting weekly or monthly earnings. Similarly, the prevalence of part-time and part-year earnings in most countries suggest that caution is needed in interpreting earnings differentials in countries, particularly between males and females.

Further references

The following additional material relevant to this indicator is available on line at:

StatLink ⌁ᵐˢᴸ http://dx.doi.org/10.1787/401781614508

- *Table A9.2b. Trends in relative earnings: male population (1997-2006)*

- *Table A9.2c. Trends in relative earnings: female population (1997-2006)*

- *Table A9.4b. Distribution of 25-to-64-year-old males by level of earnings and educational attainment (2006 or latest available year)*

- *Table A9.4c. Distribution of 25-to-64-year-old females by level of earnings and educational attainment (2006 or latest available year)*

Table A9.1a.
Relative earnings of the population with income from employment (2006 or latest available year)
By level of educational attainment and gender for 25-to-64-year-olds, 25-to-34-year-olds and 55-to-64-year-olds
(upper secondary and post-secondary non-tertiary education = 100)

			Below upper secondary education			Post-secondary non-tertiary education			All tertiary education		
			25-64	25-34	55-64	25-64	25-34	55-64	25-64	25-34	55-64
Australia	2005	Males	86	90	81	105	107	104	136	124	133
		Females	86	82	85	104	99	105	146	142	143
		M+F	81	88	74	96	98	94	131	126	124
Austria	2006	Males	72	73	66	135	117	159	155	136	157
		Females	71	68	54	123	122	129	158	147	153
		M+F	66	68	55	124	113	148	157	137	162
Belgium	2005	Males	91	95	82	98	95	108	137	124	139
		Females	81	85	68	108	105	103	134	131	128
		M+F	89	95	78	100	98	102	133	123	138
Canada	2005	Males	78	86	66	107	114	94	140	134	133
		Females	68	82	68	97	106	98	144	157	138
		M+F	77	88	68	106	111	98	138	137	137
Czech Republic	2006	Males	81	83	80	m	m	m	194	160	201
		Females	73	78	69	m	m	m	163	146	168
		M+F	74	80	72	m	m	m	183	152	192
Denmark	2004	Males	82	80	83	92	44	94	133	113	143
		Females	84	77	81	85	40	92	126	123	131
		M+F	82	81	81	97	45	104	125	112	136
Finland	2004	Males	91	90	94	m	m	m	161	139	182
		Females	97	93	94	m	m	m	146	145	158
		M+F	94	94	94	m	m	m	149	130	173
France	2006	Males	89	93	82	87	91	94	157	135	185
		Females	82	85	75	98	113	53	146	142	167
		M+F	85	93	76	87	97	78	149	133	178
Germany	2006	Males	92	85	90	115	116	155	163	142	178
		Females	83	83	81	117	114	110	153	138	150
		M+F	90	86	93	112	112	127	164	139	185
Hungary	2006	Males	75	76	73	126	112	135	259	219	277
		Females	72	77	62	116	117	114	189	180	190
		M+F	73	76	67	120	114	124	219	196	235
Ireland	2004	Males	85	84	85	100	112	92	171	158	198
		Females	68	63	61	100	112	97	168	151	145
		M+F	85	78	83	102	113	97	169	150	184
Italy	2004	Males	78	83	71	m	m	m	188	169	201
		Females	73	70	79	m	m	m	138	155	162
		M+F	79	81	74	m	m	m	165	157	194
Korea	2003	Males	73	87	71	m	m	m	127	117	169
		Females	75	126	62	m	m	m	176	148	206
		M+F	67	100	58	m	m	m	141	125	181
Luxembourg	2002	Males	79	84	78	114	209	121	149	143	185
		Females	74	70	91	120	114	m	131	128	165
		M+F	78	80	76	117	118	127	145	138	192
Netherlands	2002	Males	84	95	68	m	m	m	143	136	143
		Females	72	70	69	m	m	m	155	145	158
		M+F	84	93	68	m	m	m	148	140	141
New Zealand	2006	Males	76	87	83	99	112	98	120	114	135
		Females	88	76	83	91	105	95	123	124	128
		M+F	78	83	79	110	120	106	115	113	126
Norway	2005	Males	78	76	77	113	108	119	134	108	152
		Females	81	76	77	118	114	129	135	129	150
		M+F	78	76	76	120	115	127	129	110	154
Poland	2006	Males	86	85	79	114	110	119	194	169	216
		Females	76	82	60	116	115	112	165	157	168
		M+F	84	86	73	109	106	114	173	155	197

Source: OECD. See Annex 3 for notes (*www.oecd.org/edu/eag2008*).
Please refer to the Reader's Guide for information concerning the symbols replacing missing data.
StatLink ⟲ http://dx.doi.org/10.1787/401781614508

A9

Table A9.1a. *(continued)*

Relative earnings of the population with income from employment (2006 or latest available year)

By level of educational attainment and gender for 25-to-64-year-olds, 25-to-34-year-olds and 55-to-64-year-olds
(upper secondary and post-secondary non-tertiary education = 100)

			Below upper secondary education			Post-secondary non-tertiary education			All tertiary education		
			25-64	25-34	55-64	25-64	25-34	55-64	25-64	25-34	55-64
Portugal	2005	Males	64	73	47	m	m	m	183	167	184
		Females	66	71	51	m	m	m	173	170	178
		M+F	67	74	48	m	m	m	177	166	188
Spain	2004	Males	84	94	76	83	100	m	132	123	153
		Females	78	86	64	95	103	177	141	139	162
		M+F	85	94	74	89	104	133	132	126	155
Sweden	2005	Males	84	81	83	122	92	124	135	109	148
		Females	86	79	87	106	84	128	126	116	139
		M+F	86	81	86	121	87	131	126	108	141
Switzerland	2006	Males	78	83	72	105	93	102	138	126	138
		Females	77	77	68	116	105	127	159	148	153
		M+F	74	80	65	110	98	112	156	138	160
Turkey	2005	Males	72	77	60	m	m	m	153	171	129
		Females	43	37	49	m	m	m	154	133	307
		M+F	69	70	59	m	m	m	149	156	135
United Kingdom	2006	Males	75	74	81	m	m	m	149	141	157
		Females	69	60	68	m	m	m	177	172	165
		M+F	70	74	69	m	m	m	159	151	157
United States	2006	Males	63	71	62	109	106	106	183	162	172
		Females	63	64	64	112	109	114	170	171	177
		M+F	66	72	65	109	105	110	176	160	180
Israel	2006	Males	76	73	77	102	101	92	166	147	181
		Females	67	78	59	123	110	108	150	145	151
		M+F	78	79	74	102	94	87	151	137	165
Slovenia	2004	Males	74	76	66	m	m	m	217	180	233
		Females	71	77	51	m	m	m	190	172	184
		M+F	73	77	63	m	m	m	198	168	219

Partner countries

Source: OECD. See Annex 3 for notes (*www.oecd.org/edu/eag2008*).

Please refer to the Reader's Guide for information concerning the symbols replacing missing data.

StatLink ⌨ http://dx.doi.org/10.1787/401781614508

Table A9.1b.
Differences in earnings between females and males (2006 or latest available year)
Average annual earnings of females as a percentage of earnings of males by level of educational attainment of 30-to-44-year-olds and 55-to-64-year-olds

		Below upper secondary education		Upper secondary and post-secondary non-tertiary education		Tertiary-type B education		Tertiary-type A and advanced research programmes		All levels of education	
		30 to 44	55 to 64	30 to 44	55 to 64	30 to 44	55 to 64	30 to 44	55 to 64	30 to 44	55 to 64
Australia	2005	58	59	58	56	64	62	61	60	62	59
Austria	2006	59	50	56	61	68	77	62	55	56	53
Belgium	2005	67	64	74	77	80	80	76	72	77	69
Canada	2005	52	58	61	56	59	60	68	62	64	57
Czech Republic	2006	68	77	75	88	71	93	64	74	70	80
Denmark	2005	70	70	70	72	71	72	65	64	71	69
Finland	2004	71	78	68	78	67	74	65	71	70	73
France	2006	67	66	73	71	77	62	66	67	73	64
Germany	2006	51	51	61	57	53	40	63	48	59	49
Hungary	2006	91	96	92	114	100	90	66	78	86	90
Ireland	2004	49	47	62	66	64	77	66	45	65	27
Italy	2004	68	75	73	67	m	m	57	54	73	68
Korea	2003	49	45	44	52	59	107	76	62	51	37
Luxembourg	2002	79	83	92	71	83	105	78	131	84	56
Netherlands	2002	51	47	60	47	m	m	m	m	62	50
New Zealand	2006	66	67	60	67	63	58	61	80	63	66
Norway	2005	64	63	63	63	67	71	64	61	72	62
Poland	2006	67	74	75	97	66	74	67	75	78	90
Portugal	2005	73	73	72	67	m	m	72	65	79	68
Spain	2004	64	57	68	67	64	56	76	74	75	65
Sweden	2005	72	76	71	72	71	77	66	68	72	74
Switzerland	2006	56	50	53	53	63	59	68	57	55	48
Turkey	2005	45	30	73	37	107	m	67	85	70	45
United Kingdom	2006	52	45	53	54	56	63	64	55	58	52
United States	2006	63	62	65	60	67	69	59	62	65	59
Israel	2006	59	47	61	61	61	55	59	52	64	56
Slovenia	2004	83	84	86	108	m	m	m	m	89	106

Source: OECD. See Annex 3 for notes (*www.oecd.org/edu/eag2008*).
Please refer to the Reader's Guide for information concerning the symbols replacing missing data.
StatLink ᵐˢ⁻ http://dx.doi.org/10.1787/401781614508

A9

Table A9.2a.
Trends in relative earnings: adult population (1997-2006)
By educational attainment, for 25-to-64-year-olds (upper secondary and post-secondary non-tertiary education = 100)

		1997	1998	1999	2000	2001	2002	2003	2004	2005	2006
Australia	Below upper secondary	79	m	80	m	77	m	m	m	81	m
	Tertiary	124	m	134	m	133	m	m	m	131	m
Austria	Below upper secondary	m	m	m	m	m	m	m	m	71	66
	Tertiary	m	m	m	m	m	m	m	m	152	157
Belgium	Below upper secondary	m	m	m	92	m	91	89	90	89	m
	Tertiary	m	m	m	128	m	132	130	134	133	m
Canada	Below upper secondary	m	77	79	79	76	77	78	78	77	m
	Tertiary	m	141	141	145	146	139	140	139	138	m
Czech Republic	Below upper secondary	68	68	68	m	m	m	m	73	72	74
	Tertiary	179	179	179	m	m	m	m	182	181	183
Denmark	Below upper secondary	85	86	86	m	87	88	82	82	82	m
	Tertiary	123	124	124	m	124	124	127	126	125	m
Finland	Below upper secondary	97	96	96	95	95	95	94	94	m	m
	Tertiary	148	148	153	153	150	150	148	149	m	m
France	Below upper secondary	84	84	84	m	m	84	84	85	86	85
	Tertiary	149	150	150	m	m	150	146	147	144	149
Germany	Below upper secondary	81	78	79	75	m	77	87	88	88	90
	Tertiary	133	130	135	143	m	143	153	153	156	164
Hungary	Below upper secondary	68	68	70	71	71	74	74	73	73	73
	Tertiary	179	184	200	194	194	205	219	217	215	219
Ireland	Below upper secondary	75	79	m	89	m	76	m	86	m	m
	Tertiary	146	142	m	153	m	144	m	166	m	m
Italy	Below upper secondary	m	58	m	78	m	78	m	79	m	m
	Tertiary	m	127	m	138	m	153	m	165	m	m
Korea	Below upper secondary	m	78	m	m	m	m	67	m	m	m
	Tertiary	m	135	m	m	m	m	141	m	m	m
Luxembourg	Below upper secondary	m	m	m	m	m	78	m	m	m	m
	Tertiary	m	m	m	m	m	145	m	m	m	m
Netherlands	Below upper secondary	83	m	m	m	m	84	m	m	m	m
	Tertiary	141	m	m	m	m	148	m	m	m	m
New Zealand	Below upper secondary	77	76	76	74	74	m	76	75	78	78
	Tertiary	148	136	139	133	133	m	126	129	132	115
Norway	Below upper secondary	85	84	84	m	79	82	78	81	78	m
	Tertiary	138	132	133	m	131	134	128	133	129	m
Poland	Below upper secondary	m	m	m	m	m	m	m	78	m	84
	Tertiary	m	m	m	m	m	m	m	163	m	173
Portugal	Below upper secondary	62	62	62	m	m	m	m	60	67	m
	Tertiary	176	177	178	m	m	m	m	179	177	m
Spain	Below upper secondary	76	80	m	m	78	m	m	85	m	m
	Tertiary	149	144	m	m	129	m	m	132	m	m
Sweden	Below upper secondary	90	89	89	m	86	87	88	87	86	m
	Tertiary	129	130	131	m	131	130	130	127	126	m
Switzerland	Below upper secondary	74	75	76	78	m	77	75	75	76	74
	Tertiary	152	153	151	157	m	156	156	162	156	156
Turkey	Below upper secondary	m	m	m	m	m	m	m	65	69	m
	Tertiary	m	m	m	m	m	m	m	141	149	m
United Kingdom	Below upper secondary	64	65	65	67	67	m	69	67	69	70
	Tertiary	153	157	159	159	159	m	162	158	155	159
United States	Below upper secondary	70	67	65	65	m	66	66	65	67	66
	Tertiary	168	173	166	172	m	172	172	172	175	176
Israel	Below upper secondary	m	m	m	m	m	m	m	m	79	78
	Tertiary	m	m	m	m	m	m	m	m	151	151
Slovenia	Below upper secondary	m	m	m	m	m	m	m	73	m	m
	Tertiary	m	m	m	m	m	m	m	198	m	m

OECD countries / Partner countries

Source: OECD. See Annex 3 for notes (*www.oecd.org/edu/eag2008*).
Please refer to the Reader's Guide for information concerning the symbols replacing missing data.
StatLink ᵐˢᴸ http://dx.doi.org/10.1787/401781614508

Table A9.3.
Trends in differences in earnings between females and males (1997-2006)
Average annual earnings of females as a percentage of earnings of males by level of educational attainment of 25-to-64-year-olds

		1997	1998	1999	2000	2001	2002	2003	2004	2005	2006
Australia	Below upper secondary	60	m	66	m	62	m	m	m	61	m
	Upper secondary and post-secondary non tertiary	62	m	64	m	62	m	m	m	60	m
	Tertiary	62	m	67	m	62	m	m	m	65	m
Austria	Below upper secondary	m	m	m	m	m	m	m	m	57	58
	Upper secondary and post-secondary non tertiary	m	m	m	m	m	m	m	m	60	59
	Tertiary	m	m	m	m	m	m	m	m	62	60
Belgium	Below upper secondary	m	m	m	64	m	65	66	66	67	m
	Upper secondary and post-secondary non tertiary	m	m	m	72	m	72	74	74	75	m
	Tertiary	m	m	m	74	m	76	74	74	73	m
Canada	Below upper secondary	m	52	51	52	51	50	52	52	53	m
	Upper secondary and post-secondary non tertiary	m	59	60	60	59	61	60	59	60	m
	Tertiary	m	61	60	58	58	60	61	61	62	m
Czech Republic	Below upper secondary	66	66	66	m	m	m	m	74	74	73
	Upper secondary and post-secondary non tertiary	69	69	69	m	m	m	m	80	80	80
	Tertiary	66	65	65	m	m	m	m	67	68	67
Denmark	Below upper secondary	73	73	73	m	74	75	73	74	73	m
	Upper secondary and post-secondary non tertiary	72	71	71	m	71	73	71	71	71	m
	Tertiary	68	66	66	m	67	68	67	67	67	m
Finland	Below upper secondary	78	77	77	76	76	76	76	76	m	m
	Upper secondary and post-secondary non tertiary	74	72	72	71	71	72	72	72	m	m
	Tertiary	66	65	62	61	63	64	66	65	m	m
France	Below upper secondary	68	68	68	m	m	70	68	68	68	68
	Upper secondary and post-secondary non tertiary	75	75	75	m	m	77	75	74	75	74
	Tertiary	69	69	69	m	m	70	72	70	70	69
Germany	Below upper secondary	63	74	70	56	m	53	54	54	52	56
	Upper secondary and post-secondary non tertiary	64	67	68	63	m	61	60	60	62	62
	Tertiary	63	68	60	61	m	60	58	60	62	58
Hungary	Below upper secondary	79	80	84	83	83	85	89	89	88	93
	Upper secondary and post-secondary non tertiary	88	86	89	88	88	93	95	96	93	96
	Tertiary	64	63	62	62	62	67	71	72	69	70
Ireland	Below upper secondary	46	48	m	46	m	48	m	49	m	m
	Upper secondary and post-secondary non tertiary	59	63	m	60	m	57	m	59	m	m
	Tertiary	70	70	m	71	m	62	m	61	m	m
Italy	Below upper secondary	m	70	m	76	m	70	m	67	m	m
	Upper secondary and post-secondary non tertiary	m	62	m	65	m	66	m	71	m	m
	Tertiary	m	52	m	62	m	60	m	52	m	m
Korea	Below upper secondary	m	56	m	m	m	m	48	m	m	m
	Upper secondary and post-secondary non tertiary	m	70	m	m	m	m	47	m	m	m
	Tertiary	m	75	m	m	m	m	65	m	m	m
Luxembourg	Below upper secondary	m	m	m	m	m	80	m	m	m	m
	Upper secondary and post-secondary non tertiary	m	m	m	m	m	86	m	m	m	m
	Tertiary	m	m	m	m	m	75	m	m	m	m
Netherlands	Below upper secondary	46	m	m	m	m	49	m	m	m	m
	Upper secondary and post-secondary non tertiary	56	m	m	m	m	58	m	m	m	m
	Tertiary	57	m	m	m	m	62	m	m	m	m
New Zealand	Below upper secondary	52	61	65	61	61	m	65	66	61	72
	Upper secondary and post-secondary non tertiary	62	63	67	64	64	m	63	63	62	63
	Tertiary	60	59	61	67	67	m	62	62	60	64

Note: Data on earnings for individuals in part-time work are excluded for the Czech Republic, Hungary, Luxembourg, Poland and Portugal, while data on part-year earnings are excluded for Belgium, Hungary, Luxembourg, Poland and Portugal.
Source: OECD. See Annex 3 for notes (*www.oecd.org/edu/eag2008*).
Please refer to the Reader's Guide for information concerning the symbols replacing missing data.
StatLink http://dx.doi.org/10.1787/401781614508

A9

Table A9.3. *(continued)*
Trends in differences in earnings between females and males (1997-2006)
Average annual earnings of females as a percentage of earnings of males by level of educational attainment of 25-to-64-year-olds

		1997	1998	1999	2000	2001	2002	2003	2004	2005	2006
Norway	Below upper secondary	60	60	61	m	63	62	65	65	65	m
	Upper secondary and post-secondary non tertiary	61	61	62	m	62	63	65	64	63	m
	Tertiary	63	62	62	m	63	64	66	65	63	m
Poland	Below upper secondary	m	m	m	m	m	m	m	71	m	71
	Upper secondary and post-secondary non tertiary	m	m	m	m	m	m	m	81	m	81
	Tertiary	m	m	m	m	m	m	m	68	m	69
Portugal	Below upper secondary	72	71	71	m	m	m	m	74	73	m
	Upper secondary and post-secondary non tertiary	69	69	69	m	m	m	m	69	71	m
	Tertiary	66	66	65	m	m	m	m	67	67	m
Spain	Below upper secondary	60	61	m	m	58	m	m	63	m	m
	Upper secondary and post-secondary non tertiary	72	76	m	m	71	m	m	68	m	m
	Tertiary	68	69	m	m	64	m	m	73	m	m
Sweden	Below upper secondary	73	74	74	m	74	74	75	75	74	m
	Upper secondary and post-secondary non tertiary	72	72	73	m	71	72	73	73	73	m
	Tertiary	67	66	67	m	65	67	68	69	68	m
Switzerland	Below upper secondary	51	51	53	51	m	51	52	54	53	55
	Upper secondary and post-secondary non tertiary	55	57	58	57	m	53	54	53	56	56
	Tertiary	60	61	62	62	m	59	60	60	60	65
Turkey	Below upper secondary	m	m	m	m	m	m	m	52	47	m
	Upper secondary and post-secondary non tertiary	m	m	m	m	m	m	m	75	78	m
	Tertiary	m	m	m	m	m	m	m	89	78	m
United Kingdom	Below upper secondary	47	50	51	50	50	m	52	52	50	49
	Upper secondary and post-secondary non tertiary	53	53	53	52	52	m	54	53	52	53
	Tertiary	60	62	63	64	64	m	64	63	66	63
United States	Below upper secondary	53	60	59	59	m	63	67	63	63	65
	Upper secondary and post-secondary non tertiary	59	62	61	60	m	63	64	63	65	65
	Tertiary	59	58	59	56	m	58	61	59	59	60
Israel	Below upper secondary	m	m	m	m	m	m	m	m	57	56
	Upper secondary and post-secondary non tertiary	m	m	m	m	m	m	m	m	59	64
	Tertiary	m	m	m	m	m	m	m	m	58	57
Slovenia	Below upper secondary	m	m	m	m	m	m	m	84	m	m
	Upper secondary and post-secondary non tertiary	m	m	m	m	m	m	m	88	m	m
	Tertiary	m	m	m	m	m	m	m	77	m	m

OECD countries (Norway–United States); Partner countries (Israel, Slovenia)

Note: Data on earnings for individuals in part-time work are excluded for the Czech Republic, Hungary, Luxembourg, Poland and Portugal, while data on part-year earnings are excluded for Belgium, Hungary, Luxembourg, Poland and Portugal.
Source: OECD. See Annex 3 for notes (*www.oecd.org/edu/eag2008*).
Please refer to the Reader's Guide for information concerning the symbols replacing missing data.
StatLink ⣿⣥ http://dx.doi.org/10.1787/401781614508

Table A9.4a.
Distribution of the 25-to-64-year-old population by level of earnings and educational attainment
(2006 or latest available year)

			Level of earnings					
			At or below half of the median	More than half the median but at or below the median	More than the median but at or below 1.5 times the median	More than 1.5 times the median but at or below 2.0 times the median	More than twice the median	All categories
			%	%	%	%	%	%
Australia	2005	Below upper secondary	24.3	46.3	21.1	5.6	2.8	100
		Upper secondary and post-secondary non-tertiary	14.5	39.2	29.9	10.0	6.4	100
		Tertiary-type B education	12.9	32.6	35.2	11.3	8.0	100
		Tertiary-type A and advanced research programmes	9.1	20.5	33.1	19.5	17.9	100
		All levels of education	15.5	35.1	28.9	11.6	8.9	100
Austria	2006	Below upper secondary	35.7	40.9	16.9	4.6	1.8	100
		Upper secondary and post-secondary non-tertiary	21.2	29.0	29.1	11.9	8.9	100
		Tertiary-type B education	11.6	17.4	30.6	25.0	15.3	100
		Tertiary-type A and advanced research programmes	15.9	12.6	17.7	18.4	35.3	100
		All levels of education	22.0	28.1	26.1	12.5	11.2	100
Belgium	2005	Below upper secondary	11.4	60.5	25.9	1.6	0.6	100
		Upper secondary and post-secondary non-tertiary	5.5	55.8	33.5	4.0	1.3	100
		Tertiary-type B education	1.7	39.4	49.9	6.7	2.2	100
		Tertiary-type A and advanced research programmes	1.5	18.5	44.5	19.0	16.5	100
		All levels of education	5.4	47.1	37.0	6.6	3.9	100
Canada	2005	Below upper secondary	37.8	31.7	16.6	8.2	5.8	100
		Upper secondary and post-secondary non-tertiary	28.2	27.5	21.4	11.3	11.5	100
		Tertiary-type B education	23.3	23.7	23.8	14.8	14.4	100
		Tertiary-type A and advanced research programmes	18.3	16.2	17.3	17.1	31.2	100
		All levels of education	25.6	24.5	20.7	13.1	16.2	100
Czech Republic	2006	Below upper secondary	17.5	65.3	14.1	1.9	1.2	100
		Upper secondary and post-secondary non-tertiary	5.0	50.0	33.5	7.8	3.6	100
		Tertiary-type B education	0.9	36.4	43.1	11.4	8.1	100
		Tertiary-type A and advanced research programmes	0.3	10.5	39.3	21.5	28.4	100
		All levels of education	5.2	44.8	33.0	9.5	7.4	100
Denmark	2005	Below upper secondary	25.1	41.5	26.8	4.4	2.2	100
		Upper secondary and post-secondary non-tertiary	15.7	36.4	35.9	7.7	4.4	100
		Tertiary-type B education	12.2	23.8	43.7	13.8	6.5	100
		Tertiary-type A and advanced research programmes	13.2	21.1	38.8	15.0	12.0	100
		All levels of education	17.3	32.7	34.9	9.1	5.9	100
Finland	2004	Below upper secondary	26.2	36.7	27.4	6.8	2.8	100
		Upper secondary and post-secondary non-tertiary	22.1	36.4	30.9	7.8	2.9	100
		Tertiary-type B education	13.8	27.2	39.6	12.3	7.1	100
		Tertiary-type A and advanced research programmes	11.3	16.4	27.4	22.1	22.8	100
		All levels of education	19.2	30.8	31.1	11.3	7.7	100
France	2006	Below upper secondary	17.4	51.0	22.7	5.9	2.9	100
		Upper secondary and post-secondary non-tertiary	10.6	44.3	29.9	10.1	5.1	100
		Tertiary-type B education	6.3	27.4	35.6	17.8	12.9	100
		Tertiary-type A and advanced research programmes	7.0	18.9	26.8	20.6	26.6	100
		All levels of education	11.2	39.5	28.2	11.8	9.3	100
Germany	2006	Below upper secondary	30.7	31.4	26.8	9.2	1.9	100
		Upper secondary and post-secondary non-tertiary	23.5	34.8	28.8	8.6	4.3	100
		Tertiary-type B education	14.1	27.2	32.8	15.2	10.8	100
		Tertiary-type A and advanced research programmes	11.1	17.7	24.3	19.9	27.1	100
		All levels of education	20.5	29.5	27.7	12.0	10.3	100

OECD countries

Source: OECD. See Annex 3 for notes (*www.oecd.org/edu/eag2008*).

Please refer to the Reader's Guide for information concerning the symbols replacing missing data.

StatLink ᯲ᒲᓬᒲ http://dx.doi.org/10.1787/401781614508

A9

Table A9.4a. *(continued-1)*
Distribution of the 25-to-64-year-old population by level of earnings and educational attainment
(2006 or latest available year)

			Level of earnings					
			At or below half of the median	More than half the median but at or below the median	More than the median but at or below 1.5 times the median	More than 1.5 times the median but at or below 2.0 times the median	More than twice the median	All categories
			%	%	%	%	%	%
Hungary	2006	Below upper secondary	15.7	65.2	14.8	2.8	1.4	100
		Upper secondary and post-secondary non-tertiary	11.8	45.4	25.4	9.8	7.6	100
		Tertiary-type B education	8.5	28.9	30.7	13.9	18.0	100
		Tertiary-type A and advanced research programmes	2.2	7.7	23.5	25.2	41.3	100
		All levels of education	10.2	39.8	23.2	12.3	14.6	100
Ireland	2004	Below upper secondary	32.5	31.2	23.3	8.1	4.9	100
		Upper secondary and post-secondary non-tertiary	19.3	36.5	24.9	11.6	7.7	100
		Tertiary-type B education	12.1	30.7	26.4	16.0	14.8	100
		Tertiary-type A and advanced research programmes	8.3	17.3	20.8	18.9	34.7	100
		All levels of education	20.3	29.7	23.5	12.6	13.9	100
Italy	2004	Below upper secondary	19.5	44.4	22.3	6.4	7.4	100
		Upper secondary and post-secondary non-tertiary	10.3	33.8	32.1	9.8	14.1	100
		Tertiary-type B education	m	m	m	m	m	m
		Tertiary-type A and advanced research programmes	7.8	17.9	28.7	13.7	31.9	100
		All levels of education	13.8	36.2	27.5	8.9	13.6	100
Korea	2003	Below upper secondary	31.5	42.8	19.0	2.5	4.2	100
		Upper secondary and post-secondary non-tertiary	15.7	34.9	29.6	8.6	11.2	100
		Tertiary-type B education	14.5	30.8	31.0	11.3	12.4	100
		Tertiary-type A and advanced research programmes	8.6	17.5	29.7	17.1	27.0	100
		All levels of education	17.8	32.1	27.1	9.5	13.5	100
Luxembourg	2002	Below upper secondary	12.1	60.1	21.6	4.9	1.3	100
		Upper secondary and post-secondary non-tertiary	2.3	52.2	28.0	11.7	5.8	100
		Tertiary-type B education	0.6	28.6	41.7	17.2	11.8	100
		Tertiary-type A and advanced research programmes	0.0	14.4	36.6	24.9	24.1	100
		All levels of education	3.5	45.4	30.0	13.0	8.2	100
Netherlands	2002	Below upper secondary	26.9	37.9	29.0	5.0	1.3	100
		Upper secondary and post-secondary non-tertiary	17.4	36.5	33.2	9.3	3.6	100
		All tertiary education	8.3	20.8	30.5	21.9	18.6	100
		All levels of education	17.4	32.6	31.3	11.6	7.1	100
New Zealand	2006	Below upper secondary	22.7	46.3	22.1	6.4	2.4	100
		Upper secondary and post-secondary non-tertiary	17.4	32.0	29.8	12.9	7.9	100
		Tertiary-type B education	18.5	33.7	28.2	12.0	7.6	100
		Tertiary-type A and advanced research programmes	10.6	23.6	27.9	19.0	18.8	100
		All levels of education	17.1	33.2	27.4	12.8	9.4	100
Norway	2005	Below upper secondary	30.3	38.6	24.2	4.7	2.2	100
		Upper secondary and post-secondary non-tertiary	17.6	35.1	33.6	8.9	4.8	100
		Tertiary-type B education	8.1	15.8	35.1	22.6	18.4	100
		Tertiary-type A and advanced research programmes	12.8	22.8	39.5	13.0	12.0	100
		All levels of education	18.8	31.4	33.3	9.6	6.9	100
Poland	2006	Below upper secondary	19.2	55.2	17.7	5.4	2.5	100
		Upper secondary and post-secondary non-tertiary	13.6	45.8	26.2	8.8	5.6	100
		Tertiary-type B education	5.0	26.9	27.9	15.2	25.1	100
		Tertiary-type A and advanced research programmes	1.5	20.7	34.5	18.9	24.5	100
		All levels of education	10.5	39.2	27.6	11.4	11.3	100

Source: OECD. See Annex 3 for notes (*www.oecd.org/edu/eag2008*).
Please refer to the Reader's Guide for information concerning the symbols replacing missing data.
StatLink 🔗 http://dx.doi.org/10.1787/401781614508

Table A9.4a. *(continued-2)*
Distribution of the 25-to-64-year-old population by level of earnings and educational attainment (2006 or latest available year)

A9

			Level of earnings					
			At or below half of the median	More than half the median but at or below the median	More than the median but at or below 1.5 times the median	More than 1.5 times the median but at or below 2.0 times the median	More than twice the median	All categories
			%	%	%	%	%	%
Portugal	2005	Below upper secondary	0.1	62.2	23.3	7.3	7.2	100
		Upper secondary and post-secondary non-tertiary	0.0	34.0	28.2	14.3	23.5	100
		Tertiary-type B education	m	m	m	m	m	m
		Tertiary-type A and advanced research programmes	0.0	7.7	17.5	19.0	55.9	100
		All levels of education	0.0	50.0	23.4	10.1	16.5	100
Spain	2004	Below upper secondary	12.8	50.8	29.0	5.2	2.2	100
		Upper secondary and post-secondary non-tertiary	9.3	42.6	31.6	10.2	6.3	100
		Tertiary-type B education	7.8	43.8	30.6	10.6	7.1	100
		Tertiary-type A and advanced research programmes	3.3	22.8	33.2	19.9	20.7	100
		All levels of education	9.1	41.0	30.9	10.7	8.4	100
Sweden	2005	Below upper secondary	19.3	43.4	30.7	4.8	1.8	100
		Upper secondary and post-secondary non-tertiary	11.2	41.7	34.6	8.1	4.3	100
		Tertiary-type B education	13.1	31.2	39.1	11.4	5.2	100
		Tertiary-type A and advanced research programmes	10.5	22.5	36.1	14.9	16.0	100
		All levels of education	12.9	37.1	34.5	9.2	6.3	100
Switzerland	2006	Below upper secondary	30.8	50.4	16.6	1.5	0.7	100
		Upper secondary and post-secondary non-tertiary	21.5	35.1	32.4	7.6	3.4	100
		Tertiary-type B education	8.7	20.9	39.9	21.5	9.1	100
		Tertiary-type A and advanced research programmes	8.7	18.5	26.4	24.5	21.8	100
		All levels of education	18.2	31.5	30.1	12.3	7.9	100
Turkey	2005	Below upper secondary	27.8	38.9	21.2	7.3	4.8	100
		Upper secondary and post-secondary non-tertiary	12.1	26.7	30.7	18.7	11.8	100
		Tertiary-type B education	8.5	13.3	31.1	29.3	17.8	100
		Tertiary-type A and advanced research programmes	5.7	4.5	29.9	32.3	27.6	100
		All levels of education	20.0	30.0	25.2	14.5	10.2	100
United Kingdom	2006	Below upper secondary	38.6	41.3	14.0	4.2	1.9	100
		Upper secondary and post-secondary non-tertiary	25.7	32.7	24.3	10.5	6.8	100
		Tertiary-type B education	15.7	24.7	26.5	20.1	13.0	100
		Tertiary-type A and advanced research programmes	11.8	13.6	19.6	24.1	30.9	100
		All levels of education	22.2	28.4	22.3	14.1	12.9	100
United States	2006	Below upper secondary	42.2	41.9	10.8	3.1	1.9	100
		Upper secondary and post-secondary non-tertiary	23.8	38.6	21.4	9.2	7.0	100
		Tertiary-type B education	17.0	34.5	24.4	14.5	9.6	100
		Tertiary-type A and advanced research programmes	11.6	20.6	23.2	16.5	28.0	100
		All levels of education	20.5	31.8	21.2	11.7	14.8	100
Israel	2006	Below upper secondary	21.8	55.5	14.9	4.5	3.3	100
		Upper secondary and post-secondary non-tertiary	15.7	44.2	22.1	8.6	9.5	100
		Tertiary-type B education	15.3	37.0	21.7	11.8	14.2	100
		Tertiary-type A and advanced research programmes	11.2	24.0	20.3	13.3	31.1	100
		All levels of education	14.4	35.6	20.8	10.7	18.4	100

OECD countries (rows: Portugal, Spain, Sweden, Switzerland, Turkey, United Kingdom, United States)
Partner countries (row: Israel)

Source: OECD. See Annex 3 for notes (*www.oecd.org/edu/eag2008*).
Please refer to the Reader's Guide for information concerning the symbols replacing missing data.
StatLink ᔟᓵᔉᔍ http://dx.doi.org/10.1787/401781614508

WHAT ARE THE INCENTIVES TO INVEST IN EDUCATION?

This indicator examines incentives to invest in education by estimating the rate of return to education. The financial returns to education are calculated for investments undertaken as a part of initial education, as well as for a hypothetical 40-year-old who decides to return to education in mid-career. Private and public returns to education are given for upper secondary and tertiary education.

Key results

Chart A10.1. Private internal rates of return (IRR) for an individual obtaining upper secondary or post-secondary non-tertiary education, ISCED 3/4 and for an individual obtaining a university-level degree, ISCED 5/6 (2004)

☐ Private IRR for an individual immediately acquiring the next level of education: upper secondary or post-secondary non-tertiary education, ISCED 3/4

▲ Private IRR for an individual immediately acquiring the next level of education: tertiary level education, ISCED 5/6

In most countries, the rate of return to tertiary education is higher than for upper secondary or post-secondary non-tertiary education, except in Denmark, Spain, Sweden, the United Kingdom and the United States, where both males and females achieve returns below those for upper secondary or post-secondary non-tertiary education. Incentives to invest in tertiary education thus appear to be favourable in most countries. In all countries, the expected return to education exceeds 5% except for females investing in tertiary education in Germany and Sweden and for females investing in upper secondary or post-secondary non-tertiary education in Korea.

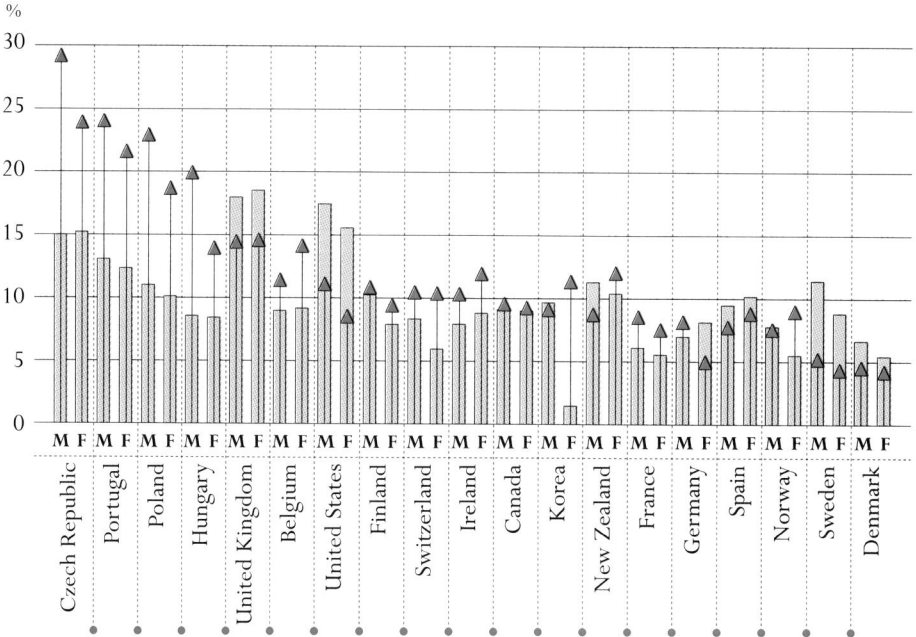

M: Male

F: Female

Countries are ranked by descending order of the private IRR for males immediately acquiring a tertiary level of education.

Source: OECD. Tables A10.1 and A10.2. See Annex 3 for notes (*www.oecd.org/edu/eag2008*).

StatLink ᵃᵢₛᴸ http://dx.doi.org/10.1787/401828118341

- Returns to education are largely driven by the earnings premium. That earnings differentials are the key drivers of returns to education suggest that it is important for educational policies to monitor and match supply to demand for education. At the tertiary level of education there is generally a trade-off between taxes and the direct costs of education, with low or no tuition fees associated with more progressive taxation when entering the labour market.

- The returns to upper secondary education or post-secondary non-tertiary education vary between 6.1% and 18% for males and 5.6% and 18.5% for females, with marginally lower returns for females. The Czech Republic, the United Kingdom and the United States are among the countries showing the highest returns for both males and females.

- On average across OECD countries, a tertiary education yields a 12 and 11% return for males and females, respectively, and returns are substantial in the Czech Republic, Hungary, Poland and Portugal. The rewards for tertiary education are relatively small in Germany, Norway, Spain, and Sweden where returns range from 5 to 8%. This suggests comparatively weaker incentives to continue education.

- At age 40, the return to an upper secondary education exceeds 13% for both males and females in the Czech Republic, Portugal and the United States. The expected rewards are large even though the individual foregoes earnings during the period of study. The rewards for investing in tertiary education are generally higher than for upper secondary education at age 40. In many countries, the returns to investment in education in mid-career are substantial enough to motivate the investment without government intervention.

- Public rates of return are higher for tertiary than for upper secondary education both for initial education and at age 40. On average across OECD countries, a tertiary education generates a return of 11% for males and 9% for females when part of initial education. At age 40, the public returns for males and females are 9.5 and 6.6%, respectively.

A10

Policy context

Economic returns to education are a key driver for individuals' decisions to invest time and money in education beyond compulsory schooling. The monetary benefits of completing higher levels of education motivate individuals to postpone consumption today for future rewards. From a policy perspective, it is crucial to be aware of the economic incentives in order to understand the flow of individuals through the education system.

A problem facing policy makers is the fact that changes in education policies generally take some time to have an impact on the labour market. Large shifts in the demand for education can drive earnings and returns up considerably before the supply catches up. This provides a strong signal both to individuals and to the education system about the need for additional investment.

Apart from the earnings differentials, which are largely determined by the labour market, major components of the returns to education are directly linked to policy: access to education, taxes and the costs of education for the individual. Very high private returns suggest that education may need to be expanded by increasing access and by making loans more readily available to individuals rather than by lowering the costs of education. Low returns indicate instead that incentives to invest in education are not in place, either because education is not rewarded in the labour market, or because costs, in terms of tuition fees, foregone earnings and taxation, are relatively high.

Economic benefits of education flow not only to the individual but also to society through additional taxes when the individual enters the labour market. The public returns to education, which take into account the costs and benefits of education for governments, provide additional information on the overall returns to education. In shaping policies it is important to consider the balance between private and public returns. This indicator takes a closer look at incentives to invest in education from the individual and the public perspective as well as incentives for males and females at different educational levels.

Evidence and explanations

Rates of return to investment in education

The relationship between education and earnings can be evaluated in an investment analysis framework. An individual incurs costs when investing in education (direct costs such as tuition fees and indirect costs such as foregone earnings while in school). The overall benefits of this investment can be assessed by estimating the economic rate of return to the investment, which measures the degree to which the costs of attaining higher levels of education translates into higher levels of earnings. The measure of return used here is the internal rate of return, basically the interest rate that an individual can expect to receive on the investment made by spending time and money to obtain an education. In this framework, the interest rate is raised to the level at which the economic benefits equal the cost of the investment. The interest rate at this point replicates the interest rate one would receive, for instance, by putting the same amount of money in the bank at the time of the investment decision.

Investments in education are not risk-free, and the interest rate applied should reflect this by means of additional percentage points. As shown in Indicator A9, variations in earnings outcomes are quite substantial within different educational groups; this uncertainty needs to be

A10

compensated for by a higher yield for those investing in education compared, for instance, to government bonds, which are generally used as a benchmark for a risk-free interest rate. In most countries, this would translate into rates of return above 5% in order to motivate investment in further education.

This indicator is analysed from two points of view: rates of return to the individual, which reflect only the individual's earnings and costs, and rates of return to government (public rate of return). The return to government includes the collection of higher income taxes and social contributions, as well as the costs borne by the government for educating the individual. These private and public returns are calculated for 19 OECD countries. The methodology of calculating rates of returns to education has changed since last year's *Education at a Glance*. Therefore, the current rates should not be compared with previous editions of *Education at a Glance* (see the section on definitions and methodologies).

Incentives for the individual to invest in education

The different costs and benefits of education make up the components of the internal rate of return and as such describe the key drivers of the returns in different countries. In order to visualise the main factors influencing the returns to education, each cost and benefit is discounted back in time with the internal rate of return. The proportionate impact of each component and the internal rates of returns are shown in Table A10.1 for investing in upper secondary or post-secondary non-tertiary education, starting from an original lower secondary level of education, and in Table A10.2 for investing in tertiary education up to an advanced research qualification, starting from an upper secondary level of education.

The returns to attaining upper secondary education or post-secondary non-tertiary education vary between 6.1 and 18% for males and 5.6 and 18.5% for females, with marginally lower returns for females. The Czech Republic, the United Kingdom and the United States are among the countries showing the highest returns to upper secondary education or post-secondary non-tertiary education for both males and females. The benefits of the additional education are quite different, however. In the United Kingdom and the United States they are largely a greater earnings potential, whereas in the Czech Republic the main benefit is lower unemployment rates.

In Denmark, France and Germany, an upper secondary or post-secondary non-tertiary education is less rewarded by the labour market, with returns for males at or below 7%. Returns for females are 6% or less in Denmark, France, Korea, Norway and Switzerland. Private direct costs for education are generally negligible at the upper secondary or post-secondary non-tertiary level so that the returns largely hinge on labour market outcomes. Policies to enhance incentives to invest would therefore in most circumstances involve tax-related interventions or in cases where tertiary education shows higher rewards, increased access to higher education.

Chart A10.2 shows the components of the rate of return to tertiary education for males in different countries. Relative to upper secondary and post-secondary non-tertiary education, the impact of unemployment benefits is less pronounced than the earnings differential, and taxes and the direct costs of education play a substantially larger role.

As with upper secondary and post-secondary non-tertiary education, the returns to tertiary education are largely driven by earnings premiums; other components are less important in explaining differences among OECD countries. This suggests that education policy needs to monitor and match the supply of and demand for education. The components illustrated in Chart A10.2 show, however, the importance of specific factors in different countries and thus indicate areas in which policy could help to improve incentives.

Tertiary education brings substantial rewards in the Czech Republic, Hungary, Poland and Portugal, with returns ranging from close to 20 to almost 30%. With tertiary attainment levels in the 25-to-64-year-old population in these countries ranging from 13 to 18%, well below the OECD average of 27%, increasing access to tertiary education appears warranted to bring supply more in line with demand. The rewards for tertiary education are relatively low in Germany, Norway, Spain, and Sweden where returns range from 5 to 8%, an indication of weak incentives to continue education. Income taxes and social contributions help to drive down returns in all countries but Spain. The pattern is similar for females in most countries (Table A10.2).

Chart A10.2. Components of the internal rate of return for a male obtaining tertiary education, ISCED 5/6 (2004)

Cash flow components discounted by the internal rate of return, in order to provide a comparable picture of their impact when costs equal benefits.

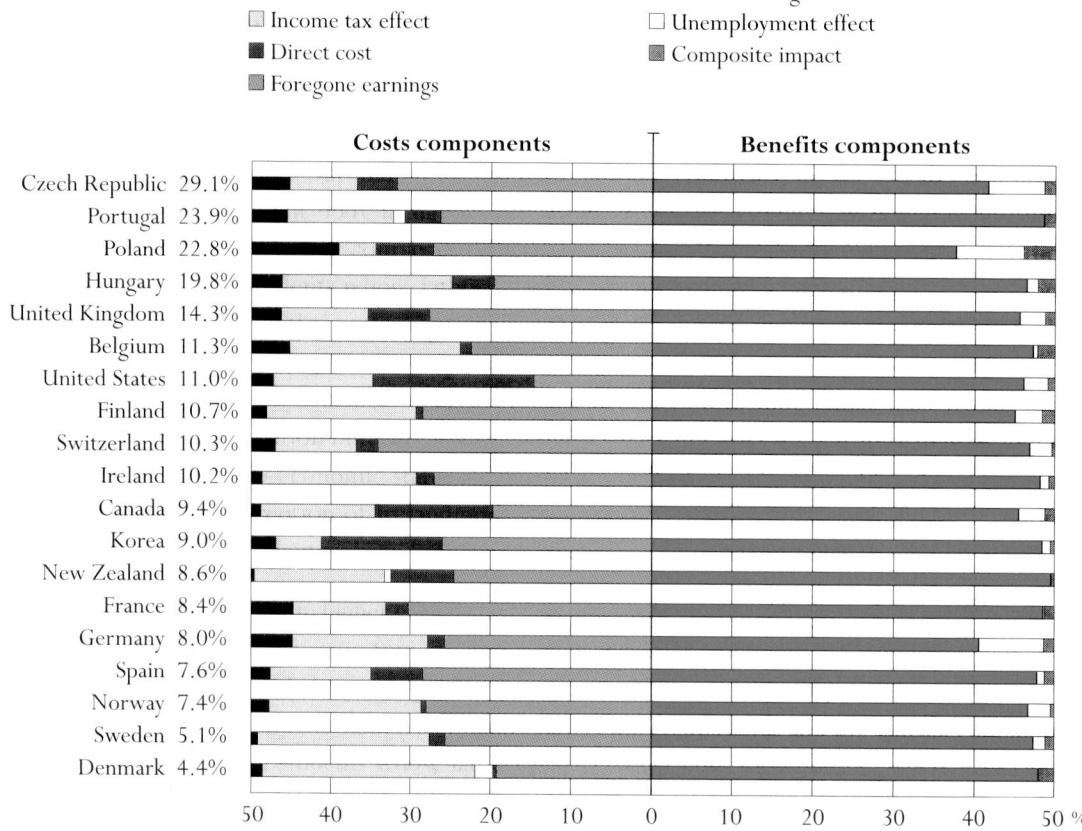

Countries are ranked by descending order of the private IRR for males immediately acquiring tertiary level of education.
Source: OECD. Tables A10.1 and A10.2. See Annex 3 for notes (*www.oecd.org/edu/eag2008*).
StatLink ⣿⣿ http://dx.doi.org/10.1787/401828118341

A10

There is generally a trade-off between taxes and the direct costs of education (tuition fees). Countries with low or no tuition fees typically let individuals pay back public subsidies later in life through progressive tax schemes. In countries in which a larger portion of the investment falls on the individual (in the form of tuition fees) a larger portion of the earnings differential is also accrued by the individual. Therefore, the stakes are higher in Canada, Korea and the United States, where tuition fees represent a large proportion of the investment cost. There is no straightforward link between tuition fees and rates of returns to education, which indicates that supply of and demand for tertiary-educated individuals is the main determinant.

Box A10.1. **Estimating returns to education**

There are essentially two main approaches to estimating the financial returns to education, founded either on investment theory, from the finance literature, or on an econometric specification, from the labour economics literature.

The basis for an investment approach is the discount rate (the time-value of money) which makes it possible to compare costs or payments (cash flows) over time. The discount rate can be estimated either by raising it to the level at which financial benefits equal costs, which is then the internal rate of return, or by setting the discount rate at a required rate that takes into consideration the risk involved in the investment, which is then a net present value calculation with the gains expressed in monetary units.

The econometric approach taken in labour economics originates from Mincer (1974) in which returns to education are estimated in a regression relating earnings to years of education, labour market experience and tenure. This basic model has been extended in subsequent work to include educational levels, employment effects and additional control variables such as gender, work characteristics (part-time, firm size, contracting arrangements, utilisation of skills, etc.) to arrive at a "net" effect of education on earnings.

The main difference between the two approaches is that the investment approach is forward-looking (although historical data are typically used) whereas an econometric approach tries to establish the actual contribution of education to earnings by controlling for other factors that can influence earnings and returns. This difference has implications for the assumptions and for interpretations of returns to education. As the investment approach focuses on the incentives at the time of the investment decision, it is prudent not to remove the effect of (controlling for) other factors as these are part of the returns that an individual can expect to receive when deciding to invest in education. In other words, it is difficult to foresee one's labour market experience, tenure with a specific firm, whether one will work part-time, for a big firm, in the public sector, or in a job which does not call for one's skills. Gender will of course be known at the time of the investment decision and is an important component in investment analysis.

Depending on the impact of the control variables, how steep the earnings curves are, and how cash flows are distributed over time, the results of the two approaches can diverge quite substantially. Depending on other underlying assumptions, returns may differ between and within a class of models as well. For instance, cash flows can be calculated differently and, depending on the method chosen, returns will vary to some degree. It is therefore generally not advisable to compare rates of return from different studies. The use of data systematically extracted from comparable sources allows a reliable cross-country comparison, even though the rates of return might differ slightly with another approach.

A10

Chart A10.3. Private internal rate of return for a female obtaining higher education at age 40 (2004)

■ ... if the foregone earnings are compensated by an arbitrary public subsidy amounting to 50% of the level she could have earned at a lower level of education

☐ ... if the foregone earnings are at a lower level of education

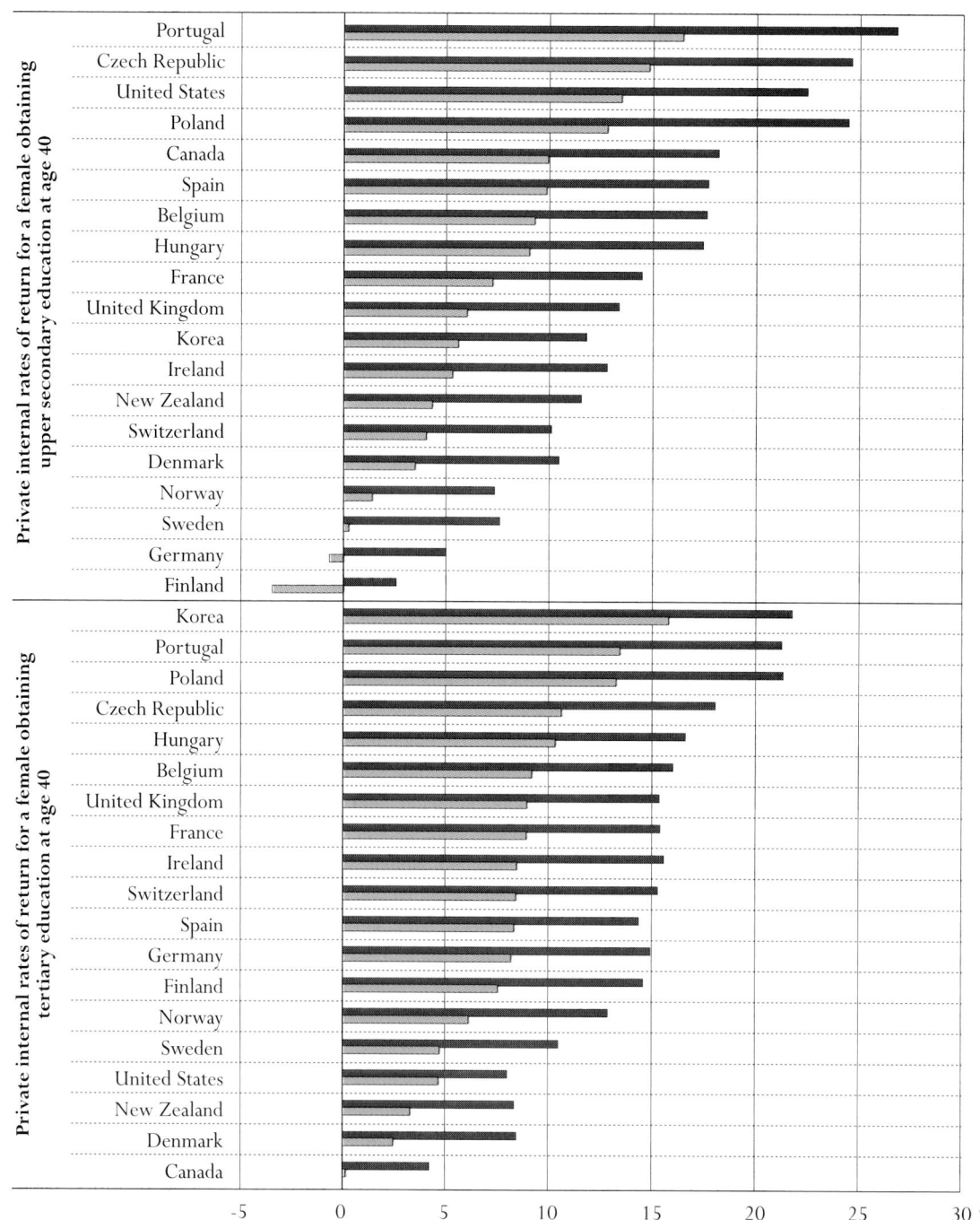

Countries are ranked in descending order of the private IRR for females acquiring a higher level of education at age 40, if the foregone earnings are at a lower level of education.
Source: OECD. Tables A10.3 and A10.4. See Annex 3 for notes (*www.oecd.org/edu/eag2008*).
StatLink ⫘ http://dx.doi.org/10.1787/401828118341

Investing in education at age 40

It is becoming increasingly important to upgrade skills and knowledge throughout working life to remain attractive in the labour market. Investment in education is not only a matter of initial education at a young age but is equally important for older workers. Tables A10.3 and A10.4 provide the returns to education undertaken at age 40 on a full-time basis for three years at the upper secondary or post-secondary non-tertiary level of education and for four years at the tertiary level. For those employed, foregone earnings constitute a major component of the costs associated with returning to education on a full-time basis. For a broad view of potential outcomes, three cases are examined: *i)* the individual bears the direct costs of tuition and foregoes earnings (net of taxes) while studying; *ii)* foregone earnings are compensated by an arbitrary public subsidy amounting to 50% of the level the individual could have earned at his/her current level of education; and *iii)* foregone earnings are compensated by a public subsidy equal to unemployment benefits.

Table A10.3 shows the returns an individual can expect to receive from upper secondary education at age 40. Most countries have incentives for returning to education at age 40 even if the individual works and entirely foregoes his/her earnings. The rate of return for both males and females exceeds 13% in the Czech Republic, Portugal and the United States; therefore, expected rewards are large even if the individual sacrifices earnings during the period of study. Returns are substantially lower, below 4% for both males and females, in Denmark, Finland, Norway and Sweden, largely because of high employment rates and earnings among those with below upper secondary education. The incentives improve considerably in most countries if foregone earnings are compensated by a public subsidy of 50% or if the government steps in and pay a subsidy amounting to unemployment benefits during the period of study.

The rewards for investing in tertiary education at age 40 are generally higher than for upper secondary education (Table A10.4). Only in Canada, Denmark and New Zealand are the returns for males and females below 4.5%. If foregone earnings are compensated by a public subsidy of 50%, returns improve everywhere to above 8%, except for females in Canada. Females are typically disadvantaged in the labour market in terms of employment owing, among other things, to cultural differences and child-rearing responsibilities. In some cases, this leaves females with an outdated stock of human capital because of labour market interruptions.

Chart A10.3 provides the financial incentives for females to return to upper secondary and to tertiary education for three and four years, respectively. As for males, the returns to a tertiary degree are generally higher in most countries. With few exceptions, they exceed 5% even if the individual foregoes all earnings. In Canada, Denmark, New Zealand, Sweden and the United States, the returns are less attractive, but in most countries they are substantial enough to motivate an investment in the absence of any government intervention.

For upper secondary education the financial returns are below 5% in Denmark, New Zealand, Norway, Sweden and Switzerland; and negative in Finland and Germany. Even if foregone earnings are compensated by 50%, the returns for a female in Finland are below 5%; this suggests that additional efforts are needed to encourage females at age 40 to invest in upper secondary education. For the majority of countries, however, the rewards are sizeable. In the Czech Republic, Poland, Portugal and the United States, the rate of return is well above 10%.

In most countries there appears to be relatively little need to improve incentives to invest in education at an older age (for both males and females). In a few countries, government subsidies in one form or another might be needed to encourage older workers to invest in education.

For an individual outside the labour market (non-employed), the foregone earnings are essentially zero. In this case, the rate of return to returning to education is generally extremely favourable in all countries. As skills requirements are constantly increasing and as staying attractive to the labour market becomes increasingly important for employment, the main message for older workers and particularly those outside the labour market is that it is not too late to invest in education at mid-career and that there are generally substantial rewards for doing so. Providing older workers with opportunities to return to education and providing information about the benefits of such a decision seem to be important areas for policy.

Public rate of return to investments in education

The public internal rate of return is one way of examining the effect on public-sector accounts of individuals' decisions to invest in education and the effect of policies that affect these investments. Similarly, to warrant an intervention by governments to improve private rates of return to education, it is important to consider public returns in order to have a complete picture of overall returns to education.

For the public sector, the costs of education include direct expenditures on education (such as direct payment of teachers' salaries, direct payments for the construction of school buildings, buying textbooks, etc.) and public-private transfers (such as public subsidies to households for scholarships and other grants and to other private entities for provision of training at the workplace, etc.). The public costs of education also include income tax revenues on students' foregone earnings. The benefits include increased revenue from income taxes on higher wages and social insurance payments.

In practice, raising levels of education will give rise to a complex set of fiscal effects on the benefit side, beyond the effects of revenue growth based on wages and payments to government. For instance, better educated individuals generally have better health, which lowers public expenditure on provision of health care and thus public expenditure. As earnings generally rise with educational attainment, there is more consumption of goods and services among the more educated, and this gives rise to fiscal effects beyond income tax and social security contributions. However, tax and expenditure data on these indirect effects of education are not readily available for inclusion in rate-of-return calculations.

Tables A10.5 and A10.6 show the public returns for individuals who obtain upper secondary education and tertiary education as part of initial education and at age 40, respectively. Chart A10.4 summarises the public returns to investment in tertiary education for both females and males. The results show that, for tertiary education during initial education, the public rate of return is generally higher than for upper secondary education. There are some exceptions. In Denmark, the return to upper secondary education is close to 10 percentage points higher than the return to tertiary education among males and in Denmark, Germany, Sweden and the United States, upper secondary education yields higher returns for females (Table A10.5).

Chart A10.4. Public internal rates of return for an individual obtaining higher education (2004)

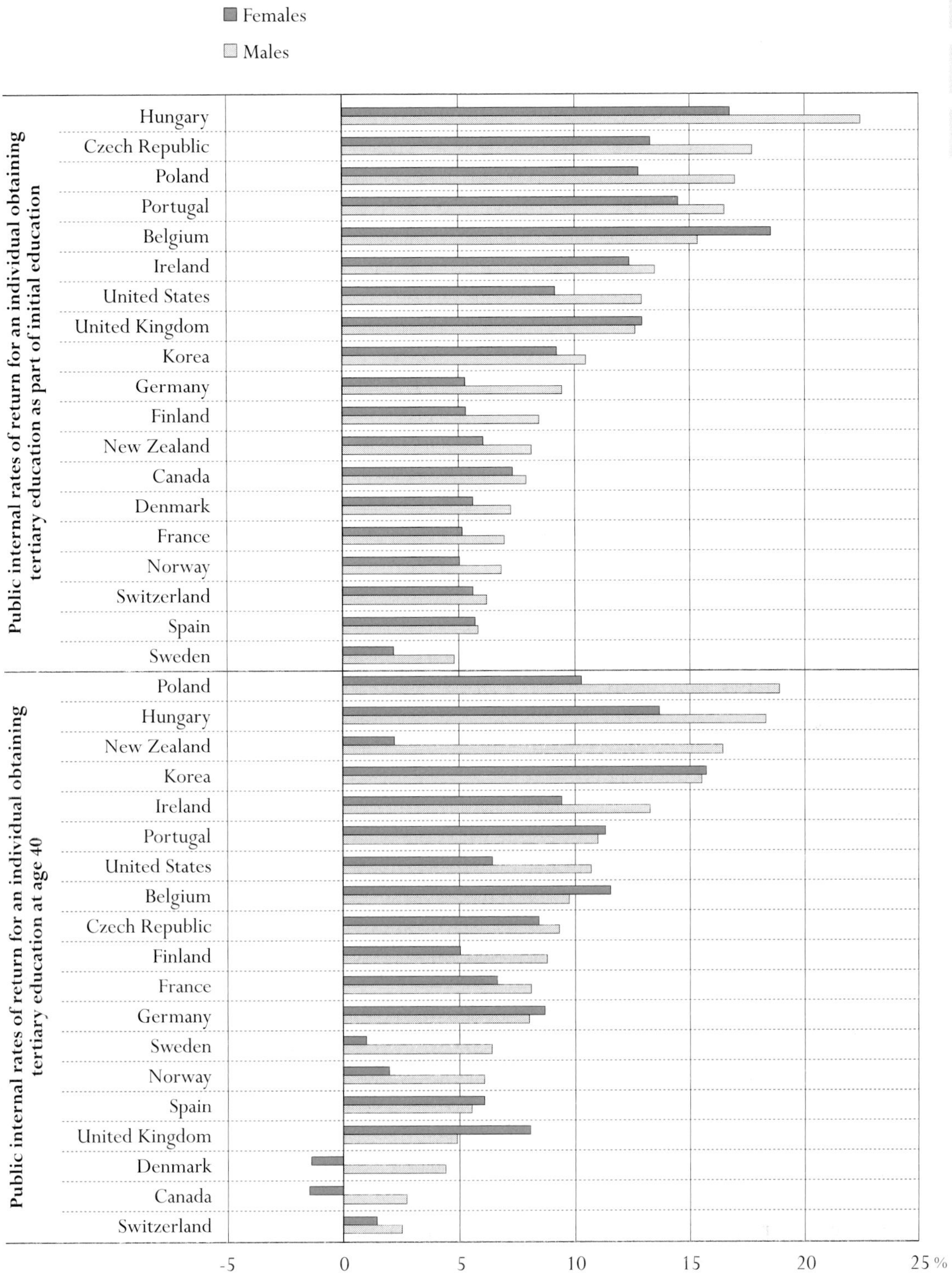

Countries are ranked in descending order of public internal rates of return for males obtaining higher education.
Source: OECD. Tables A10.5 and A10.6. See Annex 3 for notes (*www.oecd.org/edu/eag2008*).

StatLink http://dx.doi.org/10.1787/401828118341

A10

The public returns to an upper secondary education are lower when the individual returns to full-time education in mid-career, with negative returns in some countries. On average for males, the returns to upper secondary education at age 40 in OECD countries is 4%, whereas the returns to upper secondary attainment as part of initial education are close to 6.5%.

Public rates of return are substantially higher for tertiary education both as part of initial education and at age 40. On average, tertiary education generates a return of 11% for males and 9% for females as part of initial education; at age 40 the public returns are 9.5% for males and 6.6% for females. Tertiary education as part of initial education yields returns of close to 10% or more in Belgium, the Czech Republic, Hungary, Ireland, Korea, Poland, Portugal, the United Kingdom and the United States.

Part of these returns is typically redistributed among lower income groups but depending on the will to redistribute wealth, it would make sense in most countries for the government to step in and improve access and incentives to invest in education in mid-career. This is particularly true for Hungary, Korea, New Zealand and Poland where rates of return reach more than 15% for males.

Thus there seems to be room for additional expansion of higher education through either public or private financing. As upper secondary education has become the norm in many OECD countries, returns are generally lower than for tertiary education. Public as well as private rates of return to tertiary education will eventually drop in many countries with high returns as supply meets demand, but from the viewpoint of equity this may be a desirable outcome.

The interpretation of internal rates of return

For those who acquire upper secondary or tertiary education, high private internal rates of return in most countries (though not in all) indicate that investment in human capital is an attractive way for the average person to build wealth. Furthermore, and with some exceptions, policies that reduce or eliminate the direct costs of education have only a modest impact on individuals' decisions to invest in mid-career learning, because foregone earnings typically are the main cost when going back to education.

In many cases, the reported private internal rates of return are above – and in a number of countries significantly above – the risk-free real interest rate, which is typically measured with reference to rates on long-term government bonds. However, returns to human capital accumulation are not risk-free, as indicated by the wide distribution of earnings among the better educated (see Indicator A9). Moreover, not everyone who invests in a course of education actually completes the course. Rates of return will be low, and possibly negative, for individuals who drop out. Therefore, individuals contemplating an investment in education are likely to require a compensating risk premium. However, in a number of countries, the size of the premium over the real interest rate is higher than would seem warranted by considerations of risk alone. If returns to this form of investment are high, relative to investments of similar risk, it would appear that individuals perceive obstacles to making the investment. High risk-adjusted private rates of return provide initial grounds for policy intervention to alleviate the relevant constraints.

High rates of return indicate a shortage of better-educated workers which drives up earnings for these workers. The situation may be temporary; high returns to education would eventually generate enough supply response to push the rates into line with returns to other productive assets. However, the speed of adjustment would depend largely on the capacity of the education system to respond to the derived increase in demand and the capacity of the labour market to absorb the changing relative supplies of labour. The rebalancing mechanism could be accelerated by making better information about the returns to different courses of study available, as this would help individuals to make more informed choices.

Part of the high returns may also be compatible with market stability as high internal rates of return would partly reflect economic rents on scarce resources, namely ability and motivation. If the returns to education at the margin are lower, the case for public intervention to stimulate human capital accumulation is lessened if the quality of the marginal student cannot be improved. However, to the extent that the education system can improve young adults' cognitive and non-cognitive skills, education policy can make a significant contribution to efficiency and equity in the long run. The results from the OECD Programme for International Student Assessment (PISA) suggest that some countries succeed much better than others in securing high and equitable educational performances at the age of 15.

Internal rates of return to investment in education can also be viewed from a societal perspective. This perspective combines both private and public costs and benefits of additional education. For instance, the social cost of education would include foregone production of output during periods of study as well as the full cost of providing education. A social rate of return should also include a range of possible indirect benefits, which also have economic repercussions, such as better health, more social cohesion and more informed and effective citizens. While data on social costs are available for most OECD countries, information on the full range of social benefits is less readily available. Indeed, for a number of external factors possibly associated with education, current understanding of their nature and size of their effects is imperfect.

It is important to consider some of the broad conceptual limitations on the estimation of internal rates of return performed here:

- The data reported are accounting rates of return only. The results no doubt differ from econometric estimates that would rely, for example, on an earnings function approach, rather than on a lifetime stream of earnings derived from average empirical earnings.

- Estimates relate to levels of formal educational attainment only. They do not reflect the effects of learning outside of formal education.

- The approach used here estimates future earnings for individuals with different levels of educational attainment based on knowledge of how average present gross earnings vary by level of attainment and age. However, the relationship between different levels of educational attainment and earnings may differ in the future from what it is today. Technological, economic and social changes may all alter how wage levels relate to levels of educational attainment.

- As in the discussion of the interpretation of earnings dispersion data (see Indicator A9), differences in internal rates of return across countries partly reflect different institutional and non-market conditions that bear on earnings, such as institutional conditions that limit flexibility in relative earnings.

- Estimates are based on average pre-tax earnings for persons at different levels of educational attainment. However, at a given level of educational attainment, individuals who have chosen different courses of study or who come from different social groups may register different rates of return.

• In estimating benefits, the effect of education on increasing the likelihood of employment when wanting to work is taken into account. However, this also makes the estimate sensitive to the stage in the economic cycle at which the data were collected.

Definitions and methodologies

The economic returns to education are measured by the internal rate of return (IRR), which is the discount rate that makes the present value of the income stream equal to zero, or in other words, the interest rate that makes the net present value of costs of investing in education equal to the benefits.

These results are not comparable with the estimates in *Education at a Glance* 2007. Although the approach is the same, some assumptions have changed. Use of the productivity rate as a scaling factor has been abandoned because of a presumption of double counting. Foregone earnings have been standardised at the level of the legal minimum wage or the equivalent (for the calculations of upper secondary education and tertiary education as part of initial education). To facilitate comparisons, the length of time for obtaining upper secondary education and tertiary education at age 40 has been fixed at three years and four years, respectively. In order to broaden the country coverage, when information from Tables B1.3a and B1.3b were not available, the starting age of education and the duration of studies have been estimated on the basis of school expectancy (see Indicator C2) or the best estimate from the litterature.

The calculations also involve a number of restrictive assumptions needed for international comparability. In particular, it was not possible to include the effects on public accounts of changes in social transfer payments resulting from changes in wages. This is largely because the rules governing eligibility for a broad range of social entitlements vary greatly across countries as well as by marital or civil status (and sometimes other criteria). Consequently, to ensure comparability, the rates of return have been calculated on the assumption that the individual in question is single and childless.

The private internal rate of return for the individual is estimated on the basis of the additions to after-tax earnings that result from a higher level of educational attainment, net of the additional private costs (private expenditures and foregone earnings) required to attain the higher level of education. In general, living expenses of students (housing, meals, clothing, recreation, etc.) are excluded from these private expenditures.

For the individual who decides to attain upper secondary education as part of his/her initial education, the assumption concerning the estimated level of foregone earnings was the minimum wage (when no national minimum wage was available, the wage was selected from wages set in collective agreements). This assumption seeks to counterbalance the very low recorded earnings for 15-to-24-year-olds with lower secondary education that led to excessively high estimates in earlier editions of *Education at a Glance*.

For the individual who decides to return to education in mid-career, the assumptions concerned the immediate increase in earnings (10% relative to the level of earnings at the previous level of educational attainment) and the time required for convergence with the average wage of individuals already holding the next highest level of educational qualification (two years). These assumptions are somewhat *ad hoc*. Empirical evidence on the earnings of adults who return to work following part-time or full-time studies is scarce, especially for individuals attaining upper secondary qualification. However, Canadian data indicate a convergence period of just two years for 30-to-49-year-olds who obtain a university degree. It should be noted, nevertheless, that the Canadian data are derived from a small sample of individuals and do not control for the fact that those who invested in education may differ in important ways – such as motivation and inherent ability – by comparison with those who did not.

The analysis could be extended in a number of ways, subject to data availability. In particular, more differentiated and comparable data relative to costs per student and a range of social transfer payments would be useful. Estimating changes in value added tax receipts resulting from the increased earnings acquired through obtaining higher levels of education would also contribute to a more complete assessment of the impact on public accounts. The calculations do not consider the fact that those with high earnings often generate higher levels of income after age 64 owing to their superior pension arrangements.

For the methods employed for the calculation of the rates of return see Annex 3 at *www.oecd.org/edu/eag2008*.

Further references

Mincer, J. (1974), "Schooling, experience, and earnings", National Bureau of Economic Research (NBER), New York.

PISA 2006: Science Competencies for Tomorrow's World, OECD (2007c)

Education at a Glance 2007: OECD Indicators – 2007 Edition, OECD (2007a)

A10

Table A10.1.
Private internal rates of return (IRR) for an individual obtaining upper secondary or post-secondary non-tertiary education, ISCED 3/4 (2004)

	IRR Male	IRR Female	Direct cost Male	Direct cost Female	Foregone earnings Male	Foregone earnings Female	Gross earnings benefits Male	Gross earnings benefits Female	Unemployment effect Male	Unemployment effect Female	Income tax effect Male	Income tax effect Female	Social contribution effect Male	Social contribution effect Female	Composite Impact Male	Composite Impact Female
Belgium	9.0	9.2	-1.1	-1.1	-29.1	-29.9	30.8	30.2	18.7	14.1	-12.9	-12.6	-6.9	-6.4	0.5	5.7
Canada	9.1	9.0	-2.0	-2.1	-35.8	-36.5	35.1	38.9	13.8	7.4	-10.1	-8.2	-2.0	-3.2	1.1	3.7
Czech Republic	15.0	15.2	-3.8	-3.8	-39.2	-39.2	15.4	14.8	33.9	31.7	-4.3	-4.0	-2.6	-2.9	0.7	3.5
Denmark	6.7	5.4	-0.3	-0.4	-23.6	-27.8	42.7	42.6	6.2	6.3	-21.0	-16.8	-5.1	-5.1	1.1	1.0
Finland	10.2	7.9	-0.2	-0.2	-35.3	-38.1	35.4	31.1	11.4	15.0	-12.4	-9.6	-2.1	-2.1	3.2	3.8
France	6.1	5.6	-2.1	-2.1	-37.0	-37.7	31.0	31.7	18.5	16.7	-6.4	-4.6	-4.5	-5.6	0.5	1.6
Germany	7.0	8.1	-4.2	-4.3	-27.4	-28.0	26.4	36.7	23.6	11.1	-7.0	-9.6	-6.0	-8.1	-5.4	2.3
Hungary	8.6	8.4	-1.6	-1.5	-33.0	-32.5	32.0	35.9	17.0	12.3	-11.9	-11.9	-3.6	-4.1	1.0	1.8
Ireland	7.9	8.8	-0.6	-0.6	-35.9	-37.4	32.6	39.3	17.0	7.9	-11.8	-7.2	-1.8	-4.7	0.4	2.8
Korea[1]	9.7	1.5	-7.2	-7.5	-37.9	-39.3	44.6	43.3	4.7	5.1	-1.6	1.6	-3.2	-3.2	0.7	0.0
New Zealand	11.3	10.4	-3.3	-3.4	-35.2	-36.8	40.8	38.6	8.5	9.1	-11.1	-9.3	-0.4	-0.4	0.7	2.3
Norway	7.8	5.5	-1.9	-2.0	-33.7	-34.2	38.5	44.1	8.8	3.6	-11.7	-10.7	-2.6	-3.1	2.7	2.3
Poland	11.0	10.1	-0.6	-0.6	-35.8	-34.2	27.7	29.1	19.9	15.4	-3.9	-4.3	-9.7	-10.9	2.5	5.4
Portugal	13.1	12.3	0.0	0.0	-33.8	-37.3	48.7	43.2	-0.1	5.1	-11.4	-8.3	-4.5	-4.5	1.3	1.7
Spain	9.5	10.2	-2.4	-2.7	-34.9	-38.6	42.5	29.4	6.2	19.0	-10.3	-6.9	-2.4	-1.9	1.3	1.5
Sweden	11.4	8.8	0.0	0.0	-35.1	-35.8	39.6	39.1	6.4	7.2	-12.4	-11.5	-2.6	-2.7	4.0	3.7
Switzerland	8.4	6.0	-4.6	-3.7	-34.6	-27.8	34.5	36.1	15.5	10.4	-6.5	-4.8	-3.4	-13.7	-0.9	3.5
United Kingdom	18.0	18.5	-3.4	-3.6	-34.5	-36.1	31.0	34.6	15.1	8.2	-8.6	-6.6	-3.6	-3.8	3.9	7.1
United States	17.5	15.6	-3.3	-3.4	-33.6	-35.3	42.5	40.9	3.9	5.0	-9.8	-7.9	-3.3	-3.5	3.6	4.2

Note: Assuming that all individuals with a lower secondary level of education will receive the minimum wage.
1. Year of reference 2003.
Source: OECD. See Annex 3 for notes (*www.oecd.org/edu/eag2008*).
StatLink ᐧᐧ http://dx.doi.org/10.1787/401828118341

Table A10.2.
Private internal rates of return (IRR) for an individual obtaining tertiary education, ISCED 5/6 (2004)

	IRR Male	IRR Female	Direct cost Male	Direct cost Female	Foregone earnings Male	Foregone earnings Female	Gross earnings benefits Male	Gross earnings benefits Female	Unemployment effect Male	Unemployment effect Female	Income tax effect Male	Income tax effect Female	Social contribution effect Male	Social contribution effect Female	Composite Impact Male	Composite Impact Female
Belgium	11.3	14.0	-1.4	-1.5	-22.4	-24.1	47.3	40.5	0.5	5.1	-21.5	-16.1	-4.8	-8.3	2.2	4.3
Canada	9.4	9.1	-14.7	-14.7	-19.7	-19.7	45.5	46.3	3.3	2.1	-14.4	-12.3	-1.2	-3.4	1.2	1.6
Czech Republic	29.1	23.8	-5.0	-5.0	-31.7	-32.3	41.6	39.3	7.1	8.7	-8.6	-8.0	-4.7	-4.6	1.3	2.0
Denmark	4.4	4.1	-0.5	-0.6	-19.2	-26.5	48.0	47.3	-2.2	1.7	-26.7	-19.2	-1.5	-3.7	2.0	1.1
Finland	10.7	9.3	-0.9	-1.0	-28.4	-31.4	45.0	43.7	3.4	4.3	-18.8	-15.5	-1.9	-2.1	1.6	2.0
France	8.4	7.4	-2.8	-3.0	-30.2	-32.3	48.6	42.2	0.2	5.6	-11.7	-9.4	-5.3	-5.2	1.2	2.2
Germany	8.0	4.8	-2.2	-2.2	-25.6	-26.4	40.5	42.1	8.1	6.1	-17.0	-14.6	-5.2	-6.8	1.3	1.9
Hungary	19.8	13.8	-5.2	-5.0	-19.6	-18.8	46.5	45.8	1.4	2.0	-21.4	-22.6	-3.8	-3.6	2.1	2.2
Ireland	10.2	11.8	-2.3	-2.7	-27.0	-31.7	48.2	48.6	1.1	0.6	-19.4	-12.3	-1.4	-3.3	0.7	0.8
Korea[1]	9.0	11.2	-15.3	-15.1	-25.9	-29.9	48.4	49.0	1.1	0.7	-5.7	-1.6	-3.1	-3.4	0.5	0.3
New Zealand	8.6	11.9	-7.9	-9.5	-24.4	-29.2	49.5	47.7	-0.8	1.4	-16.4	-10.9	-0.4	-0.5	0.5	0.9
Norway	7.4	8.8	-0.6	-0.7	-27.9	-33.5	46.7	46.3	2.8	2.8	-19.1	-13.0	-2.3	-2.8	0.5	0.9
Poland	22.8	18.6	-7.2	-7.5	-27.1	-28.1	37.6	32.8	8.5	13.1	-4.7	-4.1	-10.9	-10.3	3.9	4.1
Portugal	23.9	21.5	-4.5	-4.3	-26.2	-24.8	48.6	49.3	-1.4	-3.5	-13.4	-12.8	-4.4	-4.6	1.4	0.7
Spain	7.6	8.7	-6.4	-6.7	-28.4	-29.5	47.8	43.3	1.0	3.9	-12.7	-11.3	-2.4	-2.5	1.2	2.9
Sweden	5.1	4.2	-2.0	-2.6	-25.5	-31.4	47.4	45.2	1.5	4.6	-21.6	-13.7	-0.8	-2.4	1.1	0.5
Switzerland	10.3	10.2	-2.7	-2.7	-34.0	-33.7	46.9	48.2	2.8	1.2	-10.2	-7.7	-3.0	-6.0	0.3	0.6
United Kingdom	14.3	14.5	-7.7	-7.6	-27.6	-27.3	45.6	45.7	3.2	2.5	-10.9	-10.8	-3.7	-4.3	1.2	1.8
United States	11.0	8.4	-20.0	-20.7	-14.7	-15.2	46.1	46.6	3.0	2.3	-12.5	-11.1	-2.8	-2.9	0.8	1.1

1. Year of reference 2003.
Source: OECD. See Annex 3 for notes (*www.oecd.org/edu/eag2008*).
StatLink ᐧᐧ http://dx.doi.org/10.1787/401828118341

Table A10.3.
Private internal rates of return for an individual obtaining upper secondary education at age 40 (2004)

	Private rate at age 40 if ...					
	... if the foregone earnings are at the level he/she could have earned with a lower secondary education		... if the foregone earnings are compensated by an arbitrary public subsidy amounting to 50% of the level he/she could have earned with a lower secondary education		... if the foregone earnings are compensated by a public subsidy amounting to unemployment benefits	
	Male	Female	Male	Female	Male	Female
Belgium	4.8	9.3	11.2	17.6	16.8	66.2
Canada	5.7	9.9	12.4	18.2	16.7	26.7
Czech Republic	13.6	14.8	24.8	24.6	29.7	29.3
Denmark	3.3	3.5	10.1	10.5	15.6	66.9
Finland	-0.8	-3.5	4.5	2.6	8.3	8.6
France	4.8	7.3	11.3	14.5	17.8	33.4
Germany	5.1	-0.7	11.1	5.0	12.6	8.5
Hungary	8.3	9.0	15.9	17.4	17.5	21.3
Ireland	2.8	5.3	9.1	12.8	5.8	13.1
Korea[1]	7.5	5.6	14.8	11.8	15.2	13.9
New Zealand	6.6	4.4	14.4	11.5	10.6	10.6
Norway	2.3	1.4	8.0	7.4	12.4	11.5
Poland	7.0	12.8	17.7	24.5	12.9	25.9
Portugal	16.8	16.4	26.8	26.8	36.0	38.3
Spain	7.3	9.9	15.1	17.6	28.1	36.0
Sweden	2.5	0.2	8.9	7.6	25.3	32.4
Switzerland	7.3	4.1	14.4	10.1	22.6	43.1
United Kingdom	9.5	6.0	18.3	13.3	12.7	11.4
United States	13.5	13.5	22.7	22.5	26.8	28.6

(OECD countries)

1. Year of reference 2003.
Source: OECD. See Annex 3 for notes (*www.oecd.org/edu/eag2008*).
StatLink ⃟⃤🔊 http://dx.doi.org/10.1787/401828118341

Table A10.4.
Private internal rates of return for an individual obtaining tertiary education at age 40 (2004)

	Private rate at age 40 if ...					
	... if the foregone earnings are at the level he/she could have earned with an upper secondary education		... if the foregone earnings are compensated by an arbitrary public subsidy amounting to 50% of the level he/she could have earned with an upper secondary education		... if the foregone earnings are compensated by a public subsidy amounting to unemployment benefits	
	Male	Female	Male	Female	Male	Female
Belgium	7.1	9.2	14.3	16.0	16.2	24.4
Canada	4.4	0.1	9.9	4.3	10.9	5.9
Czech Republic	13.3	10.6	21.6	18.0	19.7	16.9
Denmark	2.3	2.5	8.4	8.5	9.3	16.1
Finland	9.0	7.6	16.8	14.6	20.4	19.1
France	10.5	8.9	17.6	15.4	21.1	21.5
Germany	6.5	8.2	13.6	14.9	13.1	16.4
Hungary	16.1	10.3	23.9	16.6	22.1	15.6
Ireland	9.5	8.5	16.9	15.6	12.6	14.1
Korea[1]	7.1	15.8	13.0	21.8	12.8	22.2
New Zealand	4.1	3.3	10.2	8.4	8.5	8.6
Norway	4.9	6.1	11.7	12.9	16.8	17.2
Poland	15.5	13.2	24.3	21.3	19.7	19.2
Portugal	14.6	13.4	22.9	21.3	28.7	27.7
Spain	5.4	8.4	10.8	14.4	14.0	24.6
Sweden	5.1	4.7	11.5	10.5	17.8	21.1
Switzerland	6.6	8.4	13.6	15.3	20.2	38.6
United Kingdom	6.3	9.0	12.7	15.4	7.8	12.1
United States	8.3	4.7	13.1	8.0	13.2	8.7

(OECD countries)

1. Year of reference 2003.
Source: OECD. See Annex 3 for notes (*www.oecd.org/edu/eag2008*).
StatLink ⃟⃤🔊 http://dx.doi.org/10.1787/401828118341

A10

Table A10.5.
Public internal rates of return for an individual obtaining higher education as part of initial education (2004)

	Upper secondary education		Tertiary education	
	Male	Female	Male	Female
Belgium	9.7	7.9	15.4	18.5
Canada	6.5	5.1	7.9	7.3
Czech Republic	5.4	4.7	17.7	13.3
Denmark	16.7	8.9	7.2	5.6
Finland	4.1	1.0	8.4	5.3
France	1.8	0.7	6.9	5.1
Germany	5.6	5.6	9.4	5.3
Hungary	5.7	7.9	22.5	16.7
Ireland	7.0	5.1	13.5	12.4
Korea[1]	1.7	4.2	10.5	9.2
New Zealand	5.8	-3.5	8.1	6.1
Norway	3.0	1.0	6.8	5.0
Poland	6.1	5.7	17.0	12.8
Portugal	8.5	2.9	16.5	14.5
Spain	5.4	2.5	5.8	5.7
Sweden	4.4	6.3	4.8	2.2
Switzerland	3.5	4.7	6.2	5.6
United Kingdom	12.2	5.7	12.6	12.9
United States	8.1	9.2	12.9	9.1

(Left margin label: OECD countries)

1. Year of reference 2003.
Source: OECD. See Annex 3 for notes (*www.oecd.org / edu / eag2008*).
StatLink ⋙ http://dx.doi.org/10.1787/401828118341

Table A10.6.
Public internal rates of return for an individual obtaining higher education at age 40 (2004)

	Upper secondary education		Tertiary education	
	Male	Female	Male	Female
Belgium	5.6	11.5	9.7	11.5
Canada	4.8	5.8	2.7	-1.5
Czech Republic	4.3	4.2	9.3	8.4
Denmark	0.7	-1.0	4.4	-1.4
Finland	-1.9	-8.3	8.8	5.0
France	0.5	0.0	8.1	6.6
Germany	3.9	-2.4	8.0	8.7
Hungary	7.5	7.8	18.3	13.7
Ireland	5.6	4.9	13.2	9.4
Korea[1]	-0.2	-10.0	15.5	15.7
New Zealand	6.0	-1.8	16.4	2.2
Norway	-0.9	-4.6	6.1	2.0
Poland	6.3	9.7	18.9	10.3
Portugal	14.2	10.0	11.0	11.3
Spain	3.7	3.6	5.5	6.1
Sweden	-1.2	-5.5	6.4	1.0
Switzerland	1.1	-0.4	2.5	1.4
United Kingdom	7.1	3.4	4.9	8.0
United States	7.8	3.4	10.7	6.4

(Left margin label: OECD countries)

1. Year of reference 2003.
Source: OECD. See Annex 3 for notes (*www.oecd.org / edu / eag2008*).
StatLink ⋙ http://dx.doi.org/10.1787/401828118341

Chapter

B

FINANCIAL AND HUMAN RESOURCES INVESTED IN EDUCATION

Classification of educational expenditure

Educational expenditure in this chapter are classified through three dimensions:

▪ The first dimension – represented by the horizontal axis in the diagram below – relates to the location where spending occurs. Spending on schools and universities, education ministries and other agencies directly involved in providing and supporting education is one component of this dimension. Spending on education outside these institutions is another.

▪ The second dimension – represented by the vertical axis in the diagram below – classifies the goods and services that are purchased. Not all expenditure on educational institutions can be classified as direct educational or instructional expenditure. Educational institutions in many OECD countries offer various ancillary services – such as meals, transports, housing, etc. – in addition to teaching services to support students and their families. At the tertiary level spending on research and development can be significant. Not all spending on educational goods and services occurs within educational institutions. For example, families may purchase textbooks and materials themselves or seek private tutoring for their children.

▪ The third dimension – represented by the colours in the diagram below – distinguishes among the sources from which funding originates. These include the public sector and international agencies (indicated by the light blue colour), and households and other private entities (indicated by the medium-blue colour). Where private expenditure on education is subsidised by public funds, this is indicated by cells in the dark blue colour.

░ Public sources of funds	▓ Private sources of funds	▓ Private funds publicly subsidised

	Spending on educational institutions (*e.g.* schools, universities, educational administration and student welfare services)	Spending on education outside educational institutions (*e.g.* private purchases of educational goods and services, including private tutoring)
Spending on educational core services	*e.g.* public spending on instructional services in educational institutions	*e.g.* subsidised private spending on books
	e.g. subsidised private spending on instructional services in educational institutions	*e.g.* private spending on books and other school materials or private tutoring
	e.g. private spending on tuition fees	
Spending on research and development	*e.g.* public spending on university research	
	e.g. funds from private industry for research and development in educational institutions	
Spending on educational services other than instruction	*e.g.* public spending on ancillary services such as meals, transport to schools, or housing on the campus	*e.g.* subsidised private spending on student living costs or reduced prices for transport
	e.g. private spending on fees for ancillary services	*e.g.* private spending on student living costs or transport

Coverage diagrams

For Indicators **B1, B2** and **B3**

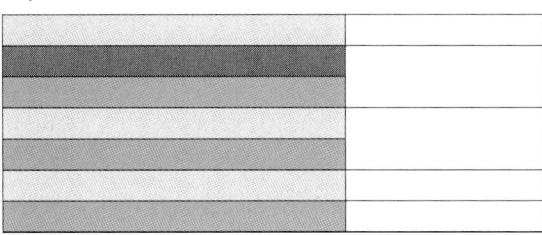

For Indicators **B4** and **B5**

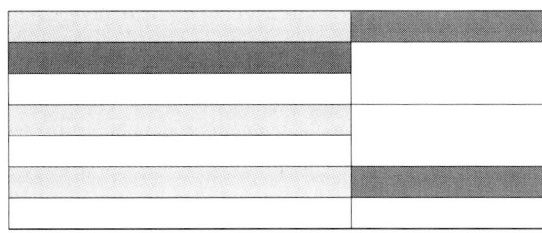

For Indicator **B6**

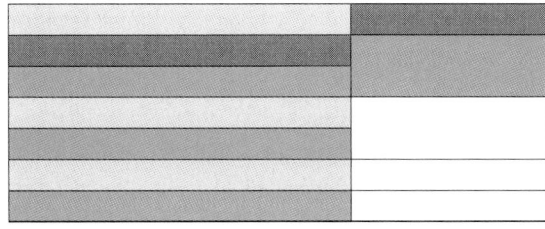

HOW MUCH IS SPENT PER STUDENT?

This indicator provides an assessment of the investment in each student. Expenditure on educational institutions per student is largely influenced by teachers' salaries (see Indicators B6 and D3), pension systems, instructional and teaching hours (see Indicators B7, D1 and D4), teaching materials and facilities, the programme orientation provided to pupils/students (see Indicator C1) and the number of students enrolled in the education system (see Indicator C2). Policies to attract new teachers or to reduce average class size or staffing patterns (see Indicator D2) have also contributed to changes in expenditure on educational institutions per student over time.

Key results

Chart B1.1. **Annual expenditure on educational institutions per student in primary through tertiary education (2005)**

Expenditure on educational institutions per student gives a measure of the unit costs of formal education. The chart shows annual expenditure on educational institutions per student in equivalent USD converted using purchasing power parities, based on full-time equivalents.

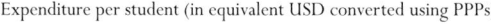

OECD countries as a whole spend USD 8 553 per student annually between primary and tertiary education: USD 6 173 per primary student, USD 7 736 per secondary student and USD 15 559 per tertiary student. However, these averages mask a broad range of expenditure across countries. As represented by the simple average of all OECD countries, countries spend nearly twice as much per student at the tertiary level as at the primary level.

Expenditure per student (in equivalent USD converted using PPPs)

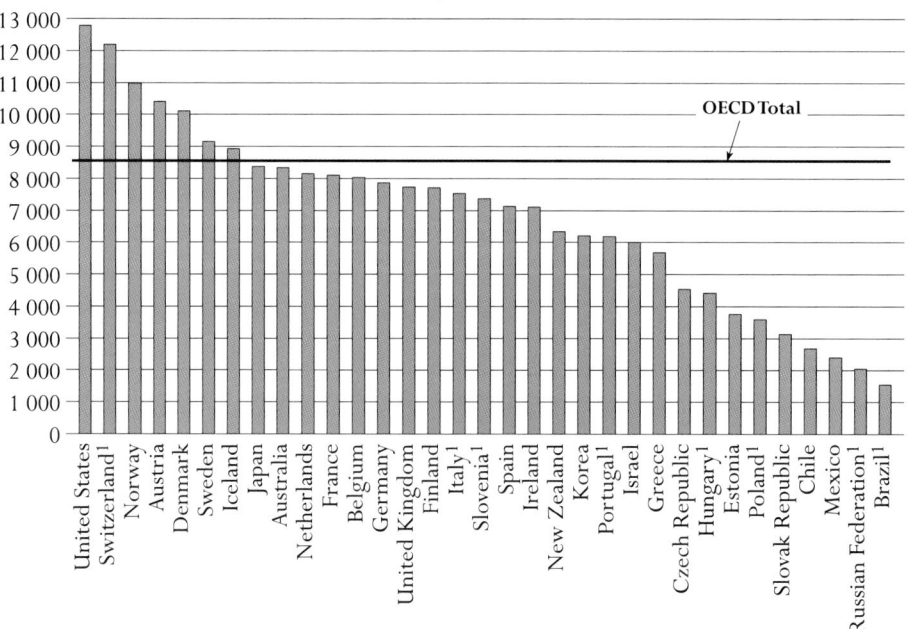

1. Public institutions only.

Countries are ranked in descending order of expenditure on educational institutions per student.

Source: OECD. Table B1.1a. See Annex 3 for notes (*www.oecd.org/edu/eag2008*).

StatLink ᛗᗵᗱ┗ http://dx.doi.org/10.1787/401862824252

Other highlights of this indicator

■ Excluding R&D activities and ancillary services, expenditure on educational core services in tertiary institutions represents on average USD 7 976 per student and ranges from USD 5 000 or less in Greece, Hungary, Poland, the Slovak Republic and the partner country Estonia to more than USD 10 000 in Canada, Switzerland and the United States.

■ OECD countries spend on average USD 87 720 per student over the theoretical duration of primary and secondary studies. The cumulative expenditure for each primary and secondary student ranges from less than USD 40 000 in Mexico and the Slovak Republic and the partner countries Brazil, Chile and the Russian Federation, to USD 100 000 or more in Austria, Denmark, Iceland, Luxembourg, Norway, Switzerland and the United States.

■ There is a clear positive relationship between spending on educational institutions per student and GDP per capita at the primary and secondary levels; it is less clear at the tertiary level. However, countries with low levels of expenditure on educational institutions per student may nevertheless have distributions of investment relative to GDP per capita similar to those of countries with high levels of spending per student. For example, at the primary, secondary and post-secondary non-tertiary level of education Korea and Portugal – with expenditure on educational institutions per student and GDP per capita below the OECD average – spend a higher proportion per student relative to GDP per capita than the OECD average.

■ Expenditure on educational institutions per tertiary student increased between 2000 and 2005 in around two-thirds of the 30 countries for which data are available, but only Australia, Austria, Denmark, Greece, Iceland, Mexico, Poland, Portugal, Spain, Switzerland and the United Kingdom had a larger increase in expenditure on educational institutions per tertiary student than in GDP per capita.

■ Expenditure on educational institutions tends to rise over time in real terms, as teachers' salaries (the main component of costs) rise in line with general earnings. However, rising unit costs that are not paralleled by increasing outcomes raise the spectre of falling productivity levels in education.

■ Expenditure on educational institutions per primary, secondary and post-secondary non-tertiary student increased in every country and on average by 35% between 1995 and 2005 during a period of relatively stable student numbers. The pattern is different at the tertiary level where spending per student has fallen in some cases, as expenditure has not kept up with the expansion in student numbers. However, from 2000 to 2005, expenditure on educational institutions per student increased by 11 percentage points on average in OECD countries after remaining stable from 1995 to 2000. This shows governments' efforts to deal with the expansion of tertiary education through massive investment.

■ Seven out of the 11 countries in which student enrolments in tertiary education increased by more than 20 percentage points between 2000 and 2005 have increased their expenditure on tertiary educational institutions by at least the same proportion over the period, whereas Hungary, Sweden and the partner countries Brazil and Chile did not.

B1

Policy context

Effective schools require the right combination of trained and talented personnel, adequate facilities and motivated students who are ready to learn. The demand for quality education, which can translate into higher costs per student, must be balanced against an undue burden on taxpayers.

As a result, the question of whether the resources devoted to education yield adequate returns to the investments made figures prominently in the public debate. Although it is difficult to assess the optimal volume of resources needed to prepare each student for life and work in modern societies, international comparisons of spending on educational institutions per student can provide a starting point for evaluating the effectiveness of different models of educational provision.

Policy makers must also balance the importance of improving the quality of educational services with the desirability of expanding access to educational opportunities, notably at the tertiary level. A comparative review of trends in expenditure on educational institutions per student shows that in many OECD countries the expansion of enrolments, particularly in tertiary education, has not always been accompanied by increased investment.

In addition, decisions on the allocation of funds among the various levels of education are important. For example, some OECD countries emphasise broad access to higher education and some invest in near-universal education for children as young as 3 or 4 years old.

Evidence and explanations

What this indicator covers and what it does not cover

The indicator shows direct public and private expenditure on educational institutions in relation to the number of full-time equivalent students enrolled.

Public subsidies for students' living expenses have been excluded to ensure international comparability of the data. Expenditure data for students in private educational institutions are not available for certain countries, and some other countries do not provide complete data on independent private institutions. Where this is the case, only the expenditure on public and government-dependent private institutions has been taken into account. Note that variations in expenditure on educational institutions per student may reflect not only variations in the material resources provided to students (*e.g.* variations in the ratio of students to teaching staff) but also variations in relative salary and price levels.

At the primary and secondary levels, educational expenditure is dominated by spending on instructional services; at the tertiary level, other services – particularly those related to R&D activities or ancillary services – can account for a significant proportion.

Expenditure on educational institutions per student in equivalent USD

Annual expenditure per student from primary through tertiary education provides a way to assess the investment made in each student. OECD countries as a whole spend on average USD 8 553 per student annually for students enrolled in primary through tertiary education. In 13 out of

33 OECD and partner countries, spending on educational institutions ranges between USD 7 000 and USD 9 000 per student. It ranges from USD 4 000 per student or less in Mexico, Poland and the Slovak Republic, and the partner countries Brazil, Chile, Estonia and the Russian Federation, to more than USD 10 000 per student in Austria, Denmark, Norway, Switzerland and the United States (Table B1.1a). The drivers of expenditure per student vary among countries (for more details see Indicator B7): among the five countries with the highest expenditure on educational institutions per student enrolled in primary through tertiary education, Switzerland is one of the countries with the highest teachers' salaries at the secondary level (see Indicator D3), the United States is one of the countries with the highest level of private expenditure at tertiary level and Austria, Denmark and Norway are among the countries with the lowest student to teaching staff ratios (see Indicator D2).

Even if overall spending per student is similar in some OECD countries, the ways in which resources are allocated among the different levels of education vary widely. OECD countries as a whole spend USD 6 173 per student at the primary level, USD 7 736 at the secondary level and USD 15 559 at the tertiary level. At the tertiary level, the totals are affected by high expenditure in a few large OECD countries, most notably Canada and the United States. Spending on educational institutions per student in a typical OECD country (as represented by the simple mean across all OECD countries) amounts to USD 6 252 at the primary level, USD 7 804 at the secondary level and USD 11 512 at the tertiary level (Table B1.1a and Chart B1.2).

These averages mask a broad range of expenditure on educational institutions per student by OECD and partner countries. At the primary level, expenditure on educational institutions varies by a factor of 10, ranging from USD 1 425 per student in the partner country Brazil to USD 14 079 in Luxembourg. Differences among countries are even greater at the secondary level, where spending on educational institutions per student varies by a factor of 16, from USD 1 186 in the partner country Brazil to USD 18 845 in Luxembourg. Expenditure on educational institutions per tertiary student ranges from USD 3 421 in the partner country the Russian Federation to more than USD 20 000 in Canada, Switzerland and the United States (Table B1.1a and Chart B1.2).

These comparisons are based on purchasing power parities for GDP, not on market exchange rates. They therefore reflect the amount of a national currency required to produce the same basket of goods and services in a given country as that produced by the USD in the United States.

Expenditure on educational core services per student

On average, OECD countries for which data are available spend USD 5 994 on core educational services at primary, secondary and post-secondary non-tertiary levels. This corresponds to 94% of the total expenditure on educational institutions per student at these levels. In 15 out of the 25 OECD and partner countries for which data are available, ancillary services provided by primary, secondary and post-secondary non-tertiary institutions account for less than 5% of the total expenditure per student. The proportion exceeds 10% of the total expenditure in Finland, France, the Slovak Republic, Sweden and the United Kingdom.

Chart B1.2. Annual expenditure on educational institutions per student for all services, by level of education (2005)

In equivalent USD converted using PPPs, based on full-time equivalents

Expenditure per student
(equivalent USD converted using PPPs)

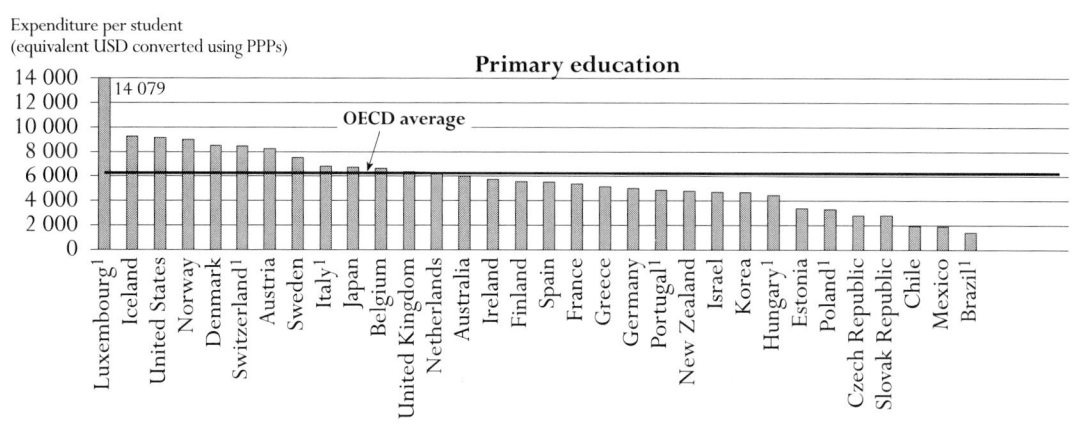

Primary education

Expenditure per student
(equivalent USD converted using PPPs)

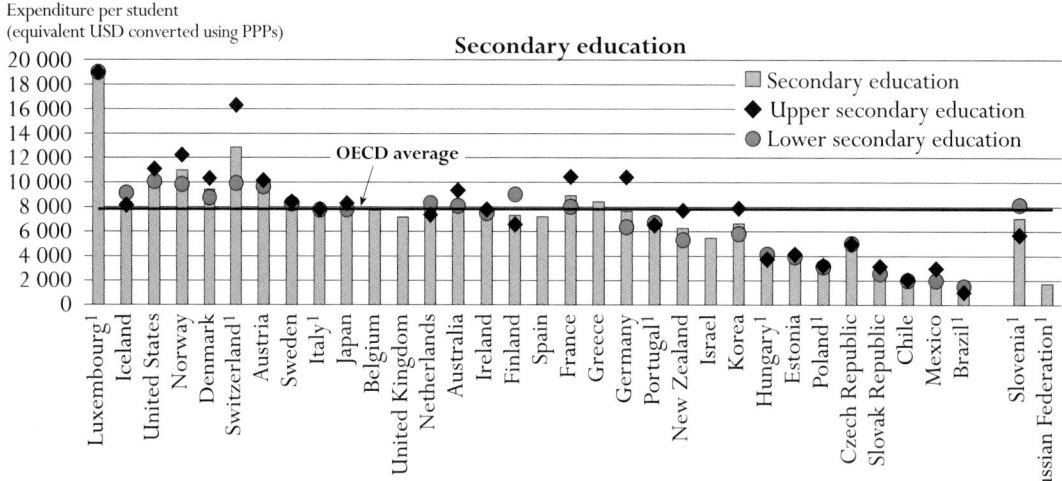

Secondary education

Expenditure per student
(equivalent USD converted using PPPs)

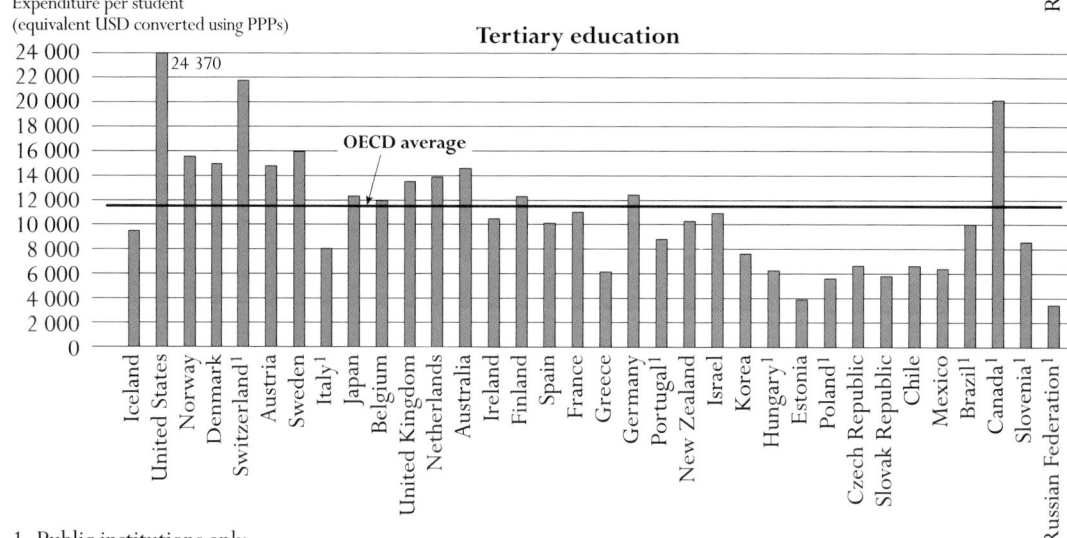

Tertiary education

1. Public institutions only.

Countries are ranked in descending order of expenditure on educational institutions per student in primary education.

Source: OECD. Table B1.1a. See Annex 3 for notes (*www.oecd.org/edu/eag2008*).

StatLink ᴴᴵᴸᴸ http://dx.doi.org/10.1787/401862824252

B1

Greater differences are observed in the proportion of total expenditure on educational institutions per student devoted to core services at the tertiary level partly because R&D expenditure can account for a significant proportion of educational spending. The OECD countries in which most R&D is performed by tertiary education institutions tend to report higher expenditure per student than those in which a large proportion of R&D is performed in other public institutions or by industry. Excluding R&D activities and ancillary services, expenditure on core educational services in tertiary institutions represents, on average, USD 7 976 per student and ranges from USD 5 000 or less in Greece, Hungary, Poland, the Slovak Republic and the partner country Estonia to more than USD 10 000 in Canada, Switzerland and the United States (Table B1.1b).

On average, expenditure on R&D and ancillary services at the tertiary level represents respectively 29 and 4% of all tertiary expenditure on educational institutions per student. In 9 out of 28 OECD and partner countries for which data on tertiary expenditure are available for every service category – Belgium, Finland, Germany, Italy, the Netherlands, Norway, Sweden, Switzerland and the United Kingdom – expenditure on R&D and ancillary services in tertiary institutions represents more than 32% of total tertiary expenditure on educational institutions per student. On a per student basis this can translate into significant amounts: in Australia, Canada, Germany, the Netherlands, Norway, Sweden, Switzerland, the United Kingdom and the United States, expenditure for R&D and ancillary services amounts to more than USD 5 000 per student (Table B1.1b).

Expenditure on educational institutions per student at different levels of education

Throughout OECD countries expenditure on educational institutions per student rises sharply from primary to tertiary education. This pattern is largely a reflection of the location and mode of educational provision. Education still essentially takes place in traditional settings with (generally) similar organisation, curriculum, teaching style and management. These shared features tended to result in similar patterns of unit expenditure. During the last decade, however, greater use of private funds at the tertiary level has increased the difference between expenditure at this level and at the other levels of education (see Indicator B3).

Comparisons of the distribution of expenditure at different levels of education indicate the relative emphasis placed on these levels as well as the relative costs of provision. Expenditure on educational institutions per student rises with the level of education in almost all OECD and partner countries, but the relative size of the differentials varies markedly (Chart B1.3). At the secondary level, the expenditure is, on average, 1.2 times that at the primary level but exceeds 1.5 in the Czech Republic, France, Germany, Greece and Switzerland. In Switzerland, this increase is mainly due to changes in teachers' salaries. In the other four countries, it is due to an increase in the number of instructional hours for students and a significant decrease, compared to the OECD average, in the number of teachers' teaching hours between primary and secondary education (see Indicators B7, D1, D3 and D4).

OECD countries spend, on average, 2.2 times as much on educational institutions per student at the tertiary level as at the primary level, but spending patterns vary widely mainly because education policies vary more among countries at the tertiary level (see Indicator B5). For example, Greece, Iceland, Italy and the partner country Estonia spend less than 1.3 times as much on a tertiary student as on a primary pupil, but Mexico and the partner countries Brazil and Chile spend more than 3 times as much (Chart B1.3).

B1

Chart B1.3. **Expenditure on educational institutions per student at various levels of education for all services relative to primary education (2005)**

Primary education = 100

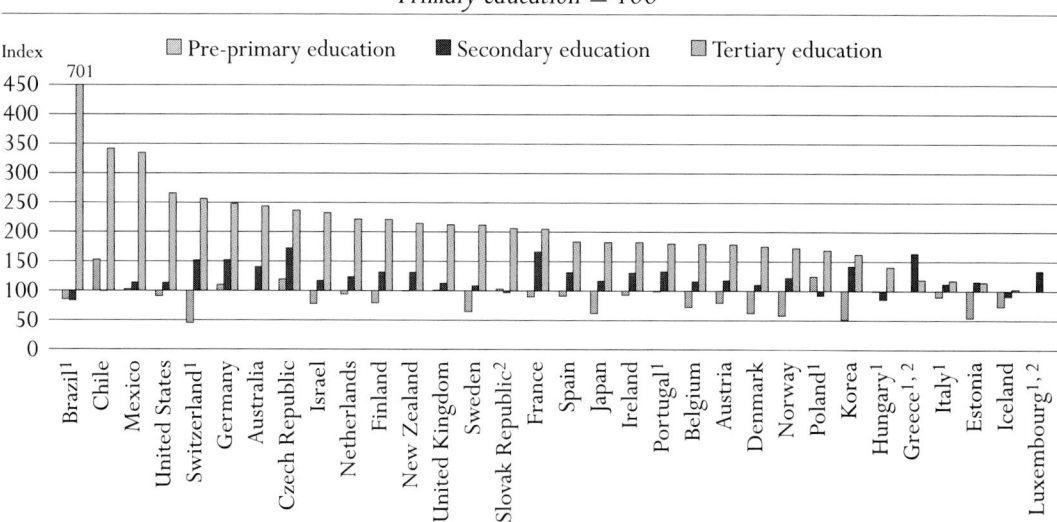

Notes: A ratio of 300 for tertiary education means that expenditure on educational institutions per tertiary student is three times the expenditure on educational institutions per primary student.

A ratio of 50 for pre-primary education means that expenditure on educational institutions per pre-primary student is half the expenditure on educational institutions per primary student.

1. Public institutions only.

2. Some levels of education are included with others. Refer to "x" code in Table B1.1a for details.

Countries are ranked in descending order of expenditure on educational institutions per student in tertiary education relative to primary education.

Source: OECD. Table B1.1a. See Annex 3 for notes (*www.oecd.org/edu/eag2008*).

StatLink ⌨ http://dx.doi.org/10.1787/401862824252

Distribution of expenditure on educational institutions relative to the number of students enrolled

Table B1.2 shows the relationship between the money invested in the education systems of OECD countries and the proportion of students enrolled at each level of education and analyses countries' strategies for allocating their expenditure to the different levels. On average among the 26 OECD countries for which data are available, two-thirds of all expenditure is allocated to primary, secondary and post-secondary non-tertiary education, which accounts for about three-quarters of students. The difference between the two figures equals or exceeds 10 percentage points in Japan, Mexico, the Slovak Republic and the United States and the partner countries Brazil, Chile and Israel (Table B1.2).

Compared to primary, secondary and post-secondary non-tertiary education, the difference between the proportion of money invested and the proportion of students enrolled in tertiary education is greater. On average among the 26 OECD countries for which data are available, 24% of all expenditure is allocated to tertiary education for only 16% of students. The difference between the two ranges from less than 7 percentage points in France, Greece, Hungary, Iceland, Italy, Korea and Portugal and the partner countries Estonia and Slovenia, to more than 13 percentage points in Switzerland and the United States and the partner countries Brazil and Chile (Table B1.2).

Educational expenditure on educational institutions per student over the theoretical duration of primary and secondary education

OECD countries spend on average USD 87 720 per student over the theoretical duration of primary and secondary studies. Although this theoretical duration is quite similar – between 12 and 13 years in 30 out of 36 OECD and partner countries – cumulative expenditure on educational institutions per student varies considerably, ranging from less than USD 40 000 in Mexico and the Slovak Republic, and the partner countries Brazil, Chile and the Russian Federation, to USD 100 000 or more in Austria, Denmark, Iceland, Luxembourg, Norway, Switzerland and the United States (Table B1.3a and Chart B1.4).

Expenditure on educational institutions per student over the average duration of tertiary studies

Both the typical duration and the intensity of tertiary education vary among OECD countries. Therefore, the differences among countries in annual expenditure on educational services per student (as shown in Chart B1.2) do not necessarily reflect the differences in the total cost of educating the typical tertiary student. Today's students can choose from a range of institutions and enrolment options to find the best fit for their degree objectives, abilities and personal interests. Many enrol on a part-time basis while others work while studying or attend more than one institution before graduating. These enrolment patterns can affect the interpretation of expenditure on educational institutions per student.

In particular, comparatively low annual expenditure on educational institutions per student can result in comparatively high overall costs of tertiary education if the typical duration of tertiary studies is long. Chart B1.5 shows the average expenditure per student throughout the course of tertiary studies. The figures account for all students for whom expenditure is incurred, including those who do not finish their studies. Although the calculations are based on a number of simplified assumptions and therefore should be treated with caution (see Annex 3 at *www.oecd.org/edu/eag2008*), there are some striking shifts between annual and aggregate expenditure in the ranking of OECD and partner countries.

For example, annual spending per tertiary student in Japan is about the same as in Germany, at USD 12 326 and USD 12 446, respectively (Table B1.1a). But because of differences in the tertiary degree structure (see Indicator A3), the average duration of tertiary studies is slightly more than one year longer in Germany than in Japan (5.4 and 4.1 years, respectively). As a consequence, the cumulative expenditure for each tertiary student is almost USD 16 000 lower in Japan than in Germany – USD 50 167 compared with USD 66 758 (Chart B1.5 and Table B1.3b).

The total cost of tertiary-type A studies in Switzerland (USD 126 160) is more than twice the cost in the other reporting countries, except Austria, Germany and the Netherlands (Table B1.3b). These differences must, of course, be interpreted in light of differences in national degree structures as well as possible differences among OECD countries in the academic level of the qualifications of students leaving university. While trends are similar in tertiary-type B studies, their total cost tends to be much lower than those of tertiary type-A programmes, largely because of their shorter duration.

Chart B1.4. Cumulative expenditure on educational institutions per student over the theoretical duration of primary and secondary studies (2005)

Annual expenditure on educational institutions per student multiplied by the theoretical duration of studies, in equivalent USD converted using PPPs

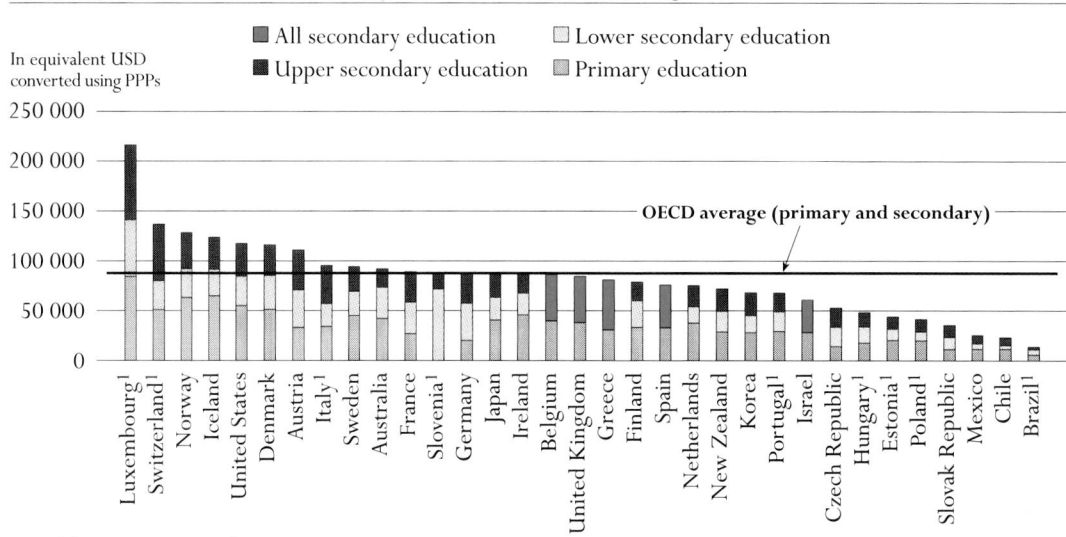

1. Public institutions only.

Countries are ranked in descending order of the total expenditure on educational institutions per student over the theoretical duration of primary and secondary studies.

Source: OECD. Table B1.3a. See Annex 3 for notes (*www.oecd.org/edu/eag2008*).

StatLink ᐉ http://dx.doi.org/10.1787/401862824252

Chart B1.5. Cumulative expenditure on educational institutions per student over the average duration of tertiary studies (2005)

Annual expenditure on educational institutions per student multiplied by the average duration of studies, in equivalent USD converted using PPPs

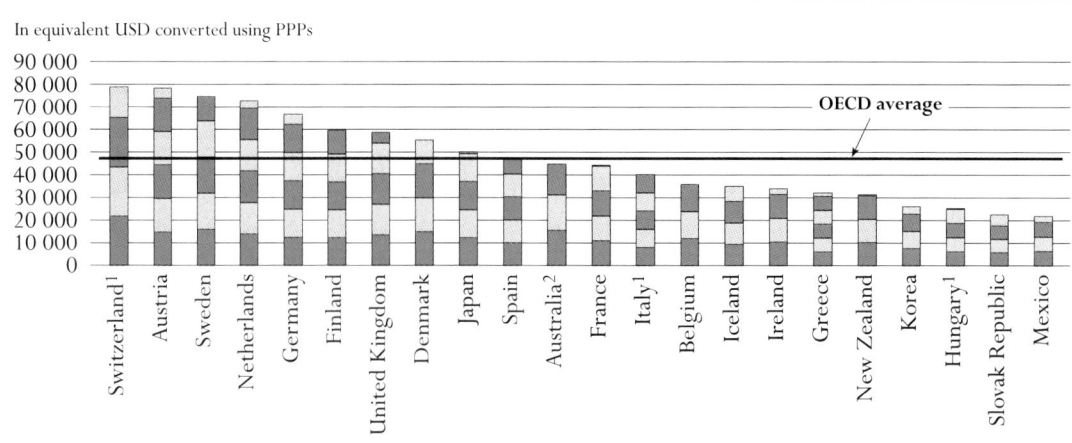

Note: Each segment of the bar represents the annual expenditure on educational institutions per student. The number of segments represents the average number of years a student remains in tertiary education.

1. Public institutions only.

2. Tertiary-type A and advanced research programmes only.

Countries are ranked in descending order of the total expenditure on educational institutions per student over the average duration of tertiary studies.

Source: OECD. Table B1.3b. See Annex 3 for notes (*www.oecd.org/edu/eag2008*).

StatLink ᐉ http://dx.doi.org/10.1787/401862824252

B1

Expenditure on educational institutions per student in relation to GDP per capita

Expenditure on educational institutions per student relative to GDP per capita is a unit spending measure that takes OECD countries' relative wealth into account. Since education is universal at lower levels, spending on educational institutions per student at the lower levels relative to GDP per capita can be interpreted as the resources spent on the school-age population relative to a country's ability to pay. At higher levels of education, this measure is affected by a combination of national income, spending and enrolment rates. At the tertiary level, for example, OECD countries can rank relatively high on this measure if a large proportion of their wealth is spent on educating a relatively small number of students.

Expenditure on educational institutions per student averages 21% of GDP per capita at the primary level, 26% at the secondary level and 40% at the tertiary level (Table B1.4). Countries with low levels of expenditure on educational institutions per student may nevertheless show distributions of investment relative to GDP per capita which are similar to those of countries with a high level of spending per student. For example, Korea and Portugal – countries with expenditure on educational institutions per student at primary, secondary and post-secondary non-tertiary level of education and GDP per capita below the OECD average – spend more per student relative to GDP per capita than the OECD average. Similarly, Canada, Mexico, Switzerland and the United States and the partner country Chile spend more than 50% of GDP per capita on each tertiary student, among the highest proportions after Brazil. Brazil has the highest proportion, spending 108% of GDP per capita on each tertiary student, but tertiary students represent only 3% of the students enrolled in all levels of education combined in Brazil (Tables B1.2 and B1.4).

The relationship between GDP per capita and expenditure on educational institutions per student is a complex one. As one would expect, there is a clear positive relationship between spending on educational institutions per student and GDP per capita at both primary and secondary levels of education; poorer OECD countries tend to spend less per student than richer ones. Although the relationship is generally positive at these levels, there are variations even for countries with similar levels of GDP per capita, especially among those in which it exceeds USD 30 000. Australia and Austria, for example, have similar levels of GDP per capita but spend very different proportions of GDP per capita at the primary and secondary levels. In Australia, the proportions are 18 and 25%, respectively, and are near the OECD average. By contrast, Austria's are 24 and 29%, respectively, and are among the highest (Table B1.4 and Chart B1.6).

There is more variation in spending on educational institutions per student at the tertiary level, and the relationship between countries' relative wealth and their expenditure levels is more variable. Canada, Iceland and Switzerland, for example, have similar levels of GDP per capita but very different levels of spending on tertiary education. The proportion of GDP per capita spent per tertiary student in Canada and Switzerland is 61% and is among the highest among OECD countries, while for Iceland (at 27%) the proportion is significantly below the OECD average (Table B1.4 and Chart B1.6).

Chart B1.6. **Annual expenditure on educational institutions per student relative to GDP per capita (2005)**

In equivalent USD converted using PPPs, by level of education

Expenditure per student
(in equivalent USD converted using PPPs)

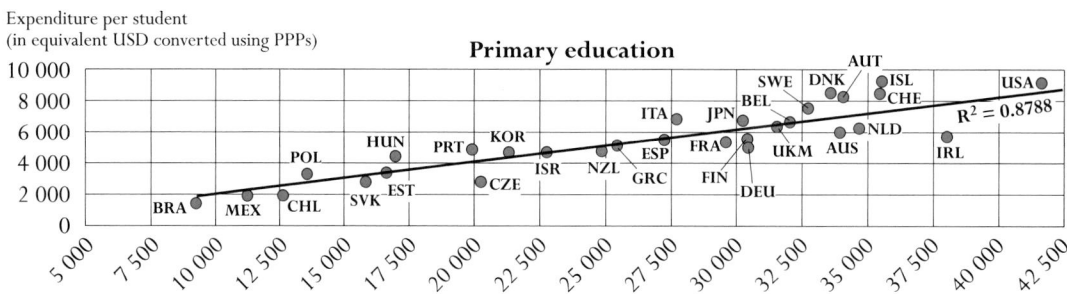

Primary education

GDP per capita (in equivalent USD converted using PPPs)

Expenditure per student
(in equivalent USD converted using PPPs)

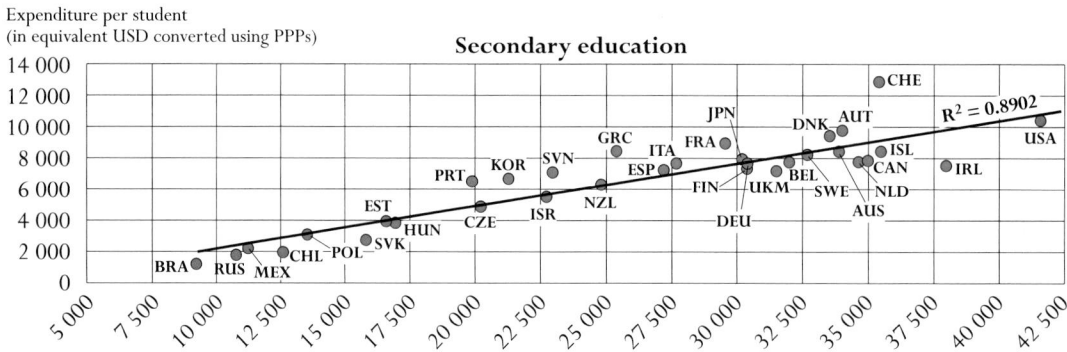

Secondary education

GDP per capita (in equivalent USD converted using PPPs)

Expenditure per student
(in equivalent USD converted using PPPs)

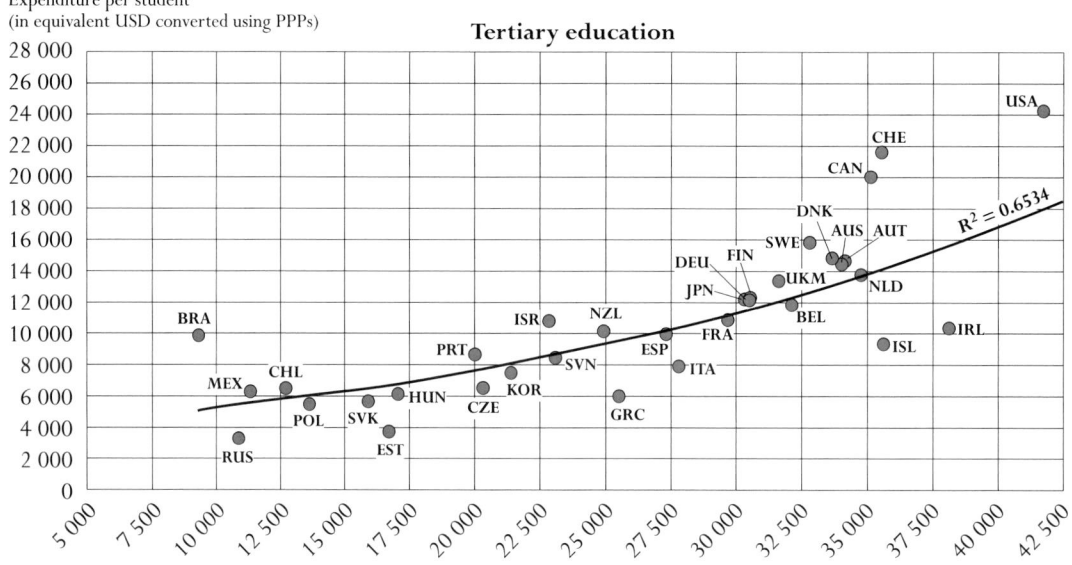

Tertiary education

GDP per capita (in equivalent USD converted using PPPs)

Note: Please refer to the Reader's Guide for the list of country codes used in this chart.
Source: OECD. Tables B1.1a, B1.4 and Annex 2. See Annex 3 for notes (*www.oecd.org/edu/eag2008*).
StatLink 🔗 http://dx.doi.org/10.1787/401862824252

Change in expenditure on educational institutions per student between 1995, 2000 and 2005

Expenditure on educational institutions tends to rise over time in real terms, as teachers' salaries (the main component of costs) rise in line with general earnings. However, rising unit costs that are not accompanied by increasing outcomes raise the spectre of falling productivity levels.

The size of the school-age population influences both enrolment rates and the amount of resources and organisational effort a country must invest in its education system. The larger the size of this population, the greater the potential demand for educational services. Table B1.5 and Chart B1.7 show the effects of changes in enrolments and total expenditure between 1995, 2000 and 2005 in indices and at constant prices.

Expenditure on educational institutions per primary, secondary and post-secondary non-tertiary student increased in every country, on average, by 35% between 1995 and 2005 during a period of relatively stable student numbers at these levels. The increase is quite similar for each five-year period; only the Czech Republic, Italy, Norway and Switzerland showed a decrease between 1995 and 2000, followed by an increase between 2000 and 2005 (Table B1.5).

Between 2000 and 2005, in 20 out of the 31 OECD and partner countries for which data are available, expenditure on educational institutions per primary, secondary and post-secondary non-tertiary student increased by at least 10% and exceeded 30% in the Czech Republic, Hungary, Iceland, Ireland, Korea and the Slovak Republic, and the partner countries Brazil and Estonia. Even with these increases, in 2005, all of these countries except Iceland had a level of expenditure on educational institutions per primary, secondary and post-secondary non-tertiary student below the OECD average. The only countries in which the increase between 2000 and 2005 in expenditure on educational institutions was 5% or less were Austria, Belgium, France, Germany, Italy and the United States, and the partner countries Chile and Israel (Table B1.5 and Chart B1.7).

Changes in enrolments do not seem to have been the main factor behind changes in expenditure on educational institutions per primary, secondary and post-secondary non-tertiary student. However, in the Czech Republic, Hungary, Japan, Poland, Portugal, the Slovak Republic and Spain and partner country Estonia, a drop of more than 5% in enrolments coincided with a significant increase in spending on educational institutions per student between 2000 and 2005. In Japan, Poland, Portugal and Spain, the decline in enrolments was concomitant with a slight rise in expenditure on educational institutions in primary, secondary and post-secondary non-tertiary education; in the other countries, it came at the same time as a sharp increase in spending (Table B1.5 and Chart B1.7).

The pattern is different at the tertiary level where spending per student between 1995 and 2005 has fallen in some cases, as expenditure failed to keep up with expanding student numbers. Expenditure on educational institutions per tertiary student remained stable over the period 1995 to 2000 but then increased by 11% on average in OECD countries from 2000 to 2005, as governments invested massively in response to the expansion of tertiary education. Australia, Austria, the Czech Republic, Finland, Mexico, Norway, Poland, the Slovak Republic and the United Kingdom followed this pattern. However, the increase in expenditure per student between 2000 and 2005 did not totally counterbalance the decrease between 1995 and 2000 in the Czech Republic, Norway and the Slovak Republic. Only in Hungary and the partner countries Estonia and Israel was there a decrease in expenditure on educational institutions per tertiary student over the two five-year-periods (Table B1.5).

B1

Chart B1.7. Changes in the number of students and changes in expenditure on educational institutions per student, by level of education (2000, 2005)

Index of change between 2000 and 2005 (2000 = 100, 2005 constant prices)

■ Change in expenditure
▨ Change in the number of students (in full-time equivalents)
◇ Change in expenditure per student

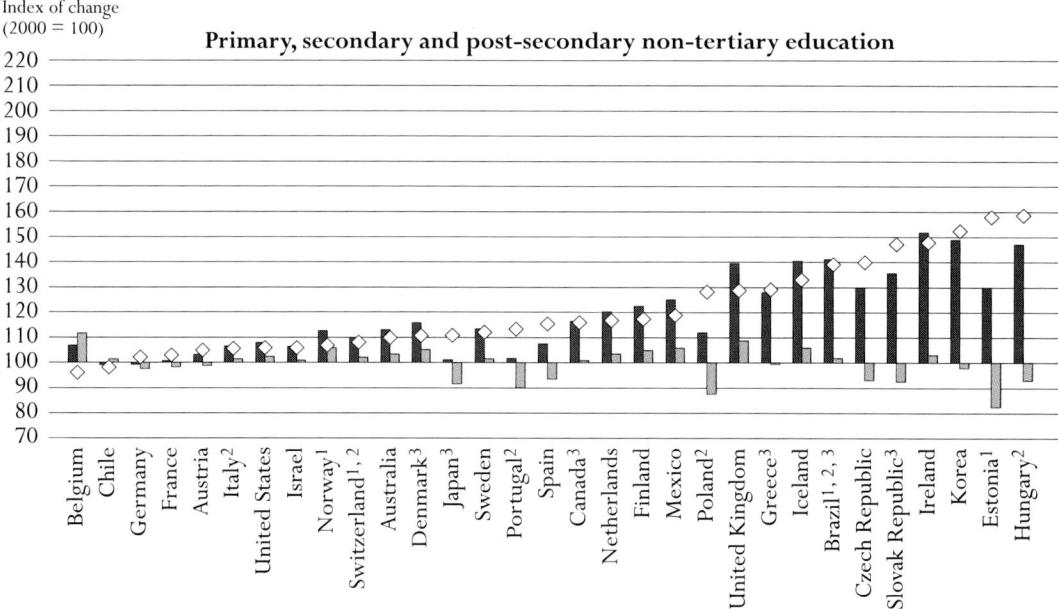

Index of change (2000 = 100)

Primary, secondary and post-secondary non-tertiary education

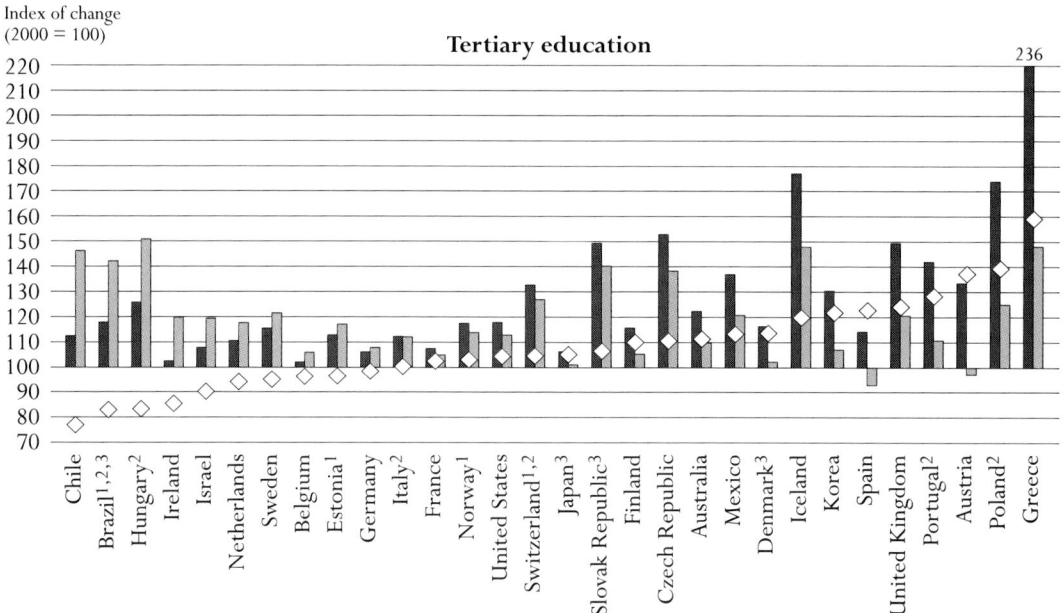

Index of change (2000 = 100)

Tertiary education

1. Public expenditure only.

2. Public institutions only.

3. Some levels of education are included with others. Refer to "x" code in Table B1.1a for details.

Countries are ranked in ascending order of change in expenditure on educational institutions per student.

Source: OECD. Table B1.5. See Annex 3 for notes (*www.oecd.org/edu/eag2008*).

StatLink ⫘ http://dx.doi.org/10.1787/401862824252

Between 2000 and 2005, out of the 30 OECD and partner countries for which data are available, Belgium, Germany, Hungary, Ireland, the Netherlands, and Sweden and the partner countries Brazil, Chile, Estonia and Israel recorded a decrease in expenditure on tertiary education per student. In all of these countries except Belgium and Germany, this decline was mainly the result of a rapid increase (of 10% or more) in the number of tertiary students (Chart B1.7). Globally, 7 out of the 11 OECD and partner countries in which the number of students enrolled in tertiary education increased by over 20% between 2000 and 2005 (the Czech Republic, Greece, Iceland, Mexico, Poland, the Slovak Republic and Switzerland) increased their expenditure on tertiary education over the period by at least the same proportion. The others – Hungary, Sweden and the partner countries Brazil and Chile – did not. Austria, Denmark and Spain were the only countries in which the number of tertiary students increased by less than 5% between 2000 and 2005, and their changes in expenditure per student between 2000 and 2005 were above the OECD average (Table B1.5 and Chart B1.7).

Change in expenditure on educational institutions per student and GDP per capita between 2000 and 2005

Chart B1.8. **Changes between 2000 and 2005 in expenditure on educational institutions per tertiary student compared with GDP per capita**

(2005 constant USD and 2005 constant PPPs)

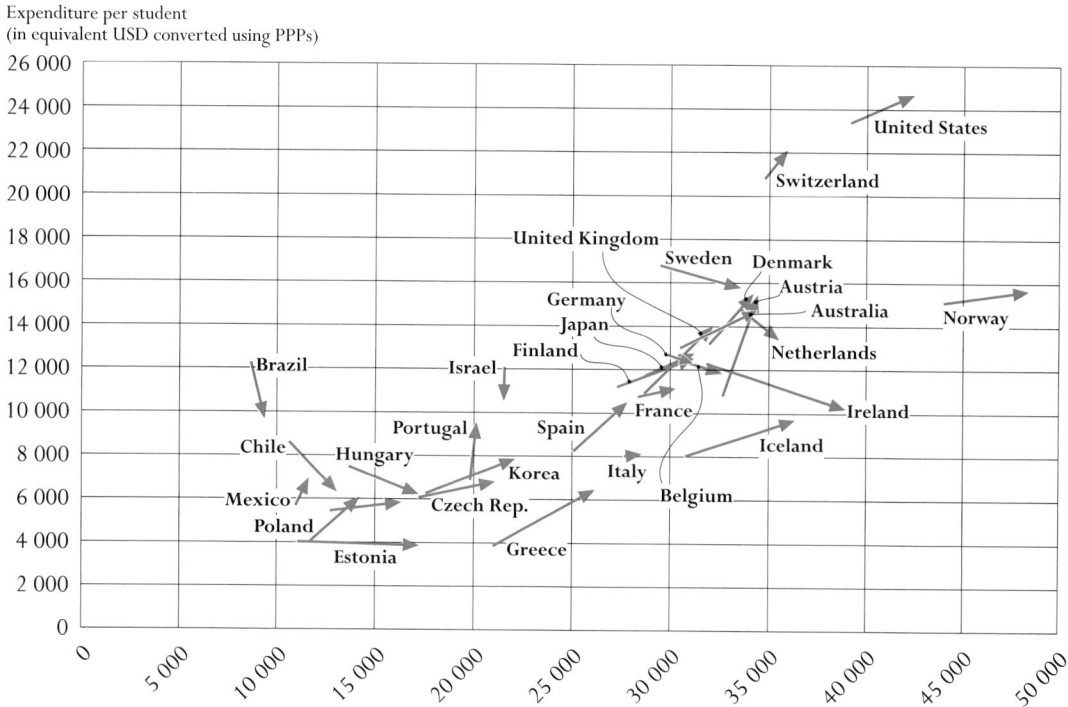

Note: The beginning of the arrow indicates expenditure per student and GDP per capita in 2000. The end of the arrow indicates corresponding values in 2005.

Source: OECD. Tables B1.1a, B1.5 and Annex 2. See Annex 3 for notes (*www.oecd.org/edu/eag2008*).

StatLink ⤨ http://dx.doi.org/10.1787/401862824252

Expenditure on educational institutions per tertiary student increased on average by 11 percentage points in OECD countries between 2000 and 2005 but not faster than GDP per capita in most countries in which expenditure per tertiary student increased. In Chart B1.8 the origin of the arrow represents GDP per capita (horizontal axis) and expenditure on educational institutions per student (vertical axis) in 2000 (at 2005 prices and 2005 purchasing power parities), and the end of each arrow shows the corresponding values for 2005. Expenditure on educational institutions per tertiary student increased in around two-thirds of the 30 countries for which data are available between 2000 and 2005 but only Australia, Austria, Denmark, Greece, Iceland, Mexico, Poland, Portugal, Spain, Switzerland and the United Kingdom had a larger increase in expenditure on educational institutions per tertiary student than in GDP per capita (Tables B1.1, B1.5 and Chart B1.8).

By contrast, in primary, secondary and post-secondary non-tertiary education, expenditure on educational institutions per student between 2000 and 2005 increased by 19% on average and faster than GDP per capita in the 22 countries (out of 31 for which data are available) with an increase in expenditure over this period. It is noteworthy that PISA performance on the reading scale tends to remain flat in the majority of countries over the period from 2000 to 2006, an indication that performance is not necessarily linked to the level of investment and that the increase in resources could be used more efficiently (see Table B1.5, PISA 2006, and Indicator B7 in *Education at a Glance 2007*).

Definitions and methodologies

Data refer to the financial year 2005 and are based on the UOE data collection on education statistics administered by the OECD in 2007 (for details see Annex 3 at *www.oecd.org/edu/eag2008*). Expenditure on educational institutions per student at a particular level of education is calculated by dividing the total expenditure on educational institutions at that level by the corresponding full-time equivalent enrolment. Only educational institutions and programmes for which both enrolment and expenditure data are available are taken into account. Expenditure in national currency is converted into equivalent USD by dividing the national currency figure by the purchasing power parity (PPP) index for GDP. The PPP exchange rate is used because the market exchange rate is affected by many factors (interest rates, trade policies, expectations of economic growth, etc.) that have little to do with current relative domestic purchasing power in different OECD countries (Annex 2 gives further details).

The OECD average is calculated as the simple average over all OECD countries for which data are available. The OECD total reflects the value of the indicator if the OECD region is considered as a whole (see the Reader's Guide for details).

Table B1.5 shows the changes in expenditure on educational institutions per student between the financial years 1995, 2000 and 2005. OECD countries were asked to collect the 1995 and 2000 data according to the definitions and the coverage of UOE 2007 data collection. All expenditure data, as well as the GDP for 1995 and 2000, are adjusted to 2005 prices using the GDP price deflator.

Expenditure on educational institutions per student relative to GDP per capita is calculated by expressing expenditure on educational institutions per student in units of national currency as a percentage of GDP per capita, also in national currency. In cases where the educational

B1

expenditure data and the GDP data pertain to different reference periods, the expenditure data are adjusted to the same reference period as the GDP data, using inflation rates for the OECD country in question (see Annex 2).

Cumulative expenditure over the average duration of tertiary studies (Table B1.3b) is calculated by multiplying current annual expenditure by the typical duration of tertiary studies. The methodology used for the estimation of the typical duration of tertiary studies is described in Annex 3 (*www.oecd.org/edu/eag2008*). For the estimation of the duration of tertiary education, data are based on a special survey carried out in OECD countries in 2005.

The ranking of OECD countries by annual expenditure on educational services per student is affected by differences in how countries define full-time, part-time and full-time equivalent enrolment. Some OECD countries count every participant at the tertiary level as a full-time student while others determine a student's intensity of participation by the credits which he or she obtains for successful completion of specific course units during a specified reference period. OECD countries that can accurately account for part-time enrolment have higher expenditure on educational institutions per full-time equivalent student than OECD countries that cannot differentiate among different modes of student attendance.

Further references

The following additional material relevant to this indicator is available on line at:
StatLink http://dx.doi.org/10.1787/401862824252

- *Table B1.1c. Annual expenditure on educational institutions per student for core services (2005)*

B1

Table B1.1a.
Annual expenditure on educational institutions per student for all services (2005)
In equivalent USD converted using PPPs for GDP, by level of education, based on full-time equivalents

| | Pre-primary education (for children aged 3 and older) | Primary education | Secondary education | | | Post-secondary non-tertiary education | Tertiary education (including R&D activities) | | | All tertiary education excluding R&D activities | Primary to tertiary education |
			Lower secondary education	Upper secondary education	All secondary education		Tertiary-type B education	Tertiary-type A & advanced research programmes	All tertiary education		
	(1)	(2)	(3)	(4)	(5)	(6)	(7)	(8)	(9)	(10)	(11)
Australia	m	5 992	7 930	9 223	8 408	7 973	8 569	15 599	14 579	10 199	8 340
Austria	6 562	8 259	9 505	10 028	9 751	x(4)	11 394	15 028	14 775	10 061	10 407
Belgium	4 816	6 648	x(5)	x(5)	7 731	x(5)	x(9)	x(9)	11 960	8 046	8 034
Canada[1, 2]	x(5)	x(5)	x(5)	x(5)	7 837	x(7)	m	20 156	m	m	m
Czech Republic	3 353	2 812	4 864	4 830	4 847	2 098	3 105	7 019	6 649	5 409	4 545
Denmark	5 320	8 513	8 606	10 197	9 407	x(4, 9)	x(9)	x(9)	14 959	m	10 108
Finland	4 395	5 557	8 875	6 441	7 324	x(5)	n	12 285	12 285	7 582	7 711
France	4 817	5 365	7 881	10 311	8 927	4 488	9 483	11 486	10 995	7 673	8 101
Germany	5 508	5 014	6 200	10 282	7 636	10 531	6 938	13 351	12 446	7 772	7 872
Greece	x(2)	5 146	x(5)	x(5)	8 423	7 266	3 417	7 661	6 130	4 928	5 692
Hungary[2]	4 402	4 438	3 993	3 613	3 806	4 731	4 549	6 328	6 244	4 837	4 423
Iceland	6 800	9 254	8 985	8 004	8 411	x(4, 9)	x(9)	x(9)	9 474	m	8 931
Ireland	5 345	5 732	7 352	7 680	7 500	5 811	x(9)	x(9)	10 468	7 386	7 108
Italy[2]	6 139	6 835	7 599	7 682	7 648	m	7 420	8 032	8 026	5 314	7 540
Japan	4 174	6 744	7 630	8 164	7 908	x(4, 9)	7 969	13 827	12 326	m	8 378
Korea	2 426	4 691	5 661	7 765	6 645	a	3 811	9 938	7 606	6 607	6 212
Luxembourg[2]	x(2)	14 079	18 844	18 845	18 845	m	m	m	m	m	m
Mexico	1 964	1 913	1 839	2 853	2 180	a	x(9)	x(9)	6 402	5 346	2 405
Netherlands	5 885	6 266	8 166	7 225	7 741	7 000	n	13 883	13 883	8 719	8 147
New Zealand	4 778	4 780	5 165	7 586	6 278	6 126	7 740	11 002	10 262	8 864	6 342
Norway	5 236	9 001	9 687	12 096	10 995	x(5)	x(9)	x(9)	15 552	9 981	10 980
Poland[2]	4 130	3 312	2 971	3 131	3 055	2 956	x(9)	x(9)	5 593	4 883	3 592
Portugal[2]	4 808	4 871	6 555	6 381	6 473	m	x(9)	x(9)	8 787	6 785	6 197
Slovak Republic	2 895	2 806	2 430	3 026	2 716	x(4)	x(4)	5 783	5 783	5 131	3 139
Spain	5 015	5 502	x(5)	x(5)	7 211	a	9 059	10 301	10 089	7 182	7 134
Sweden	4 852	7 532	8 091	8 292	8 198	2 691	x(9)	x(9)	15 946	8 281	9 156
Switzerland[2]	3 853	8 469	9 756	16 166	12 861	9 119	4 163	23 137	21 734	13 041	12 195
Turkey	m	m	m	m	m	m	m	m	m	m	m
United Kingdom	6 420	6 361	x(5)	x(5)	7 167	x(5)	x(9)	x(9)	13 506	8 842	7 741
United States	8 301	9 156	9 899	10 969	10 390	m	x(9)	x(9)	24 370	21 588	12 788
OECD average	*4 888*	*6 252*	*7 437*	*8 366*	*7 804*	*4 719*	*~*	*~*	*11 512*	*8 102*	*7 527*
OECD total	*5 254*	*6 173*	*~*	*~*	*7 736*	*~*	*~*	*~*	*15 559*	*13 141*	*8 553*
EU19 average	*4 980*	*6 055*	*7 462*	*7 864*	*7 600*	*4 757*	*~*	*~*	*10 474*	*6 990*	*7 036*
Brazil[2]	1 215	1 425	1 359	899	1 186	a	x(9)	x(9)	9 994	9 808	1 542
Chile[3]	2 953	1 936	1 865	1 956	1 924	a	3 922	7 977	6 620	m	2 694
Estonia	1 833	3 384	3 802	4 033	3 918	4 417	2 883	4 386	3 869	3 867	3 768
Israel	3 650	4 699	x(5)	x(5)	5 495	4 275	8 232	11 581	10 919	8 476	6 000
Russian Federation[2]	m	x(5)	x(5)	x(5)	1 754	x(5)	2 274	3 876	3 421	3 155	2 051
Slovenia[2]	6 364	x(3)	7 994	5 565	7 065	x(4)	x(9)	x(9)	8 573	7 037	7 378

1. Year of reference 2004.
2. Public institutions only (for Canada, in tertiary education only).
3. Year of reference 2006.
Source: OECD. See Annex 3 for notes (www.oecd.org/edu/eag2008).
Please refer to the Reader's Guide for information concerning the symbols replacing missing data.
StatLink ⌐∎⑤ http://dx.doi.org/10.1787/401862824252

Table B1.1b.
Annual expenditure per student on core services, ancillary services and R&D (2005)
In equivalent USD converted using PPPs for GDP, by level of education and type of service, based on full-time equivalents

	Primary, secondary and post-secondary non-tertiary education			Tertiary education			
	Educational core services	Ancillary services (transport, meals, housing provided by institutions)	Total	Educational core services	Ancillary services (transport, meals, housing provided by institutions)	R & D	Total
	(1)	(2)	(3)	(4)	(5)	(6)	(7)
Australia	6 856	286	**7 142**	9 544	654	4 381	**14 579**
Austria	9 046	390	**9 436**	9 952	109	4 714	**14 775**
Belgium	7 021	285	**7 306**	7 725	321	3 915	**11 960**
Canada[1, 2, 3]	7 398	439	**7 837**	13 463	1 527	5 166	**20 156**
Czech Republic	3 801	297	**4 098**	5 234	175	1 239	**6 649**
Denmark[1]	8 997	a	**8 997**	x(7)	a	x(7)	**14 959**
Finland	5 896	714	**6 610**	7 575	7	4 703	**12 285**
France	6 492	964	**7 456**	7 015	658	3 323	**10 995**
Germany	6 878	160	**7 039**	7 158	614	4 674	**12 446**
Greece[1]	5 355	138	**5 493**	4 459	470	1 202	**6 130**
Hungary[3]	3 668	359	**4 027**	4 590	247	1 407	**6 244**
Iceland[1]	x(3)	x(3)	**8 815**	x(7)	x(7)	x(7)	**9 474**
Ireland	6 269	142	**6 411**	7 386	x(7)	3 082	**10 468**
Italy[3]	7 111	298	**7 410**	5 011	303	2 712	**8 026**
Japan[1]	x(3)	x(3)	**7 343**	x(7)	x(7)	x(7)	**12 326**
Korea	5 133	505	**5 638**	6 574	33	999	**7 606**
Luxembourg[1, 3]	x(3)	x(3)	**15 930**	m	m	m	**m**
Mexico	2 025	m	**2 025**	5 346	m	1 056	**6 402**
Netherlands	6 972	72	**7 045**	8 717	2	5 164	**13 883**
New Zealand	x(3)	x(3)	**5 659**	8 864	x(7)	1 397	**10 262**
Norway	x(3)	x(3)	**9 975**	9 897	84	5 571	**15 552**
Poland[3]	3 065	99	**3 165**	4 881	1	710	**5 593**
Portugal[3]	5 606	40	**5 646**	6 785	x(7)	2 002	**8 787**
Slovak Republic[1]	2 336	404	**2 740**	4 273	858	652	**5 783**
Spain	6 152	259	**6 411**	7 182	m	2 907	**10 089**
Sweden	7 067	795	**7 861**	8 281	n	7 666	**15 946**
Switzerland[3]	x(3)	x(3)	**10 721**	13 041	x(4)	8 694	**21 734**
Turkey	m	m	**m**	m	m	m	**m**
United Kingdom	5 723	1 105	**6 888**	7 793	1 049	4 665	**13 506**
United States	9 006	763	**9 769**	18 656	2 932	2 782	**24 370**
OECD average	*5 994*	*387*	*7 065*	*7 976*	*502*	*3 391*	*11 512*
EU19 average	*5 970*	*362*	*6 840*	*6 707*	*321*	*3 220*	*10 474*
Brazil[1, 3]	x(3)	x(3)	**1 287**	9 808	x(4)	186	**9 994**
Chile[4]	1 842	88	**1 930**	x(7)	x(7)	x(7)	**6 620**
Estonia	x(3)	x(3)	**3 736**	3 867	x(4)	2	**3 869**
Israel	4 875	165	**5 041**	7 252	1 224	2 443	**10 919**
Russian Federation[3]	x(3)	x(3)	**1 754**	x(7)	x(7)	266	**3 421**
Slovenia[3]	6 770	295	**7 065**	7 016	21	1 536	**8 573**

1. Some levels of education are included with others. Refer to "x" code in Table B1.1a for details.
2. Tertiary-type A only and year of reference 2004.
3. Public institutions only (for Canada, in tertiary education only).
4. Year of reference 2006.
Source: OECD. See Annex 3 for notes (*www.oecd.org/edu/eag2008*).
Please refer to the Reader's Guide for information concerning the symbols replacing missing data.
StatLink ⫶⫶⫶ http://dx.doi.org/10.1787/401862824252

B1

Table B1.2.
Distribution of expenditure (as a percentage) on educational institutions compared to the number of students enrolled at each level of education (2005)

The table shows the distribution of educational expenditure and of students across levels of education. The number of students is adjusted to the financial year. For example, when reading the first and second columns, in the Czech Republic, 10 % of all expenditure on educational institutions is allocated to pre-primary education whereas 13.4 % of pupils/students are enrolled at this level of education.

		Pre-primary education (for children aged 3 and older)		Primary, secondary and post-secondary non-tertiary education		All tertiary education		Not allocated by level		All levels of education	
		Proportion of expenditure on educational institutions	Proportion of students enrolled, based on full-time equivalents	Proportion of expenditure on educational institutions	Proportion of students enrolled, based on full-time equivalents	Proportion of expenditure on educational institutions	Proportion of students enrolled, based on full-time equivalents	Proportion of expenditure on educational institutions	Proportion of students enrolled, based on full-time equivalents	Proportion of expenditure on educational institutions	Proportion of students enrolled, based on full-time equivalents
		(1)		(2)		(3)		(4)		(5)	
OECD countries	Australia	m	2.9	m	81.3	m	15.6	m	0.2	m	100
	Austria	8.9	13.4	67.6	70.8	23.5	15.7	a	a	100	100
	Belgium	9.8	15.6	67.7	71.2	20.5	13.2	2.0	n	100	100
	Canada	m	m	m	m	m	m	m	m	m	m
	Czech Republic	10.0	13.4	65.0	71.4	22.4	15.2	2.6	n	100	100
	Denmark[1]	10.8	19.7	60.3	65.3	23.0	15.0	6.0	n	100	100
	Finland	6.4	10.7	64.7	72.0	29.0	17.3	n	n	100	100
	France	11.3	17.6	66.8	67.4	21.9	15.0	n	n	100	100
	Germany	9.9	13.8	66.6	72.9	21.4	13.3	2.1	0.1	100	100
	Greece	x(2)	x(2)	66.5	70.2	33.5	29.8	n	n	100	100
	Hungary[2]	15.3	16.1	59.8	68.9	20.2	15.0	4.7	n	100	100
	Iceland[1]	9.5	13.1	67.4	71.4	15.5	15.2	7.7	n	100	100
	Ireland	0.1	0.1	74.7	82.8	25.3	17.2	n	n	100	100
	Italy[2]	9.6	11.6	70.0	69.7	20.4	18.7	n	n	100	100
	Japan[1]	4.1	8.4	61.7	71.7	27.1	18.8	7.0	1.1	100	100
	Korea	1.8	4.7	60.5	67.6	33.5	27.8	4.2	n	100	100
	Luxembourg	m	m	m	m	m	m	m	m	m	m
	Mexico	10.8	13.2	66.9	79.3	20.1	7.5	2.3	n	100	100
	Netherlands	7.3	9.9	67.2	75.6	25.4	14.5	n	n	100	100
	New Zealand	4.9	6.6	70.9	79.6	22.4	13.9	1.7	n	100	100
	Norway	5.8	11.9	66.7	72.2	22.9	15.9	4.6	n	100	100
	Poland[2]	10.6	9.4	64.9	74.7	24.5	16.0	n	n	100	100
	Portugal[2]	6.0	7.9	68.2	75.9	22.6	16.2	3.2	n	100	100
	Slovak Republic[1]	11.3	12.4	65.4	76.1	20.8	11.5	2.6	a	100	100
	Spain	13.1	17.7	62.7	66.1	24.2	16.2	n	n	100	100
	Sweden	8.5	14.9	66.0	71.5	25.5	13.6	n	n	100	100
	Switzerland[2]	4.0	10.5	68.6	77.5	25.8	12.0	1.6	n	100	100
	Turkey	m	m	m	m	m	m	m	m	m	m
	United Kingdom	4.8	5.7	73.9	82.2	21.6	12.2	a	a	100	100
	United States	5.8	8.7	57.1	72.5	37.1	18.9	n	n	100	100
	OECD average	*8.0*	*11.1*	*66.1*	*73.2*	*24.2*	*16.0*	*2.0*	*n*	*100*	*100*
Partner countries	Brazil[1, 2]	8.4	10.5	74.2	86.9	17.4	2.6	n	n	100	100
	Chile[3]	7.9	7.2	55.2	77.6	36.9	15.1	n	n	100	100
	Estonia	7.2	13.9	69.2	65.2	23.0	20.9	0.6	n	100	m
	Israel	10.4	17.3	55.9	67.6	23.6	13.2	10.1	1.9	100	100
	Russian Federation[2]	13.9	m	49.8	m	21.1	m	15.2	m	100	m
	Slovenia[2]	9.6	11.0	68.6	70.5	21.8	18.5	n	n	100	100

1. Some levels of education are included with others. Refer to "x" code in Table B1.1a for details.
2. Public institutions only.
3. Year of reference 2006.

Source: OECD. See Annex 3 for notes (*www.oecd.org/edu/eag2008*).
Please refer to the Reader's Guide for information concerning the symbols replacing missing data.
StatLink http://dx.doi.org/10.1787/401862824252

Table B1.3a.
Cumulative expenditure on educational institutions per student for all services over the theoretical duration of primary and secondary studies (2005)
In equivalent USD converted using PPPs for GDP, by level of education

B1

	Average theoretical duration of primary and secondary studies (in years)				Cumulative expenditure per student over the theoretical duration of primary and secondary studies (in USD)				
	Primary education	Lower secondary education	Upper secondary education	Total primary and secondary education	Primary education	Lower secondary education	Upper secondary education	All secondary education	Total primary and secondary education
	(1)	(2)	(3)	(4)	(5)	(6)	(7)	(8)	(9)
Australia	7.0	4.0	2.0	**13.0**	41 946	31 721	18 446	50 168	**92 113**
Austria	4.0	4.0	4.0	**12.0**	33 034	38 019	40 114	78 132	**111 167**
Belgium	6.0	2.0	4.0	**12.0**	39 889	x(8)	x(8)	46 385	**86 275**
Canada[1]	6.0	3.0	3.0	**12.0**	x(9)	x(9)	x(9)	x(9)	**94 040**
Czech Republic	5.0	4.0	4.0	**13.0**	14 058	19 456	19 320	38 776	**52 834**
Denmark	6.0	4.0	3.0	**13.0**	51 080	34 426	30 590	65 016	**116 096**
Finland	6.0	3.0	3.0	**12.0**	33 343	26 625	19 324	45 949	**79 292**
France	5.0	4.0	3.0	**12.0**	26 824	31 522	30 933	62 456	**89 280**
Germany	4.0	6.0	3.0	**13.0**	20 055	37 199	30 845	68 045	**88 100**
Greece	6.0	3.0	3.0	**12.0**	30 874	x(8)	x(8)	50 536	**81 410**
Hungary[2]	4.0	4.0	4.0	**12.0**	17 752	15 973	14 453	30 425	**48 177**
Iceland	7.0	3.0	4.0	**14.0**	64 778	26 955	32 016	58 972	**123 750**
Ireland	8.0	3.0	2.5	**13.5**	45 859	22 057	19 200	41 258	**87 116**
Italy[2]	5.0	3.0	5.0	**13.0**	34 175	22 796	38 408	61 203	**95 378**
Japan	6.0	3.0	3.0	**12.0**	40 463	22 890	24 492	47 382	**87 845**
Korea	6.0	3.0	3.0	**12.0**	28 143	16 984	23 296	40 280	**68 424**
Luxembourg[2]	6.0	3.0	4.0	**13.0**	84 475	56 533	75 381	131 914	**216 389**
Mexico	6.0	3.0	3.0	**12.0**	11 476	5 517	8 558	14 075	**25 551**
Netherlands	6.0	2.0	3.0	**11.0**	37 599	16 331	21 674	38 005	**75 604**
New Zealand	6.0	4.0	3.0	**13.0**	28 682	20 661	22 759	43 420	**72 102**
Norway	7.0	3.0	3.0	**13.0**	63 006	29 062	36 289	65 351	**128 357**
Poland[2]	6.0	3.0	4.0	**13.0**	19 871	8 912	12 522	21 434	**41 305**
Portugal[2]	6.0	3.0	3.0	**12.0**	29 226	19 665	19 143	38 809	**68 034**
Slovak Republic	4.0	5.0	4.0	**13.0**	11 224	12 150	12 103	24 253	**35 477**
Spain	6.0	4.0	2.0	**12.0**	33 015	x(8)	x(8)	43 268	**76 282**
Sweden	6.0	3.0	3.0	**12.0**	45 194	24 274	24 877	49 151	**94 345**
Switzerland[2]	6.0	3.0	3.5	**12.5**	50 814	29 269	56 582	85 851	**136 664**
Turkey[2]	8.0	a	3.0	**11.0**	m	a	m	m	**m**
United Kingdom	6.0	3.0	3.5	**12.5**	38 165	x(8)	x(8)	46 585	**84 750**
United States	6.0	3.0	3.0	**12.0**	54 936	29 696	32 907	62 603	**117 538**
OECD average	*5.9*	*3.3*	*3.3*	*12.4*	*36 112*	*~*	*~*	*51 374*	*87 720*
Brazil[2]	4.0	4.0	3.0	**11.0**	5 701	5 436	2 697	8 133	**13 834**
Chile[3]	6.0	2.0	4.0	**12.0**	11 614	3 730	7 825	11 555	**23 169**
Estonia	6.0	3.0	3.0	**12.0**	20 303	11 406	12 098	23 504	**43 807**
Israel	6.0	3.0	3.0	**12.0**	28 193	x(8)	x(8)	32 972	**61 165**
Russian Federation[2]	4.0	5.0	2.0	**11.0**	x(9)	x(9)	x(9)	x(9)	**19 296**
Slovenia[2]	6.0	3.0	3.0	**12.0**	x(6)	71 947	16 695	88 642	**88 642**

1. Year of reference 2004.
2. Public institutions only.
3. Year of reference 2006.
Source: OECD. See Annex 3 for notes (*www.oecd.org/edu/eag2008*).
Please refer to the Reader's Guide for information concerning the symbols replacing missing data.
StatLink ⌦⍿ http://dx.doi.org/10.1787/401862824252

B1

Table B1.3b.
Cumulative expenditure on educational institutions per student for all services
over the average duration of tertiary studies (2005)
In equivalent USD converted using PPPS for GDP, by type of programme

	Method[1]	Average duration of tertiary studies (in years)			Cumulative expenditure per student over the average duration of tertiary studies (in USD)		
		Tertiary-type B education	Tertiary-type A and advanced research programmes	All tertiary education	Tertiary-type B education	Tertiary-type A and advanced research programmes	All tertiary education
		(1)	(2)	(3)	(4)	(5)	(6)
Australia	CM	m	2.87	m	m	44 768	m
Austria	CM	2.78	5.60	5.30	31 677	84 156	78 308
Belgium	CM	2.41	3.67	2.99	x(6)	x(6)	35 761
Canada		m	m	m	m	m	m
Czech Republic		m	m	m	m	m	m
Denmark	AF	2.10	3.84	3.70	x(6)	x(6)	55 348
Finland	CM	a	4.85	4.85	a	59 582	59 582
France[2]	CM	3.00	4.74	4.02	28 448	54 444	44 202
Germany	CM	2.37	6.57	5.36	16 450	87 688	66 758
Greece	CM	5.00	5.26	5.25	17 084	40 299	32 185
Hungary[3]	CM	2.00	4.05	4.05	9 098	25 627	25 289
Iceland	CM	x(3)	x(3)	3.69	x(6)	x(6)	34 960
Ireland	CM	2.21	4.02	3.24	x(6)	x(6)	33 916
Italy[3]	AF	m	5.14	5.01	m	41 285	40 212
Japan	CM	2.11	4.51	4.07	16 815	62 359	50 167
Korea	CM	2.07	4.22	3.43	7 889	41 938	26 089
Luxembourg		m	m	m	m	m	m
Mexico	AF	x(3)	3.42	3.42	x(6)	x(6)	21 896
Netherlands	CM	a	5.24	5.24	a	72 746	72 746
New Zealand	CM	1.87	3.68	3.05	14 475	40 489	31 298
Norway	CM	m	m	m	m	m	m
Poland[3]	CM	m	3.68	m	m	m	m
Portugal		m	m	m	m	m	m
Slovak Republic	AF	2.47	3.90	3.82	m	22 555	22 555
Spain	CM	2.15	5.54	4.66	19 478	57 069	47 015
Sweden	CM	2.26	4.93	4.68	x(6)	x(6)	74 629
Switzerland[3]	CM	2.19	5.45	3.62	9 103	126 160	78 771
Turkey	CM	2.73	2.37	2.65	x(6)	x(6)	m
United Kingdom[2]	CM	3.52	5.86	4.34	x(6)	x(6)	58 654
United States		m	m	m	m	m	m
OECD average		*2.28*	*4.50*	*4.11*	*~*	*~*	*47 159*

1. Either the Chain Method (CM) or an Approximation Formula (AF) was used to estimate the duration of tertiary studies.
2. Average duration of tertiary studies is estimated based on national data.
3. Public institutions only.
Source: OECD. See Annex 3 for notes (www.oecd.org/edu/eag2008).
Please refer to the Reader's Guide for information concerning the symbols replacing missing data.
StatLink ⤳ http://dx.doi.org/10.1787/401862824252

Table B1.4.

Annual expenditure on educational institutions per student for all services relative to GDP per capita (2005)

By level of education, based on full-time equivalents

		Pre-primary education (for children aged 3 and older)	Primary education	Secondary education: Lower secondary education	Secondary education: Upper secondary education	Secondary education: All secondary education	Post-secondary non-tertiary education	Tertiary education (including R&D activities): Tertiary-type B education	Tertiary education (including R&D activities): Tertiary-type A & advanced research programmes	Tertiary education (including R&D activities): All tertiary education	All tertiary education excluding R&D activities	Primary to tertiary education
		(1)	(2)	(3)	(4)	(5)	(6)	(7)	(8)	(9)	(10)	(11)
OECD countries	Australia	m	18	23	27	25	23	25	46	43	30	25
	Austria	19	24	28	29	29	x(4)	33	44	43	29	31
	Belgium	15	21	x(5)	x(5)	24	x(5)	x(9)	x(9)	37	25	25
	Canada[1, 2]	x(5)	x(5)	x(5)	x(5)	24	x(7)	m	61	m	m	m
	Czech Republic	17	14	24	24	24	10	15	35	33	27	22
	Denmark	16	25	26	30	28	x(4, 9)	x(9)	x(9)	44	m	30
	Finland	14	18	29	21	24	x(5)	n	40	40	25	25
	France	16	18	27	35	30	15	32	39	37	26	27
	Germany	18	16	20	34	25	35	23	44	41	25	26
	Greece	x(2)	20	x(5)	x(5)	33	29	13	30	24	19	22
	Hungary[2]	26	26	23	21	22	28	27	37	37	28	26
	Iceland	19	26	25	23	24	x(4, 9)	x(9)	x(9)	27	m	25
	Ireland	14	15	19	20	20	15	x(9)	x(9)	28	19	19
	Italy[2]	22	25	27	28	28	m	27	29	29	19	27
	Japan	14	22	25	27	26	x(4, 9)	26	46	41	m	28
	Korea	11	22	27	36	31	a	18	42	36	31	29
	Luxembourg[2]	x(2)	20	27	27	27	x(5)	m	m	m	m	m
	Mexico	17	17	16	25	19	a	x(9)	x(9)	57	47	21
	Netherlands	17	18	24	21	22	20	n	40	40	25	23
	New Zealand	19	19	21	30	25	25	31	44	41	36	25
	Norway	11	19	20	25	23	x(5)	x(9)	x(9)	33	21	23
	Poland[2]	30	24	22	23	23	22	28	42	41	36	26
	Portugal[2]	24	24	33	32	32	m	x(9)	x(9)	44	34	31
	Slovak Republic	18	18	15	19	17	x(4)	x(4)	36	36	32	20
	Spain	18	20	x(5)	x(5)	26	a	33	38	37	26	26
	Sweden	15	23	25	25	25	8	x(9)	x(9)	49	25	28
	Switzerland[2]	11	24	27	46	36	26	12	65	61	37	34
	Turkey	m	m	m	m	m	m	m	m	m	m	m
	United Kingdom	20	20	x(5)	x(5)	23	x(5)	x(9)	x(9)	43	28	25
	United States	20	22	24	26	25	m	x(9)	x(9)	58	52	31
	OECD average	*18*	*21*	*24*	*27*	*26*	*17*	*22*	*42*	*40*	*29*	*26*
	EU19 average	*18*	*20*	*24*	*27*	*25*	*15*	*22*	*41*	*38*	*29*	*25*
Partner countries	Brazil[2]	13	15	15	10	13	a	x(9)	x(9)	108	106	17
	Chile[3]	23	15	15	15	15	a	31	63	52	m	21
	Estonia	11	20	23	24	24	27	17	26	23	23	23
	Israel	16	21	x(5)	x(5)	24	19	36	51	48	m	26
	Russian Federation[2]	m	x(5)	x(5)	x(5)	16	x(5)	21	36	32	m	19
	Slovenia[2]	28	x(3)	35	24	31	x(4)	x(9)	x(9)	37	31	32

1. Year of reference 2004.
2. Public institutions only (for Canada, in tertiary education only).
3. Year of reference 2006.

Source: OECD. See Annex 3 for notes (*www.oecd.org/edu/eag2008*).

Please refer to the Reader's Guide for information concerning the symbols replacing missing data.

StatLink http://dx.doi.org/10.1787/401862824252

B1

Table B1.5.
Change in expenditure on educational institutions for all services per student relative to different factors, by level of education (1995, 2000, 2005)
Index of change between 1995, 2000 and 2005 (GDP deflator 2000=100, constant prices)

	Primary, secondary and post-secondary non-tertiary education						Tertiary education					
	Change in expenditure (2000=100)		Change in the number of students (2000=100)		Change in expenditure per student (2000=100)		Change in expenditure (2000=100)		Change in the number of students (2000=100)		Change in expenditure per student (2000=100)	
	1995	2005	1995	2005	1995	2005	1995	2005	1995	2005	1995	2005
Australia	74	113	94	103	79	109	91	122	83	110	110	111
Austria	94	103	m	99	m	104	98	133	91	97	108	137
Belgium	m	107	m	112	m	96	m	102	m	106	m	96
Canada[1,2,3]	106	116	m	101	m	115	75	117	m	m	m	m
Czech Republic	116	130	107	93	109	139	101	153	64	138	159	111
Denmark[1]	84	116	96	105	87	110	91	116	96	102	95	114
Finland	89	123	93	105	96	117	90	116	89	105	101	110
France	90	101	m	98	m	103	91	107	m	105	m	102
Germany	94	99	97	98	97	102	95	106	104	108	91	98
Greece[1]	64	128	107	99	60	129	66	236	68	148	97	159
Hungary[3]	100	147	105	93	95	158	74	126	58	151	128	83
Iceland	m	140	99	106	m	133	m	177	79	148	m	120
Ireland	83	152	105	103	79	147	57	102	86	120	66	85
Italy[3]	103	107	102	101	101	105	79	112	101	112	79	100
Japan[1]	98	101	113	92	86	110	88	106	99	101	88	105
Korea	m	149	107	98	m	152	m	130	68	107	m	122
Luxembourg	m	m	m	m	m	m	m	m	m	m	m	m
Mexico	81	125	93	106	87	118	77	137	77	121	101	113
Netherlands	84	120	98	103	86	116	94	111	99	118	95	94
New Zealand[4]	71	108	m	m	m	m	105	118	m	m	m	m
Norway[4]	94	113	89	106	107	106	107	117	100	114	106	103
Poland[3]	70	112	110	88	64	128	59	174	55	125	107	139
Portugal[3]	76	102	105	90	72	113	73	142	77	111	96	128
Slovak Republic[1]	96	136	105	93	91	147	81	149	72	140	112	106
Spain	99	108	119	94	84	115	72	114	100	93	72	123
Sweden	81	113	86	102	94	112	81	116	83	121	98	95
Switzerland[3,4]	101	110	95	102	107	108	74	133	95	127	78	105
Turkey	m	m	m	m	m	m	m	m	m	m	m	m
United Kingdom	87	140	87	109	100	129	98	149	89	118	110	126
United States	80	108	95	102	83	105	70	118	92	113	77	104
OECD average	*89*	*119*	*100*	*100*	*89*	*119*	*83*	*130*	*84*	*118*	*99*	*111*
EU19 average	*89*	*119*	*101*	*99*	*88*	*120*	*82*	*131*	*83*	*118*	*101*	*111*
Brazil[1,3,4]	82	141	85	102	96	139	78	118	79	142	98	83
Chile[5]	54	99	88	101	62	98	61	112	76	146	80	77
Estonia[4]	77	130	96	83	79	158	68	113	60	117	113	96
Israel	86	106	85	101	100	105	77	108	74	119	105	90
Russian Federation	m	154	m	m	m	m	m	228	m	m	m	m
Slovenia	m	m	m	m	m	m	m	m	m	m	m	m

1. Some levels of education are included with others. Refer to "x" code in Table B1.1a for details.
2. Year of reference 2004 instead of 2005.
3. Public institutions only (for Canada, in tertiary education only).
4. Public expenditure only.
5. Year of reference 2006 instead of 2005.
Source: OECD. See Annex 3 for notes (*www.oecd.org/edu/eag2008*).
Please refer to the Reader's Guide for information concerning the symbols replacing missing data.
StatLink ⏫🖦🔧 http://dx.doi.org/10.1787/401862824252

WHAT PROPORTION OF NATIONAL WEALTH IS SPENT ON EDUCATION?

Expenditure on educational institutions as a percentage of GDP shows how a country prioritises education in relation to its overall allocation of resources. Tuition fees and investment in education from private entities other than households (see Indicator B5) have a strong impact on differences in the overall amount of financial resources that OECD countries devote to their education systems, especially at the tertiary level.

Key results

Chart B2.1. Expenditure on educational institutions as a percentage of GDP for all levels of education (1995, 2000, 2005)

This chart measures educational investment through the share of national income that each country devoted to spending on educational institutions in 1995, 2000 and 2005. It captures both direct and indirect expenditure on educational institutions from both public and private sources of funds.

☐ 2005   ■ 2000   ◆ 1995

OECD countries spend 6.1% of their collective GDP on educational institutions. The increase in spending on educational institutions between 1995 and 2005 fell behind growth in national income in nearly half of the 28 OECD countries and partner countries for which data are available.

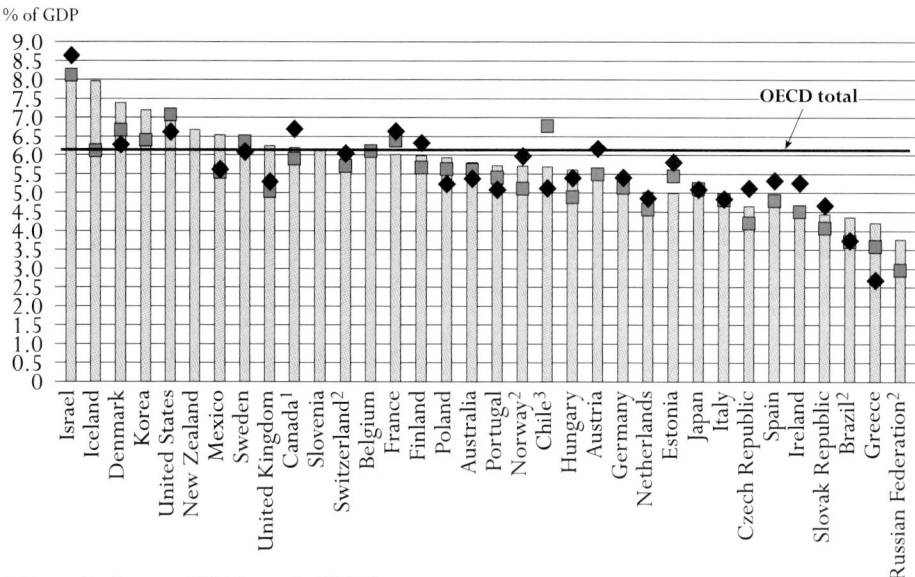

1. Year of reference 2004 instead of 2005.
2. Public expenditure only (for Switzerland, in tertiary education only).
3. Year of reference 2006 instead of 2005.
Countries are ranked in descending order of total expenditure from both public and private sources on educational institutions in 2005.
Source: OECD. Table B2.1. See Annex 3 for notes (*www.oecd.org/edu/eag2008*).
StatLink ⓢ http://dx.doi.org/10.1787/401864037554

Other highlights of this indicator

■ About 60% of expenditure on educational institutions, or 3.7% of the combined GDP in the OECD area, is devoted to primary, secondary and post-secondary non-tertiary education. Compared to their GDP, Iceland spends nearly twice as much as Greece.

■ Tertiary education accounts for nearly one-third of the combined OECD expenditure on educational institutions (2.0% of the combined GDP). In Canada and the United States expenditure at this level reaches up to 40% of expenditure on educational institutions.

■ Canada, Korea and the United States spend between 2.4 and 2.9% of their GDP on tertiary institutions. Korea, the United States, and the partner country Chile (1.8%) show the highest proportions of private expenditure at the tertiary level. Relative to GDP, the United States spends over three times more on tertiary education than Italy and the Slovak Republic and nearly four times more than the partner countries Brazil and the Russian Federation.

■ More people are completing upper secondary and tertiary education than ever before, and in many countries the expansion has been accompanied by massive financial investments. For all levels of education combined, public and private investment in education increased in all countries by at least 8% between 1995 and 2005 in real terms and increased on average by 42% in OECD countries. In two-thirds of these countries, the increase is larger for tertiary education than for primary to post-secondary non-tertiary levels combined.

■ On average in OECD countries, expenditure for all levels of education combined increased relatively more than GDP between 1995 and 2005. The increase in expenditure on educational institutions as a proportion of GDP exceeded 0.8 percentage points over this decade in Denmark, Greece, Mexico and the United Kingdom.

■ Increases in expenditure on educational institutions and in GDP did not however occur at the same pace during this period. On average, expenditure for all levels of education grew slightly less than GDP between 1995 and 2000 (17 and 20%, respectively), and significantly more than GDP between 2000 and 2005 (21 and 14%, respectively). Expenditure on educational institutions for all levels of education as a percentage of GDP increased in both of these 5-year periods in 7 of the 28 OECD and partner countries with comparable data.

■ At primary, secondary and post-secondary non tertiary levels, expenditure in most countries increased less than GDP between 1995 and 2000 but more than GDP between 2000 and 2005. On average, however, expenditure as a percentage of GDP did not vary over the ten-year period.

■ At the tertiary level, over the 1995-2005 period, expenditure increased at the same pace as GDP or faster. The increase was more pronounced from 2000 in nearly two-thirds of the 28 OECD countries with comparable data. Only Belgium, Ireland and the partner country Chile saw GDP grow faster than expenditure on educational institutions at this level from 2000 to 2005.

Policy context

This indicator provides a measure of the relative proportion of a nation's wealth that is invested in educational institutions. Expenditure on educational institutions is an investment that can help foster economic growth, enhance productivity, contribute to personal and social development, and reduce social inequality. Relative to GDP, expenditure on educational institutions shows the priority a country gives to education in terms of its overall resource allocation. The proportion of total financial resources devoted to education is a choice made by each OECD country. This is an aggregate choice, made by government, enterprises, and individual students and their families, and is partially driven by the size of the country's school-age population and enrolment in education. If the social and private returns to investment in education are sufficiently large, there is an incentive to expand enrolment and increase total investment.

The indicator also includes a comparative review of changes in educational investment over time. In deciding how much is allocated to education, governments must assess demands for increased spending in areas such as teachers' salaries and educational facilities. This indicator can provide a point of reference, as it shows how the volume of educational spending, relative to national wealth and in absolute terms, has evolved over time in various OECD countries.

Evidence and explanations

What this indicator does and does not cover

This indicator covers expenditure on schools, universities and other public and private institutions involved in delivering or supporting educational services. Expenditure on institutions is not limited to expenditure on instructional services but also includes public and private expenditure on ancillary services for students and families (such as housing and transport services), when these services are provided by educational institutions. Spending on research and development can be significant in tertiary education and is included in this indicator, to the extent that the research is performed by educational institutions.

Not all spending on educational goods and services occurs within educational institutions. For example, families may purchase textbooks and materials commercially or seek private tutoring for their children outside educational institutions. At the tertiary level, students' living costs and foregone earnings can also account for a significant proportion of the costs of education. All expenditure outside educational institutions is excluded from this indicator, even if it is publicly subsidised. Public subsidies for educational expenditure outside institutions are discussed in Indicators B4 and B5.

Overall investment relative to GDP

All OECD countries invest a substantial proportion of national resources in education. Taking into account both public and private sources of funds, OECD countries as a whole spend 6.1% of their collective GDP on educational institutions at the pre-primary, primary, secondary and tertiary levels. Given the current tight constraints on public budgets, such a large spending item is subject to close scrutiny by governments looking for ways to reduce or limit the growth of expenditure.

The highest spending on educational institutions is in Denmark, Iceland, Korea and the United States, and the partner country Israel, with at least 7% of GDP accounted for by public and private spending on educational institutions, followed by Mexico and New Zealand with more than 6.5%. Seven out of 28 OECD countries for which data are available as well as three out of six partner countries spend less than 5% of GDP on educational institutions; in Greece and in the partner country the Russian Federation, the figure is 4.2 and 3.8%, respectively (Table B2.1).

Expenditure on educational institutions by level of education

Differences in spending on educational institutions are most striking at the pre-primary level. It ranges from less than 0.2% of GDP in Australia, Ireland and Korea to 0.8% or more in Denmark, Hungary and Iceland, and the partner country Israel (Table B2.2). Differences at the pre-primary level can be explained mainly by participation rates among younger children (see Indicator C2), but are also sometimes a result of the extent to which private early childhood education is covered by this indicator. In Ireland, for example, the majority of early childhood education is delivered in private institutions that are not yet covered by the Irish data. Moreover, high-quality early childhood education and care are provided not only by the educational institutions covered by this indicator but often also in more informal settings. Inferences on access to and quality of early childhood education and care should therefore be made with caution.

On average, among OECD countries, 60% of expenditure on educational institutions goes to primary, secondary and post-secondary non-tertiary education. Because enrolment in primary and lower secondary education is almost universal in OECD countries, and participation rates in upper secondary education are high (see Indicators C1 and C2), these levels account for the bulk of expenditure on educational institutions: 3.7% of the combined OECD GDP. At the same time, significantly higher spending on educational institutions per student at the upper secondary and tertiary levels causes the overall investment in these levels to be higher than enrolment numbers alone would suggest.

Nearly one-third of combined OECD expenditure on educational institutions is accounted for by tertiary education. At this level, the pathways available to students, the duration of programmes and the organisation of teaching vary greatly among OECD countries, resulting in significant differences in the expenditure allocated to tertiary education. On the one hand, Canada, Korea and the United States spend between 2.4 and 2.9% of their GDP on tertiary institutions. Except for Canada, these countries and the partner country Chile are also those with the highest proportion of private expenditure on tertiary education. Denmark and Finland as well as the partner countries Chile and Israel, also show high levels of spending, with 1.7% or more of GDP going to tertiary institutions. On the other hand, the proportion of GDP spent on tertiary institutions in Belgium, France, Iceland, Mexico, Portugal, Switzerland and the United Kingdom is below the OECD average; these countries are among the OECD countries in which the proportion of GDP spent on primary, secondary and post-secondary non-tertiary education is above the OECD average (Chart B2.2). In Switzerland, a moderate proportion of GDP spent on tertiary institutions translates to one of the highest levels of spending per tertiary student, owing to comparatively low tertiary enrolment rates and high GDP (Tables B2.1 and B1.1a).

B2

Chart B2.2. Expenditure on educational institutions as a percentage of GDP (2005)

From public and private sources, by level of education, source of funds and year

■ Private expenditure on educational institutions
□ Public expenditure on educational institutions

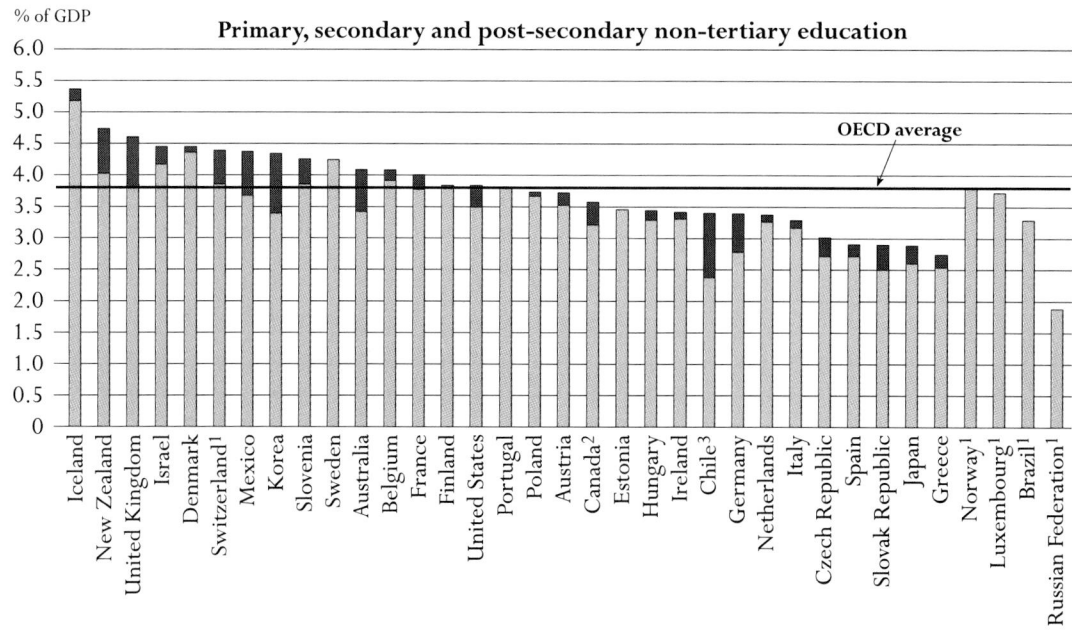

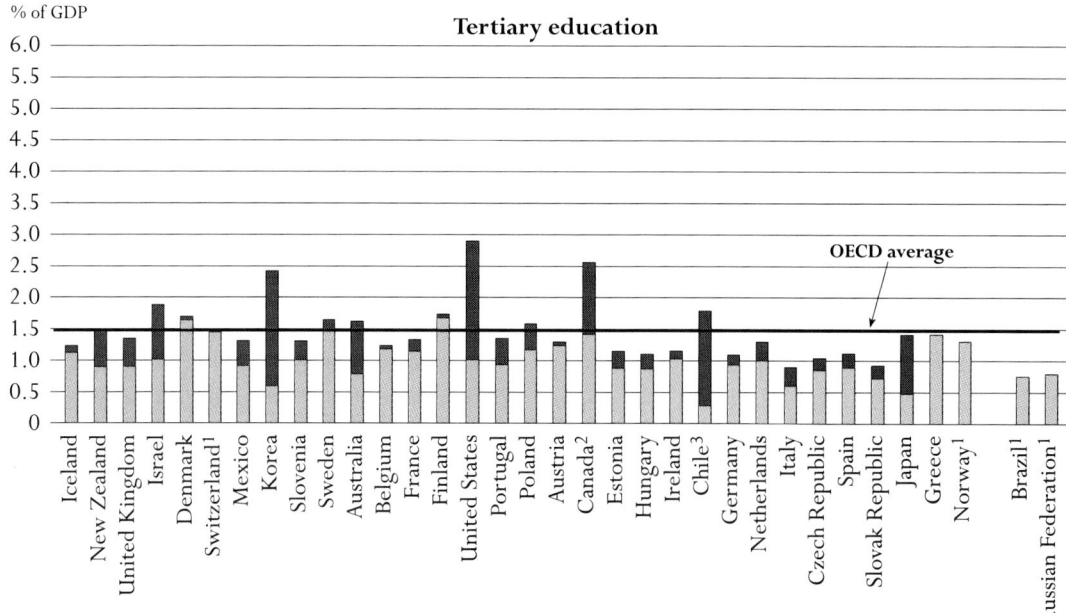

1. Public expenditure only (for Switzerland, in tertiary education only).
2. Year of reference 2004.
3. Year of reference 2006.

Countries are ranked in descending order of expenditure from both public and private sources on educational institutions in primary, secondary and post-secondary non-tertiary education.

Source: OECD. Table B2.4. See Annex 3 for notes (*www.oecd.org/edu/eag2008*).

StatLink ⫘⫘ http://dx.doi.org/10.1787/401864037554

B2

Changes in overall educational spending between 1995, 2000 and 2005

More people are completing upper secondary and tertiary education than ever before (see Indicator A1), and in many countries, this has been accompanied by massive financial investment. For all levels of education combined, public and private investment in education increased in all countries by at least 8% between 1995 and 2005 in real terms and increased on average by 42% in OECD countries. Australia, Denmark, Finland, the Netherlands, New Zealand, Portugal, the Slovak Republic, Sweden and the United States increased expenditure on educational institutions by 30 to 50% while Greece, Hungary, Ireland, Mexico, Poland and the United Kingdom, and the partner countries Brazil, Chile and Estonia, increased spending by more than 50% (Table B2.3).

The differences are partly related to the variation of the school-age population, but a sound interpretation should also take account of the trends in national income. For example, in Ireland, spending on all levels of education combined increased by more than 80% between 1995 and 2005, but GDP more than doubled (Table B2.3). On average in the 28 countries for which data are available for 1995 and 2005, expenditure for all levels of education combined increased relatively more than GDP did. The increase in expenditure on educational institutions as a proportion of GDP exceeded 0.8 percentage points over the period in Denmark (6.2% to 7.4%), Greece (2.6% to 4.2%), Mexico (5.6% to 6.5%) and the United Kingdom (5.2% to 6.2%). However, the increase in spending on educational institutions tended to lag behind the growth in national income in more than one-third of the 28 OECD and partner countries for which data are available. The most notable differences are in Austria, Canada, France, Ireland and Spain, and in partner country Estonia where the proportion of GDP spent on educational institutions decreased by 0.5 percentage point or more between 1995 and 2005 (Table B2.1), mainly as a result of the decrease in expenditure on educational institutions as a percentage of GDP at the primary, secondary and post-secondary non-tertiary levels.

From 1995 to 2005 on average, expenditure on educational institutions for all levels of education increased similarly during the two five-year periods. However, slower growth for 2000 to 2005 is particularly marked in New Zealand, Portugal and the United States and in the partner country Chile. The reverse pattern is true for the Czech Republic, Hungary, Norway, the Slovak Republic and the United Kingdom (Table B2.3 and Chart B2.3). When comparing changes in expenditure on educational institutions to changes in GDP, a clearer picture emerges: expenditure for all levels of education grew on average slightly less than GDP between 1995 and 2000 (by 17 and 20%, respectively), and significantly more than GDP between 2000 and 2005 (by 21 and 14%, respectively). In 14 out of 28 OECD and partner countries for which data are available, expenditure for all levels of education as a percentage of GDP decreased between 1995 and 2000 and then increased from 2000 to 2005. Nevertheless, expenditure on educational institutions for all levels of education as a percentage of GDP increased in both of these 5-year periods in 7 of the 28 OECD and partner countries with comparable data (all of them among the countries with the largest increases in expenditure over the period).

In two-thirds of the 28 OECD and partner countries for which data are available, expenditure on educational institutions for tertiary education between 1995 and 2005 increased proportionately more than for primary, secondary and post-secondary non-tertiary education. This is certainly associated to some extent with the significant increase in tertiary students compared to the relative stability in the number of students at lower levels (Table B1.5). In Canada, the Czech Republic,

B2

Chart B2.3. **Changes in expenditure on educational institutions and changes in GDP (2000, 2005)**

(2000 = 100, 2005 constant prices)

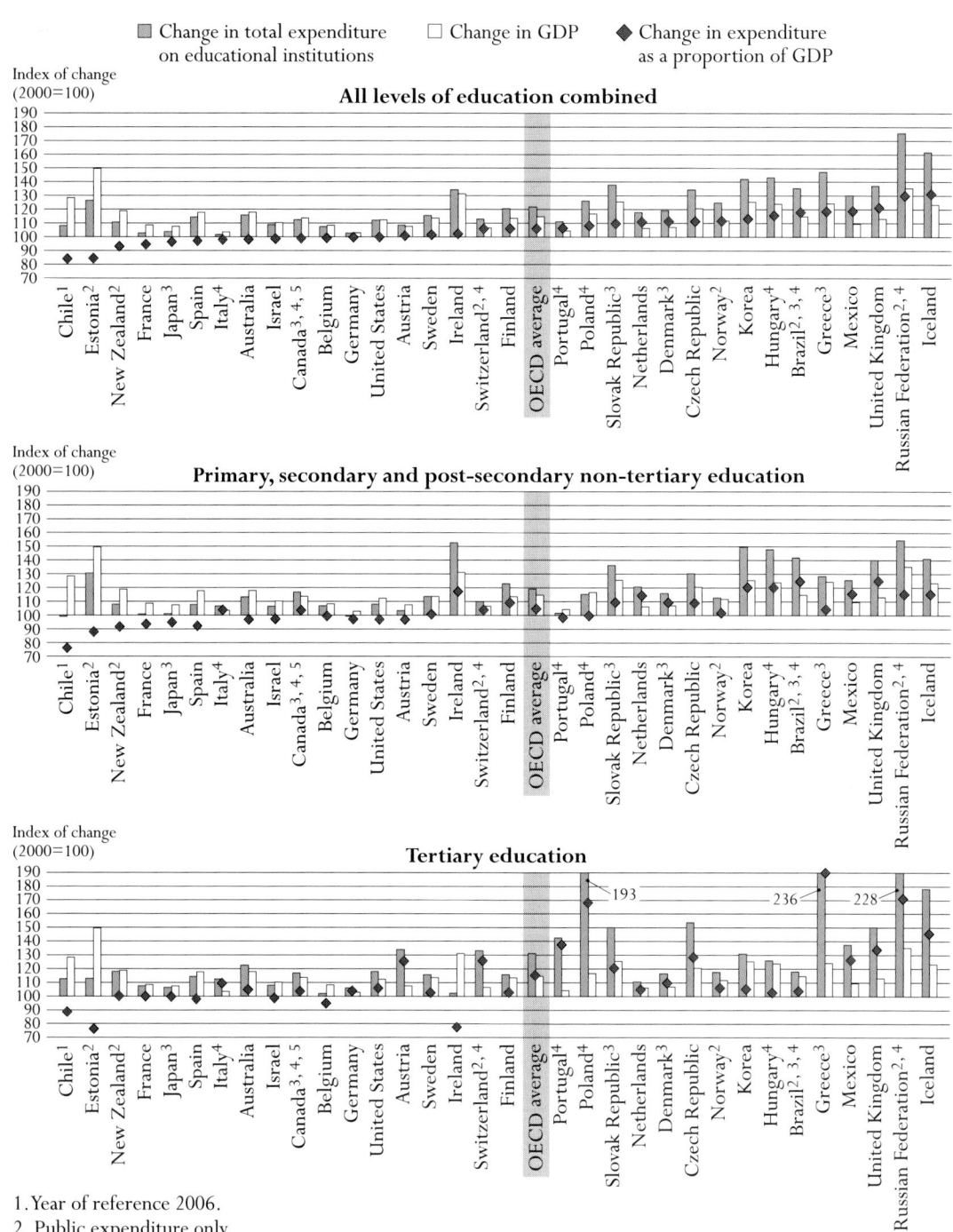

1. Year of reference 2006.
2. Public expenditure only.
3. Some levels of education are included with others.
4. Public institutions only.
5. Year of reference 2004.

Countries are ranked in ascending order of change between 2000 and 2005 in expenditure on educational institutions as a percentage of GDP for all levels of education combined.

Source: OECD. Table B2.3 and Annex 2. See Annex 3 for notes (*www.oecd.org/edu/eag2008*).

StatLink ⟶ http://dx.doi.org/10.1787/401864037554

B2

Greece, Italy, Poland, Portugal, the Slovak Republic, Spain, Switzerland and the United States, increases in spending on tertiary education surpassed increases at the primary, secondary and post-secondary non-tertiary levels by 30 percentage points or more. Ireland, Sweden and the partner countries Chile and Estonia invested additional resources in similar proportions in primary, secondary and post-secondary non-tertiary and tertiary education combined. Conversely, Australia, Denmark, Finland, the Netherlands, New Zealand, Norway, and the United Kingdom and the partner country Brazil invested most of the increases (in relative terms) in primary, secondary and post-secondary non-tertiary education (Table B2.3).

Between 1995 and 2005, spending on the various levels of education evolved quite differently. From primary to post-secondary non-tertiary education, expenditure on educational institutions as a proportion of GDP decreased in half of the countries for which data are available (15 out of 28 OECD and partner countries), but the pattern is different in the two five-year periods. In most countries, expenditure increased less than GDP between 1995 and 2000 but more than the GDP between 2000 and 2005. However, the increase from 2000 did not necessarily compensate for the preceding decrease. The opposite pattern (increase to 2000 followed by a decrease from 2000) is observed in the partner country Chile and to a lesser extent in Poland, Sweden and the United States. The main exceptions to these patterns are Austria, France, Germany, Japan, and Spain where expenditure on educational institutions from primary to post-secondary non-tertiary education (as a proportion of GDP) significantly decreased in both periods and Australia, Denmark and Greece where they significantly increased in both (Tables B2.1, B2.3 and Chart B2.3).

In tertiary education, expenditure on educational institutions as a proportion of GDP decreased from 1995 to 2005 only in Finland, France, Ireland, the Netherlands and Norway. On average, expenditure on educational institutions increased at the same pace as GDP (by 20%) during the period 1995 to 2000 and significantly more than GDP from 2000 to 2005 (by 32 and 14%, respectively). Only in Belgium, Ireland and the partner country Chile did GDP grow faster than expenditure on educational institutions at the tertiary level from 2000 to 2005. The increase in expenditure was more pronounced from 2000 in nearly two-thirds of the 28 OECD and partner countries with comparable data. However, in nine of these countries, expenditure at the tertiary level increased less than GDP before 2000 and more than GPD after 2000 (Tables B2.1, B2.3 and Chart B2.3).

Relationship between national expenditure on educational institutions and demographic patterns

National resources devoted to education depend on a number of interrelated factors of supply and demand, such as the demographic structure of the population, enrolment rates, income per capita, national levels of teachers' salaries, and the organisation and delivery of instruction. For example, OECD countries with high spending levels may enrol larger numbers of students, while countries with low spending levels may either limit access to higher levels of education or deliver educational services in a particularly efficient manner. The distribution of enrolments among sectors and fields of study may also differ, as may the duration of studies and the scale and organisation of related educational research. Finally, large differences in GDP among OECD countries mean that similar percentages of GDP spent on educational institutions can result in very different absolute amounts per student (see Indicator B1).

B2

Chart B2.4. Expenditure on educational institutions as a percentage of GDP and total enrolment in education as a percentage of total population (2005)

For all levels of education combined, based on full-time equivalents

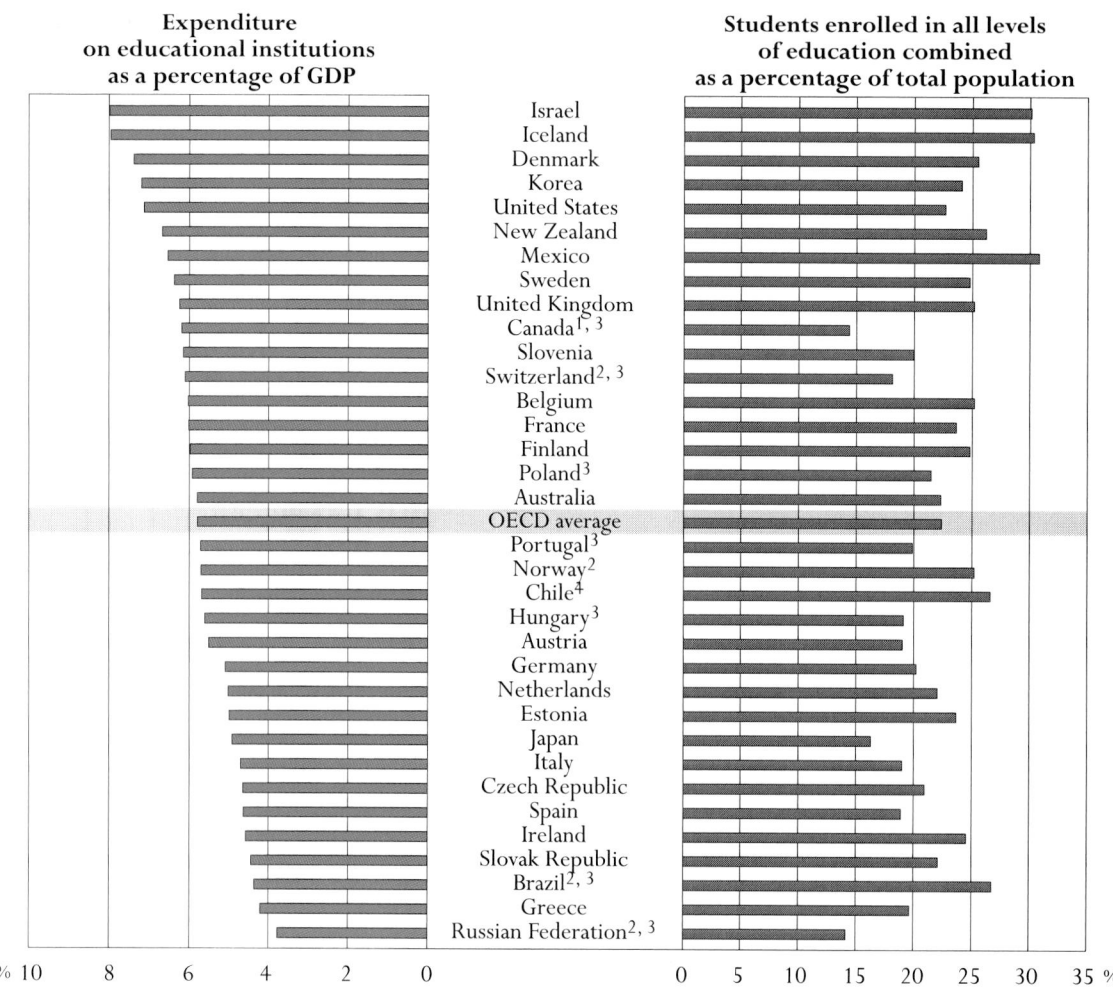

1. Year of reference 2004.
2. Public expenditure only (for Switzerland, in tertiary education only).
3. Public institutions only.
4. Year of reference 2006.

Countries are ranked in descending order of total expenditure on educational institutions as a percentage of GDP.

Source: OECD. Table B2.1 and Annex 2. See Annex 3 for notes (*www.oecd.org/edu/eag2008*).

StatLink ⊞ᵐˢᴸ http://dx.doi.org/10.1787/401864037554

The size of a country's school-age population shapes the potential demand for initial education and training: the larger this population, the greater the potential demand for educational services. Among OECD countries with comparable national income, a country in which this population is relatively large will have to spend a higher percentage of its GDP on educational institutions so that the individuals concerned have the opportunity to receive the same quantity of education as individuals in other OECD countries, based on the assumption of comparable costs for teachers and facilities. Conversely, but based on the same assumption, if this population is relatively small, the country will be required to spend less of its wealth on educational institutions in order to achieve similar results.

Comparing expenditure on educational institutions as a percentage of GDP with the proportion of the population enrolled in education shows in general that seven of the ten countries with over 25% of their population enrolled in formal education (Belgium, Denmark, Iceland, Mexico, New Zealand and the United Kingdom and the partner country Israel) are also those with expenditure on educational institutions as a percentage of GDP above the OECD average (Chart B2.4). In contrast, Austria, Canada, Greece, Hungary, Italy, Japan, Portugal, Spain and Switzerland, and the partner country the Russian Federation, have the lowest proportions of the population (less than 20%) enrolled in formal education, and except for Canada and Switzerland, they also have expenditure on educational institutions below the OECD average. Some of these countries also have the lowest shares of GDP devoted to education among OECD and partner countries.

Nevertheless, the proportion of the school-age population does not alone determine the level of expenditure. Countries with similar proportions of the population in education may spend different shares of their GDP, according to the priority they give to education or the ways in which education expenditure are distributed among levels of education. For example, the proportion of the population enrolled in education is quite similar in Mexico and the partner country Israel (30.8 and 30.1%, respectively), but Mexico spends 1.5 percentage points less of its GDP on educational institutions than Israel (6.5 and 8.0%, respectively). However, countries spending similar proportion of their GDP on educational institutions do not necessarily have the same proportion of their population enrolled in education. For example, Portugal and Norway spend 5.7% of their GDP on educational institutions, but students represent about 20% of the population in Portugal and 25% in Norway. These differences may reflect expenditure per student (Table B1.1a).

Expenditure on educational institutions by source of funding

Increased expenditure on educational institutions in response to growth in enrolments implies a heavier financial burden for society as a whole, but it does not fall entirely on public funding. On average, of the 6.1% of the combined OECD area GDP devoted to education, more than three-quarters comes from public sources (Table B2.4). The majority of funding is from public sources in all countries and is nearly the sole source of funding in Norway. However, there are greater differences among countries in the breakdown of educational expenditure by source of funding and by level of education (see Indicator B3).

Definitions and methodologies

Data refer to the financial year 2005 and are based on the UOE data collection on education statistics administered by the OECD in 2007 (for details see Annex 3 at *www.oecd.org/edu/eag2008*). Expenditure on educational institutions, as covered by this indicator, includes expenditure on both instructional and non-instructional educational institutions. Instructional educational institutions are educational institutions which directly provide instructional programmes (*i.e.* teaching) to individuals directly in an organised group setting or through distance education. Business enterprises or other institutions providing short-term courses of training or instruction to individuals on a one-to-one basis are not included. Non-instructional educational institutions provide administrative, advisory or professional services to other educational institutions but do not enrol students themselves. Examples include national, state and provincial ministries or departments of education; other bodies that administer education at various levels of government

B2

or analogous bodies in the private sector; and organisations that provide education-related services as vocational or psychological counselling, placement, testing, financial aid to students, curriculum development, educational research, building operations and maintenance services, transport of students, and student meals and housing.

This definition of institutions ensures that expenditure on services, which are provided in some OECD countries by schools and universities and in others by agencies other than schools, are covered on a comparable basis.

The distinction by source of funds is based on the initial source of funds and does not reflect subsequent public-to-private or private-to-public transfers. For this reason, subsidies to households and other entities, such as subsidies for tuition fees and other payments to educational institutions, are included in public expenditure in this indicator. Payments from households and other private entities to educational institutions include tuition and other fees, net of offsetting public subsidies. A detailed discussion of public subsidies can be found in Indicator B5.

The OECD average is calculated as the simple average of all OECD countries for which data are available. The OECD total reflects the value of the indicator if the OECD region is considered as a whole (see the Reader's Guide for details).

Tables B2.1 and B2.3 show expenditure on educational institutions for the financial years 1995, 2000 and 2005. The data on expenditure for 1995 were obtained by a special survey in 2002 and updated in 2007; expenditure for 1995 was adjusted to reflect the methods and definitions used in the 2007 UOE data collection.

Data for 1995 and 2000 are expressed in 2005 price levels. Charts B2.1 and B2.3 and Tables B2.1 and B2.3 present an index of change in expenditure on institutions and GDP between 1995, 2000 and 2005. All expenditure, as well as the 1995 and 2000 GDP, is adjusted to 2005 prices using the GDP deflator.

For comparisons over time, the OECD average accounts only for those OECD countries for which data are available for all reported reference years.

B2

Table B2.1.
Expenditure on educational institutions as a percentage of GDP, by level of education (1995, 2000, 2005)
From public and private sources, by year

	2005			2000			1995		
	Primary, secondary and post-secondary non-tertiary education	Tertiary education	Total all levels of education	Primary, secondary and post-secondary non-tertiary education	Tertiary education	Total all levels of education	Primary, secondary and post-secondary non-tertiary education	Tertiary education	Total all levels of education
Australia	4.1	1.6	**5.8**	4.0	1.5	**5.6**	3.6	1.6	**5.3**
Austria	3.7	1.3	**5.5**	3.9	1.0	**5.5**	4.2	1.2	**6.1**
Belgium	4.1	1.2	**6.0**	4.1	1.3	**6.1**	m	m	m
Canada[1,2]	3.6	2.6	**6.2**	3.3	2.3	**5.9**	4.3	2.1	**6.7**
Czech Republic	3.0	1.0	**4.6**	2.8	0.8	**4.2**	3.5	0.9	**5.1**
Denmark[2]	4.5	1.7	**7.4**	4.1	1.6	**6.6**	4.0	1.6	**6.2**
Finland	3.9	1.7	**6.0**	3.6	1.7	**5.6**	4.0	1.9	**6.3**
France	4.0	1.3	**6.0**	4.3	1.3	**6.4**	4.5	1.4	**6.6**
Germany	3.4	1.1	**5.1**	3.5	1.1	**5.1**	3.7	1.1	**5.4**
Greece[2]	2.7	1.5	**4.2**	2.7	0.8	**3.6**	2.0	0.6	**2.6**
Hungary	3.4	1.1	**5.6**	2.9	1.1	**4.9**	3.5	1.0	**5.3**
Iceland[2]	5.4	1.2	**8.0**	4.7	0.9	**6.1**	m	m	m
Ireland	3.4	1.2	**4.6**	2.9	1.5	**4.5**	3.8	1.3	**5.2**
Italy	3.3	0.9	**4.7**	3.2	0.9	**4.8**	3.6	0.7	**4.8**
Japan[2]	2.9	1.4	**4.9**	3.1	1.4	**5.1**	3.1	1.3	**5.0**
Korea	4.3	2.4	**7.2**	3.6	2.3	**6.4**	m	m	m
Luxembourg[2,3]	3.7	m	m	m	m	m	m	m	m
Mexico	4.4	1.3	**6.5**	3.8	1.0	**5.5**	4.0	1.1	**5.6**
Netherlands	3.4	1.3	**5.0**	3.0	1.2	**4.5**	3.0	1.4	**4.8**
New Zealand	4.7	1.5	**6.7**	m	m	m	m	m	m
Norway[3]	3.8	1.3	**5.7**	3.8	1.2	**5.1**	4.3	1.6	**5.9**
Poland	3.7	1.6	**5.9**	3.9	1.1	**5.6**	3.6	0.8	**5.2**
Portugal	3.8	1.4	**5.7**	3.9	1.0	**5.4**	3.6	0.9	**5.0**
Slovak Republic[2]	2.9	0.9	**4.4**	2.7	0.8	**4.0**	3.0	0.7	**4.6**
Spain	2.9	1.1	**4.6**	3.2	1.1	**4.8**	3.8	1.0	**5.3**
Sweden	4.2	1.6	**6.4**	4.3	1.6	**6.3**	4.1	1.5	**6.0**
Switzerland[3]	4.4	1.4	**6.1**	4.2	1.1	**5.7**	4.6	0.9	**6.0**
Turkey	m	m	m	2.4	1.0	**3.4**	1.7	0.7	**2.3**
United Kingdom	4.6	1.3	**6.2**	3.6	1.0	**5.0**	3.7	1.1	**5.2**
United States	3.8	2.9	**7.1**	3.9	2.7	**7.0**	3.8	2.3	**6.6**
OECD average	*3.8*	*1.5*	*5.8*	*~*	*~*	*~*	*~*	*~*	*~*
OECD total	*3.7*	*2.0*	*6.1*	*~*	*~*	*~*	*~*	*~*	*~*
EU19 average	*3.6*	*1.3*	*5.5*	*~*	*~*	*~*	*~*	*~*	*~*
OECD mean for countries with 1995, 2000 and 2005 data (24 countries)	*3.7*	*1.4*	*5.6*	*3.5*	*1.3*	*5.3*	*3.7*	*1.3*	*5.5*
Brazil[3]	3.2	0.8	**4.4**	2.6	0.7	**3.7**	2.6	0.7	**3.7**
Chile[4]	3.4	1.8	**5.7**	4.4	2.0	**6.7**	3.2	1.7	**5.1**
Estonia	3.5	1.1	**5.0**	3.9	1.0	**5.4**	4.2	1.0	**5.8**
Israel	4.5	1.9	**8.0**	4.6	1.9	**8.1**	5.0	1.9	**8.6**
Russian Federation[3]	1.9	0.8	**3.8**	1.7	0.5	**2.9**	m	m	m
Slovenia	4.3	1.3	**6.2**	m	m	m	m	m	m

Left margin labels: OECD countries (Australia–United States); Partner countries (Brazil–Slovenia)

1. Year of reference 2004 instead of 2005.
2. Some levels of education are included with others. Refer to "x" code in Table B1.1a for details.
3. Public expenditure only (for Switzerland, in tertiary education only).
4. Year of reference 2006 instead of 2005.
Source: OECD. See Annex 3 for notes (*www.oecd.org/edu/eag2008*).
Please refer to the Reader's Guide for information concerning the symbols replacing missing data.
StatLink ⌐⌐⌐ http://dx.doi.org/10.1787/401864037554

B2

Table B2.2.
Expenditure on educational institutions as a percentage of GDP, by level of education (2005)
From public and private sources[1]

	Pre-primary education (for children aged 3 and older)	Primary, secondary and post-secondary non-tertiary education				Tertiary education			All levels of education combined (including undistributed programmes)
		All primary, secondary and post-secondary non-tertiary education	Primary and lower secondary education	Upper secondary education	Post-secondary non-tertiary education	All tertiary education	Tertiary-type B education	Tertiary-type A education and advanced research programmes	
	(1)	(2)	(3)	(4)	(5)	(6)	(7)	(8)	(9)
Australia	0.1	4.1	3.1	0.9	0.1	1.6	0.1	1.5	5.8
Austria	0.5	3.7	2.4	1.3	n	1.3	0.1	1.2	5.5
Belgium[2]	0.6	4.1	1.5	2.6	x(4)	1.2	x(6)	x(6)	6.0
Canada[3]	x(2)	3.6	x(2)	x(2)	x(6, 7)	2.6	1.0	1.6	6.2
Czech Republic	0.5	3.0	1.8	1.1	0.1	1.0	n	1.0	4.6
Denmark	0.8	4.5	3.1	1.4	x(4, 6)	1.7	x(6)	x(6)	7.4
Finland	0.4	3.9	2.4	1.4	x(4)	1.7	n	1.7	6.0
France	0.7	4.0	2.6	1.4	n	1.3	0.3	1.1	6.0
Germany	0.5	3.4	2.0	1.2	0.2	1.1	0.1	1.0	5.1
Greece[2]	x(3)	2.7	1.2	1.4	0.1	1.5	0.3	1.2	4.2
Hungary	0.8	3.4	2.2	1.1	0.2	1.1	n	1.1	5.6
Iceland	0.8	5.4	3.9	x(2)	x(2)	1.2	x(6)	x(6)	8.0
Ireland	n	3.4	2.5	0.7	0.2	1.2	x(6)	x(6)	4.6
Italy	0.5	3.3	2.0	1.3	0.1	0.9	n	0.9	4.7
Japan	0.2	2.9	2.0	0.9	x(4, 6)	1.4	0.3	1.2	4.9
Korea	0.1	4.3	3.0	1.4	a	2.4	0.5	2.0	7.2
Luxembourg[4]	x(2)	3.7	2.8	0.9	m	m	m	m	m
Mexico	0.7	4.4	3.5	0.9	a	1.3	x(6)	x(6)	6.5
Netherlands	0.4	3.4	2.5	0.8	n	1.3	n	1.3	5.0
New Zealand	0.3	4.7	2.9	1.6	0.2	1.5	0.3	1.2	6.7
Norway[4]	0.3	3.8	2.6	1.2	x(4)	1.3	x(6)	x(6)	5.7
Poland	0.6	3.7	2.6	1.1	n	1.6	n	1.6	5.9
Portugal	0.4	3.8	2.8	1.0	m	1.4	x(6)	x(6)	5.7
Slovak Republic	0.5	2.9	1.8	1.1	x(4)	0.9	x(4)	0.9	4.4
Spain	0.6	2.9	x(2)	x(2)	a	1.1	x(6)	x(6)	4.6
Sweden	0.5	4.2	2.9	1.3	n	1.6	x(6)	x(6)	6.4
Switzerland[4]	0.2	4.4	2.7	1.6	0.1	1.4	n	1.4	6.1
Turkey	m	m	m	m	a	m	m	m	m
United Kingdom[2]	0.3	4.6	2.5	1.4	0.8	1.3	x(6)	x(6)	6.2
United States	0.4	3.8	2.9	1.0	m	2.9	x(6)	x(6)	7.1
OECD average	*0.4*	*3.8*	*2.5*	*1.2*	*0.1*	*1.5*	*0.2*	*1.3*	*5.8*
OECD total	*0.4*	*3.7*	*2.6*	*1.1*	*0.1*	*2.0*	*0.3*	*1.3*	*6.1*
EU19 average	*0.5*	*3.6*	*2.3*	*1.3*	*0.1*	*1.3*	*0.1*	*1.2*	*5.5*
Brazil[4]	0.4	3.2	2.7	0.5	a	0.8	x(6)	x(6)	4.4
Chile[5]	0.5	3.4	2.2	1.2	a	1.8	0.4	1.4	5.7
Estonia	0.4	3.5	2.2	1.1	0.2	1.1	0.3	0.9	5.0
Israel	0.9	4.5	2.4	2.1	n	1.9	0.4	1.5	8.0
Russian Federation[4]	0.5	1.9	x(2)	x(2)	x(2)	0.8	0.2	0.6	3.8
Slovenia	0.6	4.3	2.9	1.3	x(4)	1.3	x(6)	x(6)	6.2

OECD countries (row label at left)
Partner countries (row label at left)

1. Including international sources.
2. Column 3 only refers to primary education and column 4 refers to all secondary education.
3. Year of reference 2004.
4. Public expenditure only (for Switzerland, in tertiary education only).
5. Year of reference 2006.
Source: OECD. See Annex 3 for notes (*www.oecd.org/edu/eag2008*).
Please refer to the Reader's Guide for information concerning the symbols replacing missing data.
StatLink ⬛🖳 http://dx.doi.org/10.1787/401864037554

B2

Table B2.3.
Change in expenditure on educational institutions and in GDP (1995, 2000, 2005)

Index of change between 1995, 2000 and 2005 in expenditure on educational institutions from public and private sources and in GDP, by level of education (GDP deflator and GDP (2000=100), constant prices)

	All levels of education			Primary, secondary and post-secondary non-tertiary education			Tertiary education			Gross Domestic Product		
	1995	2000	2005	1995	2000	2005	1995	2000	2005	1995	2000	2005
	(1)	(2)	(3)	(4)	(5)	(6)	(7)	(8)	(9)	(10)	(11)	(12)
Australia	79	100	115	74	100	113	91	100	122	83	100	118
Austria	97	100	108	94	100	103	98	100	133	87	100	107
Belgium	m	100	107	m	100	107	m	100	102	88	100	108
Canada[1, 2, 3]	92	100	112	106	100	116	75	100	117	82	100	113
Czech Republic	113	100	134	116	100	130	101	100	153	93	100	120
Denmark[2]	81	100	119	84	100	116	91	100	116	87	100	107
Finland	88	100	120	89	100	123	90	100	116	79	100	113
France	90	100	103	90	100	101	91	100	107	87	100	108
Germany	95	100	103	94	100	99	95	100	106	91	100	103
Greece[2]	63	100	146	64	100	128	66	100	236	84	100	124
Hungary[3]	90	100	142	100	100	147	74	100	126	82	100	124
Iceland	m	100	161	m	100	140	m	100	177	79	100	123
Ireland	74	100	134	83	100	152	57	100	102	64	100	131
Italy[3]	91	100	102	103	100	107	79	100	112	91	100	104
Japan[2]	94	100	104	98	100	101	88	100	106	96	100	107
Korea	m	100	141	m	100	149	m	100	130	81	100	125
Luxembourg	m	100	m	m	100	m	m	100	m	74	100	120
Mexico	77	100	130	81	100	125	77	100	137	77	100	109
Netherlands	87	100	117	84	100	120	94	100	111	82	100	106
New Zealand[4]	75	100	110	71	100	108	105	100	118	88	100	118
Norway[4]	97	100	124	94	100	113	107	100	117	83	100	112
Poland[3]	80	100	126	74	100	115	89	100	193	77	100	116
Portugal[3]	77	100	111	76	100	102	73	100	142	82	100	104
Slovak Republic[2]	96	100	137	96	100	136	81	100	149	84	100	125
Spain	91	100	114	99	100	108	72	100	114	82	100	117
Sweden	81	100	115	81	100	113	81	100	116	85	100	113
Switzerland[3, 4]	95	100	113	101	100	110	74	100	133	90	100	106
Turkey[4]	57	100	m	58	100	m	56	100	m	82	100	124
United Kingdom	89	100	137	87	100	140	98	100	149	85	100	113
United States	76	100	112	80	100	108	70	100	118	82	100	112
OECD average	*86*	*100*	*121*	*88*	*100*	*119*	*83*	*100*	*131*	*84*	*100*	*114*
EU19 average	*87*	*100*	*121*	*89*	*100*	*119*	*84*	*100*	*132*	*83*	*100*	*114*
Brazil[2, 3, 4]	83	100	135	82	100	141	78	100	118	91	100	114
Chile[5]	56	100	108	54	100	99	61	100	112	82	100	128
Estonia[4]	76	100	126	77	100	130	68	100	113	76	100	149
Israel	84	100	109	86	100	106	77	100	108	80	100	110
Russian Federation[3, 4]	m	100	174	m	100	154	m	100	228	92	100	135
Slovenia	m	m	m	m	m	m	m	m	m	81	100	118

OECD countries / *Partner countries*

1. Year of reference 2004 instead of 2005.
2. Some levels of education are included with others. Refer to "x" code in Table B1.1a for details.
3. Public institutions only (for Canada, in tertiary education only).
4. Public expenditure only.
5. Year of reference 2006 instead of 2005.
Source: OECD. See Annex 3 for notes (*www.oecd.org/edu/eag2008*).
Please refer to the Reader's Guide for information concerning the symbols replacing missing data.
StatLink ⟧🔢 http://dx.doi.org/10.1787/401864037554

B2

Table B2.4.
Expenditure on educational institutions as a percentage of GDP, by source of funds and level of education (2005)
From public and private sources of funds

	Primary, secondary and post-secondary non-tertiary education			Tertiary education			Total all levels of education		
	Public[1]	Private[2]	Total	Public[1]	Private[2]	Total	Public[1]	Private[2]	Total
OECD countries									
Australia	3.4	0.7	**4.1**	0.8	0.8	**1.6**	4.3	1.5	**5.8**
Austria	3.5	0.2	**3.7**	1.2	0.1	**1.3**	5.2	0.4	**5.5**
Belgium	3.9	0.2	**4.1**	1.2	0.1	**1.2**	5.8	0.2	**6.0**
Canada[3, 4]	3.2	0.4	**3.6**	1.4	1.1	**2.6**	4.7	1.5	**6.2**
Czech Republic	2.7	0.3	**3.0**	0.8	0.2	**1.0**	4.1	0.6	**4.6**
Denmark[4]	4.4	0.1	**4.5**	1.6	0.1	**1.7**	6.8	0.6	**7.4**
Finland	3.8	n	**3.9**	1.7	0.1	**1.7**	5.9	0.1	**6.0**
France	3.8	0.2	**4.0**	1.1	0.2	**1.3**	5.6	0.5	**6.0**
Germany	2.8	0.6	**3.4**	0.9	0.2	**1.1**	4.2	0.9	**5.1**
Greece[4]	2.5	0.2	**2.7**	1.4	n	**1.5**	4.0	0.3	**4.2**
Hungary	3.3	0.2	**3.4**	0.9	0.2	**1.1**	5.1	0.5	**5.6**
Iceland[4]	5.2	0.2	**5.4**	1.1	0.1	**1.2**	7.2	0.7	**8.0**
Ireland	3.3	0.1	**3.4**	1.0	0.1	**1.2**	4.3	0.3	**4.6**
Italy	3.2	0.1	**3.3**	0.6	0.3	**0.9**	4.3	0.4	**4.7**
Japan[4]	2.6	0.3	**2.9**	0.5	0.9	**1.4**	3.4	1.5	**4.9**
Korea	3.4	0.9	**4.3**	0.6	1.8	**2.4**	4.3	2.9	**7.2**
Luxembourg[4]	3.7	m	m	m	m	m	m	m	m
Mexico	3.7	0.7	**4.4**	0.9	0.4	**1.3**	5.3	1.2	**6.5**
Netherlands	3.3	0.1	**3.4**	1.0	0.3	**1.3**	4.6	0.4	**5.0**
New Zealand	4.0	0.7	**4.7**	0.9	0.6	**1.5**	5.2	1.4	**6.7**
Norway	3.8	m	m	1.3	m	m	5.7	m	m
Poland	3.7	0.1	**3.7**	1.2	0.4	**1.6**	5.4	0.6	**5.9**
Portugal	3.8	n	**3.8**	0.9	0.4	**1.4**	5.3	0.4	**5.7**
Slovak Republic[4]	2.5	0.4	**2.9**	0.7	0.2	**0.9**	3.7	0.7	**4.4**
Spain	2.7	0.2	**2.9**	0.9	0.2	**1.1**	4.1	0.5	**4.6**
Sweden	4.2	n	**4.2**	1.5	0.2	**1.6**	6.2	0.2	**6.4**
Switzerland	3.9	0.5	**4.4**	1.4	m	m	5.6	m	m
Turkey	m	m	m	m	m	m	m	m	m
United Kingdom	3.8	0.8	**4.6**	0.9	0.4	**1.3**	5.0	1.2	**6.2**
United States	3.5	0.3	**3.8**	1.0	1.9	**2.9**	4.8	2.3	**7.1**
OECD average	*3.5*	*0.3*	*3.8*	*1.1*	*0.4*	*1.5*	*5.0*	*0.8*	*5.8*
OECD total	*3.3*	*0.4*	*3.7*	*0.9*	*1.0*	*2.0*	*4.6*	*1.5*	*6.1*
EU19 average	*3.4*	*0.2*	*3.6*	*1.1*	*0.2*	*1.3*	*5.0*	*0.5*	*5.5*
Partner countries									
Brazil	3.3	m	m	0.8	m	m	4.4	m	m
Chile[5]	2.4	1.0	**3.4**	0.3	1.5	**1.8**	3.0	2.7	**5.7**
Estonia	3.5	n	**3.5**	0.9	0.3	**1.1**	4.7	0.3	**5.0**
Israel	4.2	0.3	**4.5**	1.0	0.9	**1.9**	6.2	1.8	**8.0**
Russian Federation	1.9	m	m	0.8	m	m	3.8	m	m
Slovenia	3.9	0.4	**4.3**	1.0	0.3	**1.3**	5.3	0.8	**6.2**

1. Including public subsidies to households attributable for educational institutions, as well as including direct expenditure on educational institutions from international sources.
2. Net of public subsidies attributable for educational institutions.
3. Year of reference 2004.
4. Some levels of education are included with others. Refer to "x" code in Table B1.1a for details.
5. Year of reference 2006.
Source: OECD. See Annex 3 for notes (*www.oecd.org/edu/eag2008*).
Please refer to the Reader's Guide for information concerning the symbols replacing missing data.
StatLink ᐧᎮᔍ⅃ http://dx.doi.org/10.1787/401864037554

HOW MUCH PUBLIC AND PRIVATE INVESTMENT IS THERE IN EDUCATION?

This indicator examines the proportion of public and private funding allocated to educational institutions for each level of education. It also breaks down private funding between household expenditure and expenditure from private entities other than households. It sheds some light on the widely debated issue of how the financing of educational institutions should be shared between public entities and private ones, particularly those at the tertiary level.

Key results

Chart B3.1. **Share of private expenditure on educational institutions (2005)**

The chart shows private spending on educational institutions as a percentage of total spending on educational institutions. This includes all money transferred to educational institutions through private sources, including public funding via subsidies to households, private fees for educational services or other private spending (e.g. on accommodation) that passes through the institution.

☐ Primary, secondary and post-secondary non-tertiary education   ■ Tertiary education

On average, over 90% of primary, secondary and post-secondary non-tertiary education in OECD countries, and never less than 80% (except in Korea and in the partner country Chile), is paid for publicly. However, in tertiary education the proportion funded privately varies widely, from less than 5% in Denmark, Finland and Greece, to more than 40% in Australia, Canada, Japan, New Zealand and the United States and in the partner country Israel, and to over 75% in Korea and the partner country Chile. As with tertiary graduation and entry rates, the proportion of private funding can be influenced by the incidence of international students which form a relatively high proportion in Australia and New Zealand.

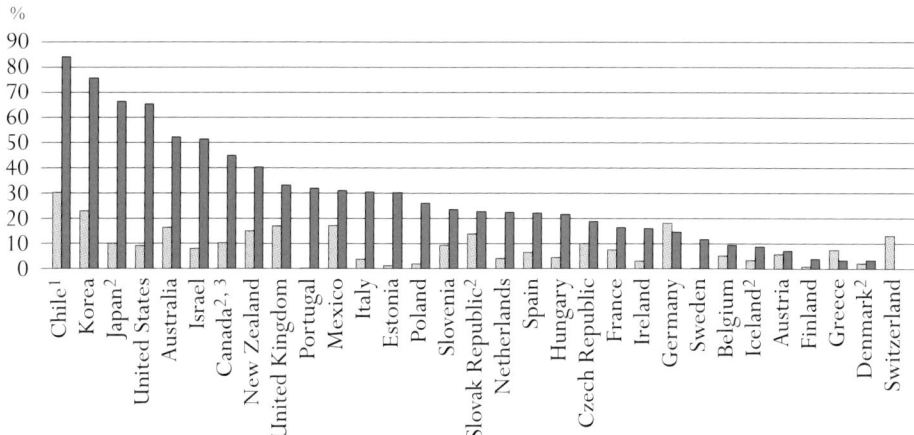

1. Year of reference 2006.
2. Some levels of education are included with others. Refer to "x" code in Table B1.1a for details.
3. Year of reference 2004.
Countries are ranked in descending order of the share of private expenditure on educational institutions for tertiary education.
Source: OECD. Tables B3.2a and B3.2b. See Annex 3 for notes (*www.oecd.org/edu/eag2008*).
StatLink ᯎᑒ﹈ http://dx.doi.org/10.1787/402017824643

Other highlights of this indicator

- In all countries for which comparable data are available, for all levels of education combined, public funding on educational institutions increased between 1995 and 2005. However, private spending increased even more in nearly three-quarters of these countries. Nevertheless, in 2005, 86% of expenditure, on average, for all levels of education combined, was still from public sources.

- The share of tertiary spending on educational institutions from private sources rose substantially in some countries between 1995 and 2005, but this was not the case for other levels of education.

- On average among the 18 OECD countries for which trend data are available, the share of public funding in tertiary institutions decreased slightly from 79% in 1995 to 77% in 2000 and to 73% in 2005. This trend is mainly influenced by non-European countries in which tuition fees are generally higher and enterprises participate more actively by providing grants to finance tertiary institutions.

- The increase in private investment has not displaced but complemented public financing. However, in eight out of the 11 OECD countries with the largest increase in public expenditure on tertiary education between 2000 and 2005, tertiary institutions charge low or no tuition fees. The exceptions are Korea, the United Kingdom and the United States.

- Compared to other levels of education, tertiary institutions and to a lesser extent pre-primary institutions obtain the largest proportions of funds from private sources, at 27 and 20%, respectively.

- In tertiary education, households account for most private expenditure in most countries for which data are available. Exceptions are Canada, Greece, Hungary, the Slovak Republic and Sweden where private expenditure from entities other than households is more significant.

B3

Policy context

Cost-sharing between participants in the education system and society as a whole is an issue under discussion in many OECD countries. It is especially relevant for pre-primary and tertiary education, for which full or nearly full public funding is less common.

As new client groups participate in a wider range of educational programmes and choose among more opportunities from increasing numbers of providers, governments are forging new partnerships to mobilise the necessary resources to pay for education and to share costs and benefits more equitably.

As a result, public funding more often provides only a part (albeit a very large part) of investment in education, and the role of private sources has become more important. Some stakeholders are concerned that this balance should not become so tilted as to discourage potential students. Thus, changes in a country's public/private funding shares can provide important information on changing patterns and levels of participation within its educational system.

Evidence and explanations

What this indicator does and does not cover

Governments can spend public funds directly on educational institutions or use them to provide subsidies to private entities for the purpose of education. When reporting on the public and private proportions of educational expenditure, it is therefore important to distinguish between the initial sources of funds and the final direct purchasers of educational goods and services.

Initial public spending includes both direct public expenditure on educational institutions and transfers to the private sector. To gauge the level of public expenditure, it is necessary to add together the components showing direct public expenditure on educational institutions and public subsidies for education. Initial private spending includes tuition fees and other student or household payments to educational institutions, less the portion of such payments offset by public subsidies.

The final public and private proportions are the percentages of educational funds spent directly by public and private purchasers of educational services. Final public spending includes direct public purchases of educational resources and payments to educational institutions and other private entities. Final private spending includes tuition fees and other private payments to educational institutions.

Not all spending on instructional goods and services occurs within educational institutions. For example, families may purchase textbooks and materials commercially or seek private tutoring for their children outside educational institutions. At the tertiary level, students' living costs and foregone earnings can also account for a significant proportion of the costs of education. All such expenditure outside educational institutions, even if publicly subsidised, is excluded from this indicator. Public subsidies for educational expenditure outside institutions are discussed in Indicators B4 and B5.

B3

Public and private expenditure on educational institutions at all levels of education

Educational institutions are still mainly publicly funded, although there is a substantial and growing degree of private funding at the tertiary level. On average in OECD countries, 86% of all funds for educational institutions come directly from public sources. In addition, 0.8% is channelled to institutions via public subsidies to households (Table B3.1).

In all OECD countries for which comparable data are available, private funding on educational institutions represents around 14% of all funds on average. This proportion varies widely among countries and only ten OECD countries and two partner countries report a share of private funding above the OECD average. Nevertheless, in Australia and Canada, as well as in the partner country Israel, private funds constitute around one-quarter of all educational expenditure. They exceed 30% in Japan, Korea and the United States and the partner country Chile (Table B3.1).

In all countries for which comparable data are available, for all levels of education combined, public funding increased between 2000 and 2005. However, private spending increased even more in nearly three-quarters of these countries. As a result, the decrease in the share of public funding on educational institutions was more than 5 percentage points in Mexico, Portugal, the Slovak Republic and the United Kingdom. This decrease is mainly due to a significant increase in tuition fees charged by tertiary educational institutions over the period 2000-2005. It is noteworthy that decreases in the share of public expenditure in total expenditure on educational institutions and, consequently increases in the share of private expenditure, have not generally gone hand in hand with cuts (in real terms) in public expenditure on educational institutions (Table B3.1). In fact, many OECD countries with the highest growth in private spending have also shown the highest increase in public funding of education. This indicates that an increase in private spending tends not to replace public investment but to complement it.

However, the share of private expenditure on educational institutions and how this varies among countries depends on the level of education.

Public and private expenditure on educational institutions in pre-primary, primary, secondary and post-secondary non-tertiary education

Investment in early childhood education is essential for building a strong foundation for lifelong learning and for ensuring equitable access to learning opportunities later in school. In pre-primary education, the private share of total payments to educational institutions is on average 20%, which is higher than the percentage for all levels of education combined. However, this proportion varies widely among countries, ranging from 5% or less in Belgium, France, the Netherlands and Sweden and the partner country Estonia, to well over 25% in Australia, Austria, Germany, Iceland and New Zealand and the partner country Chile, to over 55% in Japan and Korea. Other than in Austria and the Netherlands, the majority of private funding is covered by households (Table B3.2a).

Public funding dominates the primary, secondary and post-secondary non-tertiary levels of education in OECD and partner countries. Among OECD countries it reaches 92% on average.

B3

Chart B3.2. Distribution of public and private expenditure on educational institutions (2005)

By level of education

■ All private sources, including subsidies for payments to educational institutions received from public sources
☐ Expenditure of other private entities
▨ Household expenditure
▨ Public expenditure on educational institutions

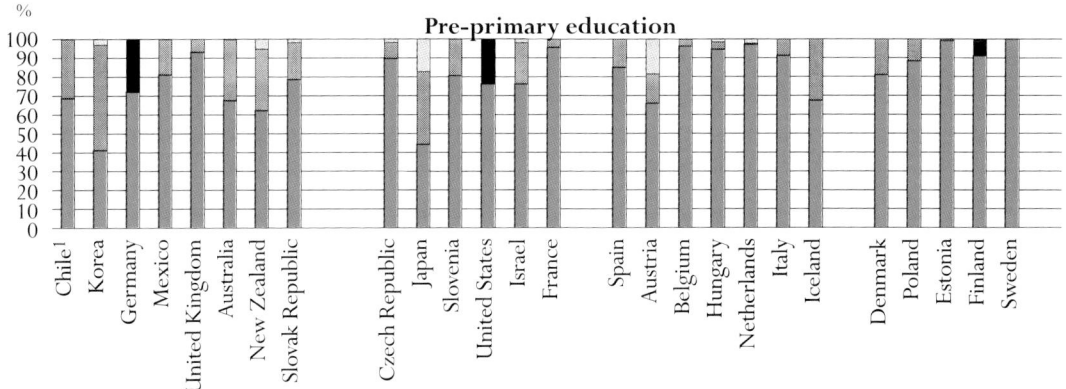

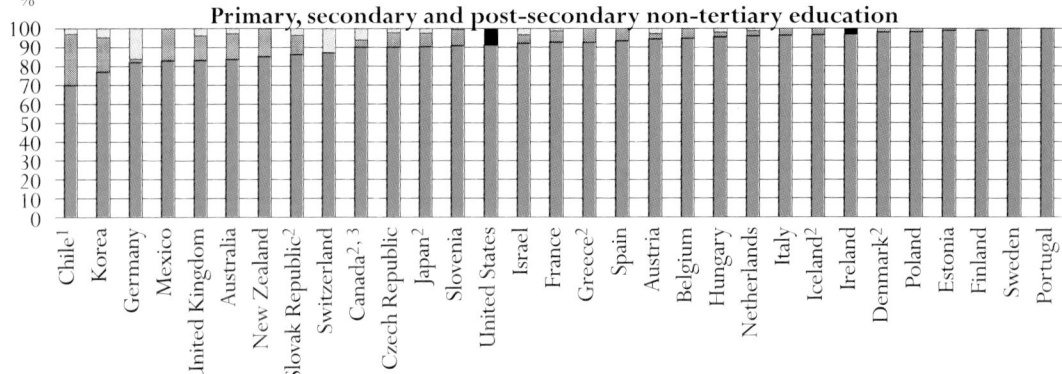

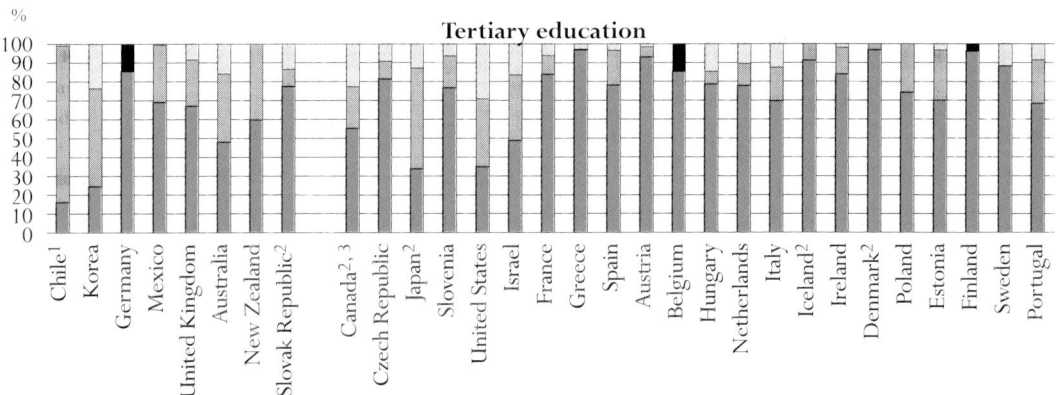

1. Year of reference 2006.
2. Some levels of education are included with others. Refer to "x" code in Table B1.1a for details.
3. Year of reference 2004.
Countries are ranked in ascending order of the proportion of public expenditure on educational institutions in primary, secondary and post-secondary non-tertiary education.
Source: OECD. Tables B3.2a and B3.2b. See Annex 3 for notes (*www.oecd.org/edu/eag2008*).
StatLink ᴬᴵˢᴸ http://dx.doi.org/10.1787/402017824643

B3

Nevertheless, private funding exceeds 10% in Australia, Canada, the Czech Republic, Germany, Korea, Mexico, New Zealand, the Slovak Republic, Switzerland and the United Kingdom, and the partner country Chile (Table B3.2a and Chart B3.2). The importance of public funding may reflect the fact that primary, secondary and post-secondary non-tertiary education are usually perceived as a public good with mainly public returns. At these levels in most countries, the largest share of private expenditure is household expenditure and goes mainly towards tuition. In Germany and Switzerland, however, most private expenditure is accounted for by contributions from the business sector to the dual system of apprenticeship at the upper secondary and post-secondary non-tertiary levels.

Between 2000 and 2005, 14 out of the 28 OECD and partner countries for which comparable data are available showed a small decrease in the share of public funding at primary, secondary and post-secondary non-tertiary levels. Among these countries, the increase in the private share is 2 percentage points or more in Canada (7.6 to 10.1%), Korea (19.2 to 23.0%), Mexico (13.9 to 17.1%), the Slovak Republic (2.4 to 13.8%), Switzerland (10.8 to 13.0%) and the United Kingdom (11.3 to 17.0%), as well as in the partner country Israel (5.9 to 8.0%). Funding shifts in the opposite direction, towards public funding, are evident in the other 14 countries; however, the share of public funding increased by 2 percentage points or more only in Hungary (from 92.7 to 95.5%) and Poland (95.4 to 98.2%) (Chart B3.3 and Table B3.2a).

In spite of such differences in the share of public funding at primary, secondary and post-secondary non-tertiary levels between 2000 and 2005, public expenditure on educational institutions increased in all countries with comparable data. Contrary to the general picture for all levels of education combined, the increase in public expenditure is accompanied by a decrease in private expenditure in Hungary, Iceland, Japan, the Netherlands, Poland, Sweden and the partner country Chile. However, the share of private expenditure on educational institutions represents less than 5% in 2005 in all countries of this group except Japan and the partner country Chile.

Public and private expenditure on educational institutions in tertiary institutions

At the tertiary level, high private returns in the form of better employment and income opportunities (see Indicator A9) suggest that a greater contribution by individuals and other private entities to the costs of tertiary education may be justified, provided, of course, that governments can ensure that funding is accessible to students irrespective of their economic background (see Indicator B5). In all OECD and partner countries except Germany and Greece, the private proportion of educational expenditure is far higher at the tertiary level than at the primary, secondary and post-secondary non-tertiary levels. It represents on average 27% of total expenditure on educational institutions at this level (Tables B3.2a and B3.2b).

The proportion of expenditure on tertiary institutions covered by individuals, businesses and other private sources, including subsidised private payments, ranges from less than 5% in Denmark, Finland and Greece, to more than 40% in Australia, Canada, Japan, New Zealand and the United States and the partner country Israel and to over 75% in Korea and the partner country Chile (Chart B3.2 and Table B3.2b). In Korea, around 80% of tertiary students are enrolled in private universities, where more than 70% of budgets derive from tuition fees. The contribution of private entities other than households to the financing of educational institutions is on average higher for tertiary education than for other levels of education.

B3

Chart B3.3.   Share of private expenditure on educational institutions (2000, 2005)

Percentage

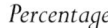 2000   ◆ 2005

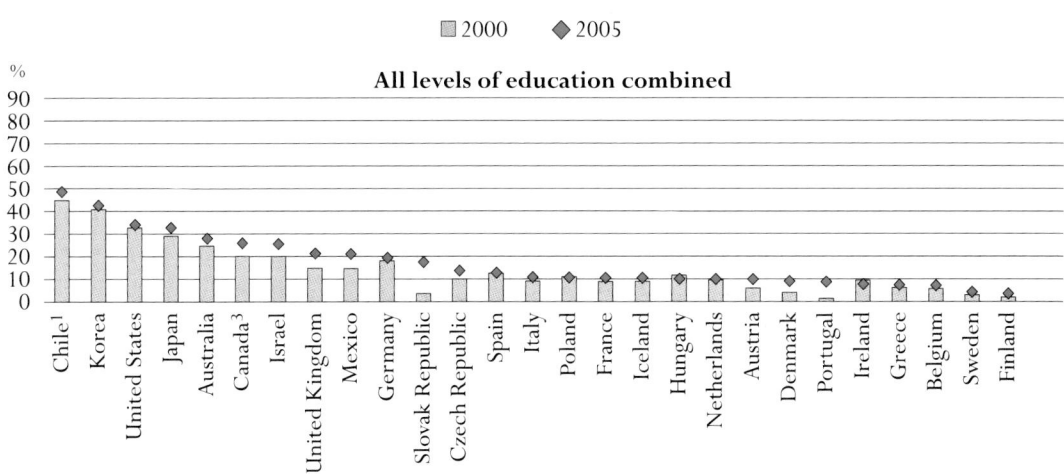

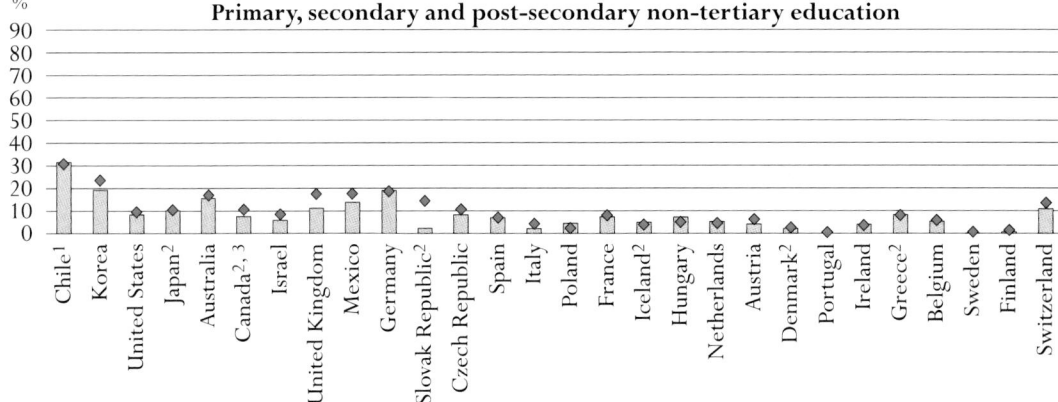

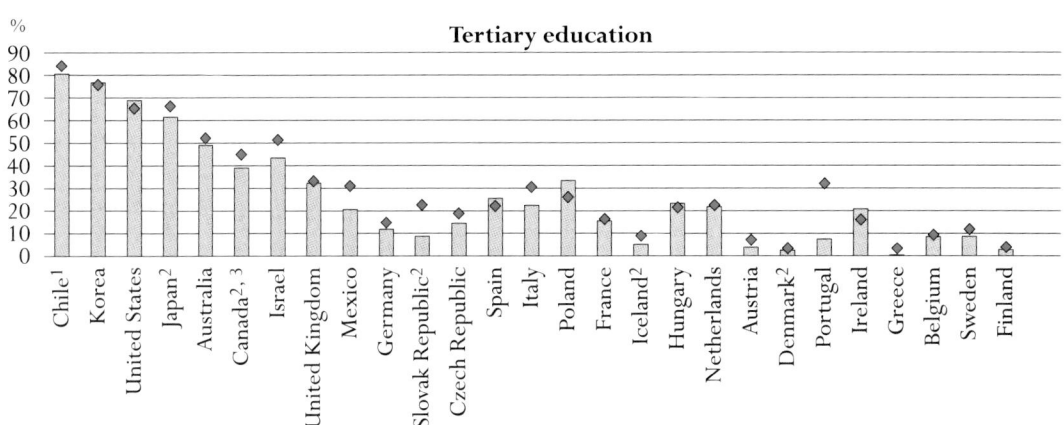

1. Year of reference 2006 instead of 2005.

2. Some levels of education are included with others. Refer to "x" code in Table B1.1a for details.

3. Year of reference 2004 instead of 2005.

Countries are ranked in descending order of the share of private expenditure on educational institutions in 2005 for all levels of education.

Source: OECD. Tables B3.1, B3.2a and B3.2b. See Annex 3 for notes (*www.oecd.org/edu/eag2008*).

StatLink ᘉᓕᔍ﹖ http://dx.doi.org/10.1787/402017824643

B3

In one-third of OECD and partner countries – Australia, Canada, Hungary, Italy, Japan, Korea, the Netherlands, the Slovak Republic, Sweden and the United States, and the partner country Israel – the proportion of expenditure on tertiary institutions covered by private entities other than households represents 10% or more.

In many OECD countries, the growth in tertiary participation (see Indicator C2) represents a response to strong demand, both individual and social. In 2005, the share of public funding at the tertiary level represented 73% on average in OECD countries. On average among the 18 OECD countries for which trend data are available, the share of public funding in tertiary institutions decreased slightly from 79% in 1995 to 77% in 2000 and to 73% in 2005. This trend is mainly affected by non-European countries in which tuition fees are generally higher and enterprises participate more actively, mainly by providing grants to finance tertiary institutions (Table B3.3 and Indicator B5).

In more than one-half of the OECD and partner countries with comparable data for 1995 and 2005, the private share increased by 3 percentage points or more. This increase exceeds 9 percentage points in Australia, Italy, Portugal, the Slovak Republic and the United Kingdom, as well as the partner countries Chile and Israel. Only the Czech Republic and Ireland – and to a lesser extent Spain – show a significant decrease in the private share allocated to tertiary educational institutions (Table B3.3 and Chart B3.3). In Australia, the main reason for the increase in the private share of spending on tertiary institutions between 1995 and 2005 was changes to the Higher Education Contribution Scheme/Higher Education Loan Programme (HECS/HELP) that took place in 1997, while the main reason for the decrease in Ireland is the abolition of tuition fees in tertiary first degree programmes which has been gradually implemented during the last decade (for more details see Indicator B5 and Annex 3).

Rises in private expenditure on educational institutions have generally gone hand in hand with rises (in real terms) in public expenditure on educational institutions at the tertiary level, as they have for all levels of education combined. Public investment in tertiary education has increased in all OECD and partner countries for which 2000 to 2005 data are available, regardless of changes in private spending (Table B3.1). Notably, in eight out of the 11 OECD countries – Austria, the Czech Republic, Greece, Hungary, Iceland, Poland, the Slovak Republic and Switzerland – with the highest increases in public expenditure on tertiary education, tertiary institutions charge low or no tuition fees and tertiary attainment is relatively low. By contrast, in Korea, the United Kingdom and in the United States where public spending has also increased significantly, there is a high reliance on private funding of tertiary education (see Table B3.3 and Indicator B5).

Definitions and methodologies

Data refer to the financial year 2005 and are based on the UOE data collection on education statistics administered by the OECD in 2007 (for details see Annex 3 at *www.oecd.org/edu/eag2008*).

The public and private proportions of expenditure on educational institutions are the percentages of total spending originating in, or generated by, the public and private sectors. Private spending includes all direct expenditure on educational institutions, whether partially covered by public subsidies or not. Public subsidies attributable to households, included in private spending, are shown separately.

B3

A portion of the budgets of educational institutions is related to ancillary services offered to students, including student welfare services (student meals, housing and transport). Part of the cost of these services is covered by fees collected from students and is included in the indicator.

Other private entities include private businesses and non-profit organisations, including religious organisations, charitable organisations and business and labour associations. Expenditure by private companies on the work-based element of school and work-based training of apprentices and students is also taken into account.

The data on expenditure for 1995 and 2000 were obtained by a special survey updated in 2007 in which expenditure for 1995 and 2000 were adjusted to the methods and definitions used in the current UOE data collection.

Table B3.1.
Relative proportions of public and private expenditure on educational institutions for all levels of education (2000, 2005)
Distribution of public and private sources of funds for educational institutions after transfers from public sources, by year

	2005					2000		Index of change between 2000 and 2005 in expenditure on educational institutions	
	Public sources	Private sources			Private: of which, subsidised	Public sources	All private sources[1]	Public sources	All private sources[1]
		Household expenditure	Expenditure of other private entities	All private sources[1]					
	(1)	(2)	(3)	(4)	(5)	(6)	(7)	(8)	(9)
OECD countries									
Australia	73.4	20.2	6.4	26.6	0.2	75.3	24.7	113	124
Austria	91.4	4.7	3.9	8.6	2.2	94.0	6.0	105	156
Belgium	94.2	4.9	1.0	5.8	1.8	94.3	5.7	107	109
Canada[2]	75.5	11.5	13.0	24.5	0.3	79.9	20.1	106	137
Czech Republic	87.6	8.6	3.8	12.4	m	89.9	10.1	130	165
Denmark	92.3	4.1	3.6	7.7	m	96.0	4.0	114	228
Finland	97.8	x(4)	x(4)	2.2	n	98.0	2.0	120	131
France	90.8	6.9	2.2	9.2	1.6	91.2	8.8	102	107
Germany	82.0	x(4)	x(4)	18.0	m	81.9	18.1	103	102
Greece	94.0	5.0	1.0	6.0	m	93.8	6.2	147	142
Hungary	91.3	3.6	5.1	8.7	n	88.3	11.7	147	105
Iceland	90.9	9.1	m	9.1	m	91.1	8.9	160	165
Ireland	93.7	5.9	0.5	6.3	m	90.5	9.5	139	90
Italy	90.5	7.0	2.4	9.5	0.9	90.9	9.1	101	105
Japan	68.6	22.0	9.3	31.4	m	71.0	29.0	100	112
Korea	58.9	29.6	11.6	41.1	1.2	59.2	40.8	140	142
Luxembourg	m	m	m	m	m	m	m	m	m
Mexico	80.3	19.5	0.2	19.7	1.0	85.3	14.7	122	174
Netherlands	91.4	4.9	3.7	8.6	0.8	90.4	9.6	119	106
New Zealand	78.4	21.2	0.4	21.6	m	m	m	110	m
Norway	m	m	m	m	m	95.0	5.0	124	m
Poland	90.7	9.3	m	9.3	m	89.0	11.0	126	104
Portugal	92.6	5.4	2.0	7.4	m	98.6	1.4	103	567
Slovak Republic	83.9	10.8	5.4	16.1	0.2	96.4	3.6	119	609
Spain	88.6	10.6	0.8	11.4	0.4	87.4	12.6	116	104
Sweden	97.0	0.1	2.9	3.0	n	97.0	3.0	115	113
Switzerland	m	m	m	m	m	92.1	7.9	113	135
Turkey	m	m	m	m	m	98.6	1.4	m	m
United Kingdom	80.0	15.3	4.7	20.0	1.6	85.2	14.8	128	184
United States	67.3	20.8	11.9	32.7	m	67.3	32.7	112	112
OECD average	85.5	~	~	14.5	0.8	~	~	119	166
EU19 average	90.5	~	~	9.5	0.9	~	~	119	179
Partner countries									
Brazil	m	m	m	m	m	m	m	135	m
Chile[3]	52.8	45.1	2.1	47.2	1.5	55.2	44.8	103	114
Estonia	92.4	6.8	0.8	7.6	1.3	m	m	126	m
Israel	75.9	17.0	7.1	24.1	2.1	80.0	20.0	103	131
Russian Federation	m	m	m	m	a	m	m	174	m
Slovenia	86.8	11.6	1.7	13.2	0.6	m	m	m	m

1. Including subsidies attributable to payments to educational institutions received from public sources.
2. Year of reference 2004 instead of 2005.
3. Year of reference 2006 instead of 2005.
Source: OECD. See Annex 3 for notes (*www.oecd.org/edu/eag2008*).
Please refer to the Reader's Guide for information concerning the symbols replacing missing data.
StatLink ⟨⟩ http://dx.doi.org/10.1787/402017824643

B3

Table B3.2a.
Relative proportions of public and private expenditure on educational institutions, as a percentage, by level of education (2000, 2005)
Distribution of public and private sources of funds for educational institutions after transfers from public sources, by year

	Pre-primary education (for children aged 3 and older) 2005					Primary, secondary and post-secondary non-tertiary education 2005					2000		Index of change between 2000 and 2005 in expenditure on educational institutions	
		Private sources					Private sources							
	Public sources	Household expenditure	Expenditure of other private entities	All private sources[1]	Private: of which, subsidised	Public sources	Household expenditure	Expenditure of other private entities	All private sources[1]	Private: of which, subsidised	Public sources	All private sources[1]	Public sources	All private sources[1]
	(1)	(2)	(3)	(4)	(5)	(6)	(7)	(8)	(9)	(10)	(11)	(12)	(13)	(14)
Australia	67.5	32.2	0.3	32.5	n	83.6	13.6	2.8	16.4	n	84.4	15.6	112	118
Austria	65.9	15.5	18.6	34.1	15.6	94.3	3.0	2.7	5.7	0.3	95.8	4.2	102	141
Belgium	96.1	3.6	0.2	3.9	0.3	94.7	5.1	0.1	5.3	1.2	94.7	5.3	107	106
Canada[2,3]	x(6)	x(7)	x(8)	x(9)	x(6)	89.9	3.9	6.2	10.1	x(6)	92.4	7.6	113	155
Czech Republic	89.6	8.5	1.9	10.4	m	89.9	7.8	2.2	10.1	m	91.7	8.3	128	158
Denmark[3]	80.8	19.2	n	19.2	m	97.9	2.1	m	2.1	m	97.8	2.2	116	112
Finland	91.1	x(4)	x(4)	8.9	n	99.2	x(9)	x(9)	0.8	n	99.3	0.7	122	154
France	95.5	4.5	n	4.5	n	92.5	6.2	1.3	7.5	1.7	92.6	7.4	101	103
Germany	72.1	x(4)	x(4)	27.9	a	81.8	2.1	16.1	18.2	m	81.0	19.0	100	95
Greece	x(6)	x(7)	x(8)	x(9)	m	92.5	7.5	n	7.5	n	91.7	8.3	129	116
Hungary	94.3	4.1	1.6	5.7	n	95.5	2.5	2.0	4.5	n	92.7	7.3	151	91
Iceland[3]	67.4	32.6	m	32.6	n	96.6	3.4	m	3.4	m	95.1	4.9	143	97
Ireland	m	m	m	m	m	96.8	x(9)	x(9)	3.2	m	96.0	4.0	153	120
Italy	91.1	8.9	n	8.9	0.2	96.3	3.7	m	3.7	m	97.8	2.2	105	180
Japan[3]	44.3	38.4	17.3	55.7	m	90.1	7.6	2.3	9.9	m	89.8	10.2	101	98
Korea	41.1	55.8	3.1	58.9	13.9	77.0	18.2	4.7	23.0	1.1	80.8	19.2	142	178
Luxembourg	m	m	m	m	m	m	m	m	m	m	m	m	m	m
Mexico	81.1	18.8	0.1	18.9	0.2	82.9	17.0	0.1	17.1	1.2	86.1	13.9	120	154
Netherlands	97.1	0.6	2.3	2.9	a	96.0	2.7	1.3	4.0	0.7	94.6	5.4	122	90
New Zealand	62.1	32.5	5.4	37.9	m	84.9	14.9	0.2	15.1	m	m	m	108	m
Norway	87.2	12.8	m	12.8	n	m	m	m	m	m	99.0	1.0	113	m
Poland	88.3	11.7	m	11.7	n	98.2	1.8	m	1.8	m	95.4	4.6	115	45
Portugal	m	m	m	m	m	99.9	0.1	m	0.1	m	99.9	0.1	102	100
Slovak Republic[3]	78.6	19.5	1.9	21.4	0.2	86.2	10.2	3.6	13.8	0.1	97.6	2.4	119	785
Spain	84.9	15.1	m	15.1	n	93.5	6.5	m	6.5	n	93.0	7.0	108	100
Sweden	100.0	n	n	n	n	99.9	0.1	m	0.1	a	99.9	0.1	113	94
Switzerland	m	m	m	m	m	87.0	n	13.0	13.0	0.8	89.2	10.8	110	135
Turkey	m	m	m	m	m	m	m	m	m	m	m	m	m	m
United Kingdom	92.9	7.1	n	7.1	n	83.0	13.1	3.9	17.0	2.0	88.7	11.3	131	210
United States	76.2	x(4)	x(4)	23.8	a	91.0	x(9)	x(9)	9.0	m	91.6	8.4	107	116
OECD average	*80.2*	*~*	*~*	*19.8*	*1.6*	*91.5*	*~*	*~*	*8.5*	*0.6*	*~*	*~*	*118*	*148*
EU19 average	*87.9*	*~*	*~*	*12.1*	*2.5*	*93.8*	*~*	*~*	*6.2*	*0.5*	*~*	*~*	*119*	*161*
Brazil	m	m	m	m	m	m	m	m	m	m	m	m	141	m
Chile[4]	68.6	31.3	0.1	31.4	m	69.8	27.3	3.0	30.2	m	68.4	31.6	101	95
Estonia	99.4	0.6	0.0	0.6	n	98.9	1.0	0.1	1.1	m	m	m	130	m
Israel	76.2	21.8	2.0	23.8	n	92.0	4.6	3.4	8.0	1.3	94.1	5.9	104	143
Russian Federation	m	m	m	m	a	m	m	m	m	a	m	m	154	m
Slovenia	80.6	19.3	0.1	19.4	n	90.7	8.8	0.5	9.3	0.9	m	m	m	m

OECD countries (Australia–United States); *Partner countries* (Brazil–Slovenia)

1. Including subsidies attributable to payments to educational institutions received from public sources.
To calculate private funds net of subsidies, subtract public subsidies (columns 5,10) from private funds (columns 4,9).
To calculate total public funds, including public subsidies, add public subsidies (columns 5,10) to direct public funds (columns 1,6).
2. Year of reference 2004 instead of 2005.
3. Some levels of education are included with others. Refer to "x" code in Table B1.1a for details.
4. Year of reference 2006 instead of 2005.
Source: OECD. See Annex 3 for notes (www.oecd.org/edu/eag2008).
Please refer to the Reader's Guide for information concerning the symbols replacing missing data.
StatLink ᴍⁱˢᴸ http://dx.doi.org/10.1787/402017824643

Table B3.2b.
Relative proportions of public and private expenditure on educational institutions, as a percentage, for tertiary education (2000, 2005)
Distribution of public and private sources of funds for educational institutions after transfers from public sources, by year

		2005					2000		Index of change between 2000 and 2005 in expenditure on educational institutions	
		Public sources	Private sources: Household expenditure	Private sources: Expenditure of other private entities	Private sources: All private sources[1]	Private: of which, subsidised	Public sources	All private sources[1]	Public sources	All private sources[1]
		(1)	(2)	(3)	(4)	(5)	(6)	(7)	(8)	(9)
OECD countries	Australia	47.8	36.3	15.9	52.2	0.7	51.0	49.0	115	130
	Austria	92.9	5.5	1.6	7.1	2.3	96.3	3.7	129	255
	Belgium	90.6	5.0	4.4	9.4	4.6	91.5	8.5	101	113
	Canada[2, 3]	55.1	22.3	22.6	44.9	0.8	61.0	39.0	105	134
	Czech Republic	81.2	9.4	9.4	18.8	m	85.4	14.6	147	199
	Denmark[3]	96.7	3.3	n	3.3	n	97.6	2.4	115	161
	Finland	96.1	x(4)	x(4)	3.9	n	97.2	2.8	114	162
	France	83.6	10.3	6.1	16.4	2.3	84.4	15.6	106	113
	Germany	85.3	x(4)	x(4)	14.7	m	88.2	11.8	102	131
	Greece	96.7	0.4	2.9	3.3	m	99.7	0.3	228	2911
	Hungary	78.5	6.9	14.6	21.5	n	76.7	23.3	129	116
	Iceland[3]	91.2	8.8	m	8.8	m	94.9	5.1	170	307
	Ireland	84.0	14.1	1.9	16.0	4.8	79.2	20.8	109	79
	Italy	69.6	18.0	12.5	30.4	4.6	77.5	22.5	100	151
	Japan[3]	33.7	53.4	12.9	66.3	m	38.5	61.5	93	115
	Korea	24.3	52.1	23.6	75.7	0.3	23.3	76.7	136	129
	Luxembourg	m	m	m	m	m	m	m	m	m
	Mexico	69.0	30.6	0.5	31.0	0.9	79.4	20.6	119	206
	Netherlands	77.6	12.0	10.4	22.4	1.2	78.2	21.8	110	114
	New Zealand	59.7	40.3	m	40.3	m	m	m	118	m
	Norway	m	m	m	m	m	96.3	3.7	117	m
	Poland	74.0	26.0	m	26.0	m	66.6	33.4	193	135
	Portugal	68.1	23.4	8.5	31.9	m	92.5	7.5	101	582
	Slovak Republic[3]	77.3	9.1	13.6	22.7	0.4	91.2	8.8	127	387
	Spain	77.9	18.7	3.4	22.1	1.8	74.4	25.6	119	99
	Sweden	88.2	n	11.8	11.8	a	91.3	8.7	111	155
	Switzerland	m	m	m	m	m	m	m	133	m
	Turkey	m	m	m	m	m	95.4	4.6	m	m
	United Kingdom	66.9	24.6	8.4	33.1	n	67.7	32.3	148	153
	United States	34.7	36.1	29.2	65.3	m	31.1	68.9	132	111
	OECD average	73.1	~	~	26.9	1.4	78	22	126	286
	EU19 average	82.5	~	~	17.5	1.3	85	15	127	334
Partner countries	Brazil	m	m	m	m	m	m	m	118	m
	Chile[4]	15.9	83.0	1.1	84.1	3.9	19.5	80.5	92	117
	Estonia	69.9	26.9	3.3	30.1	6.0	m	m	113	m
	Israel	48.7	34.9	16.5	51.3	5.3	56.5	43.5	93	127
	Russian Federation	m	m	m	m	m	m	m	228	m
	Slovenia	76.5	17.2	6.2	23.5	n	m	m	m	m

1. Including subsidies attributable to payments to educational institutions received from public sources.
To calculate private funds net of subsidies, subtract public subsidies (column 5) from private funds (column 4).
To calculate total public funds, including public subsidies, add public subsidies (column 5) to direct public funds (column 1).
2. Year of reference 2004 instead of 2005.
3. Some levels of education are included with others. Refer to "x" code in Table B1.1a for details.
4. Year of reference 2006 instead of 2005.
Source: OECD. See Annex 3 for notes (*www.oecd.org/edu/eag2008*).
Please refer to the Reader's Guide for information concerning the symbols replacing missing data.
StatLink http://dx.doi.org/10.1787/402017824643

B3

Table B3.3.
Trends in relative proportions of public expenditure[1] on educational institutions and index of change between 1995 and 2005 (2000=100), for tertiary education (1995, 2000, 2001, 2002, 2003, 2004, 2005)

		Share of public expenditure on educational institutions (%)						Index of change between 1995 and 2005 in public expenditure on educational institutions (2000=100, constant prices)						
		1995	2000	2001	2002	2003	2004	2005	1995	2000	2001	2002	2003	2004	2005
OECD countries	Australia	64.8	51.0	51.3	48.7	48.0	47.2	47.8	115	100	103	105	107	111	115
	Austria	96.1	96.3	94.6	91.6	92.7	93.7	92.9	97	100	112	103	109	119	129
	Belgium	m	91.5	89.5	86.1	86.7	90.4	90.6	m	100	99	98	97	99	101
	Canada[2]	56.6	61.0	58.6	56.4	m	55.1	m	69	100	102	98	m	105	m
	Czech Republic	71.5	85.4	85.3	87.5	83.3	84.7	81.2	86	100	108	122	138	145	147
	Denmark[2]	99.4	97.6	97.8	97.9	96.7	96.7	96.7	93	100	117	123	113	120	115
	Finland	97.8	97.2	96.5	96.3	96.4	96.3	96.1	91	100	100	104	108	114	114
	France	85.3	84.4	83.8	83.8	83.8	83.8	83.6	93	100	101	103	104	105	106
	Germany	89.2	88.2	m	m	m	m	85.3	96	100	m	m	m	m	102
	Greece[2]	m	99.7	99.6	99.6	97.9	97.9	96.7	63	100	136	154	194	196	228
	Hungary	80.3	76.7	77.6	78.7	78.5	79.0	78.5	78	100	109	124	140	122	129
	Iceland[2]	m	94.9	95.0	95.6	88.7	90.9	91.2	m	100	105	127	133	153	170
	Ireland	69.7	79.2	84.7	85.8	83.8	82.6	84.0	50	100	100	103	98	102	109
	Italy	82.9	77.5	77.8	78.6	72.1	69.4	69.6	85	100	107	111	100	101	100
	Japan[2]	35.1	38.5	36.3	35.3	36.6	36.6	33.7	80	100	94	94	101	102	93
	Korea	m	23.3	15.9	14.9	23.2	21.0	24.3	m	100	74	68	127	109	136
	Luxembourg	m	m	m	m	m	m	m	m	m	m	m	m	m	m
	Mexico	77.4	79.4	70.4	71.0	69.1	68.9	69.0	75	100	84	119	113	113	119
	Netherlands	80.6	78.2	78.2	78.8	78.6	77.6	77.6	97	100	103	105	105	107	110
	New Zealand	m	m	m	62.5	61.5	60.8	59.7	105	100	105	111	116	112	118
	Norway	93.7	96.3	m	96.3	96.7	m	m	107	100	105	117	122	124	117
	Poland	m	66.6	66.9	69.7	69.0	72.9	74.0	89	100	117	148	151	180	193
	Portugal	96.5	92.5	92.3	91.3	91.5	86.0	68.1	76	100	107	99	109	89	101
	Slovak Republic[2]	95.4	91.2	93.3	85.2	86.2	81.3	77.3	85	100	109	111	126	150	127
	Spain	74.4	74.4	75.5	76.3	76.9	75.9	77.9	72	100	107	111	117	119	119
	Sweden	93.6	91.3	91.0	90.0	89.0	88.4	88.2	84	100	102	107	111	113	111
	Switzerland	m	m	m	m	m	m	m	74	100	112	124	131	131	133
	Turkey	96.3	95.4	94.6	90.1	95.2	90.0	m	56	100	95	106	113	106	m
	United Kingdom	80.0	67.7	71.0	72.0	70.2	69.6	66.9	116	100	113	123	122	123	148
	United States	37.4	31.1	38.1	39.5	38.3	35.4	34.7	85	100	110	119	130	131	132
	OECD average	*79.7*	*78.0*	*76.6*	*76.3*	*76.6*	*74.3*	*73.8*	*85*	*100*	*105*	*112*	*120*	*121*	*127*
	OECD average for countries with data available for all reference years	*78.7*	*77.1*	*77.5*	*77.0*	*76.0*	*74.9*	*73.0*	*86*	*100*	*107*	*115*	*121*	*124*	*128*
	EU19 average for countries with data available for all reference years	*86.0*	*85.0*	*85.8*	*85.4*	*84.3*	*83.2*	*81.2*	*84*	*100*	*110*	*117*	*123*	*127*	*132*
Partner countries	Brazil	m	m	m	m	m	m	m	78	100	100	102	109	101	118
	Chile[3]	25.1	19.5	m	19.3	17.0	15.5	15.9	78	100	m	112	102	99	92
	Estonia	m	m	m	m	m	m	m	68	100	m	m	m	114	113
	Israel	59.2	56.5	56.8	53.4	59.3	49.6	48.7	81	100	103	96	107	92	93
	Russian Federation	m	m	m	m	m	m	m	m	100	120	143	171	175	228
	Slovenia	m	m	m	m	m	75.7	76.5	m	100	m	m	m	m	m

1. Excluding international funds in public and total expenditure on educational institutions.
2. Some levels of education are included with others. Refer to "x" code in Table B1.1a for details.
3. Year of reference 2006 instead of 2005.
Source: OECD. See Annex 3 for notes (www.oecd.org/edu/eag2008).
Please refer to the Reader's Guide for information concerning the symbols replacing missing data.
StatLink ⟨⟨⟨⟨ http://dx.doi.org/10.1787/402017824643

WHAT IS THE TOTAL PUBLIC SPENDING ON EDUCATION?

Public expenditure on education as a percentage of total public expenditure indicates the value placed on education relative to other public investments such as health care, social security, defence and security. It provides an important context for the other indicators on expenditure, particularly for Indicator B3 (the public and private shares of educational expenditure) and is the quantification of an important policy lever in its own right.

Key results

Chart B4.1. Total public expenditure on education as a percentage of total public expenditure (2000, 2005)

The chart shows direct public expenditure on educational institutions plus public subsidies to households (including subsidies for living costs) and other private entities, as a percentage of total public expenditure, by year. It must be recalled that public sectors differ in terms of their size and breadth of responsibility from country to country.

■ 2005   ● 2000

On average, OECD countries devote 13.2% of total public expenditure to education, but values for individual countries range from 10% or below in the Czech Republic, Germany, Italy and Japan to more than 23% in Mexico.

% of total public expenditure

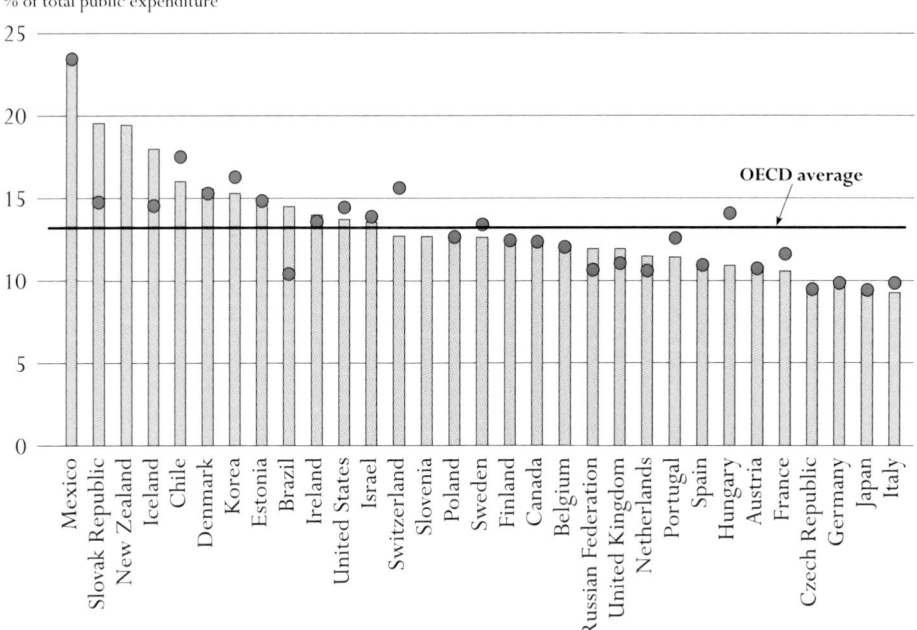

Countries are ranked in descending order of total public expenditure on education at all levels of education as a percentage of total public expenditure in 2005.
Source: OECD. Table B4.1. See Annex 3 for notes (*www.oecd.org/edu/eag2008*).
StatLink ᵐˢᴾ http://dx.doi.org/10.1787/402021027265

Other highlights of this indicator

▪ Public funding of education is a social priority, even in OECD countries with little public involvement in other areas.

▪ Between 1995 and 2005, public budgets as a percentage of GDP tended to increase slightly. Education took a growing share of total public expenditure in most countries, and on average it also grew as fast as GDP. In Denmark, the Netherlands, New Zealand, the Slovak Republic and Sweden, and the partner country Brazil, there have been particularly significant shifts in public funding in favour of education.

▪ The main increase in public expenditure on education relative to total public spending took place from 1995 to 2000, while public expenditure on education and for other public sectors increased in the same proportions from 2000 to 2005.

▪ In OECD countries, public funding of primary, secondary and post-secondary non-tertiary education is on average about three times that of tertiary education, mainly due to largely universal enrolment rates but also because the private share tends to be greater at the tertiary level. This ratio varies from less than double in Canada, Finland, Greece and Norway to more than five times in Korea and the partner country Chile. The latter figure is indicative of the relatively high proportion of private funds that go to tertiary education in these two countries.

▪ On average across OECD countries, 85% of public expenditure on education is transferred to public institutions. In two-thirds of OECD countries, as well as in the partner countries Brazil, Estonia and Slovenia, the share of public expenditure on education going to public institutions exceeds 80%. The share of public expenditure transferred to the private sector is larger at the tertiary level than at primary to post-secondary non-tertiary levels and reaches 26% on average among OECD countries for which data are available.

B4

Policy context

If the public benefits from a particular service are greater than the private benefits, markets alone may fail to provide these services adequately and governments may need to become involved. Education is one area where all governments intervene to fund or direct the provision of services. As there is no guarantee that markets will provide equal access to educational opportunities, government funding of educational services ensures that education is not beyond the reach of some members of society.

This indicator focuses on public expenditure on education but also evaluates how public expenditure has changed over time. Since the second half of the 1990s, most OECD countries have made serious efforts to consolidate public budgets. Education has had to compete for public financial support with a wide range of other areas covered by government budgets. To examine this evolution, the indicator evaluates the change in educational expenditure in absolute terms and relative to changes in the size of public budgets.

Evidence and explanations

What this indicator does and does not cover

This indicator shows total public expenditure on education, which includes direct public expenditure on educational institutions as well as public subsidies to households (*e.g.* scholarships and loans to students for tuition fees and student living costs) and to other private entities for education (*e.g.* subsidies to companies or labour organisations that operate apprenticeship programmes). Unlike the preceding indicators, this indicator also includes public subsidies that are not attributable to household payments for educational institutions, such as subsidies for student living costs.

OECD countries differ in the ways in which they use public money for education. Public funds may flow directly to schools or may be channelled to institutions via government programmes or via households; they may also be restricted to the purchase of educational services or be used to support student living costs.

Total public expenditure on all services, excluding education, includes expenditure on debt servicing (*e.g.* interest payments) that is not included in public expenditure on education. The reason for this exclusion is that some countries cannot separate interest payment outlays for education from those for other services. This means that public expenditure on education as a percentage of total public expenditure may be underestimated in countries where interest payments represent a large proportion of total public expenditure on all services.

It is important to examine public investment in education in conjunction with private investment, as shown in Indicator B3 to get a full picture of investment in education.

Overall level of public resources invested in education

On average, OECD countries devoted 13.2% of total public expenditure to education in 2005. However, the values for individual countries range from 10% or less in the Czech Republic, Germany, Italy and Japan to more than 23% in Mexico (Chart B4.1). As in the case of spending on education in relation to GDP per capita, these values must be interpreted in the light of student demography and enrolment rates.

B4

The public-sector proportion of funding of the different levels of education varies widely among OECD countries. In 2005, OECD countries and partner countries allocated between 5.9% (the Russian Federation) and 16.2% (Mexico) of total public expenditure to primary, secondary and post-secondary non-tertiary education, and between 1.6% (Italy and Japan) and 4.8% (New Zealand) on tertiary education. On average in OECD countries, public funding of primary, secondary and post-secondary non-tertiary education is nearly three times that of tertiary education, mainly owing to enrolment rates (see Indicator C2) and the demographic structure of the population or because the private share in expenditure tends to be higher at the tertiary level. This ratio varies by country from two times in Canada, Finland, Greece and Norway to more than five times in Korea and the partner country Chile. The latter figure is indicative of the relatively high proportion of private funds that goes to tertiary education in Korea and the partner country Chile (Table B4.1).

Public funding of education is a social priority, even in OECD countries with little public involvement in other areas. When public expenditure on education is considered as a proportion of total public spending, the relative sizes of public budgets (as measured by public spending in relation to GDP) must be taken into account.

When the size of public budgets relative to GDP in OECD countries is compared with the proportion of public spending on education, it is evident that even in countries with relatively low rates of public spending, education has a very high priority. For instance, the share of public spending that goes to education in Korea, Mexico, the Slovak Republic and the partner country Chile is among the highest in OECD countries (Chart B4.1), yet total public spending accounts for a relatively small proportion of GDP in these countries (Chart B4.2).

Chart B4.2. Total public expenditure as a percentage of GDP (2000, 2005)

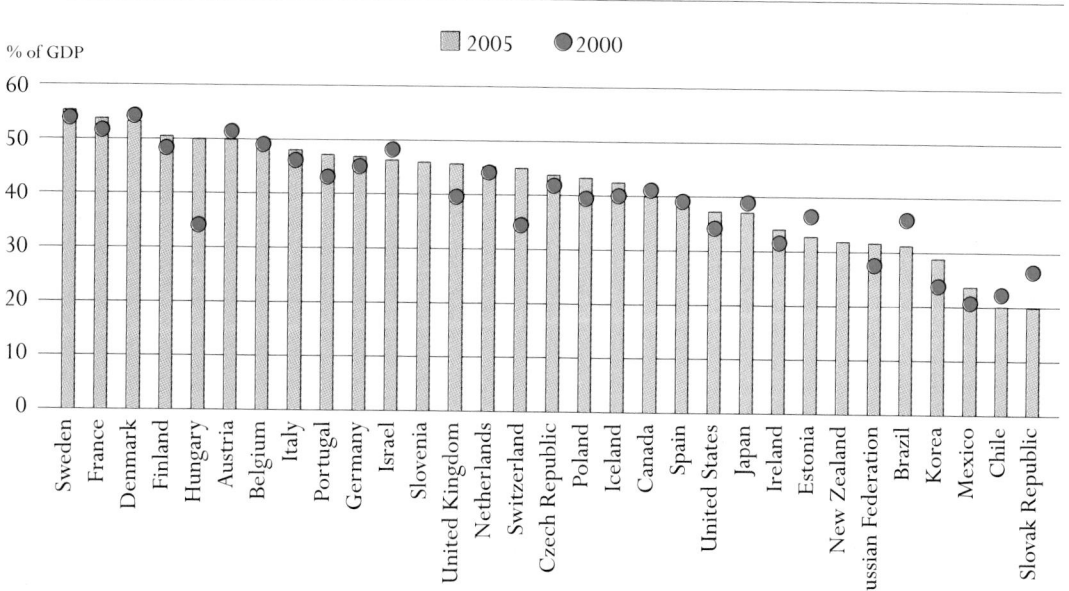

Note: This chart represents public expenditure on all services and not simply public expenditure on education.
Countries are ranked in descending order of total public expenditure as a percentage of GDP in 2005.
Source: OECD. Annex 2. See Annex 3 for notes (*www.oecd.org/edu/eag2008*).
StatLink ᕈᎢᔲᴸ http://dx.doi.org/10.1787/402021027265

B4

Although the overall pattern is not clear, there is some evidence to suggest that countries with high rates of public spending spend proportionately less on education; only one of the top ten countries for public spending on public services overall – Denmark – is among the top ten public spenders on education (Charts B4.1 and B4.2).

From 1995 to 2005, public expenditure on education typically grew faster than total public spending and as fast as national income: the average proportion of public expenditure on education increased over this period in 16 of the 21 countries with comparable data in both 1995 and 2005; simultaneously in these 21 countries, public expenditure on education as a percentage of GDP increased slightly. However, the main increase in public expenditure on education relative to total public spending took place from 1995 to 2000, while public expenditure on education and on other public sectors increased in the same proportions from 2000 to 2005. Although budget consolidation puts pressure on education along with every other service, the proportion of public budgets spent on education in OECD countries rose from 11.9% in 1995 to 13.2% in 2005. The figures suggest that the greatest relative increases in the share of public expenditure on education during this period took place in Denmark (increasing from 12.2 to 15.5%), the Netherlands (from 8.9 to 11.5%), New Zealand (16.5 to 19.4%), the Slovak Republic (14.1 to 19.5%) and Sweden (10.7 to 12.6%) and in partner country Brazil (11.2 to 14.5%).

Distribution of public expenditure to the public and private sectors

The vast majority of public funds for education – an average of 85% – are directed to public institutions: In two-thirds of OECD countries, as well as in the partner countries Brazil, Estonia and Slovenia, the share of public expenditure on education transferred to public institutions exceeds 80%. However, in a number of countries, considerable public funds are transferred to private institutions or given directly to households to spend in the institution of their choice: more than 20% of public expenditure is distributed (directly or indirectly) to the private sector in Denmark, New Zealand, Norway and the United Kingdom and in the partner countries Chile and Israel. In Belgium, most public funds go to government-dependent institutions that are managed by private bodies but otherwise operate under the aegis of the regular education system (Table B4.2).

On average among OECD countries, nearly 12% of public funding designated for education at the primary, secondary and post-secondary non-tertiary levels is spent in privately managed institutions. Belgium is the only country where the majority of public funding goes to privately managed institutions, though in the partner country Chile, the percentage is also high, at 41%. Public funding transfers to private households and other private entities are generally not a significant feature at primary, secondary and post-secondary non-tertiary levels. On average among OECD countries, these transfers represent 3.7% of public expenditure on education and exceed 10% only in Denmark.

At the tertiary level, the majority of public funds is still generally directed to public institutions, but the share of public expenditure transferred to the private sector is larger than at the primary to post-secondary non-tertiary levels and reaches an average of 26% in countries with available data. There are, however, substantial variations among countries in the share of public expenditure devoted to the private sector. In Belgium and the United Kingdom (where there are no public tertiary institutions), as well as in the partner countries Chile, Estonia and Israel,

B4

public expenditure goes mainly to privately managed institutions. The share of public expenditure indirectly transferred to the private sector (households and other private entities) is larger at the tertiary level as households/students more often receive some public funding at the tertiary level than at other levels. On average, 18% of public funding is transferred to households and other private entities at the tertiary level. This is partly due to financial aid to tertiary students through scholarships, grants and loans (see Indicator B5). The proportion of public expenditure indirectly transferred to the private sector exceeds 30% in Australia, Denmark, New Zealand and Norway and, among partner countries, in Chile.

Definitions and methodologies

The data refer to the financial year 2005 and are based on the UOE data collection on education statistics administered by the OECD in 2007 (for details see Annex 3 at *www.oecd.org/edu/eag2008*). Educational expenditure is expressed as a percentage of a country's total public sector expenditure and as a percentage of GDP. Public expenditure on education includes expenditure on educational institutions and subsidies for students' living costs and for other private expenditure outside institutions. Public expenditure on education includes expenditure by all public entities, including ministries other than ministries of education, local and regional governments and other public agencies.

Total public expenditure, also referred to as total public spending, corresponds to the non-repayable current and capital expenditure of all levels of government: central, regional and local. Current expenditure includes final consumption expenditure, property income paid, subsidies and other current transfers (*e.g.* social security, social assistance, pensions and other welfare benefits). Figures for total public expenditure have been taken from the OECD National Accounts Database (see Annex 2) and use the System of National Accounts 1993.

The glossary at *www.oecd.org/edu/eag2008* gives a definition of public, government-dependent private and independent private institutions.

Further references

The following additional material relevant to this indicator is available on line at:
StatLink ⧉🖳 http://dx.doi.org/10.1787/402021027265

- *Table B4.3a. Initial sources of public educational funds and final purchasers of educational resources by level of government for primary, secondary and post-secondary non-tertiary education (2005)*

- *Table B4.3b. Initial sources of public educational funds and final purchasers of educational resources by level of government for tertiary education (2005)*

Table B4.1.
Total public expenditure on education (1995, 2000, 2005)
Direct public expenditure on educational institutions plus public subsidies to households (which include subsidies for living costs) and other private entities, as a percentage of GDP and as a percentage of total public expenditure, by level of education and year

| | Public expenditure[1] on education as a percentage of total public expenditure | | | | | Public expenditure[1] on education as a percentage of GDP | | | | |
| | 2005 | | | 2000 | 1995 | 2005 | | | 2000 | 1995 |
	Primary, secondary and post-secondary non-tertiary education	Tertiary education	All levels of education combined	All levels of education combined	All levels of education combined	Primary, secondary and post-secondary non-tertiary education	Tertiary education	All levels of education combined	All levels of education combined	All levels of education combined
Australia	m	m	m	13.6	13.6	3.5	1.1	4.8	4.7	5.0
Austria	7.1	3.0	10.9	10.7	10.8	3.6	1.5	5.4	5.5	6.0
Belgium	8.0	2.6	12.1	12.1	m	4.0	1.3	6.0	5.9	m
Canada[2, 3]	8.2	4.2	12.3	12.4	12.7	3.3	1.7	4.9	5.1	6.2
Czech Republic	6.5	2.0	9.7	9.5	8.7	2.8	0.9	4.3	4.0	4.8
Denmark[3]	9.3	4.5	15.5	15.3	12.2	4.9	2.4	8.3	8.3	7.3
Finland	7.8	4.0	12.5	12.5	11.0	4.0	2.0	6.3	6.0	6.8
France	7.1	2.2	10.6	11.6	11.5	3.8	1.2	5.7	6.0	6.3
Germany	6.2	2.4	9.7	9.9	8.5	2.9	1.1	4.5	4.5	4.6
Greece[3]	m	m	m	7.3	5.6	2.5	1.4	4.0	3.4	2.6
Hungary[4]	6.9	2.1	10.9	14.1	12.9	3.4	1.0	5.5	4.8	5.2
Iceland[3]	12.3	3.4	18.0	13.9	m	5.2	1.5	7.6	5.8	m
Ireland	10.7	3.3	14.0	13.6	12.2	3.7	1.1	4.8	4.3	5.0
Italy	6.7	1.6	9.3	9.8	9.0	3.2	0.8	4.4	4.5	4.7
Japan[3]	7.0	1.6	9.5	9.4	m	2.6	0.6	3.5	3.7	3.6
Korea	11.8	2.1	15.3	16.3	m	3.4	0.6	4.4	3.9	m
Luxembourg[3, 4]	9.1	m	m	m	m	3.8	m	m	m	m
Mexico	16.2	4.1	23.4	23.4	22.2	3.8	1.0	5.5	4.9	4.6
Netherlands	7.7	3.0	11.5	10.6	8.9	3.5	1.4	5.2	4.7	5.0
New Zealand	13.5	4.8	19.4	m	16.5	4.3	1.5	6.2	6.8	5.6
Norway	m	m	m	14.5	15.5	4.1	2.3	7.0	5.9	7.9
Poland[4]	8.6	2.8	12.6	12.7	11.9	3.7	1.2	5.5	5.0	5.2
Portugal[4]	8.2	2.1	11.4	12.6	11.7	3.9	1.0	5.4	5.4	5.1
Slovak Republic[3]	12.9	4.1	19.5	14.7	14.1	2.6	0.8	3.9	3.9	4.6
Spain	7.2	2.5	11.1	10.9	10.3	2.8	0.9	4.2	4.3	4.6
Sweden	8.2	3.5	12.6	13.4	10.7	4.5	1.9	7.0	7.2	7.1
Switzerland[4]	8.7	3.3	12.7	15.6	13.5	3.9	1.5	5.7	5.4	5.7
Turkey	m	m	m	m	m	m	m	m	m	m
United Kingdom	8.6	2.7	11.9	11.0	11.4	3.9	1.2	5.4	4.4	5.1
United States	9.4	3.5	13.7	14.4	m	3.5	1.3	5.1	4.9	m
OECD average	*9.0*	*3.0*	*13.2*	*12.8*	*11.9*	*3.6*	*1.3*	*5.4*	*5.1*	*5.3*
EU19 average	*8.2*	*2.8*	*12.1*	*13.0*	*10.7*	*3.6*	*1.3*	*5.3*	*5.1*	*5.3*
Brazil[4]	10.6	2.8	14.5	10.4	11.2	3.3	0.9	4.5	3.8	3.9
Chile[5]	11.9	2.4	16.0	17.5	14.5	2.4	0.5	3.2	3.9	3.0
Estonia	10.9	2.8	14.9	14.9	13.9	3.6	0.9	4.9	5.4	5.8
Israel	9.0	2.2	13.5	13.9	13.5	4.2	1.0	6.3	6.7	7.0
Russian Federation[4]	5.9	2.5	11.9	10.6	m	1.9	0.8	3.8	2.9	m
Slovenia	8.8	2.8	12.7	m	m	4.1	1.3	5.8	m	m

OECD countries / Partner countries

1. Public expenditure presented in this table includes public subsidies to households for living costs, which are not spent on educational institutions. Thus the figures presented here exceed those on public spending on institutions found in Table B2.1.
2. Year of reference 2004 instead of 2005.
3. Some levels of education are included with others. Refer to "x" code in Table B1.1a for details.
4. Public institutions only.
5. Year of reference 2006 instead of 2005.
Source: OECD. See Annex 3 for notes (www.oecd.org/edu/eag2008).
Please refer to the Reader's Guide for information concerning the symbols replacing missing data.
StatLink ᔏᔍᔎ http://dx.doi.org/10.1787/402021027265

Table B4.2.
Distribution of total public expenditure on education (2005)
Public expenditure on education transferred to educational institutions and public transfers to the private sector as a percentage of total public expenditure on education, by level of education

B4

	Primary, secondary and post-secondary non-tertiary education			Tertiary education			All levels of education combined		
	Direct public expenditure on public institutions	Direct public expenditure on private institutions	Indirect public transfers and payments to the private sector	Direct public expenditure on public institutions	Direct public expenditure on private institutions	Indirect public transfers and payments to the private sector	Direct public expenditure on public institutions	Direct public expenditure on private institutions	Indirect public transfers and payments to the private sector
Australia	75.5	20.9	3.6	67.7	n	32.3	x	x	10.5
Austria	98.3	0.6	1.1	75.9	5.3	18.8	90.8	1.8	7.3
Belgium	44.2	53.2	2.6	36.2	48.6	15.2	43.7	51.2	5.1
Canada[1,2]	98.1	1.9	m	84.1	0.4	15.5	93.3	1.4	5.2
Czech Republic	91.6	3.8	4.6	93.1	1.0	5.9	92.7	2.9	4.3
Denmark[2]	81.7	6.8	11.5	69.2	a	30.8	78.2	4.3	17.5
Finland	90.1	6.8	3.1	75.5	7.4	17.1	85.6	7.0	7.4
France	84.0	12.7	3.3	86.7	5.5	7.9	85.4	10.7	3.9
Germany	84.5	10.7	4.8	79.8	1.1	19.1	80.5	11.5	7.9
Greece[2]	99.8	a	0.2	98.6	a	1.4	99.4	a	0.6
Hungary	85.8	9.6	4.6	78.9	5.4	15.7	86.5	7.5	6.0
Iceland[2]	96.8	2.0	1.1	69.7	7.2	23.1	91.7	3.1	5.2
Ireland	90.6	n	9.4	85.2	n	14.8	89.3	n	10.7
Italy	97.3	1.0	1.7	81.2	1.9	16.8	94.0	1.5	4.5
Japan[2]	96.3	3.5	0.2	65.0	13.4	21.5	89.8	6.4	3.9
Korea	82.7	15.5	1.8	75.2	21.9	2.9	80.6	15.2	4.2
Luxembourg[2]	97.8	m	2.2	m	m	m	m	m	m
Mexico	94.3	n	5.7	93.6	n	6.4	94.7	n	5.3
Netherlands	x	x	6.3	x	x	27.7	x	x	11.6
New Zealand	89.5	3.7	6.8	56.8	1.7	41.5	78.7	5.9	15.4
Norway	88.6	4.3	7.7	54.7	2.7	42.6	73.8	6.9	19.3
Poland[3]	x	x	1.8	x	x	1.6	x	x	1.6
Portugal	92.2	6.4	1.4	89.9	1.2	8.9	91.0	6.3	2.6
Slovak Republic[2]	90.4	6.6	3.1	85.9	a	14.1	90.6	4.4	5.0
Spain	84.0	14.4	1.6	90.0	1.8	8.2	85.7	11.3	3.0
Sweden	86.5	7.7	5.9	68.1	4.8	27.1	81.5	7.3	11.2
Switzerland[3]	90.4	7.3	2.2	89.6	5.4	5.0	90.3	6.7	3.0
Turkey	m	m	m	m	m	m	m	m	m
United Kingdom	75.6	22.0	2.4	a	74.2	25.8	57.8	34.0	8.2
United States	99.8	0.2	m	68.3	8.2	23.5	91.2	2.7	6.1
OECD average	*88.4*	*8.5*	*3.7*	*73.8*	*8.4*	*17.6*	*84.7*	*8.4*	*7.0*
EU19 average	*86.7*	*10.1*	*3.8*	*74.6*	*9.9*	*15.4*	*83.3*	*10.1*	*6.6*
Brazil[2,3]	98.0	n	2.0	87.9	n	12.1	96.2	n	3.8
Chile[4]	58.6	40.9	0.6	32.4	27.5	40.1	54.9	38.7	6.4
Estonia	94.7	1.3	4.0	28.6	56.0	15.4	82.4	11.8	5.8
Israel	73.8	24.8	1.4	5.5	82.9	11.6	64.3	32.6	3.1
Russian Federation	m	a	m	m	a	m	m	a	m
Slovenia	94.1	0.6	5.4	76.1	0.2	23.7	90.6	0.5	8.9

1. Year of reference 2004.
2. Some levels of education are included with others. Refer to "x" code in Table B1.1a for details.
3. Public institutions only.
4. Year of reference 2006.
Source: OECD. See Annex 3 for notes (*www.oecd.org/edu/eag2008*).
Please refer to the Reader's Guide for information concerning the symbols replacing missing data.
StatLink ⫘ http://dx.doi.org/10.1787/402021027265

HOW MUCH DO TERTIARY STUDENTS PAY AND WHAT PUBLIC SUBSIDIES DO THEY RECEIVE?

This indicator examines the relationships between annual tuition fees charged by institutions, direct and indirect public spending on educational institutions, and public subsidies to households for student living costs. It looks at whether financial subsidies for households are provided in the form of grants or loans and raises related questions: Are scholarships/grants and loans more appropriate in countries with higher tuition fees charged by institutions? Are loans an effective means for helping to increase the efficiency of financial resources invested in education and shift some of the cost of education to the beneficiaries of educational investment? Are student loans less appropriate than grants in encouraging low-income students to pursue their education?

Key results

Chart B5.1. Average annual tuition fees charged by tertiary-type A public institutions for full-time national students (academic year 2004/05)

This chart shows the annual tuition fees charged in equivalent USD converted using PPPs. Countries in bold indicate that tuition fees refer to public institutions but more than two-thirds of students are enrolled in private institutions. The net entry rate and expenditure per student (in USD) in tertiary-type A programmes are added next to country names.

There are large differences among OECD and partner countries for which data are available in the average tuition fees charged by tertiary-type A public institutions. In eight OECD countries public institutions charge no tuition fees, but in one-third of countries public institutions charge annual tuition fees for national students in excess of USD 1 500. Among the EU19 countries, only the Netherlands and the United Kingdom have annual tuition fees that represent more than USD 1 000 per full-time student; these relate to government-dependent institutions.

Average annual tuition fees in USD

5 000	United States - 64% (24 370)
	Chile - 48% (7 977)
4 500	
4 000	Australia - 82% (15 599); **Japan** - 44% (13 827); **Korea** - 51% (9 938)
3 500	Canada - m (20 156)
3 000	**Israel**[1] - 55% (11 581)
	New Zealand - 79% (11 002)
2 500	
2 000	**United Kingdom**[1] - 51% (13 506)
1 500	**Netherlands**[1] - 59% (13 883)
1 000	Italy - 56% (8 032)
	Austria - 37% (15 028); Spain - 43% (10 301)
500	Belgium (Fr. and Fl.) - 33% (11 960)
	Turkey - 27% (m); France - m (11 486)
0	Czech Republic - 41% (7 019); Denmark - 57% (14 959); Finland - 73% (12 285); Ireland - 45% (10 468); Iceland - 74% (9 474); Norway - 76% (15 552); Poland - 76% (5 593); Sweden - 76% (15 946)

Note: This chart does not take into account grants, subsidies or loans that partially or fully offset the student's tuition fees.

1. Public institutions do not exist at this level of education and most students are enrolled in government dependent institutions.

Source: OECD. Tables B1.1a, B5.1a and A2.5. See Annex 3 for notes (*www.oecd.org/edu/eag2008*).

StatLink ᠊ᡅᡋᡐ᠊ http://dx.doi.org/10.1787/402038326553

Other highlights of this indicator

- Except for Belgium, countries with quite a large difference between the fees charged for the first and last deciles of students – Australia, Canada and the United States and the partner country Chile – are also those with quite high levels of average tuition fees. The difference is partly because tertiary educational institutions in these countries have the right to differentiate the fees charged by field of education.

- In most countries, tuition fees charged by tertiary-type B institutions are lower than those charged by tertiary-type A institutions. In parallel graduates of tertiary-type A education earn substantially more than tertiary-type B graduates in all of these countries.

- When tuition fees are charged, tertiary institutions are responsible for setting tuition fee levels in almost all countries and for determining the level of tuition fees. Only Japan, the Netherlands, Spain and Switzerland have levels of tuition fees set exclusively by educational authorities (at central, regional or local levels) at least for some of their tertiary institutions.

- An average of 18% of public spending on tertiary education is devoted to supporting students, households and other private entities. In Australia, Denmark, the Netherlands, New Zealand, Norway and Sweden and the partner country Chile, public subsidies to households account for some 27% or more of public tertiary education budgets.

- Low annual tuition fees charged by tertiary-type A institutions are not systematically associated with a low proportion of students who benefit from public subsidies. In tertiary-type A education, the tuition fees charged by public institutions for national students are negligible in the Nordic countries and in the Czech Republic and are low in Turkey. And yet more than 55% of the students enrolled in tertiary-type A education in these countries can benefit from scholarships/grants and/or public loans. Moreover, Finland, Norway and Sweden are among the seven countries with the highest entry rate to tertiary-type A education.

- OECD countries in which students are required to pay tuition fees and can benefit from particularly large public subsidies do not show lower levels of access to tertiary-type A education than the OECD average. For example, Australia (82%) and New Zealand (79%) have among the highest entry rates to tertiary-type A education, and the Netherlands (59%) and the United States (64%) are above the OECD average. The United Kingdom (51%) and the partner country Chile (48%) are just below the OECD average (54%), although entry to tertiary-type A education increased by 4 and 6 percentage points, respectively, between 2000 and 2005 in these countries.

- Some studies conclude that loans are useful to support tertiary education study among middle- and upper-income students, but ineffective among lower-income students, while the converse is true for grants. Grants and loans are particularly developed in Australia, the Netherlands, New Zealand, Norway, Sweden, the United Kingdom, the United States and the partner country Chile. Globally, the cost to a government of providing public loans to a significant proportion of students is greater in countries where the average level of tuition fees charged by institutions is higher.

Policy context

Decisions taken by policy makers on the tuition fees charged by educational institutions affect both the cost of tertiary studies to students and the resources available to tertiary institutions. Subsidies to students and their families also act as policy levers which governments can use to encourage participation in education – particularly among students from low-income families – by covering part of the cost of education and related expenses. In this way, governments can seek to address issues of access and equality of opportunity. The success of such subsidies must therefore be judged, at least in part, by examining indicators of participation, retention and completion. Furthermore, public subsidies play an important role in financing educational institutions indirectly.

Channelling funding for institutions through students may also help to increase competition among institutions. Since aid for student living costs can serve as a substitute for work, public subsidies may enhance educational attainment by enabling students to study full-time and to work fewer hours or not at all.

Public subsidies come in many forms: as means-based subsidies, as family allowances for all students, as tax allowances for students or their parents, or as other household transfers. Unconditional subsidies (such as tax reductions or family allowances) may provide less of an incentive for low-income students than means-tested subsidies. However, they may still help reduce financial disparities among households with and without children in education.

Evidence and explanations

What this indicator does and does not cover

This indicator shows average tuition fees charged in public and private institutions at tertiary-type A level. It does not distinguish tuition fees by type of programmes but gives an overview of tuition fees at tertiary-type A level by type of institution and presents the proportions of students who do or do not receive scholarships/grants that fully or partially cover tuition fees. Tuition fees and associated proportions of students should be interpreted with caution as they result from the weighted average of the main tertiary-type A programmes and do not cover all educational institutions.

This indicator also shows the proportion of public spending on tertiary education transferred to students, families and other private entities. Some of these funds are spent indirectly on educational institutions – for example, when subsidies are used to cover tuition fees. Other subsidies for education do not relate to educational institutions, such as subsidies for student living costs.

The indicator distinguishes between scholarships and grants, which are non-repayable subsidies, and loans, which must be repaid. It does not, however, distinguish among different types of grants or loans, such as scholarships, family allowances and subsidies in kind.

Governments can also support students and their families by providing housing allowances, tax reductions and/or tax credits for education. These subsidies are not covered here and thus financial aid to students may be substantially underestimated in some countries.

B5

The indicator reports the full volume of student loans in order to provide information on the level of support received by current students. The gross amount of loans, including scholarships and grants, provides an appropriate measure of financial aid to current participants in education. Interest payments and repayments of principal by borrowers would be taken into account in order to assess the net cost of student loans to public and private lenders. However, such payments are not usually made by current students but by former students. In most countries, moreover, loan repayments do not flow to the education authorities, and thus the money is not available to them to cover other educational expenditures. Nevertheless, some information on repayment systems for these loans is also taken into account, as these can substantially reduce the real costs of loans. OECD indicators take the full amount of scholarships and loans (gross) into account when discussing financial aid to current students.

It is also common for governments to guarantee the repayment of loans to students made by private lenders. In some OECD countries, this indirect form of subsidy is as significant as, or more significant than, direct financial aid to students. However, for reasons of comparability, the indicator only takes into account the amounts relating to public transfers for private loans that are made to private entities (not the total value of loans generated). Some qualitative information is nevertheless presented in some of the tables to give some insight on this type of subsidy.

Some OECD countries also have difficulty quantifying the amount of loans attributable to students. Therefore, data on student loans should be treated with some caution.

Annual tuition fees charged by tertiary-type A institutions for national and foreign students

There are large differences among OECD and partner countries in the average tuition fees charged by tertiary-type A institutions for national students. No tuition fees are charged by public institutions in the five Nordic countries (Denmark, Finland, Iceland, Norway and Sweden) and in the Czech Republic, Ireland and Poland. By contrast, one-third of OECD and partner countries have annual tuition fees for national students charged by public institutions (or government-dependent private institutions) that exceed USD 1 500. In the United States, tuition fees for national students reach more than USD 5 000 in public institutions. Among the EU19 countries, only the Netherlands and the United Kingdom have annual tuition fees that exceed USD 1 100 per full-time national student, and these fees relate to government-dependent private institutions (Table B5.1a and Chart B5.1).

Tuition fees charged in tertiary-type A institutions may vary within each country for national students as a result of choices made by tertiary institutions. In Austria, there is no variation in the amount of tuition fees among national students, but in Belgium (Fr. community), Canada and the United States, and the partner country Chile, the tuition fees charged for the 10% of students with the highest fees (90th) is at least twice the level of tuition fees charged to the 10% students with the lowest fees (10th). The ratio between fees charged for these two deciles is highest in Italy at 4:1. Except for Belgium, countries with quite a large difference between the tuition fees charged for the first and last deciles of students – Australia, Canada and the United States and the partner country Chile – are also those with quite high levels of average tuition fees. The difference is mainly due to the fact that tertiary institutions in these countries have the right to differentiate the fees charged by field of education. On the contrary, in Spain, average tuition fees are moderate (around USD 800) and the fees charged vary by a ratio of less than 1.6 (Table B5.1c).

B5

National policies regarding tuition fees and financial aid to students generally cover all students studying in the country's educational institutions. Even if the focus of this indicator is mainly on national students, countries' policies also have to take international students into account. These may be a country's national students going abroad for their studies or students who enter the country for study reasons. Differentiation between national and non-national students in terms of the fees students pay or the financial help they may receive can have, along with other factors, an impact on the flows of international students, either by attracting students to some countries or by preventing students from studying in other countries (see Indicator C3).

The tuition fees charged by public educational institutions may differ among students enrolled in the same programme. Several countries make a distinction in terms of students' citizenship. In Austria, for example, the average tuition fees charged by public institutions for students who are not citizens of EU or EEA countries are twice the fees charged for citizens of these countries. This kind of differentiation also appears in Australia, Belgium, Canada, the Czech Republic, the Netherlands, New Zealand, Turkey, the United Kingdom and the United States, as well as the partner country Estonia (see Indicator C3), and appeared in Denmark from the 2006/07 academic year. In these countries, the variation in tuition fees based on citizenship is always significant. This type of policy differentiation may check the flows of international students (see Indicator C3) unless these students receive some financial support from their country of citizenship (or from their country of permanent residence as in New Zealand).

Annual tuition fees charged by private institutions

Annual tuition fees charged by private institutions vary considerably across OECD and partner countries as well as within countries themselves. Most OECD and partner countries charge higher tuition fees in private institutions. Finland and Sweden are the only countries with no tuition fees in either public or private institutions. Variation within countries tends to be highest in countries with the largest proportions of students enrolled in independent tertiary-type A private institutions. By contrast, tuition fees charged by public and government-dependent institutions differ less in most countries and are even similar in Austria. The greater autonomy of independent private institutions compared with public and government-dependent institutions partially explains this situation. For example, around three-quarters of students in Korea and Japan are enrolled in independent private institutions and these two countries also show the highest variation in the fees charged by their independent private institutions (see Indicator C2 and Table B5.1a).

Annual tuition fees charged by tertiary-type B institutions for national students

Large differences among OECD and partner countries in the average tuition fees charged by tertiary institutions are also observed in tertiary-type B education. In Nordic countries as well as in the Czech Republic, Ireland and Poland, where no tuition fees are charged in tertiary-type A institutions, there are usually no tuition fees charged in tertiary-type B institutions as well, but their tertiary-type B sector is quite small (with less than 10% of tertiary full-time students). Among other countries in which tertiary-type B institutions enrol a small proportion of full-time students (15% or less), Austria, Denmark and Spain are the only ones in which these institutions do not charge tuition fees or charge negligible fees. Australia presents the particularity of a small proportion of tertiary full-time students enrolled in tertiary-type B education (10%, nearly

B5

all of them in public institutions), but the highest average tuition fees among all OECD and partner countries (about USD 3 730), although they remain lower than those in tertiary-type A education (about USD 3 855) (Tables B5.1a and B5.1b).

In 13 OECD and partner countries, at least 15% of tertiary full-time students are enrolled in type B education. Among the nine of these countries for which data are available on tuition fees, public tertiary-type B institutions charge on average between USD 1 000 and USD 3 154 for national students, except France (maximum of USD 1 420), Ireland (no tuition fees) and Turkey (USD 166). In Japan and Korea, where 26 % and 38 % respectively of full-time tertiary students are enrolled in tertiary-type B institutions, most students are enrolled in private institutions with tuition fees amounting to more than USD 5 000 on average (Table B5.1b). In these nine OECD and partner countries except France, tuition fees charged by tertiary-type B institutions are lower than those charged by tertiary-type A institutions. This is mainly because graduates of tertiary-type A education earn substantially more than tertiary-type B graduates in all of these countries (Tables A9.1, B5.1a and B5.1b).

Decision making on fees charged by tertiary institutions

The tuition fees charged by tertiary institutions vary between type A and type B institutions but also among students in each type of education because of differentiation of the fees charged to students. There is a large degree of within-institution differentiation in countries in which fees are charged. For example, differentiation may be by level of educational programme, *e.g.* post-graduate versus undergraduate (in the United Kingdom, for example), by field of study (in Australia or Spain, for example), according to student status, in Belgium (Fl. community), for example. When tuition fees are charged, tertiary institutions have a say in determining the level of tuition fees in almost all countries (Table B5.1d). Only in Japan, the Netherlands, Spain and Switzerland are tuition fee levels set exclusively by educational authorities (at central, regional or local levels) at least for some of their tertiary institutions. However, in most countries the educational authorities do impose some restrictions. Only Korea, Mexico and the partner countries Chile and the Russian Federation face no restrictions on decisions on the level of tuition fees. Only specific areas have no restriction in Iceland, Japan, Portugal, Switzerland and the United Kingdom.

The restrictions that typically apply to the setting of tuition fees are usually upper limits. Such restrictions are used for example in Australia, Japan, New Zealand, Norway and Poland. However, restrictions may also relate to lower limits, as is the case in Australia for unsubsidised places or in some cases in the Netherlands. Both lower and upper limits may also be fixed, as in Belgium (Fl. community), the Czech Republic, Portugal and Switzerland. New Zealand and the partner country Estonia set a maximum growth rate for tuition fees (Table B5.1d and OECD [2008a]).

Country mechanisms to allocate public funding to institutions

Understanding how tertiary institutions receive public funds is relevant to the analysis of fees charged by institutions and subsidies received by students. The use of both block grants (a large sum granted without strings attached) and targeted funding (money for a particular purpose) in the allocation of public funds to institutions is widespread. Only five countries use line-item

B5

budgeting (use of funds restricted to expenditure items specified in "line-item" budget) instead of block grants: Greece, Korea, Mexico (for institutions created before 1997), Switzerland and the partner country the Russian Federation. The partner country Chile, in addition to block grants and targeted funds, uses a fairly unique mechanism in order to encourage competition for students among institutions (Table B5.1d and OECD [2008a]).

Formula funding has become the most common basis for allocating block grants or line-item budgets to institutions in participating countries. Only in Mexico is a formula not used in allocating block grants and line-item budgets; in the Netherlands, Norway, Poland and the partner countries Chile, Estonia and the Russian Federation, the basis for the allocation is a formula and historical trends. In both New Zealand and Switzerland, the basis for allocating block grants is a formula and negotiations with government authorities.

In the vast majority of countries that use targeted funding, the allocation takes place on a competitive basis. Exceptions exist in Belgium (Fl. community), the Netherlands, Sweden and Switzerland. Only Poland and Australia use formula funding for allocating targeted funds, others use direct negotiations with institutions (*e.g.* some programmes in Portugal).

Many factors enter funding formulas. As may be expected, criteria related to the size of the institution dominate: number of students enrolled (in 12 countries), number of first-year students (8 countries), or number of staff or academic staff (7 countries). In Korea the total area of buildings and facilities is also used as a proxy for size.

The allocation mechanisms are also performance-based. The main criteria relating to output or outcomes are the number of degrees awarded or the number of graduates (Belgium [Fl. community], the Czech Republic, Finland, the Netherlands, Portugal and some regions of Spain), the number of credits accumulated by students (Belgium [Fl. community], Norway, Spain, Sweden and Switzerland), the number of students completing each year of study (Spain), and average study duration (Portugal and Spain). Norway and the partner country Chile use research indicators while Korea uses an assessment of innovation efforts. Japan further uses the results of a quality evaluation by a review panel in the formula to allocate block grants to national universities.

Funding formulas are also based on criteria that relate more to the quality or type of education. For example, the field of study is used in most of the funding formulas. In Japan (the national universities) and Switzerland as well as in the partner country Estonia, an assessment of the extent to which a field of study is considered a priority influences the associated funding. The level of qualifications of academic staff is also used as an extra weight in Greece, Poland, Portugal, Spain and the partner countries Chile and the Russian Federation. A few countries reflect equity objectives in funding formulas, typically through the use of a premium in the funding formula for each student of a given under-represented group (for example in Australia and New Zealand). Also used are weights based on equity objectives (Belgium [Fl. community], Japan) and on the regional role of institutions (Finland, Japan) (Table B5.1d and OECD [2008a]).

Public subsidies to households and other private entities

OECD countries spend an average of 0.4% of their GDP on public subsidies to households and other private entities for all levels of education combined. The proportion of educational budgets spent on subsidies to households and private entities is much higher at the tertiary level than at the primary, secondary and post-secondary non-tertiary levels and represents 0.3% of GDP. The subsidies are the largest in relation to GDP at tertiary level in Norway (1.0% of GDP), followed by Denmark (0.7%), New Zealand (0.6%), Sweden (0.5%), Australia (0.4%), and the Netherlands (0.4%) (Table B5.2 and Table B5.3 available on line).

Chart B5.2. Public subsidies for education in tertiary education (2005)

Public subsidies for education to households and other private entities as a percentage of total public expenditure on education, by type of subsidy

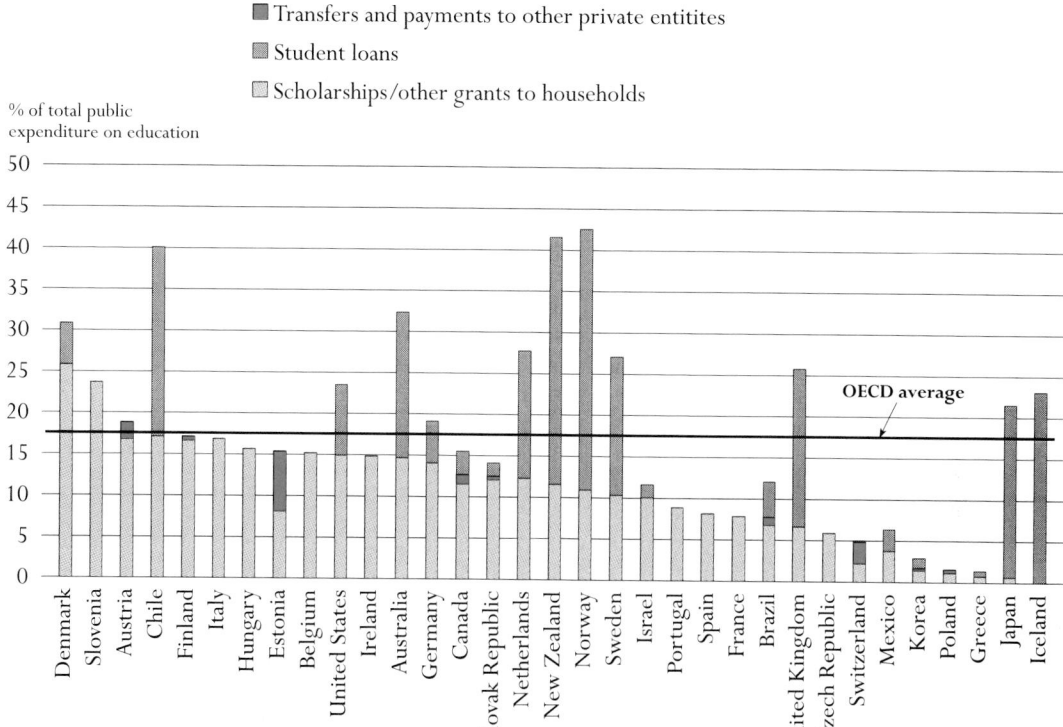

Countries are ranked in descending order of the share of scholarships/other grants to households and transfers and payments to other private entitites in total public expenditure on education.
Source: OECD. Table B5.2. See Annex 3 for notes (*www.oecd.org/edu/eag2008*).
StatLink ⪼ http://dx.doi.org/10.1787/402038326553

OECD countries spend, on average, 18% of their public budgets for tertiary education on subsidies to households and other private entities (Chart B5.2). In Australia, Denmark, the Netherlands, New Zealand, Norway and Sweden and the partner country Chile, public subsidies account for 27% or more of public spending on tertiary education. Only Greece, Korea and Poland spend less than 5% of total public spending on tertiary education on subsidies (Table B5.2).

Overall country approaches to funding tertiary education

Countries differ in their approach to funding tertiary education. This section provides a taxonomy of approaches to funding tertiary education in OECD and partner countries along with available data. Countries are grouped according to two dimensions. The first is the extent of cost-sharing, that is, the level of contribution requested from the student and/or his or her family in tertiary-type A education. The second concerns the public subsidies received by students at this level of education.

There is no single model in OECD and partner countries for the financing of tertiary-type A education. Some countries in which tertiary-type A institutions charge similar tuition fees may have differences in the proportion of students benefiting from public subsidies and/or in the average amount of these subsidies (Tables B5.1a, B5.1c, B5.2 and Chart B5.3). Nevertheless, comparing the tuition fees charged by institutions and public subsidies received by students, as well as other factors such as access to tertiary education, level of public expenditure on tertiary education or the level of taxation on income, helps to distinguish four main groups of countries. Tax revenue based on income (OECD, 2006) is highly correlated with the level of public expenditure available for education and can provide some information on the possibility of financing public subsidies to students.

Model 1: Countries with no or low tuition fees but quite generous student support systems

This group includes the Nordic countries (Denmark, Finland, Iceland, Norway, Sweden), the Czech Republic and Turkey. There are no (or low) financial barriers for tertiary studies due to tuition fees and even a high level of student aid. At 58%, the average entry rate to tertiary-type A education for this group is above the OECD average (see Indicator C2). Tuition fees charged by public educational institutions for national students are negligible (Nordic countries and the Czech Republic) or low (Turkey) in tertiary-type A education and more than 55% of students enrolled in tertiary-type A education in this group can benefit from scholarships/grants and/or public loans to finance their studies or living expenses (Tables B5.1a and B5.1c and Chart B5.3).

In the Nordic countries, net entry rates in tertiary-type A education are, on average, 71%, significantly higher than the OECD average. Also in these countries, the level of public expenditure on tertiary education as a percentage of GDP and taxation on income are among the highest among OECD and partner countries. The way tertiary education is paid for expresses a vision of these countries' societies. Public funding of tertiary education is seen as the operational expression of the weight attached to such deeply rooted social values as equality of opportunity and social equity which stand as one of the identifying traits of the Nordic countries. The notion that government should provide its citizens with tertiary education at no charge to the user is a prime feature of these countries' educational culture. In its current mode, the funding of both institutions and students is based on the principle that access to tertiary education is a right, rather than a benefit (OECD [2008a], Chapter 4).

The Czech Republic and Turkey have a different pattern: low access to tertiary-type A education compared to the OECD average – despite increases of 16 and 6 percentage points, respectively, between 2000 and 2005 – combined with low levels (compared to the OECD average) of public

B5

spending and of tax revenue on income as a percentage of GDP compared to the OECD average (see Indicators B4 and A2 and OECD [2006]). In these two countries, more than three-quarters of students enrolled in tertiary-type A programmes benefited from scholarships/grants in the Czech Republic or from a loan in Turkey, but the average amount of these public subsidies is small compared to the Nordic countries and compared to the OECD average. This indicates that these two countries are also close to those included in model 4.

Model 2: Countries with high level of tuition fees and well developed student support systems

A second group includes four Anglophone countries (Australia, New Zealand, the United Kingdom and the United States), one bilingual country (Canada), the Netherlands and the partner country Chile, which have potentially high financial barriers for entry to tertiary-type A education, but also large public subsidies to students. It is noteworthy that the average entry rate to tertiary-type A education for this group of countries is, at 67%, slightly above the OECD average and higher than most countries (except the Nordic countries) with low levels of tuition fees.

Tuition fees charged by tertiary-type A institutions exceed USD 1 500 in all these countries and more than 80% of tertiary-type A students receive public subsidies (in Australia, the Netherlands and the United States, the three countries for which data are available, see Tables B5.1a and B5.1c). Student support systems are well developed and mostly accommodate the needs of the entire student population with a proportion of public subsidies in total public expenditure on tertiary education higher than the OECD average (18%) in six out of the seven countries: Australia (32%), the Netherlands (28%), New Zealand (42%), the United Kingdom (26%) and the United States (24%) and the partner country Chile (40%) and nearly at the average for Canada (Table B5.2). Countries in this group do not have lower access to tertiary-type A education than countries from the other groups. For example, Australia (82%) and New Zealand (79%) have among the highest entry rates to tertiary-type A education, the Netherlands (59%) and the United States (64%) are above the OECD average (55%) in 2005, and the United Kingdom (51%) and the partner country Chile (48%) are just below the OECD average, although entry to tertiary-type A education in these countries increased by 4 and 6 percentage points, respectively, between 2000 and 2005 (Table A2.5). Finally, these countries spend more per tertiary student on core services than the OECD average and have a relatively high level of tax revenue based on income as a percentage of GDP compared to the OECD average. The Netherlands is an exception in terms of the level of taxation on income and the partner country Chile for both indicators (see Table B1.1b and OECD [2006]).

Model 3: Countries with high level of tuition fees but less developed student support systems

Japan and Korea present a different pattern: while cost sharing is extensive and broadly uniform across students, student support systems are somewhat less developed than in Models 1 and 2. This places a considerable financial burden on students and their families. In these two countries, tertiary-type A institutions charge high tuition fees (more than USD 3 500) but a relatively small proportion of students benefit from public subsidies (one-quarter of students receive public subsidies in Japan, and only 3% of total public expenditure on tertiary education is allocated to public subsidies in Korea). Tertiary-type A entry rates in those two countries are 41 and 51%, respectively, which is below the OECD average. In Japan, some students who excel academically but have difficulty in financing their studies may benefit from reduced tuition and/or admission fees or be entirely exempted from these fees. The below average access to tertiary-type A education is counterbalanced by an entry rate above the OECD average to tertiary-type B programmes (see Indicator C2). These two countries are among those with the lowest levels of public expenditure allocated to tertiary education as a percentage of GDP (Table B4.1). This partially explains the small proportion of students who benefit from public loans; tax revenue from income as a percentage of GDP is also among the lowest in OECD countries. However, in Japan, public subsidies for students are above the OECD average and represent 22% of total public expenditure on tertiary education and expenditure per tertiary student is also above the OECD average. Korea presents the opposite picture on both indicators (Table B5.2).

Model 4: Countries with a low level of tuition fees and less developed student support systems

The fourth and last group includes all other European countries for which data are available (Austria, Belgium, France, Ireland, Italy, Poland and Spain). These countries have relatively low financial barriers to entry to tertiary education combined with relatively low subsidies for students, mainly targeted to specific groups. There is a high level of dependence on public resources for the funding of tertiary education and participation levels are typically below the OECD average. The average tertiary-type A entry rate in this group of countries is a relatively low 48%. Similarly, expenditure per student in tertiary-type A education is also comparatively low (see Indicator B1 and Chart B5.1). While high tuition fees can raise potential barriers to student participation, this suggests that the absence of tuition fees, which is assumed to ease access to education, is not sufficient to entirely meet the challenges of access and quality of tertiary-type A education.

Tuition fees charged by public institutions in this group never exceed USD 1 100, and the proportion of student who benefit from public subsidies is below 40% in countries for which data are available (Tables B5.1a and B5.1c). In these countries students and their families can benefit from subsidies provided by sources other than the ministry of education (*e.g.* housing allowances, tax reductions and/or tax credits for education); these are not covered in this analysis. For example, in France housing allowances represent about 90% of scholarships/grants and about one-third of students benefit from these allowances. In Poland, a notable feature is that cost sharing is achieved by arrangements whereby some students have their studies fully subsidised by the public budget and the remainder pay the full costs of tuition. In other words, the burden of private contributions is borne by part of the student population rather than shared by all (see Indicator B3 and OECD [2008a]). Loan systems (public loans or loans guaranteed by the state) are not available or only available to a small proportion of student in these countries (Table B5.1c). Alongside this, the level of public spending and the tax revenue from income as a percentage of GDP vary significantly more among this group of countries than in the other groups, but policies on tuition fees and public subsidies are not necessarily the main drivers in students' decision to enter tertiary-type A education.

Chart B5.3. **Relationships between average tuition fees charged by public institutions and proportion of students who benefit from public loans AND/OR scholarships/grants in tertiary-type A education (academic year 2004/05)**

For full-time national students, in USD converted using PPPs

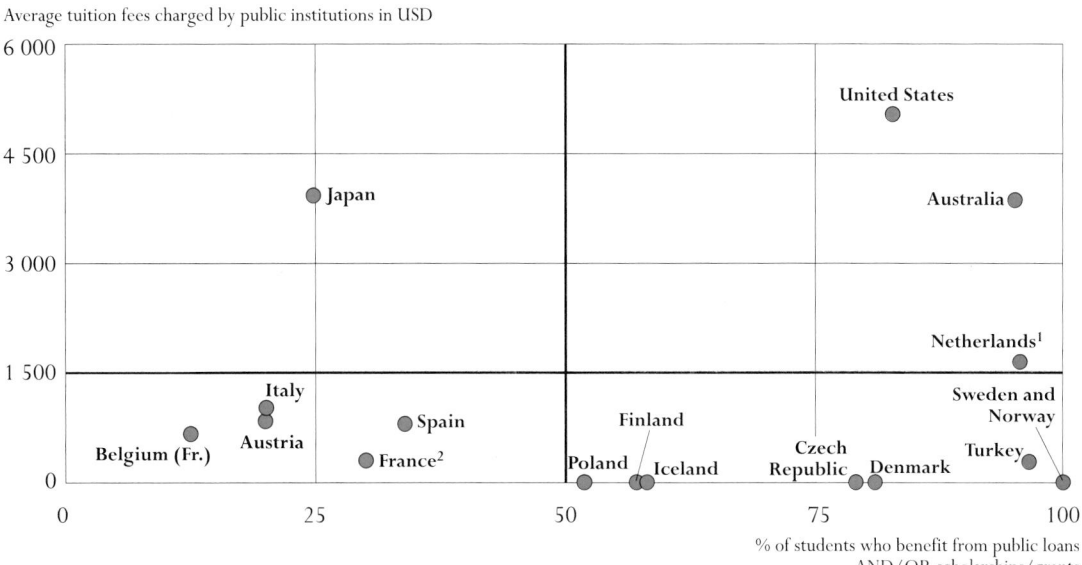

Average tuition fees charged by public institutions in USD

% of students who benefit from public loans
AND/OR scholarships/grants

1. Public institutions do not exist at this level of education and all the students are enrolled in government dependent institutions.
2. Average tuition fees from 160 to 490 USD.
Source: OECD. Tables B5.1a and B5.1c. See Annex 3 for notes (*www.oecd.org/edu/eag2008*).
StatLink ▐▒▐▒█ http://dx.doi.org/10.1787/402038326553

OECD countries use different mixes of grants and loans to subsidise students' educational costs

A key question in many OECD countries is whether financial subsidies for households should primarily be provided in the form of grants or loans. Governments subsidise students' living or educational costs through different mixes of grants and loans. Advocates of student loans argue that money spent on loans goes further: if the amount spent on grants were used to guarantee or subsidise loans instead, more aid would be available to students and overall access would increase. Loans also shift some of the cost of education to those who benefit most from educational investment. Opponents of loans argue that student loans are less effective than grants in encouraging low-income students to pursue their education. They also argue that loans may be less efficient than anticipated because of the various subsidies provided to borrowers or lenders and because of the costs of administration and servicing. Cultural differences among and within countries may also affect students' willingness to take out student loans. Thus, Usher (2006), analysing the summary of the literature on tertiary education access in the United States by St John (2003) concluded that loans are useful to support tertiary study among middle and upper-income students, but ineffective among lower-income students, while the converse is true for grants (for more details see OECD [2008a]).

Chart B5.2 presents the proportion of public educational expenditure dedicated to loans, grants and scholarships, and other subsidies to households at the tertiary level. Grants and scholarships include family allowances and other specific subsidies, but exclude tax reductions that are part of the subsidy system in Australia, Belgium (Fl. community), Canada, the Czech Republic, Finland, France, Hungary, Italy, the Netherlands, Norway, the Slovak Republic, Switzerland and the United States (see Chart B5.3 in *Education at a Glance 2006*, [OECD, 2006b]). Around one-half of the 31 reporting OECD countries and partner countries rely exclusively on scholarships/grants and transfers/payments to other private entities. The remaining OECD countries provide both scholarships/grants and loans to students (except Iceland, which relies only on student loans) and both subsidies are particularly developed in Australia, the Netherlands, New Zealand, Norway, Sweden, the United Kingdom, the United States and the partner country Chile. In general, the highest subsidies to students are provided by the countries that offer student loans; in most cases these countries also spend an above-average proportion of their budgets on grants and scholarships alone (Chart B5.2 and Table B5.2). Some other countries – Belgium (Fl. community), Finland and the partner country Estonia – do not have public loan systems but private loans that are guaranteed by the state (Table B5.1e).

Implementation of public loan systems and amount of public loans

Public loan systems are relatively recent in most of the countries that report data; their development occurred between the 1960s and 1980s, corresponding to the massive growth in enrolments at the tertiary level of education. Since then, public loan systems have developed particularly in Australia, Sweden and Turkey, where some 80% or more of students benefit from a public loan during their tertiary-type A studies. In Norway, public loans are a part of all students' tertiary-type A studies as 100% of students take out loans. Public loan systems are also quite well developed in Iceland (58% of students with a loan), one of the countries – along with Norway and Sweden – where educational institutions at this level do not charge tuition fees. In contrast, the United States has the highest tuition fees in public tertiary-type A institutions, but less than 40% of students benefit from a public loan during their studies.

The financial support that students receive from public loans during their studies cannot be solely analysed in light of the proportion of students who have loans. The support for students also depends on the amount they can receive in public loans. In countries with comparable data, the average annual gross amount of public loan available to each student is superior to USD 4 000 in about one-half of the countries and ranges from less than USD 2 000 in Belgium (Fr. community) and Turkey to more than USD 5 400 in Iceland, Japan, Mexico, the Netherlands, the United Kingdom and the United States (Table B5.1e).

A comparison of average tuition fees and average amounts of loans should be interpreted with caution because, in a given educational programme, the amount of a loan can vary widely among students even though the programme's tuition fees are usually similar. Nevertheless, it can give some insight into the possibility of a loan covering tuition fees and living expenses. The higher the average level of tuition fees charged by institutions, the greater the need for financial support to students through public loans, in order to overcome financial barriers that prevent access to tertiary education. The financial pressure on governments to support students increases with the tuition fees charged by institutions. In all of the OECD countries for which data are available on annual gross amounts of loans, the average amount of public loan is superior to the average

B5

tuition fees charged by public institutions. This shows that public loans also help to support student's living expenses during their studies.

Among the countries with average tuition fees above USD 1 500 in tertiary-type A public institutions, the average amount of the loan is more than twice the average tuition fees in the Netherlands and the United Kingdom. However, in the Netherlands, the difference in amounts should be counterbalanced by the fact that only about one-quarter of students benefit from a loan (this information is not available for the United Kingdom). The largest differences between average tuition fees and the average amount of loans are observed in the Nordic countries, in which no tuition fees are charged by institutions and a large proportion of students benefit annually from a public loan in an average amount that ranges from about USD 2 500 in Denmark to nearly USD 7 000 in Iceland to nearly USD 9 000 in Norway (Tables B5.1a and B5.1e).

The amount that students receive is not the only support related to public loans. Public loan systems also offer some financial aid through the interest rate that students may have to pay, the repayment system or even remission/forgiveness mechanisms (Table B5.1e).

Financial support through interest rates

The financial help arising from reduced interest rates on public or private loans is twofold: there may be a difference between the interest rates supported by students during and after their studies. Comparing interest rates among countries is quite difficult as the structure of interest rates (public and private) is not known and can vary significantly among countries, so that a given interest rate may be considered high in one country and low in another. However, the difference in rates during and after studies seems to aim at lowering the charge on the loan during the student's studies. For example, in Canada, Iceland, New Zealand and Norway, there is no nominal interest rate on the public loan during the period of studies but after their studies, students/graduates have an interest rate related to the cost of government borrowing or to a higher rate. For example, New Zealand charges no interest to full-time students and low-income borrowers and during 2005 made loans interest-free for borrowers while they reside in New Zealand. Nevertheless, there is no systematic difference between interest rates during and after studies, and Belgium, the Netherlands, Sweden, the United Kingdom, the United States and the partner country Estonia do not differentiate between the interest rate borne by student during and after their studies. In Australia, a real interest rate is not charged on loans. Instead, the part of a loan which has remained unpaid for 11 months or more is indexed to ensure that the real value of the loan is maintained (Table B5.1e).

Repayment of loans

Repayment of public loans can be a substantial source of income for governments and can decrease the costs of loan programmes significantly. The current reporting of household expenditure on education as part of private expenditure (see Indicator B3) does not take into account the repayment of public loans by previous recipients.

These repayments can be a substantial burden on individuals and have an impact on the decision to participate in tertiary education. The repayment period varies among countries and ranges from less than 10 years in Belgium (Fr. community), New Zealand and Turkey, and the partner country Estonia, to 20 years or more in Iceland, Norway and Sweden.

B5

Among the 13 OECD countries for which data on repayment systems are available, four Anglophone countries (Australia, New Zealand, the United Kingdom and, under specific circumstances, the United States) as well as Iceland and the Netherlands make the repayment of loans dependent on graduates' level of income (with a maximum of payback time up to 15 years in the case of the Netherlands). These are also countries in which the average tuition fees charged by their institutions are higher than USD 1 500 and the average amount of the loan is among the highest in the countries with a public loan system (Table B5.1e).

Definitions and methodologies

Data refer to the financial year 2005 and are based on the UOE data collection on education statistics administered by the OECD in 2007 (for details see Annex 3 at *www.oecd.org/edu/eag2008*). Data on tuition fees charged by educational institutions and financial aid to students (Tables B1.1a, B1.1b and B1.1c) were collected through a special survey undertaken in 2007 and refer to the academic year 2004/05. Amounts of tuition fees and amounts of loans in national currency is converted into equivalent USD by dividing the national currency figure by the purchasing power parity (PPP) index for GDP. Amounts of tuition fees and associated proportions of students should be interpreted with caution as they represent the weighted average of the main tertiary-type A programmes and do not cover all the educational institutions.

Public subsidies to households include the following categories: *i)* grants/scholarships; *ii)* public student loans; *iii)* family or child allowances contingent on student status; *iv)* public subsidies in cash or in kind, specifically for housing, transport, medical expenses, books and supplies, social, recreational and other purposes; and *v)* interest-related subsidies for private loans.

Expenditure on student loans is reported on a gross basis, that is, without subtracting or netting out repayments or interest payments from borrowers (students or households). This is because the gross amount of loans, including scholarships and grants, provides an appropriate measure of the financial aid to current participants in education.

Public costs related to private loans guaranteed by governments are included as subsidies to other private entities. Unlike public loans, only the net cost of these loans is included.

The value of tax reductions or credits to households and students is not included.

Further references

The following additional material relevant to this indicator is available on line at:
StatLink ᴬᴵˢᴸ http://dx.doi.org/10.1787/402038326553

- *Table B5.3. Public subsidies for households and other private entities as a percentage of total public expenditure on education and GDP, for primary, secondary and post-secondary non-tertiary education (2005)*

B5

Table B5.1a.
Estimated annual average tuition fees charged by tertiary-type A educational institutions[1] for national students (academic year 2004/05)
In equivalent USD converted using PPPs, by type of institutions, based on full-time students

		Percentage of tertiary-type A full-time students enrolled in:			Annual average tuition fees in USD charged by institutions (for full-time students)			
Tuition fees and associated proportions of students should be interpreted with caution as they result from the weighted average of the main tertiary-type A programmes and do not cover all educational institutions. However, the figures reported can be considered as good proxies and show the difference among countries in tuition fees charged by main educational institutions and for the majority of students.								
	Percentage of tertiary full-time students enrolled in tertiary-type A	Public institutions	Government dependent private institutions	Independent private institutions	Public institutions	Government dependent private institutions	Independent private institutions	Comment
		(1)	(2)	(3)	(4)	(5)	(6)	
Australia	87	98	a	2	3 855	a	7 452	95% of national students in public institutions are in subsidised places and pay an average USD 3 595 tuition fee, including HECS/HELP subsidies.
Austria	83	88	12	n	837	837	n	
Belgium (Fl.)	m	x(2)	100	m	x(5)	574	m	
Belgium (Fr.)[2]	m	32	68	m	661	746	m	
Canada	m	m	m	m	3 464	m	m	
Czech Republic	83	93	a	7	No tuition fees	a	3 145	The average fee in public institutions is negligible because fees are paid only by students studying too long (more than standard length of the programme plus 1 year): about 4% of students.
Denmark[3]	89	100	n	a	No tuition fees	m	a	
Finland	100	89	11	a	No tuition fees	No tuition fees	a	Excluding membership fees to student unions.
France	72	87	1	12	From 160 to 490	m	m	University programmes dependent from the Ministry of Education.
Germany	87	98	2	x(2)	m	m	m	
Greece	61	100	a	a	m	m	m	
Hungary	90	88	12	a	m	m	m	
Iceland	97	87	13	a	No tuition fees	From 1 750 to 4 360	a	Excluding registration fees for all students.
Ireland	74	99.6	a	0.4	No tuition fees	a	No tuition fees	The tuition fees charged by institutions are in average of USD 4 470 [1 870 to 20 620] in public institutions and of USD 4 630 [3 590 to 6 270] in private institutions but the government gives the money directly to institutions and the students do not have to pay these fees.
Italy	97	93.7	a	6.3	1 017	a	3 520	The annual average tuition fees do not take into account the scholarships/grants that fully cover tuition fees but partial reductions of fees cannot be excluded.
Japan	72	25.0	a	75.0	3 920	a	6 117	Excludes admission fee charged by the school for the first year (USD 2 267 on average for public, USD 2 089 on average for private institutions) and subscription fee for using facilities (USD 1 510 on average) for private institutions.

1. Scholarships/grants that the student may receive are not taken into account.
2. Tuition fees charged for programmes are the same in public as in private institutions but the distribution of students differs between public and private institutions so that the weighted average is not the same.
3. Weighted average for all tertiary education.
4. Year of reference 2006.
Source: OECD. See Annex 3 for notes (*www.oecd.org/edu/eag2008*).
Please refer to the Reader's Guide for information concerning the symbols replacing missing data.
StatLink ᵐˢᴸ http://dx.doi.org/10.1787/402038326553

B5

Table B5.1a. *(continued)*

Estimated annual average tuition fees charged by tertiary-type A educational institutions[1] for national students (academic year 2004/05)

In equivalent USD converted using PPPs, by type of institutions, based on full-time students

Tuition fees and associated proportions of students should be interpreted with caution as they result from the weighted average of the main tertiary-type A programmes and do not cover all educational institutions. However, the figures reported can be considered as good proxies and show the difference among countries in tuition fees charged by main educational institutions and for the majority of students.

	Percentage of tertiary full-time students enrolled in tertiary-type A	Percentage of tertiary-type A full-time students enrolled in:			Annual average tuition fees in USD charged by institutions (for full-time students)			Comment
		Public institutions	Government dependent private institutions	Independent private institutions	Public institutions	Government dependent private institutions	Independent private institutions	
		(1)	(2)	(3)	(4)	(5)	(6)	
Korea	61	22	a	78	3 883	a	7 406	Tuition fees in first degree programme only. Excludes admission fees to university, but includes supporting fees. Student receiving a scholarship twice a year are counted as two students.
Luxembourg	m	m	m	m	m	m	m	
Mexico	96	66.2	a	33.8	m	a	11 359	
Netherlands	100	a	100	a	a	1 646	a	
New Zealand	78	98.4	1.6	x(2)	2 671	x(4)	x(4)	
Norway	96	87.0	13.0	a	No tuition fees	From 4 800 to 5 800	a	
Poland	96	86.6	a	13.4	No tuition fees	a	2 710	
Portugal	94	74	a	26	m	m	m	
Slovak Republic	96	99	n	1	m	m	m	
Spain	81	90.9	a	9.1	795	a	m	
Sweden	89	92.9	7.1	n	No tuition fees	No tuition fees	m	Excluding mandatory membership fees to student unions.
Switzerland	84	95	5	n	m	m	m	
Turkey	69	91.9	a	8.1	276	a	14 430 [9 020 to 20 445]	For public institutions, only undergraduate and master levels.
United Kingdom	88	a	100	n	a	1 859	1 737	
United States	81	68.5	a	31.5	5 027	a	18 604	Including non national students.
Brazil	94	28	a	72	m	m	m	
Chile[4]	67	39	16	44	4 863	4 444	5 644	
Estonia	62	a	86.0	14.0	a	From 2 190 to 4 660	From 1 190 to 9 765	
Israel	76	a	87	13	a	From 2 658 to 3 452	From 6 502 to 8 359	Tuition fees charged by institutions are higher for 2nd degree than for 1st degree programmes.
Russian Federation	73	91	a	9	m	a	m	
Slovenia	64	99	n	n	m	m	m	

(OECD countries: Korea through United States. Partner countries: Brazil through Slovenia.)

1. Scholarships/grants that the student may receive are not taken into account.
2. Tuition fees charged for programmes are the same in public as in private institutions but the distribution of students differs between public and private institutions so that the weighted average is not the same.
3. Weighted average for all tertiary education.
4. Year of reference 2006.
Source: OECD. See Annex 3 for notes (*www.oecd.org/edu/eag2008*).
Please refer to the Reader's Guide for information concerning the symbols replacing missing data.
StatLink ⌨ http://dx.doi.org/10.1787/402038326553

B5

Table B5.1b.
Estimated annual average tuition fees charged by tertiary-type B educational institutions[1] for national students (academic year 2004/05)
In equivalent USD converted using PPPs, by type of institutions, based on full-time students

		Percentage of tertiary-type B full-time students enrolled in:			Annual average tuition fees in USD charged by institutions (for full-time students)			
	Percentage of tertiary full-time students enrolled in tertiary-type B	Public institutions	Government dependent private institutions	Independent private institutions	Public institutions	Government dependent private institutions	Independent private institutions	Comment
		(1)	(2)	(3)	(4)	(5)	(6)	
Australia	10	97	1	2	3 734	a	5 991	
Austria	10	69	31	n	No tuiton fees	No tuiton fees	No tuiton fees	Refers only to post-secondary colleges of three years duration.
Belgium (Fl.)	m	m	m	m	m	m	m	
Belgium (Fr.)[2]	m	m	m	m	191	192	m	
Canada	m	m	m	m	m	m	m	
Czech Republic	10	67	33	a	171	1 137	a	
Denmark[3]	9	100	n	a	No tuiton fees	m	a	
Finland	n	a	a	a	a	a	a	ISCED 5B education is being phased out.
France	24	72	8	20	From 0 to 1 420	m	m	
Germany	13	62	38	x(2)	m	m	m	
Greece	35	100	n	n	m	m	m	
Hungary	8	69	31	a	m	m	m	
Iceland	2	72	28	a	No tuiton fees	From 1 750 to 4 360	a	
Ireland	23	95	a	5	No tuiton fees	a	m	
Italy	1	86	a	14	272	a	1 886	
Japan	26	7	a	93	1 682	a	5 014	Average tuition fees exclude the admission fee charged by the school for the first year (USD 621 on average in public, USD 1 024 in independent private institutions) and the subscription fee for using facilities (USD 1 178 on average) for private institutions.

OECD countries

1. Scholarships/grants that the student may receive are not taken into account.
2. Tuition fees charged for programmes are the same in public as in private institutions but the distribution of students differs between public and private institutions so that the weighted average is not the same.
3. Weighted average for all tertiary education.
4. Year of reference 2006.
Source: OECD. See Annex 3 for notes (*www.oecd.org/edu/eag2008*).
Please refer to the Reader's Guide for information concerning the symbols replacing missing data.
StatLink 🔗 http://dx.doi.org/10.1787/402038326553

B5

Table B5.1b. *(continued)*
Estimated annual average tuition fees charged by tertiary-type B educational institutions[1]
for national students (academic year 2004/05)
In equivalent USD converted using PPPs, by type of institutions, based on full-time students

		Tuition fees and associated proportions of students should be interpreted with caution as they result from the weighted average of the main Tertiary-type B programmes and do not cover all educational institutions. However, the figures reported can be considered good proxies and show the difference among countries in tuition fees charged by main educational institutions and for the majority of students.						
	Percentage of tertiary full-time students enrolled in tertiary-type B	Percentage of tertiary-type B full-time students enrolled in:			Annual average tuition fees in USD charged by institutions (for full-time students)			
		Public institutions	Government dependent private institutions	Independent private institutions	Public institutions	Government dependent private institutions	Independent private institutions	Comment
		(1)	(2)	(3)	(4)	(5)	(6)	
OECD countries								
Korea	38	16	a	84	2 696	a	5 653	Tuition fees in first degree programme only. Excludes admission fees to university, but includes supporting fees. Student receiving a scholarship twice a year, are counted as two students.
Luxembourg	m	m	m	m	m	m	m	
Mexico	3	96	a	4	m	a	m	
Netherlands	a	a	a	a	a	a	a	
New Zealand	19	63	33	4	2 489	x(4)	x(4)	Weighted average fees on the whole tertiary level.
Norway	1	53	47	x(2)	m	m	m	
Poland	2	78	a	22	No tuition fees	a	m	Full-time students in public institutions do not pay fees
Portugal	1	m	m	m	m	m	m	
Slovak Republic	2	94	6	a	m	m	a	
Spain	15	78	16	6	n	n	m	
Sweden	7	61	39	n	No tuition fees	No tuition fees	a	
Switzerland	5	49	25	26	m	m	m	
Turkey	29	98	a	2	166	a	6.010 [4 210 to 10 820]	
United Kingdom	9	a	100	n	a	m	m	
United States	17	76	a	24	1 850	a	12 120	
Partner countries								
Brazil	4	30	a	70	m	a	m	
Chile[4]	33	7	3	8	3 154	3 767	2 506	
Estonia	35	51	13	36	From 1 060 to 3 060	From 1 600 to 3 990	From 1 200 to 4 100	Many public institutions do not charge tuition fees.
Israel	20	34	66	a	m	m	m	
Russian Federation	27	97	a	3	m	m	m	
Slovenia	36	96	4	n	m	m	m	

1. Scholarships/grants that the student may receive are not taken into account.
2. Tuition fees charged for programmes are the same in public as in private institutions but the distribution of students differs between public and private institutions so that the weighted average is not the same.
3. Weighted average for all tertiary education.
4. Year of reference 2006.
Source: OECD. See Annex 3 for notes (*www.oecd.org/edu/eag2008*).
Please refer to the Reader's Guide for information concerning the symbols replacing missing data.
StatLink ⫘ http://dx.doi.org/10.1787/402038326553

B5

Table B5.1c.
Distribution of financial aid to students compared to amount of tuition fees charged
in tertiary-type A education (academic year 2004/05)

	Amount of tuition fees charged by tertiary-type A educational institutions			Distribution of financial aid to students: Percentage of students that			
	10th percentile	Average	90th percentile	benefit from public loans only	benefit from scholarships/ grants only	benefit from public loans AND scholarships/ grants	DO NOT benefit from public loans OR scholarships/ grants
	(1)	(2)	(3)	(4)	(5)	(6)	(7)
Australia[1]	2 712	3 855	4 718	71	17	7	5
Austria	837	837	837	n	20	n	80
Belgium (Fl.)	m	574	m	m	m	m	m
Belgium (Fr.)	357	746	820	n	12	n	88
Canada	1 516	3 464	4 045	m	m	m	m
Czech Republic	n	n	m	a	79	a	21
Denmark[2]	No tuition fees	No tuition fees	No tuition fees	1	39	41	19
Finland	No tuition fees	No tuition fees	No tuition fees	a	57	a	43
France[2]	m	m	m	n	30	n	70
Germany	m	m	m	m	m	m	m
Greece	m	m	m	m	m	m	m
Hungary	m	m	m	m	m	m	m
Iceland	No tuition fees	No tuition fees	No tuition fees	58	n	m	42
Ireland	No tuition fees	No tuition fees	No tuition fees	a	m	m	m
Italy	443	1 017	1 733	n	20	n	80
Japan	m	5 568	m	24	1	a	75
Korea	m	m	m	m	m	m	m
Luxembourg	m	m	m	m	m	m	m
Mexico[2]	m	m	m	1	10	m	90
Netherlands	m	1 646	m	13	68	15	4
New Zealand[2]	m	2 671	m	m	m	m	m
Norway	No tuition fees	No tuition fees	No tuition fees	m	m	100	n
Poland	No tuition fees	No tuition fees	No tuition fees	a	52	n	48
Portugal	m	m	m	m	m	m	m
Slovak Republic	m	m	m	m	m	m	m
Spain	638	795	988	a	34	n	66
Sweden[2]	No tuition fees	No tuition fees	No tuition fees	n	20	80	n
Switzerland	m	m	m	m	m	m	m
Turkey	m	276	m	88	6	3	3
United Kingdom	m	1 859	m	m	m	m	m
United States[2]	2 880	5 027	7 542	38	44	m	17
Brazil	m	m	m	m	m	m	m
Chile[2]	3 032	6 762	9 402	23	m	m	m
Estonia	m	From 2 190 to 4 660	m	m	m	m	m
Israel	m	m	m	m	m	m	m
Russian Federation	m	m	m	m	m	m	m
Slovenia	m	m	m	m	m	m	m

OECD countries / *Partner countries*

1. Excludes foreign students.
2. Distribution of students in total tertiary education.
Source: OECD. See Annex 3 for notes (*www.oecd.org/edu/eag2008*).
Please refer to the Reader's Guide for information concerning the symbols replacing missing data.
StatLink ᘈᶆ᠋ http://dx.doi.org/10.1787/402038326553

B5

Table B5.1d.
Governance of tertiary institutions (academic year 2004/05)

	Responsibility for determining the level of tuition fees (domestic students) in:		Government restrictions to setting of tuition fees (for domestic students) by:	
	Public institutions	Government dependent private institutions	Public institutions	Government dependent private institutions
	(1)	(2)	(3)	(4)
Australia	TEI[1]	TEI	Lower limit (unsubsidised places); upper limit (publicly subsidised places)	Lower limit (unsubsidised places); upper limit (publicly subsidised places)
Belgium (Fl.)	TEI	TEI	Within a range	Within a range
Czech Republic	TEI	TEI	Within a range (ISCED 5B); lower limit (ISCED 5A)	None
Finland	a	a	a	a
Greece	TEI	a	Governement approval required	a
Iceland	a	TEI	a	None
Japan	National universities/ public university corporations: TEIs, in all cases Public universities: Local governments	a	National universities: government sets standard tuition fee level and the upper limit of 110% of it. Public university corporations: no restrictions by central government	a
Korea	TEI	TEI	None	None
Mexico	TEI	a	None	a
Netherlands	TEI only in certain cases (students above 30; dual programme, part-time students)	TEI only in certain cases (students above 30; dual programme, part-time students)	Lower limit	Lower limit
New Zealand	TEI	TEI	Upper limit; maximum growth rate (5% each year)	Upper limit; maximum growth rate (5% each year)
Norway	a	TEI	a	May not exceed the cost of providing the programme; upper limit on programme costs
Poland	TEI	a	May not exceed the cost of providing the programme	a
Portugal	TEI	a	Within a range for some programmes (1st cycle programme, integrated programme; 2nd cycle programme. Providing access to professional activity); no restrictions on others	a
Spain	Educational authorities	a	a	a
Sweden	a	a	a	a
Switzerland	Educational authorities (universities), TEI in other cases	TEI or negotiations between TEI and educational authorities	None (except for Federal Institute of Technology where fees must be "socially acceptable")	None, or within a range (higher VET study programmes and courses)
United Kingdom	a	TEI (in Scotland, only in certain cases)	a	Upper limit generally; no restrictions for postgraduate and part-time students
Chile	TEI	TEI	None	None
Estonia	TEI	TEI	Maximum growth rate (10% each year)	Maximum growth rate (10% each year)
Russian Federation	TEI	a	None	a

OECD countries / *Partner countries*

1. TEI : Tertiary educational institutions
Source: OECD (2008a).
StatLink ⟐⟐⟐ http://dx.doi.org/10.1787/402038326553

Table B5.1d. *(continued-1)*
Governance of tertiary institutions (academic year 2004/05)

B5

	Mechanisms to allocate public funds to educational institutions for teaching and learning activities, and bases for allocation		
	Block grants	**Targeted funds**	**Other**
	(5)	(6)	(7)
OECD countries			
Australia	Funding formula, historical trends	Competitive basis, funding formula	Mix of block grant and targeted funds, funded on funding formula mainly
Belgium (Fl.)	Funding formula, historical trends	No competition (evaluation of teaching development plan and performance)	a
Czech Republic	Funding formula	Competitive basis	a
Finland	Funding formula	Competitive basis	a
Greece	a	a	Line-item budget: funded based on funding formula
Iceland	Funding formula	a	a
Japan	Funding formula	Competitive basis	a
Korea	no	Competitive basis	Line-item budget funded based on funding formula
Mexico	m	Competitive basis	Line-item budget funded based on historical trends
Netherlands	Funding formula, historical trends	Competitive basis, at the discretion of the ministry depending on given fund	a
New Zealand	Funding formula; negociation with government	Competitive basis, funding formula	a
Norway	Funding formula, historical trends	a	a
Poland	Funding formula, historical trends	Funding formula	a
Portugal	Funding formula	Competition, negotiations with government authorities	a
Spain	Funding formula (negotiations with government authorities in some autonomous regions)	a	a
Sweden	Funding formula	No competition	a
Switzerland	Funding formula, negotiations with government authorities and intermediate agencies	Negotiations with government authorities and intermediate agencies, funding formulas, competitive basis, no competition	Line-item budget funded based on negotiations with government authorities and intermediate agencies, funding formulas
United Kingdom	Funding formula	Competitive basis	a
Partner countries			
Chile	Funding formula (5%), historical trends (95%)	Competitive basis	Indirect funding on competitive basis
Estonia	Historical trends (main part), funding formula, priority fields of study	a	a
Russian Federation	a	Competitive basis	Line-item budget funded based on historical trends and funding formulas

1. TEI : Tertiary educational institutions
Source: OECD (2008a).
StatLink ⸻ http://dx.doi.org/10.1787/402038326553

B5

Table B5.1d. *(continued-2)*
Governance of tertiary institutions (academic year 2004/05)

	Criteria for funding formulas			
	Criteria related to volume of education provided		Criteria related to outputs/ outcomes of education	
	Number of students	**Number of staff**	**Student results/ behaviour**	**Number of degrees awarded/graduates**
	(8)	(9)	(10)	(11)
Australia	Student load, mode of study	Full-time employment	Progress rate; commencing bachelor students' retention rate	
Belgium (Fl.)	First-year students		Number of credits accumulated by students	Yes
Czech Republic	Yes			Number of graduates
Finland	Agreed number of entry places			Number of graduates; target number of degrees
Greece	First-year students	Number of staff		
Iceland	Full-time equivalent students			
Japan	Yes, number of first-year students	Number of staff and academic staff		
Korea	Yes	Number of staff		
Mexico	m	m	m	m
Netherlands	First-year students		Number of students leaving institutions with/ without diploma	Number of degrees awarded
New Zealand	FTE students; number of international student exchange		Number of credits accumulated by students	
Norway				Number of credits accumulated by students
Poland	FTE students; number of international student exchange	Number of academic staff		
Portugal	Yes	Number of staff and academic staff		Number of graduates
Spain	First-year students, number of students		Number of credits accumulated by students; number of students completing each year of study	Number of graduates
Sweden	Number of students		Number of credits accumulated by students	
Switzerland	Number of students		Number of credits accumulated by students	
United Kingdom	Number of students, mode of study			
Chile	Number of students	FTE academic staff		
Estonia	Agreed number of state-commissionned places per field			
Russian Federation	Number of students per teacher			

1. TEI : Tertiary educational institutions
Source: OECD (2008a).
StatLink ᠁ http://dx.doi.org/10.1787/402038326553

B5

Table B5.1d. *(continued-3)*
Governance of tertiary institutions (academic year 2004/05)

	Criteria for funding formulas				Criteria relating to cost
	Criteria relating to quality/type of education provided				
	Equity	Field of study	Qualification of	Other	
	(12)	(13)	(14)	(15)	(16)
OECD countries					
Australia	Domestic students with low SES, disability…)			Student satisfaction with generic skills and with teaching	
Belgium (Fl.)	Yes	Yes			
Czech Republic		Yes			Cost per student
Finland				Regional role	
Greece		Yes	Staff		Cost per student, expenditure on renovation and infrastructure
Iceland		Yes			
Japan	Yes	High priority field		Quality evaluation; regional role	Cost per student; income from non-public sources
Korea		Yes		Degree of innovation	Total area of buidings and facilities
Mexico	m	m	m		m
Netherlands					
New Zealand	Yes	Yes			Cost per student, institutions' fixed costs, type of institutions
Norway				Number of international student exchange programmes – based indicators	
Poland		Yes	Staff		
Portugal			Academic staff		Average study duration
Spain		Yes	Academic staff		Cost per student, income from non-public sources, average study duration
Sweden		Yes			
Switzerland		Yes, high priority fields			Cost per student
United Kingdom		Yes			
Partner countries					
Chile			Academic staff	Number of indexed jounal articles published, research programmes ongoing	Number of programmes offered
Estonia		Yes			Cost per student
Russian Federation		Yes	Academic staff		

1. TEI : Tertiary educational institutions
Source: OECD (2008a).
StatLink [icon] http://dx.doi.org/10.1787/402038326553

B5

Table B5.1e.
Financial support to students through public loans in tertiary-type A education (academic year 2004/05)
National students, in USD converted using PPPs

| | Year of creation of a public loan system in the country | Proportion of students who have a loan (in %) | Average annual gross amount of loan available to each student (in USD) | Subsidy through reduced interest rate | |
				Interest rate during studies	Interest rate after studies
	(1)	(2)	(3)	(4)	(5)
Australia[1]	1989	79	3 450	No nominal interest rate	No real interest rate (2.4%)
Belgium (Fl.)[2]	m	m	m	1/3 of the interest rate supported by the students (2%)	1/3 of the interest rate supported by the students (2%)
Belgium (Fr.)[3]	1983	1	1 380	4.0%	4.0%
Canada[4]	1964	m	3 970	No nominal interest rate	Interest rates paid by the student (6.7%)
Denmark[5]	1970	42	2 500	4.0%	Flexible rate set by the Central Bank plus percentage point
Finland[2]	1969	26	Up to 2 710 per year	1.0%	Full interest rate agreed with the private bank; interest assistance for low-income persons
Hungary[2]	2001	m	1 717	11.95	11.95
Iceland	1961	58	6 950	No nominal interest rate	1.0%
Japan[6]	1943	24	5 950	No nominal nor real interest rate	Maximum of 3%, rest paid by government
Mexico[7]	1970	1	10 480	m	m
Netherlands	1986	28	5 730	Cost of government borrowing (3.05%), but repayment delayed until the end of studies	Cost of government borrowing (3.05%)
New Zealand	1992	m	4 320	No nominal interest rate	Cost of government borrowing (max. 7%)
Norway	m	100	Maximum 8 960	No nominal interest rate	Cost of government borrowing
Poland[2]	1998	26	Maximum 3 250	No nominal interest rate	Cost of government borrowing (2.85 to 4.2%)
Sweden	1965	80	4 940	2.80%	2.80%
Turkey	1961	91	1 800	m	m
United Kingdom[8]	1990	m	5 480	No real interest rate (2.6%)	No real interest rate (2.6%)
United States	1970s	38	6 430	5% (interest assistance for low-income students)	5% (interest assistance for low-income students)
Estonia[2]	1995	m	2 260	5%, rest paid by government	5%, rest paid by government

1. Including Commonwealth countries.
2. Loan guaranted by the state rather than public loan.
3. Loan made by the student's parents. Only the parents have to reimburse the loan.
4. Loan outside Quebec. In Quebec, there are only private loans guaranteed by the government.
5. The proportion of students refers to all tertiary education. Average amount of loan includes foreign students.
6. Average amount of loan for students in ISCED 5A first qualification programme.
7. Average amount of loan for students in tertiary education.
8. Annual gross amount of loan refers to students in England.
Source: OECD. See Annex 3 for notes (www.oecd.org/edu/eag2008).
Please refer to the Reader's Guide for information concerning the symbols replacing missing data.
StatLink http://dx.doi.org/10.1787/402038326553

Table B5.1e. *(continued)*

Financial support to students through public loans in tertiary-type A education (academic year 2004/05)

National students, in USD converted using PPPs

		Repayment				Debt at graduation	
		Repayment system	Annual minimum income threshold (in USD)	Duration of typical amortisation period (in years)	Average annual amount of repayment (in USD)	Percentage of graduates with debt (in %)	Average debt at graduation (in USD)
		(6)	(7)	(8)	(9)	(10)	(11)
OECD countries	Australia[1]	Income contingent	25 750	m	m	67 % (domestic graduates)	m
	Belgium (Fl.)[2]	m	m	m	m	m	m
	Belgium (Fr.)[3]	Mortgage style	-	5	250	a	a
	Canada[4]	Mortgage style	-	10	950	m	m
	Denmark[5]	Mortgage style	-	10-15	830	49	10 430
	Finland[2]	Mortgage style	-	m	1 330	39	6 160
	Hungary[2]	Mortgage style	-	m	640	m	m
	Iceland	A fixed part and a part that is income contingent	-	22	3.75% of income	m	m
	Japan[6]	Mortgage style	-	15	1 270	m	m
	Mexico[7]	m	m	m	m	m	m
	Netherlands	Income contingent	17 490	15	m	m	12 270
	New Zealand	Income contingent	10 990	6.7	10% of income amount above income threshold	57% (domestic graduates)	15 320
	Norway	m	-	20	m	m	20 290
	Poland[2]	Mortgage style	-	m (twice as long as benefiting period)	1 950 (+interest)	11	3 250-19 510
	Sweden	Income contingent	4 290	25	860	83	20 590
	Turkey	Mortgage style	-	1-2	1 780	20	3 560
	United Kingdom[8]	Income contingent	24 240	m	9% of income amount above income threshold	79% of eligible students	14 220
	United States	Mortgage style	-	10	m	65	19 400
Partner countries	Estonia[2]	Mortgage style	a	7-8	m	m	m

1. Including Commonwealth countries.
2. Loan guaranted by the state rather than public loan.
3. Loan made by the student's parents. Only the parents have to reimburse the loan.
4. Loan outside Quebec. In Quebec, there are only private loans guaranteed by the government.
5. The proportion of students refers to all tertiary education. Average amount of loan includes foreign students.
6. Average amount of loan for students in ISCED 5A first qualification programme.
7. Average amount of loan for students in tertiary education.
8. Annual gross amount of loan refers to students in England.

Source: OECD. See Annex 3 for notes (*www.oecd.org/edu/eag2008*).

Please refer to the Reader's Guide for information concerning the symbols replacing missing data.

StatLink http://dx.doi.org/10.1787/402038326553

B5

Table B5.2.
Public subsidies for households and other private entities as a percentage of total public expenditure on education and GDP, for tertiary education (2005)

Direct public expenditure on educational institutions and subsidies for households and other private entities

	Direct public expenditure for institutions	Public subsidies for education to private entities						Subsidies for education to private entities as a percentage of GDP
		Financial aid to students			Scholarships/ other grants to households attributable for educational institutions	Transfers and payments to other private entities	Total	
		Scholarships/ other grants to households	Student loans	Total				
	(1)	(2)	(3)	(4)	(5)	(6)	(7)	(8)
OECD countries								
Australia	67.7	14.7	17.7	32.3	1.0	n	32.3	0.37
Austria	81.2	16.8	m	16.8	m	2.0	18.8	0.28
Belgium	84.8	15.2	n	15.2	4.3	n	15.2	0.20
Canada[1]	84.5	11.5	2.8	14.4	m	1.2	15.5	0.26
Czech Republic	94.1	5.9	a	5.9	m	n	5.9	0.05
Denmark	69.2	25.8	5.0	30.8	n	n	30.8	0.73
Finland	82.9	16.6	n	16.6	n	0.5	17.1	0.34
France	92.1	7.9	a	7.9	m	a	7.9	0.09
Germany	80.9	14.1	5.1	19.1	m	n	19.1	0.22
Greece	98.6	0.8	0.7	1.4	m	a	1.4	0.02
Hungary	84.3	15.7	m	15.7	n	n	15.7	0.16
Iceland[2]	76.9	m	23.1	23.1	m	n	23.1	0.34
Ireland	85.2	14.8	n	14.8	4.8	n	14.8	0.16
Italy	83.2	16.8	n	16.8	5.5	n	16.8	0.13
Japan[2]	78.5	0.7	20.9	21.5	m	n	21.5	0.13
Korea	97.1	1.4	1.2	2.7	0.8	0.3	2.9	0.02
Luxembourg	m	m	m	m	m	m	m	m
Mexico	93.6	3.7	2.7	6.4	1.2	n	6.4	0.06
Netherlands	72.3	12.3	15.5	27.7	1.2	n	27.7	0.38
New Zealand	58.5	11.6	30.0	41.5	m	n	41.5	0.63
Norway	57.4	10.9	31.7	42.6	m	n	42.6	0.97
Poland[3]	98.4	1.1	a	1.1	m	0.4	1.6	0.02
Portugal	91.1	8.9	a	8.9	m	m	8.9	0.09
Slovak Republic[2]	85.9	12.1	1.6	13.7	a	0.4	14.1	0.12
Spain	91.8	8.2	n	8.2	2.2	n	8.2	0.08
Sweden	72.9	10.3	16.8	27.1	a	a	27.1	0.52
Switzerland[3]	95.0	2.2	0.2	2.4	m	2.6	5.0	0.07
Turkey	m	m	m	m	m	m	m	m
United Kingdom	74.2	6.7	19.1	25.8	x(4)	n	25.8	0.31
United States	76.5	14.9	8.6	23.5	m	m	23.5	0.31
OECD average	*82.4*	*10.4*	*7.8*	*17.3*	*1.6*	*0.3*	*17.6*	*0.25*
Partner countries								
Brazil[2, 3]	87.9	6.8	4.3	11.1	x(2)	1.0	12.1	0.10
Chile[4]	59.9	17.1	22.9	40.1	14.8	m	40.1	0.19
Estonia[3]	84.6	8.2	a	8.2	m	7.2	15.4	0.14
Israel	88.4	10.0	1.6	11.6	9.6	n	11.6	0.12
Russian Federation[3]	m	m	a	m	a	m	m	m
Slovenia	76.3	23.7	n	23.7	m	n	23.7	0.30

1. Year of reference 2004.
2. Some levels of education are included with others. Refer to "x" code in Table B1.1a for details.
3. Public institutions only.
4. Year of reference 2006.
Source: OECD. See Annex 3 for notes (*www.oecd.org/edu/eag2008*).
Please refer to the Reader's Guide for information concerning the symbols replacing missing data.
StatLink ⬛ http://dx.doi.org/10.1787/402038326553

ON WHAT RESOURCES AND SERVICES IS EDUCATION FUNDING SPENT?

This indicator compares OECD countries with respect to the division of spending between current and capital expenditure and the distribution of current expenditure. It is affected by teachers' salaries (see Indicator D3), pension systems, the age distribution of teachers, the size of the non-teaching staff employed in education (see Indicator D2 in *Education at a Glance 2005*) and the degree to which expanded enrolments require the construction of new buildings. It also compares how OECD countries' spending is distributed among the different functions of educational institutions.

Key results

Chart B6.1. Distribution of current expenditure on educational institutions for primary, secondary and post-secondary non-tertiary education (2005)

The chart shows the distribution of current spending on educational institutions by resource category. Spending on educational institutions can be broken down into capital and current expenditure. Within current expenditure, one can distinguish between spending on instruction compared to ancillary and R&D services. The biggest item in current spending – teachers' compensation – is examined further in Indicator D3.

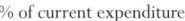 Compensation of all staff   ■ Other current expenditure

In primary, secondary and post-secondary non-tertiary education, taken together, current expenditure accounts for an average of 92% of total spending in OECD countries. In all but four OECD and partner countries, more than 70% of current expenditure on primary, secondary and post-secondary non-tertiary educational institutions is for staff salaries.

% of current expenditure

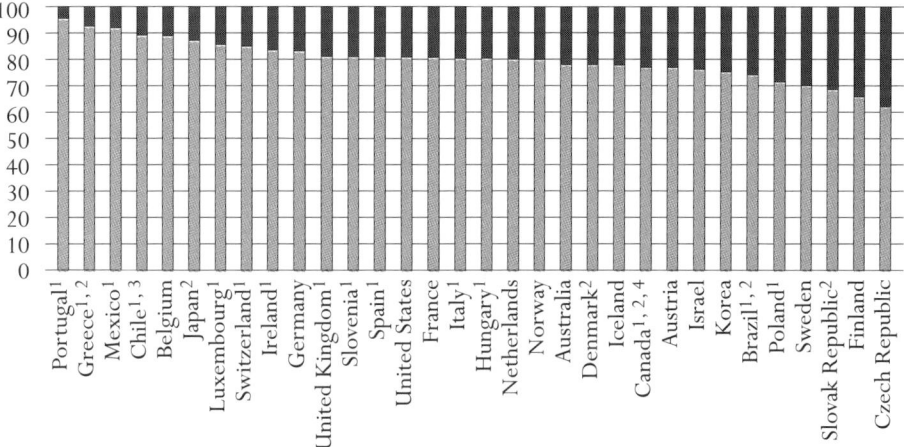

1. Public institutions only.
2. Some levels of education are included with others. Refer to "x" code in Table B1.1a for details.
3. Year of reference 2006.
4. Year of reference 2004.
Countries are ranked in descending order of the share of compensation of all staff in primary, secondary and post-secondary non-tertiary education.
Source: OECD. Table B6.2b. See Annex 3 for notes (*www.oecd.org/edu/eag2008*).
StatLink 🔗 http://dx.doi.org/10.1787/402057518843

Other highlights of this indicator

■ At primary, secondary and post-secondary non-tertiary levels of education, OECD countries spend an average of 20% of current expenditure on purposes other than the compensation of educational personnel.

■ The difference between primary and secondary education in terms of the proportion of current expenditure for purposes other than compensation exceeds 5 percentage points only in Austria, France, Ireland and Spain and is mainly due to significant variations in teachers' salaries, size of non-teaching staff, class size, instruction hours received by pupils and teaching time given by teachers.

■ Compensation of teaching staff is a smaller share of current and capital spending at the tertiary level than at other levels because of the higher cost of facilities and equipment and the construction of new buildings owing to the expansion in enrolments. At the tertiary level, OECD countries spend an average of 32% of current expenditure on purposes other than compensation of educational personnel.

■ On average, OECD countries spend 0.2% of GDP on ancillary services provided by primary, secondary and post-secondary non-tertiary institutions. This represents 6% of total spending on educational institutions. At the high end, Finland, France, the Slovak Republic, Sweden and the United Kingdom allocate some 10% or more of total expenditure on educational institutions to ancillary services.

■ High spending on R&D is a distinctive feature of tertiary institutions and averages over one-quarter of expenditure. The fact that some countries spend much more than others (Switzerland and Sweden spend up to 40% or more) helps explain wide differences in overall tertiary spending as do significant differences among OECD countries in their emphasis on R&D in tertiary institutions.

B6

Policy context

The distribution of spending among categories of expenditure can affect the quality of services (such as teachers' salaries), the condition of educational facilities (such as school maintenance) and the education system's capacity to adjust to changing demographic and enrolment trends (such as construction of new schools).

Comparisons of how different OECD countries apportion educational expenditure among the various categories can also provide insight into the organisation and operation of their educational institutions. Decisions on the allocation of budgetary and structural resources at the system level eventually feed through to the classroom and affect the nature of instruction and the conditions under which it is provided.

Educational institutions offer a range of services in addition to instruction, and this indicator also compares how spending is distributed among their various functions. At the primary, secondary and post-secondary non-tertiary levels, they may offer meals and free transport to and from school or boarding facilities. At the tertiary level, they may offer housing and often perform a wide range of research activities.

Evidence and explanations

What this indicator does and does not cover

This indicator breaks down educational expenditure by current and capital expenditure and the three main functions typically fulfilled by educational institutions. It includes costs directly attributable to instruction, such as teachers' salaries or school materials, and costs indirectly related to the provision of instruction, such as expenditure on administration, instructional support services, teachers' professional development, student counselling, or the construction and/or provision of school facilities. It also includes spending on ancillary services such as the student welfare services provided by educational institutions. Finally, it includes spending on research and development (R&D) performed at tertiary institutions, in the form either of separately funded R&D activities or of the proportion of salaries and current expenditure in general education budgets that is attributable to the research activities of staff.

The indicator does not include public and private R&D spending outside educational institutions, such as R&D spending in industry. A review of R&D spending in sectors other than education is provided in the *Main OECD Science and Technology Indicators*. Expenditure on student welfare services at educational institutions only includes public subsidies for those services; expenditure by students and their families on services that are provided by institutions on a self-funding basis is not included.

Expenditure on instruction, R&D and ancillary services

Below the tertiary level, educational expenditure is dominated by spending on educational core services. At the tertiary level, other services – particularly those related to R&D activities – can account for a significant proportion of educational spending. Differences among OECD countries in expenditure on R&D activities therefore explain a significant part of the differences in overall educational expenditure per tertiary-level student (Chart B6.2). For example, high levels of R&D spending (between 0.4 and 0.8% of GDP) in tertiary educational institutions in Australia,

B6

Chart B6.2. Expenditure on educational core services, R&D and ancillary services in tertiary educational institutions as a percentage of GDP (2005)

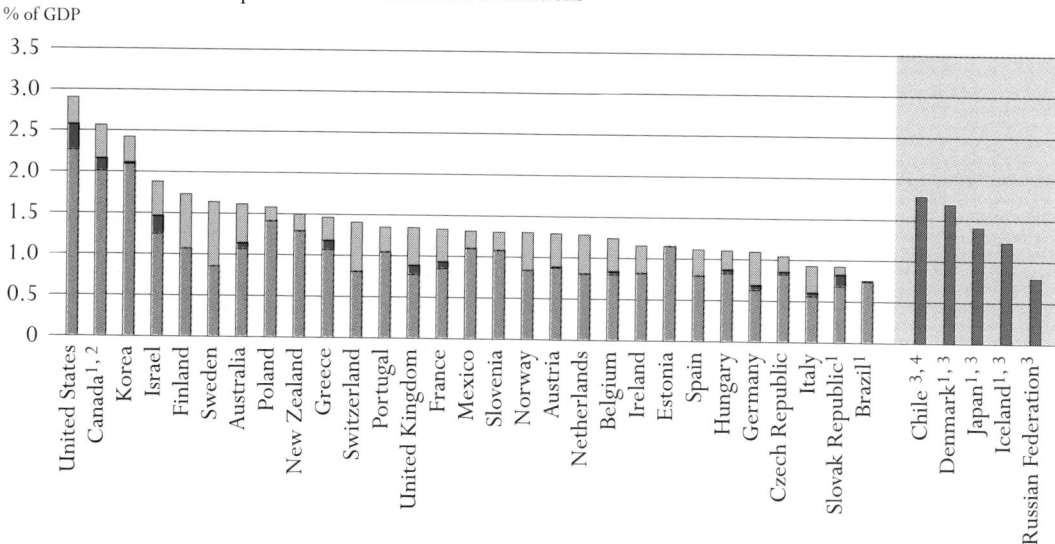

- Research and development (R&D)
- Ancillary services (transport, meals, housing provided by institutions)
- Educational core services
- Total expenditure on educational institutions

1. Some levels of education are included with others. Refer to "x" code in Table B1.1a for details.
2. Year of reference 2004.
3. Total expenditure at tertiary level including expenditure on research and development (R&D).
4. Year of reference 2006.
Countries are ranked in descending order of total expenditure on educational institutions in tertiary institutions.
Source: OECD. Table B6.1. See Annex 3 for notes (*www.oecd.org/edu/eag2008*).
StatLink ⬛⬛⬛ http://dx.doi.org/10.1787/402057518843

Austria, Belgium, Canada, Finland, France, Germany, the Netherlands, Norway, Sweden, Switzerland and the United Kingdom, and the partner country Israel, imply that spending on educational institutions per student in these countries would be considerably lower if the R&D component were excluded (Table B1.1b).

Student welfare services

Student welfare services (and in some cases services for the general public) are an integral function of schools and universities in many OECD countries. Countries finance these ancillary services with different combinations of public expenditure, public subsidies and fees paid by students and their families.

On average, OECD countries spend 0.2% of GDP on ancillary services provided by primary, secondary and post-secondary non-tertiary institutions. This represents 6% of total spending on these institutions. At the high end, Finland, France, the Slovak Republic, Sweden and the United Kingdom spend some 10% or more of their total spending on educational institutions on ancillary services (Table B6.1).

Chart B6.3. Distribution of current and capital expenditure on educational institutions (2005)

By resource category and level of education

☐ Current expenditure   ■ Capital expenditure

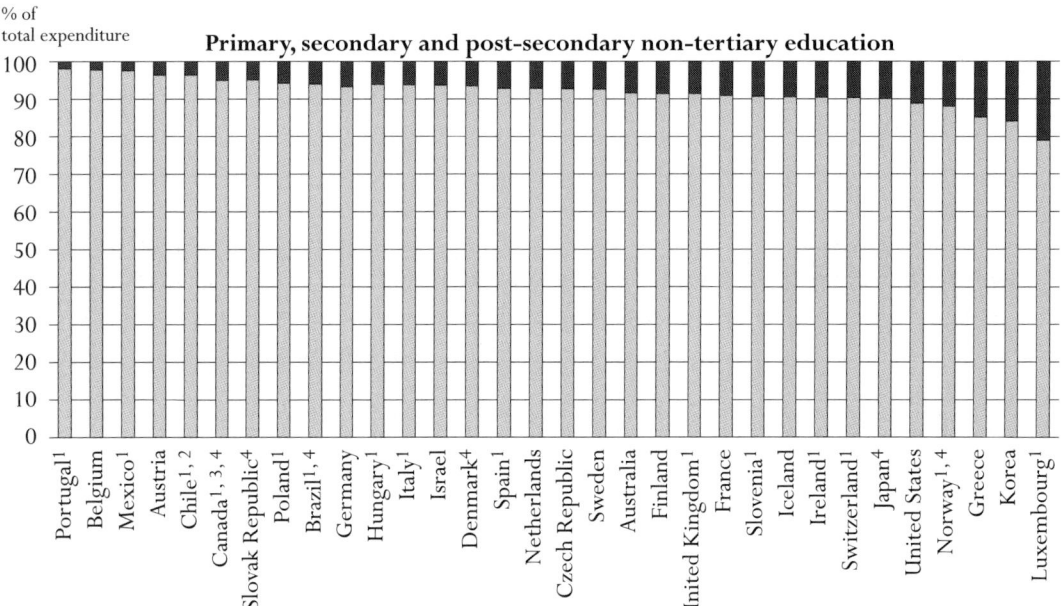

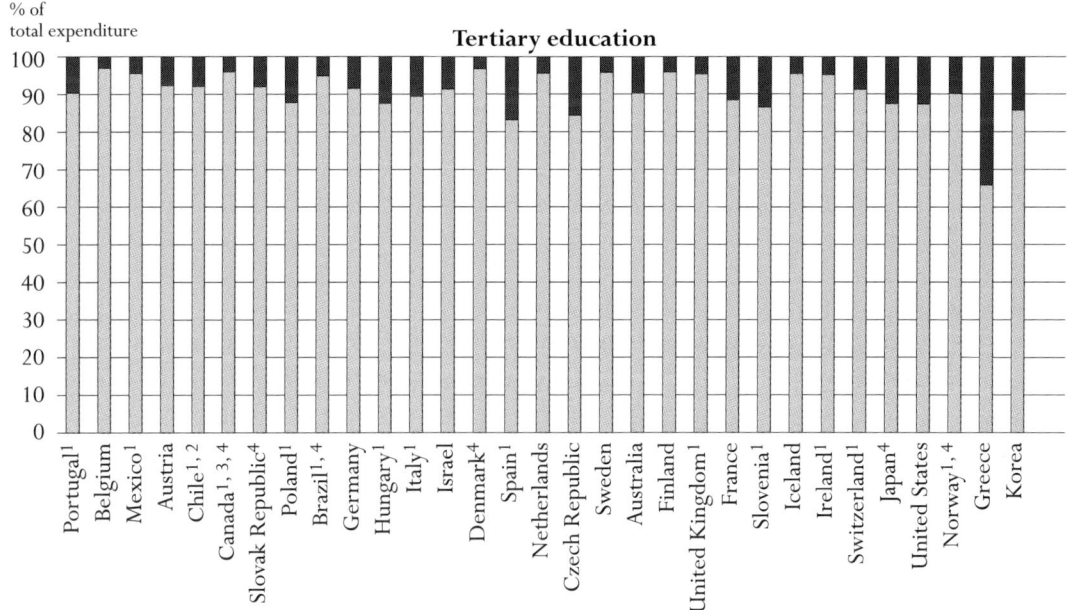

1. Public institutions only.

2. Year of reference 2006.

3. Year of reference 2004.

4. Some levels of education are included with others. Refer to "x" code in Table B1.1a for details.

Countries are ranked in descending order of the share of current expenditure on primary, secondary and post-secondary non-tertiary education.

Source: OECD. Table B6.2b. See Annex 3 for notes (*www.oecd.org/edu/eag2008*).

StatLink ᐧᐧᐧᒪ http://dx.doi.org/10.1787/402057518843

At the tertiary level, ancillary services are more often self-financed. On average, expenditure on subsidies for ancillary services at the tertiary level amounts to less than 0.1% of GDP but represents up to 0.3% in the United States (Table B6.1).

Current and capital expenditure and the distribution of current expenditure

Educational expenditure can be divided into current and capital expenditure. Capital expenditure on educational institutions covers spending on assets that last longer than one year and includes spending on the construction, renovation and major repair of buildings. Current expenditure on educational institutions comprises spending on school resources used each year for the operation of schools.

Education mostly takes place in school and university settings. Its labour-intensive nature explains the large proportion of current spending in total educational expenditure. In primary, secondary, and post-secondary non-tertiary education, taken together, current expenditure accounts on average for nearly 92% of total spending across all OECD countries.

There is significant variation among OECD countries in the proportions of current and capital expenditure: at the primary, secondary and post-secondary non-tertiary levels, taken together, the proportion of current expenditure ranges from less than 80% in Luxembourg to 97% or more in Belgium, Mexico and Portugal (Table B6.2b and Chart B6.3).

Proportion of current expenditure on educational institutions allocated to compensation of teachers and other staff

Current expenditure on educational institutions can be further subdivided into three broad functional categories: compensation of teachers, compensation of other staff and other current expenditures (teaching materials and supplies, maintenance of school buildings, preparation of students' meals, and rental of school facilities). The amount allocated to each of these functional categories depends partly on current and projected changes in enrolments, on salaries of educational personnel, and on the costs of maintenance and construction of educational facilities.

The salaries of teachers and other staff employed in education account for the largest proportion of current expenditure in all OECD countries. Expenditure on compensation of educational personnel accounts on average for 80% of current expenditure at the primary, secondary and post-secondary non-tertiary levels of education, taken together. In all countries except the Czech Republic, Finland and the Slovak Republic, 70% or more of current expenditure at the primary, secondary and post-secondary non-tertiary levels is spent on staff salaries. The proportion devoted to the compensation of educational personnel is 90% or more in Greece, Mexico and Portugal (Chart B6.1).

There is very little difference in the average proportion of expenditure on compensation of personnel between primary and secondary levels of education. The only exceptions to this pattern are Austria, France, Ireland and Spain where the difference between the two exceeds 5 percentage points (Table B6.2a). This is mainly due to significant variations in teachers' salaries, class size, size of non-teaching staff, instruction hours received by pupils and teaching time given by teachers (see Indicators B7, D1, D2, D3 and D4).

OECD countries with relatively small education budgets, such as Mexico, Portugal and Turkey, tend to spend a larger proportion of current educational expenditure on compensation of personnel and a smaller proportion on sub-contracted services such as support services (*e.g.* maintenance of school buildings), ancillary services (*e.g.* preparation of students' meals), and rental of school buildings and other facilities.

In Austria, Denmark, France, the United Kingdom and the United States, and the partner country Slovenia, more than 20% of current expenditure in primary, secondary and post-secondary non-tertiary education, taken together, goes towards compensation of non-teaching staff, while in Ireland, Korea and the partner country Chile, the figure is 10% or less. These differences are likely to reflect the degree to which educational personnel such as principals, guidance counsellors, bus drivers, school nurses, janitors and maintenance workers are included in this category (Table B6.2b).

OECD countries spend, on average, 32% of current expenditure at the tertiary level on purposes other than the compensation of educational personnel. This is due to the higher cost of facilities and equipment in higher education (Table B6.2b).

Proportions of capital expenditure

At the tertiary level, the proportion of total expenditure for capital outlays is larger than at the primary, secondary and post-secondary non-tertiary levels (9.5 versus 8.2%), generally because of more differentiated and advanced teaching facilities. In 11 out of the 31 OECD and partner countries for which data are available, the proportion spent on capital expenditure at the tertiary level is 10% or more and in the Czech Republic, Greece and Spain it is above 15% (Chart B6.3).

Differences are likely to reflect how tertiary education is organised in each country as well as the degree to which the expansion in enrolments requires the construction of new buildings.

Definitions and methodologies

Data refer to the financial year 2005 and are based on the UOE data collection on education statistics administered by the OECD in 2007 (for details see Annex 3 at *www.oecd.org/edu/eag2008*).

The distinction between current and capital expenditure on educational institutions is taken from the standard definition used in national income accounting. Current expenditure refers to goods and services consumed within the current year and requiring recurrent production in order to sustain the provision of educational services. Capital expenditure refers to assets which last longer than one year, including spending on construction, renovation or major repair of buildings and new or replacement equipment. The capital expenditure reported here represents the value of educational capital acquired or created during the year in question – that is, the amount of capital formation – regardless of whether the capital expenditure was financed from current revenue or by borrowing. Neither current nor capital expenditure includes debt servicing.

Calculations cover expenditure by public institutions or, where available, that of both public and private institutions.

Current expenditure on educational institutions other than on compensation of personnel includes expenditure on sub-contracted services such as support services (*e.g.* maintenance of

B6

school buildings), ancillary services (*e.g.* preparation of meals for students) and rental of school buildings and other facilities. These services are obtained from outside providers, unlike the services provided by the education authorities or by the educational institutions themselves using their own personnel.

Expenditure on R&D includes all expenditure on research performed at universities and other tertiary education institutions, regardless of whether the research is financed from general institutional funds or through separate grants or contracts from public or private sponsors. The classification of expenditure is based on data collected from the institutions carrying out R&D rather than on the sources of funds.

Ancillary services are those provided by educational institutions that are peripheral to the main educational mission. The two main components of ancillary services are student welfare services and services for the general public. At primary, secondary and post-secondary non-tertiary levels, student welfare services include meals, school health services and transport to and from school. At the tertiary level, it includes residence halls (dormitories), dining halls and health care. Services for the general public include museums, radio and television broadcasting, sports and recreational and cultural programmes. Expenditure on ancillary services, including fees from students or households, is excluded.

Educational core services are estimated as the residual of all expenditure, that is, total expenditure on educational institutions net of expenditure on R&D and ancillary services.

B6

Table B6.1.

Expenditure on educational institutions by service category as a percentage of GDP (2005)

Expenditure on instruction, R&D and ancillary services in educational institutions and private expenditure
on educational goods purchased outside educational institutions

| | Primary, secondary and post-secondary non-tertiary education | | | | Tertiary education | | | | |
| | Expenditure on educational institutions | | | Private payments on instructional services/goods outside educational institutions | Expenditure on educational institutions | | | | Private payments on instructional services/goods outside educational institutions |
	Core educational services	Ancillary services (transport, meals, housing provided by institutions)	Total		Core educational services	Ancillary services (transport, meals, housing provided by institutions)	Research & development at tertiary institutions	Total	
	(1)	(2)	(3)	(4)	(5)	(6)	(7)	(8)	(9)
Australia	3.93	0.16	**4.09**	0.13	1.07	0.07	0.48	**1.62**	0.16
Austria	3.57	0.15	**3.72**	m	0.87	0.01	0.41	**1.30**	m
Belgium	3.92	0.16	**4.08**	0.12	0.80	0.03	0.41	**1.24**	0.17
Canada[1,2]	3.43	0.20	**3.63**	m	2.01	0.15	0.41	**2.56**	0.14
Czech Republic	2.80	0.22	**3.02**	0.04	0.82	0.03	0.19	**1.04**	0.03
Denmark[2]	x(3)	x(3)	**4.45**	0.57	x(8)	a	x(8)	**1.69**	0.73
Finland	3.45	0.42	**3.87**	m	1.07	n	0.66	**1.73**	m
France	3.49	0.52	**4.01**	0.19	0.86	0.08	0.40	**1.33**	0.07
Germany	3.32	0.08	**3.40**	0.14	0.63	0.05	0.41	**1.09**	0.08
Greece[2]	2.67	0.07	**2.74**	0.93	1.07	0.11	0.29	**1.46**	0.10
Hungary[3]	3.17	0.28	**3.44**	m	0.83	0.04	0.24	**1.11**	m
Iceland[2]	x(3)	x(3)	**5.36**	m	x(8)	x(8)	x(8)	**1.23**	m
Ireland	3.34	0.08	**3.42**	m	0.82	x(8)	0.34	**1.16**	m
Italy	3.16	0.13	**3.29**	0.37	0.56	0.04	0.33	**0.93**	0.14
Japan[2]	x(3)	x(3)	**2.89**	0.78	x(8)	x(8)	x(8)	**1.41**	0.04
Korea	3.95	0.39	**4.34**	m	2.09	0.01	0.32	**2.42**	m
Luxembourg[3]	x(3)	x(3)	**3.73**	m	m	m	m	**m**	m
Mexico	4.37	m	**4.37**	0.23	1.10	m	0.22	**1.31**	0.06
Netherlands	3.34	0.03	**3.38**	0.21	0.80	n	0.48	**1.28**	0.07
New Zealand	x(3)	x(3)	**4.74**	n	1.29	x(8)	0.20	**1.50**	n
Norway	x(3)	x(3)	**3.81**	m	0.84	n	0.47	**1.31**	m
Poland[3]	3.62	0.12	**3.74**	0.17	1.41	n	0.17	**1.58**	0.05
Portugal[3]	3.78	0.03	**3.80**	0.05	x(8)	x(8)	0.31	**1.35**	0.00
Slovak Republic[2]	2.47	0.43	**2.90**	0.45	0.68	0.14	0.10	**0.92**	0.20
Spain	2.79	0.12	**2.90**	m	0.79	m	0.32	**1.12**	m
Sweden	3.82	0.43	**4.25**	m	0.85	n	0.79	**1.64**	m
Switzerland[3]	x(3)	x(3)	**4.39**	m	0.80	x(8)	0.61	**1.41**	m
Turkey	m	m	**m**	m	m	m	m	**m**	m
United Kingdom	3.86	0.75	**4.60**	m	0.78	0.11	0.47	**1.35**	0.15
United States	3.53	0.31	**3.84**	a	2.26	0.31	0.33	**2.90**	a
OECD average	*3.44*	*0.24*	*3.80*	*0.27*	*1.05*	*0.06*	*0.37*	*1.46*	*0.13*
Brazil[3]	x(3)	x(3)	**3.23**	m	0.74	x(5)	0.01	**0.76**	m
Chile[4]	3.26	0.14	**3.41**	0.02	x(8)	x(8)	x(8)	**1.79**	n
Estonia	x(3)	x(3)	**3.46**	m	x(8)	x(8)	n	**1.15**	m
Israel	4.32	0.15	**4.47**	0.31	1.25	0.21	0.42	**1.88**	n
Russian Federation[3]	x(3)	x(3)	**1.88**	m	x(8)	x(8)	x(8)	**0.79**	m
Slovenia[3]	4.08	0.18	**4.25**	m	1.08	n	0.23	**1.31**	m

1. Year of reference 2004.
2. Some levels of education are included with others. Refer to "x" code in Table B1.1a for details.
3. Public institutions only.
4. Year of reference 2006.
Source: OECD. See Annex 3 for notes (*www.oecd.org/edu/eag2008*).
Please refer to the Reader's Guide for information concerning the symbols replacing missing data.
StatLink ᐸᔑᒪ http://dx.doi.org/10.1787/402057518843

B6

Table B6.2a.
Expenditure on educational institutions by resource category in primary and secondary education (2005)
Distribution of total and current expenditure on educational institutions from public and private sources

	Primary education						Secondary education					
	Percentage of total expenditure		Percentage of current expenditure				Percentage of total expenditure		Percentage of current expenditure			
	Current	Capital	Compensation of teachers	Compensation of other staff	Compensation of all staff	Other current expenditure	Current	Capital	Compensation of teachers	Compensation of other staff	Compensation of all staff	Other current expenditure
	(1)	(2)	(3)	(4)	(5)	(6)	(7)	(8)	(9)	(10)	(11)	(12)
Australia	91.8	8.2	64.0	16.1	80.1	19.9	91.4	8.6	59.1	17.4	76.5	23.5
Austria	95.0	5.0	53.5	20.0	73.5	26.5	97.0	3.0	58.2	20.9	79.1	20.9
Belgium	97.2	2.8	69.5	20.0	89.6	10.4	98.0	2.1	70.7	17.8	88.5	11.5
Canada[1]	m	m	m	m	m	m	m	m	m	m	m	m
Czech Republic	90.9	9.1	47.5	17.6	65.1	34.9	93.2	6.8	48.7	12.8	61.5	38.5
Denmark[2]	92.2	7.8	51.0	27.5	78.4	21.6	94.4	5.6	52.4	25.0	77.5	22.5
Finland	90.8	9.2	58.2	9.5	67.7	32.3	91.7	8.3	52.3	12.4	64.7	35.3
France	93.7	6.3	53.1	22.8	75.9	24.1	89.7	10.3	59.5	23.2	82.7	17.3
Germany	92.3	7.7	x(5)	x(5)	83.0	17.0	93.5	6.5	x(11)	x(11)	83.4	16.6
Greece[2,3]	86.5	13.5	x(5)	x(5)	91.3	8.7	85.2	14.8	x(11)	x(11)	95.0	5.0
Hungary[3]	95.2	4.8	x(5)	x(5)	81.0	19.0	93.5	6.5	x(11)	x(11)	80.2	19.8
Iceland	88.2	11.8	x(5)	x(5)	79.0	21.0	93.0	7.0	x(11)	x(11)	76.6	23.4
Ireland[3]	90.0	10.0	76.3	11.8	88.1	11.9	90.8	9.2	74.8	5.7	80.5	19.5
Italy[3]	93.6	6.4	64.9	16.8	81.7	18.3	94.1	5.9	64.7	16.5	81.2	18.8
Japan[2]	90.0	10.0	x(5)	x(5)	87.6	12.4	90.2	9.8	x(11)	x(11)	86.9	13.1
Korea	82.8	17.2	64.7	10.7	75.4	24.6	85.0	15.0	68.3	6.7	75.0	25.0
Luxembourg[3]	75.6	24.4	74.2	10.6	84.8	15.2	83.0	17.0	73.8	12.6	86.5	13.5
Mexico[3]	97.7	2.3	84.1	9.5	93.6	6.4	97.3	2.7	74.9	15.0	89.9	10.1
Netherlands	91.5	8.5	x(5)	x(5)	78.5	21.5	93.7	6.3	x(11)	x(11)	81.0	19.0
New Zealand	m	m	m	m	m	m	m	m	m	m	m	m
Norway	88.4	11.6	x(5)	x(5)	79.6	20.4	87.7	12.3	x(11)	x(11)	80.2	19.8
Poland[3]	93.7	6.3	x(5)	x(5)	72.9	27.1	94.6	5.4	x(11)	x(11)	70.6	29.4
Portugal[3]	99.1	0.9	85.4	11.1	96.5	3.5	97.3	2.7	81.5	13.2	94.7	5.3
Slovak Republic[2]	92.3	7.7	52.7	14.0	66.7	33.3	96.3	3.7	53.7	15.4	69.0	31.0
Spain[3]	92.2	7.8	72.5	11.6	84.1	15.9	93.2	6.8	69.7	9.3	79.0	21.0
Sweden	92.6	7.4	53.7	18.3	72.1	27.9	92.6	7.4	50.6	17.8	68.5	31.5
Switzerland[3]	88.6	11.4	71.6	13.0	84.7	15.3	91.7	8.3	71.9	13.2	85.2	14.8
Turkey	m	m	m	m	m	m	m	m	m	m	m	m
United Kingdom[3]	90.5	9.5	53.4	26.2	79.6	20.4	92.8	7.2	60.0	21.3	81.4	18.6
United States	88.8	11.2	55.1	25.8	80.8	19.2	88.8	11.2	55.1	25.8	80.8	19.2
OECD average	*91.1*	*8.9*	*63.5*	*16.5*	*80.5*	*19.5*	*92.2*	*7.8*	*63.2*	*15.9*	*79.9*	*20.1*
Brazil[2,3]	93.2	6.8	x(5)	x(5)	74.2	25.8	94.6	5.4	x(11)	x(11)	74.0	26.0
Chile[3,4]	96.6	3.4	85.1	4.9	89.9	10.1	96.1	3.9	83.4	4.8	88.2	11.8
Estonia	m	m	m	m	m	m	m	m	m	m	m	m
Israel	92.8	7.2	x(5)	x(5)	75.4	24.6	94.6	5.4	x(11)	x(11)	77.1	23.0
Russian Federation	m	m	m	m	m	m	m	m	m	m	m	m
Slovenia[3]	m	m	m	m	m	m	m	m	m	m	m	m

1. Year of reference 2004.
2. Some levels of education are included with others. Refer to "x" code in Table B1.1a for details.
3. Public institutions only.
4. Year of reference 2006.
Source: OECD. See Annex 3 for notes (*www.oecd.org/edu/eag2008*).
Please refer to the Reader's Guide for information concerning the symbols replacing missing data.
StatLink ᴴ᎑ᵐ http://dx.doi.org/10.1787/402057518843

B6

Table B6.2b.
Expenditure on educational institutions by resource category and level of education (2005)
Distribution of total and current expenditure on educational institutions from public and private sources

	Primary, secondary and post-secondary non-tertiary education						Tertiary education					
	Percentage of total expenditure		Percentage of current expenditure				Percentage of total expenditure		Percentage of current expenditure			
	Current	Capital	Compensation of teachers	Compensation of other staff	Compensation of all staff	Other current expenditure	Current	Capital	Compensation of teachers	Compensation of other staff	Compensation of all staff	Other current expenditure
	(1)	(2)	(3)	(4)	(5)	(6)	(7)	(8)	(9)	(10)	(11)	(12)
OECD countries												
Australia	91.6	8.4	60.9	17.0	77.9	22.1	90.2	9.8	32.4	28.0	60.4	39.6
Austria	96.4	3.6	56.1	20.8	76.9	23.1	92.3	7.7	42.5	15.8	58.3	41.7
Belgium	97.7	2.3	70.3	18.6	88.9	11.1	96.9	3.1	54.1	23.8	77.9	22.1
Canada[1, 2, 3]	95.0	5.0	63.8	13.5	77.3	22.7	95.9	4.1	33.0	34.6	67.5	32.5
Czech Republic	92.7	7.3	48.2	13.8	62.0	38.0	81.9	15.2	36.0	24.4	60.4	39.6
Denmark[2]	93.4	6.6	51.8	26.1	77.9	22.1	96.6	3.4	51.7	24.9	76.6	23.4
Finland	91.4	8.6	54.3	11.4	65.7	34.3	95.8	4.2	35.4	28.2	63.6	36.4
France	90.9	9.1	57.5	23.1	80.6	19.4	88.4	11.6	52.7	28.5	81.2	18.8
Germany	93.3	6.7	x(5)	x(5)	83.1	16.9	91.5	8.5	x(11)	x(11)	70.4	29.6
Greece[2, 3]	85.1	14.9	x(5)	x(5)	92.5	7.5	65.8	34.2	x(11)	x(11)	70.2	29.8
Hungary[3]	93.9	6.1	x(5)	x(5)	80.3	19.7	87.6	12.4	x(11)	x(11)	69.9	30.1
Iceland	90.6	9.4	x(5)	x(5)	77.7	22.3	95.4	4.6	x(11)	x(11)	80.0	20.0
Ireland[3]	90.4	9.6	74.9	8.6	83.5	16.5	95.1	4.9	49.2	24.8	74.0	26.0
Italy[3]	93.7	6.3	64.0	16.4	80.4	19.6	89.4	10.6	43.4	23.3	66.7	33.3
Japan[2]	90.1	9.9	x(5)	x(5)	87.2	12.8	87.4	12.6	x(11)	x(11)	61.7	38.3
Korea	84.1	15.9	66.8	8.4	75.1	24.9	85.7	14.3	35.3	15.6	50.9	49.1
Luxembourg[3]	79.0	21.0	74.0	11.6	85.6	14.4	m	m	m	m	m	m
Mexico[3]	97.5	2.5	80.1	11.9	92.0	8.0	95.5	4.5	57.0	14.7	71.7	28.3
Netherlands	92.8	7.2	x(5)	x(5)	79.9	20.1	95.5	4.5	x(11)	x(11)	74.3	25.7
New Zealand	m	m	m	m	m	m	m	m	m	m	m	m
Norway	88.1	12.0	x(5)	x(5)	79.9	20.1	90.1	9.9	x(11)	x(11)	64.1	35.9
Poland[3]	94.2	5.8	x(5)	x(5)	71.4	28.6	87.8	12.2	x(11)	x(11)	60.5	39.5
Portugal[3]	98.1	1.9	83.2	12.3	95.5	4.5	90.4	9.6	x(11)	x(11)	69.8	30.2
Slovak Republic[2]	95.2	4.8	53.4	15.0	68.4	31.6	92.0	8.0	30.9	21.9	52.7	47.3
Spain[3]	92.8	7.2	70.8	10.2	80.9	19.1	83.2	16.8	59.3	21.5	80.8	19.2
Sweden	92.6	7.4	52.0	18.1	70.0	30.0	95.7	4.3	x(11)	x(11)	62.8	37.2
Switzerland[3]	90.3	9.7	71.7	13.2	84.9	15.1	91.2	8.8	53.6	23.1	76.7	23.3
Turkey	m	m	m	m	m	m	m	m	m	m	m	m
United Kingdom[3]	91.4	8.6	57.4	23.6	81.0	19.0	95.2	4.8	m	m	m	m
United States	88.8	11.2	55.1	25.8	80.8	19.2	87.3	12.7	28.9	36.5	65.4	34.6
OECD average	**91.8**	**8.2**	**63.3**	**16.0**	**79.9**	**20.1**	**90.4**	**9.5**	**43.5**	**24.3**	**68.0**	**32.0**
Partner countries												
Brazil[2, 3]	93.9	6.1	x(5)	x(5)	74.1	25.9	94.8	5.2	x(11)	x(11)	77.9	22.1
Chile[3, 4]	96.4	3.6	84.3	4.8	89.1	10.9	92.1	7.9	x(11)	x(11)	64.5	35.5
Estonia	m	m	m	m	m	m	m	m	m	m	m	m
Israel	93.7	6.3	x(5)	x(5)	76.1	23.9	91.3	8.7	x(11)	x(11)	75.8	24.2
Russian Federation	m	m	m	m	m	m	m	m	m	m	m	m
Slovenia[3]	90.6	9.4	47.6	33.4	81.0	19.0	86.4	13.6	37.0	34.0	71.0	29.0

1. Year of reference 2004.
2. Some levels of education are included with others. Refer to "x" code in Table B1.1a for details.
3. Public institutions only.
4. Year of reference 2006.
Source: OECD. See Annex 3 for notes (*www.oecd.org/edu/eag2008*).
Please refer to the Reader's Guide for information concerning the symbols replacing missing data.
StatLink 🖳 http://dx.doi.org/10.1787/402057518843

HOW EFFICIENTLY ARE RESOURCES USED IN EDUCATION?

This indicator examines the relationship between resources invested and outcomes achieved in upper secondary education in OECD countries and thus raises questions about the efficiency of education systems.

Key results

Chart B7.1. Contribution of various factors to salary cost per student as a percentage of GDP per capita, at the upper secondary level of education (2004)

The chart shows the contribution (in percentage points) of the factors to the difference between salary cost per student (as a percentage of GDP per capita) in the country and the OECD average, at the upper secondary level of education. For example, in Portugal, the salary cost per student is 10 percentage points higher than the average salary cost per student. This is because Portugal has higher salaries (compared to GDP per capita) than the average, a smaller number of teaching hours for teachers than the average and smaller class sizes than the average. However these effects are slighltly dampened by below average instruction time for students.

- ■ Salary as % of GDP/capita
- ■ 1/class size
- ▨ Instruction time
- ◇ Difference with OECD average
- ▢ 1/teaching time

Teacher compensation cost per student varies from 3.9% of GDP per capita in the Slovak Republic (less than half the OECD average rate of 10.9%) to over five times that rate in Portugal (20.9%, nearly twice the OECD average). Four factors influence these trends – salary level, instruction time for students, teaching time of teachers and average class size – so that a given level of compensation cost per student can result from quite different combinations of the four factors. For example, in Korea and Luxembourg, the compensation cost per student (as a percentage of GDP per capita) is 15.5 and 15.2%, respectively, both notably higher than the OECD average. However, whereas in Korea higher than average teacher salary levels coupled with relatively large class sizes are the main influence on this, in Luxembourg, relatively low class size is the main factor which results in such a high teacher compensation cost per student (as a proportion of GDP per capita) compared to the OECD average.

Percentage points

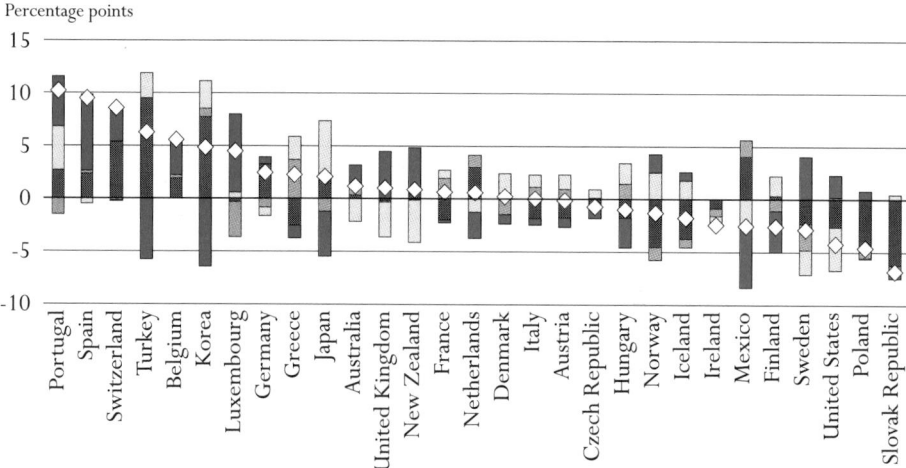

Countries are ranked in descending order of the difference between the salary cost in percentage of GDP per capita and the OECD average.

Source: OECD. Table B7.2. See Annex 3 for notes (www.oecd.org/edu/eag2008).

StatLink ᴹˢᴾ http://dx.doi.org/10.1787/402072442032

Other highlights of this indicator

■ In countries with the lowest compensation cost per student (as a percentage of GDP per capita) at the upper secondary level, low salary levels as a proportion of GDP is usually the main driver. This is the case in Iceland, Ireland, Norway, Poland, the Slovak Republic and Sweden. The main exception to this pattern is Mexico where teacher salary costs relative to GDP per capita are well above the OECD average but this is more than compensated for by large class sizes.

■ In contrast, among countries with the highest levels of compensation cost per student (Portugal, Spain, Switzerland), no single factor determines this position, but rather each of the four factors act to increase costs to varying degrees.

■ High spending per student cannot automatically be equated with strong performance by education systems. Spending per student up to the age of 15 in the Czech Republic is roughly one-third of, and in Korea roughly one-half of, spending levels in the United States. However, while both the Czech Republic and Korea are among the top ten performers in the PISA 2006 assessment of science achievement among 15-year-olds, the United States performs below the OECD average. Similarly, Spain and the United States perform almost equally well, but while the United States spends roughly USD 95 600 per student up to the age of 15 years, Spain only spends USD 61 860.

■ Clustering countries according to the characteristics of their education system shows that similar education systems can have very different outcomes. For example, Finland and the Czech Republic and, to a lesser extent, Sweden perform well above the OECD average on the PISA science scale but the other countries in the same cluster (Denmark, Iceland, Norway and the Slovak Republic) perform below the OECD average.

Policy context

The relationship between the resources devoted to education and the outcomes achieved has been the focus of much education policy interest in recent years as governments seek to achieve more and better education for the whole population. However, given the increasing pressures on public budgets, there is intense interest in ensuring that funding – public funding in particular – is well directed, in order to achieve the desired outcomes in the most effective way possible. Internationally, much attention is of course paid to which education systems achieve most in terms of the quality and equity of learning outcomes, but there is also considerable interest in knowing which systems achieve most given the inputs provided. Could the same outputs be achieved with fewer inputs? Could better outputs be achieved with the same inputs? What are the main factors that drive investment in education? Would better performances be achieved if one of these factors is modified?

Evidence and explanations

This indicator begins with an examination of the correlation between spending and performance and considers what this says about the efficiency of education systems, referring also to analyses conducted by the OECD Economics Department in the context of its "Public Spending Efficiency" project and published in *Education at a Glance 2007*. Finally, the indicator describes the main variables accounting for differences among countries in the level of expenditure per student allocated by countries to upper secondary education and groups countries with similarities in their input variables at the upper secondary level of education to see whether similar education systems can expect similar levels of outcomes.

Student performance and spending per student

Table B7.1 compares countries' actual cumulative spending per student between the ages of 6 and 15 in 2005 on average, with their average student performance on the science literacy scale of PISA 2006 and with other economic and social indicators. Cumulative spending per student is approximated by multiplying public and private expenditure on educational institutions per student in 2005 at each level of education by the theoretical duration of education at these levels between the ages of 6 and 15 years. The results are expressed in USD using purchasing power parities.

Chart B7.2 shows a positive relationship between cumulative spending per student and mean science performance. As cumulative expenditure per student on educational institutions increases, so does a country's mean PISA performance in science. However, the relationship is not a strong one; cumulative expenditure per student in fact explains merely 15% of the variation in mean performance between countries. The relation between PISA performance in science and national income is similarly weak, though the correlation is stronger when the performance of countries with comparatively low levels of national income and cumulative expenditure per student between the ages of 6 and 15 years are taken into account (Mexico, the Slovak Republic and the partner countries Brazil, Chile and the Russian Federation) (Table B7.1 and Chart B7.2).

However, many countries deviate from the trend line. In other words, spending levels per student cannot automatically be equated with the performance of the education system as measured by PISA. To illustrate this, spending per student up to the age of 15 years in the Czech Republic is roughly one-third of, and in Korea roughly one-half of, spending levels in the United States,

Chart B7.2. Relationship between PISA performance in science at age 15 and cumulative expenditure per student between 6 and 15 year-olds (2005, 2006)

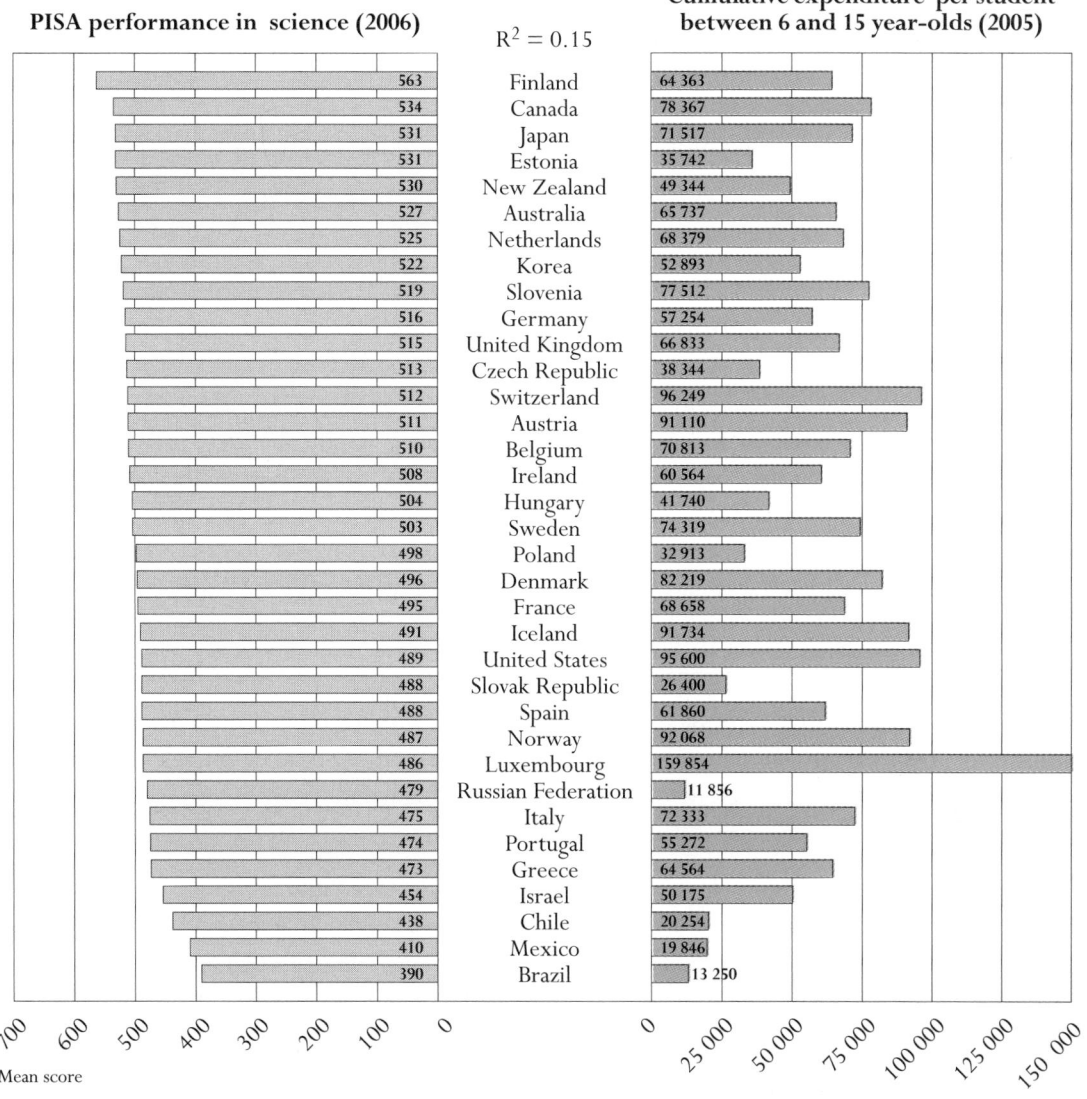

Countries are ranked in descending order of the PISA performance in science at age 15.
Source: Table B7.1 and PISA 2006 databases. See Annex 3 for notes (www.oecd.org/edu/eag2008).
StatLink http://dx.doi.org/10.1787/402072442032

but while both the Czech Republic and Korea are among the top ten performers in PISA, the United States performs below the OECD average. Similarly, Spain and the United States perform almost equally well, but while the United States spends roughly USD 95 600 per student up to the age of 15, Spain spends only USD 61 860 (Table B7.1 and Chart B7.2).

Table B7.1 also shows that spending per student up to the age of 15 is more closely correlated with the proportion of low performers at 15 years of age (level of proficiency 1 or below) than with the proportion of best achievers on the PISA science scale (level of proficiency 5 or above), though the correlations are both relatively weak: cumulative expenditure per student explains 17% of the variation in the proportion of low performers and only 8% of the variation in the proportion of the best performers. However, these figures should be interpreted with caution given that they are influenced by a small group of countries with the highest proportion of low achievers on the PISA scale combined with the lowest cumulative spending per student between 6 and 15 years of age.

In summary, the results suggest that, while spending on education is a necessary prerequisite for high-quality education, it is not sufficient to achieve high levels of outcomes. Effective use of resources is necessary to achieve good outcomes. This is not surprising as countries with the same level of expenditure can allocate their spending to different aspects of their education system.

What factors account for performance differences among countries with similar levels of investments?

Many factors affect the relationship between spending per student and student performance. They include the organisation and management of schooling within the system (*e.g.* layers of management and distribution of decision making, geographic dispersion of the population), the organisation of the immediate learning environment of the students (*e.g.* class size, hours of instruction), the quality of the teaching workforce as well as characteristics of the students themselves, most notably their socio-economic background.

Countries with similar levels of spending on education may reach different performance levels and some results suggest that there are possibilities for reducing inputs while holding outputs constant, or, on the contrary, for maximising outputs while holding inputs constant. In *Education at a Glance 2007*, for instance, indicator B7 showed that among OECD countries, there is the potential for increasing learning outcomes by 22% while maintaining current levels of resources (output efficiency).

The level of expenditure is therefore not the sole factor to be taken into account when analysing the efficiency of the resources used in education. As a given level of expenditure may result from differences in education systems, analysis of differences among countries that have an impact on the level of expenditure may help to understand differences in performance.

A relationship exists between expenditure per student and structural and institutional factors that relate to the organisation of the school and curriculum. Expenditure can be broken down into the compensation of teachers and other expenditure (defined as all expenditure other than compensation of teachers). Compensation of teachers usually constitutes the largest part of expenditure on education. Then, compensation of teachers divided by the number of students (referred to here as "compensation cost per student" or "salary cost per student") is the main proportion of expenditure per student.

Compensation of teachers is a function of instruction time of students, teaching time of teachers, teachers' salaries and the number of teachers needed to teach students, which depends on class size (see Definitions and methodologies). As a consequence, differences among countries in these four factors may explain differences in the level of expenditure per student. In the same way, a given level of expenditure may result from a different combination of these factors; for example, teachers' salaries may be higher in some countries than in others or the amount of students' instruction time may differ.

B7

The first part of Table B7.2 presents the level of teacher compensation cost as well as the contribution of these four factors to the difference from the OECD average at the upper secondary level of education. Compensation cost per student varies from USD 570 in the Slovak Republic to about USD 9 850 in Luxembourg. However, as the level of salary, and as a consequence, the level of the compensation cost also depends on the country's relative wealth, the second part of the table presents compensation cost as a percentage of GDP per capita to exclude the effect of relative wealth on compensation cost. This table also shows the contribution (in percentage points) of the four factors to the difference from the OECD average.

Teacher compensation cost per student varies from 3.9% of GDP per capita in the Slovak Republic (less than half the OECD average rate of 10.9%) to over five times that rate in Portugal (20.9%, nearly twice the OECD average). The four factors influencing teacher compensation costs interact in contrasting ways between countries to reveal the different policy choices that governments make (Table B7.2 and Chart B7.1).

For example, in Korea and Luxembourg, compensation cost per student (as a percentage of GDP per capita) are both well above the OECD average (15.5% and 15.2% respectively) but these rates result from quite different combinations of instruction time, teaching time, class size and teachers' salaries (as a proportion of GDP per capita). In Korea, of the four factors, relatively large class size is the only one that acts to reduce compensation cost per student relative to the OECD average. Here, despite the size of this effect, it is more than counter-balanced by relatively high teacher salaries (as a proportion of GDP per capita), which together with above-average instruction time and below-average teaching time produce a compensation cost per student that is much higher than the OECD average. In contrast, higher than average compensation costs per student in Luxembourg are almost entirely attributable to very low class sizes, which outweigh the counter influences of slightly below average teacher salaries as a percentage of GDP per capita and above average instruction time (Table B7.2).

Alongside such contrasts, there are also striking similarities in the policy choices made by countries. In Australia, New Zealand and the United Kingdom, the compensation cost per student as a percentage of GDP per capita is close to the OECD average, which is the result in each of the countries of the balancing of two opposite effects: above-average teaching time, acting to reduce compensation cost per student relative to the OECD average and relatively low class sizes, which act to increase compensation cost per student relative to the OECD average.

In countries with the lowest compensation cost per student (as a percentage of GDP per capita) at the upper secondary level, low salary levels as a proportion of GDP per capita is usually the main driver. This is the case in Iceland, Ireland, Norway, Poland, the Slovak Republic and Sweden. The main exception to this pattern is Mexico where teacher salary costs relative to GDP per capita are well above the OECD average but this is more than compensated for by large class sizes.

In contrast, among countries with the highest levels of compensation cost per student (Portugal, Spain, Switzerland), no single factor dictates this position, but rather each of the four factors act to increase costs to varying degrees (Table B7.2 and Chart B7.1).

The fact that similar levels of expenditure between countries can mask a variety of contrasting policy choices made by countries goes some way to explaining why simplistic comparisons of student performance and expenditure levels fail to show strong correlations. It remains for further analysis to examine what influence these different policy choices actually have on quality and equity of learning outcomes.

Moreover, this analysis only considers the reasons for the variation in compensation costs per student (as a proportion of GDP per capita). However, as noted previously, compensation cost is only part of expenditure on education. To quantify the relative impact that each of the factors has on total expenditure per student (rather than on the compensation cost per student) requires a different approach. The regression analysis discussed in the next section attempts to do this by seeking to determine the factors that have a statistically significant impact on expenditure per student and to isolate their effects.

What are the main factors accounting for differences among countries in expenditure per student in upper secondary education?

Table B7.3 presents the results of the regression analysis. In addition to instruction time, teaching time, teachers' salaries and class size, more than ten other quantitative explanatory variables have been included to take into account characteristics related to the school context, the teacher context, the student context as well as general investment in education (for a list of these variables, see Definitions and methodologies). Variables considered for the regression analysis were those that seemed, *a priori*, to have a strong relationship with educational expenditure and which, in most cases, could be derived from data published in *Education at a Glance*. The final choice of variables to be included in the regression analysis was made on the basis of their correlation with expenditure per student. As expenditure per student (and the level of salaries) is closely correlated with GDP per capita (coefficient of 0.90), and to avoid multicolinearity, the dependent variable in the model is expenditure per student as a percentage of GDP per capita (rather than expenditure per student on its own). Similarly, statutory salaries have been divided by GDP per capita as well.

Testing alternative models concluded that a regression containing 10 out of the 13 variables (see Table B7.3 and Definitions and methodologies for excluded variables) resulted in the model with most explanatory power. In this case, 83% of the variation in expenditure per student as a proportion of GDP per capita is accounted for. However, only four of the variables have a significant impact on expenditure per student as a proportion of GDP per capita at the 5% threshold, with one other significant at the 10% threshold.

In terms of general investment in education, two variables are significantly linked to expenditure per student. As expected, other things being equal, the proportion of GDP devoted to education is positively linked to expenditure per student as a proportion of GDP. Moreover, the proportion of educational expenditure from private sources is also positively linked to expenditure per student. Thus public and private sources of funds are complementary sources of funds, as an increase of private funds goes with an increase in expenditure per student.

In terms of the school context, only the student-teacher ratio has a significant relationship with expenditure per student as a proportion of GDP per capita. As expected, the relationship is negative: other things being equal, an increase in the number of students per teacher should lead to a decrease in the number of teachers necessary to teach all students, and this should then

B7

result in a decrease in expenditure per student. Another way to vary the number of teachers necessary for a given population of students would be to change the number of teaching hours for teachers and/or the number of hours of instruction to students. However, this analysis does not show that these factors have a significant relationship with expenditure per student. This may be because the relationship is investigated at national level whereas changes in the annual number of teaching hours may have an impact (other things being equal) on the number of teachers needed for teaching at school or local level.

In terms of the teacher context, only statutory salaries as a proportion of GDP per capita are significantly linked to expenditure per student as a proportion of GDP per capita. As expected the relationship is positive.

In terms of the student context, no factor seems to be statistically significantly linked to expenditure per student as a proportion of GDP per capita.

This regression analysis (as well as the analysis of the contribution of instruction time, teaching time, class size and teachers' salary on compensation cost per student) shows the complex relationship between the level of expenditure per student and factors that may have an impact on the level of expenditure. The complexity of the relationship may also explain the lack of a direct relationship between the level of expenditure and the level of performance, as each of the factors that explains the level of expenditure may affect performance. Nevertheless, the different combinations of the characteristics of the education system appear to be as important as the level of expenditure for analysing their effect on students' performance. Therefore, a complementary analysis seeks to distinguish between different combinations of characteristics of the education system in OECD countries.

What are the main profiles of countries in upper secondary education?

For this purpose, Chart B7.3 presents clusters of countries according to their similarities at the upper secondary level of education. As shown above, countries' performance and more generally countries' outcomes are not necessarily linked to expenditure per student. Thus, countries with similar investments in education can have very different education systems. However, the question is whether countries with similarities in their education system have similar level of outcomes. To answer this question, *Education at a Glance* has many indicators that rank and compare countries according to their economic and financial, student, system level, school or teacher contexts. Countries are grouped here into six profiles or clusters, based on their similarities relative to the 14 variables that represent the main indicators for upper secondary education published in *Education at a Glance 2007*. The distribution of these clusters is based on four dimensions:

• **Student context**: These variables include the percentage of students who repeated at least one grade before the age of 15, the instruction time between 12 and 14 years of age, the percentage of student enrolled in vocational programmes in upper secondary education, and the enrolment rates at 16 years of age.

• **Teacher context**: These variables include the ratio of statutory salary after 15 years of experience relative to GDP per capita, annual variation in salary from starting to top statutory salary scale, proportion of teachers aged 50 or more and instruction time in upper secondary education.

- **General investment in education**: These variables include expenditure per student as a percentage of GDP per capita, educational expenditure as a percentage of GDP, and the proportion of private expenditure in upper secondary education.

- **School context**: These variables include the proportion of 5-to-25-year-olds in the population, the ratio of students to teaching staff, the proportion of expenditure devoted to other than compensation of teachers in upper secondary education.

Six main country profiles can be defined for the 25 OECD countries for which data on the 14 variables are available.

Cluster 1 includes Australia, Ireland, the Netherlands, New Zealand, Poland and the United States. They have similar patterns in terms of teacher and school contexts. In these countries teaching time is above the OECD average and the ratio of student to teaching staff is also generally above the OECD average. However, whereas the level of teachers' salaries differs markedly among these countries, teachers' salaries have large increases between starting and top salaries compared to the OECD average which reward over time the high level of teaching time compared to the OECD average. All of these countries except New Zealand have both enrolment rates at 16 years of age well above the OECD average and expenditure on upper secondary education as a percentage of GDP below the OECD average. Other factors vary and have less influence on their grouping.

Cluster 2 includes all Nordic countries (Denmark, Finland, Iceland, Norway, and Sweden) and two eastern European countries (the Czech Republic and the Slovak Republic). They have moderate figures on general investment in education, school, student and teacher contexts. The education systems are globally less demanding in these countries at this level of education for all the actors of education (*i.e.* government, students and teachers). Thus, educational expenditure as a proportion of GDP is below or at the OECD average, educational expenditure relies less than the average on private funds, students usually receive fewer instruction hours than the average and teaching time and salaries as a percentage of GDP per capita are also below the OECD average. In these countries, few or no students have repeated at least one grade before the age of 15.

Cluster 3 includes Austria, France, Hungary and Italy. This group is mainly influenced by student and teacher contexts and are among the countries with the highest number of hours of instruction (more than 1 000 hours per year in all against an average of 959). More than 10% of pupils have repeated at least one grade before the age of 15. Moreover, net teaching time is well below the OECD average, so that the ratio of instruction relative to teaching time is well above the OECD average and the students to teaching staff ratios are below the OECD average. Teachers' salaries are also below the OECD average.

Cluster 4 includes Portugal and Luxembourg. Like the countries in cluster 3, they are mainly influenced by student and teacher contexts but have relatively low instruction time and a small proportion of 16-year-olds enrolled in education. Other similarities with cluster 3 are a relatively low teaching hours combined with a high level of repeaters. They have quite a young teacher population relative to the OECD average. They spend 1% or less of their GDP on educational expenditure in upper secondary education, whereas cluster 3 countries spend proportionally more on education (at least 1.2% of their GDP).

Chart B7.3. Groupings of countries according to their similarities/dissimilarities, at the upper secondary level of education (2004, 2005)

Cluster analysis of 25 countries and 14 variables
retated to general investment in education, school, student and teacher contexts

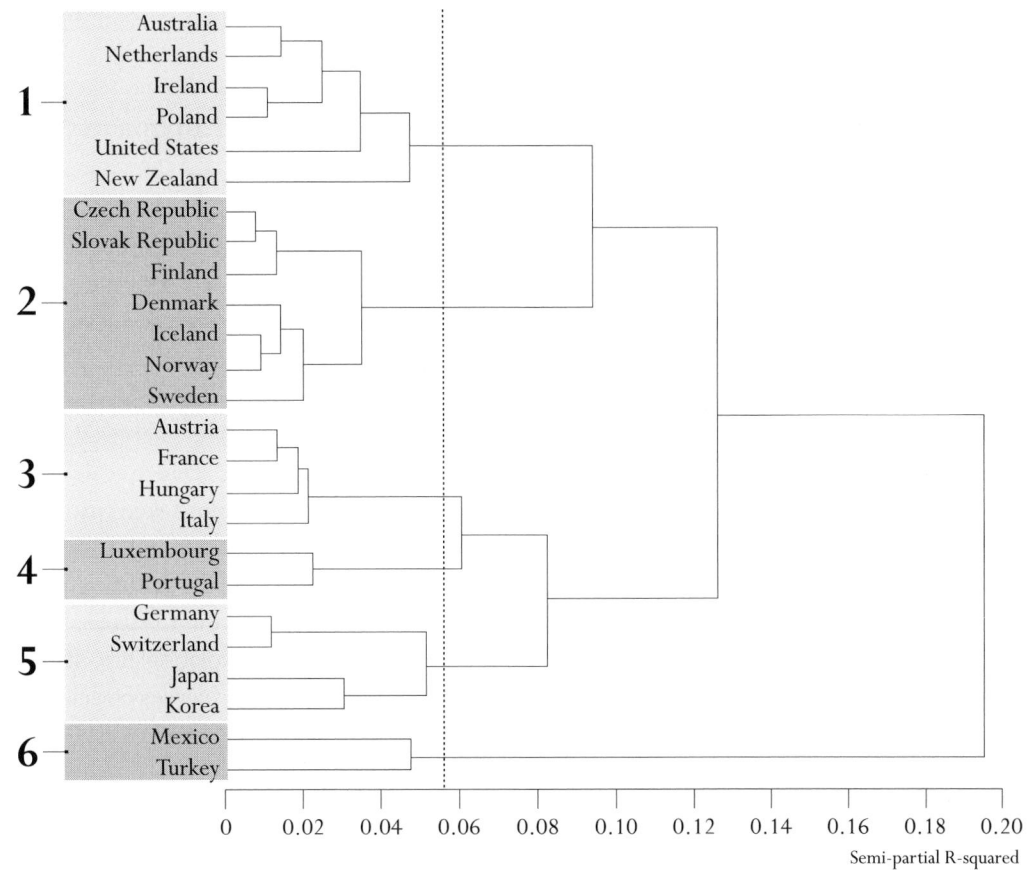

Semi-partial R-squared

Source: OECD. See Annex 3 for notes (*www.oecd.org/edu/eag2008*).
StatLink ᴍ⫯ᴚᴸ http://dx.doi.org/10.1787/402072442032

Countries in Cluster 5 (Germany, Japan, Korea and Switzerland) have similar patterns in terms of general investment in education and teacher context. They have the highest levels of expenditure per student as a proportion of GDP per capita (from 35 to 44% of GDP per capita except in Japan, which has 27%, at the OECD average), and among the largest proportions of private expenditure in OECD countries (from 24% in Japan and 35% in Korea, mainly because of tuition fees paid by households, to more than 36% in Switzerland and Germany, mainly because of their dual systems). This last characteristic, together with teachers' salaries as a proportion of GDP per capita well above average, may explain the high level of expenditure per student in upper secondary education. Nevertheless, Japan and Korea differ from Germany and Switzerland in terms of the proportion of students enrolled in vocational programmes (less than 30% versus more than 60%), the proportion of teachers more than 50 years old (28% or less versus 35% or more) and teaching time (550 hours or less versus 670 or more).

Countries in Cluster 6 (Mexico and Turkey) differ from others especially in terms of school context and financial investment in education. Compared to other countries, a large proportion of their population is between 5 and 25 years old (about 40% or above) and they have the highest ratios of students to teaching staff (with Finland) among OECD countries. They have low economic resources for meeting educational needs and the lowest proportion of GDP devoted to education (0.9% or less). In spite of this, teachers' salaries as a proportion of GDP per capita in upper secondary education in Turkey (in lower secondary for Mexico) are among the highest in the OECD countries (over twice the level of GDP per capita).

Can we identify a relation between secondary profiles and PISA performance?

Grouping countries by their main features at the upper secondary level of education can provide insight into the relationship between the organisation of the education system at upper secondary level and performance on the PISA science scale. However, the cluster analysis tends to show that similar education systems can have quite different outcomes. Three out of the six clusters presented show this. In cluster 3, Finland, the Czech Republic and to a lesser extent Sweden perform well above the OECD average on the PISA science scale whereas Denmark, Iceland, Norway and the Slovak Republic do not. Similarly, Australia (cluster 6) and Austria (cluster 4) perform well above the OECD average on the PISA science scale whereas the United States (cluster 6) and Italy (cluster 3) at 489 and 475, respectively, on the science scale perform significantly below the OECD average. This indicates that other factors not taken into account in this classification have better explanatory value as regards the performance of 15-year-olds. Among these, the socio-economic context, the quality of the teachers, the teaching methods and the content of the curriculum may affect outcomes. Taking into account features at lower secondary level of education could also give some more insight into this relationship. Moreover, this analysis of the relationship between clusters and student performance focuses on science, the results may be different for a similar analysis of another field of study.

Definitions and methodologies

Table B7.2 shows the compensation cost of teachers. The compensation of teachers divided by the number of students or "the compensation cost per student" (CCS) is estimated through:

$$CCS = SAL \times instT \times \frac{1}{teachT} \times \frac{1}{ClassSize} = \frac{SAL}{Ratiostud/teacher}$$

SAL: teachers' salaries (estimated by statutory salary after 15 years of experience).
instT: instruction time of students (estimated as the annual number of instruction time for students).
teachT: teaching time of teachers (estimated as the annual number of teaching hours for teachers).
ClassSize: a proxy for class size.
Ratiostud/teacher: the ratio of students to teaching staff.

With the exception of class size (which was not computed at upper secondary level, as class sizes are difficult to define and compare as students may attend several classes depending on the subject area), values for the different variables can be obtained from the indicators published in chapter D of *Education at a Glance 2007*. However, for the purpose of the analysis, a "theoretical" class size or proxy class size is estimated based on the ratio of students to teaching staff and the number of teaching hours and instruction hours. This should be interpreted with caution as a proxy.

Further details on the analysis of these factors are available in Annex 3.

For the regression analysis shown in Table B7.3, a multilinear regression analysis was carried out on expenditure per student as a percentage of GDP/capita and 13 explanatory variables related to general, school, teacher and student contexts, at the upper secondary level of education. The following variables were used:

• From general investment in education: GDP per capita, educational expenditure as a percentage of GDP, proportion of educational expenditure from private sources.

• From school context: the ratio of students to teaching staff, the proportion of 5-to-25-year-olds in the population, the proportion of expenditure for other than compensation of teachers.

• From teacher context: teachers' statutory salaries after 15 years of experience (or ratio of statutory salary to GDP per capita), proportion of teachers aged 50 or more, annual variation of salary from the beginning of the statutory salary scale to the top of the statutory salary scale; teaching time.

• From student context: instruction time, enrolment rate at 16, proportion of repeaters among 15-year-olds, proportion of students enrolled in prevocational/vocational programmes.

The enrolment rate for 16-year-olds students, the proportion of students enrolled in prevocational/vocational programmes, and the proportion of repeaters among 15 year-olds have been excluded from the final model because the coefficient of the regression was of better quality without these three variables.

In most cases, the values for the variables are derived from *Education at a Glance 2007* and refer to the school year 2004/05 and the calendar year 2004 for indicators related to finance. However, in order to compensate for missing values for some variables, some data have been estimated on the basis of data published in previous editions of *Education at a Glance*. When there was no possibility for estimating and no knowledge of a proxy figure, the missing values have been replaced by the average for all OECD countries.

Among the 30 OECD countries, Canada was excluded from the analysis because of the amount of missing data for the reference year. Four other countries (Belgium, Greece, Spain and the United Kingdom) were also excluded as data on expenditure per student were not available separately for upper secondary level of education (but only for total secondary level of education) (see Annex 3).

A cluster analysis was performed for Chart B7.3 to determine whether countries were similar enough to fall into groups or clusters showing general investment in education and student, school and teacher contexts in upper secondary education. It used Ward's method which uses an analysis of variance approach to evaluate the distance between clusters. This method attempts to minimise the sum of the squares of any two hypothetical clusters that can be formed at each step. Cluster analysis was also calculated using the four other main agglomerative methods: the single linkage (nearest neighbour approach); the complete linkage (furthest neighbour); the average linkage; and the Centroid method. Results from the Ward method were most meaningful. The semi-partial r-square (or within-class variance) measures the loss of homogeneity of joined clusters: the lower the semi-partial r-square, the higher is the homogeneity within clusters.

B7

Table B7.1.

Economic and social indicators and the relationship with performance in science (2005, 2006)

	PISA performance at 15-year-olds (2006)			Economic and social indicators			
	Science performance	Percentage of students at level of proficiency 1 or below on the science scale (below 409.54 score points)	Percentage of students at level of proficiency 5 or above on the science scale (above 633.33 score points)	GDP per capita (2005, in USD)	Cumulative expenditure per student aged between 6 and 15 (2005, in USD)	Percentage of the population aged 35 to 44 that has attained at least upper secondary education (2006)	Percentage of the variance in PISA performance in science explained by the PISA index of economic, social and cultural status[1] (2006)
OECD countries							
Australia	527	13	15	33 983	65 737	66	11.3
Austria	511	16	10	34 107	91 110	84	15.4
Belgium	510	17	10	32 077	70 813	72	19.4
Canada	534	10	14	32 929	78 367	88	8.2
Czech Republic	513	16	12	20 280	38 344	93	15.6
Denmark	496	18	7	33 626	82 219	83	14.1
Finland	563	4	21	30 468	64 363	87	8.3
France	495	21	8	29 644	68 658	71	21.2
Germany	516	15	12	30 496	57 254	85	19.0
Greece	473	24	3	25 472	64 564	65	15.0
Hungary	504	15	7	17 014	41 740	81	21.4
Iceland	491	21	6	35 571	91 734	67	6.7
Ireland	508	16	9	38 061	60 564	70	12.7
Italy	475	25	5	27 750	70 126	54	10.0
Japan	531	12	15	30 290	71 517	m	7.4
Korea	522	11	10	21 342	52 893	88	8.1
Luxembourg	486	22	6	69 984	159 854	68	21.7
Mexico	410	51	0	11 299	19 846	23	16.8
Netherlands	525	13	13	34 724	68 379	76	16.7
New Zealand	530	14	18	24 882	49 344	82	16.4
Norway	487	21	6	47 620	92 068	78	8.3
Poland	498	17	7	13 573	32 913	50	14.5
Portugal	474	24	3	19 967	55 272	26	16.6
Slovak Republic	488	20	6	15 881	26 400	92	19.2
Spain	488	20	5	27 270	61 860	54	13.9
Sweden	503	16	8	32 770	74 327	90	10.6
Switzerland	512	16	10	35 500	96 249	85	15.7
Turkey	424	47	1	7 786	m	25	16.5
United Kingdom	515	17	14	31 580	66 833	67	13.9
United States	489	24	9	41 674	95 600	88	17.9
OECD average	*500*	*19*	*9*	*29 587*	*67 895*	*71*	*14.4*
Partner countries							
Brazil	390	61	1	8 586	12 442	32	17
Chile	438	40	2	12 655	20 254	52	23
Estonia	531	8	11	16 660	m	95	9
Israel	454	36	5	21 474	50 175	82	11
Russian Federation	479	22	4	10 846	11 132	95	8
Slovenia	519	14	13	23 043	77 512	84	17
Correlation (R) between cumulative expenditure and other factors:	*0.39*	*-0.41*	*0.28*	*0.94*	*1.00*	*0.26*	*-0.05*

1. This index is derived from the occupational status of the father or the mother (whichever is higher), the level of education of the father or the mother (whichever is higher) and from the index of home possessions. For more details see PISA website (*www.pisa.oecd.org*).

Source: OECD. See Annex 3 for notes (*www.oecd.org/edu/eag2008*).

Please refer to the Reader's Guide for information concerning the symbols replacing missing data.

StatLink ⟶ http://dx.doi.org/10.1787/402072442032

Table B7.2.
Contribution of various factors to salary cost per student at the upper secondary level of education (2004)

	Salary cost per student	Difference from OECD average	Contribution (in USD) of school factors to salary cost per student			
			Contribution to the difference from the OECD average			
			Salary	Instruction time	1/teaching time	1/class size
Australia	3 668	596	389	209	-646	644
Austria	3 502	430	-13	291	425	-272
Belgium	5 202	2 129	1 070	99	-6	966
Czech Republic	1 936	-1 136	-1 152	22	205	-212
Denmark	3 530	458	587	-448	593	-274
Finland	2 411	-661	246	-315	550	-1 141
France	3 284	212	-497	565	221	-77
Germany	3 938	865	1 154	-242	-239	192
Greece	3 592	520	-790	1 035	611	-337
Hungary	1 600	-1 473	-1 621	336	451	-639
Iceland	2 963	-109	-657	-241	545	245
Ireland	3 013	-59	498	-232	-283	-42
Italy	2 971	-101	-577	323	328	-175
Japan	3 695	623	650	-351	1 539	-1 214
Korea	3 222	149	842	192	616	-1 501
Luxembourg	9 848	6 776	4 712	-1 601	262	3 403
Mexico	827	-2 245	-1 063	292	-421	-1 053
Netherlands	3 786	714	1 519	364	-396	-774
New Zealand	2 869	-203	-221	-35	-1 059	1 113
Norway	3 926	854	-173	-412	860	579
Poland	797	-2 275	-2 285	-161	-21	191
Portugal	4 038	965	-747	-351	954	1 109
Slovak Republic	570	-2 502	-2 323	-130	119	-167
Spain	5 247	2 175	288	75	-139	1 951
Sweden	2 430	-642	-425	-730	-684	1 197
Switzerland	6 690	3 618	2 643	-56	-30	1 061
Turkey	1 223	-1 849	-1 394	-6	357	-806
United Kingdom	3 722	649	343	-40	-999	1 346
United States	2 562	-510	97	56	-1 365	702

Source: OECD. Data from *Education at a Glance 2007* (*www.oecd.org/edu/eag2007*). See Annex 3 for notes (*www.oecd.org/edu/eag2008*).
StatLink ᐧᒥᔕᐧ http://dx.doi.org/10.1787/402072442032

B7

Table B7.2. *(continued)*
Contribution of various factors to salary cost per student at the upper secondary level of education (2004)

	Salary cost per student as % of GDP/capita	Difference from OECD average	Contribution (in percentage points) of school factors to salary cost per student as a percentage of GDP per capita			
			Contribution to the difference from the OECD average			
			Salary as % of GDP per capita	Instruction time	1/teaching time	1/class size
Australia	11.9	1.0	0.3	0.7	-2.2	2.2
Austria	10.5	-0.3	-1.8	1.0	1.4	-0.9
Belgium	16.3	5.4	1.9	0.3	0.0	3.2
Czech Republic	10.0	-0.9	-0.9	0.1	0.8	-0.9
Denmark	10.9	0.1	0.5	-1.5	2.0	-0.9
Finland	8.1	-2.8	0.3	-1.1	1.9	-3.9
France	11.3	0.5	-2.0	2.0	0.8	-0.3
Germany	13.2	2.3	3.3	-0.8	-0.8	0.7
Greece	13.0	2.1	-2.6	3.7	2.2	-1.2
Hungary	9.7	-1.2	-1.8	1.5	2.0	-2.8
Iceland	8.9	-1.9	-3.8	-0.8	1.8	0.8
Ireland	8.2	-2.6	-0.9	-0.7	-0.9	-0.1
Italy	10.7	-0.1	-1.8	1.2	1.2	-0.6
Japan	12.8	1.9	2.0	-1.2	5.4	-4.2
Korea	15.5	4.7	7.7	0.8	2.6	-6.4
Luxembourg	15.2	4.3	-0.3	-3.3	0.6	7.4
Mexico	8.2	-2.7	4.1	1.6	-2.3	-6.0
Netherlands	11.3	0.4	3.0	1.2	-1.3	-2.5
New Zealand	11.6	0.7	0.7	-0.1	-4.0	4.2
Norway	9.4	-1.5	-4.5	-1.2	2.6	1.7
Poland	6.1	-4.8	-4.8	-0.7	-0.1	0.8
Portugal	20.9	10.0	2.7	-1.5	4.1	4.8
Slovak Republic	3.9	-7.0	-6.2	-0.5	0.5	-0.7
Spain	20.2	9.3	2.3	0.3	-0.5	7.2
Sweden	7.8	-3.0	-2.3	-2.5	-2.3	4.1
Switzerland	19.3	8.4	5.4	-0.2	-0.1	3.3
Turkey	17.0	6.1	9.5	0.0	2.4	-5.7
United Kingdom	11.7	0.9	-0.2	-0.1	-3.3	4.5
United States	6.5	-4.4	-2.6	0.2	-4.1	2.1

Source: OECD. Data from *Education at a Glance 2007* (*www.oecd.org/edu/eag2007*). See Annex 3 for notes (*www.oecd.org/edu/eag2008*).
StatLink ᏔᎥᏚᏞ http://dx.doi.org/10.1787/402072442032

Table B7.3.
**Relationships between expenditure per student as a percentage of GDP per capita
and 10 explanatory variables, at the upper secondary level of education (2005, 25 OECD countries)**

	Variables	Coefficient	Standard error	t value	pr > t
General context	**Expenditure as % of GDP**	9.33126	2.71578	**3.43594**	0.00402
	5-to-25 year-olds in population	-0.15898	0.16764	-0.94830	0.35906
	Proportion of private expenditure	0.17596	0.06359	**2.76701**	0.01513
School context	Instruction time	-0.00005	0.00636	-0.00788	0.99383
	Teaching time	0.00681	0.00520	1.30921	0.21154
	Ratio student/teachers	-0.57713	0.28026	**-2.05927**	0.05857
	Expenditure other than teachers' compensation	-0.17095	0.10712	-1.59588	0.13283
Teacher context	**Salaries as % of GDP/capita**	4.55855	1.78904	**2.54804**	0.02321
	Annual variation in salaries	-0.35682	0.39721	-0.89831	0.38421
Student context	Repeaters	0.01579	0.06579	0.24003	0.81379
	Intercept	21.38996	8.16527	**2.61963**	0.02019
	$R^2 = 0.8329$ (F = 6.978; Pr > F = 0.00064)				

Note: Bold figures relate to variables that are statistically significant at a 5% or 10% threshold.
Source: OECD. See Annex 3 for notes (*www.oecd.org/edu/eag2008*).
StatLink ᴹˢᴸ http://dx.doi.org/10.1787/402072442032

Access to Education, Participation and Progression

HOW PREVALENT ARE VOCATIONAL PROGRAMMES?

This indicator shows the participation of students in vocational education and training (VET) at the upper secondary level and the distribution of upper secondary and post-secondary non-tertiary vocational graduates across fields of education. It compares the levels of educational expenditure per student for general programmes and VET at the upper secondary level. It also compares educational outcomes of 15-year-old students enrolled in general and in vocational education.

Key results

Chart C1.1. **Difference in science performance associated with students' programme orientation (2006)**

■ ▨ Differences in science performance between general programme students and pre-vocational and vocational programme students
Statistically significant differences are marked in darker tone

▨ ▨ Differences in science performance between general programme students and pre-vocational and vocational programme students, with accounting for the economic, social and cultural status of students (ESCS)
Statistically significant differences are marked in darker tone

PISA 2006 shows that 15-year-olds in pre-vocational and vocational programmes have statistically significant lower performance in science compared to students enrolled in general programmes in 12 out of the 14 OECD countries for which data are available. On average, 15-year-olds enrolled in general programmes score 35 points higher and after adjusting for socio-economic factors a difference of 24 points still remains.

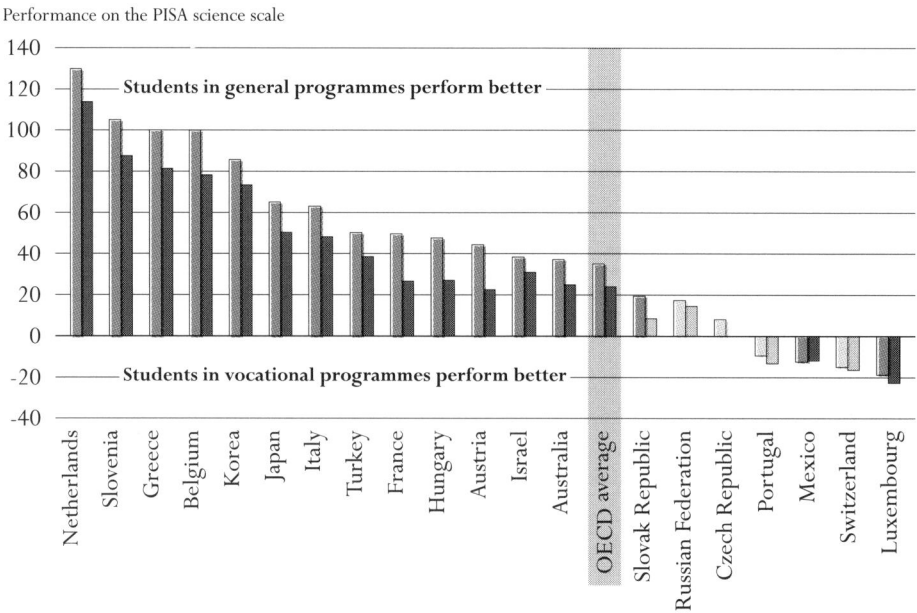

Performance on the PISA science scale

Note: This chart shows data for countries with more than 3% of students in the aggregated category of pre-vocational and vocational programmes.
Countries are ranked in descending order of performance advantage for students enrolled in general programmes versus students enrolled in vocational programmes.
Source: OECD PISA 2006 database. Table C1.4. See Annex 3 for notes (*www.oecd.org/edu/eag2008*).
StatLink ▨▨▨ http://dx.doi.org/10.1787/402134482176

Other highlights of this indicator

■ In 13 out of 28 OECD countries and the partner country Slovenia, most upper secondary students are enrolled in pre-vocational and vocational programmes. In most OECD countries, a significant proportion of upper secondary vocational education is school-based.

■ In OECD countries with available data, vocational qualification is concentrated in engineering, manufacturing and construction at both the upper secondary (34%) and post-secondary non-tertiary (22%) levels.

■ The 14 OECD countries for which data are available spend, on average, USD 925 more per student on upper secondary vocational programmes than on general programmes.

C1

Policy context

A range of factors – including better employment outcomes for the more educated – has strengthened the incentive for young people to remain in school beyond the end of compulsory education and to graduate from upper secondary education. The continued rise in participation in upper secondary education means that countries have to cater to a more diverse student population at that level.

Countries have taken various approaches to meeting these demands. Some have comprehensive lower secondary systems with non-selective general/academic programmes so that all students have similar opportunities for learning; others provide more distinctive education programmes (academic, pre-vocational and/or vocational programmes) in both lower and upper secondary education. Vocational programmes differ from academic ones not only in terms of their curricula but also because they generally prepare students for specific types of occupations and, in some cases, for direct entry into the labour market.

Countries must continuously review their educational systems to ensure that graduates meet the changing demands of the labour market, and they must also anticipate future requirements. VET-related issues with which countries are wrestling include increasing the supply of apprentices, dealing with specific skill shortages in the work force, enhancing the status of VET and upgrading its quality.

Today VET encompasses both formal education – secondary programmes (pre-vocational and vocational), post-secondary programmes and even university programmes – and non-formal job-related continuing education and training (see Indicator C5). This indicator focuses on formal education (pre-vocational and vocational programmes) at the upper secondary and post-secondary non-tertiary level.

Evidence and explanations

Participation in upper secondary vocational education

In most OECD countries, students do not follow a uniform curriculum at the upper secondary level. Programmes at this level can be subdivided into three categories based on the degree to which they are oriented towards a specific class of occupations or trades and lead to a qualification that is relevant to the labour market:

• General education programmes are not designed explicitly to prepare participants for specific occupations or trades, or for entry into further vocational or technical education programmes (less than 25% of programme content is vocational or technical).

• Pre-vocational or pre-technical education programmes are mainly designed to introduce participants to the world of work and to prepare them for entry into further vocational or technical education programmes. Successful completion of such programmes does not lead to a vocational or technical qualification that is directly relevant to the labour market. (At least 25% of programme content is vocational or technical.)

• Vocational or technical education programmes prepare participants for direct entry into specific occupations without further training. Successful completion of such programmes leads to a vocational or technical qualification that is relevant to the labour market.

C1

Vocational and pre-vocational programmes are further divided into two categories (school-based and combined school- and work-based programmes) on the basis of the amount of training provided in school as opposed to the work place:

• In school-based programmes, instruction takes place (either partially or exclusively) in educational institutions. They include special training centres run by public or private authorities or enterprise-based special training centres if these qualify as educational institutions. These programmes can have an on-the-job training component involving some practical work experience at the workplace. Programmes are classified as school-based if at least 75% of the programme curriculum is presented in the school environment; this may include distance education.

• In combined school- and work-based programmes, less than 75% of the curriculum is presented in the school environment or through distance education. These programmes can be organised in conjunction with educational authorities or educational institutions and include apprenticeship programmes, that involve concurrent school-based and work-based training, and programmes that involve alternating periods of attendance at educational institutions and of participation in work-based training (sometimes referred to as "sandwich" programmes).

The degree to which a programme has a vocational or general orientation does not necessarily determine whether participants have access to tertiary education. In several OECD countries, vocationally oriented programmes are designed to prepare students for further study at the tertiary level, and in some countries general programmes do not always provide direct access to further education.

For 13 OECD countries and the partner country Slovenia for which data is available, the majority of upper secondary students pursue pre-vocational and vocational programmes. In most OECD countries with dual-system apprenticeship programmes (Austria, Germany, Luxembourg, the Netherlands and Switzerland) and in Australia, Belgium, the Czech Republic, Finland, Italy, Norway, the Slovak Republic and Sweden, and the partner country Slovenia, 55% or more of upper secondary students are enrolled in pre-vocational or vocational programmes. However, in Canada, Greece, Hungary, Iceland, Ireland, Japan, Korea, Mexico, Portugal and Turkey, and the partner countries Brazil, Chile, Estonia and Israel, 60% or more of upper secondary students are enrolled in general programmes even though pre-vocational and/or vocational programmes are offered (Table C1.1).

In many OECD countries, upper secondary vocational education is school-based. In Austria, the Czech Republic, Iceland and the Slovak Republic, however, about 40% of the students participate in vocational programmes which combine school- and work-based elements. In Denmark, Germany, Hungary, Ireland and Switzerland and the partner country Estonia, around 75% or more of students are enrolled in vocational programmes which have both school-based and work-based elements.

Upper secondary students in many education systems can enrol in vocational programmes, but some OECD countries delay vocational training until after graduation from upper secondary education. While vocational programmes are offered as advanced upper secondary programmes in some OECD countries (*e.g.* Austria, Hungary and Spain), similar programmes are offered as post-secondary education in others (*e.g.* Canada and the United States).

Apprenticeship programmes

Table C1.1 includes enrolments in apprenticeship programmes that are a recognised part of the education system in countries. This section provides information on the typical characteristics of these programmes and other work-based learning programmes.

In most OECD countries (Australia, Austria, Belgium, the Czech Republic, Denmark, Finland, France, Germany, Hungary, Ireland, Luxembourg, Mexico, the Netherlands, New Zealand, Norway, Poland, the Slovak Republic, Switzerland, Turkey and the United Kingdom) and partner countries (Israel, the Russian Federation and Slovenia), some form of apprenticeship system exists. In some countries (*e.g.* Austria, Germany and Hungary), apprenticeship contracts are established between a student (not the vocational training school) and a company. For the most part, the majority of countries have combined school and work-based apprenticeship programmes. In contrast, apprenticeship systems do not exist in Japan, Korea, Spain and Sweden. In the United States, there are apprenticeship programmes, but they are not part of the formal education system.

The minimum entry requirement for apprenticeship programmes varies but is typically the completion of lower secondary education (Canada, the Czech Republic, Denmark, Finland, France, Germany, Ireland, Luxembourg, Mexico, the Netherlands, Norway, Poland and the Slovak Republic, and the partner countries Israel and Slovenia). In Austria, the minimum entry requirement is the completion of nine years of compulsory schooling. In Australia, Belgium, the Netherlands, the United Kingdom and the United States, entry is governed (in full or in part) by age criteria, while in New Zealand, participants must be employed. In Turkey, the minimum requirement is completion of primary education, but entrants must be at least 14 years old and have a contract with a workplace. The Russian Federation has no legal framework for entry into apprenticeship programmes.

In some countries the duration of apprenticeship programmes is standardised; it ranges from one to four years in Canada, the Czech Republic, Denmark, France, Germany, Ireland, New Zealand, Norway, Poland and the United Kingdom, and the partner countries Israel and Slovenia. In other countries (*e.g.* Austria and Belgium), it varies according to subject, specific qualification sought, previous knowledge and/or experience.

In most countries, the successful completion of an apprenticeship programme usually results in the awarding of an upper secondary or post-secondary qualification. In some countries, higher qualifications are possible (such as an advanced diploma in Australia).

Differences in graduation rates in general and vocational programmes

Although average graduation rates for general, pre-vocational and vocational programmes are similar at the upper secondary level (47% and 45%, respectively), graduation rates in general programmes exceed those in pre-vocational and vocational programmes in 15 of 27 OECD countries, and in 5 of 6 partner countries. The exceptions are Austria, Belgium, the Czech Republic, Finland, Germany, Italy, Luxembourg, the Netherlands, the Slovak Republic, Sweden and Switzerland, and the partner country Slovenia (Table A2.1).

Gender differences in vocational programmes

For all OECD countries and partner countries for which comparable data are available, there is no clear gender trend for pre-vocational and vocational upper secondary graduation rates.

Although 47% of males and 44% of females graduate from vocational programmes in OECD countries, female graduates in such programmes outnumber males in Australia, Belgium, Denmark, Finland, Ireland, the Netherlands and Spain and the partner country Brazil (Table A2.1 and Chart C1.2).

C1

Chart C1.2. **Upper secondary graduation rates for pre-vocational/vocational programmes, by gender (2006)**

Percentage of graduates to the population at the typical age of graduation

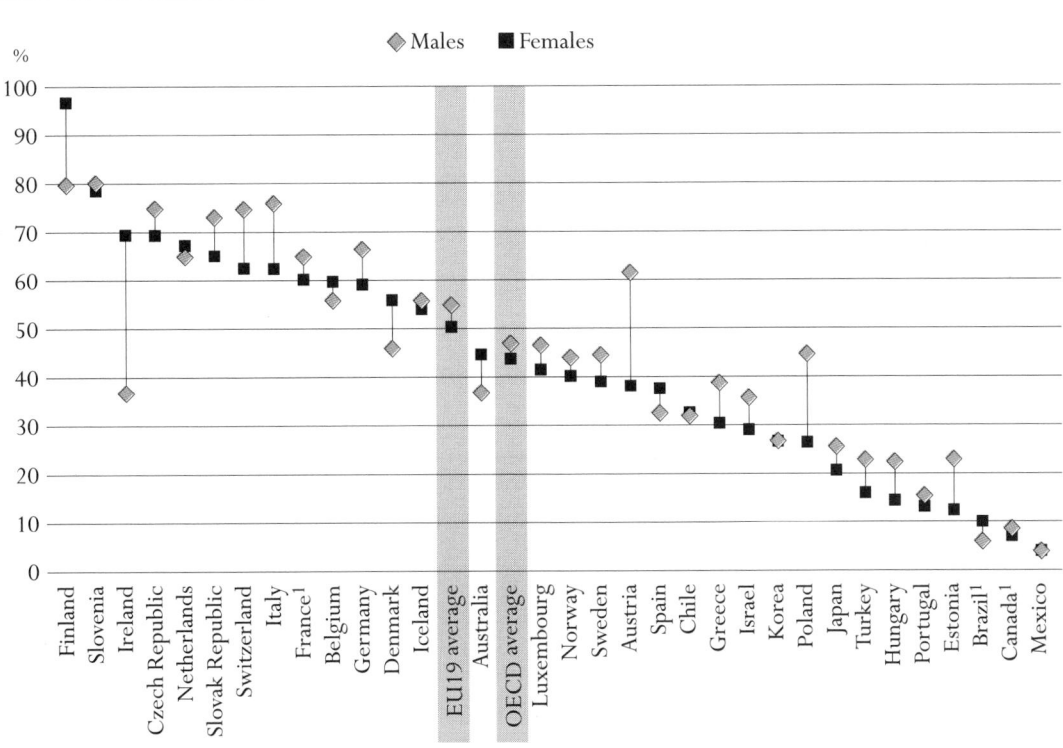

1. Year of reference 2005.
Countries are ranked in descending order of upper secondary graduation rates for pre-vocational/vocational programmes for females.
Source: OECD. Table A2.1. See Annex 3 for notes (*www.oecd.org/edu/eag2008*).
StatLink ⧉ http://dx.doi.org/10.1787/402134482176

Vocational graduates by field of education

Changing opportunities in the job market, differences in earnings among occupations and sectors, and government policies (such as those that attempt to align VET provision with labour market requirements) affect students' choice of fields of education. In turn, the relative popularity of various fields affects the supply of new graduates and the demand for courses and teaching staff (VET teachers and trainers). The distribution of upper secondary and post-secondary non-tertiary vocational graduates across fields sheds light on the relative importance of different fields from country to country. This knowledge helps policy makers ensure that the demand for qualified skilled VET trainers (who are also adequately prepared for the teaching part of their jobs) is met.

They must also ensure that policies are in place to ensure that VET teachers, trainers and training institutions continue to develop and update their skills and equipment to meet current and future labour market needs. Efficient and effective delivery of VET is necessary to raise the status of VET and can help minimise dropout.

For the 21 OECD countries and 2 partner countries for which data are available, the vast majority of graduates from upper secondary vocational programmes have occupationally oriented qualifications (Table C1.2). More than 78% of qualifications are in four categories: engineering, manufacturing and construction (34%), social sciences, business and law (21%), services (13%) and health and welfare (11%). Engineering, manufacturing and construction lead in Belgium, the Czech Republic, Finland, France, Hungary, Iceland, Japan, Korea, Norway, Poland, the Slovak Republic, Spain, Sweden and Turkey and in the partner country Estonia. Social sciences, business and law lead in Australia, Luxembourg, Switzerland and the partner country Slovenia; health and welfare lead in the Netherlands; and mathematics and statistics lead in Denmark. In Germany, both engineering and social science, business and law account for the most graduates.

The picture is similar at the post-secondary non-tertiary level. Engineering, manufacturing and construction account for the most graduates (22%), followed closely by social sciences, business and law (20%), services (19%), and health and welfare (13%) (Table C1.2). Engineering, manufacturing and construction lead in Ireland, Luxembourg and the Netherlands; social sciences, business and law in Australia, the Czech Republic, Finland, Germany, Hungary, Norway and Sweden and the partner country Slovenia; services in Denmark, Iceland, Poland and the Slovak Republic and in the partner country Estonia; and health and welfare in France. Computing takes the lead in Greece, Portugal and Switzerland and humanities and arts in New Zealand.

Differences in educational expenditure per student between general and vocational programmes

In most OECD countries, expenditure per student varies between general and vocational programmes. In the 14 OECD countries for which data are available, expenditure per student in upper secondary vocational programmes in 2005 was, on average, USD 925 higher than in general programmes (Table C1.3).

In countries with dual-system apprenticeship programmes at the upper secondary level (*e.g.* Austria, Germany, Luxembourg, the Netherlands and Switzerland) the difference between expenditure per student in general and in vocational programmes tends to be larger. For example, Germany and Switzerland spend USD 6 284 and USD 7 118 more per student, respectively, in vocational than in general programmes, with employers contributing a large part. This difference is smaller in Austria (USD 793). The Netherlands has higher expenditure per student in general programmes than in vocational programmes, while Luxembourg's expenditure per student is similar for both. Among the four other countries – Australia, the Czech Republic, Finland and the Slovak Republic – with 60% or more of upper secondary students enrolled in vocational programmes, the Czech Republic and Finland spend more per student enrolled in vocational programmes than in general programmes (Table C1.1 and Table C1.3).

C1

Learning outcomes from vocational education

Is there a difference in the performance of students enrolled in vocational versus general programmes? The analysis below is limited to student performance in science at age 15. Similar patterns were found for PISA 2006 performance in reading and mathematics, but those findings are not reported here in order to simplify the presentation and avoid repetition.

The PISA 2006 results on student performance in science at age 15 show that in OECD countries, students in pre-vocational and vocational programmes score on average 35 points below students in general programmes before socio-economic factors are taken into account (Table C1.4). The largest differences are observed in Belgium, Greece, Korea and the Netherlands. In the Netherlands, the performance of students in general programmes (565 score points) is significantly higher than the overall OECD average for all students (509 score points), while the performance of students in vocational programmes (434 score points) is lower than the overall OECD average. A similar pattern is found in Belgium, Italy and Korea and the partner country Slovenia. On the other hand, students enrolled in both general and pre-vocational/vocational programmes performed below the OECD average in Greece and Turkey and in the partner countries Chile, Israel and the Russian Federation. Luxembourg and Mexico are the only countries in which students enrolled in pre-vocational and vocational programmes have a statistically significant advantage (19 and 12 score points, respectively), although in Mexico, students enrolled in general and in pre-vocational and vocational programmes perform below the OECD average (406 and 418 score points, respectively).

Given the influence that socio-economic factors can have on student performance, it is important to examine differences in performance after adjusting for these factors. After adjusting for socio-economic factors, the performance difference in pre-vocational and vocational programmes is lowered by 11 score points, to remain at 24 score points on average across OECD countries. For 13 OECD countries, there is a statistically significant difference between performance levels of students in general programmes and in pre-vocational and vocational programmes, even after adjusting for socio-economic factors. In Luxembourg and Mexico, students enrolled in pre-vocational and vocational programmes still have a statistically significant advantage (23 and 12 score points, respectively). For the other countries, students enrolled in pre-vocational and vocational programmes have a disadvantage ranging from 23 score points in Austria to 114 score points in the Netherlands (Table C1.4 and Chart C1.1). Nevertheless, this weaker performance does not necessarily mean pre-vocational and vocational programmes have an adverse impact on such students' future careers. In The Netherlands, all 15 year old students are enrolled in either pre-vocational or general programmes. At the age of 16 at the earliest, students can be enrolled in vocational programmes.

In addition to job-related skills, today's VET programmes must also equip students with basic skills (literacy and numeracy) and general competencies (social and communication skills), as employers are increasingly emphasising those skills.

Definitions and methodologies

The student performance data are based on assessments administered as part of the Programme for International Student Assessment (PISA) undertaken by the OECD in 2006.

C1

Data on enrolments is for the school year 2005-2006 and data on finance refer to the financial year 2005 and both are based on the UOE data collection on educational systems administered annually by the OECD.

Data on apprenticeship programmes are based on a special survey carried out by the OECD in the autumn of 2006.

Further references

The following additional material relevant to this indicator is available on line at:
StatLink ᵐˢ⊑ http://dx.doi.org/10.1787/402134482176

- *Table C1.5. Differences in science performance between the different programme orientations (2006)*

- *Table C1.6. Performance of 15-year-old students on the mathematics, reading and science scales by programme orientation (2006)*

Table C1.1.
Upper secondary enrolment patterns (2006)
Enrolment in upper secondary programmes in public and private institutions by programme destination and programme orientation

C1

	Distribution of enrolment by programme destination			Distribution of enrolment by programme orientation			
	ISCED 3A	ISCED 3B	ISCED 3C	General	Pre-vocational	Vocational	Combined school and work-based
	(1)	(2)	(3)	(4)	(5)	(6)	(7)
OECD countries							
Australia	38.4	x(1)	61.6	38.4	a	61.6	m
Austria	44.1	46.7	9.2	22.1	6.2	71.8	33.0
Belgium	49.4	a	50.6	30.6	a	69.4	3.5
Canada[1]	94.6	a	5.4	94.6	x(6)	5.4	a
Czech Republic	71.5	0.4	28.1	20.7	0.1	79.2	34.8
Denmark	52.2	a	47.8	52.2	a	47.8	47.6
Finland	100.0	a	a	34.6	a	65.4	10.9
France	56.9	11.1	32.0	56.9	a	43.1	11.6
Germany	40.6	59.0	0.4	40.6	a	59.4	44.2
Greece	66.1	a	33.9	66.1	a	33.9	5.1
Hungary	77.2	a	22.8	76.3	10.7	12.9	12.9
Iceland	50.5	0.6	48.9	63.3	1.5	35.2	16.7
Ireland	72.0	a	28.0	66.6	31.0	2.4	2.4
Italy	80.6	2.9	16.5	39.5	35.6	24.9	a
Japan	75.4	0.9	23.7	75.4	0.9	23.7	a
Korea	72.2	a	27.8	72.2	a	27.8	a
Luxembourg	59.3	15.6	25.1	37.1	a	62.9	13.8
Mexico	90.2	a	9.8	90.2	a	9.8	m
Netherlands	62.8	a	37.2	32.5	a	67.5	18.3
New Zealand	m	m	m	m	m	m	m
Norway	40.0	a	60.0	40.0	a	60.0	13.9
Poland	88.1	a	11.9	56.0	a	44.0	6.3
Portugal	100.0	x(1)	x(1)	68.5	19.9	11.6	m
Slovak Republic	81.5	a	18.5	26.3	a	73.7	30.9
Spain	57.5	n	42.5	57.5	n	42.5	2.2
Sweden	94.6	n	5.4	44.9	0.9	54.2	n
Switzerland	30.7	63.4	5.9	35.8	n	64.2	57.8
Turkey[2]	100.0	a	m	63.7	a	36.3	n
United Kingdom[3]	77.2	x(1)	22.8	58.3	x(6)	41.7	m
United States	100.0	x(1)	x(1)	100.0	x(4)	x(4)	x(4)
OECD average	*69.8*	*8.0*	*26.0*	*53.8*	*4.1*	*44.0*	*15.2*
EU 19 average	*70.1*	*8.0*	*24.1*	*46.7*	*5.8*	*47.8*	*16.3*
Partner countries							
Brazil[1]	100.0	a	a	93.5	a	6.5	a
Chile	100.0	a	a	64.5	a	35.5	a
Estonia	100.0	a	n	69.1	a	30.9	30.9
Israel	95.8	a	4.2	65.6	a	34.4	4.2
Russian Federation	55.7	14.4	29.9	55.7	14.4	29.9	m
Slovenia	33.8	44.4	21.8	33.8	n	66.2	5.4

1. Year of reference 2005.
2. Excludes ISCED 3C.
3. Includes post-secondary, non-tertiary education.
Source: OECD. See Annex 3 for notes (*www.oecd.org/edu/eag2008*).
Please refer to the Reader's Guide for information concerning the symbols replacing missing data.
StatLink ⫘⫘ http://dx.doi.org/10.1787/402134482176

C1

Table C1.2.
Percentage of upper secondary and post-secondary non-tertiary pre-vocational/vocational graduates, by field of education (2006)

	ISCED level	Education	Humanities and arts	Social sciences, business and law	Services	Engineering, manufacturing and construction	Agriculture	Health and welfare	Life sciences	Physical sciences	Mathematics and statistics	Computing	Not known or unspecified
	(1)	(2)	(3)	(4)	(5)	(6)	(7)	(8)	(9)	(10)	(11)	(12)	(13)
Australia	3	1.1	4.0	27.5	15.4	24.0	4.0	17.7	0.5	n.	n	1.8	4.1
	4	26.0	6.1	30.4	6.1	5.5	1.9	15.8	0.6	n.	n	4.7	2.8
Austria	3	m	m	m	m	m	m	m	m	m	m	m	n
	4	m	m	m	m	m	m	m	m	m	m	m	m
Belgium	3	n	15.1	17.3	11.9	19.8	1.7	16.5	0.3	0.3	n	1.1	16.1
	4	n	4.4	14.2	7.1	16.8	1.3	23.4	n.	n	n	0.3	32.4
Canada	3	m	m	m	m	m	m	m	m	m	m	m	m
	4	m	m	m	m	m	m	m	m	m	m	m	m
Czech Republic	3	1.0	3.1	23.6	18.3	43.3	4.0	6.6	n	n	n	n	0.1
	4	n	30.3	40.1	10.5	18.5	0.4	0.2	n	n	n	n	n
Denmark	3	n	12.7	21.8	4.4	18.1	1.9	14.6	n	n	26.4	n	n
	4	n	n	n	65.6	28.7	n	n	n	n	5.7	n	n
Finland	3	0.1	5.9	16.2	21.6	30.8	5.2	16.4	n	n	n	3.7	n
	4	n	0.4	59.9	14.0	16.3	2.0	7.0	n	n	n	0.5	n
France[1]	3	n	2.0	26.0	16.7	37.8	4.7	12.8	n	n	n	n	n
	4	0.6	23.2	12.0	7.0	0.7	n	54.4	0.6	0.1	n	1.4	n
Germany	3	0.5	2.4	28.7	10.9	28.3	2.3	10.8	0.1	n.	n.	3.0	13.1
	4	0.2	2.6	36.5	11.2	32.5	2.6	7.3	0.1	n.	n.	2.7	4.4
Greece	3	m	m	m	m	m	m	m	m	m	m	m	n
	4	6.4	n	21.6	17.2	18.9	1.5	10.7	n	n	n	23.7	n
Hungary	3	0.4	1.5	14.0	24.7	49.1	4.5	3.2	n	n	n	2.6	n
	4	1.4	6.7	27.7	18.4	19.0	1.8	11.5	n	n	0.3	13.1	n
Iceland	3	0.8	9.9	17.1	15.2	37.6	3.1	12.9	n	n	n	1.4	n
	4	8.0	2.9	1.9	38.9	33.8	5.9	5.1	n	n	n	3.5	n
Ireland	3	m	m	m	m	m	m	m	m	m	m	m	m
	4	n	1.2	3.6	12.5	65.1	14.3	2.6	n	n	n	0.7	n
Italy	3	m	m	m	m	m	m	m	m	m	m	m	m
	4	m	m	m	m	m	m	m	m	m	m	m	m
Japan	3	n	0.2	29.7	7.5	35.5	11.2	4.5	n	n	n	0.1	11.3
	4	m	m	m	m	m	m	m	m	m	m	m	m
Korea	3	0.3	20.5	11.3	3.6	50.8	1.7	0.2	0.3	n.	n	11.3	n
	4	a	a	a	a	a	a	a	a	a	a	a	n
Luxembourg	3	7.8	2.5	41.7	4.4	31.0	3.5	6.6	n	0.6	n	2.0	n
	4	2.4	6.0	n	11.9	63.1	3.6	13.1	n	n	n	n	n
Mexico	3	m	m	m	m	m	m	m	m	m	m	m	m
	4	a	a	a	a	a	a	a	a	a	a	a	a
Netherlands	3	3.0	2.2	21.1	17.7	20.5	3.9	26.7	0.1	n.	n	4.8	n
	4	7.0	n	15.0	2.7	43.4	15.8	n	n	n	n	16.1	n

Note: Column 1 specifies the level of education: 3 equals upper secondary education and 4 equals post-secondary non-tertiary education.
1. Year of reference 2005.
Source: OECD. See Annex 3 for notes (*www.oecd.org/edu/eag2008*).
Please refer to the Reader's Guide for information concerning the symbols replacing missing data.
StatLink ⌧ http://dx.doi.org/10.1787/402134482176

Table C1.2. *(continued)*

Percentage of upper secondary and post-secondary non-tertiary pre-vocational/vocational graduates, by field of education (2006)

	ISCED level	Education	Humanities and arts	Social sciences, business and law	Services	Engineering, manufacturing and construction	Agriculture	Health and welfare	Life sciences	Physical sciences	Mathematics and statistics	Computing	Not known or unspecified
	(1)	(2)	(3)	(4)	(5)	(6)	(7)	(8)	(9)	(10)	(11)	(12)	(13)
New Zealand	3	0.6	13.8	11.1	5.0	5.1	3.0	2.5	0.3	n.	n	3.3	56.5
	4	2.1	35.4	22.7	11.1	8.0	4.2	11.4	0.3	0.5	n	2.4	2.4
Norway	3	n	1.6	6.6	15.0	42.1	3.0	29.0	n	n	n	2.7	n
	4	n	19.0	24.3	19.6	21.3	8.8	2.7	n	0.5	n	3.6	0.5
Poland	3	n.	1.4	24.0	17.5	53.1	3.6	n.	n	0.2	n	0.1	n
	4	0.2	3.2	26.5	29.7	3.9	0.7	18.8	n	0.1	n	16.8	0.1
Portugal	3	m	m	m	m	m	m	m	m	m	m	m	m
	4	n	25.3	19.7	6.9	12.4	n	0.9	n	n	n	34.8	n
Slovak Republic	3	0.8	3.3	23.6	21.7	38.0	3.8	4.4	n	n	n	4.3	a
	4	4.7	0.3	14.6	61.2	1.7	0.9	15.6	n	n	n	1.1	a
Spain	3	n	17.0	22.7	12.0	30.8	2.9	12.6	n	n	n	2.1	n
	4	a	a	a	a	a	a	a	a	a	a	a	a
Sweden	3	n	23.8	5.8	10.5	34.1	5.7	11.5	0.1	n	n	n.	8.4
	4	0.9	9.8	30.2	14.7	29.3	4.0	9.3	n	n	n	1.9	n
Switzerland	3	n	3.5	37.7	9.0	32.2	3.9	6.4	n	n	n	2.8	4.3
	4	1.6	0.1	n	7.4	n	n	42.5	n	n	n	48.4	n
Turkey	3	n	2.3	18.2	3.2	38.4	0.1	10.4	n	n	n	9.5	17.9
	4	a	a	a	a	a	a	a	a	a	a	a	a
United Kingdom	3	m	m	m	m	m	m	m	m	m	m	m	m
	4	m	m	m	m	m	m	m	m	m	m	m	m
United States	3	a	a	a	a	a	a	a	a	a	a	a	a
	4	m	m	m	m	m	m	m	m	m	m	m	m
OECD average	*3*	*0.8*	*7.1*	*21.3*	*12.7*	*33.5*	*3.7*	*10.8*	*0.1*	*0.1*	*1.3*	*2.7*	*5.8*
	4	*3.1*	*8.8*	*20.0*	*18.7*	*21.9*	*3.5*	*12.6*	*0.1*	*0.1*	*0.3*	*8.8*	*2.1*
Partner countries													
Brazil	3	m	m	m	m	m	m	m	m	m	m	m	m
	4	a	a	a	a	a	a	a	a	a	a	a	a
Chile	3	m	m	m	m	m	m	m	m	m	m	m	m
	4	a	a	a	a	a	a	a	a	a	a	a	a
Estonia	3	n	3.0	6.2	19.3	62.4	5.3	n	n	n	n	3.7	n
	4	n	3.5	23.5	29.1	24.4	5.0	8.7	n	n	n	5.9	n
Israel	3	m	m	m	m	m	m	m	m	m	m	m	m
	4	m	m	m	m	m	m	m	m	m	m	m	m
Russian Federation	3	m	m	m	m	m	m	m	m	m	m	m	m
	4	m	m	m	m	m	m	m	m	m	m	m	m
Slovenia	3	3.0	0.5	36.0	13.1	31.6	4.4	9.5	n	n	n	1.8	n
	4	12.5	0.2	34.7	14.6	32.5	2.9	2.7	n	n	n	n	n

Note: Column 1 specifies the level of education: 3 equals upper secondary education and 4 equals post-secondary non-tertiary education.

1. Year of reference 2005.

Source: OECD. See Annex 3 for notes (*www.oecd.org/edu/eag2008*).

Please refer to the Reader's Guide for information concerning the symbols replacing missing data.

StatLink http://dx.doi.org/10.1787/402134482176

Table C1.3.

Annual expenditure on educational institutions per student for all services, by programme orientation (2005)

In equivalent USD converted using purchasing power parities for GDP, by level of education, based on full-time equivalent

		Secondary education								Post-secondary non-tertiary education		
		Lower secondary education			Upper secondary education			All secondary education				
		All programmes	General programmes	Vocational/ pre-vocational programmes	All programmes	General programmes	Vocational/ pre-vocational programmes	All programmes	General programmes	Vocational/ pre-vocational programmes	All programmes	General programmes	Vocational/ pre-vocational programmes
		(1)	(2)	(3)	(4)	(5)	(6)	(7)	(8)	(9)	(10)	(11)	(12)
OECD countries	Australia	7 930	7 951	7 679	9 223	9 852	7 864	8 408	8 526	7 810	7 973	a	7 973
	Austria	9 505	9 505	a	10 028	9 429	10 222	9 751	9 491	10 222	x(7)	x(8)	x(9)
	Belgium	x(7)	x(7)	x(7)	x(7)	x(7)	x(7)	7 731	x(7)	x(7)	x(7)	x(7)	x(7)
	Canada[1, 2]	x(7)	x(7)	x(7)	x(7)	x(7)	x(7)	7 837	x(7)	x(7)	x(7)	m	m
	Czech Republic	4 864	4 836	10 466	4 830	4 316	4 963	4 847	4 747	4 998	2 098	1 757	2 139
	Denmark	8 606	8 606	a	10 197	x(4)	x(4)	9 407	x(7)	x(7)	m	m	m
	Finland	8 875	8 875	a	6 441	5 545	6 895	7 324	7 638	6 895	x(7)	a	x
	France	7 881	7 881	a	10 311	10 127	10 609	8 927	8 596	10 609	4 488	x(10)	x(10)
	Germany	6 200	6 200	a	10 282	6 451	12 735	7 636	6 244	12 735	10 531	7 611	11 081
	Greece	x(7)	x(7)	x(7)	x(7)	x(7)	x(7)	8 423	x(7)	x(7)	7 266	a	7 266
	Hungary[3]	3 993	x(1)	x(1)	3 613	3 536	3 829	3 806	3 798	3 858	4 731	a	4 731
	Iceland	8 985	m	a	8 004	m	m	8 411	m	x(7)	x(7)	x(7)	x(7)
	Ireland	7 352	x(1)	x(1)	7 680	x(4)	x(4)	7 500	x(7)	x(7)	5 811	x(10)	x(10)
	Italy	7 599	7 587	m	7 682	x(4)	x(4)	7 648	x(7)	x(7)	m	m	m
	Japan	7 630	7 630	a	8 164	x(4)	x(4)	7 908	x(7)	x(7)	x(7)	m	m
	Korea	5 661	5 661	a	7 765	x(4)	x(4)	6 645	x(7)	x(7)	a	a	a
	Luxembourg[3]	18 844	18 844	a	18 845	18 846	18 845	18 845	18 845	18 845	m	m	m
	Mexico	1 839	2 148	264	2 853	2 762	3 659	2 180	2 365	1 068	a	a	a
	Netherlands	8 166	8 301	7 901	7 225	7 747	6 980	7 741	8 143	7 327	7 000	a	7 000
	New Zealand	5 165	x(1)	x(1)	7 586	x(4)	x(4)	6 278	x(7)	x(7)	6 126	m	m
	Norway	9 687	9 687	a	12 096	x(4)	x(4)	10 995	x(7)	x(7)	x(4)	x(4)	x(4)
	Poland[3]	2 971	2 971	a	3 131	x(4)	x(4)	3 055	x(7)	x(7)	2 956	a	2 956
	Portugal[3]	6 555	x(1)	x(1)	6 381	x(4)	x(4)	6 473	x(7)	x(7)	m	m	m
	Slovak Republic	2 430	2 430	a	3 026	3 390	2 890	2 716	2 622	2 890	x(7)	x(8)	x(9)
	Spain	x(7)	x(7)	x(7)	x(7)	x(7)	x(7)	7 211	x(7)	x(7)	a	a	a
	Sweden	8 091	8 091	a	8 292	8 107	8 454	8 198	8 097	8 454	2 691	8 456	655
	Switzerland[3]	9 756	9 756	a	16 166	11 534	18 652	12 861	10 195	18 652	9 119	4 716	12 808
	Turkey[3]	m	a	a	m	m	m	m	m	m	a	a	a
	United Kingdom	x(7)	x(7)	x(7)	x(7)	x(7)	x(7)	7 167	x(7)	x(7)	x(7)	x(7)	x(7)
	United States	9 899	9 899	a	10 969	10 969	a	10 390	10 390	a	m	a	m
	OECD average	*7 437*	*7 343*	*6 578*	*8 366*	*8 044*	*8 969*	*7 804*	*7 835*	*8 797*	*4 719*	*5 635*	*6 290*
Partner countries	Brazil[3]	1 359	1 359	a	899	x(4)	x(4)	1 186	x(7)	x(7)	a	a	a
	Chile[4]	1 865	1 865	a	1 956	2 081	1 700	1 924	1 983	1 700	a	a	a
	Estonia[3]	3 802	x(1)	x(1)	4 033	4 325	3 402	3 918	x(7)	x(7)	4 417	a	4 417
	Israel	x(7)	x(7)	x(7)	x(7)	x(7)	x(7)	5 495	4 355	9 168	4 275	4 275	a
	Russian Federation[3]	x(8)	x(8)	a	x(7)	x(8)	1 856	1 754	1 741	1 856	x(7)	a	x(9)
	Slovenia[3, 5]	7 994	7 994	a	5 565	x(4)	x(4)	7 065	x(7)	x(7)	x(7)	x(7)	x(7)

1. Year of reference 2004.
2. All secondary includes pre-primary and primary educaton.
3. Public institutions only.
4. Year of reference 2006.
5. Lower secondary includes primary education.

Source: OECD. See Annex 3 for notes (*www.oecd.org/edu/eag2008*).

Please refer to the Reader's Guide for information concerning the symbols replacing missing data.

StatLink http://dx.doi.org/10.1787/402134482176

Table C1.4.
Performance of 15-year-old students on the PISA science scale by programme orientation (2006)
Distinction between programme orientation is based on students' self-reports

		Performance in general programmes		Performance in pre-vocational and vocational programmes		Differences in science performance between general programme students and pre-vocational and vocational programme students		Differences in science performance between general programme students and pre-vocational and vocational programme students, accounting for their economic, social and cultural status (ESCS)	
		Mean score	S.E.	Mean score	S.E.	Mean score	S.E.	Mean score	S.E.
OECD countries	Australia	531	2.3	494	5.2	**37**	5.3	**25**	4.9
	Austria	542	7.7	498	4.5	**45**	9.1	**23**	8.3
	Belgium	558	2.8	458	3.3	**100**	4.5	**78**	4.2
	Canada	534	2.0	a	a	a	a	a	a
	Czech Republic	516	4.1	508	6.4	8	7.7	0	7.2
	Denmark	496	3.1	a	a	a	a	a	a
	Finland	563	2.0	a	a	a	a	a	a
	France	500	3.4	450	9.2	**50**	9.7	**27**	7.6
	Germany	c	c	c	c	c	c	c	c
	Greece	487	3.0	387	6.1	**100**	6.7	**82**	5.9
	Hungary	531	4.9	483	2.7	**48**	5.5	**27**	5.1
	Iceland	c	c	c	c	c	c	c	c
	Ireland	c	c	c	c	c	c	c	c
	Italy	511	3.5	448	2.4	**63**	4.2	**48**	4.2
	Japan	548	3.6	482	7.8	**65**	8.9	**51**	8.9
	Korea	542	3.6	456	7.4	**86**	8.1	**74**	7.5
	Luxembourg	484	1.1	503	3.0	**-19**	3.2	**-23**	3.4
	Mexico	406	3.7	418	2.6	**-12**	4.5	**-12**	3.6
	Netherlands	565	2.1	434	3.3	**130**	3.8	**114**	3.2
	New Zealand	530	2.7	a	a	a	a	a	a
	Norway	487	3.1	a	a	a	a	a	a
	Poland	498	2.3	a	a	a	a	a	a
	Portugal	473	2.9	482	8.1	-9	7.8	-13	6.8
	Slovak Republic	497	4.5	477	5.1	**19**	8.0	9	6.5
	Spain	488	2.6	a	a	a	a	a	a
	Sweden	c	c	c	c	c	c	c	c
	Switzerland	511	3.2	525	9.0	-15	9.0	-16	8.7
	Turkey	444	5.4	394	4.8	**51**	7.3	**39**	5.9
	United Kingdom	515	2.3	a	a	a	a	a	a
	United States	489	4.2	a	a	a	a	a	a
	OECD average	*509*		*473*		*35*		*24*	
Partner countries	Brazil	390	2.8	a	a	a	a	a	a
	Chile	c	c	c	c	c	c	c	c
	Estonia	531	2.5	a	a	a	a	a	a
	Israel	461	4.3	422	13.0	**39**	14.7	**31**	13.6
	Russian Federation	482	3.7	464	10.7	17	10.9	15	9.7
	Slovenia	574	2.1	468	1.2	**105**	2.4	**88**	2.8

Note: The classification of students into programme type is based on self-reports of 15-year-old students, whereas the classification of students into programme type in Table C1.1 is based on national statistics of upper seconday students and may differ.
Two symbols are used to denote missing data:
a: Because the category does not apply in the country concerned, there are no data.
c: There are too few observations to provide reliable estimates (fewer than 3% of students or too few schools). However, these statistics were included in the calculation of cross-country averages.
Source: OECD PISA 2006 database. See Annex 3 for notes (*www.oecd.org/edu/eag2008*).
StatLink http://dx.doi.org/10.1787/402134482176

WHO PARTICIPATES IN EDUCATION?

This indicator examines access to education and its evolution using information on enrolment rates and on enrolment trends from 1995 to 2006. It also shows patterns of participation at the secondary level of education and the percentage of the youth cohort that will enter different types of tertiary education during their lifetime. Participation rates reflect both the accessibility of tertiary education and the perceived value of attending tertiary programmes. For information on vocational education and training in secondary education, see Indicator C1.

Key results

Chart C2.1. Enrolment rates of 20-to-29-year-olds (1995, 2000 and 2006)

Full-time and part-time students in public and private institutions

☐ 2006   ● 2000   ◆ 1995

In Australia, Denmark, Finland, Greece, Iceland, Norway, Poland and Sweden, and in the partner country Slovenia, more than 30% of the population aged 20 to 29 is enrolled in education. From 1995 to 2006, enrolment rates of 20-to-29-year-olds increased by 8 percentage points.

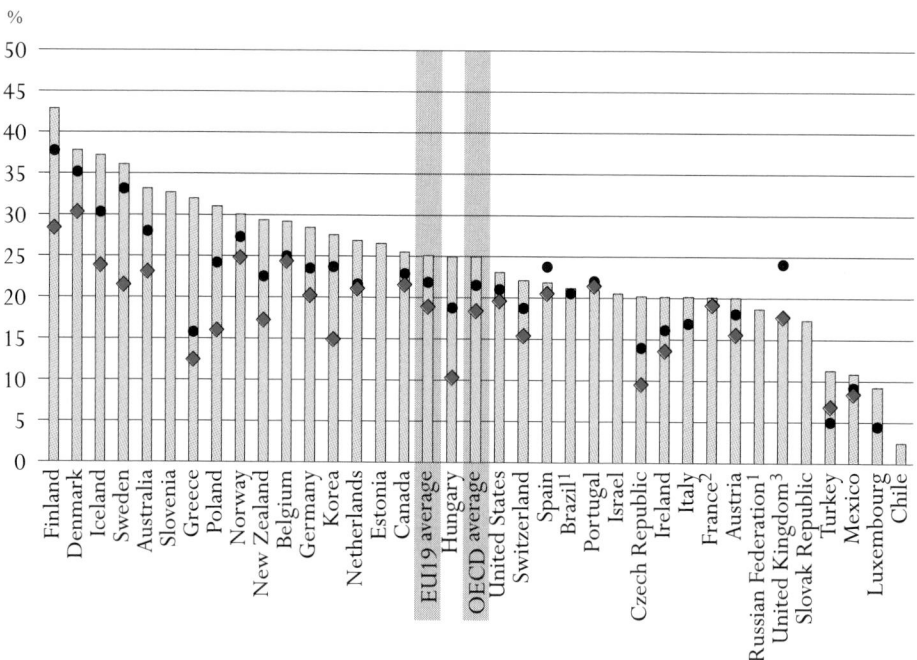

1. Year of reference 2005.
2. Excludes overseas departments for 1995 and 2000.
3. Break in time series following methodological change from 2006.
Countries are ranked in descending order of the enrolment rates of 20-to-29-year-olds in 2006.
Source: OECD. Table C2.2. See Annex 3 for notes (*www.oecd.org/edu/eag2008*).
StatLink ⌸ http://dx.doi.org/10.1787/402156412821

Other highlights of this indicator

- In most OECD countries today, virtually everyone has access to at least 12 years of formal education. At least 90% of students are enrolled in education in an age range spanning 14 or more years in Belgium, France, Germany, Hungary, Iceland, Japan, Norway and Spain. In contrast, Mexico and Turkey have enrolment rates exceeding 90% for only nine and six years, respectively; the corresponding figure for the partner country the Russian Federation is nine years.

- In more than one-half of OECD countries, more than 70% of 3-to-4-year-olds are enrolled in either pre-primary or primary programmes. A child is more likely to be enrolled at age 4 and under in the 19 European Union countries that are members of the OECD than in other OECD countries. The enrolment rate for 3-to-4-year-olds averages 76.7% for the EU19, while the OECD average is 69.4%.

- Enrolment rates for 15-to-19-year-olds increased on average from 74 to 81% from 1995 to 2006. In Belgium, Greece and Poland, and the partner country Slovenia, they reached more than 90% in 2006 (in Belgium they had already reached this level in 1995). The pattern is similar for 20-to-29-year-olds, an age group in which most students are enrolled in tertiary education; between 1995 and 2006, their enrolment rates increased in all OECD countries except Portugal.

C2

Policy context

A well-educated population is essential to a country's economic and social development. Societies therefore have an intrinsic interest in ensuring that children and adults have access to a wide variety of educational opportunities. Early childhood programmes prepare children for primary education; they provide opportunities to enhance and complement their educational experience at home and can help combat linguistic and social disadvantages. Primary and secondary education lay the foundation for a broad range of competencies and prepare young people to become lifelong learners and productive members of society. Tertiary education, either directly after initial schooling or later in life, provides a range of options for acquiring advanced knowledge and skills.

Various factors, including increased risks of unemployment and other forms of exclusion for young adults with insufficient education, have strengthened the incentive to remain in school beyond the end of compulsory education and graduate from upper secondary education. In most OECD countries, graduation from upper secondary education is becoming the norm, and most upper secondary programmes prepare students for tertiary studies (see Indicator A2).

High tertiary participation rates help to ensure the development and maintenance of a highly educated population and labour force. Moreover, tertiary education programmes are generally associated with better access to employment (see Indicator A8) and higher earnings (see Indicator A9). Rates of entry into tertiary education are a partial indication of the degree to which a population is acquiring the high-level skills and knowledge valued by the labour market in today's knowledge society (see Indicator A2).

As students have become more aware of the economic and social benefits of tertiary education, graduation rates for tertiary-type A programmes have risen (see Indicator A3). Tertiary-type A programmes dominate tertiary enrolments and absorb a large proportion of the available resources as they tend to be longer than other tertiary programmes (see Indicator B1, Table B1.3).

The continuing rise in participation and the widening diversity of backgrounds and interests among those aspiring to tertiary studies mean that tertiary institutions need to expand admissions and adapt their programmes to the needs of these new generations of students. In addition, the internationalisation of tertiary education means that some educational institutions may also have to adapt their curriculum and teaching methods to a culturally and linguistically diverse student body (see Indicator C3).

Evidence and explanations

Virtually all young people in OECD countries have access to at least 12 years of formal education. At least 90% of students are enrolled in an age range spanning 14 or more years in Belgium, France, Germany, Hungary, Iceland, Japan, Norway and Spain. By contrast, Mexico and Turkey, and the partner country the Russian Federation, have enrolment rates exceeding 90% for only nine, six and nine years, respectively (Table C2.1). However, patterns of participation in education throughout people's lives vary widely among countries. Enrolment rates in the United Kingdom appear to be lower than in previous years, however this is due to a break in time series following methodological change from 2006.

Participation in early childhood education

A child is more likely to be enrolled at age 4 and under in the EU19 countries than in other OECD countries. On average, the enrolment rate for 3-to-4-year-olds is 76.7% for the EU19 countries, whereas the OECD average is 69.4%.

C2

In the majority of OECD and partner countries, full enrolment (defined here as enrolment rates exceeding 90%) begins between the ages of 5 and 6. However, in Belgium, the Czech Republic, Denmark, France, Germany, Hungary, Iceland, Italy, Japan, Luxembourg, New Zealand, Norway, Portugal, the Slovak Republic, Spain, Sweden and the United Kingdom, and in the partner countries Estonia, Israel and Slovenia, at least 70% of 3-to-4-year-olds are enrolled in either pre-primary or primary programmes. Enrolment rates for early childhood education range from less than 25% in Korea and Turkey to over 90% in Belgium, Denmark, France, Germany, Iceland, Italy, New Zealand, Spain and the United Kingdom (Table C2.1).

Given the importance of early childhood education and care in building a strong foundation for lifelong learning and in ensuring equitable access to later learning opportunities, pre-primary education is very valuable. Many countries have recognised this by making pre-primary education by 3 years of age almost universal. However, institutionally based pre-primary programmes covered by this indicator are not the only available form of effective early childhood education and care. Inferences about access to and quality of pre-primary education and care should therefore be made with caution.

Participation towards the end of compulsory education and beyond

Several factors influence the decision to stay enrolled beyond the end of compulsory education, particularly the limited prospects of young adults with insufficient education; in many countries they are at greater risk of unemployment and other forms of exclusion than their well-educated peers. In many OECD countries, the transition from education to employment has become longer and more complex, providing the opportunity, or the obligation, to combine learning and work to develop marketable skills (see Indicator C4).

The age at which compulsory education ends ranges from 14 in Korea, Portugal and Turkey and the partner countries Brazil and Slovenia to 18 in Belgium, Germany and the Netherlands and the partner country Chile. All other countries lie between these two extremes (Table C2.1). However, the statutory age at which compulsory education ends does not always correspond to the age at which enrolment is universal.

Participation rates tend to be high up to the end of compulsory education in most OECD and partner countries. However, in Germany, Mexico, the Netherlands, New Zealand, Turkey, the United Kingdom and the United States and the partner country Chile, they drop below 90% before the end of compulsory education (Table C2.1 and Table C2.3). In Germany, the Netherlands and the United States and the partner country Chile, this may be due, in part, to the fact that compulsory education ends relatively late at age 18 (age 17, on average, in the United States).

In most OECD and partner countries, enrolment rates decline gradually during the last years of upper secondary education. More than 20% of the population aged 15 to 19 is not enrolled in education in Luxembourg, Mexico, New Zealand, Portugal, Turkey, the United Kingdom and the United States, and in the partner countries Brazil, Chile, Israel and the Russian Federation (Table C2.1).

C2

There has been an average increase of 8 percentage points in the proportion of 15-to-19-year-olds enrolled in education in OECD countries between 1995 and 2006. Enrolment rates for this age group increased on average from 74 to 81% from 1995 to 2006 and reached more than 90% in 2006 in Belgium, Greece, Poland and the partner country Slovenia (Belgium had already reached 90% or more in 1995) (Table C2.2). However, while enrolment rates for 15-to-19-year-olds have improved by more than 20 percentage points during the past 11 years in the Czech Republic, Greece and Hungary, they remained virtually unchanged in Australia, Belgium, Canada, France, Germany, Luxembourg, the Netherlands, Norway and Switzerland. Of these, all except Luxembourg have a high proportion of their population of 15-to-19-year-olds enrolled in education (Table C2.2).

Chart C2.2. **Enrolment rates of 15-to-19-year-olds (1995, 2000 and 2006)**

Full-time and part-time students in public and private institutions

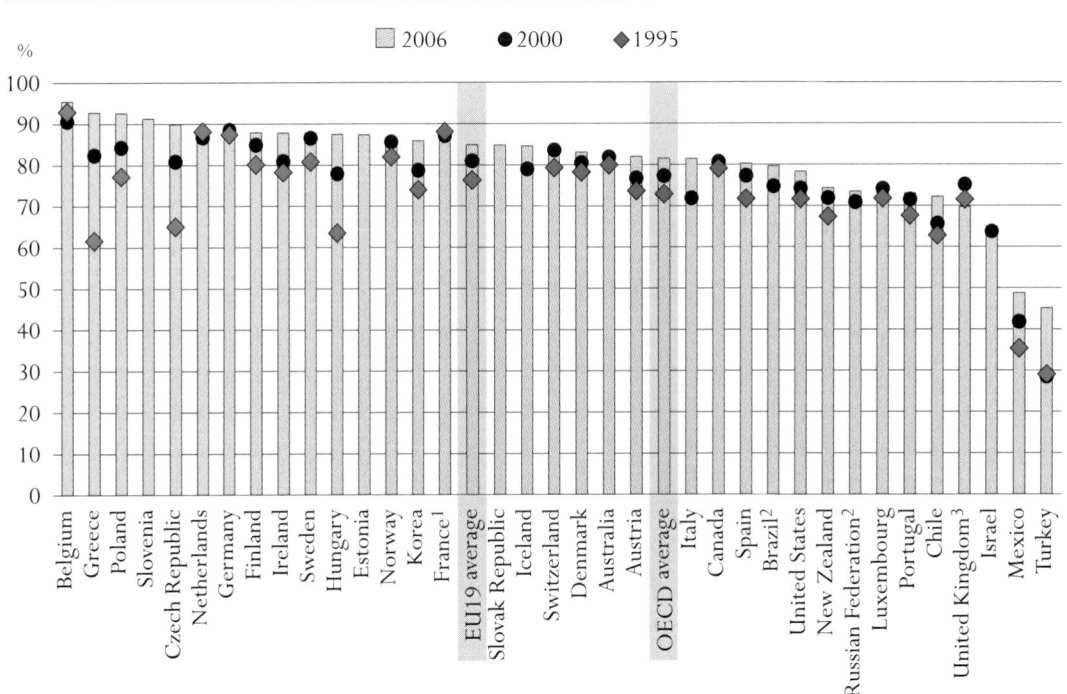

1. Excludes overseas departments for 1995 and 2000.
2. Year of reference 2005.
3. Break in time series following methodological change from 2006.
Countries are ranked in descending order of the enrolment rates of 15-to-19-year-olds in 2006.
Source: OECD. Table C2.2. See Annex 3 for notes (*www.oecd.org/edu/eag2008*).
StatLink ⛗⛗ http://dx.doi.org/10.1787/402156412821

The transition to post-secondary education

Upper secondary students in many education systems can enrol in relatively short programmes (less than two years) to prepare for a certain trade or specific vocational field. Some OECD countries delay vocational training until after graduation from upper secondary education. While these programmes are offered as advanced upper secondary programmes in some OECD countries

C2

(*e.g.* Austria, Hungary and Spain), they are offered as post-secondary education in others (*e.g.* Canada and the United States), although the latter often resemble upper secondary level programmes.

From an internationally comparable point of view, these programmes straddle upper secondary and tertiary education and are therefore classified as a distinct level of education (post-secondary non-tertiary education).

End of compulsory education and decline in enrolment rates

An analysis of the participation rates by level of education and single year of age shows that there is no close relationship between the end of compulsory education and the decline in enrolment rates. In most OECD and partner countries, the sharpest decline in enrolment rates occurs not at the end of compulsory education but at the end of upper secondary education. After the age of 16, however, enrolment rates begin to decline in all OECD and partner countries. Enrolment rates in secondary education fall from 91% on average at age 16 to 82% at age 17, 52% at age 18 and 27% at age 19. In Belgium, the Czech Republic, Finland, Germany, Hungary, Japan, Korea, Norway, Poland, the Slovak Republic and Sweden, and in the partner countries Estonia, Israel and Slovenia, 90% or more of all 17-year-olds are still enrolled at this level, even though compulsory education ends at less than 17 years of age in most of these countries (Table C2.3).

Participation in tertiary education

Enrolment rates indicate the number of individuals participating in tertiary education. On average in OECD countries, 25% of 20-to-29-year-olds are enrolled in education. Enrolment rates are 30% or more in Australia, Denmark, Finland, Greece, Iceland, Norway, Poland and Sweden, and in the partner country Slovenia (Table C2.1).

Policies to expand education have led to greater access to tertiary education in many OECD and partner countries. This has so far more than compensated the declines in cohort sizes which had led, until recently, to predictions of stable or declining demand in several OECD countries. While some OECD countries (Ireland, New Zealand and Portugal) now show signs of a levelling of demand for tertiary education, the overall trend remains upwards. On average, in all OECD countries with comparable data, participation rates in tertiary education grew by 8 percentage points from 1995 to 2006. All OECD and partner countries except Portugal have seen participation by 20-to-29-year-olds increase. This growth is particularly significant in the Czech Republic, Greece and Hungary, which were earlier at the bottom of the scale of OECD countries but have moved up to the middle (Table C2.2 and Chart C2.1).

The relative size of the public and the private sectors

In OECD and partner countries, education at the primary and secondary levels is still predominantly publicly provided. On average, 91% of primary education students in OECD countries are enrolled in public institutions; the figures decline slightly in secondary education, with 85% of lower secondary students and 83% of upper secondary students taught in public institutions. Japan and Mexico are an exception at the upper secondary level, as independent private providers (those that receive less than 50% of their funds from government sources) take in 31 and 20%, respectively, of upper secondary students (Table C2.4).

At the tertiary level, the pattern is quite different. Private providers generally play a more significant role. In tertiary-type B programmes, the private sector accounts for one third of students, and in tertiary-type A and advanced research programmes it accounts for one fifth of students. In the United Kingdom, all tertiary education is provided through government-dependent private institutions. Such providers also receive more than half of tertiary-type B students in the partner country Israel (66%). Government-dependent private providers also take a significant share of tertiary-type A and advanced research programmes in the partner countries Estonia (86%) and Israel (78%). Independent private providers are more prominent at the tertiary level than at pre-tertiary levels (an average of 14% of tertiary students attend such institutions), particularly in Japan, Korea and the partner country Brazil, where more than 70% of students are enrolled in such institutions (Table C2.5).

Definitions and methodologies

Data on enrolments is for the school year 2005-2006 and data on finance refer to the financial year 2005 and both are based on the UOE data collection on educational systems administered annually by the OECD.

Except where otherwise noted, figures are based on head counts; that is, they do not distinguish between full-time and part-time study because the concept of part-time study is not recognised by some countries. In some OECD countries, part-time education is only partially covered in the reported data.

Net enrolment rates, expressed as percentages in Table C2.1 and Table C2.2, are calculated by dividing the number of students of a particular age group enrolled in all levels of education by the size of the population of that age group.

In Table C2.2, data on trends in enrolment rates for the years 1995, 2000, 2001, 2002, 2003 and 2004 are based on a special survey carried out in OECD countries and four out of six partner countries in January 2007.

Further references

The following additional material relevant to this indicator is available on line at:

StatLink ⫶ http://dx.doi.org/10.1787/402156412821

• *Table C2.6. Education expectancy (2006)*

• *Table C2.7. Expected years in tertiary education (2006)*

Table C2.1.
Enrolment rates, by age (2006)
Full-time and part-time students in public and private institutions

C2

	Ending age of compulsory education	Number of years at which over 90% of the population are enrolled	Age range at which over 90% of the population are enrolled	Students aged:					
				4 and under as a percentage of the population aged 3 to 4	5 to 14 as a percentage of the population aged 5 to 14	15 to 19 as a percentage of the population aged 15 to 19	20 to 29 as a percentage of the population aged 20 to 29	30 to 39 as a percentage of the population aged 30 to 39	40 and over as a percentage of the population aged 40 and over
	(1)	(2)	(3)	(4)	(5)	(6)	(7)	(8)	(9)
OECD countries									
Australia	15	12	5 - 16	41.7	99.6	82.7	33.2	13.8	5.9
Austria	15	13	5 - 17	67.9	98.1	82.0	20.0	3.3	0.3
Belgium[1]	18	16	3 - 18	125.4	99.4	95.5	29.2	8.7	3.7
Canada[2]	16-18	m	m	m	m	80.2	26.0	5.6	1.7
Czech Republic	15	13	5 - 17	79.5	99.9	89.9	20.2	4.2	0.3
Denmark	16	13	3 - 16	93.6	97.4	83.1	37.8	7.9	1.5
Finland	16	13	6 - 18	44.0	95.1	87.9	42.9	13.8	3.2
France[1]	16	15	3 - 17	112.1	101.0	85.9	20.1	2.6	n
Germany	18	14	4 - 17	96.8	98.8	88.6	28.5	2.5	0.1
Greece	14.5	13	6 - 19	27.9	98.1	92.8	32.0	1.1	n
Hungary	16	14	4 - 17	82.2	100.3	87.5	24.9	6.0	0.6
Iceland	16	14	3 - 16	94.2	98.8	84.6	37.2	12.5	3.4
Ireland	16	12	5 - 16	23.6	101.2	87.8	20.2	5.8	0.1
Italy[1]	15	13	3 - 15	104.9	100.7	81.5	20.2	3.4	0.1
Japan	15	14	4 - 17	83.4	100.7	m	m	m	m
Korea	14	12	6 - 17	24.4	94.9	85.9	27.6	2.1	0.5
Luxembourg[3]	15	12	4 - 15	80.7	96.2	73.5	9.2	0.8	0.1
Mexico	15	9	5 - 13	53.1	100.9	48.8	10.9	3.5	0.6
Netherlands	18	13	5 - 17	37.3	99.6	88.7	26.9	2.7	0.7
New Zealand	16	12	4 - 15	90.8	101.0	74.4	29.4	12.3	5.4
Norway	16	14	4 - 17	89.3	98.8	86.3	30.0	6.9	1.6
Poland	16	13	6 - 18	37.3	94.5	92.6	31.0	4.4	x(8)
Portugal	14	11	5 - 15	71.8	103.8	73.0	20.9	3.5	0.5
Slovak Republic	16	12	6 - 17	74.8	96.8	84.8	17.3	3.3	0.5
Spain[1]	16	14	3 - 16	122.8	101.0	80.2	21.8	3.8	1.1
Sweden	16	13	6 - 18	84.2	98.8	87.8	36.1	13.2	3.0
Switzerland	15	12	5 - 16	26.2	100.3	83.5	22.1	3.7	0.4
Turkey	14	6	7 - 12	4.6	82.9	45.2	11.3	1.6	0.2
United Kingdom	16	12	4 - 15	90.1	100.7	69.7	17.3	5.8	1.8
United States	17	11	6 - 16	48.4	98.0	78.4	23.1	5.4	1.4
OECD average	*16*	*13*		*69.4*	*98.5*	*81.5*	*25.1*	*5.7*	*1.4*
EU19 average	*16*	*13*		*76.7*	*99.0*	*84.9*	*25.1*	*5.1*	*1.0*
Partner countries									
Brazil[2]	14	10	7 - 16	41.6	93.1	79.6	21.2	8.1	2.4
Chile	18	10	7 - 16	35.2	91.2	72.2	2.5	0.7	0.3
Estonia	15	12	6 - 17	83.3	102.2	87.4	26.6	7.0	0.8
Israel[4]	15	13	5 - 17	76.7	95.8	65.0	20.6	5.2	0.9
Russian Federation[2]	15	9	7 - 15	m	81.5	73.5	18.7	0.7	n
Slovenia	14	12	6 - 17	74.4	96.4	91.3	32.7	6.2	0.7

Note: Ending age of compulsory education is the age at which compulsory schooling ends. For example, an ending age of 18 indicates that all students under 18 are legally obliged to participate in education. Mismatches between the coverage of the population data and the student/graduate data mean that the participation/graduation rates may be underestimated for countries such as Luxembourg that are net exporters of students and may be overestimated for those that are net importers.

1. The rates "4 and under as a percentage of the population of 3-to-4-year-olds" are overestimated. A significant number of students are younger than 3 years old. The net rates between 3 and 5 are around 100%.

2. Year of reference 2005.

3. Underestimated because many resident students go to school in the neighborhood countries.

4. Excludes programmes for children younger than 3 years old, resulting in substantially lower figures than in previous years.

Source: OECD. See Annex 3 for notes (*www.oecd.org/edu/eag2008*).

Please refer to the Reader's Guide for information concerning the symbols replacing missing data.

StatLink ⬛⬛⬛⬛ http://dx.doi.org/10.1787/402156412821

Table C2.2.
Trends in enrolment rates (1995-2006)
Full-time and part-time students in public and private institutions in 1995, 2000, 2001, 2002, 2003, 2004, 2005, 2006

	15-to-19-year-olds as a percentage of the population aged 15 to 19 years								20-to-29-year-olds as a percentage of the population aged 20 to 29 years							
	1995	2000	2001	2002	2003	2004	2005	2006	1995	2000	2001	2002	2003	2004	2005	2006
	(1)	(2)	(3)	(4)	(5)	(6)	(7)	(8)	(9)	(10)	(11)	(12)	(13)	(14)	(15)	(16)
Australia	81	82	81	83	82	82	82	83	23	28	28	33	33	33	33	33
Austria	75	77	77	77	77	79	80	82	16	18	19	17	18	19	19	20
Belgium[1]	94	91	91	92	94	95	94	95	24	25	26	27	29	30	29	29
Canada	80	81	81	80	80	79	80	81	22	23	24	25	25	25	26	26
Czech Republic	66	81	87	90	90	91	90	90	10	14	15	16	17	19	20	20
Denmark	79	80	83	82	85	85	85	83	30	35	36	36	36	36	38	38
Finland	81	85	85	85	86	87	87	88	28	38	39	40	40	41	43	43
France[2]	89	87	86	86	87	87	86	86	19	19	20	20	20	20	20	20
Germany	88	88	90	89	89	89	89	89	20	24	24	26	27	28	28	28
Greece	62	82	74	83	83	86	97	93	13	16	22	25	26	28	24	32
Hungary	64	78	79	81	83	85	87	88	10	19	20	21	22	24	24	25
Iceland	m	79	79	81	83	84	85	85	24	31	30	32	36	37	37	37
Ireland	79	81	82	83	84	87	89	88	14	16	18	19	19	23	21	20
Italy	m	72	73	76	78	79	80	81	m	17	17	18	20	20	20	20
Japan	m	m	m	m	m	m	m	m	m	m	m	m	m	m	m	m
Korea	75	79	79	80	81	84	86	86	15	24	25	27	27	28	27	28
Luxembourg	73	74	75	75	75	75	72	73	m	5	6	6	6	7	6	9
Mexico	36	42	42	44	45	47	48	49	8	9	9	10	10	11	11	11
Netherlands	89	87	86	87	85	86	86	89	21	22	23	23	25	26	26	27
New Zealand	68	72	72	74	74	74	74	74	17	23	25	28	30	31	30	29
Norway	83	86	85	85	85	86	86	86	25	28	26	26	29	29	29	30
Poland	78	84	86	87	88	90	92	93	16	24	26	28	29	30	31	31
Portugal	68	71	73	71	72	73	73	73	22	22	22	22	23	23	22	21
Slovak Republic	m	m	74	76	80	83	85	85	m	m	12	13	13	15	16	17
Spain	73	77	78	78	78	80	81	80	21	24	23	23	22	22	22	22
Sweden	82	86	86	86	87	87	87	88	22	33	33	34	34	36	36	36
Switzerland	80	83	83	83	83	83	83	84	15	19	20	20	21	21	22	22
Turkey	30	28	30	34	35	40	41	45	7	5	5	6	6	10	10	11
United Kingdom[3]	72	75	75	77	75	79	79	70	18	24	24	27	26	28	29	17
United States	73	74	76	75	75	76	79	78	20	21	22	23	22	23	23	23
OECD average	*74*	*77*	*78*	*79*	*79*	*81*	*81*	*82*	*18*	*22*	*22*	*23*	*24*	*25*	*25*	*25*
OECD average for countries with 1995 and 2006 data	*74*							*81*	*18*							*26*
EU19 average	*77*	*81*	*81*	*82*	*83*	*84*	*85*	*85*	*19*	*22*	*22*	*23*	*24*	*25*	*25*	*25*
Brazil	m	75	71	74	80	79	80	m	m	21	23	22	22	23	21	m
Chile	64	66	m	66	68	70	74	72	m	m	m	m	m	m	m	2
Estonia	m	m	m	m	m	m	87	87	m	m	m	m	m	m	27	27
Israel	m	64	63	65	66	65	65	65	m	m	m	21	21	20	20	21
Russian Federation	m	71	71	74	m	m	74	m	m	m	m	13	m	m	19	m
Slovenia	m	m	m	m	m	m	91	91	m	m	m	m	m	m	32	33

1. Excludes the German-speaking Community of Belgium for 2004, 2005 and 2006.
2. Excludes overseas departments (DOM) from 1995 to 2004.
3. Break in time series following methodological change from 2006.
Source: OECD. See Annex 3 for notes (*www.oecd.org/edu/eag2008*).
Please refer to the Reader's Guide for information concerning the symbols replacing missing data.
StatLink 📊 http://dx.doi.org/10.1787/402156412821

Table C2.3.
Transition characteristics from age 15 to 20, by level of education (2006)
Net enrolment rates (based on head counts)

C2

	Graduation age at the upper secondary level of education	Age 15	Age 16			Age 17			Age 18			Age 19			Age 20		
		Secondary education	Secondary education	Post-secondary non-tertiary	Tertiary education	Secondary education	Post-secondary non-tertiary	Tertiary education	Secondary education	Post-secondary non-tertiary	Tertiary education	Secondary education	Post-secondary non-tertiary	Tertiary education	Secondary education	Post-secondary non-tertiary	Tertiary education
		(1)	(2)	(3)	(4)	(5)	(6)	(7)	(8)	(9)	(10)	(11)	(12)	(13)	(14)	(15)	(16)
Australia	17	99	94	n	n	80	1	4	39	3	27	26	3	35	21	2	36
Austria	17-18	96	93	n	n	78	15	n	47	26	5	18	16	14	6	6	21
Belgium	18	102	103	n	n	101	n	1	48	7	36	24	8	47	14	5	49
Canada[1]	17-18	95	93	x(4)	1	82	x(7)	7	30	x(10)	36	9	x(13)	47	4	x(16)	47
Czech Republic	18-19	100	100	n	n	96	n	n	82	4	1	37	10	20	7	7	35
Denmark	19	96	91	n	n	84	n	n	80	n	n	58	n	4	35	n	14
Finland	19	99	96	n	n	96	n	n	93	n	1	32	n	20	18	n	33
France	17-20	97	96	n	n	89	n	2	50	n	27	25	1	39	10	1	41
Germany	19-20	97	96	n	n	91	n	1	83	n	3	43	17	10	22	14	19
Greece	18	93	102	a	a	73	n	14	19	2	69	15	5	72	6	6	74
Hungary	19	98	96	n	n	92	n	n	61	9	12	21	16	32	11	11	36
Iceland	20	99	94	n	n	84	n	n	73	n	n	68	n	2	36	n	17
Ireland	18-19	100	95	1	n	75	6	6	29	26	34	4	17	43	1	13	41
Italy	19	94	89	a	a	83	a	a	74	a	12	20	n	35	6	1	37
Japan	18	99	98	a	a	94	a	m	3	m	m	1	m	m	m	m	m
Korea	17	93	94	a	n	93	a	1	7	a	66	1	a	74	n	a	67
Luxembourg	18-19	88	84	n	n	77	n	n	69	n	1	41	1	5	24	1	7
Mexico	18	64	54	a	a	43	a	3	19	a	13	27	a	18	4	a	19
Netherlands	17-20	99	98	n	n	85	n	6	61	n	21	42	n	30	27	n	35
New Zealand	17-18	96	87	1	1	69	3	4	25	6	26	11	5	34	8	4	37
Norway	18-20	99	94	n	n	92	n	n	86	n	n	41	1	15	20	2	30
Poland	19-20	98	97	a	a	95	a	n	92	n	1	35	9	35	13	10	45
Portugal	17-18	88	81	n	a	73	n	a	47	n	20	27	n	27	15	n	29
Slovak Republic	19-20	99	95	n	n	91	n	n	79	n	3	35	n	24	7	1	34
Spain	17	98	93	a	n	82	a		42	a	28	23	a	35	13	a	38
Sweden	19	99	99	n	n	97	n	n	93	n	1	30	1	14	19	1	23
Switzerland	18-20	97	91	n	n	86	1	n	76	2	2	46	3	8	20	4	16
Turkey	16	60	57	a	n	34	a	6	21	a	18	m	a	24	m	a	24
United Kingdom	16	100	86	x(2)	n	71	x(5)	2	23	x(8)	25	10	x(11)	32	6	x(14)	33
United States	18	94	93	m	n	82	m	4	23	m	40	5	m	49	n	m	50
OECD average		*94*	*91*	*n*	*n*	*82*	*1*	*2*	*52*	*3*	*18*	*27*	*4*	*29*	*13*	*3*	*34*
EU19 average		*97*	*94*	*n*	*n*	*86*	*1*	*2*	*62*	*4*	*16*	*29*	*6*	*28*	*14*	*4*	*34*
Brazil[1]	18	88	86	a	n	82	a	1	62	a	7	42	a	10	24	a	12
Chile	18	93	94	a	m	89	a	m	61	a	m	19	a	m	5	a	m
Estonia	19	103	96	n	n	93	n	n	68	2	10	19	8	37	8	8	41
Israel	17	96	94	n	n	90	n	3	19	n	7	2	n	11	1	1	12
Russian Federation	17	83	74	x(2)	m	35	x(5)	m	13	x(8)	m	4	x(11)	m	1	x(14)	m
Slovenia	18-19	98	97	n	n	96	n	n	84	1	4	29	3	45	m	m	52

Note: Mismatches between the coverage of the population data and the student/graduate data mean that the participation/graduation rates may be underestimated for countries such as Luxembourg that are net exporters of students and may be overestimated for those that are net importers.

1. Year of reference 2005.

Source: OECD. See Annex 3 for notes (*www.oecd.org/edu/eag2008*).

Please refer to the Reader's Guide for information concerning the symbols replacing missing data.

StatLink ⓘ http://dx.doi.org/10.1787/402156412821

Table C2.4.
Students in primary and secondary education by type of institution or mode of study (2006)
Distribution of students, by mode of enrolment and type of institution

		Type of institution									Mode of enrolment	
		Primary			Lower secondary			Upper secondary			Primary and secondary	
		Public	Government-dependent private	Independent private	Public	Government-dependent private	Independent private	Public	Government-dependent private	Independent private	Full-time	Part-time
		(1)	(2)	(3)	(4)	(5)	(6)	(7)	(8)	(9)	(10)	(11)
OECD countries	Australia	70.5	29.5	a	67.5	32.5	a	78.6	21.3	0.1	77.5	22.5
	Austria	95.1	4.9	x(2)	92.3	7.7	x(5)	88.5	11.5	x(8)	m	m
	Belgium	45.9	54.1	m	43.6	56.4	m	42.5	57.5	m	79.8	20.2
	Canada[1]	94.2	x(1)	5.8	94.2	x(1)	5.8	94.5	x(1)	5.5	100.0	a
	Czech Republic	98.8	1.2	a	97.9	2.1	a	86.8	13.2	a	100.0	n
	Denmark	87.9	12.1	n	75.7	24.0	0.3	97.4	2.6	n	96.4	3.6
	Finland	98.7	1.3	a	95.9	4.1	a	85.9	14.1	a	100.0	a
	France	85.0	14.5	0.5	78.6	21.1	0.3	69.6	29.5	0.9	100.0	xr
	Germany	96.7	3.3	x(2)	92.1	7.9	x(5)	91.4	8.6	x(8)	99.7	0.3
	Greece	92.9	a	7.1	94.7	a	5.3	94.1	a	5.9	97.5	2.5
	Hungary	93.2	6.8	a	92.5	7.5	a	83.8	16.2	a	94.8	5.2
	Iceland	98.8	1.2	n	99.3	0.7	n	90.3	9.3	0.4	91.6	8.4
	Ireland	99.2	a	0.8	100.0	a	n	99.3	a	0.7	99.9	0.1
	Italy	93.2	a	6.8	96.4	a	3.6	94.5	0.8	4.7	99.2	0.8
	Japan	99.0	a	1.0	93.3	a	6.7	69.2	a	30.8	98.8	1.2
	Korea	98.7	a	1.3	81.2	18.8	a	51.5	48.5	a	m	m
	Luxembourg	92.9	0.6	6.5	79.9	11.9	8.2	83.7	8.1	8.3	100.0	n
	Mexico	91.9	a	8.1	87.6	a	12.4	79.9	a	20.1	100.0	a
	Netherlands	m	m	m	m	m	m	m	m	m	98.9	1.1
	New Zealand	87.9	10.1	2.1	83.5	11.6	5.0	74.4	21.0	4.7	90.8	9.2
	Norway	97.7	2.3	x(2)	97.2	2.8	x(5)	91.4	8.6	x(8)	99.1	0.9
	Poland	98.1	0.5	1.4	97.3	0.8	2.0	90.7	0.8	8.5	95.0	5.0
	Portugal	89.2	2.6	8.3	88.2	6.6	5.2	81.3	5.3	13.4	100.0	a
	Slovak Republic	94.9	5.1	n	94.2	5.8	n	87.8	12.2	n	98.9	1.1
	Spain	68.5	28.2	3.4	68.1	28.9	3.0	78.3	11.1	10.6	91.6	8.4
	Sweden	93.5	6.5	n	92.4	7.6	n	91.2	8.8	n	89.3	10.7
	Switzerland	96.1	1.2	2.7	92.9	2.5	4.6	92.9	3.0	4.1	99.8	0.2
	Turkey	98.2	a	1.8	a	a	a	97.6	a	2.4	100.0	n
	United Kingdom	94.7	a	5.3	93.7	0.9	5.4	52.2	41.9	5.9	96.2	3.8
	United States	90.2	a	9.8	91.6	a	8.4	92.0	a	8.0	100.0	a
	OECD average	*91.1*	*6.6*	*2.9*	*84.9*	*9.4*	*3.0*	*83.2*	*12.6*	*5.4*	*96.2*	*3.9*
	EU19 average	*89.9*	*7.9*	*2.7*	*87.4*	*10.7*	*2.2*	*83.3*	*13.4*	*3.9*	*96.5*	*3.7*
Partner countries	Brazil[1]	90.8	a	9.2	90.5	a	9.5	84.9	a	15.1	m	m
	Chile	47.2	46.8	6.0	51.4	42.7	5.9	44.3	49.0	6.7	100.0	a
	Estonia	97.4	a	2.6	98.4	a	1.6	97.3	a	2.7	96.3	3.6
	Israel	100.0	a	a	100.0	a	a	100.0	a	a	100.0	a
	Russian Federation	99.4	a	0.6	99.6	a	0.4	99.0	a	1.0	99.9	0.1
	Slovenia	99.9	0.1	n	99.9	0.1	n	96.4	3.5	0.2	93.5	6.5

1. Year of reference 2005.
Source: OECD. See Annex 3 for notes (www.oecd.org/edu/eag2008).
Please refer to the Reader's Guide for information concerning the symbols replacing missing data.
StatLink ⌷⌸⌷ http://dx.doi.org/10.1787/402156412821

Table C2.5.
Students in tertiary education by type of institution or mode of study (2006)
Distribution of students, by mode of enrolment, type of institution and programme destination

C2

	Type of institution						Mode of study			
	Tertiary-type B education			Tertiary-type A and advanced research programmes			Tertiary-type B education		Tertiary-type A and advanced research programmes	
	Public	Government-dependent private	Independent private	Public	Government-dependent private	Independent private	Full-time	Part-time	Full-time	Part-time
	(1)	(2)	(3)	(4)	(5)	(6)	(7)	(8)	(9)	(10)
Australia	96.7	1.7	1.6	98.0	n	2.0	40.0	60.0	68.3	31.7
Austria	67.3	32.7	x(2)	88.8	11.2	n	m	m	m	m
Belgium	46.6	53.4	a	42.5	57.5	a	64.6	35.4	87.6	12.3
Canada[1]	m	m	m	m	m	m	m	m	74.8	25.2
Czech Republic	67.2	31.9	0.9	91.7	n	8.3	93.6	6.4	96.1	3.9
Denmark	98.2	1.8	n	98.1	1.9	n	64.1	35.9	92.3	7.7
Finland	100.0	n	a	89.5	10.5	a	100.0	a	57.1	42.9
France	72.1	8.3	19.6	87.1	0.7	12.3	100.0	a	100.0	a
Germany[2]	62.6	37.4	x(2)	95.9	4.1	x(5)	84.3	15.7	96.0	4.0
Greece	100.0	a	a	100.0	a	a	100.0	a	100.0	a
Hungary	59.5	40.5	a	86.5	13.5	a	76.1	23.9	53.9	46.1
Iceland	53.0	47.0	n	81.0	19.0	n	27.0	73.0	78.7	21.3
Ireland	93.3	a	6.7	91.6	a	8.4	62.1	37.9	83.4	16.6
Italy	88.6	a	11.4	92.8	a	7.2	100.0	n	100.0	n
Japan	7.1	a	92.9	24.1	a	75.9	96.8	3.2	88.7	11.3
Korea	15.9	a	84.1	22.2	a	77.8	m	m	m	m
Luxembourg	m	m	m	m	m	m	m	m	m	m
Mexico	95.0	a	5.0	66.4	a	33.6	100.0	a	100.0	a
Netherlands	n	n	n	m	m	m	n	n	83.4	16.6
New Zealand	71.0	29.0	m	98.1	1.9	m	36.6	63.4	60.0	40.0
Norway	56.4	43.6	x(2)	86.7	13.3	x(5)	62.2	37.8	72.9	27.1
Poland	77.7	n	22.3	69.1	a	30.9	100.0	a	55.5	44.5
Portugal	68.1	a	31.9	75.1	a	24.9	m	m	m	m
Slovak Republic	86.5	13.5	n	95.7	n	4.3	74.0	26.0	61.9	38.1
Spain	79.1	15.6	5.3	87.7	n	12.3	98.1	1.9	88.2	11.8
Sweden	61.7	38.3	n	93.8	6.2	n	91.7	8.3	49.2	50.8
Switzerland	29.9	39.5	30.6	92.2	5.7	2.2	23.3	76.7	90.4	9.6
Turkey	97.5	a	2.5	94.3	a	5.7	100.0	n	100.0	n
United Kingdom	a	100.0	n	a	100.0	n	24.4	75.6	71.7	28.3
United States	84.3	a	15.7	71.9	a	28.1	49.0	51.0	65.1	34.9
OECD average	*65.5*	*19.1*	*13.8*	*78.5*	*9.1*	*13.9*	*70.7*	*25.3*	*79.8*	*20.2*
EU19 average	*68.3*	*20.7*	*6.1*	*81.5*	*12.1*	*6.8*	*77.1*	*16.7*	*79.8*	*20.2*
Brazil[1]	25.5	a	74.5	28.3	a	71.7	m	m	m	m
Chile	7.1	3.0	89.9	32.3	22.2	45.5	100.0	a	100.0	a
Estonia	47.8	18.3	33.9	n	86.0	14.0	91.5	8.5	88.9	11.1
Israel	33.7	66.3	a	8.4	78.4	12.5	100.0	a	78.1	21.9
Russian Federation[2]	95.4	a	4.6	85.0	a	15.0	71.9	28.1	54.9	45.1
Slovenia	82.7	6.2	11.2	97.5	1.1	1.4	47.6	52.4	76.2	23.8

1. Year of reference 2005.
2. Excludes advanced research programmes.
Source: OECD. See Annex 3 for notes (*www.oecd.org/edu/eag2008*).
Please refer to the Reader's Guide for information concerning the symbols replacing missing data.
StatLink ᐁᔑᓬ http://dx.doi.org/10.1787/402156412821

WHO STUDIES ABROAD AND WHERE?

INDICATOR C3

This indicator provides a picture of student mobility and of the internationalisation of tertiary education in OECD and partner countries. It shows global trends and highlights the main destinations of international students and trends in market shares of the international student pool. Some of the factors underlying students' choice of country of study are also examined. It shows the extent of student mobility to different destinations and presents international student intake in terms of the distribution by countries and regions of origin, types of programmes, and fields of education. The distribution of students enrolled outside of their country of citizenship by destination is also examined, along with the immigration implications for host countries. The proportion of international students in tertiary enrolments provides a good indication of the magnitude of student mobility in different countries.

Key results

Chart C3.1. **Student mobility in tertiary education (2006)**

This chart shows the percentage of international students in tertiary enrolments. According to country-specific immigration legislations and data availability constraints, student mobility is either defined on the basis of students' country of residence or the country where students received their prior education.

Student mobility – *i.e.* international students who travelled to a country different from their own for the purpose of tertiary study – ranges from below 1 to almost 18% of tertiary enrolments. International students are most numerous in tertiary enrolments in Australia, Austria, New Zealand, Switzerland and the United Kingdom.

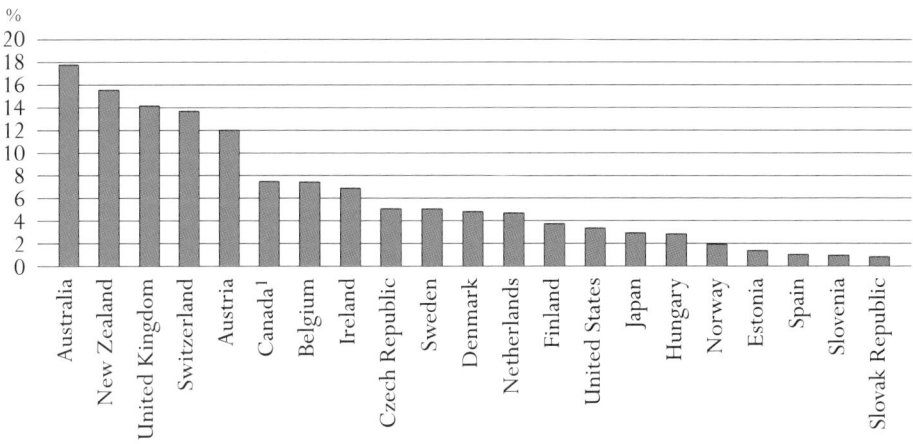

Note: The data presented in this chart are not comparable with data on foreign students in tertiary education presented in editions prior to *Education at a Glance 2006* or elsewhere in this chapter.
1. Year of reference 2005.
Countries are ranked in descending order of the percentage of international students in tertiary education.
Source: OECD. Table C3.1. See Annex 3 for notes (*www.oecd.org/edu/eag2008*).
StatLink ᴍᴤᴾ http://dx.doi.org/10.1787/402158641726

Other highlights of this indicator

- In 2006, over 2.9 million tertiary students were enrolled outside their country of citizenship. This represented a 3% increase from the previous year in total foreign student intake reported to the OECD and the UNESCO Institute for Statistics.

- France, Germany, the United Kingdom and the United States receive 49% of all foreign students worldwide. The largest absolute numbers of international students from OECD countries are from France, Germany, Japan and Korea. Students from China and India comprise the largest numbers of international students from partner countries.

- International students make up 15% or more of the enrolments in tertiary education in Australia and New Zealand. International students make up more than 20% of enrolments in advanced research programmes in Belgium, Canada, New Zealand, Switzerland, the United Kingdom and the United States.

- 30% or more of international students are enrolled in sciences, agriculture or engineering in Finland, Germany, Hungary, Sweden, Switzerland and the United States.

C3

Policy context

The general trend towards freely circulating capital, goods and services – coupled with changes in the openness of labour markets – has increased demand for new kinds of educational provision in OECD countries. Governments as well as individuals are looking to higher education to play a role in broadening students' horizons and allowing them to develop a deeper understanding of the world's languages, cultures and business methods. One way for students to expand their knowledge of other societies and languages and hence to leverage their labour market prospects is to study in tertiary educational institutions in countries other than their own. Indeed, several OECD governments – especially in countries of the European Union (EU) – have set up schemes and policies to promote mobility as a way to foster intercultural contacts and help to build social networks for the future.

From a macroeconomic perspective, international negotiations on liberalisation of trade in services highlight the trade implications of the internationalisation of education services. Some OECD countries already show signs of specialisation in education exports. The long-term trend towards greater internationalisation of education (Box C3.1) is likely to have a growing impact on countries' balance of payments as a result of revenue from tuition fees and domestic consumption by international students. It is worth noting that, in addition to student mobility, the cross-border electronic delivery of flexible educational programmes and campuses abroad are also relevant to the trade dimension of international tertiary education, although no comparable data yet exist.

The internationalisation of tertiary education has many economic impacts in addition to the short-term monetary costs and benefits that are reflected in the current account balance. It can also provide an opportunity for smaller and/or less-developed educational systems to improve the cost efficiency of their education provision. Indeed, training opportunities abroad may constitute a cost-efficient alternative to national provision and allow countries to focus limited resources on educational programmes for which economies of scale can be generated, or to expand participation in tertiary education despite bottlenecks in provision.

In addition, the rapid expansion of tertiary education in OECD countries – and more recently in most emerging countries (OECD, 2005a) – has intensified the financial pressures on education systems and has led to greater interest in recruiting foreign students. As tertiary institutions increasingly relied on revenues from foreign tuition fees, some countries actively recruited foreign students. In others, education abroad was encouraged as a way to address unmet demand resulting from bottlenecks caused by the rapid expansion of tertiary education. In the past few years, the rise of the knowledge economy and global competition for skills have provided a new driver for the internationalisation of education systems in many OECD countries, with the recruitment of foreign students part of a broader strategy to recruit highly skilled immigrants.

At the institutional level, the additional revenues that foreign students may generate – either through differentiated tuition fees or public subsidies – help drive international education. But tertiary education institutions also have academic incentives to engage in international activities to build or maintain their reputation in increasingly global academic competition.

At the same time, from the perspective of educational institutions, international enrolments constrain instructional settings and processes insofar as they have to adapt their curriculum and teaching methods to a culturally and linguistically diverse student body. These constraints are,

C3

however, outweighed by numerous benefits to host institutions. A potential international client base compels institutions to offer programmes that stand out among competitors and may contribute to the development of highly reactive, client-driven quality tertiary education that responds to changing needs. International enrolments can also help institutions to reach the critical mass needed to diversify the range of their educational programmes and to increase their financial resources when foreign students bear the full cost of their education (Box C3.3). Given these advantages, institutions may favour the enrolment of international students, thereby restricting access to domestic students. There is little evidence of this, except in some prestigious programmes of elite institutions that are in high demand (OECD, 2004a).

For individuals, the returns to studying abroad depend to a large extent both on the policies of sending countries regarding financial aid to students going abroad and the tuition fee policies of countries of destination (Box C3.3) and their financial support for international students. The cost of living in countries of study and exchange rates also affect the cost of international education. In addition, the long-term returns to international education depend greatly on how international degrees are recognised and valued by local labour markets.

The numbers of students enrolled in other countries can provide some ideas of the extent of the internationalisation of tertiary education. In the future, it will also be important to develop ways to quantify and measure other components of cross-border education.

Evidence and explanations

Concepts and terminology used in this indicator

The concepts and terminology used in this indicator have changed from those used in editions of *Education at a Glance* produced before 2006. Previously, Indicator C3 focused on foreign students in tertiary education, defined as non-citizens of the country in which they study. This concept was inappropriate for measuring student mobility in that not all foreign students come for the express purpose of studying. In particular, foreign students who are permanent residents in their country of study as a result of immigration – their own or that of their parents – are included in the total. This results in an overestimate of numbers of foreign students in countries with comparatively low rates of naturalisation of their immigrant populations. Moreover, citizens of the country in which they study may be mobile students (*i.e.* nationals who have lived abroad and return to their country of citizenship to study). Therefore, in an effort to improve the measurement of student mobility and the comparability of data on internationalisation, the OECD – together with Eurostat and the UNESCO Institute for Statistics – revised in 2005 the instruments used to gather data on student mobility. According to this new concept, the term "international students" refers to students who have crossed borders expressly with the intention to study.

The measurement of student mobility depends to a large extent on country-specific immigration legislation and constraints on the availability of data. For instance, the free mobility of individuals within the EU and the broader European Economic Area (EEA) makes it impossible to derive numbers of international students from visa statistics. The OECD therefore allows countries to define as international students those who are not permanent residents of their country of study or, alternatively, those who received their prior education in another country (regardless of citizenship), depending on which operational definition is most appropriate in their national context. Overall, the country of prior education is considered a better operational criterion for EU countries so as not to omit intra-EU student mobility (Kelo *et al.*, 2005), while the residence criterion is usually a good proxy in countries that require a student visa to enter the country for educational purposes.

The convention adopted here is to use the term "international student" when referring to student mobility and the term "foreign student" for non-citizens enrolled in a country (*i.e.* including some permanent residents and therefore an overestimate of actual student mobility). However since not all countries are yet able to report data on student mobility on the basis of students' country of residence or of prior education, some tables and charts present indicators on both international and foreign students, albeit separately to emphasise the need for caution in interpreting the results.

In this indicator, data on total foreign enrolments worldwide are based on the number of foreign students enrolled in countries reporting data to the OECD and to the UNESCO Institute for Statistics and thus may be underestimated. In addition, all trend analyses in this indicator are based on numbers of foreign students at different points in time, as time series on student mobility are not yet available. Work is under way to fill this gap and develop retrospective time series on student mobility for future editions of *Education at a Glance*.

Trends in foreign student numbers

In 2006, 2.9 million tertiary students were enrolled outside their country of citizenship, of whom 2.4 million (83.5%) in the OECD area. This represented a 2.7% increase of 77 000 additional individuals in total foreign enrolments worldwide since the previous year. In the OECD area the increase was 3.0%. Since 2000, the number of foreign tertiary students enrolled in the OECD area and worldwide increased by 54.1 and 54.4%, respectively, for an average annual increase of 7.5% (Table C3.6).

Compared to 2000, the number of foreign students enrolled in tertiary education more than doubled in the Czech Republic, Korea, the Netherlands, New Zealand and Spain, and in the partner country Estonia. In contrast, the number of foreign students enrolled in Belgium, the Slovak Republic, Turkey and the United States, grew by about 25% or less (Table C3.1). Changes in foreign student numbers between 2000 and 2006 indicate that, on average, the number of foreign student has grown faster in the OECD area than in the 19 EU countries of the OECD, by 111 and 78%, respectively (Table C3.1).

The combination of OECD and UNESCO Institute for Statistics data makes it possible to examine longer-term trends and illustrates the dramatic growth in foreign enrolments (Box C3.1). Over the past three decades, the number of students enrolled outside their country of citizenship has risen dramatically, from 0.6 million worldwide in 1975 to 2.9 million in 2006, a more than four-fold increase. Growth in the internationalisation of tertiary education has accelerated during the past eleven years, mirroring the growing globalisation of economies and societies.

The rise in the number of students enrolled abroad since 1975 stems from various factors. During the early years, public policies aimed at promoting and nurturing academic, cultural, social and political ties between countries played a key role, especially in the context of the European construction: building mutual understanding among young Europeans was a major policy objective. North American policies of academic co-operation had similar rationales. Over time, however, economic factors played an increasing role. Decreasing transport costs, the spread of new technologies, and faster, cheaper communication made economies and societies increasingly interdependent through the

1980s and 1990s. The trend was particularly marked in the high-technology sector and in the labour market, with the internationalisation of labour markets for the highly skilled giving individuals an incentive to gain international experience as part of their studies. The spread of information and communication technology (ICT) lowered the information and transaction costs of study abroad and boosted demand for international education.

C3

Box C3.1. Long term growth in the number of students enrolled outside their country of citizenship

Growth in internationalisation of tertiary education (1975-2006)

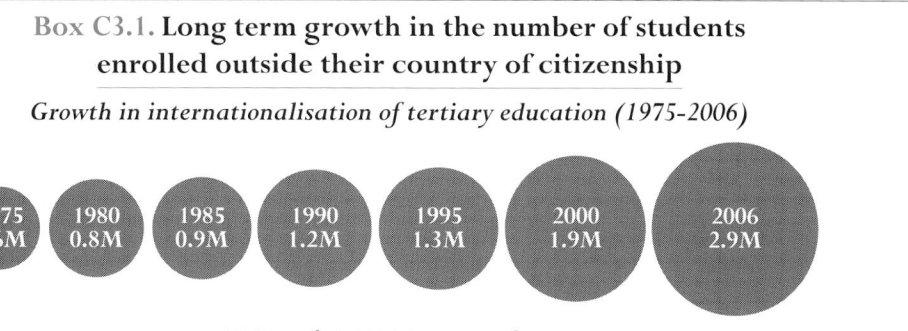

Source: OECD and UNESCO Institute for Statistics.

Data on foreign enrolment worldwide comes from both the OECD and the UNESCO Institute for Statistics (UIS). UIS provided the data on all countries for 1975-1995 and most of the partner countries for 2000 and 2006. The OECD provided the data on OECD countries and the other partner countries in 2000 and 2006. Both sources use similar definitions, thus making their combination possible. Missing data were imputed with the closest data reports to ensure that breaks in data coverage do not result in breaks in time series.

Chart C3.2. Distribution of foreign students in tertiary education, by country of destination (2006)

Percentage of foreign tertiary students reported to the OECD who are enrolled in each country of destination

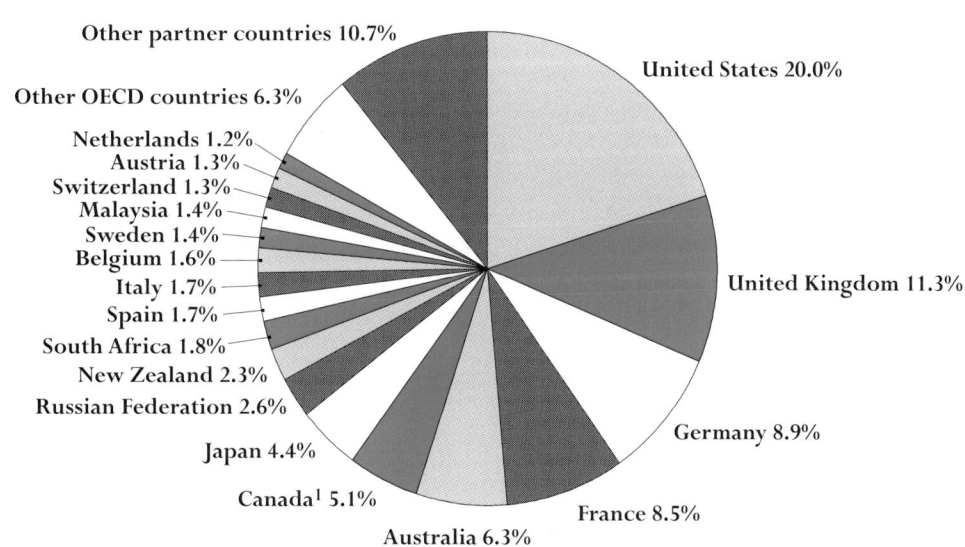

1. Year of reference 2005.
Source: OECD and UNESCO Institute for Statistics for most data on partner countries. Table C3.7 (available on line at the link below). See Annex 3 for notes (*www.oecd.org/edu/eag2008*).
StatLink ⏴🖵🖴 http://dx.doi.org/10.1787/402158641726

Major destinations of foreign students

In 2006, five out of ten foreign students went to the four countries that host the majority of foreign students enrolled outside of their country of citizenship. The United States received the most (in absolute terms) with 20% of all foreign students worldwide, followed by the United Kingdom (11%), Germany (9%) and France (8%). Altogether, these destinations account for 49% of all tertiary students pursuing their studies abroad (Chart C3.2). Besides these four major destinations, significant numbers of foreign students were enrolled in Australia (6%), Canada (5%), Japan (4%) and New Zealand (2%), and in the partner country the Russian Federation (3%), in 2006.

Trends in market shares show the emergence of new players on the international education market

The examination of country-specific trends in market shares of the international education market – measured as a percentage of all foreign students worldwide enrolled in a given destination – sheds light on the dynamics of internationalisation of tertiary education. Over a six-year period, the share of the United States as a preferred destination dropped from 25.1 to 20.0%. For Germany the decline was around 1 percentage point, and for Belgium and the United Kingdom, it was about one-half of a percentage point. In contrast, the market shares of Australia, Japan and South Africa expanded by around 1 percentage point. The impressive growth in France (1.2%) and New Zealand (1.9%) keeps them among the big players in the international education market (Chart C3.3).

These trends underline the dynamics of international education in OECD and partner countries, and reflect differences in internationalisation policies; these range from proactive marketing in the Asia-Pacific region to a more passive approach in the traditionally dominant United States,

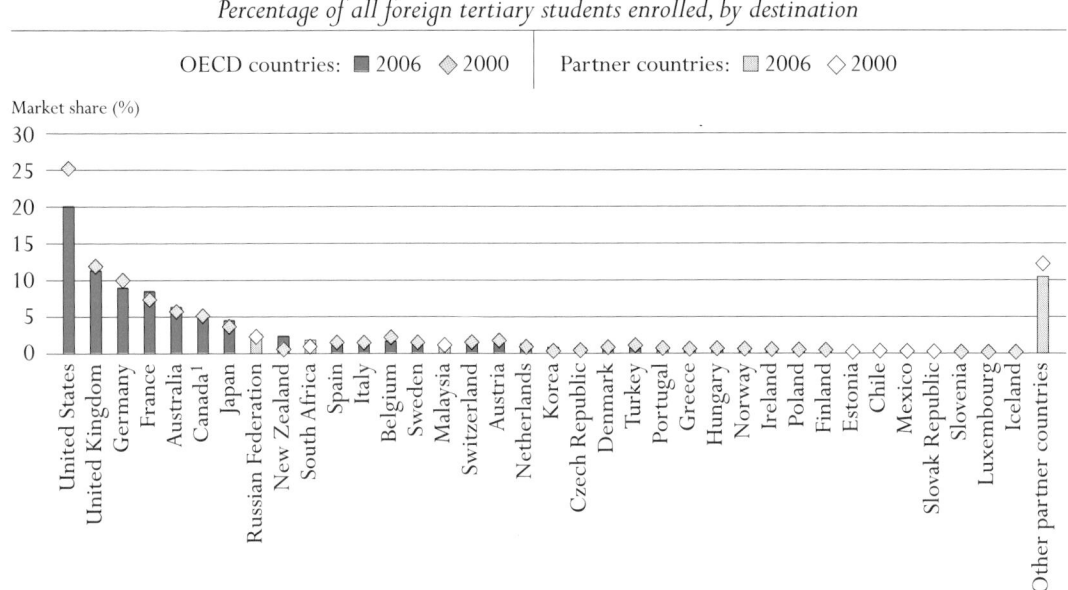

Chart C3.3. **Trends in international education market shares (2000, 2006)**

Percentage of all foreign tertiary students enrolled, by destination

1. Year of reference 2005.

Countries are ranked in descending order of 2006 market shares.

Source: OECD and UNESCO Institute for Statistics for most data on partner countries. Table C3.7 (available on line at the link below). See Annex 3 for notes (*www.oecd.org/edu/eag2008*).

StatLink ⬛ᵐˢ⬛ http://dx.doi.org/10.1787/402158641726

where the intake of foreign students was also affected by the tightening of the conditions of entry for international students in the aftermath of the events of 11 September 2001 (see Indicator C3 [OECD, 2005a]).

Underlying factors in students' choice of a country of study

Language of instruction: a critical factor

The language spoken and used in instruction is an essential element in the choice of a foreign country in which to study. Therefore, countries whose language of instruction is widely spoken and read (*e.g.* English, French, and German) are leading destinations of foreign students, both in absolute and relative terms. Japan is a notable exception: despite a less widespread language of instruction it enrols large numbers of foreign students, 94.2% of whom are from Asia (Table C3.2 and Chart C3.3).

The dominance (in absolute numbers) of English-speaking destinations (Australia, Canada, New Zealand, the United Kingdom and the United States) may be largely due to the fact that students intending to study abroad are likely to have learned English in their home country and/or wish to improve their English language skills through immersion and study abroad. The rapid increase in foreign enrolments in Australia (index change of 175), Canada (157) and, most importantly, New Zealand (825) between 2000 and 2006 can be partly attributed to linguistic considerations (Table C3.1).

Given this pattern, an increasing number of institutions in non-English-speaking countries now offer courses in English to overcome their linguistic disadvantage in terms of attracting foreign students. This trend is especially noticeable in the Nordic countries (Box C3.2).

Box C3.2. **OECD and partner countries offering tertiary programmes in English (2006)**

Use of English in instruction	OECD and partner countries
All or nearly all programmes offered in English	Australia, Canada[1], Ireland, New Zealand, United Kingdom, United States
Many programmes offered in English	Denmark, Finland, Netherlands, Sweden
Some programmes offered in English	Belgium (Fl.), Czech Republic, France, Germany, Hungary, Iceland, Japan, Korea, Norway, Poland, Portugal, Slovak Republic, Switzerland, Turkey
No or nearly no programmes offered in English	Austria, Belgium (Fr.), Greece, Italy, Luxembourg, Mexico, Portugal, Spain, Brazil, Chile, Israel, Russian Federation

Note: Assessing the extent to which a country offers a few or many programmes in English is subjective. In doing so, country size has been taken into account, hence the classification of France and Germany among countries with comparatively few English programmes, although they have more English programmes than Sweden in absolute terms.

1. In Canada, tertiary institutions are either French- (mostly Quebec) or English-speaking.

Source: OECD, compiled from brochures for prospective international students by OAD (Austria), CHES and NARIC (Czech Republic), Cirius (Denmark), CIMO (Finland), EduFrance (France), DAAD (Germany), Campus Hungary (Hungary), University of Iceland (Iceland), JPSS (Japan), NIIED (Korea), NUFFIC (Netherlands), SIU (Norway), CRASP (Poland), Swedish Institute (Sweden) and Middle-East Technical University (Turkey).

C3

Impact of tuition fees and cost of living on foreign students' destinations

Tuition fees and cost of living are also important factors in prospective international students' choice of country. In Denmark, Finland, Iceland, Norway and Sweden, there are no tuition fees for either domestic or international students (Box C3.3). This, associated with the existence of programmes in English, probably explains part of the robust growth between 2000 and 2006 in the number of foreign students enrolled in some of these countries (Table C3.1). However, in the absence of fees, the high unit costs of tertiary education mean that international students place a high monetary burden on their countries of destination (Table B1.1). As a result, Denmark adopted tuition fees for non-EU and non-EEA international students, as of 2006/07. Similar options are currently being discussed in Finland, Norway and Sweden, where foreign enrolments grew by more than 50% between 2000 and 2006.

Box C3.3. Level of tuition fees charged for international students in public universities (2004/05)

Tuition fee structure	Countries
Higher tuition fees for international students than for domestic students	Australia, Austria[1], Belgium[1,2], Canada, Czech Republic, Estonia[1], Netherlands[1], New Zealand, Turkey, United Kingdom[1], United States[3]
Same tuition fees for international and domestic students	France, Italy, Japan, Korea, Mexico[2], Spain
No tuition fees for either international or domestic students	Denmark, Finland, Iceland, Norway, Sweden

Annual average tuition fees charged to international students by public tertiary-type A institutions (2004)

USD PPPs

- 13 000 — United States
- 11 500 — Australia
- 10 000 — Canada
- 9 500 — New Zealand
- 3 700 — Japan, Korea
- 1 700 — Austria
- 1 100 — Italy
- 900 — Belgium, Czech Republic, France, Spain, Turkey
- 0 — Denmark, Finland, Iceland, Norway, Sweden

1. For non-European Union or non-European Economic Area students.
2. Some institutions charge higher tuition fees for international students.
3. International students pay the same fees as domestic out-of-state students. However since most domestic students are enrolled in-state, international students pay higher tuition fees than most domestic students in practice.
Source: OECD. Indicator B5. See Annex 3 for notes (*www.oecd.org/edu/eag2008*).

C3

Countries that charge their international students the full cost of education reap significant trade benefits. Several countries in the Asia-Pacific region have actually made international education an explicit part of their socio-economic development strategies and have initiated policies to attract international students on a revenue-generating or at least self-financing basis. Australia and New Zealand have successfully adopted differentiated tuition fees for international students. In Japan and Korea, with high tuition fees that are the same for domestic and international students, foreign enrolments nevertheless grew robustly between 2000 and 2006 (see Indicator B5). This shows that tuition costs do not necessarily discourage prospective international students as long as the quality of education provided and its likely returns make the investment worthwhile. However, in choosing between similar educational opportunities, cost considerations may play a role, especially for students originating from developing countries. In this respect, the comparatively low rise in foreign enrolments in the United Kingdom and the United States between 2000 and 2006 and the deterioration of the United States' market share may be attributed to the comparatively high tuition fees charged to international students in a context of fierce competition from other primarily English-speaking destinations offering similar educational opportunities at a lower cost (Box C3.3).

Impact of immigration policy on foreign student destinations

In recent years, several OECD countries have softened their immigration policies to encourage the temporary or permanent immigration of their international students. Australia, Canada and New Zealand, for example, make it easy for foreign students who have studied in their universities to settle by granting them additional points for their immigration file. This makes these countries more attractive to students and strengthens their knowledge economy. As a result, immigration considerations may also affect some international students' choice between alternative educational opportunities abroad. In addition, the total freedom of movement of workers within Europe explains part of the high level of student mobility in Europe compared to that between the countries of North America, as the North America Free Trade Agreement (NAFTA) does not include the free movement of workers within a common labour market.

Other factors

Other important factors for foreign students include the academic reputation of particular institutions or programmes; the flexibility of programmes with respect to counting time spent abroad towards degree requirements; the limitations of tertiary education provision in the home country; restrictive university admission policies at home; geographical, trade or historical links between countries; future job opportunities; cultural aspirations; and government policies to facilitate transfer of credits between home and host institutions. The transparency and flexibility of courses and degree requirements also count.

Extent of student mobility in tertiary education

The foregoing analysis has focused on trends in absolute numbers of foreign students and their distribution by countries of destination since time series or global aggregates on student mobility do not exist. It is also possible to measure the extent of student mobility in each country of destination by examining the proportion of international students in total tertiary enrolments. This has the advantage of taking the size of different tertiary education systems into account and highlighting those that are highly internationalised regardless of their size and the importance of their absolute market share.

C3

Wide variations in the proportion of international students enrolled in OECD and partner countries

Among countries for which data on student mobility are available, Australia, Austria, New Zealand, Switzerland and the United Kingdom display the highest levels of incoming student mobility, measured as the proportion of international students in their total tertiary enrolment. In Australia, 17.8% of tertiary students have come to the country in order to pursue their studies. Similarly, international students represent 12.0% of total tertiary enrolments in Austria, 15.5% in New Zealand, 13.7% in Switzerland and 14.1% in the United Kingdom. In contrast, incoming student mobility is 1% or less of total tertiary enrolments in the Slovak Republic, Spain and the partner country Slovenia (Table C3.1 and Chart C3.1).

Among countries for which data on student mobility are not available, foreign enrolments constitute a large group of tertiary students in France (11.2%) and Luxembourg (42.2%), an indication of significant levels of incoming student mobility. However foreign enrolments represent 1% or less of total tertiary enrolments in Korea, Poland, Turkey and the partner country the Russian Federation (Table C3.1).

Student mobility at different levels of tertiary education

The proportion of international students at different levels of tertiary education in each country of destination also sheds light on patterns of student mobility. A first observation is that, with the exception of Japan, New Zealand and Norway, tertiary-type B programmes are far less internationalised than tertiary-type A programmes, suggesting that international students are mostly attracted to traditional academic programmes for which degree transferability is often easier. With the exception of Italy and Portugal, this observation also holds true for countries for which data on student mobility are not available (Table C3.1).

In Australia, Austria, the Czech Republic, the Slovak Republic and Sweden, the proportions of international students are roughly the same in tertiary-type A and advanced research programmes, an indication that these countries of destination are successful at attracting students from abroad from the start of their tertiary education and keeping or attracting them beyond their first degrees. In contrast, other countries display significantly higher incoming student mobility relative to total enrolments in advanced research programmes than in tertiary-type A programmes. This pattern is clear in Belgium, Canada, Finland, Hungary, Japan, New Zealand, Norway, Spain, Switzerland, the United Kingdom and the United States, and in the partner country Slovenia, as well as in France, Iceland, Italy, Korea, Poland and Turkey, countries for which data on student mobility are not available. It may reflect the attractiveness of advanced research programmes in these countries or a preference for recruitment of international students at higher levels of education to capitalise on their contribution to domestic research and development or in anticipation of their subsequent recruitment as highly qualified immigrants.

Profile of international student intake in different destinations

Asia leads among regions of origin

Asian students form the largest group of international students enrolled in countries reporting data to the OECD or the UNESCO Institute for Statistics: 45.3 % of the total in all reporting destinations (42.8% of the total in OECD countries, and 58.3% of the total in partner countries).

Their predominance is greatest in Australia, Japan, Korea and New Zealand, where more than 73% of international or foreign students originate from Asia. In OECD countries, the Asian group is followed by Europeans (23.0%), particularly EU citizens (15.7%). Students from Africa account for 9.9% of all international students, while those from North America account for only 3.5%. Finally, students from South America represent 5.0% of the total. Altogether, 29.3% of international students enrolled in the OECD area originate from another OECD country (Table C3.2).

Main countries of origin of international students

The predominance of students from Asia and Europe is also clear when looking at individual countries of origin. Students from France, Germany, Japan and Korea represent the largest groups of international students enrolled in OECD countries, at 2.2%, 2.8%, 2.4% and 4.1% of the total respectively, followed by students from Canada and the United States at 1.7% and 1.8%, respectively (Table C3.2).

Among international students originating from partner countries, students from China represent by far the largest group, with 15.4% of all international students enrolled in the OECD area (not including an additional 1.3% from Hong Kong, China) (Table C3.2). Their destination of choice is the United States, followed closely by Japan, with 20.7% and 19.1%, respectively, of all international Chinese students studying abroad. Students from China are followed by those from India (5.4%), Morocco (1.6%), and Malaysia (1.6%) and the Russian Federation (1.2%). A significant number of Asian students studying abroad also come from Indonesia, the Islamic Republic of Iran, Kazakhstan, Pakistan , Thailand, Uzbekistan and Vietnam (Table C3.3 and Table C3.7, available on line).

The proportion of international students by level and type of tertiary education highlights specialisations

In some countries a comparatively large proportion of international students are enrolled in tertiary-type B programmes. This is the case in Belgium (31.8%), Japan (24.1%), New Zealand (27.5%) and the partner country Slovenia (21.9%). In Korea, for which data on student mobility are not available, foreign enrolments in tertiary-type B programmes also constitute a large group of foreign students (24.9%) (Table C3.4).

In other countries, a large proportion of their international students enrol in advanced research programmes. This is particularly true in Spain (36.0%) and Switzerland (27.3%). Such patterns suggest that these countries offer attractive advanced programmes to prospective international graduate students. This concentration can also be observed – to a more limited extent – in Canada (9.8%), Finland (14.3%), Japan (10.1%), the United Kingdom (11.6%) and the United States (15.7%). Among countries for which data on student mobility are not available, foreign enrolments in advanced research programmes constitute a large group of foreign students in France (10.1%). All of these countries are likely to benefit from the contribution of these high-level international students to domestic research and development. In addition, this specialisation can also generate higher tuition revenue per international student in the countries charging full tuition costs to foreign students (Box C3.3).

C3

The proportion of international students by field of education underlines magnet centres

As shown in Table C3.5, sciences attract about one in six international students in Germany (17.1%), New Zealand (17.4%), Switzerland (16.6%) and the United States (18.7%), but fewer than one in fifty in Japan (1.3%). However, the picture changes slightly when agriculture, engineering, manufacturing and construction programmes are included among scientific disciplines. Finland receives 41.9% of its international students in these fields. The proportion of international students enrolled in agriculture, sciences or engineering is also high in Canada (29.0%), Germany (38.3%), Hungary (30.2%), Sweden (39.6%), Switzerland (34.2%), the United Kingdom (29.8%) and the United States (34.6%). Similarly, among countries for which data on student mobility are not available, agriculture, sciences and engineering attract at least 27% of foreign students in France (27.0%), Portugal (27.2%) and the Slovak Republic (28.3%). In contrast, few foreign students are enrolled in agriculture, sciences and engineering in Poland (Chart C3.4).

Most countries that enrol large proportions of their international students in agriculture, sciences and engineering deliver programmes in English. In Germany, the large proportion of foreign students in scientific disciplines may also reflect its strong tradition in these fields.

Non-anglophone countries tend to enrol a higher proportion of their international students in the humanities and the arts, areas that are favoured by over 20% of the international students in Austria (23.6%), Germany (22.0%), Japan (24.5%), Norway (20.1%) and the partner country Slovenia (21.5%). Among countries for which data on student mobility are not available, this is also the case in France (20.7%), Iceland (44.3%) and Poland (20.0%).

Social sciences, business and law programmes also attract international students in large numbers. In Australia, New Zealand and the partner country Estonia, these fields enrol around half of all international students (at 52.7, 49.0 and 53.4%, respectively). The proportion is also high in the Netherlands (45.3%) and the United Kingdom (40.8%). Among countries for which data on student mobility are not available, France (40.6%) and Portugal (46.6%) have the largest proportion of their foreign students enrolled in social sciences, business and law.

The situation of health and welfare is fairly specific since it depends to a large extent on national policies relating to recognition of medical degrees. Health and welfare programmes attract large proportions of international students in EU countries, most notably in Belgium (43.5%), the Czech Republic (23.5%), Denmark (19.9%), Hungary (30.0%) and Spain (30.7%). Among countries for which data on student mobility are not available, health and welfare programmes are also chosen by one-fifth to one-quarter of foreign students in Italy (21.6%), Poland (26.0%) and the Slovak Republic (30.5%). This pattern relates to the quotas imposed in many European countries which restrict access to educational programmes in the medical field. This increases the demand for training in other EU countries to bypass quotas and take advantage of EU countries' automatic recognition of medical degrees under the European Medical Directive.

Overall, the concentration of international students in various disciplines in countries of destination highlights magnet programmes that attract students from abroad in large numbers. This attraction results from many factors on both the supply and demand side.

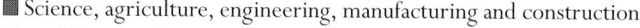

Chart C3.4. Distribution of international students by field of education (2006)

Percentage of international tertiary students enrolled in different fields of education

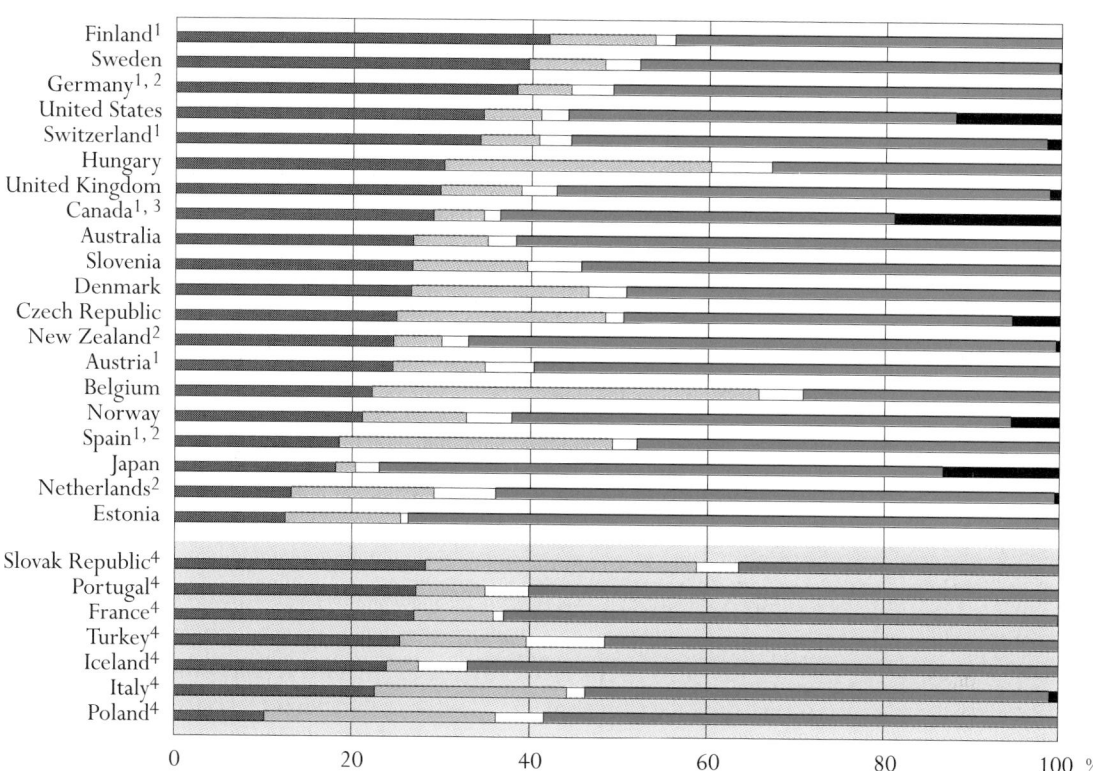

■ Science, agriculture, engineering, manufacturing and construction
▨ Health and welfare
□ Education
▤ Humanities, arts, services, social sciences, business and law
■ Unknown

1. Excludes tertiary-type B programmes.
2. Excludes advanced research programmes.
3. Year of reference 2005.
4. Distribution of foreign students by field of education. These data are not comparable with data on international students and are therefore presented separately.
Countries are ranked in descending order of the proportion of international students enrolled in sciences, agriculture, engineering, manufacturing and construction.
Source: OECD. Table C3.5. See Annex 3 for notes (*www.oecd.org/edu/eag2008*).
StatLink ⛁ http://dx.doi.org/10.1787/402158641726

On the supply side, some destinations offer centres of excellence or traditional expertise able to attract students from other countries in large numbers (*e.g.* Finland and Germany in sciences and engineering). In the humanities and arts, some destinations also have a natural monopoly on some programmes. This is especially obvious for linguistic or cultural studies (*e.g.* Austria, Germany and Japan).

On the demand side, the characteristics of international students can help to explain their concentration in certain fields of education. For instance, students in scientific disciplines are usually less likely to be fluent in many different languages, which may explain their stronger propensity to study in countries offering education programmes in English, and their lesser propensity to enrol in countries where these are less common (*e.g.* Japan). Similarly, the demand of many Asian students for business training may explain the strong concentration of international students in social sciences, business and law in neighbouring Australia and New Zealand and to a lesser extent in Japan. Finally, EU provisions for the recognition of medical degrees clearly drive the concentration of international students in health and welfare programmes in EU countries.

Destinations of citizens enrolled abroad

When studying in tertiary education outside of their country of citizenship, OECD students enrol predominantly in another country of the OECD area. On average, only 3.2% of foreign students from OECD countries are enrolled in a partner country. The proportion of foreign students from partner countries enrolled in another partner country is significantly higher, with more than 22% of foreign students from Chile, Estonia, Israel and the Russian Federation enrolled in another partner country. In contrast, students from the Czech Republic (0.9%), France (0.8%), Iceland (0.2%), Ireland (0.2%), Poland (0.8%), the Slovak Republic (0.2%) and most notably, Luxembourg (0.1%) display an extremely low propensity to study outside of the OECD area (Table C3.3).

Language considerations, geographic proximity and similarity of education systems are all important determinants of the choice of destination. Geographic considerations and differences in entry requirements are likely explanations of the concentration of students from Austria in Germany, from Belgium in France and the Netherlands, from France in Belgium, from Canada in the United States, from New Zealand in Australia, from China in Japan, etc. Language issues as well as academic traditions also shed light on the propensity for anglophone students to concentrate in other countries of the Commonwealth or in the United States, even those that are geographically distant. Migration networks also play a role, as illustrated by the concentration of students with Portuguese citizenship in France, students from Turkey in Germany or from Mexico in the United States.

Finally, international students' destinations also highlight the attractiveness of specific education systems, whether due to considerations of academic reputation or subsequent immigration opportunities. In this respect, it is noteworthy that students from China are mostly in Australia, Germany, Japan, New Zealand, the United Kingdom and the United States, most of which have schemes to facilitate the immigration of international students. Similarly, students from India favour Australia, the United Kingdom and the United States; these three destinations attract 81.5% of Indian citizens enrolled abroad (Table C3.3).

Definitions and methodologies

Data sources, definitions and reference period

Data on international and foreign students refer to the academic year 2005/06 and are based on the UOE data collection on education statistics administered by the OECD in 2007 (for details see Annex 3 at *www.oecd.org/edu/eag2008*). Additional data from the UNESCO Institute for Statistics are also included.

Students are classified as international students if they left their country of origin and moved to another country for the purpose of study. Depending on country-specific immigration legislation, mobility arrangements (*e.g.* free mobility of individuals within the EU and EEA areas) and data availability, international students may be defined as students who are not permanent or usual residents of their country of study or alternatively as students who obtained their prior education in a different country (*e.g.* EU countries).

Permanent or usual residence in the reporting country is defined according to national legislation. In practice, this means holding a student visa or permit, or electing a foreign country of domicile in the year prior to entering the education system of the country reporting data. The country of prior education is defined as the country in which students obtained the qualification required to enrol in their current level of education, *i.e.* the country in which they obtained their upper secondary or post-secondary non-tertiary education for international students enrolled in tertiary-type A and tertiary-type B programmes and the country in which they obtained their tertiary-type A education for international students enrolled in advanced research programmes. Country-specific operational definitions of international students are indicated in the tables as well as in Annex 3 (*www.oecd.org/edu/eag2008*).

Students are classified as foreign students if they are not citizens of the country in which the data are collected. While pragmatic and operational, this classification is inappropriate for capturing student mobility because of differing national policies regarding the naturalisation of immigrants. For instance, while Australia and Switzerland report similar intakes of foreign students relative to their tertiary enrolments – 20.9 and 19.2%, respectively – these proportions reflect significant differences in the actual levels of student mobility – 17.8% of tertiary enrolments in Australia and 13.7% in Switzerland (Table C3.1). This is because Australia has a higher propensity to grant permanent residence to its immigrant populations than Switzerland. Therefore, interpretations of data based on the concept of foreign students in terms of student mobility and bilateral comparisons need to be made with caution.

Methodologies

Data on international and foreign students are obtained from enrolments in their countries of destination. The method of obtaining data on international and foreign students is therefore the same as that used for collecting data on total enrolments, *i.e.* records of regularly enrolled students in an educational programme. Domestic and international students are usually counted on a specific day or period of the year. This procedure makes it possible to measure the proportion of international enrolments in an education system, but the actual number of individuals involved may be much higher since many students study abroad for less than a full academic year, or participate in exchange programmes that do not require enrolment (*e.g.* inter-university exchange or advanced research short-term mobility). Moreover, the international student body comprises some distance-learning students who are not, strictly speaking, mobile students. This pattern of distance enrolments is fairly common in the tertiary institutions of Australia and the United Kingdom (OECD, 2004a).

Since data on international and foreign students are obtained from tertiary enrolments in their country of destination, the data relate to incoming students rather than to students going abroad. Countries of destination covered by this indicator include all of the OECD countries (with the exception of Mexico) and the partner countries Estonia, the Russian Federation and Slovenia, as well as partner countries reporting similar data to the UNESCO Institute for Statistics in order to derive global figures and to examine the destinations of students and trends in market shares.

Data on students enrolled abroad as well as trend analyses are not based on the numbers of international students but on the number of foreign citizens on whom data consistent across countries and over time are readily available. Yet the data do not include students enrolled in OECD and partner countries that did not report foreign students to the OECD or to the UNESCO Institute for Statistics. All statements on students enrolled abroad may therefore underestimate the real number of citizens studying abroad (Table C3.3), especially in cases where many citizens study in countries that do not report their foreign students to the OECD or UNESCO Institute for Statistics (*e.g.* China, India).

Table C3.1 displays international as well as foreign enrolments as a proportion of total enrolment at each level of tertiary education. Total enrolment, used as a denominator, comprises all persons studying in the country (including domestic and international students) but excludes students from that country who study abroad. The table also exhibits changes between 2000 and 2006 in foreign enrolments for all tertiary education.

Tables C3.2, C3.4 and C3.5 show the distribution of international students enrolled in an education system – or foreign students for countries that do not have information on student mobility – according to their country of origin in Table C3.2, according to their level and type of tertiary education in Table C3.4, and according to their field of education in Table C3.5.

Table C3.3 presents the distribution of citizens of a given country enrolled abroad according to their country of destination (or country of study). As mentioned above, the total number of students enrolled abroad, which is used as a denominator, covers only students enrolled in other countries reporting data to the OECD or the UNESCO Institute for Statistics. Therefore, the resulting proportions may be biased and overestimated for countries with large numbers of students studying in non-reporting countries.

Table C3.6 shows trends in the absolute numbers of foreign students reported by OECD countries and worldwide between 2000 and 2006, and the indexes of change between 2006 and the years from 2000 to 2005. The figures are based on the number of foreign students enrolled in countries reporting data to the OECD and to the UNESCO Institute for Statistics. Since data for partner countries that did not report to the OECD were not included in the past, the figures are not strictly comparable with those published in editions of *Education at a Glance* prior to 2006.

Table C3.7 (available on line) provides the matrix of foreign students' numbers by country of origin and country of destination.

Further references

The relative importance of international students in the education system affects tertiary entry and graduation rates and may artificially increase them in some fields or levels of education (see Indicators A2 and A3). It may also affect the mix recorded between public and private expenditure (see Indicator B3).

In countries in which differentiated tuition fees are applied to international students, student mobility may boost the financial resources of tertiary educational institutions and contribute to the financing of the education system. On the other hand, international students may represent a high financial burden for countries in which tertiary tuition fees are low or inexistent given the high level of unit costs in tertiary education (see Indicator B5).

International students enrolled in a country different from their own are only one aspect of the internationalisation of tertiary education. New forms of cross-border education have emerged in the last decade, including the mobility of educational programmes and institutions across borders. Yet, cross-border tertiary education has developed quite differently and in response to different rationales in different world regions. For a detailed analysis of these issues, as well as the trade and policy implications of the internationalisation of tertiary education see OECD (2004a).

The following additional material relevant to this indicator is available on line at:

StatLink ᵐˢ▇ http://dx.doi.org/10.1787/402158641726

• *Table C3.7. Number of foreign students in tertiary education, by country of origin and destination (2006) and market shares in international education (2000, 2006)*

Table C3.1.
Student mobility and foreign students in tertiary education (2000, 2006)
International mobile students enrolled as a percentage of all students (international plus domestic), foreign enrolments as a percentage of all students (foreign and national) and index of change in the number of foreign students

Reading the first column: 17.8% of all students in tertiary education in Australia are international students and 13.7% of all students in tertiary education in Switzerland are international students. According to country-specific immigration legislation and data availability constraints, student mobility is either defined on the basis of students' country of residence (*i.e.* Australia) or the country where students received their prior education (*i.e.* Switzerland). The data presented in this table on student mobility represent the best available proxy of student mobility for each country.

Reading the fifth column: 20.9% of all students in tertiary education in Australia are not Australian citizens, and 19.2% of all students in tertiary education in Switzerland are not Swiss citizens.

		Student mobility				Foreign enrolments				
		International students as a percentage of all tertiary enrolment				Foreign students as a percentage of all tertiary enrolment				Index of change in the number of foreign students, total tertiary (2000=100)
		Total tertiary	Tertiary-type B programmes	Tertiary-type A programmes	Advanced research programmes	Total tertiary	Tertiary-type B programmes	Tertiary-type A programmes	Advanced research programmes	
		(1)	(2)	(3)	(4)	(5)	(6)	(7)	(8)	(9)
OECD countries	Australia[1]	17.8	7.4	19.7	19.1	20.9	7.6	23.0	29.7	175
	Austria[1, 2]	12.0	m	13.1	15.1	15.5	m	16.9	20.9	129
	Belgium[1]	7.4	5.4	8.5	20.5	12.1	9.5	13.5	31.0	121
	Canada[1, 2, 3, 4]	7.4	m	6.9	21.4	14.6	m	13.8	38.3	157
	Czech Republic[1]	5.1	0.7	5.4	6.4	6.3	1.1	6.8	8.0	391
	Denmark[1]	4.8	3.7	4.9	7.3	8.4	10.3	7.8	19.2	149
	Finland[5]	3.7	n	3.4	7.4	2.9	n	2.5	7.5	161
	France	m	m	m	m	11.2	4.8	12.3	35.8	181
	Germany[5]	m	m	10.6	m	11.4	3.9	12.7	m	140
	Greece[2]	m	m	m	m	2.5	0.8	3.7	1.8	192
	Hungary[1]	2.8	0.3	2.9	7.1	3.3	0.5	3.4	8.1	146
	Iceland	m	m	m	m	4.5	1.3	4.6	12.2	177
	Ireland[5]	6.8	m	m	m	m	m	m	m	172
	Italy	m	m	m	m	2.4	6.2	2.3	5.0	196
	Japan[1]	2.9	3.0	2.6	16.1	3.2	3.0	2.9	16.8	195
	Korea	m	m	m	m	0.7	0.5	0.7	4.7	660
	Luxembourg	m	m	m	m	42.2	m	m	m	174
	Mexico	m	m	m	m	m	m	m	m	m
	Netherlands[2]	4.7	n	4.7	m	6.1	n	6.2	m	260
	New Zealand[1]	15.5	16.0	15.1	22.2	28.5	27.6	28.3	42.8	825
	Norway[1]	1.9	8.2	1.8	4.6	6.7	11.2	6.2	22.3	164
	Poland	m	m	m	m	0.5	0.1	0.5	2.9	186
	Portugal	m	m	m	m	4.6	5.9	4.5	7.7	161
	Slovak Republic[1]	0.8	0.5	0.8	0.7	0.9	0.5	0.9	0.7	110
	Spain[1, 2]	1.0	m	0.8	8.5	2.9	3.8	1.8	19.2	200
	Sweden[1]	5.0	0.5	5.3	5.3	9.8	4.5	9.5	20.6	162
	Switzerland[2, 5]	13.7	m	13.4	44.4	19.2	16.5	17.0	44.2	152
	Turkey	m	m	m	m	0.8	0.2	1.1	2.7	108
	United Kingdom[1]	14.1	5.5	15.2	40.8	17.9	11.6	18.4	42.7	148
	United States[1]	3.3	2.0	3.1	23.7	m	m	m	m	123
	OECD average	*6.9*	*3.8*	*7.3*	*15.9*	*9.6*	*5.5*	*8.5*	*18.5*	*210.9*
	EU 19 average	*5.7*	*1.9*	*6.3*	*11.9*	*8.9*	*4.0*	*7.3*	*15.4*	*177.8*
Partner countries	Brazil	m	m	m	m	m	m	m	m	m
	Chile	m	m	m	m	m	m	m	m	m
	Estonia[1]	1.4	0.1	2.0	2.8	3.1	3.1	3.1	3.4	249
	Israel	m	m	m	m	m	m	m	m	m
	Russian Federation[4]	m	m	m	m	0.9	0.4	1.0	m	188
	Slovenia[1]	0.9	0.5	1.3	4.4	1.2	0.8	1.5	5.5	179

1. For the purpose of measuring student mobility, international students are defined on the basis of their country of residence.
2. Percentage in total tertiary underestimated because of the exclusion of certain programmes.
3. Year of reference 2005.
4. Excludes private institutions.
5. For the purpose of measuring student mobility, international students are defined on the basis of their country of prior education.

Source: OECD. See Annex 3 for notes (*www.oecd.org/edu/eag2008*).
Please refer to the Reader's Guide for information concerning the symbols replacing missing data.
StatLink http://dx.doi.org/10.1787/402158641726

Table C3.2.

Distribution of international and foreign students in tertiary education, by country of origin (2006)

Number of international and foreign students enrolled in tertiary education from a given country of origin as a percentage of all international or foreign students in the country of destination, based on head counts

The table shows for each country the proportion of international students in tertiary education who are residents of or had their prior education in a given country of origin. When data on student mobility are not available, the table shows the proportion of foreign students in tertiary education that have citizenship of a given country of origin.
Reading the third column: 1.4% of international tertiary students in Canada are German residents, 0.1% of international tertiary students in Canada are Greek residents, etc.
Reading the sixth column: 5.6% of international tertiary students in Ireland had their prior education in Germany, 0.5% of international tertiary students in Ireland had their prior education in Greece, etc.
Reading the 15th column: 25.9% of foreign tertiary students in Austria are German citizens, 0.6% of foreign tertiary students in Austria are Greek citizens, etc.

	Australia[1]	Belgium[1,2]	Canada[1,3,4,5]	Denmark[1]	Germany[3,6,7]	Ireland[6]	Netherlands[7]	New Zealand[1]	Slovak Republic[1]	Spain[1,3]	Sweden[1]	Switzerland[1,6]	United Kingdom[1]	United States[1]	Austria[3,8]	Czech Republic[8]	Finland[8]	France[8]
	(1)	(2)	(3)	(4)	(5)	(6)	(7)	(8)	(9)	(10)	(11)	(12)	(13)	(14)	(15)	(16)	(17)	(18)
Australia	a	n	0.6	2.2	0.2	0.4	0.0	7.5	n	n	1.1	0.2	0.5	0.5	0.1	n	0.4	0.1
Austria	0.1	0.1	0.2	0.6	2.3	0.5	0.1	0.1	0.4	n	1.5	2.0	0.4	0.1	a	0.2	0.4	0.2
Belgium	n	a	0.3	1.4	0.7	0.6	1.9	n	n	n	0.9	0.7	0.8	0.1	0.2	n	0.3	1.1
Canada	2.0	0.2	a	0.9	0.3	3.3	0.1	1.2	0.5	n	1.3	0.9	1.4	5.0	0.1	0.2	0.8	0.5
Czech Republic	0.1	0.1	0.1	0.2	1.0	0.3	0.1	0.1	29.0	n	0.8	0.4	0.3	0.2	1.3	a	0.7	0.3
Denmark	0.1	n	0.2	a	0.3	0.2	0.1	0.1	n	n	0.7	0.2	0.5	0.2	0.2	n	0.5	0.1
Finland	n	n	0.1	0.7	0.4	0.6	0.1	0.1	0.1	n	3.0	0.3	0.5	0.1	0.5	n	a	0.1
France	0.4	36.9	8.3	4.4	2.9	6.3	0.5	0.9	0.4	0.3	6.0	14.8	3.8	1.2	1.1	0.1	1.8	a
Germany	0.9	0.8	1.4	8.3	a	5.6	15.4	3.2	1.0	0.3	9.2	21.6	4.0	1.6	25.9	1.0	3.6	2.7
Greece	n	0.3	0.1	0.4	1.3	0.5	0.2	n	6.0	n	0.4	0.7	5.4	0.4	0.6	0.5	0.6	0.8
Hungary	n	0.1	0.1	0.1	1.1	0.1	0.2	n	1.4	n	0.3	0.6	0.2	0.1	2.9	0.2	1.0	0.3
Iceland	n	n	0.1	7.6	n	0.1	0.1	n	n	n	0.2	n	0.1	0.1	0.1	n	0.3	n
Ireland	0.1	0.1	0.2	1.0	0.2	a	0.1	0.1	0.1	n	0.3	0.1	5.1	0.2	0.1	0.2	0.4	0.2
Italy	0.1	0.3	0.4	1.3	1.8	1.8	0.3	0.1	0.1	0.4	1.9	6.1	1.7	0.6	15.7	0.1	1.5	1.8
Japan	1.8	0.2	2.1	0.2	1.0	0.5	0.1	2.8	0.1	n	0.5	0.7	1.9	6.9	0.7	0.1	1.1	0.9
Korea	2.4	0.1	0.4	0.1	1.8	0.1	0.1	0.1	0.2	n	0.3	0.3	1.2	10.5	0.8	0.1	0.4	1.0
Luxembourg	n	4.4	n	0.6	1.1	0.1	n	n	n	n	n	1.0	0.3	n	1.1	n	0.1	0.7
Mexico	0.2	0.1	1.7	0.5	0.6	0.1	0.1	0.2	0.1	0.7	0.5	0.5	0.5	2.5	0.1	n	0.5	0.6
Netherlands	0.1	7.4	0.3	1.0	0.4	0.6	a	0.1	n	0.1	2.3	0.5	0.8	0.3	0.3	0.1	0.9	0.2
New Zealand	1.1	n	0.1	0.6	0.1	0.1	n	a	n	n	0.1	0.1	0.2	0.2	n	n	0.1	n
Norway	1.0	0.1	0.3	15.2	0.3	1.4	0.2	0.6	5.7	n	0.8	0.2	0.9	0.2	0.2	0.9	0.7	0.1
Poland	0.1	0.3	0.3	1.3	6.4	1.4	0.7	n	1.2	0.1	1.8	1.4	1.3	0.5	3.4	1.1	1.7	1.4
Portugal	n	0.2	0.1	0.2	0.3	0.1	0.1	n	n	0.6	0.6	0.4	0.9	0.1	0.2	0.7	0.3	1.0
Slovak Republic	0.1	0.1	0.1	0.1	0.6	0.1	0.1	n	a	n	0.1	0.5	0.2	0.1	3.1	68.5	0.2	0.2
Spain	0.1	0.1	0.3	2.7	2.1	3.0	0.4	n	0.2	a	4.2	1.5	1.9	0.6	1.0	0.1	1.4	1.5
Sweden	0.5	0.1	0.4	6.7	0.3	0.6	0.1	0.5	0.6	n	a	0.6	1.0	0.6	0.5	0.3	6.3	0.2
Switzerland	0.2	0.1	0.4	1.4	0.9	0.2	0.1	0.1	n	0.1	0.9	a	0.5	0.2	0.7	0.1	0.4	0.7
Turkey	0.1	0.3	0.7	0.4	3.4	0.1	0.3	0.1	0.4	n	0.4	1.6	0.6	2.1	5.3	0.2	0.8	1.0
United Kingdom	0.8	0.1	1.6	13.0	0.9	9.4	0.3	1.1	0.7	0.2	1.2	0.8	a	1.5	0.5	1.7	2.1	1.0
United States	1.6	0.5	10.4	5.1	1.7	16.1	0.2	5.6	1.5	0.1	2.2	1.5	4.5	a	0.8	0.6	2.3	1.1
Total from OECD countries	*13.9*	*52.9*	*31.1*	*78.2*	*34.5*	*54.3*	*22.2*	*24.6*	*49.7*	*3.2*	*43.4*	*60.1*	*41.3*	*36.5*	*67.5*	*77.2*	*31.6*	*19.7*
Brazil	0.2	0.1	0.6	0.3	0.9	0.1	0.1	0.1	0.1	0.3	0.1	1.0	0.4	1.2	0.2	n	0.4	0.9
Chile	0.1	n	0.2	0.1	0.3	n	n	0.1	0.1	0.2	0.1	0.3	0.1	0.3	n	n	0.2	0.2
China	22.7	2.2	23.7	7.9	11.6	13.5	3.7	50.9	0.2	n	0.9	2.2	15.4	16.0	3.4	0.3	16.1	6.9
Estonia	n	0.1	n	0.2	0.3	0.1	n	n	n	n	0.1	0.1	0.1	0.1	0.1	n	7.0	0.0
India	12.1	0.5	3.7	1.3	1.7	3.5	0.1	4.8	0.4	n	0.2	0.9	5.8	13.5	0.3	0.4	1.9	0.3
Israel	0.1	n	0.4	0.4	0.6	0.1	0.1	n	9.5	n	n	0.2	0.3	0.6	0.1	0.7	0.2	0.1
Russian Federation	0.2	0.3	0.5	0.6	5.8	0.8	0.4	0.7	0.9	0.1	0.2	1.8	0.7	0.9	1.1	3.7	12.4	1.2
Slovenia	n	0.2	n	n	0.1	0.1	n	n	0.1	n	0.2	0.1	0.1	n	1.4	0.1	0.1	n
Total from Africa	*3.2*	*2.7*	*10.6*	*2.3*	*8.7*	*5.7*	*1.5*	*0.6*	*3.5*	*0.8*	*0.6*	*7.7*	*9.4*	*6.4*	*1.5*	*1.9*	*12.6*	*45.2*
Total from Asia	*78.7*	*5.3*	*50.1*	*13.7*	*30.9*	*34.1*	*6.8*	*73.4*	*21.0*	*0.2*	*3.3*	*9.2*	*46.1*	*63.6*	*14.3*	*8.4*	*29.9*	*18.5*
Total from Europe	*5.1*	*53.2*	*16.8*	*71.5*	*46.4*	*36.3*	*22.9*	*8.0*	*72.5*	*2.7*	*38.7*	*64.0*	*33.1*	*12.5*	*82.0*	*86.6*	*51.1*	*20.8*
of which, from EU19 countries	*3.5*	*51.4*	*14.4*	*44.1*	*24.2*	*31.8*	*20.9*	*6.5*	*41.2*	*2.2*	*35.1*	*54.0*	*28.9*	*8.5*	*58.5*	*74.9*	*23.7*	*13.8*
Total from North America	*3.6*	*0.7*	*11.0*	*6.0*	*2.0*	*19.4*	*0.3*	*6.8*	*2.0*	*0.1*	*3.5*	*2.4*	*5.9*	*5.1*	*1.0*	*0.8*	*3.2*	*1.6*
Total from Oceania	*2.1*	*0.1*	*0.7*	*2.8*	*0.3*	*0.5*	*0.1*	*10.5*	*n*	*n*	*1.2*	*0.3*	*0.7*	*0.8*	*0.2*	*n*	*0.5*	*0.1*
Total from South America	*1.1*	*0.9*	*7.3*	*1.9*	*3.8*	*0.7*	*1.0*	*0.7*	*1.0*	*3.2*	*1.0*	*5.4*	*2.6*	*11.5*	*1.1*	*0.8*	*2.3*	*4.4*
Not specified	*6.2*	*37.1*	*2.5*	*1.9*	*7.8*	*3.3*	*67.4*	*n*	*n*	*93.0*	*51.6*	*10.9*	*2.3*	*n*	*0.1*	*1.5*	*0.4*	*9.3*
Total from all countries	*100.0*	*100.0*	*100.0*	*100.0*	*100.0*	*100.0*	*100.0*	*100.0*	*100.0*	*100.0*	*100.0*	*100.0*	*100.0*	*100.0*	*100.0*	*100.0*	*100.0*	*100.0*

1. International students are defined on the basis of their country of residence.
2. Excludes data for social advancement education.
3. Excludes tertiary-type B programmes.
4. Year of reference 2005.
5. Excludes private institutions.
6. International students are defined on the basis of their country of prior education.
7. Excludes advanced research programmes.
8. Foreign students are defined on the basis of their country of citizenship; these data are not comparable with data on international students and are therefore presented separately in the table.
Source: OECD. See Annex 3 for notes (*www.oecd.org/edu/eag2008*).
Please refer to the Reader's Guide for information concerning the symbols replacing missing data.
StatLink ᓂᔕᒪ http://dx.doi.org/10.1787/402158641726

Table C3.2. *(continued)*

Distribution of international and foreign students in tertiary education, by country of origin (2006)

Number of international and foreign students enrolled in tertiary education from a given country of origin as a percentage of all international or foreign students in the country of destination, based on head counts

The table shows for each country the proportion of international students in tertiary education who are residents of or had their prior education in a given country of origin. When data on student mobility are not available, the table shows the proportion of foreign students in tertiary education that have citizenship of a given country of origin.

Reading the third column: 1.4% of international tertiary students in Canada are German residents, 0.1% of international tertiary students in Canada are Greek residents, etc.

Reading the sixth column: 5.6% of international tertiary students in Ireland had their prior education in Germany, 0.5% of international tertiary students in Ireland had their prior education in Greece, etc.

Reading the 15th column: 25.9% of foreign tertiary students in Austria are German citizens, 0.6% of foreign tertiary students in Austria are Greek citizens, etc.

						Countries of destination											
	OECD countries												Partner countries				
	Foreign students												International		Foreign		
Countries of origin	Greece[8]	Hungary[8]	Iceland[8]	Italy[8]	Japan[8]	Korea[8]	Luxembourg[8]	Norway[8]	Poland[8]	Portugal[8]	Turkey[8]	Total OECD destinations	Estonia[1]	Slovenia[1]	Russian Fed.[5,7,8]	Total partner country destinations	Total all reporting destinations
	(19)	(20)	(21)	(22)	(23)	(24)	(25)	(26)	(27)	(28)	(29)	(30)	(31)	(32)	(33)	(34)	(35)
Australia	0.2	n	0.1	0.1	0.3	0.2	n	0.2	0.1	0.1	0.2	0.4	n	0.1	m	0.1	0.3
Austria	n	0.4	2.4	0.4	n	n	0.2	0.3	0.3	0.1	0.1	0.4	0.1	1.3	m	0.1	0.3
Belgium	0.2	n	0.7	0.4	n	n	14.1	0.2	0.1	0.5	n	0.4	0.2	0.1	m	n	0.3
Canada	0.2	0.8	2.7	0.3	0.2	0.7	0.1	0.6	2.3	0.6	0.1	1.7	0.2	0.1	m	0.1	1.5
Czech Republic	0.1	0.1	1.1	0.3	n	n	0.4	0.3	2.3	0.2	n	0.3	n	0.2	m	n	0.2
Denmark	n	n	8.1	0.1	n	n	0.2	6.0	0.1	n	n	0.2	0.9	0.1	m	n	0.2
Finland	0.1	0.2	4.3	0.2	n	n	0.2	2.0	0.1	0.1	n	0.2	42.9	0.1	m	0.2	0.2
France	0.2	0.3	3.9	1.9	0.3	n	34.0	1.1	0.7	4.4	0.1	2.2	0.3	0.1	m	0.1	1.8
Germany	2.1	9.7	13.7	3.4	0.3	0.3	9.8	4.1	3.0	1.8	1.1	2.8	0.9	0.7	m	0.2	2.4
Greece	a	1.1	0.1	11.2	n	n	0.5	0.1	0.2	0.2	5.2	1.3	n	n	m	0.7	1.2
Hungary	0.1	a	0.3	0.5	0.1	n	0.2	0.2	0.6	0.1	n	0.3	0.3	1.2	m	n	0.2
Iceland	n	0.2	a	n	n	n	0.2	1.7	n	n	n	0.1	n	n	m	n	0.1
Ireland	n	0.3	0.3	0.1	n	n	0.4	0.2	0.1	0.1	n	0.8	n	n	m	n	0.7
Italy	0.4	0.2	3.4	a	0.1	n	4.2	0.5	0.4	1.4	0.1	1.2	0.5	8.4	m	0.1	1.0
Japan	0.1	0.1	1.5	0.7	a	5.4	n	0.4	0.2	n	n	2.4	0.3	n	m	0.2	2.0
Korea	n	0.1	0.1	0.7	17.2	a	n	0.2	0.4	n	0.1	4.1	0.1	0.1	m	0.3	3.4
Luxembourg	n	n	n	0.1	n	n	a	n	n	0.3	n	0.3	n	0.1	m	n	0.2
Mexico	n	0.1	0.4	0.5	0.1	0.1	n	0.3	0.1	0.1	n	1.0	n	0.1	m	0.2	0.8
Netherlands	0.1	0.1	1.0	0.1	0.0	n	0.5	1.1	0.1	1.4	0.1	0.4	n	0.1	m	n	0.3
New Zealand	n	n	0.1	n	0.1	0.1	n	0.1	n	0.1	n	0.2	n	n	m	n	0.1
Norway	n	5.2	5.5	0.2	n	n	n	a	6.5	0.1	n	0.5	n	0.1	m	n	0.4
Poland	0.5	0.4	2.5	2.7	0.1	0.1	0.9	1.2	a	0.8	0.1	1.2	0.1	0.5	m	0.1	1.0
Portugal	n	0.1	0.3	0.2	n	n	15.9	0.3	0.3	a	n	0.4	n	0.1	m	n	0.3
Slovak Republic	0.1	16.0	0.8	0.4	n	n	0.4	0.3	1.4	0.1	n	0.9	n	0.4	m	n	0.8
Spain	0.1	0.2	5.2	1.0	0.1	n	1.1	0.8	0.3	4.0	n	0.9	0.5	n	m	0.1	0.8
Sweden	0.1	1.5	7.4	0.3	0.1	n	0.2	8.2	2.8	0.1	n	0.5	1.1	0.2	m	0.1	0.5
Switzerland	0.1	0.1	1.1	2.6	n	n	0.3	0.3	n	0.5	n	0.4	0.1	n	m	0.1	0.3
Turkey	0.7	0.3	0.1	0.6	0.1	0.2	0.3	0.3	0.4	0.1	a	1.2	0.1	0.1	m	1.8	1.3
United Kingdom	0.5	0.4	3.2	0.6	0.3	0.1	0.4	2.4	0.4	0.5	0.6	0.9	0.2	n	m	0.1	0.8
United States	0.6	1.5	6.9	0.8	1.3	2.2	n	2.4	6.7	0.9	0.1	1.8	1.0	0.1	m	0.8	1.6
Total from OECD countries	**6.5**	**39.5**	**77.3**	**30.3**	**20.8**	**9.7**	**84.2**	**36.0**	**30.0**	**18.5**	**8.0**	**29.3**	**49.9**	**14.0**	**m**	**5.6**	**25.4**
Brazil	n	n	0.4	1.7	0.4	0.1	0.4	0.4	0.3	11.2	n	0.7	0.1	0.3	m	0.3	0.7
Chile	n	n	0.3	0.4	n	n	n	0.5	n	n	n	0.2	n	n	m	0.4	0.2
China	0.2	1.0	2.1	2.0	66.4	68.7	1.3	4.4	2.7	0.5	0.6	15.4	12.2	0.2	m	10.8	14.6
Estonia	0.1	0.1	0.8	0.1	n	n	n	0.5	0.1	n	n	0.1	a	0.2	1.0	0.3	0.1
India	n	0.3	0.1	0.8	0.3	1.2	0.1	1.0	1.5	0.1	n	5.4	1.1	0.8	m	1.9	4.8
Israel	0.4	5.3	0.1	2.2	n	n	n	0.1	0.3	n	0.1	0.4	n	n	m	0.8	0.4
Russian Federation	1.3	1.6	2.8	1.6	0.3	1.1	0.6	5.4	4.0	0.4	3.2	1.2	7.2	1.0	a	3.0	1.5
Slovenia	n	0.2	n	0.8	n	n	n	n	0.1	0.1	n	0.1	n	a	m	n	0.1
Total from Africa	*4.3*	*1.8*	*1.4*	*9.4*	*0.7*	*0.8*	*7.1*	*9.7*	*4.1*	*63.1*	*1.8*	*9.9*	*0.4*	*n*	*m*	*17.8*	*11.2*
Total from Asia	*63.9*	*14.7*	*7.1*	*13.2*	*94.2*	*93.1*	*2.5*	*15.9*	*18.5*	*1.8*	*53.4*	*42.8*	*14.7*	*1.8*	*40.4*	*58.3*	*45.3*
Total from Europe	*30.4*	*80.8*	*78.9*	*66.9*	*2.2*	*2.2*	*89.2*	*45.5*	*67.3*	*18.6*	*29.7*	*23.0*	*83.5*	*97.0*	*23.2*	*15.9*	*21.8*
of which, from EU19 countries	*4.6*	*31.1*	*58.7*	*23.8*	*1.5*	*0.7*	*83.4*	*29.4*	*13.2*	*16.0*	*7.5*	*15.7*	*48.1*	*13.4*	*m*	*m*	*m*
Total from North America	*0.8*	*2.3*	*9.5*	*1.1*	*1.5*	*2.9*	*0.1*	*3.0*	*9.0*	*1.6*	*0.2*	*3.5*	*1.2*	*0.2*	*m*	*1.0*	*3.1*
Total from Oceania	*0.2*	*0.1*	*0.3*	*0.2*	*0.4*	*0.4*	*n*	*0.3*	*0.2*	*0.1*	*0.2*	*0.7*	*n*	*0.1*	*m*	*0.1*	*0.6*
Total from South America	*0.3*	*0.3*	*2.7*	*8.7*	*1.0*	*0.7*	*0.7*	*2.6*	*0.8*	*14.8*	*n*	*5.0*	*0.2*	*0.9*	*m*	*6.9*	*5.3*
Not specified	*n*	*n*	*0.1*	*0.6*	*n*	*n*	*0.4*	*23.2*	*0.1*	*n*	*14.6*	*15.1*	*n*	*n*	*36.3*	*n*	*12.6*
Total from all countries	*100.0*	*100.0*	*100.0*	*100.0*	*100.0*	*100.0*	*100.0*	*100.0*	*100.0*	*100.0*	*100.0*	*100.0*	*100.0*	*100.0*	*100.0*	*100.0*	*100.0*

1. International students are defined on the basis of their country of residence.
2. Excludes data for social advancement education.
3. Excludes tertiary-type B programmes.
4. Year of reference 2005.
5. Excludes private institutions.
6. International students are defined on the basis of their country of prior education.
7. Excludes advanced research programmes.
8. Foreign students are defined on the basis of their country of citizenship; these data are not comparable with data on international students and are therefore presented separately in the table.
Source: OECD. See Annex 3 for notes (www.oecd.org/edu/eag2008).
Please refer to the Reader's Guide for information concerning the symbols replacing missing data.
StatLink ᵐˢᴸ http://dx.doi.org/10.1787/402158641726

Table C3.3.

Citizens studying abroad in tertiary education, by country of destination (2006)

Number of students enrolled in tertiary education in a given country of destination as a percentage of all students enrolled abroad, based on head counts

The table shows for each country the proportion of students studying abroad in tertiary education in a given country of destination.
Reading the second column: 6.7% of Czech citizens enrolled in tertiary education abroad study in Austria, 13.0% of German citizens enrolled in tertiary education abroad study in Austria, etc.
Reading the first row: 2.5% of Australian citizens enrolled in tertiary education abroad study in France, 3.3% of Australian citizens enrolled in tertiary education abroad study in Germany, etc.

Countries of origin	Australia[1] (1)	Austria[2] (2)	Belgium[3] (3)	Canada[2,4,5] (4)	Czech Republic (5)	Denmark (6)	Finland (7)	France (8)	Germany[6] (9)	Greece (10)	Hungary (11)	Iceland (12)	Ireland[7,8] (13)	Italy (14)	Japan (15)	Korea (16)	Luxembourg (17)	Mexico (18)	Netherlands[6] (19)	New Zealand (20)
Australia	a	0.5	0.2	6.4	n	0.4	0.3	2.5	3.3	0.3	0.1	n	0.5	0.5	3.3	0.5	n	m	0.6	27.7
Austria	1.3	a	0.3	1.5	0.3	0.3	0.3	3.4	51.3	0.1	0.4	0.1	0.5	1.7	0.4	n	n	m	1.6	0.3
Belgium	0.7	0.6	a	3.7	0.1	0.2	0.2	23.6	8.5	0.3	0.1	n	0.7	1.8	0.5	0.1	1.4	m	18.9	n
Canada	8.7	0.1	0.3	a	0.1	0.3	0.2	3.0	1.4	0.1	0.3	n	1.0	0.3	0.7	0.4	n	m	0.3	1.0
Czech Republic	1.5	6.7	0.8	1.7	a	0.6	0.8	9.2	30.5	0.1	0.2	0.1	0.5	2.2	0.5	0.1	0.1	m	1.5	0.3
Denmark	2.0	1.1	0.8	3.2	n	a	0.7	3.9	9.3	0.1	n	0.9	0.4	0.8	0.3	0.1	n	m	2.1	0.8
Finland	0.8	1.9	0.5	1.5	0.1	1.9	a	3.0	9.3	0.1	0.3	0.3	0.8	0.9	0.5	n	n	m	1.7	0.3
France	1.1	0.7	26.9	12.0	n	0.3	0.2	a	9.6	0.1	0.1	n	1.2	1.4	0.6	n	0.6	m	1.1	0.5
Germany	2.0	13.0	0.7	2.0	0.3	1.4	0.4	8.4	a	0.4	1.8	0.1	0.9	2.1	0.5	0.1	0.1	m	15.2	1.5
Greece	0.1	0.6	1.2	0.4	0.3	0.1	0.1	5.0	15.4	a	0.4	n	0.2	13.5	0.1	n	n	m	1.1	n
Hungary	0.7	13.9	1.1	1.7	0.4	0.8	1.1	8.1	33.6	0.2	a	n	0.2	2.8	1.1	n	n	m	4.3	0.1
Iceland	0.8	0.6	0.4	1.2	0.1	44.5	0.8	1.3	3.0	0.2	0.9	a	0.2	0.5	0.4	n	0.1	m	2.3	0.3
Ireland	0.9	0.2	0.3	1.3	0.2	0.3	0.2	2.5	2.2	n	0.2	n	a	0.2	0.1	n	n	m	0.6	0.1
Italy	0.6	15.4	5.8	1.1	0.1	0.4	0.3	11.1	18.8	0.2	0.1	0.1	0.6	a	0.3	n	0.1	m	1.3	0.1
Japan	5.4	0.5	0.3	3.0	n	0.1	0.2	3.5	3.9	n	n	n	0.1	0.5	a	2.0	n	m	0.4	1.7
Korea	4.3	0.3	0.1	0.7	n	n	n	2.3	5.0	n	n	n	n	0.3	21.5	a	n	m	0.3	n
Luxembourg	0.2	5.8	21.8	0.4	n	n	0.1	22.4	31.2	n	n	n	0.2	0.5	n	n	a	m	0.6	n
Mexico	1.4	0.2	0.3	7.0	n	0.3	0.2	5.5	4.7	n	n	n	0.1	0.9	0.5	0.1	n	a	0.6	0.2
Netherlands	1.7	1.0	25.1	3.3	0.1	1.4	0.6	4.6	12.3	0.1	0.1	0.1	0.6	0.2	0.5	n	n	m	a	0.4
New Zealand	47.6	0.1	n	3.6	n	0.5	0.2	1.3	1.5	n	n	n	0.4	0.1	1.8	0.6	n	m	0.5	a
Norway	12.7	0.4	0.2	2.0	1.4	15.4	0.4	2.4	4.7	n	5.3	0.3	1.3	0.8	0.3	n	n	m	1.8	1.5
Poland	0.5	3.7	1.3	2.0	0.7	1.8	0.4	9.5	44.6	0.2	0.2	n	0.5	3.7	0.3	0.1	n	m	2.4	n
Portugal	0.3	0.4	6.5	2.0	1.1	0.3	0.2	18.7	11.6	n	0.1	n	0.1	0.7	0.3	n	1.3	m	2.1	0.1
Slovak Republic	0.5	5.3	0.3	0.5	63.8	0.1	0.1	1.8	7.4	n	10.1	n	0.1	0.8	0.1	n	n	m	0.5	n
Spain	0.4	1.5	4.0	1.0	0.1	0.6	0.5	13.6	19.9	n	0.1	0.1	1.4	1.9	0.3	n	n	m	3.0	0.1
Sweden	6.1	1.3	0.3	2.4	0.4	9.2	3.9	3.8	4.8	0.1	1.5	0.4	0.6	0.9	0.7	n	n	m	1.2	1.2
Switzerland	2.7	2.8	0.7	4.2	0.1	0.6	0.4	15.4	20.6	0.2	0.1	0.1	0.2	12.0	0.4	n	n	m	1.5	0.4
Turkey	0.4	3.6	0.6	1.3	0.1	0.4	0.1	4.2	44.3	0.2	0.1	n	0.5	0.3	0.1	n	n	m	1.2	n
United Kingdom	6.2	0.8	0.8	11.4	1.5	1.9	0.8	10.3	7.5	0.3	0.2	0.1	4.8	1.1	1.4	0.1	n	m	3.1	1.7
United States	5.9	0.7	0.4	19.2	0.3	0.7	0.4	5.6	6.6	0.2	0.4	0.1	4.2	0.8	3.5	1.0	n	m	1.0	4.2
Total from OECD countries	3.0	3.1	3.6	3.9	2.0	1.1	0.3	5.8	12.7	0.1	0.7	0.1	0.8	1.7	3.2	0.3	m	m	2.7	1.1
Brazil	2.0	0.3	0.7	3.5	n	0.4	0.2	9.9	9.2	n	n	n	0.1	4.0	2.2	0.1	n	m	0.5	0.2
Chile	1.7	0.2	1.2	3.6	0.1	0.4	0.2	7.9	8.2	n	n	n	n	2.8	0.4	0.1	n	m	0.4	0.7
China	9.3	0.3	0.3	6.8	n	0.5	0.3	3.8	6.1	n	n	n	0.4	0.2	19.1	3.4	n	m	0.8	4.2
Estonia	0.2	0.7	0.5	0.6	0.1	2.7	14.5	2.8	18.4	0.4	0.2	0.1	0.3	1.4	0.5	n	n	m	1.2	n
India	15.1	0.1	0.1	4.8	n	0.2	0.1	0.5	2.8	n	n	n	0.3	0.3	0.3	0.2	n	m	0.2	1.2
Israel	1.6	0.3	0.3	7.0	1.1	0.4	0.1	2.1	9.2	0.5	5.4	n	n	7.5	0.3	n	n	m	1.5	n
Russian Federation	0.9	0.8	0.9	3.2	1.6	0.9	2.3	6.3	25.7	0.4	0.5	n	0.2	1.6	0.7	0.5	n	m	1.0	0.5
Slovenia	0.4	19.5	4.4	0.8	0.8	0.3	0.3	3.6	21.0	n	0.8	n	0.2	14.1	0.5	n	n	m	1.9	0.1

Note: The proportion of students abroad is based only on the total of students enrolled in countries reporting data to the OECD and UNESCO Institute for Statistics.

1. Data by country of origin relate to international students defined on the basis of their country of residence.
2. Excludes tertiary-type B programmes.
3. Excludes data for social advancement education.
4. Year of reference 2005.
5. Excludes private institutions.
6. Excludes advanced research programmes.
7. Data by country of origin relate to international students defined on the basis of their country of prior education.
8. Excludes part-time students.
Source: OECD. See Annex 3 for notes (*www.oecd.org/edu/eag2008*).
Please refer to the Reader's Guide for information concerning the symbols replacing missing data.

StatLink ᴀᴍˢᴾ http://dx.doi.org/10.1787/402158641726

C3

Table C3.3. *(continued)*
Citizens studying abroad in tertiary education, by country of destination (2006)
Number of students enrolled in tertiary education in a given country of destination as a percentage of all students enrolled abroad, based on head counts

The table shows for each country the proportion of students studying abroad in tertiary education in a given country of destination.
Reading the second column: 6.7% of Czech citizens enrolled in tertiary education abroad study in Austria, 13.0% of German citizens enrolled in tertiary education abroad study in Austria, etc.
Reading the first row: 2.5% of Australian citizens enrolled in tertiary education abroad study in France, 3.3% of Australian citizens enrolled in tertiary education abroad study in Germany, etc.

	Norway	Poland	Portugal	Slovak Republic	Spain	Sweden	Switzerland	Turkey	United Kingdom[1]	United States[1]	Total OECD destinations	Brazil	Chile	Estonia	Israel	Russian Federation[5,6]	Slovenia	Total partner country destinations	Total all reporting destinations
Countries of origin	(21)	(22)	(23)	(24)	(25)	(26)	(27)	(28)	(29)	(30)	(31)	(32)	(33)	(34)	(35)	(36)	(37)	(38)	(39)
OECD countries																			
Australia	0.3	0.1	0.2	n	0.4	3.2	0.7	0.3	16.0	28.9	97.6	m	m	n	m	m	n	2.4	100.0
Austria	0.3	0.3	0.2	0.1	1.2	3.9	7.7	0.2	11.0	7.0	95.8	m	m	n	m	m	0.1	4.2	100.0
Belgium	0.3	0.1	0.7	n	3.2	2.1	2.9	n	21.5	6.8	98.6	m	m	n	m	m	n	1.4	100.0
Canada	0.2	0.6	0.2	n	0.2	1.0	0.6	n	10.6	67.0	98.4	m	m	n	m	m	n	1.6	100.0
Czech Republic	0.6	3.5	0.4	6.4	1.5	2.9	2.2	n	11.6	12.7	99.1	m	m	n	m	m	n	0.9	100.0
Denmark	13.5	0.2	0.1	n	1.1	15.3	1.6	0.1	25.1	14.6	98.2	m	m	n	m	m	n	1.8	100.0
Finland	2.9	0.1	0.1	n	1.1	38.9	1.2	0.1	17.9	6.3	92.4	m	m	4.0	m	m	n	7.6	100.0
France	0.2	0.1	1.1	n	2.7	2.5	6.6	n	18.9	10.5	99.2	m	m	n	m	m	n	0.8	100.0
Germany	0.7	0.4	0.4	n	2.1	3.9	11.1	0.3	17.0	11.7	98.5	m	m	n	m	m	n	1.5	100.0
Greece	n	0.1	0.1	0.2	0.5	0.7	0.7	2.4	43.5	5.3	92.1	m	m	n	m	m	n	7.9	100.0
Hungary	0.4	0.8	0.2	0.4	0.5	2.2	2.5	n	9.8	10.5	97.6	m	m	0.1	m	m	0.2	2.4	100.0
Iceland	6.7	n	n	n	0.3	13.0	0.4	n	9.4	12.3	99.8	m	m	n	m	m	n	0.2	100.0
Ireland	0.1	0.1	n	n	0.3	0.7	0.2	n	83.4	5.7	99.8	m	m	n	m	m	n	0.2	100.0
Italy	0.2	0.1	0.6	n	6.7	1.8	11.3	n	13.6	8.3	98.8	m	m	n	m	m	0.2	1.2	100.0
Japan	0.1	n	n	n	0.2	0.4	0.4	n	10.2	65.7	98.6	m	m	n	m	m	n	1.4	100.0
Korea	n	n	n	n	0.4	0.1	0.2	n	3.9	58.9	98.4	m	m	n	m	m	n	1.6	100.0
Luxembourg	n	n	0.6	n	0.1	0.1	3.8	n	11.3	0.7	99.9	m	m	n	m	m	n	0.1	100.0
Mexico	0.2	n	0.1	n	12.1	0.8	0.5	n	6.5	53.9	96.2	m	m	n	m	m	n	3.8	100.0
Netherlands	1.2	0.1	1.9	n	2.2	5.4	2.7	0.1	20.5	12.4	98.5	m	m	n	m	m	n	1.5	100.0
New Zealand	0.2	0.2	n	n	0.1	1.1	0.5	n	13.4	22.9	96.9	m	m	n	m	m	n	3.1	100.0
Norway	a	5.2	0.1	0.6	0.4	10.2	0.6	n	21.5	9.5	99.0	m	m	n	m	m	n	1.0	100.0
Poland	0.5	a	0.4	0.1	1.6	2.6	1.5	n	12.0	8.7	99.2	m	m	n	m	m	n	0.8	100.0
Portugal	0.3	0.3	a	n	17.0	1.4	6.3	n	20.8	6.3	98.4	m	m	n	m	m	n	1.6	100.0
Slovak Republic	0.2	0.7	0.1	a	0.4	0.2	0.8	n	2.8	3.1	99.8	m	m	n	m	m	n	0.2	100.0
Spain	0.4	0.1	2.5	n	a	4.3	5.9	n	23.2	13.3	98.4	m	m	n	m	m	n	1.6	100.0
Sweden	8.1	2.2	0.1	0.1	1.3	a	1.8	n	22.9	22.9	98.2	m	m	0.1	m	m	n	1.8	100.0
Switzerland	0.4	n	0.8	n	2.9	2.7	a	n	15.9	12.5	97.5	m	m	n	m	m	n	2.5	100.0
Turkey	0.1	0.1	n	n	0.1	0.5	1.4	a	3.7	21.1	84.5	m	m	n	m	m	n	15.5	100.0
United Kingdom	1.4	0.2	0.3	n	2.5	3.0	1.5	0.5	a	34.2	97.5	m	m	n	m	m	n	2.5	100.0
United States	0.7	1.5	0.3	0.1	1.3	1.9	0.9	0.1	29.9	a	92.0	m	m	n	m	m	n	8.0	100.0
Total from OECD countries	0.6	0.4	0.4	0.1	1.9	2.4	3.1	0.2	16.1	25.3	96.8	m	m	0.1	n	m	n	3.2	100.0
Partner countries																			
Brazil	0.3	0.2	9.0	n	9.3	0.6	1.4	n	5.5	34.1	93.7	a	m	n	m	m	n	6.3	100.0
Chile	0.9	n	0.1	n	17.8	3.4	1.3	n	4.6	20.6	76.7	m	a	n	m	m	n	23.3	100.0
China	0.1	n	n	n	0.1	0.3	0.2	n	11.2	20.7	88.4	m	m	n	m	m	n	11.6	100.0
Estonia	1.8	0.3	n	n	1.9	5.9	0.6	n	8.3	7.7	71.4	m	m	a	m	18.7	n	28.6	100.0
India	0.1	0.1	n	n	n	0.5	0.2	n	13.0	53.5	93.7	m	m	n	m	m	n	6.3	100.0
Israel	0.1	0.2	n	1.1	0.8	0.3	0.5	0.2	6.6	25.0	72.2	m	m	n	a	m	n	27.8	100.0
Russian Federation	1.6	0.9	0.1	n	1.1	1.5	1.3	1.2	4.4	10.1	70.6	m	m	2.3	m	a	n	29.4	100.0
Slovenia	0.1	0.3	0.7	0.1	1.9	1.9	1.7	n	10.4	8.0	93.7	m	m	n	m	m	a	6.3	100.0

Note: The proportion of students abroad is based only on the total of students enrolled in countries reporting data to the OECD and UNESCO Institute for Statistics.
1. Data by country of origin relate to international students defined on the basis of their country of residence.
2. Excludes tertiary-type B programmes.
3. Excludes data for social advancement education.
4. Year of reference 2005.
5. Excludes private institutions.
6. Excludes advanced research programmes.
7. Data by country of origin relate to international students defined on the basis of their country of prior education.
8. Excludes part-time students.
Source: OECD. See Annex 3 for notes (*www.oecd.org/edu/eag2008*).
Please refer to the Reader's Guide for information concerning the symbols replacing missing data.
StatLink ᵐˢᵖ http://dx.doi.org/10.1787/402158641726

Table C3.4.
Distribution of international and foreign students in tertiary education, by level and type of tertiary education (2006)

C3

	Tertiary-type B programmes	Tertiary-type A programmes	Advanced research programmes	Total tertiary programmes
	(1)	(2)	(3)	(4)
International students by level and type of tertiary education				
Australia[1]	6.4	89.4	4.2	100
Austria[1,2,3]	m	91.7	8.3	100
Belgium[1]	31.8	62.0	6.2	100
Canada[1,3,4,5]	m	90.2	9.8	100
Czech Republic[1]	1.4	90.3	8.5	100
Denmark[1]	9.6	87.2	3.2	100
Finland[3,6]	m	85.7	14.3	100
Hungary[1]	0.7	94.7	4.6	100
Ireland	m	m	m	m
Japan[1]	24.1	65.8	10.1	100
Luxembourg	m	m	m	m
Mexico	m	m	m	m
Netherlands[7]	n	100.0	m	100
New Zealand[1]	27.5	69.3	3.2	100
Norway[1]	3.9	90.5	5.6	100
Slovak Republic[1]	0.8	94.9	4.3	100
Spain[1,3]	m	64.0	36.0	100
Sweden[1]	0.5	94.2	5.3	100
Switzerland[3,6]	m	72.7	27.3	100
United Kingdom[1]	8.6	79.8	11.6	100
United States[1]	12.7	71.6	15.7	100
Brazil	m	m	m	m
Chile	m	m	m	m
Estonia[1]	3.3	90.6	6.0	100
Israel	m	m	m	m
Slovenia[1]	21.9	73.9	4.2	100
Foreign students by level and type of tertiary education				
France[8]	*10.4*	*79.5*	*10.1*	*100*
Germany[7,8]	*5.1*	*94.9*	*m*	*100*
Greece[8]	11.9	85.6	2.5	100
Iceland[8]	0.7	96.6	2.7	100
Italy[8]	1.8	94.3	3.9	100
Korea[8]	24.9	66.0	9.1	100
Poland[8]	0.1	91.6	8.3	100
Portugal[8]	1.5	89.3	9.2	100
Turkey[8]	5.6	89.8	4.6	100
Russian Federation[5,7,8]	10.3	89.7	m	100

OECD countries / Partner countries (row groupings)

1. International students are defined on the basis of their country of residence.
2. Based on the number of registrations, not head-counts.
3. Excludes tertiary-type B programmes.
4. Year of reference 2005.
5. Excludes private institutions.
6. International students are defined on the basis of their country of prior education.
7. Excludes advanced research programmes.
8. Foreign students are defined on the basis of their country of citizenship, these data are not comparable with data on international students and are therefore presented separately in the table.
Source: OECD. See Annex 3 for notes (*www.oecd.org/edu/eag2008*).
Please refer to the Reader's Guide for information concerning the symbols replacing missing data.
StatLink http://dx.doi.org/10.1787/402158641726

C3

Table C3.5.
Distribution of international and foreign students in tertiary education, by field of education (2006)

		Agriculture	Education	Engineering, manufacturing and construction	Health and welfare	Humanities and arts	Sciences	Services	Social sciences, business and law	Not known or unspecified	Total all fields of education
		(1)	(2)	(3)	(4)	(5)	(6)	(7)	(8)	(9)	(10)
	International students by field of education										
OECD countries	Australia[1]	0.7	3.2	11.0	8.3	7.4	15.0	1.6	52.7	n	100
	Austria[1, 2]	2.3	5.5	11.5	10.3	23.6	10.8	1.5	34.5	n	100
	Belgium[1]	9.0	5.0	6.6	43.5	13.0	6.6	2.2	14.1	n	100
	Canada[1, 2, 3]	1.1	1.8	12.9	5.6	9.0	15.0	1.2	34.3	19.0	100
	Czech Republic[1]	1.7	2.0	11.7	23.5	7.4	11.5	1.6	35.1	5.4	100
	Denmark[1]	2.2	4.3	16.6	19.9	16.6	7.8	0.8	31.9	n	100
	Finland[2, 4]	2.2	2.3	29.9	12.0	16.4	9.8	3.7	23.7	n	100
	Germany[2, 4, 5]	1.4	4.7	19.8	6.1	22.0	17.1	1.3	27.4	0.1	100
	Greece	m	m	m	m	m	m	m	m	m	m
	Hungary[1]	11.5	6.9	12.0	30.0	11.4	6.7	1.8	19.7	n	100
	Ireland	m	m	m	m	m	m	m	m	m	m
	Japan[1]	2.4	2.7	14.5	2.2	24.5	1.3	2.5	36.6	13.4	100
	Korea	m	m	m	m	m	m	m	m	m	m
	Luxembourg	m	m	m	m	m	m	m	m	m	m
	Mexico	m	m	m	m	m	m	m	m	m	m
	Netherlands[5]	1.9	6.9	5.4	16.0	13.1	5.8	5.0	45.3	0.5	100
	New Zealand[1, 5]	0.9	3.0	6.2	5.4	14.7	17.4	2.9	49.0	0.4	100
	Norway[1]	1.9	5.1	4.9	11.6	20.1	14.3	3.6	32.9	5.5	100
	Spain[1, 2, 5]	1.7	2.7	9.5	30.7	13.2	7.4	2.8	31.9	n	100
	Sweden[1]	1.0	3.9	24.1	8.6	15.7	14.5	1.5	30.4	0.3	100
	Switzerland[2, 4]	0.9	3.6	16.7	6.6	18.2	16.6	2.6	33.2	1.6	100
	United Kingdom[1]	0.8	3.9	14.8	9.1	13.9	14.1	1.2	40.8	1.2	100
	United States[1]	0.3	3.0	15.6	6.5	11.0	18.7	1.8	31.0	12.0	100
Partner countries	Brazil	m	m	m	m	m	m	m	m	m	m
	Chile	m	m	m	m	m	m	m	m	m	m
	Estonia[1]	8.3	0.9	1.0	12.9	19.5	3.2	0.8	53.4	n	100
	Israel	m	m	m	m	m	m	m	m	m	m
	Russian Federation	m	m	m	m	m	m	m	m	m	m
	Slovenia[1]	1.2	6.1	16.4	12.9	21.5	9.1	3.4	29.5	n	100
	Foreign students by field of education										
OECD countries	France[6]	0.2	1.2	11.5	8.9	20.7	15.4	1.6	40.6	0.1	100
	Iceland[6]	0.4	5.5	5.6	3.6	44.3	17.9	1.4	21.3	n	100
	Italy[6]	1.8	2.1	14.4	21.6	18.6	6.5	1.8	32.3	1.0	100
	Poland[6]	0.7	5.4	4.3	26.0	20.0	5.3	3.6	34.8	n	100
	Portugal[6]	1.2	4.9	18.6	7.7	8.5	7.4	5.0	46.6	n	100
	Slovak Republic[6]	9.8	4.7	11.3	30.5	14.8	7.3	5.4	16.3	a	100
	Turkey[6]	2.3	8.8	14.3	14.2	9.8	8.9	3.2	38.5	n	100

1. International students are defined on the basis of their country of residence.
2. Excludes tertiary-type B programmes.
3. Year of reference 2005.
4. International students are defined on the basis of their country of prior education.
5. Excludes advanced research programmes.
6. Foreign students are defined on the basis of their country of citizenship; these data are not comparable with data on international students and are therefore presented separately in the table and chart.

Source: OECD. See Annex 3 for notes (*www.oecd.org/edu/eag2008*).
Please refer to the Reader's Guide for information concerning the symbols replacing missing data.
StatLink http://dx.doi.org/10.1787/402158641726

Table C3.6.
Trends in the number of foreign students enrolled outside their country of origin (2000 to 2006)
Number of foreign students enrolled in tertiary education outside their country of origin, head counts

	Number of foreign students						
	2006	2005	2004	2003	2002	2001	2000
Foreign students enrolled worldwide	2 924 679	2 847 536	2 697 759	2 507 931	2 267 627	1 972 111	1 894 792
Foreign students enrolled in OECD countries	2 440 657	2 368 931	2 265 135	2 085 263	1 897 866	1 642 676	1 583 744

	Index of change (2006)					
	2005=100	2004=100	2003=100	2002=100	2001=100	2000=100
Foreign students enrolled worldwide	103	108	117	129	148	154
Foreign students enrolled in OECD countries	103	108	117	129	149	154

Note: Figures are based on the number of foreign students enrolled in OECD and partner countries reporting data to the OECD and UNESCO Institute for Statistics, in order to provide a global picture of foreign students worldwide. The coverage of these reporting countries has evolved over time, therefore missing data have been imputed wherever necessary to ensure the comparability of time series over time. Given the inclusion of UNESCO data for partner countries and the imputation of missing data, the estimates of the number of foreign students may differ from those published in previous editions of *Education at a Glance.*
Source: OECD and UNESCO Institute for Statistics for most data on partner countries. See Annex 3 for notes (*www.oecd.org/edu/eag2008*).
StatLink ⫘ http://dx.doi.org/10.1787/402158641726

HOW SUCCESSFUL ARE STUDENTS IN MOVING FROM EDUCATION TO WORK?

This indicator shows the number of years that young adults are expected to spend in education, employment and non-employment and examines their education and employment status by gender. During the past decade, individuals have spent more time in initial education, delaying their entry into the workforce. Part of this additional time is spent combining work and education, a practice that is widespread in some countries. Once students have completed their initial education, access to the labour market is often impeded by periods of unemployment or non-employment, although males and females are affected differently. This indicator is based on the current situation of persons between the ages of 15 and 29 and gives a picture of major trends in the transition from school to work.

Key results

Chart C4.1. **Change in the proportion of 15-to-19-year-olds in education and change in the proportion not in education and not employed among 15-to-19-year-olds between 1995 and 2005**

This chart relates the increase in the proportion of 15-to-19-year-olds in education to the decrease in the proportion of 15-to-19-year-olds not in education and not employed.

Most OECD countries have expanded their education system to accommodate more of the younger cohorts. For 15-to-19-year-olds, recruitment to education has largely taken place among individuals outside the labour market (not in education or employment) and to a lesser extent among employed individuals. With few exceptions, policies to expand education systems have thus helped to lower unemployment and inactivity among young adults.

Change in the proportion of 15-to-19-year-olds
not in education and not employed between 1995-2005 (%)

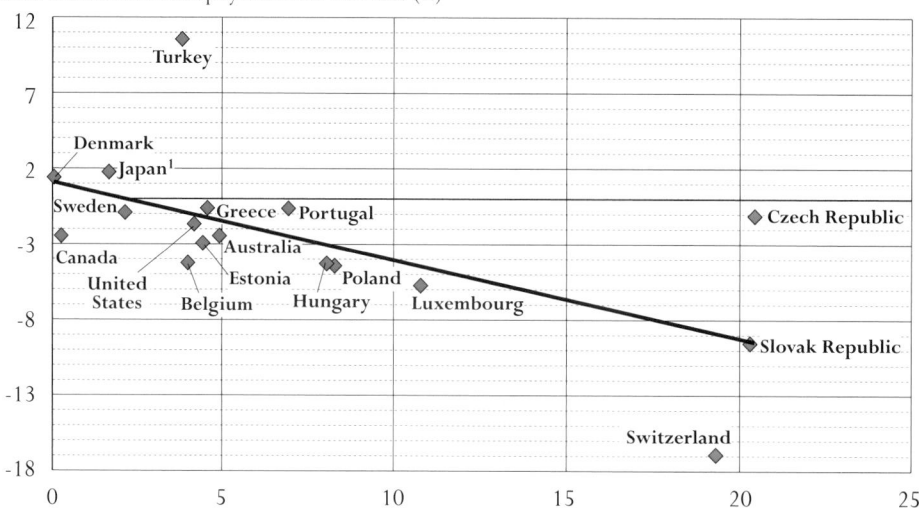

Change in the proportion of 15-to-19-year-olds in
education between 1995 and 2005 (%)

1. Data for Japan refer to 15-to-24-year-olds.
Source: OECD. Table C4.1b. See Annex 3 for notes (*www.oecd.org/edu/eag2008*).
StatLink ⧉ http://dx.doi.org/10.1787/402165765880

Other highlights of this indicator

- On average across OECD countries, a young person aged 15 in 2006 can expect to continue in formal education for about 6.7 years. In 20 of the 29 OECD countries and 3 partner countries for which data are available, this period is from 5 to 7.5 years. However, it ranges from 3.1 years (Turkey) to a high of 8.7 years (Denmark and Iceland).

- In addition to the expected number of years spent in education, a young person aged 15 can expect to hold a job for 6.2 of the 15 subsequent years, to be unemployed for a total of 0.8 years and to be out of the labour market (not employed, not in education and not looking for a job) for 1.3 years on average across OECD countries.

- Among 15-to-19-year-olds, the proportion of individuals in school in OECD countries has increased by 5.1 percentage points, from 80.4 to 85.6%, between 2000 and 2006. Growth has been greatest in the Netherlands and the Slovak Republic with increases exceeding 11 and 23 percentage points, respectively.

- The 15-to-19-year-old population that is not in education is generally associated with being unemployed or out of the labour force. Some countries are better able than others to provide employment for young adults with relatively low educational attainment. In Iceland, Japan and Norway, more than 70% of this age group not in education have employment.

- On average, completing upper secondary education reduces unemployment among 20-to-24-year-olds by 7.4 percentage points and that of 25-to-29-year-olds by 6.8 percentage points. The lack of an upper secondary qualification is clearly a serious impediment to finding employment, and a tertiary qualification further increases the likelihood of job seekers finding employment.

C4

Policy context

All OECD countries are experiencing rapid social and economic changes that make the transition to working life more uncertain for younger individuals. In some OECD countries, education and work are largely consecutive, while in others they may be concurrent. The ways in which education and work are combined can significantly affect the transition process. Of particular interest is the extent to which working while studying (beyond students' usual summer jobs) may facilitate entry into the labour force.

The transition from education to work is a complex process that depends not only on the length and quality of the schooling received but also on a country's general labour market and economic conditions. High general unemployment rates make the transition substantially more difficult. Unemployment rates among those entering the labour market typically reflect this situation through rates that are above those of the more experienced workforce.

General labour market conditions also influence the schooling decisions of younger individuals: when labour markets are poor, younger individuals tend to remain longer in education; the opposite applies when they are good. It is logical that employment prospects should influence the length and timing of schooling, since high unemployment rates drive down the opportunity costs of education, such as foregone earnings, which tend to be the most prominent component of the cost of education in most countries.

Taken together, the interaction between the education system and the labour market makes it difficult to understand the school-to-work transition, but educational policies can make a substantial contribution towards facilitating it. Most countries have extended their educational systems not only by expanding tertiary education but also by increasing the proportion of young adults receiving an upper secondary education. These policies have aimed at forming a competitive labour force but also at bringing down unemployment rates and inactivity among the younger population.

Evidence and explanations

On average, a person aged 15 in 2006 can expect to continue in education for 6.7 years (Table C4.1a). Some will continue longer than others. In 20 of the 29 countries studied, including the partner country Israel, a 15-year-old can expect to spend on average from five to seven and a half additional years in education. However, the gap between the two extremes is large: eight years or more in Denmark, Finland, Iceland and the Netherlands and the partner country Slovenia, but less than five years in Mexico and Turkey.

In addition to the average 6.7 years spent in education, a person aged 15 can expect to hold a job for 6.2 of the following 15 years, to be unemployed for a total of 0.8 years and to be out of the labour market for 1.3 years, neither in education nor seeking work (Table C4.2).

The average cumulative duration of unemployment varies significantly among countries, owing to differences in general unemployment rates as well as differences in the duration of education. The cumulative average duration of unemployment is six months or less in Australia, Denmark, Iceland, Ireland, Japan, Mexico, the Netherlands, New Zealand, Norway, Switzerland and the United States but around one and a half years in Poland and the Slovak Republic, a large improvement over recent years for these two countries, however.

Chart C4.2. Expected years in education and not in education for 15-to-29-year-olds (2006)

Number of years, by work status

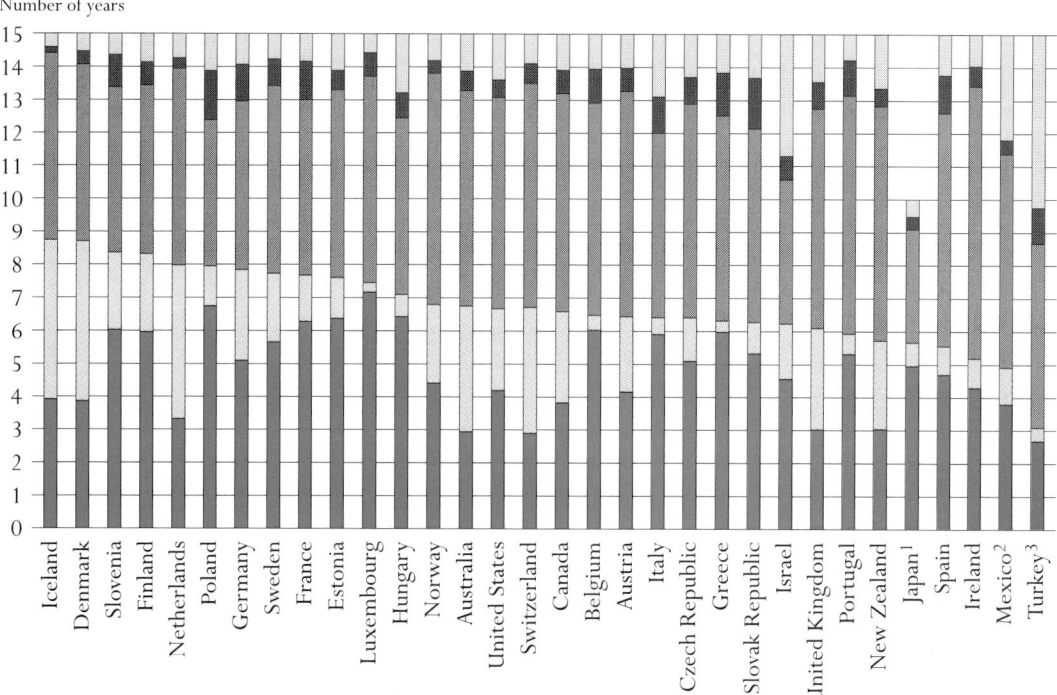

☐ Not in education, not in the labour force
◼ Not in education, unemployed
▨ Not in education, employed
▧ In education, employed (including work study programmes)
◼ In education, not employed

C4

1. Data refer to 15-to-24-year-olds.
2. Year of reference 2004.
3. Year of reference 2005.
Countries are ranked in descending order of the expected years in education of the youth population.
Source: OECD. Table C4.1a. See Annex 3 for notes (*www.oecd.org/edu/eag2008*).
StatLink ᴬᴵˢᴾ http://dx.doi.org/10.1787/402165765880

The average overall number of expected years in education is higher for females (6.9 years compared to 6.5 for males). In all countries except Austria, Germany, Japan, Mexico, the Netherlands, Switzerland and Turkey, females spend more years in education than males. In Turkey, female students can expect to spend nearly one year less in education than their male counterparts; in Finland, Ireland, Italy, Norway and the partner country Estonia, the opposite applies (Chart C4.3). However, up to age 29, males are likely to be employed much more than females, a difference of one and a half years in OECD countries. This reflects the fact that females are more likely to be outside both the education system and the labour market (not in education, not employed and not looking for a job).

Chart C4.3. Gender difference in expected years in education and not in education for 15-to-29-year-olds (2006)

■ In education   ■ Not in education, employed   ▨ Not in education, not employed

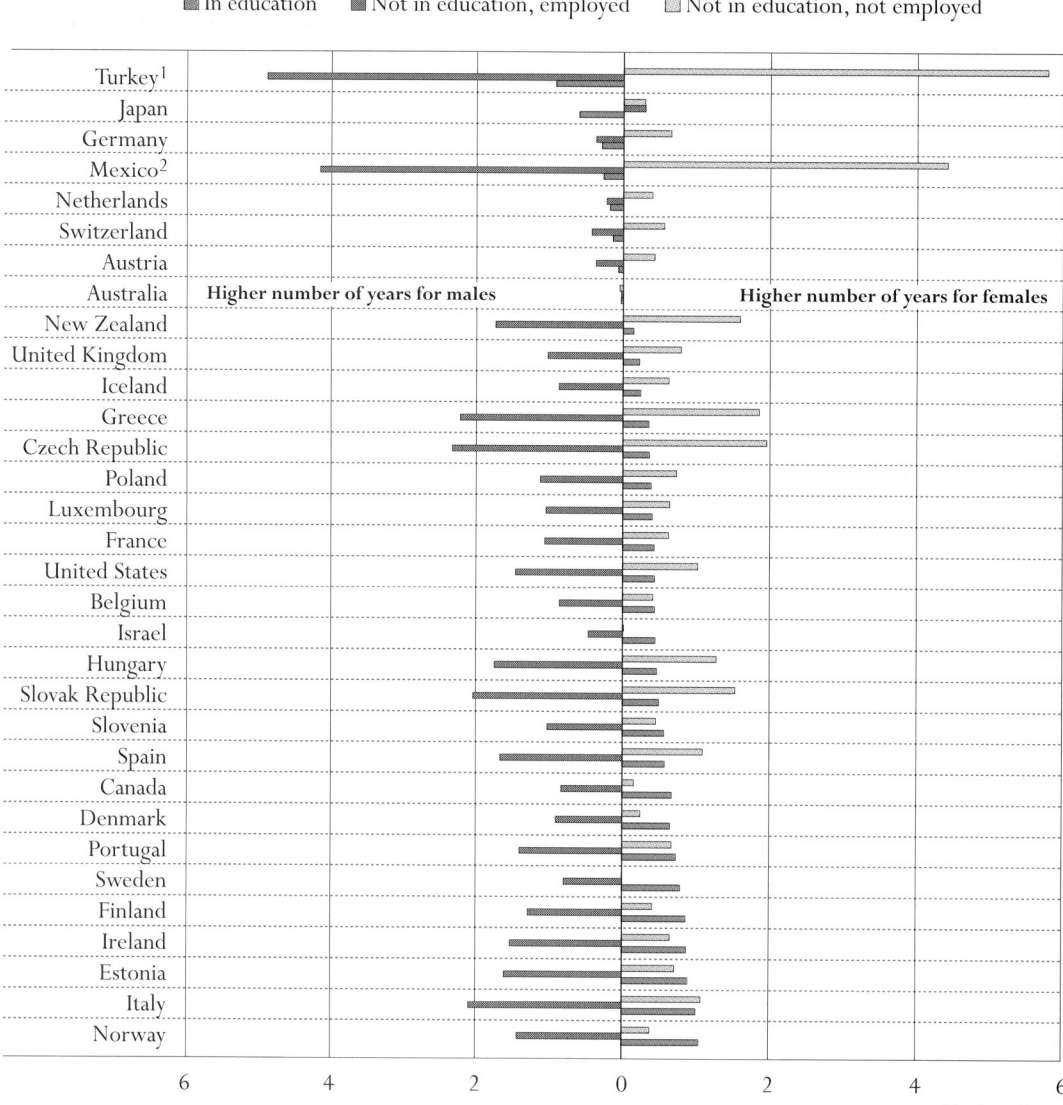

1. Year of reference 2005.
2. Year of reference 2004.

Countries are ranked in descending order of the difference between females and males in expected years in education of the 15- to-29-year-olds.

Source: OECD. Table C4.1a. See Annex 3 for notes (*www.oecd.org/edu/eag2008*).
StatLink Ꮭ᎒ᎽᏚᏓ http://dx.doi.org/10.1787/402165765880

However, males and females differ very little in terms of the expected number of years in unemployment, even though expected periods of unemployment tend to be marginally longer for males (0.9 for males, 0.7 for females). While the situation is similar for both in many countries, females appear to be at a particular advantage in Canada, Germany, the Slovak Republic, Turkey and the United Kingdom. Periods of unemployment for females exceed those for males in Denmark, Greece, Portugal, Spain and the partner country Slovenia (Table C4.1a).

Whereas young males can expect to spend 1.6 years neither in education nor in employment between the ages of 15 and 29, the average figure for females is 2.7 years. In the Czech Republic, Hungary, Mexico, the Slovak Republic and Turkey, there is a much stronger tendency for young females to leave the labour market and to spend time out of the educational system and not working. In Austria, Belgium, Canada, Denmark, Finland, Japan, the Netherlands, Norway, Sweden and Switzerland, young males and young females do not differ by more than half a year in this measure.

Conversely, relative to males, females between the ages of 15 and 29 in all OECD countries can expect a shorter duration of employment after education; this is partly a consequence of the time spent in education, but is also attributable to other factors such as time spent in child-bearing and child-rearing (Table C4.1a).

Unemployment and inactivity among young non-students

Young adults represent the principal source of new skills. In most OECD countries, education policy seeks to encourage them to complete at least upper secondary education. Since many jobs in the current labour market require ever higher general skill levels, persons with low attainment are often penalised.

Both unemployment and non-employment (unemployment and not in the labour force) rise with the proportion of individuals not in education. The 15-to-19-year-old population that is not in education is generally associated with being unemployed or out of the labour force. Approximately half of those not in education are out of the labour force or unemployed (Chart C4.4).

Chart C4.4. Percentage of 15-to-19-year-olds not in education and unemployed or not in the labour force

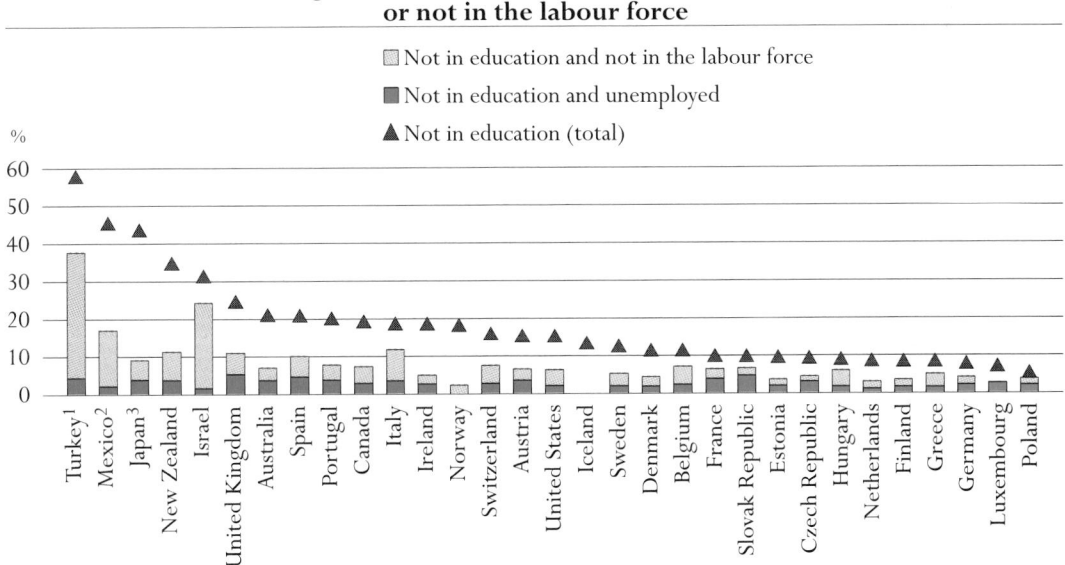

Note: Missing bars refer to cells below reliability thresholds.
1. Year of reference 2005.
2. Year of reference 2004.
3. Data refer to 15-to-24-year-olds.
Countries are ranked in descending order of the percentage of 15-to-19-year-olds not in education.
Source: OECD. Table C4.2a. See Annex 3 for notes (*www.oecd.org/edu/eag2008*).
StatLink http://dx.doi.org/10.1787/402165765880

Some countries are better able than others to provide employment for young adults with relatively low educational attainment (indicated by the difference between the bars and the triangles). In Iceland, Japan and Norway, more than 70% of those not in education find employment. Low unemployment levels among the working age population in general (25-to-64-year-olds) typically contribute to a smoother transition from school to work for young adults with low levels of education.

The group of young adults not currently engaged in employment, education or training (NEET) has attracted considerable attention in some countries. This group is out of both the labour market and the education system and receives little or no support from the welfare system in most countries. The proportion of 15-to-19-year-olds not in education and not in the labour force ranges from over 30% in Turkey to 1% in Poland. On average across OECD countries, 4.3% of this cohort are not in education and not in the labour force. Obviously, their lack of education contributes to the fact that they are inactive, as their skills are likely to be inadequate for finding a suitable job (Table C4.2a).

Differences in unemployment rates among young non-students by level of educational attainment are an indicator of the degree to which further education improves the economic opportunities of young adults. On average, completing upper secondary education reduces this unemployment ratio (unemployment among non-students as a percentage of the age cohort) among 20-to-24-year-olds by 7.4 percentage points and that of 25-to-29-year-olds by 6.2 percentage points (Table C4.3).

Chart C4.5. Share of 25-to-29-year-olds who are unemployed and not in education, by level of educational attainment (2006)

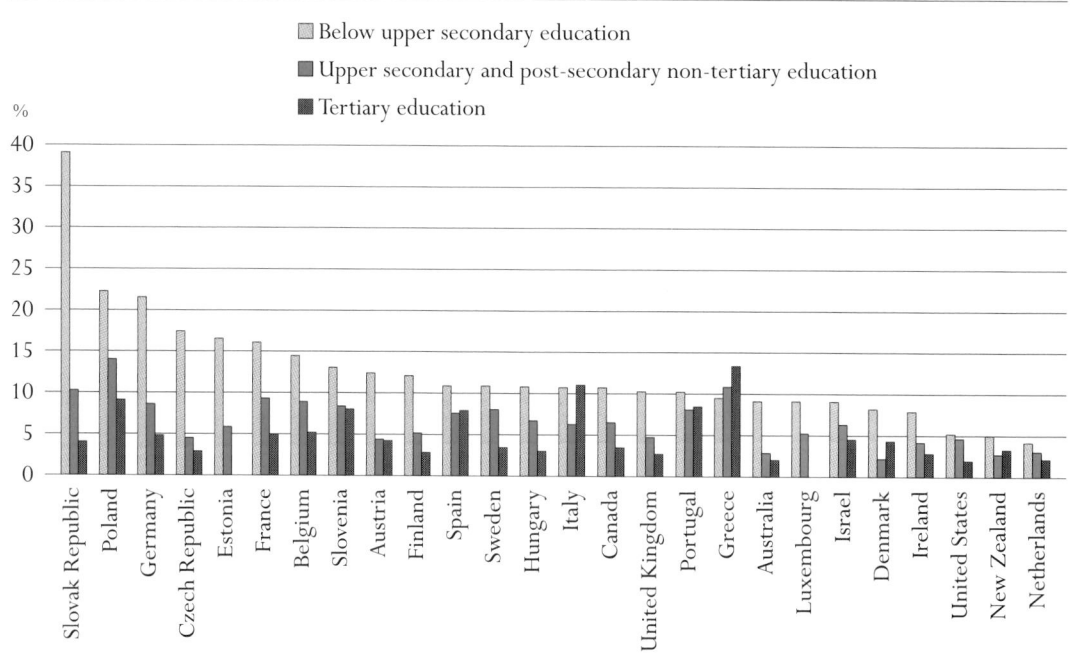

Countries are ranked in descending order of the ratio of the population not in education and unemployed to the 25- to-29-year-old population having attained below upper secondary education.
Source: OECD. Table C4.3. See Annex 3 (www.oecd.org/edu/eag2008).
StatLink ⌨️🔢 http://dx.doi.org/10.1787/402165765880

C4

Since it has become the norm in most OECD countries to complete upper secondary education, those who do not complete this level of education are much more likely to have difficulty finding employment when they enter the labour market. Countries with unemployment levels of 15% or more, for 20-to-24-year-olds with less than upper secondary education attainment, include Belgium, the Czech Republic, France, Poland, the Slovak Republic and Sweden. At the end of the transition period, between the ages of 25 and 29 when most young adults have finished their studies, differences in access to employment are linked to the education level attained. The lack of an upper secondary qualification is clearly a serious handicap. Conversely, for most job seekers tertiary education offers a premium (Chart C4.5).

In 15 OECD countries and 3 partner countries, for upper secondary graduates aged 25 to 29, the ratio of persons not in education and unemployed to the cohort population is at or above 5%. In a few OECD countries, even young adults who have completed tertiary education are subject to considerable unemployment risk when they enter the labour market. Unemployment rates for 25-to-29-year-olds with tertiary education exceed 10% in Greece and Italy. In these two countries and in Denmark, New Zealand, Portugal and Spain, upper secondary and post-secondary non-tertiary unemployment rates are lower than tertiary unemployment rates.

Among 20-to-24-year-olds with tertiary attainment, the ratio of unemployed non-students to the cohort population is 10% or more – and in some cases significantly more – in Greece, Poland and Portugal (Table C4.3). Countries with high unemployment rates among young tertiary educated individuals are also those with high unemployment rates for tertiary educated individuals in the total population (25-to-64-year-olds). Unemployment rates among young adults largely mirrors those of the labour market in general (see Indicator A8).

Entry into the labour market after initial education

The transition from education to work occurs at different points in time in OECD countries, depending on a range of educational and labour market characteristics. As they grow older, young adults spend less time in education and more in the labour force. On average, 83% of 15-to-19-year-olds are in education, a proportion that drops to 39.7% for 20-to-24-year-olds and to 13.8% for 25-to-29-year-olds (Table C4.2a). Since 1995 the proportion of 15-to-19-year-olds in education has expanded rapidly in most OECD countries, with increases of 20% or more in the Czech Republic, Iceland and the Slovak Republic. Young adults thus begin their transition to work later, and in some cases the transition is longer. This reflects not only the demand for education, but also the general state of the labour market, the length and orientation of educational programmes in relation to the labour market and the prevalence of part-time education (Table C4.4a).

Overall, older non-students are much more likely to be employed than non-students aged 15 to 19, and a higher percentage of male than female non-students are employed. A significantly higher share of females than males are out of the labour force. This is particularly true of the 25-to-29-year-old age group and is likely to reflect, in part, time spent in child-bearing and child-rearing (Tables C4.2b and C4.2c on line).

Employment-to-population ratios among young adults not in education provide information on the effectiveness of transition frameworks and thus help policy makers to evaluate transition policies. In 2006 in 9 out of 26 OECD countries (the Czech Republic, Finland, France, Germany,

C4

Hungary, Luxembourg, the Netherlands, Poland, the Slovak Republic), and in the partner countries Estonia and Slovenia, 90% or more of 15-to-19-year-olds were in education. This indicates that few leave school early. While the average of employment-to-population ratios for 20-to-24-year-olds not in education exceeds 44.3%, the ratios in some OECD countries such as Hungary and Poland are considerably lower (Table C4.4a).

The recruiting ground for the expansion of education among 15-to-19-year-olds between 1995 and 2005 has generally been the ranks of the unemployed and those out of the labour force (Chart C4.1). A comparison of the expansion of education between 1995 and 2000 among 15-to-19-year-olds and changes in the proportion of those not in education and not employed among 20-to-24-year-olds from 2000 to 2005 suggests further that most countries have suffered little or no negative spillover effects to the labour market at the later stage (Table C4.4a). For 20-to-24-year-olds and 25-to-29-year-olds, the effect on employment has been greater than on non-employed across OECD countries.

Education systems have continued to expand since the start of the decade. Between 2000 and 2006 in OECD countries, the proportion of individuals in school has increased by more than 5 percentage points among 15-to-19-year-olds. During the key transition period (*i.e.* ages 20 to 24) the proportion of individuals in education has increased by 6 percentage points. Important changes have occurred in several countries (Table C4.4a). The proportion of 20-to-24-year-olds in education has risen by more than 10 percentage points in the Czech Republic, Germany, Greece, Hungary, the Netherlands, Poland and the Slovak Republic; at the same time, the proportion of 20-to-24-year-olds not employed has fallen in all of these countries. In OECD countries, the number of individuals in employment has decreased by 3.5 percentage points, largely because a large proportion of the students are those with better employment prospects.

In OECD countries, the proportion of 25-to-29-year-olds in education increased between 2000 and 2006 by 2.2 percentage points on average, reinforcing the earlier trend towards remaining longer in education. On average, however, only 15% of 25-to-29-year-olds were in education in 2006, 69% were employed and an additional 17% were not in the labour market and not employed. The non-employed ratio has dropped marginally in OECD countries (from 19 to 16.9%) during the period. In Greece, Hungary and the Slovak Republic, non-employment decreased by around 5 percentage points.

The lengthening of education has contributed to lower non-employment rates in most OECD countries, and this is particularly clear among 15-to-19-year-olds). Even if the expansion of education among 20-to-24-year-olds and 25-to-29-year-olds has led, on average, to lower employment rates, the positive effects for individuals and society typically far exceed the lost productivity of the extra years of schooling. The returns to education are substantial in most OECD countries and earnings foregone during studies are outweighed by the benefits later in working life (see Indicator A10).

Definition and methodologies

The statistics presented here are calculated from labour force survey data on age-specific proportions of young people in each of the specified categories. These proportions are then totalled over the 15-to-29-year-old age group to yield the expected number of years spent in various situations. For countries providing data only from age 16, it is assumed that all 15-year-

C4

olds are in education and out of the labour force. This assumption tends to increase the average number of expected years in education compared to (OECD, 2004b).

Persons in education include part-time as well as full-time students, as the coverage should be as close as possible to that of formal education in administrative sources on enrolment. Therefore, non-formal education or educational activities of very short duration (for example, at the work place) are excluded.

Data for this indicator are collected as part of the annual OECD Labour Force Survey (for certain European countries the data come from the annual European Labour Force Survey, see Annex 3) and usually refer to the first quarter, or the average of the first three months of the calendar year, thereby excluding summer employment. The labour force status categories shown in this indicator are defined according to International Labour Organisation (ILO) guidelines, with one exception. For the purposes of this indicator, persons in work-study programmes (see below) have been classified separately as being in education and employed, without reference to their ILO labour force status during the survey reference week, since they may not necessarily be in the work component of their programmes during that week and may therefore not be employed then. The category *other employed* includes individuals employed according to the ILO definition, but excludes those attending work-study programmes who are already counted as employed. Finally, the category *not in the labour force* includes individuals who are not working and who are not unemployed, *i.e.* individuals who are not looking for a job.

Work-study programmes combine work and education as part of an integrated, formal education or training activity, such as the dual system in Germany; *apprentissage* or *formation en alternance* in France and Belgium; internship or co-operative education in Canada; and apprenticeship in Ireland. Vocational education and training take place both in school settings and working environments. Students or trainees can be paid or not, usually depending on the type of job and the course or training.

Participation rates in education and training are here estimated on the basis of self-reports collected during labour force surveys which often correspond imprecisely to enrolments obtained from administrative sources shown elsewhere in this publication, for several reasons. First, age may not be measured in the same way. For example, in administrative data, both enrolment and age are measured on 1 January in OECD countries in the northern hemisphere, whereas in some labour force surveys, both participation in education and age are measured in the reference week, which does not make a significant difference with the administrative measure. However, in other surveys, the age recorded is the age to be attained at the end of the calendar year, even if the survey is conducted early in the year; in this case, the rates of participation in education reflect a population that is one year younger than the specified age range. At ages when movements out of education may be significant, this affects the recorded rates of participation in education and training, which are overestimated. From 2003, the French data take into account the age measured in the reference week. Second, young people may be enrolled in several programmes and may sometimes be counted twice in administrative statistics but only once in a labour force survey. Moreover, not all enrolments may be captured in administrative statistics, particularly in profit-making institutions. Third, the programme classification used in self-reports in labour force surveys does not always correspond to the qualification standards used for administrative data collections.

C4

The principle behind the estimation of expected years in education is that knowledge of the proportion of young adults in or out of education is used as a basis for assumptions about how long a typical individual will spend in different labour and educational situations.

The unemployment-to-population and the employment-to-population ratios are calculated by dividing the total number of individuals unemployed or employed by the number of individuals in that population.

With respect to Table C4.4b, there is a break in the time series for Finland. In 2004, military conscripts in Finland were not included in the data, but in previous years they were included in the category "Not in education, not employed".

Further references

Education at a Glance: OECD Indicators – 2004 Edition, OECD (2004b).

The following additional material relevant to this indicator is available on line at:
StatLink ￼ http://dx.doi.org/10.1787/402165765880

- *Percentage of the youth population in education and not in education (2006)*
  Table C4.2b. Young males
  Table C4.2c. Young females

- *Trends in the percentage of young population in education and not in education (1995-2006)*
  Table C4.4b. Trends for young males
  Table C4.4c. Trends for young females

Table C4.1a.
Expected years in education and not in education for 15-to-29-year-olds (2006)
By gender and work status

		Expected years in education			Expected years not in education			
		Not employed	Employed (including work study programmes)	Sub-total	Employed	Unemployed	Not in the labour force	Sub-total
		(1)	(2)	(3)	(4)	(5)	(6)	(7)
Australia	Males	2.9	3.8	6.8	7.0	0.7	0.5	8.2
	Females	2.9	3.8	6.7	6.1	0.5	1.7	8.3
	M+F	2.9	3.8	6.8	6.5	0.6	1.1	8.2
Austria	Males	3.9	2.6	6.5	7.0	0.8	0.7	8.5
	Females	4.4	2.0	6.4	6.6	0.6	1.4	8.6
	M+F	4.1	2.3	6.4	6.8	0.7	1.0	8.6
Belgium	Males	5.8	0.4	6.3	6.9	1.1	0.8	8.7
	Females	6.2	0.5	6.7	6.0	0.9	1.4	8.3
	M+F	6.0	0.5	6.5	6.4	1.0	1.1	8.5
Canada	Males	3.9	2.3	6.3	7.0	0.9	0.8	8.7
	Females	3.7	3.2	6.9	6.2	0.5	1.4	8.1
	M+F	3.8	2.8	6.6	6.6	0.7	1.1	8.4
Czech Republic	Males	4.7	1.6	6.2	7.6	0.8	0.3	8.8
	Females	5.5	1.0	6.6	5.3	0.8	2.3	8.4
	M+F	5.1	1.3	6.4	6.5	0.8	1.3	8.6
Denmark	Males	3.6	4.8	8.4	5.8	0.4	0.4	6.6
	Females	4.1	4.9	9.0	4.9	0.4	0.6	6.0
	M+F	3.8	4.8	8.7	5.4	0.4	0.5	6.3
Finland	Males	5.8	2.1	7.9	5.7	0.8	0.5	7.1
	Females	6.1	2.7	8.8	4.5	0.5	1.2	6.2
	M+F	6.0	2.4	8.3	5.1	0.7	0.9	6.7
France	Males	6.0	1.4	7.5	5.9	1.2	0.4	7.5
	Females	6.5	1.4	7.9	4.8	1.1	1.2	7.1
	M+F	6.3	1.4	7.7	5.3	1.2	0.8	7.3
Germany	Males	5.1	2.9	8.0	5.3	1.3	0.4	7.0
	Females	5.1	2.6	7.7	4.9	0.9	1.5	7.3
	M+F	5.1	2.7	7.8	5.1	1.1	0.9	7.2
Greece	Males	5.8	0.4	6.1	7.3	1.0	0.6	8.9
	Females	6.2	0.3	6.5	5.1	1.6	1.8	8.5
	M+F	6.0	0.3	6.3	6.2	1.3	1.2	8.7
Hungary	Males	6.3	0.6	6.9	6.2	0.9	1.0	8.1
	Females	6.6	0.8	7.3	4.5	0.7	2.5	7.7
	M+F	6.4	0.7	7.1	5.3	0.8	1.8	7.9
Iceland	Males	4.5	4.1	8.6	6.1	0.2	0.1	6.4
	Females	3.3	5.6	8.9	5.2	0.2	0.7	6.1
	M+F	3.9	4.8	8.7	5.7	0.2	0.4	6.3
Ireland	Males	4.0	0.8	4.8	9.0	0.7	0.5	10.2
	Females	4.6	1.0	5.6	7.5	0.5	1.4	9.4
	M+F	4.3	0.9	5.2	8.3	0.6	1.0	9.8
Italy	Males	5.5	0.4	5.9	6.6	1.2	1.3	9.1
	Females	6.3	0.6	6.9	4.5	1.1	2.5	8.1
	M+F	5.9	0.5	6.4	5.6	1.1	1.9	8.6
Japan[1]	Males	5.2	0.7	6.0	3.3	0.4	0.3	4.0
	Females	4.6	0.7	5.4	3.6	0.4	0.7	4.6
	M+F	4.9	0.7	5.7	3.4	0.4	0.5	4.3
Luxembourg	Males	6.9	0.4	7.2	6.8	0.7	0.2	7.8
	Females	7.5	0.2	7.7	5.7	0.7	0.9	7.3
	M+F	7.2	0.3	7.4	6.3	0.7	0.6	7.6
Mexico[2]	Males	3.7	1.4	5.0	8.6	0.5	0.8	10.0
	Females	3.9	0.9	4.8	4.5	0.3	5.4	10.2
	M+F	3.8	1.1	4.9	6.5	0.4	3.2	10.1
Netherlands	Males	3.3	4.8	8.1	6.1	0.4	0.5	6.9
	Females	3.4	4.5	7.9	5.9	0.3	1.0	7.1
	M+F	3.3	4.6	8.0	6.0	0.3	0.7	7.0

1. Data refer to 15-to-24-year-olds.
2. Year of reference 2004.
3. Year of reference 2005.
Source: OECD. See Annex 3 for notes (*www.oecd.org/edu/eag2008*).
StatLink ᵐˢ┖ http://dx.doi.org/10.1787/402165765880

C4

Table C4.1a. *(continued)*
Expected years in education and not in education for 15-to-29-year-olds (2006)
By gender and work status

		Expected years in education			Expected years not in education			
		Not employed	Employed (including work study programmes)	Sub-total	Employed	Unemployed	Not in the labour force	Sub-total
		(1)	(2)	(3)	(4)	(5)	(6)	(7)
New Zealand	Males	3.1	2.6	5.6	8.0	0.6	0.8	9.4
	Females	3.0	2.8	5.8	6.2	0.5	2.5	9.2
	M+F	3.0	2.7	5.7	7.1	0.5	1.6	9.3
Norway	Males	4.4	1.8	6.3	7.7	0.4	0.6	8.7
	Females	4.4	2.9	7.3	6.3	0.4	1.0	7.7
	M+F	4.4	2.4	6.8	7.0	0.4	0.8	8.2
Poland	Males	6.5	1.3	7.7	5.0	1.6	0.6	7.3
	Females	7.0	1.1	8.1	3.9	1.3	1.6	6.9
	M+F	6.7	1.2	7.9	4.4	1.5	1.1	7.1
Portugal	Males	5.0	0.6	5.6	7.9	1.0	0.6	9.4
	Females	5.6	0.7	6.3	6.5	1.2	1.0	8.7
	M+F	5.3	0.6	5.9	7.2	1.1	0.8	9.1
Slovak Republic	Males	5.0	1.0	6.0	6.9	1.8	0.4	9.0
	Females	5.7	0.8	6.5	4.8	1.3	2.3	8.5
	M+F	5.3	0.9	6.3	5.9	1.5	1.3	8.7
Spain	Males	4.5	0.8	5.3	7.9	1.0	0.8	9.7
	Females	5.0	0.9	5.9	6.2	1.3	1.7	9.1
	M+F	4.7	0.9	5.6	7.1	1.2	1.2	9.4
Sweden	Males	5.6	1.8	7.3	6.1	0.9	0.7	7.7
	Females	5.7	2.4	8.1	5.3	0.7	0.9	6.9
	M+F	5.7	2.1	7.7	5.7	0.8	0.8	7.3
Switzerland	Males	2.8	4.0	6.8	7.0	0.6	0.6	8.2
	Females	3.0	3.7	6.6	6.6	0.6	1.2	8.4
	M+F	2.9	3.8	6.7	6.8	0.6	0.9	8.3
Turkey[3]	Males	3.0	0.6	3.5	8.0	1.5	1.9	11.5
	Females	2.4	0.3	2.6	3.1	0.7	8.6	12.4
	M+F	2.7	0.4	3.1	5.6	1.1	5.2	11.9
United Kingdom	Males	3.0	2.9	6.0	7.2	1.0	0.8	9.0
	Females	3.0	3.2	6.2	6.1	0.6	2.0	8.8
	M+F	3.0	3.1	6.1	6.6	0.8	1.4	8.9
United States	Males	4.2	2.3	6.4	7.1	0.6	0.8	8.6
	Females	4.2	2.7	6.9	5.7	0.5	2.0	8.1
	M+F	4.2	2.5	6.7	6.4	0.5	1.4	8.3
OECD average	*Males*	*4.6*	*1.9*	*6.5*	*6.9*	*0.9*	*0.7*	*8.5*
	Females	*4.8*	*2.1*	*6.9*	*5.5*	*0.7*	*1.9*	*8.1*
	M+F	*4.7*	*2.0*	*6.7*	*6.2*	*0.8*	*1.3*	*8.3*
EU19 average	*Males*	*5.1*	*1.7*	*6.7*	*6.7*	*1.0*	*0.6*	*8.3*
	Females	*5.5*	*1.7*	*7.2*	*5.4*	*0.9*	*1.5*	*7.8*
	M+F	*5.3*	*1.7*	*6.9*	*6.1*	*0.9*	*1.1*	*8.1*
Estonia	Males	6.0	1.2	7.2	6.5	0.7	0.7	7.8
	Females	6.8	1.3	8.1	4.9	0.5	1.5	6.9
	M+F	6.4	1.2	7.6	5.7	0.6	1.1	7.4
Israel	Males	4.5	1.5	6.0	4.6	0.7	3.7	9.0
	Females	4.6	1.8	6.5	4.1	0.7	3.7	8.5
	M+F	4.6	1.7	6.2	4.4	0.7	3.7	8.8
Slovenia	Males	5.8	2.3	8.1	5.5	0.8	0.6	6.9
	Females	6.3	2.4	8.6	4.5	1.1	0.7	6.4
	M+F	6.0	2.3	8.4	5.0	1.0	0.6	6.6

OECD countries / *Partner countries*

1. Data refer to 15-to-24-year-olds.
2. Year of reference 2004.
3. Year of reference 2005.
Source: OECD. See Annex 3 for notes (*www.oecd.org/edu/eag2008*).
StatLink ⫶ᔕ⌐ http://dx.doi.org/10.1787/402165765880

Table C4.1b.
Trends in expected years in education and not in education for 15-to-29-year-olds (1998-2006)
By gender

		1998		1999		2000		2001		2002		2003		2004		2005		2006	
		In education	Not in education	In education	Not in education	In education	Not in education	In education	Not in education	In education	Not in education	In education	Not in education	In education	Not in education	In education	Not in education	In education	Not in education
		(1)	(2)	(3)	(4)	(5)	(6)	(7)	(8)	(9)	(10)	(11)	(12)	(13)	(14)	(15)	(16)	(17)	(18)
Australia	Males	6.0	9.0	6.4	8.6	6.4	8.6	6.6	8.4	6.7	8.3	6.7	8.3	6.8	8.2	6.7	8.3	6.8	8.2
	Females	6.0	9.0	6.2	8.8	6.5	8.5	6.4	8.6	6.7	8.3	6.9	8.1	6.8	8.2	6.8	8.2	6.7	8.3
	M+F	6.0	9.0	6.3	8.7	6.4	8.6	6.5	8.5	6.7	8.3	6.8	8.2	6.8	8.2	6.8	8.2	6.8	8.2
Austria[1]	Males	m	m	m	m	m	m	m	m	5.9	9.1	6.2	8.8	6.2	8.8	6.2	8.8	6.5	8.5
	Females	m	m	m	m	m	m	m	m	6.0	9.0	6.2	8.8	6.2	8.8	6.2	8.8	6.4	8.6
	M+F	m	m	m	m	m	m	m	m	5.9	9.1	6.2	8.8	6.2	8.8	6.2	8.8	6.4	8.6
Belgium	Males	6.4	8.6	7.0	8.0	6.9	8.1	7.3	7.7	6.3	8.7	6.6	8.4	6.7	8.3	6.4	8.6	6.3	8.7
	Females	6.5	8.5	7.3	7.7	7.2	7.8	7.2	7.8	6.7	8.3	6.8	8.2	6.7	8.3	6.9	8.1	6.7	8.3
	M+F	6.5	8.5	7.1	7.9	7.0	8.0	7.2	7.8	6.5	8.5	6.7	8.3	6.7	8.3	6.7	8.3	6.5	8.5
Canada	Males	6.3	8.7	6.2	8.8	6.1	8.9	6.2	8.8	6.1	8.9	6.1	8.9	6.1	8.9	6.3	8.7	6.3	8.7
	Females	6.6	8.4	6.6	8.4	6.6	8.4	6.8	8.2	6.8	8.2	6.8	8.2	6.8	8.2	6.9	8.1	6.9	8.1
	M+F	6.5	8.5	6.4	8.6	6.3	8.7	6.5	8.5	6.5	8.5	6.5	8.5	6.5	8.5	6.6	8.4	6.6	8.4
Czech Republic	Males	4.7	10.3	4.6	10.4	4.7	10.3	5.0	10.0	5.1	9.9	5.3	9.7	5.6	9.4	5.8	9.2	6.2	8.8
	Females	4.8	10.2	4.7	10.3	4.8	10.2	5.1	9.9	5.2	9.8	5.4	9.6	5.7	9.3	6.1	8.9	6.6	8.4
	M+F	4.7	10.3	4.6	10.4	4.8	10.2	5.1	9.9	5.2	9.8	5.4	9.6	5.7	9.3	5.9	9.1	6.4	8.6
Denmark	Males	8.6	6.4	8.1	6.9	8.3	6.7	8.1	6.9	8.4	6.6	7.4	7.6	8.1	6.9	8.0	7.0	8.4	6.6
	Females	8.8	6.2	8.8	6.2	9.0	6.0	8.4	6.6	8.8	6.2	8.3	6.7	8.6	6.4	8.7	6.3	9.0	6.0
	M+F	8.7	6.3	8.5	6.5	8.7	6.3	8.3	6.7	8.6	6.4	7.9	7.1	8.3	6.7	8.3	6.7	8.7	6.3
Finland	Males	m	m	m	m	m	m	m	m	m	m	8.1	6.9	8.0	7.0	8.0	7.0	7.9	7.1
	Females	m	m	m	m	m	m	m	m	m	m	8.6	6.4	8.5	6.5	8.6	6.4	8.8	6.2
	M+F	m	m	m	m	m	m	m	m	m	m	8.3	6.7	8.3	6.7	8.3	6.7	8.3	6.7
France[2]	Males	7.8	7.2	7.8	7.2	7.9	7.1	7.8	7.2	7.8	7.2	m	m	7.5	7.5	7.4	7.6	7.5	7.5
	Females	8.0	7.0	8.0	7.0	8.1	6.9	8.1	6.9	8.2	6.8	m	m	7.7	7.3	7.9	7.1	7.9	7.1
	M+F	7.9	7.1	7.9	7.1	8.0	7.0	8.0	7.0	8.0	7.0	m	m	7.6	7.4	7.7	7.3	7.7	7.3
Germany	Males	m	m	6.8	8.2	6.8	8.2	6.9	8.1	7.3	7.7	7.6	7.4	8.0	7.0	7.9	7.1	8.0	7.0
	Females	m	m	6.7	8.3	6.7	8.3	6.9	8.1	7.2	7.8	7.6	7.4	7.7	7.3	7.7	7.3	7.7	7.3
	M+F	m	m	6.7	8.3	6.7	8.3	6.9	8.1	7.3	7.7	7.6	7.4	7.8	7.2	7.8	7.2	7.8	7.2
Greece	Males	5.6	9.4	5.9	9.1	5.8	9.2	6.1	8.9	5.9	9.1	5.7	9.3	5.6	9.4	5.9	9.1	6.1	8.9
	Females	5.6	9.4	5.8	9.2	6.0	9.0	6.1	8.9	6.2	8.8	6.2	8.8	5.8	9.2	6.2	8.8	6.5	8.5
	M+F	5.6	9.4	5.8	9.2	5.9	9.1	6.1	8.9	6.0	9.0	6.0	9.0	5.7	9.3	6.0	9.0	6.3	8.7
Hungary	Males	5.6	9.4	5.6	9.4	6.1	8.9	6.1	8.9	6.1	8.9	6.6	8.4	6.6	8.4	6.8	8.2	6.9	8.1
	Females	5.7	9.3	5.9	9.1	6.1	8.9	6.4	8.6	6.5	8.5	6.8	8.2	7.0	8.0	7.1	7.9	7.3	7.7
	M+F	5.7	9.3	5.7	9.3	6.1	8.9	6.2	8.8	6.3	8.7	6.7	8.3	6.8	8.2	6.9	8.1	7.1	7.9
Iceland	Males	8.2	6.8	8.3	6.7	8.4	6.6	7.6	7.4	8.1	6.9	8.5	6.5	8.6	6.4	8.2	6.8	8.6	6.4
	Females	8.4	6.6	8.1	6.9	8.4	6.6	8.8	6.2	9.0	6.0	9.2	5.8	8.7	6.3	8.9	6.1	8.9	6.1
	M+F	8.3	6.7	8.2	6.8	8.4	6.6	8.2	6.8	8.5	6.5	8.8	6.2	8.7	6.3	8.6	6.4	8.7	6.3
Ireland	Males	m	m	5.4	9.6	5.3	9.7	5.2	9.8	5.4	9.6	5.5	9.5	5.4	9.6	5.2	9.8	4.8	10.2
	Females	m	m	5.9	9.1	6.1	8.9	6.0	9.0	6.0	9.0	6.0	9.0	5.9	9.1	5.7	9.3	5.6	9.4
	M+F	m	m	5.7	9.3	5.7	9.3	5.6	9.4	5.7	9.3	5.7	9.3	5.7	9.3	5.4	9.6	5.2	9.8
Italy	Males	5.7	9.3	5.8	9.2	5.7	9.3	5.8	9.2	5.9	9.1	6.7	8.3	5.8	9.2	5.8	9.2	5.9	9.1
	Females	6.2	8.8	6.2	8.8	6.2	8.8	6.3	8.7	6.5	8.5	7.3	7.7	6.6	8.4	6.6	8.4	6.9	8.1
	M+F	5.9	9.1	6.0	9.0	6.0	9.0	6.0	9.0	6.2	8.8	7.0	8.0	6.2	8.8	6.2	8.8	6.4	8.6
Japan[3]	Males	9.4	5.6	9.3	5.7	9.7	5.3	9.9	5.1	9.0	6.0	9.0	6.0	9.2	5.8	9.3	5.7	9.0	6.0
	Females	8.6	6.4	8.7	6.3	8.9	6.1	8.9	6.1	8.6	6.4	8.5	6.5	8.5	6.5	8.6	6.4	8.1	6.9
	M+F	9.0	6.0	9.0	6.0	9.3	5.7	9.4	5.6	8.8	6.2	8.8	6.2	8.9	6.1	9.0	6.0	8.5	6.5
Luxembourg	Males	6.5	8.5	7.0	8.0	6.9	8.1	7.2	7.8	7.3	7.7	7.0	8.0	6.9	8.1	7.2	7.8	7.2	7.8
	Females	6.2	8.8	6.2	8.8	6.7	8.3	6.8	8.2	7.2	7.8	6.8	8.2	7.1	7.9	7.3	7.7	7.7	7.3
	M+F	6.3	8.7	6.6	8.4	6.8	8.2	7.0	8.0	7.3	7.7	6.9	8.1	7.0	8.0	7.3	7.7	7.4	7.6
Mexico	Males	3.9	11.1	4.1	10.9	4.0	11.0	4.2	10.8	4.5	10.5	4.5	10.5	4.5	10.5	m	m	5.0	10.0
	Females	3.5	11.5	3.8	11.2	3.6	11.4	3.9	11.1	4.1	10.9	4.1	10.9	4.2	10.8	m	m	4.8	10.2
	M+F	3.7	11.3	4.0	11.0	3.8	11.2	4.0	11.0	4.3	10.7	4.3	10.7	4.4	10.6	m	m	4.9	10.1
Netherlands	Males	8.0	7.0	8.0	7.0	5.8	9.2	7.2	7.8	7.4	7.6	7.4	7.6	7.7	7.3	7.9	7.1	8.1	6.9
	Females	7.4	7.6	7.5	7.5	5.7	9.3	6.8	8.2	7.1	7.9	7.2	7.8	7.5	7.5	7.7	7.3	7.9	7.1
	M+F	7.7	7.3	7.8	7.2	5.7	9.3	7.0	8.0	7.2	7.8	7.3	7.7	7.6	7.4	7.8	7.2	8.0	7.0

1. Breaks in time series are due to a change in survey methodology from 2003 to 2004.
2. Breaks in time series are due to a change in methodology: age is measured in the reference week from 2004, as is participation in education.
3. Data refer to 15-to-24-year-olds.
Source: OECD. See Annex 3 for notes (*www.oecd.org/edu/eag2006*).
Please refer to the Reader's Guide for information concerning the symbols replacing missing data.
StatLink ⌐ᵐˢ⌐ http://dx.doi.org/10.1787/402165765880

C4

Table C4.1b. *(continued)*

Trends in expected years in education and not in education for 15-to-29-year-olds (1998-2006)
By gender

		1998 In education	1998 Not in education	1999 In education	1999 Not in education	2000 In education	2000 Not in education	2001 In education	2001 Not in education	2002 In education	2002 Not in education	2003 In education	2003 Not in education	2004 In education	2004 Not in education	2005 In education	2005 Not in education	2006 In education	2006 Not in education
		(1)	(2)	(3)	(4)	(5)	(6)	(7)	(8)	(9)	(10)	(11)	(12)	(13)	(14)	(15)	(16)	(17)	(18)
New Zealand	Males	m	m	m	m	m	m	m	m	m	m	m	m	m	m	6.1	8.9	5.6	9.4
	Females	m	m	m	m	m	m	m	m	m	m	m	m	m	m	6.1	8.9	5.8	9.2
	M+F	m	m	m	m	m	m	m	m	m	m	m	m	m	m	6.1	8.9	5.7	9.3
Norway	Males	6.5	8.5	6.6	8.4	6.7	8.3	6.2	8.8	6.2	8.8	6.5	8.5	6.7	8.3	6.8	8.2	6.3	8.7
	Females	7.4	7.6	7.5	7.5	7.8	7.2	7.2	7.8	7.3	7.7	7.4	7.6	7.6	7.4	7.8	7.2	7.3	7.7
	M+F	7.0	8.0	7.0	8.0	7.3	7.7	6.7	8.3	6.7	8.3	6.9	8.1	7.1	7.9	7.3	7.7	6.8	8.2
Poland	Males	6.3	8.7	6.3	8.7	6.5	8.5	7.2	7.8	7.8	7.2	7.9	7.1	7.8	7.2	8.1	6.9	7.7	7.3
	Females	6.4	8.6	6.5	8.5	6.6	8.4	7.5	7.5	8.1	6.9	8.4	6.6	8.4	6.6	8.6	6.4	8.1	6.9
	M+F	6.4	8.6	6.4	8.6	6.6	8.4	7.4	7.6	7.9	7.1	8.1	6.9	8.1	6.9	8.4	6.6	7.9	7.1
Portugal	Males	5.2	9.8	5.5	9.5	5.4	9.6	5.4	9.6	5.2	9.8	5.4	9.6	5.5	9.5	5.5	9.5	5.6	9.4
	Females	5.8	9.2	6.0	9.0	6.0	9.0	6.1	8.9	6.0	9.0	6.2	8.8	6.0	9.0	6.2	8.8	6.3	8.7
	M+F	5.5	9.5	5.7	9.3	5.7	9.3	5.7	9.3	5.6	9.4	5.8	9.2	5.7	9.3	5.8	9.2	5.9	9.1
Slovak Republic	Males	4.5	10.5	4.5	10.5	4.4	10.6	4.3	10.7	5.0	10.0	5.1	9.9	5.7	9.3	6.0	9.0	6.0	9.0
	Females	4.8	10.2	4.6	10.4	4.4	10.6	4.5	10.5	5.4	9.6	5.5	9.3	6.0	9.0	6.3	8.7	6.5	8.5
	M+F	4.6	10.4	4.5	10.5	4.4	10.6	4.4	10.6	5.2	9.8	5.4	9.6	5.8	9.2	6.2	8.8	6.3	8.7
Spain	Males	6.3	8.7	6.1	8.9	6.3	8.7	6.3	8.7	6.1	8.9	6.1	8.9	5.9	9.1	5.2	9.8	5.3	9.7
	Females	7.4	7.6	7.2	7.8	7.2	7.8	7.2	7.8	7.1	7.9	7.0	8.0	6.8	8.2	5.9	9.1	5.9	9.1
	M+F	6.8	8.2	6.7	8.3	6.7	8.3	6.8	8.2	6.6	8.4	6.5	8.5	6.3	8.7	5.6	9.4	5.6	9.4
Sweden	Males	7.3	7.7	7.3	7.7	7.2	7.8	7.1	7.9	7.2	7.8	7.4	7.6	7.3	7.7	7.5	7.5	7.3	7.7
	Females	8.1	6.9	8.0	7.0	7.9	7.1	7.8	7.2	7.9	7.1	7.9	7.1	8.2	6.8	8.4	6.6	8.1	6.9
	M+F	7.7	7.3	7.7	7.3	7.5	7.5	7.4	7.6	7.5	7.5	7.6	7.4	7.7	7.3	7.9	7.1	7.7	7.3
Switzerland	Males	6.7	8.3	6.8	8.2	7.2	7.8	7.3	7.7	6.9	8.1	6.7	8.3	6.9	8.1	6.9	8.1	6.8	8.2
	Females	5.8	9.2	6.1	8.9	6.3	8.7	6.6	8.4	6.5	8.5	6.2	8.8	6.6	8.4	6.6	8.4	6.6	8.4
	M+F	6.3	8.7	6.4	8.6	6.8	8.2	7.0	8.0	6.7	8.3	6.4	8.6	6.8	8.2	6.8	8.2	6.7	8.3
Turkey	Males	3.6	11.4	3.8	11.2	3.2	11.8	3.3	11.7	3.4	11.6	3.9	11.1	3.4	11.6	3.5	11.5	m	m
	Females	2.3	12.7	2.5	12.5	2.3	12.7	2.3	12.7	2.4	12.6	2.6	12.4	2.5	12.5	2.6	12.4	m	m
	M+F	3.0	12.0	3.2	11.8	2.8	12.2	2.8	12.2	2.9	12.1	3.3	11.7	3.0	12.0	3.1	11.9	m	m
United Kingdom	Males	m	m	m	m	5.9	9.1	5.8	9.2	5.4	9.6	6.1	8.9	6.0	9.0	6.1	8.9	6.0	9.0
	Females	m	m	m	m	6.2	8.8	6.2	8.8	6.5	8.5	6.3	8.7	6.1	8.9	6.3	8.7	6.2	8.8
	M+F	m	m	m	m	6.0	9.0	6.0	9.0	5.9	9.1	6.2	8.8	6.1	8.9	6.2	8.8	6.1	8.9
United States	Males	6.4	8.6	6.5	8.5	6.4	8.6	6.5	8.5	6.6	8.4	m	m	6.5	8.5	6.5	8.5	6.4	8.6
	Females	6.6	8.4	6.4	8.6	6.6	8.4	6.7	8.3	6.9	8.1	m	m	7.0	8.0	7.0	8.0	6.9	8.1
	M+F	6.5	8.5	6.5	8.5	6.5	8.5	6.6	8.4	6.8	8.2	m	m	6.7	8.3	6.8	8.2	6.7	8.3
OECD average	*Males*	*6.2*	*8.8*	*6.3*	*8.7*	*6.2*	*8.8*	*6.3*	*8.7*	*6.3*	*8.7*	*6.4*	*8.6*	*6.5*	*8.5*	*6.6*	*8.4*	*6.6*	*8.4*
	Females	*6.3*	*8.7*	*6.4*	*8.6*	*6.4*	*8.6*	*6.5*	*8.5*	*6.6*	*8.4*	*6.7*	*8.3*	*6.8*	*8.2*	*6.9*	*8.1*	*7.0*	*8.0*
	M+F	*6.2*	*8.8*	*6.3*	*8.7*	*6.3*	*8.7*	*6.4*	*8.6*	*6.5*	*8.5*	*6.6*	*8.4*	*6.6*	*8.4*	*6.8*	*8.2*	*6.8*	*8.2*
EU19 average	*Males*	*6.3*	*8.7*	*6.4*	*8.6*	*6.2*	*8.8*	*6.4*	*8.6*	*6.4*	*8.6*	*6.6*	*8.4*	*6.6*	*8.4*	*6.7*	*8.3*	*6.7*	*8.3*
	Females	*6.6*	*8.4*	*6.6*	*8.4*	*6.5*	*8.5*	*6.7*	*8.3*	*6.8*	*8.2*	*6.9*	*8.1*	*7.0*	*8.0*	*7.1*	*7.9*	*7.2*	*7.8*
	M+F	*6.4*	*8.6*	*6.5*	*8.5*	*6.4*	*8.6*	*6.5*	*8.5*	*6.6*	*8.4*	*6.7*	*8.3*	*6.8*	*8.2*	*6.9*	*8.1*	*6.9*	*8.1*
Estonia	Males	m	m	m	m	m	m	m	m	m	m	6.9	8.1	7.5	7.5	8.1	6.9	7.2	7.8
	Females	m	m	m	m	m	m	m	m	m	m	8.6	6.4	8.4	6.6	8.1	6.9	8.1	6.9
	M+F	m	m	m	m	m	m	m	m	m	m	7.7	7.3	8.0	7.0	8.1	6.9	7.6	7.4
Israel	Males	m	m	m	m	m	m	m	m	5.8	9.2	5.9	9.1	5.9	9.1	5.9	9.1	6.0	9.0
	Females	m	m	m	m	m	m	m	m	6.0	9.0	6.0	9.0	6.2	8.8	6.1	8.9	6.5	8.5
	M+F	m	m	m	m	m	m	m	m	5.9	9.1	6.0	9.0	6.0	9.0	6.0	9.0	6.2	8.8
Slovenia	Males	m	m	m	m	m	m	m	m	m	m	8.1	6.9	8.2	6.8	8.0	7.0	8.1	6.9
	Females	m	m	m	m	m	m	m	m	m	m	9.1	5.9	9.4	5.6	8.7	6.3	8.6	6.4
	M+F	m	m	m	m	m	m	m	m	m	m	8.6	6.4	8.8	6.2	8.3	6.7	8.4	6.6

OECD countries (New Zealand through United States); *Partner countries* (Estonia, Israel, Slovenia)

1. Breaks in time series are due to a change in survey methodology from 2003 to 2004.
2. Breaks in time series are due to a change in methodology: age is measured in the reference week from 2004, as is participation in education.
3. Data refer to 15-to-24-year-olds.
Source: OECD. See Annex 3 for notes (*www.oecd.org/edu/eag2006*).
Please refer to the Reader's Guide for information concerning the symbols replacing missing data.
StatLink ⌖ http://dx.doi.org/10.1787/402165765880

Table C4.2a.
Percentage of the youth population in education and not in education (2006)
By age group and work status

	Age group	In education					Not in education				Total in education and not in education
		Students in work-study programmes[1]	Other employed	Unemployed	Not in the labour force	Sub-total	Employed	Unemployed	Not in the labour force	Sub-total	
		(1)	(2)	(3)	(4)	(5)	(6)	(7)	(8)	(9)	(10)
Australia	15-to-19	7.3	29.5	5.3	37.2	79.3	13.7	3.7	3.4	20.7	100
	20-to-24	6.2	21.0	1.2	10.6	39.0	49.5	4.2	7.2	61.0	100
	25-to-29	1.3	10.9	0.5	3.8	16.6	67.7	3.7	12.0	83.4	100
Austria	15-to-19	25.1	2.5	1.8	55.6	85.0	8.5	3.6	3.0	15.0	100
	20-to-24	2.2	9.1	1.1	20.3	32.6	54.8	5.1	7.4	67.4	100
	25-to-29	c	7.6	0.7	5.3	13.7	71.0	5.3	10.0	86.3	100
Belgium	15-to-19	c	1.4	c	86.1	88.9	4.0	2.4	4.7	11.1	100
	20-to-24	c	3.0	1.1	31.1	35.6	47.6	9.9	7.0	64.4	100
	25-to-29	c	3.3	c	2.9	7.2	75.3	8.2	9.4	92.8	100
Canada	15-to-19	a	29.5	5.1	46.5	81.1	11.6	2.9	4.5	18.9	100
	20-to-24	a	19.3	1.5	17.7	38.4	48.6	5.9	7.1	61.6	100
	25-to-29	a	6.8	0.4	5.1	12.4	72.1	5.3	10.2	87.6	100
Czech Republic	15-to-19	21.2	0.4	c	69.4	91.0	4.5	3.1	1.4	9.0	100
	20-to-24	0.9	2.9	0.3	35.9	40.0	45.8	7.9	6.2	60.0	100
	25-to-29	c	3.0	0.1	4.5	7.7	71.0	5.0	16.3	92.3	100
Denmark	15-to-19	a	46.1	5.3	37.4	88.9	6.7	1.9	2.5	11.1	100
	20-to-24	a	33.3	2.5	19.5	55.3	38.8	2.4	3.4	44.7	100
	25-to-29	a	17.6	0.9	10.8	29.4	62.2	3.7	4.6	70.6	100
Finland	15-to-19	a	11.4	6.1	74.4	91.8	4.6	1.7	1.9	8.2	100
	20-to-24	a	20.6	4.4	26.8	51.7	35.0	6.9	6.4	48.3	100
	25-to-29	a	15.1	2.3	8.2	25.6	60.4	5.1	8.8	74.4	100
France	15-to-19	4.9	1.9	0.5	83.0	90.4	3.2	3.8	2.6	9.6	100
	20-to-24	5.0	6.8	1.4	33.7	47.0	36.5	11.0	5.5	53.0	100
	25-to-29	5.0	4.3	1.0	4.3	14.6	68.1	8.5	8.8	85.4	100
Germany	15-to-19	17.0	6.4	1.6	67.5	92.4	3.3	2.2	2.0	7.6	100
	20-to-24	13.5	9.0	0.7	22.3	45.5	37.8	9.9	6.8	54.5	100
	25-to-29	1.8	7.4	0.5	8.7	18.5	61.5	10.1	9.9	81.5	100
Greece	15-to-19	a	1.5	c	83.8	85.7	5.4	2.8	6.0	14.3	100
	20-to-24	a	3.6	1.6	40.5	45.7	36.9	10.7	6.8	54.3	100
	25-to-29	a	1.9	c	5.5	7.8	71.1	11.2	9.9	92.2	100
Hungary	15-to-19	a	0.4	c	90.9	91.3	2.7	1.8	4.2	8.7	100
	20-to-24	a	4.6	1.1	42.1	47.8	33.7	6.8	11.7	52.2	100
	25-to-29	a	7.6	0.6	5.3	13.5	62.2	6.4	17.8	86.5	100
Iceland	15-to-19	a	49.1	6.2	31.7	86.9	9.9	c	c	13.1	100
	20-to-24	a	31.3	c	20.9	53.6	41.9	c	c	46.4	100
	25-to-29	a	15.9	c	17.0	33.7	62.3	c	c	66.3	100
Ireland	15-to-19	a	10.2	c	71.0	81.7	13.3	2.6	2.4	18.3	100
	20-to-24	a	7.5	c	18.6	26.5	61.7	5.1	6.7	73.5	100
	25-to-29	a	1.5	c	3.9	5.6	81.1	4.0	9.3	94.4	100
Italy	15-to-19	c	1.6	0.7	79.4	81.6	6.6	3.5	8.3	18.4	100
	20-to-24	0.2	4.2	1.6	34.2	40.2	37.0	10.1	12.7	59.8	100
	25-to-29	c	3.9	1.1	10.2	15.2	60.7	8.3	15.8	84.8	100
Japan	15-to-24	a	7.2	0.1	49.3	56.7	34.2	3.9	5.2	43.3	100
Luxembourg	15-to-19	a	2.9	c	89.9	93.1	2.8	2.7	c	6.9	100
	20-to-24	a	2.2	c	47.9	50.3	39.4	5.9	4.4	49.7	100
	25-to-29	a	c	c	8.5	9.2	79.6	5.6	5.6	90.8	100
Mexico[2]	15-to-19	a	7.1	0.5	47.3	54.9	28.0	2.2	14.9	45.1	100
	20-to-24	a	4.7	0.4	15.2	20.3	52.3	3.2	24.2	79.7	100
	25-to-29	a	1.9	0.1	2.4	4.4	65.4	2.7	27.6	95.6	100
Netherlands	15-to-19	a	46.3	5.5	39.9	91.7	5.2	1.2	1.9	8.3	100
	20-to-24	a	33.7	1.8	14.8	50.3	42.4	2.1	5.2	49.7	100
	25-to-29	a	13.3	0.4	4.3	18.1	71.2	3.1	7.7	81.9	100

OECD countries (side label)

1. Students in work-study programmes are considered to be both in education and employed, irrespective of their labour market status according to the ILO definition.
2. Year of reference 2004.
3. Year of reference 2005.
Source: OECD. See Annex 3 for notes (*www.oecd.org/edu/eag2008*).
StatLink ⬛ http://dx.doi.org/10.1787/402165765880

C4

Table C4.2a. *(continued)*
Percentage of the youth population in education and not in education (2006)
By age group and work status

	Age group	In education					Not in education				Total in education and not in education
		Students in work-study programmes[1]	Other employed	Unemployed	Not in the labour force	Sub-total	Employed	Unemployed	Not in the labour force	Sub-total	
		(1)	(2)	(3)	(4)	(5)	(6)	(7)	(8)	(9)	(10)
New Zealand	15-to-19	a	25.2	4.1	36.2	65.6	23.2	3.7	7.5	34.4	100
	20-to-24	a	18.1	2.1	10.0	30.1	54.8	3.8	11.2	69.9	100
	25-to-29	a	8.9	0.5	4.6	14.0	68.0	3.3	14.7	86.0	100
Norway	15-to-19	a	23.7	3.9	54.4	82.1	14.5	c	2.4	17.9	100
	20-to-24	a	17.8	c	19.7	39.2	51.7	3.3	5.7	60.8	100
	25-to-29	a	5.6	c	6.1	12.2	76.3	3.3	8.1	87.8	100
Poland	15-to-19	a	3.7	0.8	90.4	94.9	1.3	2.2	1.6	5.1	100
	20-to-24	a	12.9	5.2	36.9	55.1	24.2	13.8	6.8	44.9	100
	25-to-29	a	7.0	1.3	3.9	12.2	61.2	13.2	13.4	87.8	100
Portugal	15-to-19	a	1.5	c	78.4	80.2	12.0	3.8	4.0	19.8	100
	20-to-24	a	4.9	1.1	31.8	37.7	48.9	7.7	5.7	62.3	100
	25-to-29	a	5.5	0.7	6.0	12.2	72.9	9.2	5.6	87.8	100
Slovak Republic	15-to-19	13.6	c	c	76.5	90.5	2.9	4.7	1.9	9.5	100
	20-to-24	c	2.5	0.6	31.9	35.4	41.9	14.6	8.2	64.6	100
	25-to-29	c	2.9	c	2.7	5.7	67.9	11.0	15.4	94.3	100
Spain	15-to-19	a	3.9	1.4	74.2	79.5	10.5	4.6	5.5	20.5	100
	20-to-24	a	7.7	1.8	25.0	34.5	48.6	8.9	8.0	65.5	100
	25-to-29	a	5.5	1.0	4.3	10.9	70.1	8.8	10.3	89.1	100
Sweden	15-to-19	a	20.3	8.3	59.1	87.7	7.0	2.0	3.3	12.3	100
	20-to-24	a	11.6	5.0	26.4	43.0	41.8	8.2	7.0	57.0	100
	25-to-29	a	8.9	2.2	9.8	20.9	67.5	6.2	5.4	79.1	100
Switzerland	15-to-19	35.2	7.6	1.6	40.1	84.4	8.0	2.8	4.8	15.6	100
	20-to-24	11.4	12.1	c	12.5	36.9	52.3	5.3	5.5	63.1	100
	25-to-29	c	10.0	c	3.7	14.7	73.8	4.0	7.5	85.3	100
Turkey[3]	15-to-19	a	2.2	0.4	39.9	42.5	19.9	4.4	33.3	57.5	100
	20-to-24	a	3.9	1.2	10.2	15.2	37.7	9.6	37.6	84.8	100
	25-to-29	a	2.5	0.4	1.4	4.3	53.5	8.0	34.2	95.7	100
United Kingdom	15-to-19	3.7	30.9	4.8	36.2	75.7	13.4	5.3	5.6	24.3	100
	20-to-24	2.7	13.2	1.6	12.6	30.2	51.6	6.8	11.5	69.8	100
	25-to-29	1.2	9.1	0.4	3.5	14.1	69.5	4.4	12.0	85.9	100
United States	15-to-19	a	21.7	3.0	60.3	85.0	8.6	2.1	4.2	15.0	100
	20-to-24	a	19.3	1.1	14.6	35.0	49.4	5.2	10.4	65.0	100
	25-to-29	a	8.3	c	3.1	11.7	71.5	3.6	13.2	88.3	100
OECD average	*15-to-19*		*14.4*	*3.3*	*62.0*	*83.0*	*9.1*	*3.0*	*5.3*	*17.1*	*100*
	20-to-24		*12.2*	*1.8*	*24.4*	*39.7*	*44.2*	*7.3*	*9.1*	*60.1*	*100*
	25-to-29		*7.3*	*0.8*	*5.7*	*13.8*	*68.3*	*6.5*	*11.9*	*86.1*	*100*
EU19 average	*15-to-19*		*10.7*	*3.3*	*70.7*	*87.5*	*6.2*	*2.9*	*3.5*	*12.5*	*100*
	20-to-24		*10.2*	*1.9*	*29.1*	*42.3*	*42.4*	*8.1*	*7.2*	*57.7*	*100*
	25-to-29		*7.0*	*0.9*	*5.9*	*13.8*	*68.7*	*7.2*	*10.3*	*86.2*	*100*
Estonia	15-to-19	a	2.4	1.6	86.8	90.7	5.6	2.0	1.7	9.3	100
	20-to-24	a	15.1	c	31.5	47.6	37.0	4.9	10.4	52.4	100
	25-to-29	a	7.2	c	2.2	9.4	75.0	5.2	10.5	90.6	100
Israel	15-to-19	a	5.0	1.1	62.9	69.0	6.8	1.6	22.6	31.0	100
	20-to-24	a	12.3	1.5	15.5	29.3	30.1	6.9	33.7	70.7	100
	25-to-29	a	16.4	1.0	7.5	24.8	51.8	6.0	17.4	75.2	100
Slovenia	15-to-19	a	7.9	0.8	84.0	92.7	3.1	2.5	1.7	7.3	100
	20-to-24	a	20.3	2.8	32.7	55.8	30.5	7.5	6.2	44.2	100
	25-to-29	a	17.3	2.6	6.5	26.3	60.3	8.6	4.7	73.7	100

1. Students in work-study programmes are considered to be both in education and employed, irrespective of their labour market status according to the ILO definition.
2. Year of reference 2004.
3. Year of reference 2005.
Source: OECD. See Annex 3 for notes (*www.oecd.org/edu/eag2008*).
StatLink ⌗⌗ http://dx.doi.org/10.1787/402165765880

C4

Table C4.3.
Percentage of the cohort population not in education and unemployed (2006)
By level of educational attainment, age group and gender

		Below upper secondary education			Upper secondary and post-secondary non-tertiary education			Tertiary education		All levels of education			
		15 to 19	20 to 24	25 to 29	15 to 19[1]	20 to 24	25 to 29	20 to 24[1]	25 to 29	15 to 19	20 to 24	25 to 29	15 to 29
		(1)	(2)	(3)	(4)	(5)	(6)	(7)	(8)	(9)	(10)	(11)	(12)
Australia	Males	4.4	11.6	11.3	3.7	3.9	2.7	c	c	4.1	5.6	4.1	4.6
	Females	2.7	6.8	6.6	4.0	1.9	3.1	c	2.3	3.2	2.8	3.4	3.1
	M+F	3.6	9.7	9.1	3.8	2.9	2.9	3.0	2.0	3.7	4.2	3.7	3.9
Austria	Males	3.6	17.6	16.6	c	4.3	5.4	c	c	3.7	6.5	6.3	5.5
	Females	3.1	9.7	9.4	c	2.6	3.4	c	c	3.5	3.8	4.3	3.8
	M+F	3.4	13.9	12.4	4.8	3.4	4.4	c	4.3	3.6	5.1	5.3	4.7
Belgium	Males	2.4	18.4	15.2	c	9.3	6.9	10.3	6.5	2.8	11.4	8.3	7.5
	Females	c	11.8	13.5	c	7.6	11.5	8.3	4.3	2.0	8.4	8.3	6.3
	M+F	1.8	15.5	14.4	4.2	8.5	8.9	9.1	5.2	2.4	9.9	8.3	6.9
Canada	Males	2.7	15.0	14.1	5.4	6.6	7.5	4.9	4.1	3.6	7.3	6.7	5.9
	Females	1.9	7.9	5.9	2.5	4.4	5.0	3.4	3.1	2.1	4.4	3.9	3.5
	M+F	2.3	12.1	10.7	3.9	5.6	6.5	4.1	3.5	2.9	5.9	5.3	4.7
Czech Republic	Males	1.5	21.0	21.0	17.0	7.1	4.3	c	3.1	3.7	8.3	5.0	5.6
	Females	1.1	14.4	14.6	11.6	6.9	4.8	7.8	2.8	2.5	7.5	5.1	5.1
	M+F	1.3	18.1	17.4	14.5	7.0	4.5	7.5	2.9	3.1	7.9	5.0	5.4
Denmark	Males	1.8	c	c	c	c	c	c	4.9	2.0	1.9	3.5	2.5
	Females	1.9	c	c	m	2.5	c	m	3.8	1.8	2.9	3.9	2.9
	M+F	1.9	c	8.2	c	2.1	2.2	c	4.3	1.9	2.4	3.7	2.7
Finland	Males	1.9	9.6	10.3	c	8.9	5.1	c	c	2.3	9.1	5.3	5.6
	Females	c	c	c	c	4.6	5.2	c	c	c	4.8	5.0	3.6
	M+F	1.3	7.8	12.1	c	6.8	5.2	c	2.8	1.7	6.9	5.1	4.6
France	Males	4.0	25.9	17.6	5.3	8.0	9.3	8.5	5.8	4.2	11.4	9.5	8.3
	Females	2.9	18.9	14.2	5.1	9.5	9.3	8.4	4.2	3.4	10.5	7.5	7.1
	M+F	3.5	22.8	16.1	5.2	8.7	9.3	8.4	4.9	3.8	11.0	8.5	7.7
Germany	Males	2.1	16.6	26.4	11.1	10.4	9.4	c	5.3	2.5	12.2	11.4	8.6
	Females	1.5	10.6	17.3	8.5	6.6	7.7	c	4.5	2.0	7.5	8.8	6.1
	M+F	1.8	13.8	21.6	9.5	8.5	8.6	6.0	4.8	2.2	9.9	10.1	7.4
Greece	Males	c	c	8.4	c	6.5	7.3	c	11.2	3.1	7.3	8.4	6.6
	Females	c	c	c	c	11.5	14.7	27.1	15.1	c	14.1	14.3	10.8
	M+F	c	12.2	9.5	6.2	9.0	10.8	21.0	13.4	2.8	10.7	11.2	8.6
Hungary	Males	1.8	13.6	12.2	6.2	5.8	7.1	c	3.6	2.4	7.7	7.2	5.9
	Females	c	10.3	9.1	c	4.7	6.3	8.1	2.6	1.2	6.0	5.6	4.4
	M+F	1.2	12.1	10.8	5.0	5.3	6.7	9.8	3.0	1.8	6.8	6.4	5.2
Iceland	Males	c	m	c	c	m	m	m	m	c	m	c	c
	Females	c	c	m	m	m	m	m	m	c	c	c	c
	M+F	c	c	c	c	m	m	m	m	c	c	m	c
Ireland	Males	3.1	14.0	9.4	3.7	4.5	4.6	4.2	3.4	3.3	5.9	4.8	4.7
	Females	c	9.1	c	3.0	3.2	3.6	3.8	2.4	2.1	4.0	3.1	3.1
	M+F	2.3	12.1	7.9	3.3	3.9	4.2	3.9	2.8	2.7	5.0	3.9	3.9
Italy	Males	3.1	14.6	11.1	12.3	8.6	6.0	4.5	12.1	4.1	10.2	8.5	7.7
	Females	1.8	15.2	10.1	10.5	8.3	6.6	12.1	10.3	2.9	10.1	8.1	7.2
	M+F	2.5	14.9	10.7	11.3	8.5	6.3	9.2	11.0	3.5	10.1	8.3	7.5
Luxembourg	Males	c	11.2	c	c	c	c	c	c	c	7.3	4.6	4.9
	Females	c	c	c	c	c	c	c	c	c	4.5	6.6	4.6
	M+F	2.4	8.8	9.1	c	4.3	5.3	c	c	2.7	5.9	5.6	4.7
Mexico	Males	m	m	m	m	m	m	m	m	m	m	m	3.6
	Females	m	m	m	m	m	m	m	m	m	m	m	2.2
	M+F	m	m	m	m	m	m	m	m	m	m	m	2.8
Netherlands	Males	1.2	3.1	5.7	m	0.7	3.0	m	2.1	1.4	2.3	3.5	2.4
	Females	0.6	3.3	2.9	m	1.1	2.8	m	2.2	0.8	1.9	2.7	1.8
	M+F	0.9	3.9	4.2	1.1	1.3	3.1	m	2.1	1.1	2.1	3.1	2.1

OECD countries

1. Differences between countries in these columns reflect in part the fact that the average age of graduation varies across countries. For instance, in some countries a smaller share of 15-to-19-year-olds attain upper secondary education simply because graduation typically occurs at 19. This means that the denominator in the ratio for the reported columns will be smaller than those for which graduation occurs at an earlier age.

Source: OECD. See Annex 3 for notes (*www.oecd.org/edu/eag2008*).

Please refer to the Reader's Guide for information concerning the symbols replacing missing data.

StatLink ᵐˢᴸ http://dx.doi.org/10.1787/402165765880

C4

Table C4.3. *(continued)*
Percentage of the cohort population not in education and unemployed (2006)
By level of educational attainment, age group and gender

		Below upper secondary education			Upper secondary and post-secondary non-tertiary education			Tertiary education		All levels of education			
		15 to 19	20 to 24	25 to 29	15 to 19[1]	20 to 24	25 to 29	20 to 24[1]	25 to 29	15 to 19	20 to 24	25 to 29	15 to 29
		(1)	(2)	(3)	(4)	(5)	(6)	(7)	(8)	(9)	(10)	(11)	(12)
New Zealand	Males	5.2	5.6	5.7	2.8	2.3	3.2	4.9	2.7	3.9	3.6	3.5	3.7
	Females	3.6	9.1	c	3.2	2.9	c	3.6	3.7	3.5	4.0	3.1	3.5
	M+F	4.5	7.2	5.0	3.0	2.6	2.7	4.2	3.3	3.7	3.8	3.3	3.6
Norway	Males	c	c	c	c	c	c	c	c	c	c	3.6	2.7
	Females	c	c	c	c	c	c	c	c	c	c	c	2.3
	M+F	c	7.4	c	c	c	c	c	c	c	3.3	3.3	2.5
Poland	Males	1.1	30.1	24.1	9.8	14.7	13.5	15.3	10.1	2.0	16.4	13.6	10.9
	Females	0.8	21.2	19.6	12.7	10.3	14.6	13.3	8.4	2.3	11.2	12.7	9.0
	M+F	1.0	27.1	22.3	11.4	12.5	14.0	14.0	9.1	2.2	13.8	13.2	10.0
Portugal	Males	4.2	8.6	8.0	c	4.4	7.8	c	c	4.2	6.9	7.6	6.4
	Females	3.2	10.7	13.1	c	5.1	8.3	15.6	10.0	3.3	8.5	10.9	8.0
	M+F	3.7	9.4	10.2	c	4.8	8.1	13.0	8.5	3.8	7.7	9.2	7.2
Slovak Republic	Males	3.0	47.4	51.0	26.0	13.8	11.6	c	c	5.7	16.6	12.4	11.7
	Females	2.5	27.2	30.4	13.4	11.8	8.8	c	4.3	3.8	12.5	9.6	8.8
	M+F	2.7	38.4	39.1	19.7	12.8	10.3	c	4.0	4.7	14.6	11.0	10.3
Spain	Males	4.9	11.7	8.2	3.7	5.0	5.2	7.4	6.8	4.8	8.4	6.9	6.8
	Females	4.7	13.3	14.8	3.1	6.9	10.1	8.7	8.9	4.5	9.4	10.8	8.6
	M+F	4.8	12.4	10.9	3.4	6.0	7.6	8.2	7.9	4.6	8.9	8.8	7.7
Sweden	Males	c	17.4	c	c	9.4	9.6	c	c	2.5	8.9	7.4	6.1
	Females	c	c	c	c	9.2	5.9	c	c	c	7.6	5.0	4.6
	M+F	c	16.8	10.9	8.8	9.3	8.0	c	3.5	2.0	8.2	6.2	5.4
Switzerland	Males	c	c	c	c	4.7	3.7	c	c	3.1	5.6	3.7	4.1
	Females	c	c	c	c	3.9	c	c	c	2.4	5.0	4.2	3.9
	M+F	1.7	7.5	c	10.1	4.3	3.4	c	c	2.8	5.3	4.0	4.0
Turkey	Males	m	m	m	m	m	m	m	m	m	m	m	m
	Females	m	m	m	m	m	m	m	m	m	m	m	m
	M+F	m	m	m	m	m	m	m	m	m	m	m	m
United Kingdom	Males	5.0	20.0	16.5	7.3	7.6	5.1	7.6	3.5	6.4	8.6	5.5	6.8
	Females	2.6	7.4	c	4.8	4.8	4.5	4.8	2.1	4.1	5.0	3.5	4.2
	M+F	3.9	13.7	10.3	6.0	6.2	4.8	6.0	2.7	5.3	6.8	4.4	5.5
United States	Males	c	8.3	5.8	6.1	5.4	4.7	5.5	2.2	2.3	5.9	4.0	4.0
	Females	c	11.3	c	4.3	3.9	4.6	c	1.7	1.9	4.5	3.3	3.2
	M+F	0.9	9.6	5.2	5.2	4.7	4.6	3.9	1.9	2.1	5.2	3.6	3.6
OECD average	*Males*	*3.0*	*16.3*	*14.9*	*8.6*	*6.9*	*6.5*	*7.3*	*5.5*	*3.4*	*8.1*	*6.6*	*5.9*
	Females	*2.3*	*12.1*	*13.0*	*6.7*	*5.8*	*7.0*	*9.6*	*5.1*	*2.7*	*6.7*	*6.4*	*5.1*
	M+F	*2.4*	*13.6*	*12.5*	*7.0*	*6.2*	*6.3*	*8.2*	*4.9*	*3.0*	*7.3*	*6.4*	*5.5*
EU19 average	*Males*	*2.8*	*17.7*	*16.4*	*10.2*	*7.6*	*7.1*	*8.3*	*6.0*	*3.4*	*8.8*	*7.3*	*6.6*
	Females	*2.2*	*13.1*	*14.1*	*8.1*	*6.5*	*7.5*	*10.7*	*5.7*	*2.7*	*7.4*	*7.1*	*5.8*
	M+F	*2.4*	*15.2*	*13.6*	*7.6*	*6.8*	*7.0*	*9.7*	*5.4*	*2.9*	*8.1*	*7.2*	*6.2*
Estonia	Males	c	c	19.3	c	3.9	6.8	m	m	c	4.1	7.6	4.4
	Females	c	m	c	c	6.9	c	c	m	c	5.8	c	3.6
	M+F	c	c	16.6	c	5.4	5.9	c	m	2.0	4.9	5.2	4.0
Israel	Males	1.2	9.0	10.9	3.0	6.3	5.1	c	5.0	1.7	6.5	6.0	4.7
	Females	c	12.7	c	3.3	7.3	8.0	c	4.2	1.5	7.3	6.0	4.8
	M+F	1.0	10.1	9.1	3.2	6.8	6.3	4.0	4.5	1.6	6.9	6.0	4.8
Slovenia	Males	1.8	14.0	14.4	5.3	4.5	6.4	c	6.0	2.5	6.1	7.1	5.4
	Females	c	9.3	c	9.9	8.2	10.8	25.4	9.0	2.5	9.1	10.1	7.5
	M+F	1.3	12.2	13.0	7.4	6.2	8.4	25.0	8.1	2.5	7.5	8.6	6.4

1. Differences between countries in these columns reflect in part the fact that the average age of graduation varies across countries. For instance, in some countries a smaller share of 15-to-19-year-olds attain upper secondary education simply because graduation typically occurs at 19. This means that the denominator in the ratio for the reported columns will be smaller than those for which graduation occurs at an earlier age.
Source: OECD. See Annex 3 for notes (*www.oecd.org/edu/eag2008*).
Please refer to the Reader's Guide for information concerning the symbols replacing missing data.
StatLink ⫶⫶⫶ http://dx.doi.org/10.1787/402165765880

Table C4.4a.
Trends in the percentage of the youth population in education and not in education (1995, 1998-2006)
By age group and work status

	Age group	1995 In education Total (1)	1995 Not in education Employed (2)	1995 Not in education Not employed (3)	1998 In education Total (4)	1998 Not in education Employed (5)	1998 Not in education Not employed (6)	1999 In education Total (7)	1999 Not in education Employed (8)	1999 Not in education Not employed (9)	2000 In education Total (10)	2000 Not in education Employed (11)	2000 Not in education Not employed (12)	2001 In education Total (13)	2001 Not in education Employed (14)	2001 Not in education Not employed (15)
Australia	15-to-19	73.4	16.7	9.9	77.3	13.8	8.8	78.2	14.4	7.4	79.5	13.7	6.8	79.5	13.0	7.6
	20-to-24	27.0	56.1	16.9	32.7	51.3	16.0	34.9	50.6	14.5	35.9	50.9	13.3	36.5	49.6	13.9
	25-to-29	11.4	67.1	21.5	13.7	67.1	19.2	15.0	66.5	18.5	15.5	65.5	19.0	15.8	67.0	17.2
Austria[1]	15-to-19	m	m	m	m	m	m	m	m	m	m	m	m	m	m	m
	20-to-24	m	m	m	m	m	m	m	m	m	m	m	m	m	m	m
	25-to-29	m	m	m	m	m	m	m	m	m	m	m	m	m	m	m
Belgium	15-to-19	86.1	3.3	10.5	85.3	3.9	10.8	89.4	3.7	6.8	89.9	3.6	6.5	89.7	4.1	6.2
	20-to-24	37.5	43.6	19.0	40.6	42.5	16.9	43.7	38.6	17.7	43.8	40.2	16.0	44.2	42.8	13.0
	25-to-29	6.8	74.2	19.0	9.3	72.4	18.2	14.4	67.7	17.9	11.8	72.5	15.7	15.0	69.5	15.5
Canada	15-to-19	79.9	10.5	9.5	81.5	9.9	8.5	80.8	10.9	8.3	80.6	11.2	8.2	81.3	11.4	7.3
	20-to-24	33.9	47.3	18.7	36.7	45.4	17.8	37.1	47.2	15.7	35.7	48.5	15.7	36.5	47.9	15.7
	25-to-29	10.3	67.7	22.1	10.8	70.1	19.1	10.7	71.2	18.2	10.6	72.3	17.1	11.6	72.1	16.3
Czech Republic	15-to-19	69.8	23.7	6.5	77.1	15.8	7.2	75.6	14.8	9.7	82.1	10.0	7.9	87.0	6.2	6.8
	20-to-24	13.1	67.1	19.8	17.1	64.3	18.5	19.6	59.8	20.6	19.7	60.0	20.3	23.1	58.9	18.1
	25-to-29	1.1	76.1	22.9	1.8	75.1	23.1	2.4	71.7	25.9	2.4	72.1	25.6	3.0	72.1	25.0
Denmark	15-to-19	88.4	8.7	3.0	90.3	7.9	1.8	85.8	10.8	3.4	89.9	7.4	2.7	86.8	9.4	3.8
	20-to-24	50.0	39.3	10.7	55.0	38.0	7.0	55.8	36.6	7.6	54.8	38.6	6.6	55.3	38.1	6.6
	25-to-29	29.6	59.0	11.4	34.5	57.8	7.7	35.5	56.7	7.8	36.1	56.4	7.5	32.4	60.0	7.6
Finland	15-to-19	m	m	m	m	m	m	m	m	m	m	m	m	m	m	m
	20-to-24	m	m	m	m	m	m	m	m	m	m	m	m	m	m	m
	25-to-29	m	m	m	m	m	m	m	m	m	m	m	m	m	m	m
France[2]	15-to-19	96.2	1.3	2.5	95.6	1.3	3.1	95.7	1.0	3.3	95.3	1.5	3.3	94.9	1.7	3.4
	20-to-24	51.2	31.3	17.5	53.5	30.0	16.5	53.1	29.4	17.5	54.2	31.7	14.1	53.6	33.1	13.4
	25-to-29	11.4	67.5	21.0	11.4	66.5	22.1	11.9	66.6	21.4	12.2	69.2	18.6	11.4	70.3	18.3
Germany	15-to-19	m	m	m	m	m	m	89.5	6.0	4.5	87.4	6.8	5.7	88.5	6.4	5.1
	20-to-24	m	m	m	m	m	m	34.3	49.0	16.7	34.1	49.0	16.9	35.0	48.7	16.4
	25-to-29	m	m	m	m	m	m	13.6	68.2	18.1	12.7	69.8	17.5	13.5	68.5	18.0
Greece	15-to-19	80.0	9.6	10.5	80.1	10.2	9.7	81.8	8.0	10.3	82.7	8.3	9.0	85.4	7.1	7.6
	20-to-24	29.2	43.0	27.8	28.2	44.7	27.1	30.3	43.7	26.0	31.5	43.7	24.9	35.1	40.9	24.0
	25-to-29	4.7	65.2	30.2	4.2	66.8	28.9	5.6	66.9	27.5	5.3	66.9	27.8	6.4	67.4	26.3
Hungary	15-to-19	82.5	6.7	10.8	78.2	10.0	11.8	79.3	9.2	11.6	83.7	7.7	8.6	85.0	6.7	8.3
	20-to-24	22.5	44.4	33.1	26.5	45.9	27.6	28.6	47.7	23.6	32.3	45.7	22.0	35.0	45.1	20.0
	25-to-29	7.3	56.8	35.9	7.4	58.9	33.7	8.7	60.1	31.3	9.4	61.4	29.2	9.4	63.4	27.1
Iceland	15-to-19	59.5	25.7	14.8	82.2	15.1	c	81.6	17.0	c	83.1	14.8	c	79.5	19.0	c
	20-to-24	33.3	52.6	14.0	47.8	45.9	6.3	44.8	48.4	6.8	48.0	47.7	c	50.3	45.6	c
	25-to-29	24.1	64.7	11.1	32.8	57.4	9.8	34.7	58.8	6.5	34.9	59.2	5.9	33.8	61.5	c
Ireland	15-to-19	m	m	m	m	m	m	79.4	15.4	5.2	80.0	15.6	4.4	80.3	15.5	4.1
	20-to-24	m	m	m	m	m	m	24.6	64.6	10.8	26.7	63.6	9.7	28.3	62.4	9.3
	25-to-29	m	m	m	m	m	m	3.1	82.4	14.5	3.3	83.4	13.3	3.3	83.1	13.5
Italy	15-to-19	m	m	m	75.4	9.5	15.2	76.9	8.3	14.8	77.1	9.8	13.1	77.6	9.8	12.6
	20-to-24	m	m	m	35.8	34.1	30.1	35.6	34.5	29.9	36.0	36.5	27.5	37.0	36.9	26.1
	25-to-29	m	m	m	16.5	54.1	29.4	17.7	53.4	28.9	17.0	56.1	26.9	16.4	58.0	25.6
Japan	15-to-24	58.0	34.9	7.1	60.0	32.4	7.6	60.0	31.0	9.0	62.1	29.2	8.8	62.6	28.9	8.4
Luxembourg	15-to-19	82.7	9.3	8.0	88.6	5.3	6.1	89.2	5.8	5.0	92.2	6.1	c	91.2	7.0	c
	20-to-24	36.5	52.7	10.8	40.4	50.1	9.5	47.2	43.2	9.6	42.8	48.9	8.2	46.7	44.2	9.0
	25-to-29	8.3	71.6	20.1	11.9	74.0	14.1	11.3	74.1	14.6	11.6	75.5	12.9	11.6	75.9	12.5
Mexico	15-to-19	45.0	31.8	23.2	46.9	33.8	19.3	49.6	32.7	17.7	47.9	33.8	18.3	50.3	31.9	17.8
	20-to-24	15.9	53.4	30.7	17.1	55.4	27.4	19.1	54.8	26.1	17.7	55.2	27.1	19.1	53.8	27.1
	25-to-29	4.6	62.0	33.4	4.2	65.2	30.6	4.9	65.0	30.1	4.0	65.8	30.2	4.1	64.9	31.0
Netherlands	15-to-19	m	m	m	89.7	7.6	2.7	88.2	8.9	3.0	80.6	15.7	3.7	86.5	9.9	3.6
	20-to-24	m	m	m	50.5	42.0	7.5	50.7	42.5	6.7	36.5	55.2	8.2	44.2	47.8	8.0
	25-to-29	m	m	m	24.4	64.9	10.7	25.0	65.2	9.8	5.0	83.0	12.1	15.3	73.7	11.0

Note: Due to incomplete data, some averages have not been calculated.
1. Breaks in time series are due to a change in survey methodology from 2003 to 2004.
2. Breaks in time series are due to a change in methodology: age is measured in the reference week from 2003, as is participation in education.
Source: OECD. See Annex 3 for notes (www.oecd.org/edu/eag2008).
Please refer to the Reader's Guide for information concerning the symbols replacing missing data.
StatLink ᵐˢᴸ http://dx.doi.org/10.1787/402165765880

C4

Table C4.4a. *(continued-1)*

Trends in the percentage of the youth population in education and not in education (1995, 1998-2006)

By age group and work status

	Age group	1995 In education Total (1)	1995 Not in education Employed (2)	1995 Not in education Not employed (3)	1998 In education Total (4)	1998 Not in education Employed (5)	1998 Not in education Not employed (6)	1999 In education Total (7)	1999 Not in education Employed (8)	1999 Not in education Not employed (9)	2000 In education Total (10)	2000 Not in education Employed (11)	2000 Not in education Not employed (12)	2001 In education Total (13)	2001 Not in education Employed (14)	2001 Not in education Not employed (15)
New Zealand	15-to-19	m	m	m	m	m	m	m	m	m	m	m	m	m	m	m
	20-to-24	m	m	m	m	m	m	m	m	m	m	m	m	m	m	m
	25-to-29	m	m	m	m	m	m	m	m	m	m	m	m	m	m	m
Norway	15-to-19	m	m	m	92.1	6.0	1.9	91.9	6.4	c	92.4	5.9	c	85.8	11.1	3.0
	20-to-24	m	m	m	40.2	51.4	8.4	38.4	53.8	7.8	41.7	50.3	8.0	39.6	51.7	8.7
	25-to-29	m	m	m	14.4	76.1	9.6	17.2	74.4	8.3	17.5	72.1	10.4	13.9	75.9	10.2
Poland	15-to-19	89.6	4.2	6.2	91.0	4.2	4.8	93.2	2.3	4.6	92.8	2.6	4.5	91.8	2.4	5.8
	20-to-24	23.7	42.5	33.8	30.8	45.3	23.9	33.1	39.7	27.2	34.9	34.3	30.8	45.2	27.7	27.1
	25-to-29	3.1	67.5	29.4	5.7	70.5	23.8	5.4	68.0	26.6	8.0	62.9	29.1	11.4	59.9	28.7
Portugal	15-to-19	72.4	18.5	9.1	71.6	20.1	8.3	72.3	19.6	8.1	72.6	19.7	7.7	72.8	19.8	7.4
	20-to-24	37.8	46.6	15.6	32.4	55.7	12.0	34.9	53.2	11.9	36.5	52.6	11.0	36.3	53.3	10.4
	25-to-29	11.6	70.9	17.4	9.5	74.8	15.8	11.5	75.1	13.4	11.0	76.6	12.5	11.2	77.3	11.6
Slovak Republic	15-to-19	70.1	14.0	15.9	69.4	12.3	18.3	69.6	10.1	20.4	67.3	6.4	26.3	67.3	6.3	26.4
	20-to-24	14.8	54.9	30.3	17.4	56.3	26.3	17.4	51.2	31.4	18.1	48.8	33.1	19.4	45.7	34.9
	25-to-29	1.6	65.5	32.9	1.1	71.6	27.2	1.6	70.2	28.2	1.3	66.9	31.8	2.3	65.0	32.7
Spain	15-to-19	77.3	11.2	11.5	80.2	9.9	9.8	79.3	11.3	9.4	80.6	11.4	8.0	81.4	11.6	6.9
	20-to-24	40.0	34.2	25.8	44.3	35.7	20.1	43.6	38.8	17.6	44.6	40.3	15.0	45.0	40.7	14.2
	25-to-29	14.6	51.5	33.9	15.3	57.3	27.5	15.2	59.6	25.1	16.2	62.4	21.4	17.0	63.1	19.8
Sweden	15-to-19	87.4	6.9	5.6	90.9	4.3	4.7	91.5	4.9	3.7	90.6	5.8	3.6	88.4	7.3	4.3
	20-to-24	38.8	43.7	17.5	42.6	44.3	13.1	43.8	45.2	11.0	42.1	47.2	10.7	41.2	48.2	10.6
	25-to-29	19.9	67.0	13.2	24.9	65.0	10.0	22.5	68.1	9.5	21.9	68.9	9.2	22.7	70.0	7.2
Switzerland	15-to-19	65.6	10.2	24.2	85.5	9.6	4.8	84.4	8.0	7.6	84.6	7.5	7.9	85.7	7.5	6.8
	20-to-24	29.5	59.2	11.3	34.8	54.2	11.0	35.8	55.8	8.4	37.4	56.7	5.9	39.3	52.3	8.4
	25-to-29	10.6	76.2	13.2	10.1	77.9	12.1	10.4	79.3	10.3	15.0	73.9	11.1	13.5	75.1	11.4
Turkey	15-to-19	38.7	34.2	27.2	40.2	32.1	27.7	42.9	30.2	26.9	39.2	29.6	31.2	41.0	26.7	32.3
	20-to-24	10.3	46.5	43.2	13.4	44.7	42.0	13.1	45.6	41.4	12.7	43.1	44.2	12.7	43.1	44.2
	25-to-29	2.7	59.6	37.8	2.9	60.4	36.7	3.4	57.7	38.8	2.9	58.8	38.3	2.6	57.1	40.2
United Kingdom	15-to-19	m	m	m	m	m	m	m	m	m	77.0	15.0	8.0	76.1	15.7	8.2
	20-to-24	m	m	m	m	m	m	m	m	m	32.4	52.2	15.4	33.5	51.7	14.8
	25-to-29	m	m	m	m	m	m	m	m	m	13.3	70.3	16.3	13.7	70.6	16.0
United States	15-to-19	81.5	10.7	7.8	82.2	10.5	7.3	81.3	11.3	7.4	81.3	11.7	7.0	81.2	11.4	7.5
	20-to-24	31.5	50.7	17.8	33.0	52.6	14.4	32.8	52.1	15.1	32.5	53.1	14.4	33.9	50.5	15.6
	25-to-29	11.6	71.4	17.0	11.9	72.7	15.4	11.1	73.2	15.7	11.4	72.8	15.8	11.8	70.5	17.7
OECD average	15-to-19				79.6	11.5	9.2	80.3	11.3	9.0	80.4	11.3	9.2	80.6	11.2	8.8
	20-to-24				35.0	46.8	18.2	35.5	46.9	17.6	35.3	47.8	17.5	37.0	46.4	17.1
	25-to-29				12.7	67.1	20.2	13.0	67.5	19.5	12.4	68.6	19.0	12.9	68.5	19.2
EU19 average	15-to-19				83.1	8.7	8.2	83.5	8.7	7.7	83.6	9.0	7.7	84.2	8.6	7.5
	20-to-24				36.8	44.9	18.3	37.3	44.9	17.9	36.5	46.4	17.1	38.7	45.1	16.2
	25-to-29				12.7	66.4	20.9	12.8	67.1	20.0	11.7	69.1	19.3	12.7	68.7	18.6
Estonia	15-to-19	m	m	m	m	m	m	m	m	m	m	m	m	m	m	m
	20-to-24	m	m	m	m	m	m	m	m	m	m	m	m	m	m	m
	25-to-29	m	m	m	m	m	m	m	m	m	m	m	m	m	m	m
Israel	15-to-19	m	m	m	m	m	m	m	m	m	m	m	m	m	m	m
	20-to-24	m	m	m	m	m	m	m	m	m	m	m	m	m	m	m
	25-to-29	m	m	m	m	m	m	m	m	m	m	m	m	m	m	m
Slovenia	15-to-19	m	m	m	m	m	m	m	m	m	m	m	m	m	m	m
	20-to-24	m	m	m	m	m	m	m	m	m	m	m	m	m	m	m
	25-to-29	m	m	m	m	m	m	m	m	m	m	m	m	m	m	m

OECD countries / Partner countries

Note: Due to incomplete data, some averages have not been calculated.

1. Breaks in time series are due to a change in survey methodology from 2003 to 2004.

2. Breaks in time series are due to a change in methodology: age is measured in the reference week from 2003, as is participation in education.

Source: OECD. See Annex 3 for notes (*www.oecd.org/edu/eag2008*).

Please refer to the Reader's Guide for information concerning the symbols replacing missing data.

StatLink ᵐˢᵖ http://dx.doi.org/10.1787/402165765880

Table C4.4a. *(continued-2)*

Trends in the percentage of the youth population in education and not in education (1995, 1998-2006)
By age group and work status

C4

	Age group	2002 In education Total	2002 Not in education Employed	2002 Not in education Not employed	2003 In education Total	2003 Not in education Employed	2003 Not in education Not employed	2004 In education Total	2004 Not in education Employed	2004 Not in education Not employed	2005 In education Total	2005 Not in education Employed	2005 Not in education Not employed	2006 In education Total	2006 Not in education Employed	2006 Not in education Not employed
		(1)	(2)	(3)	(4)	(5)	(6)	(7)	(8)	(9)	(10)	(11)	(12)	(13)	(14)	(15)
Australia	15-to-19	79.7	13.3	7.0	79.6	13.6	6.8	78.4	14.1	7.5	78.3	14.3	7.4	79.3	13.7	7.1
	20-to-24	38.7	48.1	13.2	39.7	47.0	13.3	39.0	48.7	12.3	39.4	49.0	11.6	39.0	49.5	11.5
	25-to-29	16.5	65.7	17.8	17.7	64.7	17.6	17.7	65.0	17.3	16.6	68.0	15.4	16.6	67.7	15.7
Austria[1]	15-to-19	81.5	12.1	6.3	83.6	10.7	5.6	83.3	9.3	7.3	84.4	8.7	6.9	85.0	8.5	6.6
	20-to-24	29.4	58.9	11.7	30.3	59.3	10.4	30.3	56.8	12.9	30.4	57.2	12.4	32.6	54.8	12.5
	25-to-29	10.3	77.3	12.4	12.5	75.2	12.3	13.0	72.6	14.4	12.0	74.6	13.4	13.7	71.0	15.3
Belgium	15-to-19	89.6	3.6	6.8	89.1	3.8	7.1	92.1	3.1	4.9	90.1	3.7	6.2	88.9	4.0	7.1
	20-to-24	38.2	44.4	17.4	39.9	43.0	17.1	38.8	44.4	16.9	38.1	43.6	18.3	35.6	47.6	16.9
	25-to-29	5.8	77.0	17.2	8.9	72.8	18.3	6.0	74.3	19.7	7.4	74.9	17.7	7.2	75.3	17.5
Canada	15-to-19	80.2	11.9	8.0	80.0	11.9	8.1	79.0	12.2	8.8	80.2	12.8	7.0	81.1	11.6	7.3
	20-to-24	36.4	48.3	15.3	36.7	49.0	14.3	38.2	47.6	14.2	39.2	46.3	14.4	38.4	48.6	13.0
	25-to-29	12.7	69.8	17.5	12.7	71.2	16.1	11.9	71.9	16.2	12.5	71.7	15.8	12.4	72.1	15.5
Czech Republic	15-to-19	88.3	5.7	6.0	89.0	5.2	5.8	89.9	4.4	5.7	90.3	4.4	5.3	91.0	4.5	4.5
	20-to-24	25.7	56.2	18.1	28.7	53.3	18.0	32.3	49.2	18.5	35.9	47.5	16.6	40.0	45.8	14.1
	25-to-29	2.9	73.3	23.8	3.0	73.0	24.1	3.8	71.6	24.5	4.4	72.4	23.2	7.7	71.0	21.4
Denmark	15-to-19	88.7	8.9	2.4	89.8	7.7	2.5	89.5	8.4	2.1	88.4	7.3	4.3	88.9	6.7	4.4
	20-to-24	55.3	37.4	7.3	52.1	36.1	11.8	54.0	34.8	11.3	54.4	37.2	8.3	55.3	38.8	5.9
	25-to-29	35.0	58.3	6.7	23.9	64.6	11.5	28.3	59.8	11.9	27.0	61.3	11.6	29.4	62.2	8.4
Finland	15-to-19	m	m	m	88.1	5.7	6.2	88.9	5.2	5.9	90.2	4.5	5.2	91.8	4.6	3.6
	20-to-24	m	m	m	52.5	33.1	14.4	53.1	31.5	15.4	52.8	34.1	13.0	51.7	35.0	13.3
	25-to-29	m	m	m	27.2	58.7	14.1	25.7	58.8	15.5	25.7	60.3	14.0	25.6	60.4	13.9
France[2]	15-to-19	94.6	1.9	3.4	m	m	m	91.7	3.2	5.1	91.0	3.0	6.0	90.4	3.2	6.4
	20-to-24	53.2	32.5	14.4	m	m	m	45.2	38.8	16.0	46.7	37.5	15.8	47.0	36.5	16.5
	25-to-29	11.7	70.1	18.2	m	m	m	13.5	68.2	18.3	13.2	69.6	17.2	14.6	68.1	17.3
Germany	15-to-19	90.1	5.2	4.7	91.2	4.1	4.7	93.4	3.0	3.6	92.9	2.7	4.4	92.4	3.3	4.2
	20-to-24	38.1	46.0	15.9	41.2	43.1	15.6	44.0	38.5	17.5	44.2	37.1	18.7	45.5	37.8	16.7
	25-to-29	16.3	66.3	17.4	17.9	63.7	18.4	17.6	62.8	19.6	18.5	60.3	21.2	18.5	61.5	20.0
Greece	15-to-19	86.6	7.1	6.3	84.2	6.3	9.5	83.5	6.5	10.0	84.5	5.7	9.8	85.7	5.4	8.8
	20-to-24	35.6	41.8	22.6	38.4	39.9	21.7	36.3	41.9	21.8	42.6	37.3	20.1	45.7	36.9	17.4
	25-to-29	5.7	68.7	25.5	7.0	68.8	24.3	5.8	68.9	25.3	6.8	70.2	23.0	7.8	71.1	21.1
Hungary	15-to-19	87.5	4.5	8.0	89.7	3.5	6.8	90.4	3.4	6.2	90.6	3.0	6.4	91.3	2.7	6.0
	20-to-24	36.9	42.6	20.5	40.5	39.6	19.9	43.8	37.6	18.6	46.6	34.5	18.9	47.8	33.7	18.5
	25-to-29	8.6	63.1	28.3	12.6	59.9	27.5	12.9	63.2	23.9	13.1	63.0	24.0	13.5	62.2	24.3
Iceland	15-to-19	80.9	14.8	c	88.5	7.6	c	85.4	11.8	c	86.4	10.7	c	86.9	9.9	c
	20-to-24	53.8	40.1	6.2	57.1	35.1	7.8	56.1	37.5	6.4	53.0	37.1	10.0	53.6	41.9	c
	25-to-29	36.5	58.8	c	26.8	61.7	11.5	30.2	64.0	5.8	30.9	61.5	7.6	33.7	62.3	c
Ireland	15-to-19	81.5	13.6	4.9	81.2	13.5	5.3	83.3	11.8	4.9	82.4	13.1	4.5	81.7	13.3	5.0
	20-to-24	28.9	60.1	10.9	30.5	58.0	11.5	29.0	59.4	11.6	27.7	60.0	12.3	26.5	61.7	11.8
	25-to-29	3.6	81.4	15.0	5.0	79.7	15.3	4.8	80.1	15.1	5.3	80.9	13.8	5.6	81.1	13.3
Italy	15-to-19	80.8	8.7	10.5	83.8	6.9	9.3	81.2	7.8	11.0	81.8	7.0	11.2	81.6	6.6	11.8
	20-to-24	38.2	37.5	24.3	44.1	34.2	21.7	37.7	38.7	23.6	38.6	37.3	24.1	40.2	37.0	22.8
	25-to-29	15.6	59.5	24.8	22.8	54.7	22.5	15.4	59.8	24.8	14.4	59.8	25.8	15.2	60.7	24.1
Japan	15-to-24	58.6	32.0	9.5	58.4	31.7	9.8	59.1	31.7	9.2	59.7	31.5	8.8	56.7	34.2	9.1
Luxembourg	15-to-19	91.3	5.7	3.0	92.2	5.7	2.1	91.4	5.5	3.2	93.4	4.4	2.2	93.1	2.8	4.1
	20-to-24	47.8	45.2	7.0	46.0	45.9	8.1	49.1	40.8	10.1	47.4	43.3	9.3	50.3	39.4	10.3
	25-to-29	13.9	74.5	11.6	7.6	82.2	10.2	6.1	81.5	12.4	8.6	81.2	10.3	9.2	79.6	11.2
Mexico	15-to-19	53.4	29.0	17.5	54.0	28.2	17.8	54.9	28.0	17.0	m	m	m	m	m	m
	20-to-24	20.8	52.6	26.6	19.8	52.6	27.6	20.3	52.3	27.4	m	m	m	m	m	m
	25-to-29	4.6	64.8	30.6	4.2	64.8	31.0	4.4	65.4	30.3	m	m	m	m	m	m
Netherlands	15-to-19	86.7	9.5	3.8	87.0	8.7	4.3	89.2	7.5	3.3	89.2	7.0	3.9	91.7	5.2	3.0
	20-to-24	45.1	47.7	7.3	44.2	46.5	9.4	46.6	44.2	9.3	49.1	41.8	9.1	50.3	42.4	7.3
	25-to-29	16.2	71.6	12.2	16.5	71.4	12.1	16.9	71.2	11.9	18.2	70.2	11.6	18.1	71.2	10.8

Note: Due to incomplete data, some averages have not been calculated.

1. Breaks in time series are due to a change in survey methodology from 2003 to 2004.

2. Breaks in time series are due to a change in methodology: age is measured in the reference week from 2003, as is participation in education.

Source: OECD. See Annex 3 for notes (www.oecd.org/edu/eag2008).

Please refer to the Reader's Guide for information concerning the symbols replacing missing data.

StatLink ⟋⟍ http://dx.doi.org/10.1787/402165765880

C4

Table C4.4a. *(continued-3)*
Trends in the percentage of the youth population in education and not in education (1995, 1998-2006)
By age group and work status

	Age group	2002 In education Total	2002 Not in education Employed	2002 Not in education Not employed	2003 In education Total	2003 Not in education Employed	2003 Not in education Not employed	2004 In education Total	2004 Not in education Employed	2004 Not in education Not employed	2005 In education Total	2005 Not in education Employed	2005 Not in education Not employed	2006 In education Total	2006 Not in education Employed	2006 Not in education Not employed
		(1)	(2)	(3)	(4)	(5)	(6)	(7)	(8)	(9)	(10)	(11)	(12)	(13)	(14)	(15)
New Zealand	15-to-19	m	m	m	m	m	m	m	m	m	70.0	21.5	8.5	65.6	23.2	11.3
	20-to-24	m	m	m	m	m	m	m	m	m	32.9	50.5	16.7	30.1	54.8	15.0
	25-to-29	m	m	m	m	m	m	m	m	m	15.4	67.9	16.7	14.0	68.0	18.0
Norway	15-to-19	85.3	11.5	3.2	86.9	10.4	2.7	87.2	9.9	2.8	87.4	10.1	2.5	82.1	14.5	3.4
	20-to-24	38.5	51.8	9.7	38.7	50.8	10.6	40.6	49.6	9.8	41.5	48.9	9.6	39.2	51.7	9.1
	25-to-29	14.2	75.0	10.7	15.4	71.9	12.7	15.4	71.5	13.1	15.7	72.0	12.3	12.2	76.3	11.5
Poland	15-to-19	95.9	1.0	3.1	95.6	1.1	3.3	96.5	0.9	2.6	97.9	0.4	1.7	94.9	1.3	3.8
	20-to-24	53.8	20.8	25.4	55.7	18.8	25.5	57.5	18.4	24.1	62.7	17.2	20.1	55.1	24.2	20.7
	25-to-29	14.9	53.3	31.8	17.3	52.4	30.2	15.5	53.7	30.8	16.4	54.3	29.3	12.2	61.2	26.6
Portugal	15-to-19	72.4	20.3	7.3	74.8	16.4	8.8	75.1	15.1	9.8	79.3	12.2	8.4	80.2	12.0	7.8
	20-to-24	34.7	53.3	12.0	35.2	52.5	12.3	38.7	47.8	13.5	37.4	48.4	14.1	37.7	48.9	13.3
	25-to-29	10.7	77.1	12.2	11.7	73.7	14.6	11.0	75.0	14.0	11.5	73.6	14.9	12.2	72.9	14.9
Slovak Republic	15-to-19	78.6	5.8	15.6	82.2	5.2	12.6	87.8	4.3	7.9	90.4	3.3	6.3	90.5	2.9	6.7
	20-to-24	22.1	44.0	33.9	24.0	46.4	29.6	27.5	44.7	27.8	31.0	43.8	25.2	35.4	41.9	22.8
	25-to-29	2.9	66.6	30.5	2.6	68.3	29.1	4.5	66.6	28.9	6.1	64.9	29.0	5.7	67.9	26.4
Spain	15-to-19	81.9	11.0	7.2	82.6	10.1	7.3	82.2	10.1	7.6	78.2	11.0	10.8	79.5	10.5	10.1
	20-to-24	43.4	41.5	15.1	43.5	41.8	14.8	41.3	43.2	15.6	35.1	45.5	19.4	34.5	48.6	16.9
	25-to-29	16.1	64.2	19.8	15.4	65.0	19.5	15.3	66.2	18.5	10.9	69.3	19.8	10.9	70.1	19.1
Sweden	15-to-19	88.4	7.0	4.6	88.7	7.0	4.2	89.4	5.8	4.8	89.6	5.8	4.7	87.7	7.0	5.3
	20-to-24	41.7	47.0	11.2	42.3	46.0	11.8	42.8	43.6	13.6	42.5	44.1	13.4	43.0	41.8	15.2
	25-to-29	22.4	69.5	8.1	22.8	67.9	9.4	21.5	68.0	10.5	23.6	66.5	10.0	20.9	67.5	11.6
Switzerland	15-to-19	86.2	8.0	5.8	83.6	8.4	8.0	84.9	7.9	7.2	84.9	7.9	7.2	84.4	8.0	7.6
	20-to-24	38.0	52.3	9.7	35.8	51.5	12.7	37.3	51.7	11.0	37.3	51.7	11.0	36.9	52.3	10.8
	25-to-29	12.7	74.7	12.6	12.2	73.6	14.2	15.6	72.3	12.1	15.6	72.3	12.1	14.7	73.8	11.5
Turkey	15-to-19	42.2	24.8	32.9	45.9	21.3	32.8	43.5	21.2	35.3	42.5	19.9	37.7	m	m	m
	20-to-24	14.1	40.6	45.3	15.8	36.5	47.8	13.0	39.1	47.8	15.2	37.7	47.1	m	m	m
	25-to-29	3.0	56.2	40.7	3.7	53.2	43.1	3.1	54.0	42.8	4.3	53.5	42.2	m	m	m
United Kingdom	15-to-19	75.3	16.2	8.6	76.3	14.3	9.4	74.3	16.7	9.0	76.0	14.6	9.3	75.7	13.4	10.9
	20-to-24	31.0	53.7	15.3	32.6	52.1	15.3	31.1	54.1	14.8	32.1	51.0	16.8	30.2	51.6	18.2
	25-to-29	13.3	70.7	16.0	15.0	68.7	16.3	14.2	69.0	16.8	13.3	70.1	16.6	14.1	69.5	16.4
United States	15-to-19	82.9	10.2	7.0	m	m	m	83.9	9.2	6.9	85.6	8.3	6.1	85.0	8.6	6.3
	20-to-24	35.0	48.5	16.5	m	m	m	35.2	47.9	16.9	36.1	48.4	15.5	35.0	49.4	15.6
	25-to-29	12.3	70.3	17.4	m	m	m	13.0	68.7	18.4	11.9	70.0	18.1	11.7	71.5	16.8
OECD average	*15-to-19*	*81.9*	*10.4*	*7.8*	*82.7*	*9.5*	*8.0*	*83.3*	*9.1*	*7.7*	*84.3*	*8.4*	*7.5*	*85.6*	*8.0*	*6.5*
	20-to-24	*37.5*	*45.9*	*16.6*	*38.6*	*44.5*	*16.9*	*39.2*	*43.8*	*17.0*	*40.4*	*43.3*	*16.4*	*41.4*	*44.3*	*14.6*
	25-to-29	*13.0*	*68.4*	*19.2*	*13.7*	*67.3*	*19.0*	*13.4*	*67.6*	*19.0*	*14.0*	*67.9*	*18.0*	*14.5*	*69.1*	*16.9*
EU19 average	*15-to-19*	*85.5*	*8.2*	*6.3*	*86.1*	*7.5*	*6.4*	*87.0*	*6.9*	*6.0*	*87.4*	*6.4*	*6.2*	*87.5*	*6.2*	*6.3*
	20-to-24	*38.8*	*45.0*	*16.1*	*40.1*	*43.9*	*16.0*	*41.0*	*42.5*	*16.5*	*41.9*	*42.0*	*16.1*	*42.3*	*42.4*	*15.3*
	25-to-29	*12.6*	*69.0*	*18.4*	*13.9*	*67.8*	*18.3*	*13.3*	*68.0*	*18.8*	*13.5*	*68.3*	*18.2*	*13.8*	*68.7*	*17.5*
Estonia	15-to-19	m	m	m	94.4	2.3	3.3	91.0	1.4	7.6	92.0	2.9	5.2	90.7	5.6	3.7
	20-to-24	m	m	m	39.7	42.3	18.0	48.6	31.9	19.5	50.9	32.7	16.3	47.6	37.0	15.4
	25-to-29	m	m	m	14.7	59.8	25.5	14.9	65.3	19.8	14.2	61.8	24.0	9.4	75.0	15.6
Israel	15-to-19	69.4	6.0	24.6	69.0	5.7	25.2	68.9	5.6	25.6	68.9	6.3	24.7	69.0	6.8	24.3
	20-to-24	26.8	31.7	41.6	28.1	27.7	44.2	28.6	30.5	40.9	28.3	31.4	40.3	29.3	30.1	40.6
	25-to-29	19.1	52.2	28.7	19.6	52.7	27.7	20.9	53.9	25.3	21.4	54.3	24.2	24.8	51.8	23.4
Slovenia	15-to-19	m	m	m	92.8	2.4	4.8	92.2	3.5	4.3	92.4	2.7	4.9	92.7	3.1	4.2
	20-to-24	m	m	m	56.8	30.2	13.0	60.9	27.9	11.2	55.7	31.3	13.0	55.8	30.5	13.7
	25-to-29	m	m	m	25.3	63.1	11.5	26.6	61.8	11.5	24.6	63.9	11.5	26.3	60.3	13.3

Note: Due to incomplete data, some averages have not been calculated.

1. Breaks in time series are due to a change in survey methodology from 2003 to 2004.

2. Breaks in time series are due to a change in methodology: age is measured in the reference week from 2003, as is participation in education.

Source: OECD. See Annex 3 for notes (*www.oecd.org/edu/eag2008*).

Please refer to the Reader's Guide for information concerning the symbols replacing missing data.

StatLink ⫶ http://dx.doi.org/10.1787/402165765880

DO ADULTS PARTICIPATE IN TRAINING AND EDUCATION AT WORK?

This indicator examines the participation of the adult population in non-formal job-related education and training in terms of the expected number of hours of such education and training. It focuses particularly on the time a hypothetical individual is expected to spend in such education and training over a typical working life (of 40 years) and the intensity of this education and training towards the end of the working life.

Key results

Chart C5.1. Number of hours in non-formal job-related education and training for 55-to-64-year-olds relative to 25-to-34-year-olds by level of educational attainment (2003)

This chart shows the intensity of training for the age group nearing retirement age (55-to-64-year-olds) relative to the cohort that has just entered the labour market (25-34-year-olds).

■ Tertiary education (ISCED 5/6)

□ Upper secondary education (ISCED 3/4)

■ Below upper secondary education (ISCED 0/1/2)

There are major differences among countries in the time older workers can expect to spend in non-formal job-related education and training. The relative intensity (number of hours) of non-formal job-related education and training typically increases with educational attainment (except in the United Kingdom, Italy and the Netherlands) but decreases with age. An older worker with tertiary education can expect to receive at least 70% of the education and training of a young worker in Denmark, Sweden and the United States, but the proportion falls below 20% in France, Hungary and the Netherlands.

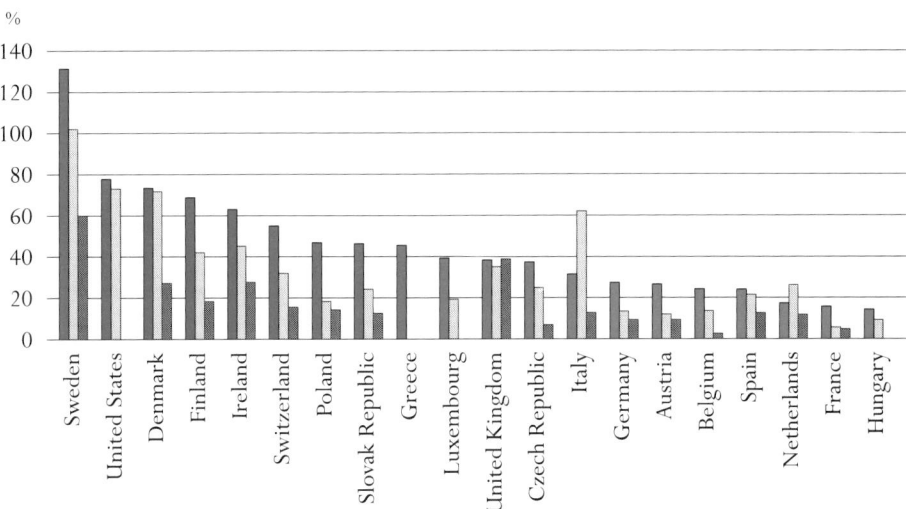

Countries are ranked by relative number of hours in training for those with tertiary education.
Source: OECD. Table C5.1b. See Annex 3 for notes (*www.oecd.org/edu/eag2008*).
StatLink ᴍᴉ̅ˢ⅃ http://dx.doi.org/10.1787/402178012235

Other highlights of this indicator

- Adults with higher levels of educational attainment are more likely to participate in non-formal job-related continuing education and training than adults with lower educational attainment.

- There are major differences among countries in the number of hours that individuals can expect to spend in non-formal job-related education and training over a typical working life. At the tertiary level, it ranges from less than 350 hours in Greece, Italy and the Netherlands to more than 1 000 in Denmark, Finland, France and Switzerland.

- Males can expect to spend more hours in non-formal job-related education and training than females. Gender differences in participation rates are generally less pronounced. Females with tertiary educational attainment are more likely to participate in non-formal job-related education and training in 15 out 22 OECD countries.

- The number of hours of non-formal job-related education and training generally decreases with age and in most countries the drop is dramatic. There are, however, some indications that equitable training opportunities for older workers (55-to-64-year-olds) with tertiary education are associated with better employment rates for this age group.

Policy context

The ageing of the population and the demand for skills associated with new technologies, globalisation and organisational change are among the main reasons why lifelong learning occupies a prominent place on today's policy agenda. Many observers also hold that changes in workplace organisation are leading to shifts in the demand for different types of skills and to greater emphasis on continuing education and training.

For the growing number of workers nearing retirement age, it is important to continue to invest in updating their knowledge and skills. Increasing life expectancy means that there is mounting pressure to continue to work beyond the current retirement age, yet in most countries employment rates drop long before the stipulated retirement age, in part, because older workers' knowledge and skills are in less demand.

Education and training among 55-to-64-year-olds constitute an important indicator of skill acquisition and potential employability up to retirement age and beyond. The complex relation between education and training, employment rates, and national retirement and pension systems makes it difficult to disentangle statistically the effect of investing in education and training for older age cohorts. Even so, as the acquisition of new skills become more critical for all workers, it is likely that, with age, this will become not less but more important for employment.

Evidence and explanations

Variation in participation rates

There is substantial cross-country variation in participation in non-formal job-related continuing education and training. Four OECD countries – Denmark, Finland, Sweden and the United States – take the lead, with more than 35% of 25-to-64-year-olds having participated in some type of non-formal job-related continuing education and training over the previous 12 months. The participation rate is less than 10% in Greece, Hungary, Italy, the Netherlands, Poland, Portugal and Spain. Between these two extremes, participation in education and training varies greatly; it is about 11% in the Czech Republic and Ireland but over twice that in Canada and the United Kingdom (Table C5.1a).

Training leads to further training

Adult education and training increase with the level of initial education (Table C5.1a). In all countries, it is striking that participation rates vary significantly depending on prior levels of educational attainment. For the OECD countries surveyed, participation in adult non-formal job-related education and training is 14 percentage points higher on average among individuals with tertiary education than among those with only an upper secondary or post-secondary non-tertiary education. Similarly, participation is 10 percentage points higher for those with an upper secondary and post-secondary non-tertiary education than for those with below upper secondary level of education. Better understanding of the underlying causes of these differentials could help to promote lifelong learning among the less qualified.

Gender difference in training

Employed males can expect to spend more hours in non-formal job-related education and training than employed females in all OECD countries except in France, Finland, Hungary, the Netherlands, and Portugal (Table C5.1a). Switzerland has by far the largest gender difference, with employed males registering almost 360 more expected hours of non-formal job-related education and training than employed females. However, gender differences in participation rates are less pronounced (Chart C5.2). That gender differences in participation rates are less pronounced than for hours spent in education and training suggest that males typically have longer training episodes than females, perhaps due to differences in their occupations.

Chart C5.2. **Gender difference in participation in non-formal job-related education and training for 25-to- 64-year-olds, by level of educational attainment (2003)**

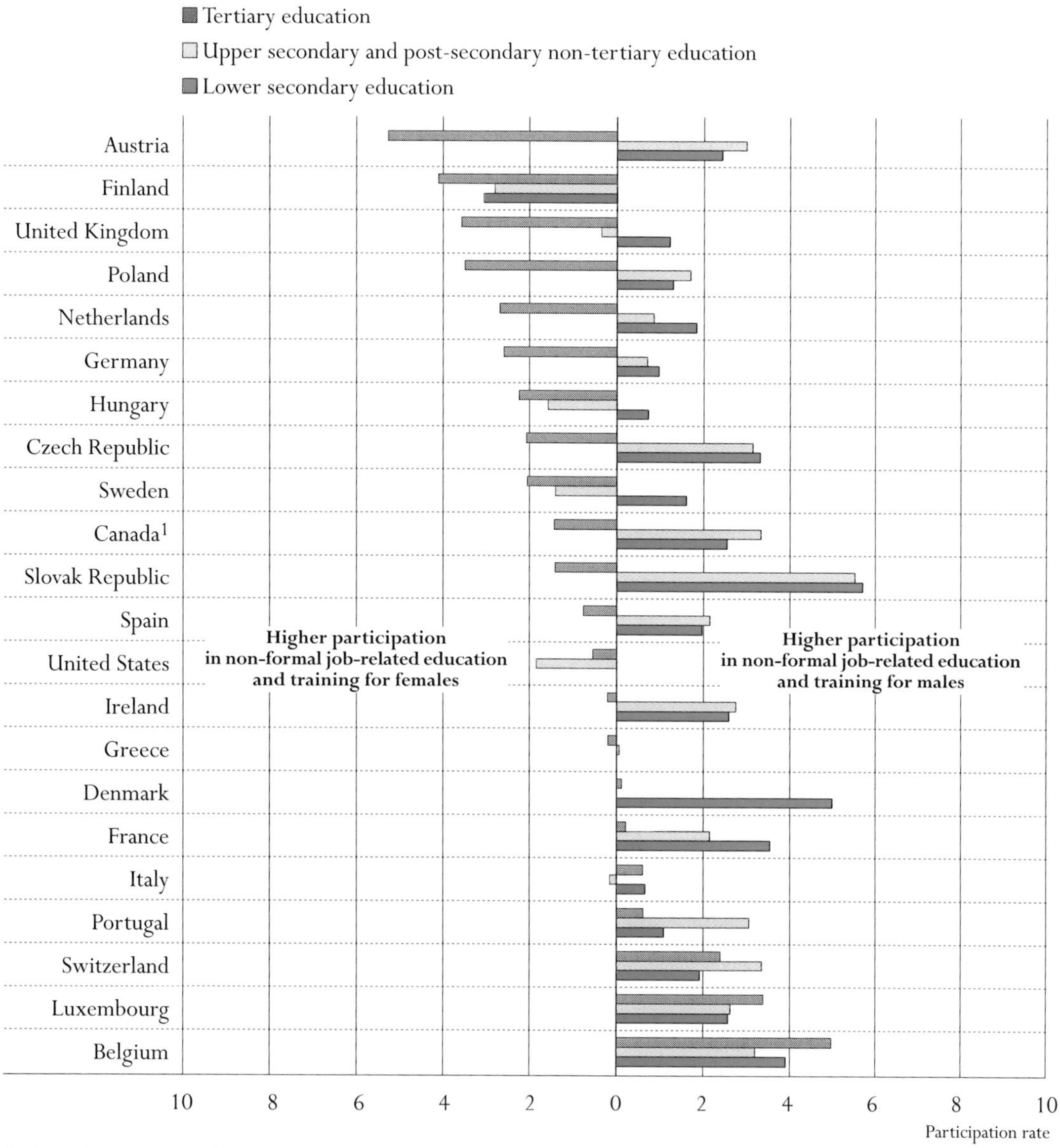

■ Tertiary education
□ Upper secondary and post-secondary non-tertiary education
■ Lower secondary education

(Chart: horizontal diverging bar chart. Left side labelled "Higher participation in non-formal job-related education and training for females"; right side labelled "Higher participation in non-formal job-related education and training for males". Countries listed top to bottom: Austria, Finland, United Kingdom, Poland, Netherlands, Germany, Hungary, Czech Republic, Sweden, Canada¹, Slovak Republic, Spain, United States, Ireland, Greece, Denmark, France, Italy, Portugal, Switzerland, Luxembourg, Belgium. Horizontal axis: 10, 8, 6, 4, 2, 0, 2, 4, 6, 8, 10. Axis label: Participation rate.)

1. Year of reference 2002.
Countries are ranked in descending order of the difference between male and female with tertiary education.
Source: OECD. Table C5.1a. See Annex 3 for notes (*www.oecd.org/edu/eag2008*).
StatLink ⌐┌╥╙╜ http://dx.doi.org/10.1787/402178012235

In 15 out of 22 countries, females with tertiary educational attainment can expect to participate more than their male counterparts in education and training, but the opposite is true among those with lower secondary education and upper secondary and post-secondary non-tertiary education. In Belgium, France, Luxembourg and Switzerland females are disadvantaged at all three levels of educational attainment, while in Finland females have an advantage at all three levels. On the other hand, differences in participation rates are relatively small and do not exceed 6 percentage points in any OECD country.

Box C5.1. Benefits of education and training for individuals

The major portion of all non-formal job-related education and training is sponsored by the employer, and employer-sponsored training is the single most important source of further education and training for the working age population. Much recent research suggests that employers finance training whether specific to the firm or general in nature and that individuals only contribute to the investment to a minor extent.

Although the employer pays the lion's share of the investment, empirical literature from various countries suggests that training generates significant wage returns for those who participate. A part of the return to education and training is typically captured by the employer financing the training, that is, the productivity effects from the investment are larger than what is normally detected in wage returns.

While employers benefit from investing in education and training, most studies also suggest that employer-financed training generates larger wage returns than self-financed training. There are also some indications that training initiated by firms and training more closely related to the job yield higher wage returns for the individual. It seems that individuals with poor employment prospects (older and less educated employees) have relatively modest wage returns to training but gain more stable employment prospects, with less risk of job loss and better prospects for re-employment when laid off.

Research also indicates that training for female workers is more rationed (females want more training than they receive) and that they finance their own training more than males. However, there is no clear evidence that females have lower returns to training than males.

For further information on the effects of job-related training, see OECD (2008d).

Expected hours of non-formal job-related education and training

Table C5.1a shows the expected number of hours of non-formal job-related education and training by level of educational attainment. In Switzerland, workers with tertiary education can expect to receive over 1 300 hours of non-formal job-related education and training over a typical working life, the highest figure among all OECD countries (Table C5.1a). This implies that, over their working life, they can expect to spend the equivalent of over 84% of an average year of work in continuing education and training. Considering all levels of education together, lifetime hours of non-formal job-related education and training as a percentage of an average year of work range from below 10% in the Czech Republic, Greece, Italy and Poland to 40% and above in Denmark, France, Sweden and Switzerland.

Chart C5.3 shows major differences among countries in the number of hours that workers with different levels of educational attainment can expect to spend in non-formal job-related education and training over a typical working life. At the tertiary level of attainment, it ranges from less than 350 hours in Greece, Italy and the Netherlands to more than 1 000 in Denmark, Finland, France and Switzerland. In Denmark, France and Finland, workers whose educational attainment is below the upper secondary level can expect to spend considerably more hours in non-formal job-related continuing education and training than those with tertiary education in other countries.

Chart C5.3. Expected hours of non-formal job-related education and training, by level of educational attainment (2003)

Expected number of hours of non-formal job-related education and training for 25-to-64-year-olds in the population by level of educational attainment

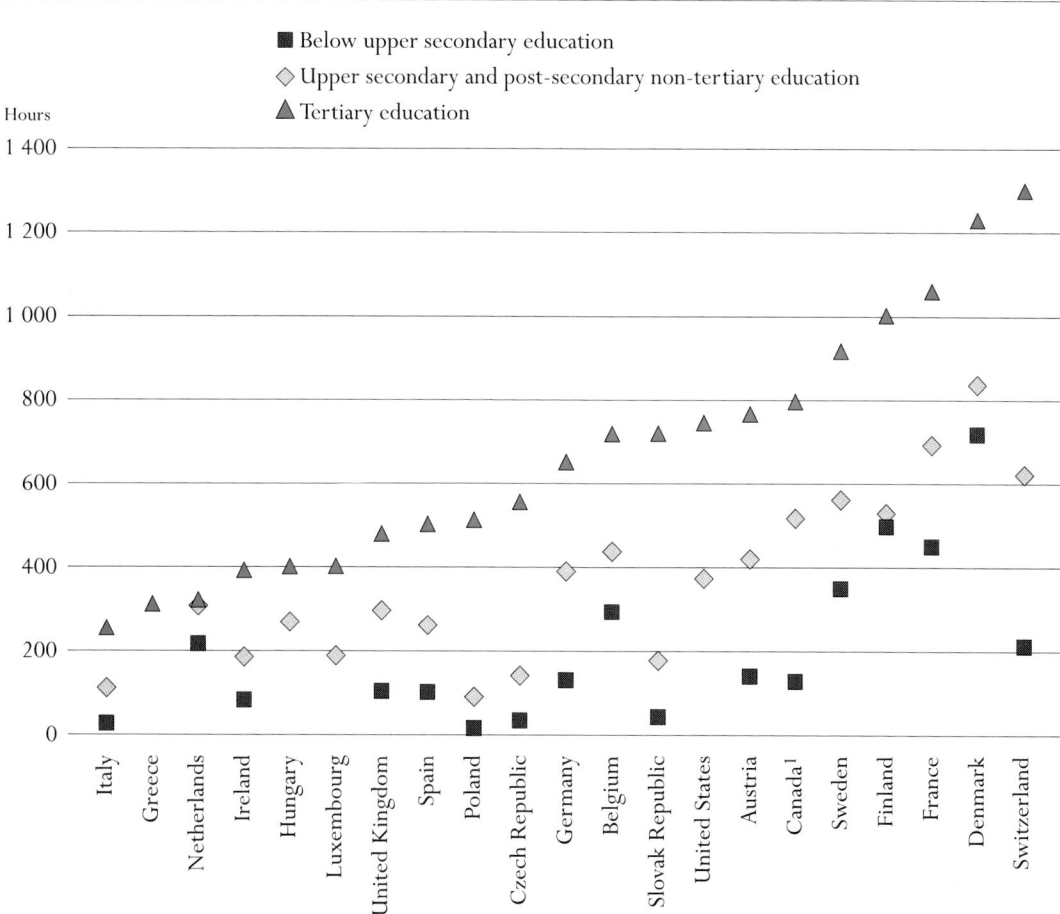

1. Year of reference 2002.
Countries are ranked in ascending order of expected hours of non-formal job-related training at the tertiary level of education.
Source: OECD. Table C5.1a. See Annex 3 for notes (*www.oecd.org/edu/eag2008*).
StatLink ⌖ﬁ⎙ http://dx.doi.org/10.1787/402178012235

C5

Expected hours in non-formal job-related education and training by age

Participation in non-formal job-related education and training declines with age, although the extent of the decline varies across countries. As shown in Chart C5.1 there are substantial differences in how education and training efforts are distributed across age groups. Countries such as France and Belgium, with relatively large investments in education and training, orient most of their investments to those entering the labour market (initial job-related education and training) whereas Denmark, Finland, Sweden, and United States, also with large investments in education and training, spread them more evenly over the working life. Denmark, Sweden, and Switzerland are exceptional as regards the high number of expected hours of non-formal learning among tertiary educated in the oldest age group, with over 200 hours (Table C5.1b).

The decline in non-formal job-related education and training may occur because older adults place less value on investment in training and/or because employers propose training less frequently to older workers (possibly in light of the shorter time available for capturing returns to this investment). By presenting data on how hours in training are distributed across age cohorts, Table C5.1b sheds light on whether a country is putting the concept of lifelong learning into practice (it is important to look at both the absolute number of hours of training and their distribution). For a complete picture of lifelong learning, information on employment rates among older workers is also important.

Employment rates typically rise with educational attainment but for all levels of educational attainment employment rates generally drop before retirement age. At all levels of educational attainment, employment rates generally drop before retirement age and so do participation in non-formal job-related education and training. Chart C5.4 shows the relationship between the relative number of hours of non-formal job-related education and training for 55-to-64-year-olds to 25-to-34-year-olds with tertiary education and employment rates for the older age group with tertiary education. Employment rates among the oldest age cohort increases in countries where older workers are less disadvantaged in receiving education and training compared with the younger cohort. The pattern is similar with respect to the absolute number of hours of non-formal job-related education and training received by 55-to-64-year-olds with tertiary education. Whether the link is due to interaction with retirement and pension schemes in different countries or whether education and training generate these employment effects is difficult to ascertain. However, the positive impact of adult education and training on employment has been documented in a number of studies, such as the *OECD Employment Outlook* (OECD 2004c).

Job-related education and training may also be effective in combating unemployment by helping workers to develop skills that make them more attractive to employers. In the face of changing technologies, work practices and markets, policy makers in many countries are promoting more general work-related training and informal learning. However, employed workers accumulate many more hours of non-formal job-related education and training than unemployed workers. In all countries, employed workers have significantly higher expected hours of job-related education and training than the unemployed (Table C5.1b). This is mainly because the time spent in unemployment is generally much shorter than the time spent in employment, but the incidence and intensity of education and training are typically lower among the unemployed as well.

Chart C5.4. **Training efforts and employment rates for 55-to-64-year-olds with tertiary education**

Number of hours of non-formal job-related education and training for 55-to-64-year-olds relative to 25-to-34-year-olds (2003) and employment rate for the 55-to-64-year-old population (2003)

C5

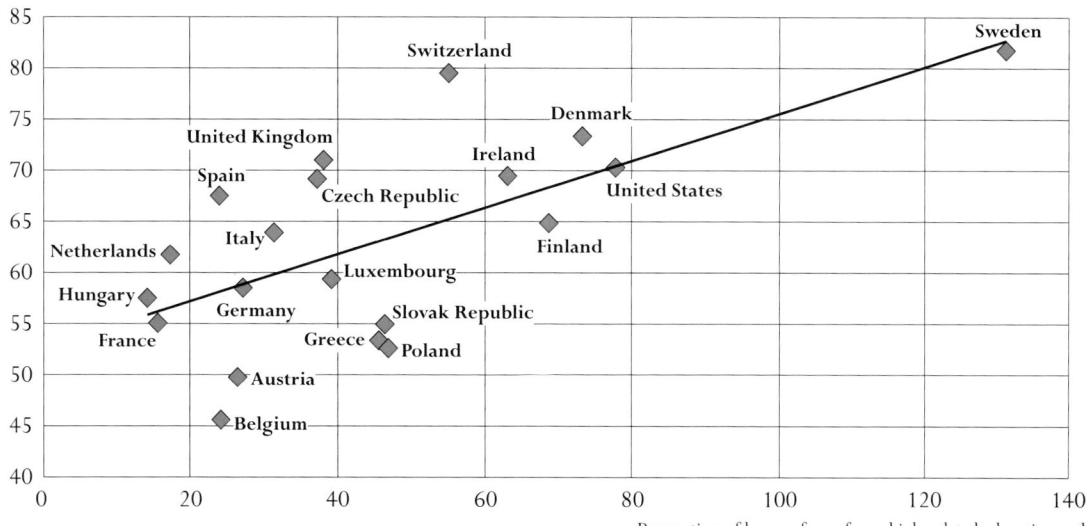

Employment rate of the 55-to-64-year-old population (%)

Proportion of hours of non-formal job-related education and training for 55-to-64-year-olds relative to 25-to-34-year-olds (%)

Source: OECD. Table C5.1b. See Annex 3 for notes (*www.oecd.org/edu/eag2008*).

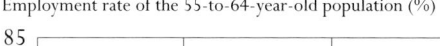 StatLink http://dx.doi.org/10.1787/402178012235

Definition and methodologies

Data for non-European countries were calculated from country-specific household surveys (see Annex 3 at *www.oecd.org/edu/eag2008*). Data for countries in the European statistical system come from the European Labour Force Survey *ad hoc* module "Lifelong Learning 2003". The reference period of the LLL ad hoc module was the whole of 2003 in some countries, for some it was Q2 (April-June) and for others it was Spring (March-May). For most European countries, data on training hours in job-related activities are available for up to the three most recent non-formal learning activities. Data for Canada cover up to five job-related training activities per participant. Data for the United States cover up to four job-related training activities per participant.

The analysis in this indicator focuses on non-formal job-related continuing education and training. Non-formal education is defined as any organised and sustained educational activity that cannot be considered as formal education according to ISCED and does not lead to a qualification. Non-formal education may therefore take place both within and outside educational institutions and may cater to persons of any age. Depending on the country, it may cover educational programmes for adult literacy, basic education for out-of-school children, life skills, work skills and general culture. Non-formal education programmes do not follow the educational ladder. The term "job-related" refers to education and training activities intended mainly for work reasons as opposed to personal or social reasons. That is, the respondent takes part in the activity in order to obtain knowledge and/or learn new skills for a current or a future job, increase earnings, improve career opportunities and generally improve his or her opportunities for advancement and promotion.

C5

The calculation of time spent in non-formal job-related learning activities by labour force status (Table C5.1b) is weighted by the time a hypothetical individual is expected to spend as "employed", "unemployed" and "inactive". For most countries the data refer to labour force status during a reference week, while the time spent in learning activities refers to all activities during a one-year reference period (prior to the interview), regardless of the labour force status when participating in the learning activity.

Further references

OECD (2004c), *Employment Outlook 2004 – Improving skills for more and better jobs: Does training make a difference?*, OECD, Paris.

OECD (2008d), "Job-related training and benefits for individuals: A review of evidence and explanations", OECD Education Working Paper Series, No. 19, OECD publishing, Paris.

C5

Table C5.1a.
Participation rate and expected number of hours in non-formal job-related education and training, by level of educational attainment (2003)
Participation rate and expected number of hours in non-formal job-related education and training for a 40-year period for 25-to-64-year-olds in the population, by gender and educational attainment

		Participation rate during one year				Expected hours in non-formal job-related education and training between the ages of 25 and 64				Average hours of work	Ratio (%) of hours in training to annual hours of work
		Lower secondary education	Upper secondary and post-secondary non-tertiary education	Tertiary education	All levels of education	Lower secondary education	Upper secondary and post-secondary non-tertiary education	Tertiary education	All levels of education		
		(1)	(2)	(3)	(4)	(5)	(6)	(7)	(8)	(9)	(10)
Austria	M+F	5	19	37	19	140	420	767	422	1550	27
	Males	7	20	34	21	157	468	722	470	m	m
	Females	4	17	40	17	131	366	834	374	m	m
Belgium	M+F	6	15	30	16	293	437	719	469	1542	30
	Males	8	17	33	18	353	543	768	540	m	m
	Females	4	14	28	14	230	327	668	397	m	m
Canada[1]	M+F	6	20	35	25	128	517	796	586	1740	34
	Males	8	22	35	25	126	486	863	590	m	m
	Females	5	19	36	25	c	549	738	582	m	m
Czech Republic	M+F	3	10	21	11	34	142	556	182	1986	9
	Males	6	12	20	13	28	134	562	186	m	m
	Females	2	9	22	9	39	150	553	179	m	m
Denmark	M+F	22	36	54	39	719	836	1 230	934	1475	63
	Males	25	36	54	39	726	884	1 197	946	m	m
	Females	20	36	54	39	722	780	1 260	922	m	m
Finland	M+F	20	32	54	36	497	530	1 003	669	1718	39
	Males	18	31	52	33	503	514	975	637	m	m
	Females	21	33	56	39	486	545	1 035	701	m	m
France	M+F	9	19	33	19	450	692	1 061	713	1441	49
	Males	11	20	34	20	458	567	1 093	664	m	m
	Females	8	17	33	17	440	833	1 039	760	m	m
Germany	M+F	3	10	24	12	130	390	650	398	1441	28
	Males	3	10	23	12	149	431	672	447	m	m
	Females	3	9	25	11	114	348	626	348	m	m
Greece	M+F	n	3	11	4	c	c	312	106	1936	5
	Males	1	3	11	4	c	c	316	106	m	m
	Females	n	3	11	3	c	c	c	106	m	m
Hungary	M+F	1	4	9	4	c	270	402	253	m	m
	Males	2	3	8	4	c	177	384	192	m	m
	Females	1	5	10	5	c	370	422	312	m	m
Ireland	M+F	5	10	20	11	82	185	392	203	1646	12
	Males	6	12	20	11	98	c	401	209	m	m
	Females	3	9	20	10	c	190	385	197	m	m
Italy	M+F	1	6	12	4	26	111	254	82	1591	5
	Males	2	6	13	4	31	113	264	87	m	m
	Females	1	6	12	4	21	110	244	77	m	m

1. Year of reference 2002.
Source: OECD. See Annex 3 for notes (*www.oecd.org/edu/eag2008*).
Please refer to the Reader's guide for information concerning the symbols replacing missing data.
StatLink ᐧᔕᒲ http://dx.doi.org/10.1787/402178012235

Table C5.1a. *(continued)*

Participation rate and expected number of hours in non-formal job-related education and training, by level of educational attainment (2003)

Participation rate and expected number of hours in non-formal job-related education and training for a 40-year period for 25-to-64-year-olds in the population, by gender and educational attainment

			Participation rate during one year				Expected hours in non-formal job-related education and training between the ages of 25 and 64					
			Lower secondary education	Upper secondary and post-secondary non-tertiary education	Tertiary education	All levels of education	Lower secondary education	Upper secondary and post-secondary non-tertiary education	Tertiary education	All levels of education	Average hours of work	Ratio (%) of hours in training to annual hours of work
			(1)	(2)	(3)	(4)	(5)	(6)	(7)	(8)	(9)	(10)
OECD countries	**Luxembourg**	M+F	3	12	27	12	c	189	402	176	1592	11
		Males	4	13	29	13	c	212	436	207	m	m
		Females	2	11	26	10	c	c	c	c	m	m
	Netherlands	M+F	5	11	13	9	216	308	322	283	1354	21
		Males	6	11	12	10	227	292	298	277	m	m
		Females	4	10	14	9	211	328	357	289	m	m
	Poland	M+F	1	7	29	9	16	90	513	139	1984	7
		Males	2	8	27	9	c	104	531	147	m	m
		Females	1	6	31	9	c	76	495	131	m	m
	Portugal	M+F	4	15	27	7	232	c	c	343	1678	20
		Males	4	17	27	8	159	c	c	316	m	m
		Females	3	14	27	7	302	c	c	367	m	m
	Slovak Republic	M+F	6	19	37	19	43	178	721	225	1931	12
		Males	10	21	37	22	c	190	741	240	m	m
		Females	4	16	38	16	c	165	699	212	m	m
	Spain	M+F	3	7	14	6	102	261	503	237	1800	13
		Males	4	9	14	7	116	265	503	247	m	m
		Females	2	6	14	6	87	257	506	226	m	m
	Sweden	M+F	24	37	57	40	350	562	917	622	1563	40
		Males	24	36	56	39	368	617	932	641	m	m
		Females	23	38	58	42	324	502	911	603	m	m
	Switzerland	M+F	8	27	44	29	212	621	1 301	723	1556	46
		Males	9	29	45	33	256	760	1 422	912	m	m
		Females	7	26	43	26	184	514	1 085	551	m	m
	United Kingdom	M+F	7	26	46	27	103	297	480	315	1672	19
		Males	8	26	45	28	131	323	494	344	m	m
		Females	7	27	48	26	81	272	471	287	m	m
	United States	M+F	12	32	56	37	c	374	746	471	1822	26
		Males	c	32	58	37	c	c	790	499	m	m
		Females	c	34	58	39	c	351	704	446	m	m
	OECD average	***M+F***	***7***	***17***	***31***	***18***	***210***	***371***	***669***	***389***	***1668***	***25***
		Males	***8***	***18***	***31***	***19***	***243***	***393***	***684***	***405***	***m***	***m***
		Females	***6***	***17***	***32***	***17***	***241***	***370***	***686***	***384***	***m***	***m***

Source: OECD. See Annex 3 for notes (*www.oecd.org/edu/eag2008*).

Please refer to the Reader's guide for information concerning the symbols replacing missing data.

StatLink http://dx.doi.org/10.1787/402178012235

Table C5.1b.
Expected number of hours in non-formal job-related education and training,
by level of educational attainment (2003)
Expected number of hours in non-formal job-related education and training, by age group and labour force status

C5

| | | Expected hours in non-formal job-related education and training between the ages of 25 and 64 | | | | | | | |
| | | Age group | | | | Labour force status | | | |
	Level of education	25 to 34	35 to 44	45 to 54	55 to 64	Employed	Unemployed	Inactive	Total
Austria	Below upper secondary (0/1/2)	58	48	29	5	110	c	c	140
	Upper secondary (3/4)	175	136	89	21	368	22	29	420
	Tertiary (5/6)	241	250	212	64	714	c	c	767
Belgium	Below upper secondary (0/1/2)	127	115	49	3	186	59	48	293
	Upper secondary (3/4)	151	171	95	21	340	57	41	437
	Tertiary (5/6)	286	205	159	69	640	43	37	719
Canada[1]	Below upper secondary (0/1/2)	m	m	m	m	m	m	m	m
	Upper secondary (3/4)	m	m	m	m	m	m	m	m
	Tertiary (5/6)	m	m	m	m	m	m	m	m
Czech Republic	Below upper secondary (0/1/2)	14	7	12	1	23	c	c	34
	Upper secondary (3/4)	47	45	38	12	129	9	4	142
	Tertiary (5/6)	186	186	114	70	546	c	c	556
Denmark	Below upper secondary (0/1/2)	239	243	171	65	455	c	184	719
	Upper secondary (3/4)	205	284	199	147	685	86	65	836
	Tertiary (5/6)	282	379	362	207	1 011	116	103	1 230
Finland	Below upper secondary (0/1/2)	194	149	118	36	273	c	c	497
	Upper secondary (3/4)	147	175	146	62	389	102	39	530
	Tertiary (5/6)	247	309	277	170	889	c	51	1 003
France	Below upper secondary (0/1/2)	245	118	75	12	247	107	96	450
	Upper secondary (3/4)	324	227	123	18	470	106	116	692
	Tertiary (5/6)	488	291	206	76	809	105	146	1 061
Germany	Below upper secondary (0/1/2)	54	39	32	5	46	59	24	130
	Upper secondary (3/4)	162	120	87	22	230	109	52	390
	Tertiary (5/6)	243	187	153	66	522	86	42	650
Greece	Below upper secondary (0/1/2)	11	c	c	c	12	c	c	15
	Upper secondary (3/4)	48	26	15	c	76	10	8	94
	Tertiary (5/6)	98	91	79	45	285	15	c	312
Hungary	Below upper secondary (0/1/2)	45	31	11	c	56	c	c	90
	Upper secondary (3/4)	118	99	42	11	170	21	79	270
	Tertiary (5/6)	176	120	81	25	337	c	49	402
Ireland	Below upper secondary (0/1/2)	29	28	18	8	66	c	c	82
	Upper secondary (3/4)	60	56	43	27	161	c	c	185
	Tertiary (5/6)	109	113	102	69	371	c	c	392
Italy	Below upper secondary (0/1/2)	10	9	5	1	25	c	c	26
	Upper secondary (3/4)	27	34	32	17	102	5	3	111
	Tertiary (5/6)	90	72	65	28	222	12	21	254
Luxembourg	Below upper secondary (0/1/2)	17	6	10	c	33	c	c	34
	Upper secondary (3/4)	64	56	57	12	165	c	c	189
	Tertiary (5/6)	128	126	98	50	396	c	c	402

1. Year of reference 2002.
Source: OECD. See Annex 3 for notes (*www.oecd.org/edu/eag2008*).
Please refer to the Reader's Guide for information concerning the symbols replacing missing data.
StatLink 🔢📊 http://dx.doi.org/10.1787/402178012235

Table C5.1b. *(continued)*
**Expected number of hours in non-formal job-related education and training,
by level of educational attainment (2003)**
Expected number of hours in non-formal job-related education and training, by age group and labour force status

| | | Expected hours in non-formal job-related education and training between the ages of 25 and 64 | | | | | | | |
| | | Age group | | | | Labour force status | | | |
	Level of education	25 to 34	35 to 44	45 to 54	55 to 64	Employed	Unemployed	Inactive	Total
Netherlands	Below upper secondary (0/1/2)	92	73	41	11	134	c	78	216
	Upper secondary (3/4)	131	87	55	34	254	17	37	308
	Tertiary (5/6)	130	103	67	22	294	c		322
Poland	Below upper secondary (0/1/2)	6	6	3	1	12	c	c	16
	Upper secondary (3/4)	32	32	20	6	78	10	c	90
	Tertiary (5/6)	145	169	132	68	497	10	c	513
Portugal	Below upper secondary (0/1/2)	88	92	41	10	149	c	c	232
	Upper secondary (3/4)	261	145	79	c	463	c	c	529
	Tertiary (5/6)	336	226	169	c	764	c	c	835
Slovak Republic	Below upper secondary (0/1/2)	11	21	10	1	27	c	c	43
	Upper secondary (3/4)	61	58	44	15	159	15	c	178
	Tertiary (5/6)	217	218	185	101	703	c	c	721
Spain	Below upper secondary (0/1/2)	48	29	19	6	73	22	7	102
	Upper secondary (3/4)	86	83	73	18	188	40	33	261
	Tertiary (5/6)	180	151	129	43	409	62	32	503
Sweden	Below upper secondary (0/1/2)	106	73	107	64	325	c	c	350
	Upper secondary (3/4)	123	164	149	125	504	46	12	562
	Tertiary (5/6)	183	249	244	241	889	18	10	917
Switzerland	Below upper secondary (0/1/2)	108	62	25	17	126	56	c	212
	Upper secondary (3/4)	214	175	164	68	552	35	34	621
	Tertiary (5/6)	407	352	317	225	1 171	76	54	1 301
United Kingdom	Below upper secondary (0/1/2)	30	35	27	12	56	c	c	103
	Upper secondary (3/4)	101	93	67	35	254	16	27	297
	Tertiary (5/6)	161	140	117	62	442	10	27	480
United States	Below upper secondary (0/1/2)	c	c	c	c	c	c	c	c
	Upper secondary (3/4)	98	107	97	72	337	c	c	374
	Tertiary (5/6)	190	186	223	148	695	c	c	746

OECD countries (side label)

C5 (side tab)

Source: OECD. See Annex 3 for notes (*www.oecd.org/edu/eag2008*).
Please refer to the Reader's Guide for information concerning the symbols replacing missing data.
StatLink ⬛📊 http://dx.doi.org/10.1787/402178012235

Chapter

D

The Learning Environment and Organisation of Schools

HOW MUCH TIME DO STUDENTS SPEND IN THE CLASSROOM?

This indicator examines the amount of instruction time students are expected to receive between the ages of 7 and 15. It also discusses the relationship between instruction time and student learning outcomes.

INDICATOR D1

Key results

Chart D1.1. Total number of intended instruction hours in public institutions between the ages of 7 and 14 (2006)

■ Ages 7 to 8   ▨ Ages 9 to 11   ▨ Ages 12 to 14

> Students in OECD countries are expected to receive, on average, 6 907 hours of instruction between the ages of 7 and 14, of which 1 591 between ages 7 and 8, 2 518 between ages 9 and 11, and 2 798 between ages 12 and 14. The large majority of intended hours of instruction are compulsory.

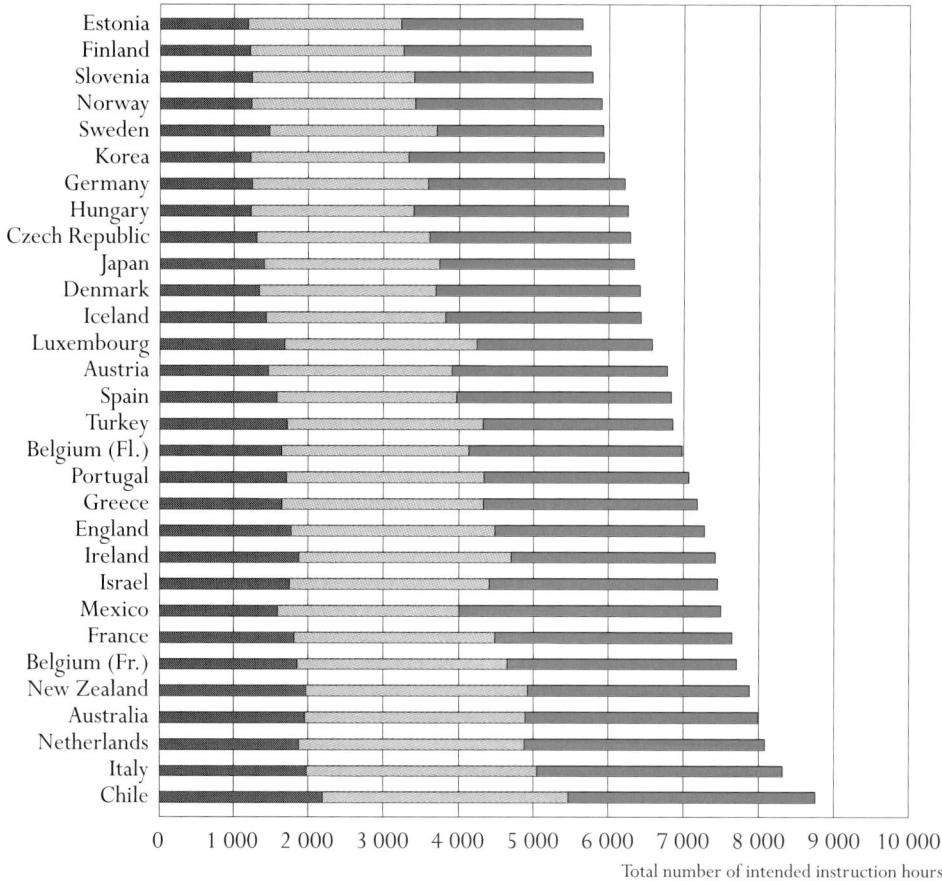

Countries are ranked in ascending order of total number of intended instruction hours.
Source: OECD. Table D1.1. See Annex 3 for notes (*www.oecd.org/edu/eag2008*).
StatLink ⣍⣫ http://dx.doi.org/10.1787/402183135853

Other highlights of this indicator

▪ In OECD countries, 7-to-8-year-olds receive an average of 770 hours per year of compulsory instruction time and 796 hours per year of intended instruction time in the classroom. Those aged 9 to 11 receive about 40 compulsory hours more per year than 7-to-8-year-olds and those aged 12 to 14 receive just over 86 hours more per year than 9-to-11-year-olds.

▪ On average across OECD countries, the teaching of reading, writing and literature, mathematics and science represents nearly 50% of the compulsory instruction time for 9-to-11-year-olds and 40% for 12-to-14-year-olds. For 9-to-11-year-olds, the proportion of compulsory curriculum devoted to reading, writing and literature varies widely from 13% in Australia to 30% or more in France, Mexico and the Netherlands.

INDICATOR D1

D1

Policy context

Instruction time in formal classroom settings comprises a large element of the public investment in student learning and is a central component of effective schooling. The amount of instruction time available to students can determine the amount of classroom teaching they receive and therefore their opportunities for effective learning. Instruction time is the main factor in schools' operations. It is also central to education policy decision making. Matching resources with students' needs and making optimal use of time, from the perspective of both learner and public investment, are major challenges for education policy. The main costs of education are teachers' work, institutional maintenance and other educational resources. The length of time during which these resources are made available to students (as partly shown in this indicator) is thus an important factor in the allocation of funding.

Countries make various choices concerning the overall length of time devoted to instruction and the subjects that are compulsory. These choices reflect national priorities and preferences for the education students receive at different ages and the emphasis placed on different subject areas. Countries usually have statutory or regulatory requirements regarding hours of instruction. These are most often stipulated as the minimum number of hours of instruction that a school must offer. Central to the setting of minimum levels is the view that sufficient teaching time is essential to productive learning outcomes.

Evidence and explanations

What this indicator shows

Intended instruction time is an important indicator of students' opportunity to learn and of the public resources invested in education. This indicator captures intended instruction time as a measure of exposure to learning in formal classroom settings as established in public regulations. It does not show the actual number of hours of instruction received by students and does not cover learning outside of the formal classroom setting. Discrepancies may exist across countries between the regulatory minimum hours of instruction and the actual hours of instruction received by students. There exists research showing that due to factors such as school timetable decisions, lesson cancellations and teacher absenteeism the regulatory minimum instruction time may not be reached on all occasions (see Box D1.1 of *Education at a Glance 2007*).

The indicator also illustrates how minimum instruction times are allocated to different curricular areas. It shows the intended net hours of instruction for the grades in which the majority of students are from 7 to 15 years of age. Although the data are difficult to compare among countries because of different curriculum policies, they nevertheless provide an indication of how much formal instruction time is considered necessary for students to achieve the desired educational goals.

Total intended instruction time: an average of 6 907 hours between the ages of 7 and 14

Total intended instruction time is an estimate of the number of hours during which students are taught both compulsory and non-compulsory parts of the curriculum as per public regulations.

In OECD countries, the total number of instruction hours that students are intended to receive between the ages of 7 and 14 averages 6 907 hours. However, formal requirements range from 5 644 hours in the partner country Estonia to over 8 000 hours in Italy and the Netherlands and the partner country Chile. These include the compulsory and non-compulsory hours during which schools are obliged to offer instruction to students. The total intended instruction time for this age range is a good indicator of students' theoretical workload, but it cannot be interpreted as the actual instruction students receive during the years they spend in initial education. In some countries with a heavier student workload, the age band of compulsory education is smaller and students drop out of the school system earlier; in other countries a more even distribution of study time over more years ultimately means a larger number of total instruction hours for all. Table D1.1 shows the age range for which over 90% of the population is in education and Chart D1.1 shows the total amount of intended instruction time students should receive between the ages of 7 and 14.

In some countries, intended instruction time varies considerably among regions or types of schools. In many countries, local education authorities or schools can determine the number and allocation of hours of instruction. Additional teaching time is often planned for individual remedial teaching or enhancement of the curriculum. On the other hand, time may be lost owing to a lack of qualified substitutes to replace absent teachers or to student absences.

Annual instruction time should also be examined together with the length of compulsory education, which measures the time during which young people receive full-time educational support from public resources, and during which more than 90% of the population participates in education (see Indicator C2). Intended instruction time does not capture the quality of learning opportunities provided or the level or quality of the human and material resources involved. (For some insight into human resources, see Indicator D2, which shows the number of teachers relative to the student population.)

Compulsory instruction time: an average of 6 657 hours between the ages of 7 and 14

Total compulsory instruction time is an estimate of the number of hours during which students are taught both the compulsory core and compulsory flexible parts of the curriculum.

For 7-to-8-year-olds and 9-to-11-year-olds, total intended instruction time equals the total compulsory instruction time in most countries; this is less often the case for older age groups. However, intended instruction time is fully compulsory for all age groups between 7 and 14 years in Belgium (Fl.), the Czech Republic, Denmark, Germany, Greece, Iceland, Japan, Korea, Luxembourg, Mexico, the Netherlands, Norway, Spain and Sweden, as well as the partner countries Chile, Estonia and Slovenia. Except for Belgium (Fl.), Greece, Mexico, the Netherlands and the partner country Chile, these countries have a total length of intended instruction time that is below the OECD average. Except for Greece and Mexico (as well as for Japan and the Netherlands: the two countries for which data are missing), intended instruction time is also fully compulsory at age 15 in these countries.

Within the formal education system, OECD countries show an average annual amount of total compulsory instruction time in classroom settings of 770 hours for 7-to-8-year-olds, 810 hours for 9-to-11-year-olds and 896 hours for 12-to-14-year-olds. The average annual number of compulsory instruction hours is 910 for the typical programme in which most 15-year-olds are enrolled (Table D1.1).

D1

Teaching of reading and writing, mathematics and science: at least 40% of compulsory instruction time, on average, for 12-to-14-year-olds

In OECD countries, for 9-to-11-year-olds study areas are not necessarily organised as separate classes. They spend an average of nearly 50% of the compulsory curriculum on three basic subject areas: reading, writing and literature (23%), mathematics (16%) and science (9%). On average, an additional 7% of the compulsory curriculum is devoted to modern foreign languages. Together with social studies, the arts and physical education, these seven study areas form part of the curriculum in all OECD and partner countries for these age cohorts (Table D1.2a and Chart D1.2a).

On average, reading and writing account for the greatest proportion of the curriculum for 9-to-11-year-olds, but the differences among countries are greater than for other subjects; this subject area accounts for 13% of instruction time in Australia, compared with 30% or more in France, Mexico and the Netherlands. There is also sizeable variation in modern foreign languages, which account for 1% or less of compulsory instruction time in Australia, England, Japan, Mexico and the Netherlands but 21% of total compulsory instruction time in Luxembourg and over 10% in the Czech Republic, Portugal, Spain and Sweden and in the partner countries Estonia, Israel and Slovenia.

Chart D1.2a. Instruction time per subject as a percentage of total compulsory instruction time for 9-to-11-year-olds (2006)

Percentage of intended instruction time devoted to various subject areas within the total compulsory curriculum

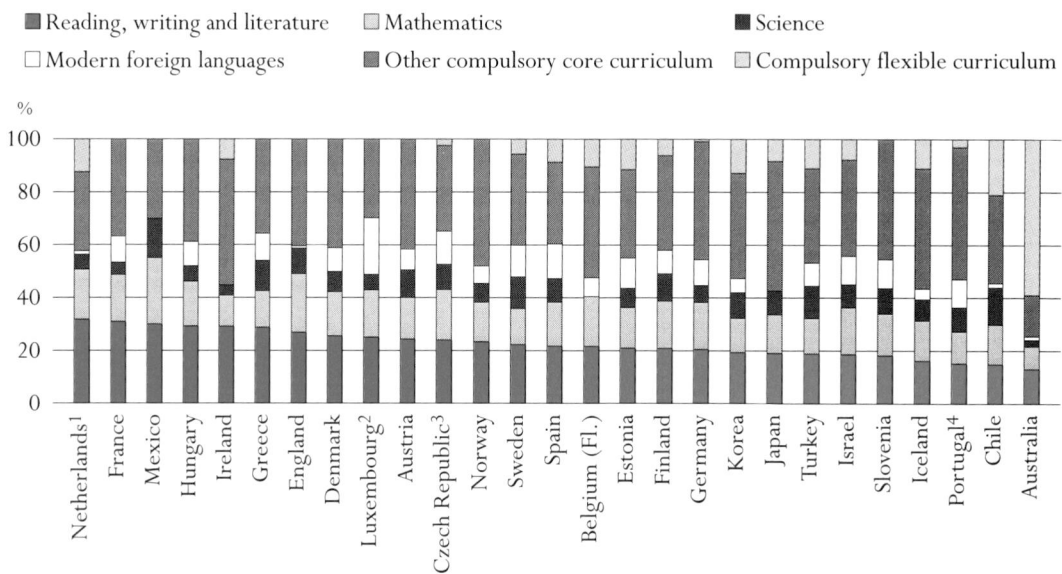

1. Includes 11-year-olds only.
2. German as a language of instruction is included in "Reading, writing and literature" in addition to the mother tongue Luxemburgish.
3. For 9-to-10-year-olds, social studies is included in science.
4. Includes 10-to-11-year-olds only.
Countries are ranked in descending order of number of intended instruction hours devoted to reading, writing and literature.
Source: OECD. Table D1.2a. See Annex 3 for notes (*www.oecd.org/edu/eag2008*).
StatLink 🔗 http://dx.doi.org/10.1787/402183135853

In OECD countries, an average of nearly 40% of the compulsory curriculum for 12-to-14-year-olds is devoted to three subject areas: reading, writing and literature (15%), mathematics (13%) and science (11%). For this age cohort, a relatively larger part of the curriculum is devoted to modern foreign languages (12%) and social studies (12%), and somewhat less time is devoted to the arts (8%). Together with physical education, these seven study areas form part of the compulsory curriculum for lower secondary students in all OECD countries and partner countries (Table D1.2b and Chart D1.2b).

D1

**Chart D1.2b. Instruction time per subject as a percentage
of total compulsory instruction time for 12-to-14-year-olds (2006)**

Percentage of intended instruction time devoted to various subject areas within the total compulsory curriculum

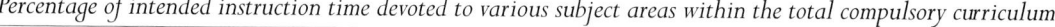

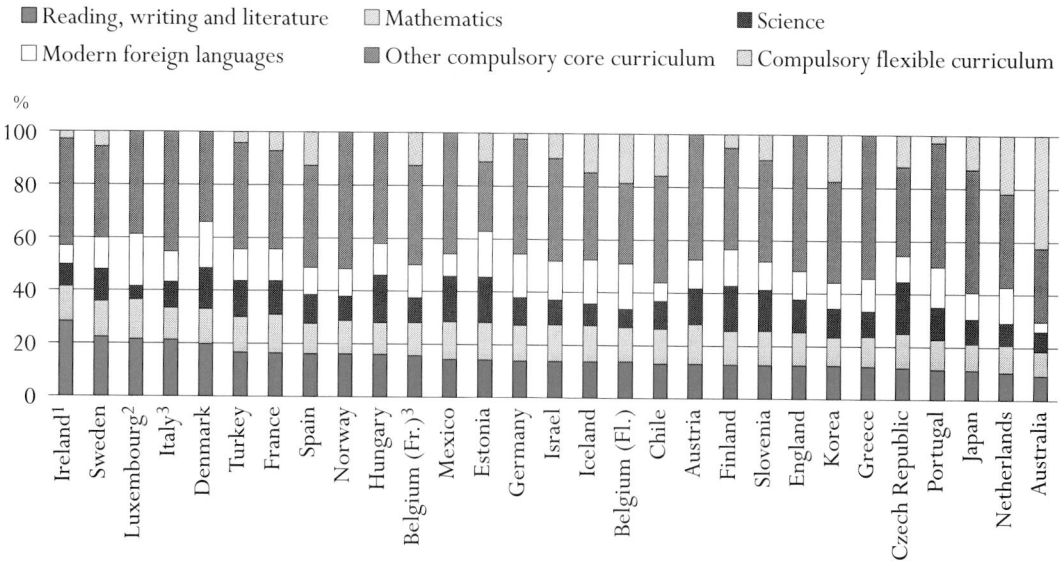

1. For 13-to-14-year-olds, arts is included in non-compulsory curriculum.
2. German as a language of instruction is included in "Reading, writing and literature" in addition to the mother tongue Luxemburgish.
3. Includes 12-to-13-year-olds only.
Countries are ranked in descending order of number of intended instruction hours devoted to reading, writing and literature.
Source: OECD. Table D1.2b. See Annex 3 for notes (*www.oecd.org/edu/eag2008*).
StatLink ᐊᔑᐢᔆ http://dx.doi.org/10.1787/402183135853

Among countries, the percentage share of subjects within the curriculum for 12-to-14-year-olds varies less than for 9-to-11-year-olds. Differences in the amounts of instruction time can reflect different national and curriculum priorities. The greatest variation is again in reading and writing with a range from 10% or less in Australia and the Netherlands to 28% in Ireland (where reading and writing includes work in both English and Irish).

There is also substantial variation in the percentage of compulsory instruction time devoted to particular subjects for 9-to-11-year-olds compared to 12-to-14-year-olds. On average among OECD countries, one-third less time is devoted to reading, writing and literature for 12-to-14-year-olds than for 9-to-11-year-olds. However, the reverse is true for social studies and modern foreign languages.

These differences are larger in some countries than in others. The percentage of compulsory instruction time given to reading, writing and literature for 12-to-14-year-olds is equal to or less than one-half of that for 9-to-11-year-olds in the Czech Republic, England, Greece, Mexico and the Netherlands. Yet in Ireland and Sweden, the difference is less than 5%. Clearly, countries place different emphases both on subjects and on when they should be taught to students.

Among OECD countries, the non-compulsory part of the curriculum comprises on average 4 to 5% of the total intended instruction time for 9-to-11-year-olds as well as for 12-to-14-year-olds. Nevertheless, a considerable amount of additional non-compulsory instruction time is sometimes provided. For 9-to-11-year-olds, all intended instruction time is compulsory in most countries, but additional non-compulsory time is as much as 15% in Italy and 20% in Hungary and Turkey. For 12-to-14-year-olds, non-compulsory instruction time is a feature in Australia, Austria, Belgium (Fr.), England, Finland, France, Hungary, Ireland, Italy, Portugal and Turkey, and ranges from 3% in Portugal to 37% in Hungary (Tables D1.2a and D1.2b).

On average, 4% of compulsory instruction time belongs to the flexible part of the curriculum in the grades where most students are 9 to 11 years of age; the corresponding proportion is 8% for students aged 12 to 14.

Most OECD countries define the number of hours of compulsory instruction. Within the compulsory part of the curriculum, students have varying degrees of freedom to choose the subjects they want to study. Australia has the highest degree of flexibility in the compulsory curriculum with up to 59% for 9-to-11-year-olds and 43% for 12-to-14-year-olds. Several other countries allow 10% or more of flexibility in the compulsory curriculum for 12-to-14-year olds (Belgium, the Czech Republic, Iceland, Japan, Korea, the Netherlands and Spain, and the partner countries Chile, Estonia and Slovenia) (Tables D1.2a and D1.2b).

Definitions and methodologies

Data on instruction time are from the 2007 OECD-INES Survey on Teachers and the Curriculum and refer to the school year 2005/06.

Instruction time for 7-to-15-year-olds refers to the formal number of 60-minute hours per school year organised by the school for class instructional activities for students in the reference school year 2005/06. For countries with no formal policy on instruction time, the number of hours was estimated from survey data. Hours lost when schools are closed for festivities and celebrations, such as national holidays, are excluded. Intended instruction time does not include non-compulsory time outside the school day, homework, individual tutoring, or private study done before or after school.

The compulsory curriculum refers to the amount and allocation of instruction time that almost every public school must provide and almost all public-sector students must attend. The measurement of the time devoted to specific study areas (subjects) focuses on the minimum common core rather than on the average time spent, since the data sources (policy documents) do not allow for more precise measurement. The total compulsory curriculum comprises the compulsory core curriculum as well as the compulsory flexible curriculum.

D1

The non-compulsory part of the curriculum refers to the average time of instruction to which students are entitled beyond the compulsory hours of instruction. These subjects often vary from school to school or from region to region, and may take the form of non-compulsory (elective) subjects.

Intended instruction time refers to the number of hours per year during which students receive instruction in the compulsory and non-compulsory parts of the curriculum.

In Table D1.1, typical instruction time for 15-year-olds refers to the programme in which most 15-year-olds are enrolled. The programme may take place in lower or upper secondary education, and in most countries consists of a general programme. If the system channels students into different programme types at this age, the average instruction time may have been estimated for the most important mainstream programmes and weighted by the proportion of students in the grade in which most 15-year-olds are enrolled. When vocational programmes are also taken into account in typical instruction time, only the school-based part of the programme should be included in the calculations.

Instruction time for the least demanding programme refers to programmes for students who are least likely to continue studying beyond the mandatory school age or beyond lower secondary education. Such programmes may or may not exist in a country depending on streaming and selection policies. In many countries students are offered the same amount of instruction time in all or most programmes, but there is flexibility in the choice of study areas or subjects. Often such choices have to be made quite early if programmes are long and differ substantially.

Further references

Specific notes for each country on definitions and methodologies regarding this indicator are given in Annex 3 at *www.oecd.org/edu/eag2008*. In addition, a more comprehensive analysis of decision making is available in Indicator D6.

Table D1.1.
Compulsory and intended instruction time in public institutions (2006)
*Average number of hours per year of total compulsory and non-compulsory instruction time in the curriculum
for 7-to-8, 9-to-11, 12-to-14 and 15-year-olds*

	Age range at which over 90% of the population is enrolled	Average number of hours per year of total compulsory instruction time					Average number of hours per year of total intended instruction time				
		Ages 7 to 8	Ages 9 to 11	Ages 12 to 14	Age 15 (typical programme)	Age 15 (least demanding programme)	Ages 7 to 8	Ages 9 to 11	Ages 12 to 14	Age 15 (typical programme)	Age 15 (least demanding programme)
	(1)	(2)	(3)	(4)	(5)	(6)	(7)	(8)	(9)	(10)	(11)
OECD countries											
Australia	5 to 16	978	978	989	968	968	978	978	1033	1024	1024
Austria	5 to 17	690	767	913	1005	960	735	812	958	1050	1005
Belgium (Fl.)	3 to 18	826	826	949	949	445	826	826	949	949	445
Belgium (Fr.)[1]	3 to 18	840	840	960	m	m	930	930	1020	m	m
Czech Republic	5 to 17	655	766	892	960	392	655	766	892	960	392
Denmark	3 to 16	671	783	910	900	900	671	783	910	900	900
England	4 to 15	880	900	900	760	a	890	900	933	950	a
Finland	6 to 18	608	640	777	856	a	608	683	829	913	a
France	3 to 17	910	887	963	1033	a	910	887	1056	1138	a
Germany	4 to 17	622	782	875	900	m	622	782	875	900	m
Greece	6 to 19	828	889	953	1117	958	828	889	953	1330	1170
Hungary	4 to 17	555	601	694	763	763	614	724	953	1106	1106
Iceland	3 to 16	720	792	872	888	a	720	792	872	888	a
Ireland	5 to 16	941	941	848	802	713	941	941	907	891	891
Italy	3 to 15	891	891	990	1089	m	990	1023	1089	1089	m
Japan	4 to 17	707	774	868	m	a	707	774	868	m	a
Korea	6 to 17	612	703	867	1020	a	612	703	867	1020	a
Luxembourg	4 to 15	847	847	782	750	a	847	847	782	750	a
Mexico	5 to 13	800	800	1167	1058	a	800	800	1167	1124	a
Netherlands	5 to 17	940	1000	1067	m	a	940	1000	1067	m	a
New Zealand	4 to 15	m	m	m	m	m	985	985	985	985	985
Norway	4 to 17	620	728	827	855	a	620	728	827	855	a
Poland	6 to 18	m	m	m	m	m	m	m	m	m	m
Portugal	5 to 15	860	854	887	826	m	860	871	913	980	m
Scotland	4 to 15	m	m	m	a	a	m	m	m	a	a
Slovak Republic	6 to 17	m	m	m	m	m	m	m	m	m	m
Spain	3 to 16	793	794	956	979	978	793	794	956	979	978
Sweden	6 to 18	741	741	741	741	a	741	741	741	741	a
Switzerland	5 to 16	m	m	m	m	m	m	m	m	m	m
Turkey	7 to 12	720	720	750	810	a	864	864	846	810	a
United States	6 to 16	m	m	m	m	m	m	m	m	m	m
OECD average		*770*	*810*	*896*	*910*	*786*	*796*	*839*	*933*	*971*	*890*
EU 19 average		*783*	*819*	*892*	*902*	*763*	*800*	*844*	*932*	*977*	*861*
Partner countries											
Brazil	7 to 16	m	m	m	m	m	m	m	m	m	m
Chile	7 to 16	1094	1094	1094	1210	1210	1094	1094	1094	1210	1210
Estonia	6 to 17	595	683	802	840	m	595	683	802	840	m
Israel	5 to 17	878	867	966	1040	1015	878	884	1016	1089	1064
Russian Federation	7 to 15	m	m	m	m	m	m	m	m	m	m
Slovenia	6 to 17	621	721	791	908	888	621	721	791	908	888

1. "Ages 12 to 14" covers ages 12 to 13 only.
Source: OECD. See Annex 3 for notes (*www.oecd.org/edu/eag2008*).
Please refer to the Reader's Guide for information concerning the symbols replacing missing data.
StatLink 🔗 http://dx.doi.org/10.1787/402183135853

Table D1.2a.
Instruction time per subject as a percentage of total compulsory instruction time for 9-to-11-year-olds (2006)
Percentage of intended instruction time devoted to various subject areas within the total compulsory curriculum

D1

| | Compulsory core curriculum | | | | | | | | | | | | Compulsory flexible curriculum | TOTAL compulsory curriculum | Non-compulsory curriculum |
	Reading, writing and literature	Mathematics	Science	Social studies	Modern foreign languages	Technology	Arts	Physical education	Religion	Practical and vocational skills	Other	TOTAL compulsory core curriculum			
	(1)	(2)	(3)	(4)	(5)	(6)	(7)	(8)	(9)	(10)	(11)	(12)	(13)	(14)	(15)
OECD countries															
Australia[1]	13	9	2	3	1	2	4	4	1	n	1	41	59	100	n
Austria	24	16	10	3	8	n	18	10	8	x(12)	3	100	x(12)	100	6
Belgium (Fl.)[1]	22	19	x(11)	x(11)	7	n	10	7	7	n	18	89	11	100	n
Belgium (Fr.)[1]	x(11)	x(11)	x(11)	x(11)	5	x(11)	x(11)	7	7	x(11)	81	100	n	100	11
Czech Republic[2]	24	19	9	11	13	n	14	8	n	n	n	97	3	100	n
Denmark	26	17	8	4	9	n	20	10	4	n	3	100	n	100	n
England	27	22	10	8	1	9	8	7	5	n	3	100	n	100	n
Finland	21	18	10	2	9	n	19	9	5	n	n	94	6	100	7
France	31	18	5	10	10	3	11	13	n	n	n	100	n	100	n
Germany	20	18	6	7	10	1	15	11	7	n	3	99	1	100	n
Greece	29	14	11	11	10	n	8	7	7	n	2	100	n	100	n
Hungary	29	17	6	7	9	n	14	12	n	5	2	100	n	100	20
Iceland	16	15	8	8	4	6	12	9	3	5	2	89	11	100	n
Ireland	29	12	4	8	x(13)	n	12	4	10	n	14	92	8	100	n
Italy[3]	a	a	a	a	a	a	a	a	a	a	a	a	a	100	15
Japan	19	15	9	9	n	n	10	9	n	n	21	92	8	100	m
Korea	19	13	10	10	5	2	13	10	n	2	3	87	13	100	n
Luxembourg[4]	25	18	6	2	21	n	11	10	7	n	n	100	n	100	n
Mexico	30	25	15	20	n	n	5	5	n	n	n	100	n	100	n
Netherlands[5]	32	19	6	6	1	n	9	7	5	3	n	88	13	100	n
New Zealand	a	a	a	a	a	a	a	a	a	a	a	a	a	a	a
Norway	23	15	7	8	7	n	15	7	9	n	9	100	n	100	n
Poland	m	m	m	m	m	m	m	m	m	m	m	m	m	m	m
Portugal[6]	15	12	9	6	11	x(7)	18	9	n	n	17	97	3	100	3
Scotland	a	a	a	a	a	a	a	a	a	a	a	a	a	a	a
Slovak Republic	m	m	m	m	m	m	m	m	m	m	m	m	m	m	m
Spain	22	17	9	9	13	n	11	11	x(13)	n	n	91	9	100	n
Sweden	22	14	12	13	12	x(3)	7	8	x(4)	7	n	94	6	100	n
Switzerland	m	m	m	m	m	m	m	m	m	m	m	m	m	m	m
Turkey	19	13	12	10	9	n	7	4	7	2	6	89	11	100	20
United States	m	m	m	m	m	m	m	m	m	m	m	m	m	m	m
OECD average[1]	*23*	*16*	*9*	*8*	*7*	*1*	*12*	*8*	*4*	*1*	*4*	*91*	*4*	*100*	*4*
EU 19 average[1]	*25*	*17*	*9*	*7*	*9*	*1*	*13*	*9*	*4*	*1*	*3*	*97*	*3*	*100*	*4*
Partner countries															
Brazil	m	m	m	m	m	m	m	m	m	m	m	m	m	m	m
Chile	15	15	14	4	2	7	10	7	5	n	1	79	21	100	n
Estonia	21	15	7	6	12	6	10	10	n	n	n	88	12	100	n
Israel	19	18	9	6	11	n	6	6	6	4	9	92	8	100	2
Russian Federation	m	m	m	m	m	m	m	m	m	m	m	m	m	m	m
Slovenia	18	16	10	8	11	2	11	11	n	3	10	100	n	100	n

1. Australia, Belgium (Fl.) and Belgium(Fr.) are not included in the averages.
2. For 9-to-10-year-olds, social studies is included in science.
3. For 9 and 10-year-olds the curriculum is largely flexible, for 11-year-olds it is about the same as for 12 and 13-year-olds.
4. German as a language of instruction is included in "Reading, writing and literature" in addition to the mother tongue Luxemburgish.
5. Includes 11-year-olds only.
6. Includes 10-to-11-year-olds only.
Source: OECD. See Annex 3 for notes (*www.oecd.org/edu/eag2008*).
Please refer to the Reader's Guide for information concerning the symbols replacing missing data.
StatLink ⌗═ http://dx.doi.org/10.1787/402183135853

D1

Table D1.2b.

Instruction time per subject as a percentage of total compulsory instruction time for 12-to-14-year-olds (2006)

Percentage of intended instruction time devoted to various subject areas within the total compulsory curriculum

		Compulsory core curriculum														
		Reading, writing and literature	Mathematics	Science	Social studies	Modern foreign languages	Technology	Arts	Physical education	Religion	Practical and vocational skills	Other	TOTAL compulsory core curriculum	Compulsory flexible curriculum	TOTAL compulsory curriculum	Non-compulsory curriculum
		(1)	(2)	(3)	(4)	(5)	(6)	(7)	(8)	(9)	(10)	(11)	(12)	(13)	(14)	(15)
OECD countries	**Australia**	9	9	7	7	4	5	6	6	1	n	3	**57**	43	**100**	4
	Austria	13	15	13	12	11	n	16	10	7	2	n	**100**	x(12)	**100**	5
	Belgium (Fl.)	14	13	7	9	17	4	4	6	6	1	n	**81**	19	**100**	n
	Belgium (Fr.)[1]	16	13	9	13	13	3	3	9	6	n	3	**88**	13	**100**	6
	Czech Republic	12	13	20	16	10	3	8	7	n	n	n	**88**	12	**100**	n
	Denmark	20	13	15	9	18	n	11	8	3	n	3	**100**	n	**100**	n
	England	13	12	12	13	11	12	11	8	4	n	4	**100**	n	**100**	4
	Finland	13	13	17	7	14	n	15	7	5	4	n	**95**	5	**100**	7
	France	16	15	13	13	12	6	7	11	n	n	n	**93**	7	**100**	10
	Germany	14	14	10	12	17	3	10	9	5	2	2	**98**	2	**100**	n
	Greece	12	11	10	10	12	5	6	8	6	1	19	**100**	n	**100**	n
	Hungary	16	12	18	11	12	3	11	9	n	3	5	**100**	n	**100**	37
	Iceland	14	14	8	6	17	4	7	8	2	4	3	**85**	15	**100**	n
	Ireland[2]	28	13	8	17	7	x(15)	4	5	9	x(15)	5	**97**	3	**100**	7
	Italy[1]	21	12	10	15	12	7	13	7	4	n	n	**100**	n	**100**	16
	Japan	11	10	9	9	10	3	7	9	n	n	18	**87**	13	**100**	m
	Korea	13	11	11	10	10	4	8	8	n	4	5	**82**	18	**100**	n
	Luxembourg[3]	22	15	5	10	20	n	10	8	6	n	5	**100**	n	**100**	n
	Mexico	14	14	17	26	9	n	6	6	n	9	n	**100**	n	**100**	n
	Netherlands	10	10	8	11	14	5	7	9	n	3	n	**78**	22	**100**	n
	New Zealand	a	a	a	a	a	a	a	a	a	a	a	a	a	a	a
	Norway	16	13	9	11	10	n	8	10	7	n	16	**100**	n	**100**	n
	Poland	m	m	m	m	m	m	m	m	m	m	m	m	m	m	m
	Portugal	11	11	12	13	15	x(7)	11	9	n	n	14	**97**	3	**100**	3
	Scotland	a	a	a	a	a	a	a	a	a	a	a	a	a	a	a
	Slovak Republic	m	m	m	m	m	m	m	m	m	m	m	m	m	m	m
	Spain	16	11	11	10	10	8	11	7	x(13)	x(13)	3	**87**	13	**100**	n
	Sweden	22	14	12	13	12	x(3)	7	8	x(4)	7	n	**94**	6	**100**	n
	Switzerland	m	m	m	m	m	m	m	m	m	m	m	m	m	m	m
	Turkey	17	13	14	12	12	n	4	7	5	4	7	**96**	4	**100**	13
	United States	m	m	m	m	m	m	m	m	m	m	m	m	m	m	m
	OECD average	*15*	*13*	*11*	*12*	*12*	*3*	*8*	*8*	*3*	*2*	*5*	**92**	*8*	**100**	*5*
	EU 19 average	*16*	*13*	*12*	*12*	*13*	*4*	*9*	*8*	*4*	*1*	*4*	**94**	*6*	**100**	*6*
Partner countries	**Brazil**	m	m	m	m	m	m	m	m	m	m	m	m	m	m	m
	Chile	13	13	11	11	7	5	10	5	5	n	4	**84**	16	**100**	m
	Estonia	14	14	17	7	17	5	7	7	n	n	n	**89**	11	**100**	m
	Israel	14	14	9	7	15	5	5	5	5	5	6	**91**	9	**100**	m
	Russian Federation	m	m	m	m	m	m	m	m	m	m	m	m	m	m	m
	Slovenia	13	13	15	15	11	2	6	6	n	n	9	**90**	10	**100**	m

1. Includes 12-to-13-year-olds only.
2. For 13-to-14-year-olds, arts is included in non-compulsory curriculum.
3. German as a language of instruction is included in "Reading, writing and literature" in addition to the mother tongue Luxemburgish.

Source: OECD. See Annex 3 for notes (*www.oecd.org/edu/eag2008*).

Please refer to the Reader's Guide for information concerning the symbols replacing missing data.

StatLink http://dx.doi.org/10.1787/402183135853

WHAT IS THE STUDENT-TEACHER RATIO AND HOW BIG ARE CLASSES?

This indicator examines the number of students per class at the primary and lower secondary levels and the ratio of students to teaching staff at all levels; it distinguishes between public and private institutions. Class size and student-teacher ratios are much discussed aspects of the education students receive and – along with students' total instruction time (see Indicator D1), teachers' average working time (see Indicator D4) and the division of teachers' time between teaching and other duties – are among the determinants of the size of countries' teaching force.

Key results

Chart D2.1. **Average class size in primary education (2000, 2006)**

▦ 2006   ◆ 2000

The average class size in primary education is slightly more than 21 students per class, but varies from 32 in Korea to fewer than half that number in Luxembourg and the partner country the Russian Federation. From 2000 to 2006, average class size did not vary significantly, but differences in class size among OECD countries seem to have diminished. Class size tends to have decreased in countries that had relatively large class sizes in 2000 (such as Japan, Korea and Turkey) whereas it tends to have increased in countries with relatively small class sizes (such as Iceland).

Number of students per classroom

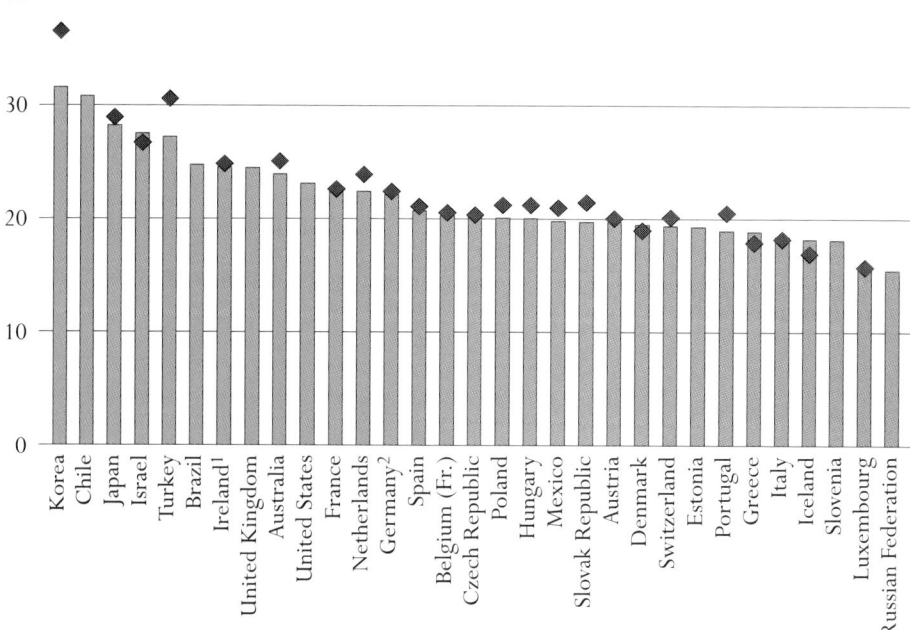

1. Public institutions only.
2. Years of reference 2001 and 2006.
Countries are ranked in descending order of average class size in primary education in 2006.
Source: OECD. 2006 data: Table D2.1. 2000 data: Table D2.4 on line. See Annex 3 for notes (*www.oecd.org/ edu/eag2008*).
StatLink ▦ᵃˢ▟ http://dx.doi.org/10.1787/402267680060

Other highlights of this indicator

■ The average class size in lower secondary education is 24 students per class, but varies from about 30 or more in Japan, Korea and Mexico and the partner countries Brazil, Chile and Israel, to 20 or fewer in Denmark, Iceland, Ireland (public institutions), Luxembourg and Switzerland and the partner country the Russian Federation.

■ The number of students per class increases by an average of nearly three between primary and lower secondary education, but ratios of students to teaching staff tend to decrease with increasing levels of education owing to more annual instruction time, though this pattern is not uniform among countries.

■ On average in OECD countries, the availability of teaching resources relative to student numbers in secondary education is more favourable in private than in public institutions. This is most striking in Mexico where, at the secondary level, there are around 14 more students per teacher in public institutions than in private ones. At the lower secondary level, there is one student more per class on average across OECD countries in public than in private institutions.

Policy context

Class size, education quality and education systems

Class size is a hotly debated topic and an important element of education policy in many OECD countries. Smaller classes are often perceived to allow teachers to focus more on the individual needs of students and to reduce the amount of class time they spend dealing with disruptions. Smaller class sizes may also influence parents when they choose schools for their children. In this respect, class size would be viewed as an indicator of the quality of the school system.

Yet evidence on the effects of differences in class size upon student performance is mixed. In what has evolved as a contentious area of research, and one which has produced little in the way of consistent results, there is some evidence that smaller classes may have an impact upon specific groups of students (*e.g.* Krueger, 2002).

A further reason for the mixed evidence on the impact of class size may be that class size does not vary enough to estimate the true effects of this variable on student performance. In addition, policies that group students who perform less satisfactorily into smaller classes in order to devote more attention to them may reduce the observed performance gains that may otherwise be expected from smaller classes. Finally, the fact that the relationship between class size and student performance is often non-linear makes the effects difficult to estimate.

Many factors influence the interaction between teachers and students, and class size is only one of them. Other influences include the number of classes or students for which a teacher is responsible, the subject taught, the division of the teacher's time between teaching and other duties, the grouping of students within classes, the pedagogical approach employed and the practice of team teaching.

The ratio of students to teaching staff is also an important indicator of the resources devoted to education. A smaller ratio of students to teaching staff may have to be weighted against higher salaries for teachers, increased professional development and teacher training, greater investment in teaching technology, or more widespread use of assistant teachers and other paraprofessionals whose salaries are often considerably lower than those of qualified teachers. Moreover, as larger numbers of children with special educational needs are integrated into normal classes, more use of specialised personnel and support services may limit the resources available for reducing the ratio of students to teaching staff.

The ratio of students to teaching staff is obtained by dividing the number of full-time equivalent students at a given level of education by the number of full-time equivalent teachers at that level and in similar types of institutions. However, this ratio does not take into account instruction time compared to the length of a teacher's working day, nor how much time teachers spend teaching and therefore it cannot be interpreted in terms of class size (Box D2.1).

Evidence and explanations

Average class size in primary and lower secondary education

At the primary level, the average class size in OECD countries is slightly more than 21 students per class, but varies widely. It ranges from 32 students per primary class in Korea to fewer than 20 in Austria, Denmark, Greece, Iceland, Italy, Luxembourg, Mexico, Portugal, the Slovak Republic and

D2

Switzerland and the partner countries Estonia, the Russian Federation and Slovenia. At the lower secondary level, the average class size in OECD countries is 24 students per class and varies from 36 students per class in Korea to 20 or fewer in Denmark, Iceland, Ireland (public institutions), Luxembourg and Switzerland and the partner country the Russian Federation (Table D2.1).

D2

Box D2.1. **Relationship between class size and ratio of students to teaching staff**

The number of students per class results from a number of different elements: the ratio of students to teaching staff, the number of classes or students for which a teacher is responsible, the instruction time of students compared to the length of teachers' working days, the proportion of time teachers spend teaching, the grouping of students within classes and team teaching.

For example, in a school of 48 full-time students and 8 full-time teachers, the ratio of students to teaching staff is 6. If teachers' working week is estimated to be 35 hours including 10 hours teaching, and if instruction time for each student is 40 hours per week, then whatever the grouping of students in this school, average class size can be estimated as follows:

Estimated class size = 6 students per teacher * (40 hours of instruction time per student/ 10 hours of teaching per teacher) = 24 students.

Compared to this estimated figure, the class size presented in Table D2.1 is defined as the division of students who are following a common course of study, based on the highest number of common courses (usually compulsory studies), and excludes teaching in subgroups. Thus, the estimated class size will be close to the average class size of Table D2.1 where teaching in sub-groups is less frequent (as is the case in primary and lower secondary education).

Because of these definitions, similar student-teacher ratios between countries can result in different class sizes. For example, in lower secondary education, Austria and the United States have similar average class sizes (23.9 students in Austria and 24.3 in the United States – see Table D2.1), but the ratio of students to teaching staff differs substantially with 10.4 students per teaching staff in Austria compared to 14.7 in the United States (Table D2.2). The explanation may lie in the higher number of teaching hours required of teachers in the United States (607 in Austria and 1 080 in the United States – Table D4.1).

The number of students per class tends to increase, on average, by nearly three students between primary and lower secondary education. In Austria, Japan, Korea, Luxembourg, Mexico, Poland and Spain, and the partner countries Brazil and Israel, the increase in average class size exceeds four students, while Switzerland and the United Kingdom show a small drop in the number of students per class between these two levels (Chart D2.2). The indicator on class size is limited to primary and lower secondary education because class sizes are difficult to define and compare at higher levels, where students often attend several different classes, depending on the subject area.

However data collected in the context of PISA 2006 give some insight into class size in a specific area (national language of instruction classes) for the grade attended by most of the students aged 15 in the country (Box D2.2).

Box D2.2. National language of instruction class size in the grade attended by most 15-year-olds

The 2006 PISA survey analysed the performance of 15-year-old students, with a focus on science. As part of the contextual information collected, principals of institutions were asked to give the actual number of students in classes in the national language of instruction, for the grade attended by most of the country's students aged 15. As the survey is representative of 15-year-old students, the size of classes is representative of class sizes in each country for this group of students.

Principals were asked to specify the size of classes according to the 9 following categories: 15 students or fewer, from 16 to 20, from 21 to 25, from 26 to 30, from 31 to 35, from 36 to 40, from 41 to 45, from 46 to 50, and more than 50. From these categories, average class size was computed using the middle class size value for each category and the values 15 and 51 for the two extremes. Average class sizes, as well as the difference in class size between the smallest 10% of classes and largest 10% of classes are shown on the chart below.

In OECD countries, the average class size corresponding to the grade attended by most of the country's 15-year-olds is 26 students. The average size of these classes is two more than that reported in this indicator for lower secondary level of education, but the difference should be interpreted with caution owing to differences in methodology. There are large differences in class sizes for 15-year-olds as there are at the lower secondary level. For the grade attended by most 15-year-olds, average class sizes vary from fewer than 20 students in Switzerland to nearly twice this number in the partner country Chile (38.6). From the six countries with the smallest class sizes for 15-year-olds (Belgium, Denmark, Finland, Luxembourg and Switzerland and the partner country the Russian Federation), four are among those reported here with the smallest class sizes at the lower secondary level. Similarly, among the 8 countries with more than 30 students in the grade attended by most of the country's 15-year-olds (Greece, Japan, Korea, Mexico, Turkey and the partner countries Brazil, Chile and Israel), 6 are among those with the largest class sizes at lower secondary level.

Average class size in the grade attended by most 15-year-olds varies widely among countries, but the distribution of class sizes within each country also varies. In some countries such as Finland and Luxembourg, the average class size is below the OECD average and the difference between the smallest 10% of classes and the largest 10% is about 8.5 students. However the difference between the smallest 10% and largest 10% of classes reaches at least twice this number in Austria, Turkey and in the partner countries Brazil and the Russian Federation, and about three times this number or more in Spain and in the partner country Estonia. In Greece and Mexico, the difference can even be about five times or more the difference shown in Finland and Luxembourg. However, the variation between the smallest and largest class sizes in each country is not necessarily linked to average class size. In Korea, the average class size is among the largest in OECD countries, but the difference between the smallest 10% and the largest 10% of class sizes is about 10 students, only slightly more than the average across OECD countries. In Austria, instead, the average class size is, at nearly 24 students, below the OECD average, but there are more variations in class sizes than on average in OECD countries (19 and 9 students, respectively).

Average class size in national language of instruction classes for 15-year-olds

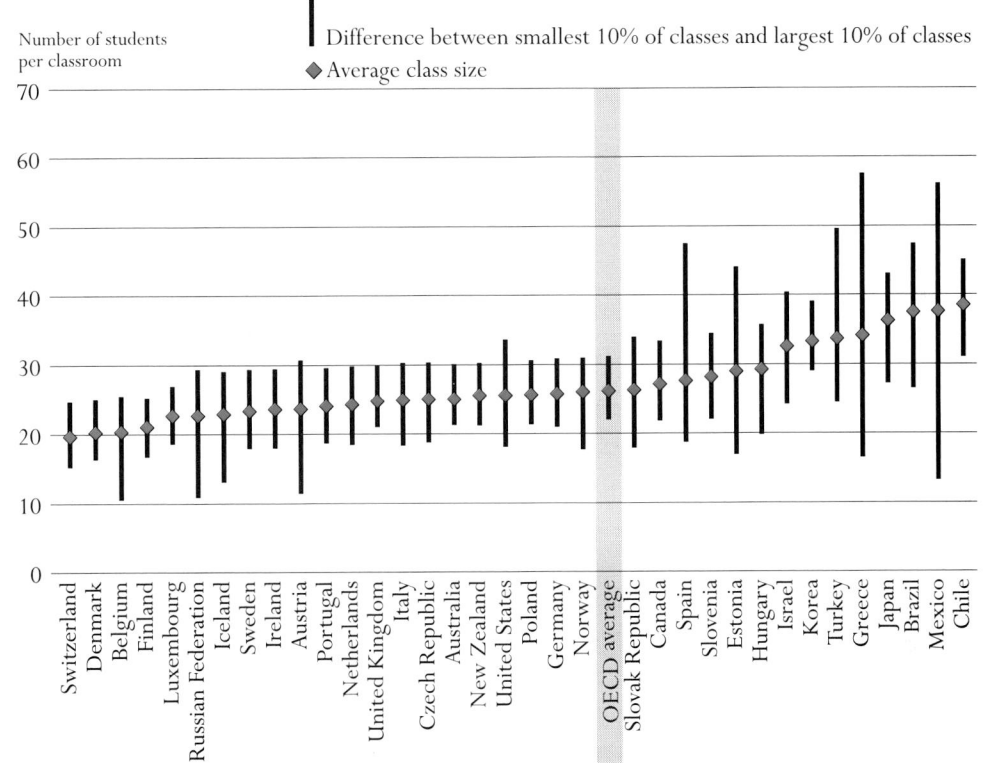

Countries are ranked in ascending order of average class size in national language of instruction classes.
Source: OECD PISA 2006 database. See Annex 3 for notes (*www.oecd.org/edu/eag2008*).
StatLink ⌐ℤℤℤ http://dx.doi.org/10.1787/402267680060

Although the data on class size do not refer to science classes, it is interesting to look at the relationship between PISA performance in science and average class size. The class size in the language of instruction does not seem to have a direct impact on PISA performance in science. For example a country like Finland has both a small average class size in the language of instruction and holds the top ranking for performance in science. However, countries like Japan and the partner country Estonia, which are also among the top five OECD and partner countries for PISA performance in science, have average class sizes that are larger than the OECD average. Estonia's average class size exceeds the OECD average by only three students while Japan's exceeds it by ten. Large average class sizes in Korea and in the partner country Slovenia do not prevent these countries from having above average PISA performance in science. Japan has also large average class size and above average PISA performance, but on the other hand, attempts small-group teaching to improve achievement of students.

D2

Between 2000 and 2006, average class size in primary education did not vary significantly (21.5 in 2006 against 22.0 in 2000). However, among countries with comparable data, class size decreased in countries that had larger class sizes in 2000 (Korea, Japan and Turkey), whereas class size increased (or stayed constant) in countries that had the smallest class sizes in 2000 (Iceland, Italy, Greece and Luxembourg). At the secondary level of education, variations in class sizes between 2000 and 2006 follow a similar trend, leading to a narrowing of the range of class sizes (Table D2.1 and Table D2.4 available on line).

Chart D2.2. **Average class size in educational institutions, by level of education (2006)**

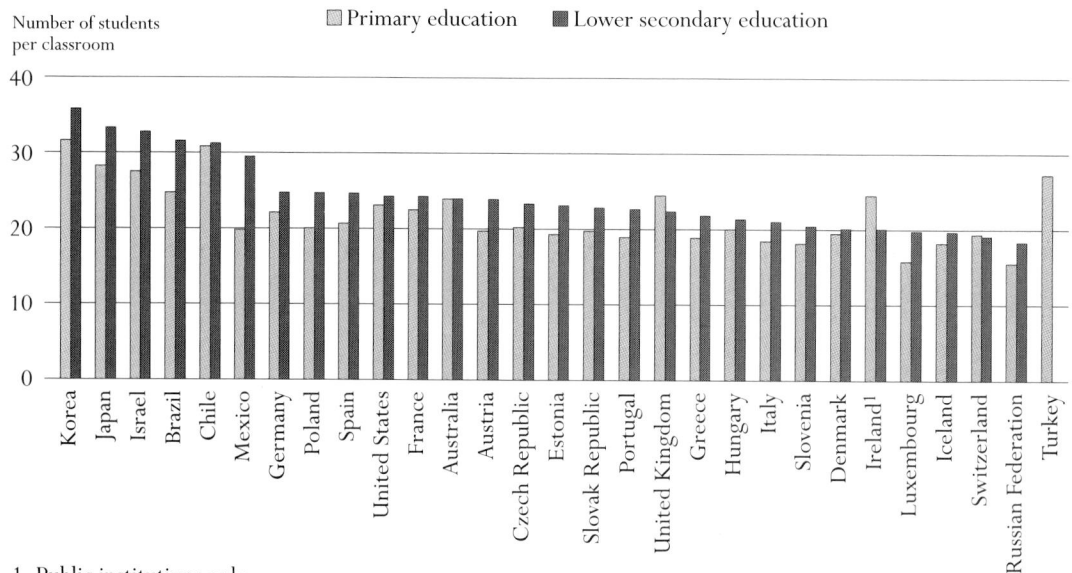

1. Public institutions only.
Countries are ranked in descending order of average class size in lower secondary education.
Source: OECD. Table D2.1. See Annex 3 for notes (*www.oecd.org/edu/eag2008*).
StatLink ▰▱▰ http://dx.doi.org/10.1787/402267680060

Ratio of students to teaching staff

In primary education, the ratio of students to teaching staff, expressed in full-time equivalents, ranges from 26 students or more per teacher in Korea, Mexico and Turkey to fewer than 11 in Greece, Hungary, Italy, Norway and Portugal. The OECD average in primary education is 16 students per teacher (Chart D2.3).

There is similar variation among countries in the ratio of students to teaching staff at the secondary level, ranging from 30 students per full-time equivalent teacher in Mexico to fewer than 11 in Austria, Belgium, Greece, Iceland, Italy, Luxembourg, Norway, Portugal and Spain and in partner country the Russian Federation. On average among OECD countries, the ratio of students to teaching staff at the secondary level is 13, which is close to the ratios in Australia (12), the Czech Republic (12), Finland (13), France (12), Japan (14), Poland (13), the Slovak Republic (14), Sweden (13), Switzerland (12) and the United Kingdom (14), and the partner countries Estonia (13), Israel (13) and Slovenia (13) (Table D2.2).

Chart D2.3. Ratio of students to teaching staff in educational institutions, by level of education (2006)

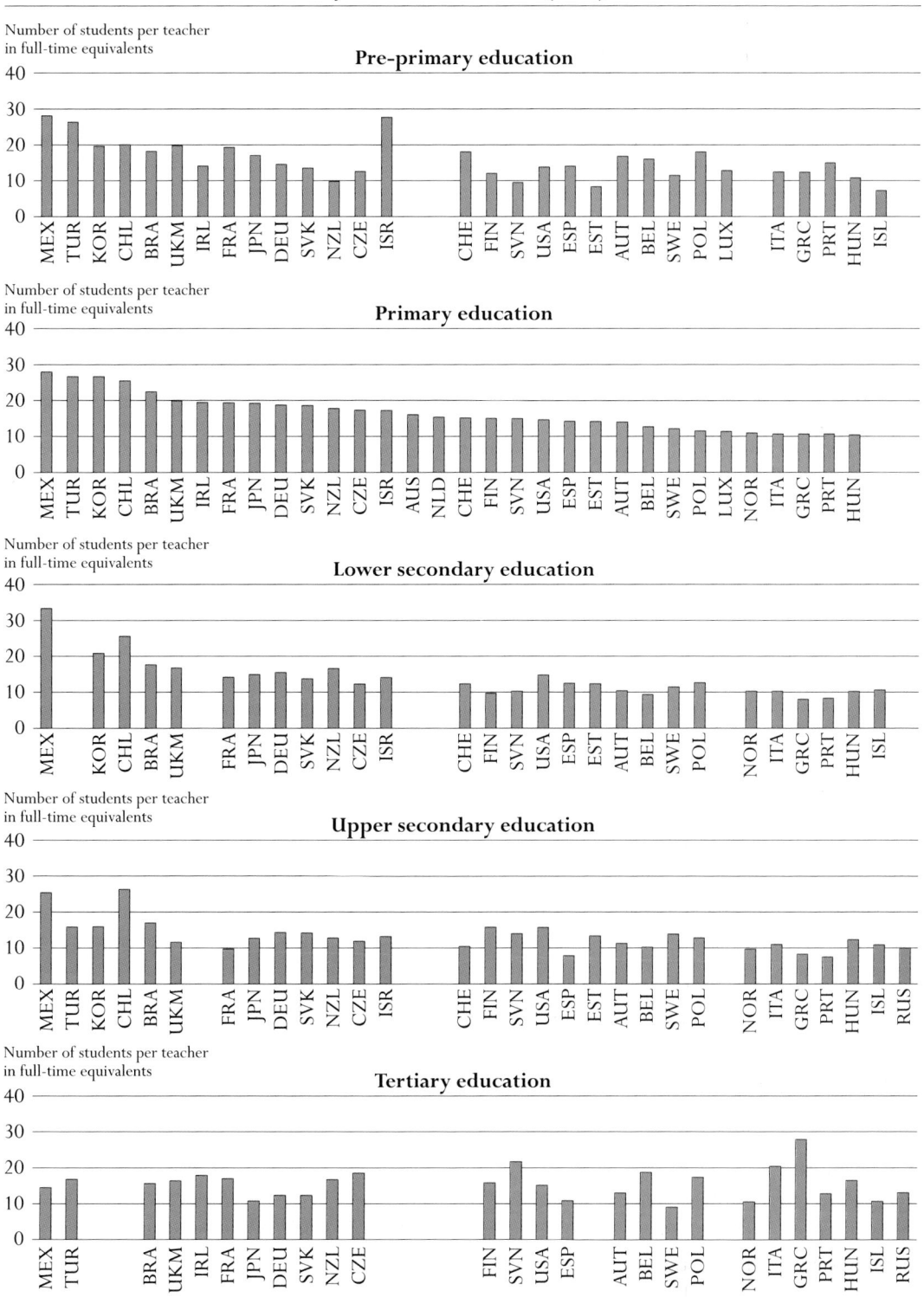

Note: Please refer to the Reader's Guide for the list of country codes for country names used in this chart.

Countries are ranked in descending order of average class size in primary education.

Source: OECD. Table D2.2. See Annex 3 for notes (*www.oecd.org/edu/eag2008*).

StatLink ⫘᠊᠊ http://dx.doi.org/10.1787/402267680060

D2

As the difference in the mean ratios of students to teaching staff between primary and secondary education indicates, there are fewer full-time equivalent students per full-time equivalent teacher at higher levels of education. The ratio of students to teaching staff decreases between primary and secondary levels of education, despite a tendency for class sizes to increase. This was found to be true in all but seven OECD countries (Hungary, Italy, Mexico, the Netherlands, Poland, Sweden and the United States), and the partner country Chile.

The decrease in the ratio of students to teaching staff from the primary to the secondary level reflects differences in annual instruction time, which tends to increase with the level of education. It may also result from delays in matching the teaching force to demographic changes, or from differences in teaching hours for teachers at different levels. The general trend is consistent among countries, but it is not obvious from an educational perspective why a smaller ratio of students to teaching staff should be more desirable at higher levels of education (Table D2.2).

The ratios of students to teaching staff in pre-primary education are shown in Table D2.2. For the pre-primary level, information is also presented on the ratio of students to contact staff (teachers and teachers' aides). Some countries make extensive use of teachers' aides at the pre-primary level. Ten OECD countries and three partner countries reported smaller ratios of students to contact staff (column 1 of Table D2.2) than of students to teaching staff. For countries such as the Czech Republic, the Slovak Republic, Sweden and the United Kingdom, this difference is not substantial. However, in Austria, France, Germany, Ireland and the United States, as well as in the partner countries Chile, Estonia and Israel, there are larger numbers of teachers' aides. As a result, the ratios of students to contact staff are substantially lower than ratios of students to teaching staff, particularly in France and Ireland and in partner country Israel.

At the tertiary level, the ratio of students to teaching staff ranges from 28 students per teacher in Greece to 11 or fewer in Iceland, Japan, Norway, Spain and Sweden (Table D2.2). Such comparisons in tertiary education should be made with caution, however, since it is still difficult to calculate full-time equivalent students and teachers on a comparable basis at this level.

In 14 out of the 15 OECD and partner countries with comparable data, the ratio of students to teaching staff is lower in the more occupationally specific tertiary-type B programmes than in tertiary-type A and advanced research programmes (Table D2.2). Turkey is the only country with a higher ratio in tertiary-type B programmes.

Teaching resources in public and private institutions

Table D2.3 focuses on the secondary level and illustrates comparative teaching resources between public and private institutions by comparing the ratio of students to teaching staff for the two types of providers. On average among OECD countries and partner countries for which data are available, the ratios of students to teaching staff are smaller in private institutions at both lower secondary and upper secondary levels, with slightly more than two more students per teacher in public institutions than in private institutions at total secondary level. The most striking examples are Mexico and the United Kingdom where, at the lower secondary level, there are at least 12 more students per teacher in public than in private institutions. The difference in Mexico at the upper secondary level is similarly large. However, this is not true in all countries.

In some countries, ratios of students to teaching staff are smaller in the public sector than in the private sector. This is most pronounced at the lower secondary level in Spain where there are some 16 students per teacher in private institutions compared with only 11 in public institutions.

In terms of class size (Chart D2.4 and Table D2.1), on average among OECD countries for which data are available, average class sizes do not differ between public and private institutions by more than one or two students per class for both primary and lower secondary education. However, this disguises marked differences among countries. At the primary level, in Poland, Turkey, the United Kingdom and the United States, and in the partner countries Brazil, Estonia and the Russian Federation, for example, average class sizes in public institutions are higher by four students or more per class. However, in all these countries except the partner country Brazil, the private sector is relatively small (at most 5% of students at the primary level). In contrast, class sizes in private institutions exceed those in public institutions to at least a similar degree in Japan and Spain.

D2

Chart D2.4. **Average class size in public and private institutions, by level of education (2006)**

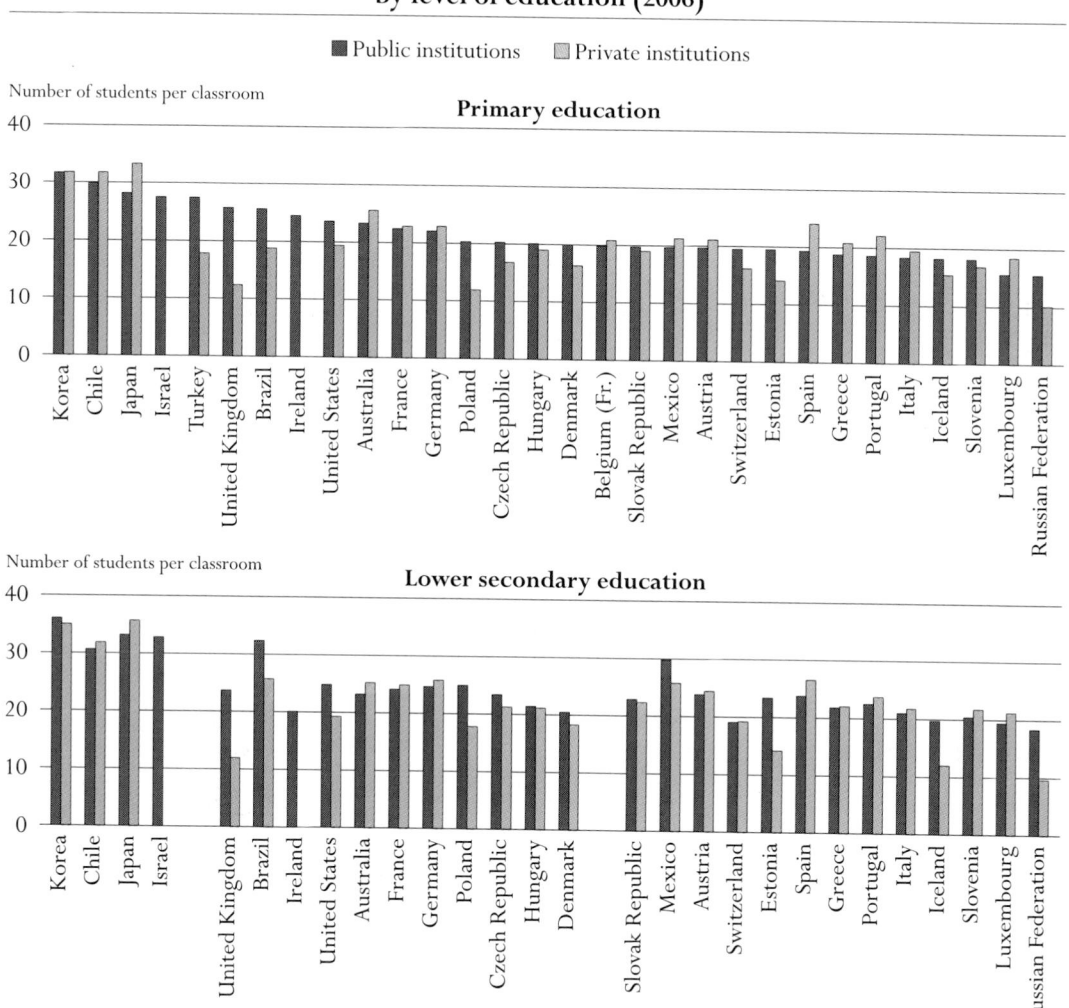

Countries are ranked in descending order of average class size in public institutions in primary education.
Source: OECD. Table D2.1. See Annex 3 for notes (*www.oecd.org/edu/eag2008*).
StatLink ⟡⟡⟡ http://dx.doi.org/10.1787/402267680060

D2

The comparison of class size between public and private institutions shows a mixed picture at the lower secondary level, where private education is more prevalent. Lower secondary average class sizes are larger in private institutions than in public institutions in 11 OECD and 2 partner countries, although differences tend to be smaller than in primary education.

Countries encourage and provide resources for public and private schools for various reasons. In many countries, one reason is to broaden the choice of schooling available to students and their families. Considering the importance of class size in discussions of schooling in many countries, differences in class sizes between public and private schools and institutions may be a driver of differences in enrolment. It is interesting that in Australia, Belgium (Fr.), Denmark, Korea, and Luxembourg and the partner country Chile, countries with a substantial private sector in primary and lower secondary education (Table C2.4), there are, on average, only marginal differences in class size between public and private institutions. Where large differences do exist, they tend to show that private institutions have more students per class than public ones. This indicates that in countries where a substantial proportion of students and families have decided to choose private education institutions, class size is not a major determinant of their decisions.

Definitions and methodologies

Data refer to the academic year 2005/06 and are based on the UOE data collection on education statistics administered by the OECD in 2007 (for details see Annex 3 at *www.oecd.org/edu/eag2008*).

Class sizes have been calculated by dividing the number of students enrolled by the number of classes. In order to ensure comparability among countries, special needs programmes have been excluded. Data include only regular programmes at primary and lower secondary levels of education and exclude teaching in sub-groups outside the regular classroom setting.

The ratio of students to teaching staff has been calculated by dividing the number of full-time equivalent students at a given level of education by the number of full-time equivalent teachers at that level and in the specified type of institution.

The breakdown of the ratio of students to teaching staff by type of institution distinguishes between students and teachers in public institutions and in private institutions (government-dependent private institutions and independent private institutions). In some countries the proportion of students in private institutions is small (Table C2.4).

Instructional personnel:

• Teaching staff refers to professional personnel directly involved in teaching students. The classification includes classroom teachers, special education teachers and other teachers who work with a whole class of students in a classroom, in small groups in a resource room, or in one-to-one teaching situations inside or outside a regular class. Teaching staff also includes department chairpersons whose duties include some teaching, but excludes non-professional personnel who support teachers in providing instruction to students, such as teachers' aides and other paraprofessional personnel.

• Teachers' aides and teaching/research assistants include non-professional personnel or students who support teachers in providing instruction to students.

Further references

The following additional material relevant to this indicator is available on line at:

StatLink 🖼️🔗 http://dx.doi.org/10.1787/402267680060

• *Table D2.4. Average class size, by type of institution and level of education (2000)*

Specific notes on definitions and methodologies regarding this indicator for each country are given in Annex 3 at *www.oecd.org/edu/eag2008*.

D2

Table D2.1.
Average class size, by type of institution and level of education (2006)
Calculations based on number of students and number of classes

D2

	Primary education					Lower secondary education (general programmes)				
		Private institutions					Private institutions			
	Public institutions	Total private institutions	Government-dependent private institutions	Independent private institutions	Total: Public and private institutions	Public institutions	Total private institutions	Government-dependent private institutions	Independent private institutions	Total: Public and private institutions
	(1)	(2)	(3)	(4)	(5)	(6)	(7)	(8)	(9)	(10)
OECD countries										
Australia	23.3	25.6	25.6	a	**23.9**	23.2	25.3	25.3	a	**24.0**
Austria	19.6	21.1	x(2)	x(2)	**19.7**	23.9	24.4	x(7)	x(7)	**23.9**
Belgium	m	m	m	m	**m**	m	m	m	m	**m**
Belgium (Fr.)	19.9	20.9	20.9	a	**20.3**	m	m	m	a	**m**
Canada	m	m	m	m	**m**	m	m	m	m	**m**
Czech Republic	20.3	16.8	16.8	a	**20.2**	23.4	21.2	21.2	a	**23.3**
Denmark	20.0	16.3	16.3	a	**19.5**	20.5	18.3	18.3	a	**20.1**
Finland	m	m	m	a	**m**	m	m	m	a	**m**
France	22.4	22.8	x(2)	x(2)	**22.5**	24.1	24.9	25.1	13.4	**24.3**
Germany	22.1	22.9	22.9	x(3)	**22.1**	24.7	25.7	25.7	x(8)	**24.7**
Greece	18.7	20.8	a	20.8	**18.9**	21.8	22.1	a	22.1	**21.8**
Hungary	20.1	19.0	19.0	a	**20.0**	21.4	21.1	21.1	a	**21.4**
Iceland	18.3	15.5	15.5	n	**18.2**	19.8	12.0	12.0	n	**19.7**
Ireland	24.5	m	a	m	**m**	20.1	m	a	m	**m**
Italy	18.4	19.5	a	19.5	**18.4**	21.0	21.8	a	21.8	**21.0**
Japan	28.2	33.3	a	33.3	**28.3**	33.2	35.7	a	35.7	**33.3**
Korea	31.6	31.7	a	31.7	**31.6**	36.0	35.0	35.0	a	**35.8**
Luxembourg	15.6	18.5	18.1	18.5	**15.8**	19.5	21.2	20.5	22.4	**19.8**
Mexico	19.7	21.3	a	21.3	**19.8**	29.8	25.8	a	25.8	**29.5**
Netherlands	x(5)	x(5)	x(5)	a	**22.4**	m	m	m	m	**m**
New Zealand	m	m	m	m	**m**	m	m	m	m	**m**
Norway	a	a	a	a	**a**	a	a	a	a	**a**
Poland	20.3	11.9	11.9	11.9	**20.1**	25.0	17.8	26.3	15.8	**24.7**
Portugal	18.6	22.1	24.6	21.4	**19.0**	22.5	23.7	23.8	23.5	**22.7**
Slovak Republic	19.8	19.0	19.0	n	**19.7**	22.9	22.3	22.3	n	**22.8**
Spain	19.3	24.1	24.1	24.0	**20.7**	23.8	26.6	26.9	24.1	**24.7**
Sweden	m	m	m	m	**m**	m	m	m	m	**m**
Switzerland	19.5	16.1	16.0	16.1	**19.4**	19.1	19.2	21.3	18.7	**19.1**
Turkey	27.5	17.9	a	17.9	**27.2**	a	a	a	a	**a**
United Kingdom	25.8	12.3	a	12.3	**24.5**	23.7	12.0	17.8	11.4	**22.4**
United States	23.6	19.4	a	19.4	**23.1**	24.9	19.3	a	19.3	**24.3**
OECD average	*21.5*	*20.4*	*19.3*	*20.6*	*21.5*	*23.8*	*22.6*	*22.8*	*21.2*	*24.0*
EU19 average	*20.3*	*19.2*	*19.4*	*18.3*	*20.2*	*22.5*	*21.6*	*22.6*	*19.3*	*22.7*
Partner countries										
Brazil	25.6	18.8	a	18.8	**24.7**	32.4	25.8	a	25.8	**31.6**
Chile	29.9	31.7	33.4	23.6	**30.8**	30.7	31.9	33.3	24.7	**31.2**
Estonia	19.5	14.1	a	14.1	**19.3**	23.4	14.2	a	14.2	**23.1**
Israel	27.5	a	a	a	**27.5**	32.8	a	a	a	**32.8**
Russian Federation	15.5	10.1	a	10.1	**15.5**	18.4	9.7	a	9.7	**18.3**
Slovenia	18.2	16.9	16.9	n	**18.1**	20.5	21.8	21.8	n	**20.5**

Source: OECD. See Annex 3 for notes (*www.oecd.org/edu/eag2008*).
Please refer to the Reader's Guide for information concerning the symbols replacing missing data.
StatLink ⫸ http://dx.doi.org/10.1787/402267680060

Table D2.2.
Ratio of students to teaching staff in educational institutions (2006)
By level of education, calculations based on full-time equivalents

D2

	Pre-primary education			Secondary education				Tertiary education		
	Students to contact staff (teachers and teachers aides)	Students to teaching staff	Primary education	Lower secondary education	Upper secondary education	All secondary education	Post-secondary non-tertiary education	Tertiary-type B	Tertiary-type A and advanced research programmes	All tertiary education
	(1)	(2)	(3)	(4)	(5)	(6)	(7)	(8)	(9)	(10)
OECD countries										
Australia[1,2]	m	m	16.0	x(6)	x(6)	12.2	m	m	14.9	m
Austria	14.2	16.8	13.9	10.4	11.3	10.7	10.7	7.3	13.5	13.0
Belgium	16.0	16.0	12.6	9.4	10.2	9.9	x(5)	x(10)	x(10)	18.7
Canada[2]	m	x(6)	x(6)	x(6)	x(6)	15.9	m	m	m	m
Czech Republic	12.3	12.5	17.3	12.3	11.9	12.1	17.5	13.4	19.3	18.5
Denmark	m	6.3	x(4)	11.4	m	m	m	m	m	m
Finland	m	12.0	15.0	9.7	15.8	12.9	x(5)	x(5)	15.8	15.8
France[3]	13.7	19.3	19.3	14.1	9.7	11.9	m	16.8	17.1	17.0
Germany	11.2	14.5	18.7	15.5	14.3	15.1	15.1	11.9	12.5	12.4
Greece	12.4	12.4	10.6	8.0	8.3	8.2	5.9	26.9	28.4	27.8
Hungary	m	10.7	10.4	10.2	12.3	11.2	11.9	15.7	16.5	16.5
Iceland	7.2	7.2	x(4)	10.6	10.8	10.7	x(5, 10)	x(10)	x(10)	10.7
Ireland[2]	7.1	14.1	19.4	x(6)	x(6)	14.6	x(6)	x(10)	x(10)	17.9
Italy	12.4	12.4	10.7	10.3	11.0	10.7	m	8.4	20.6	20.4
Japan	16.4	17.0	19.2	14.9	12.7	13.7	x(5, 10)	8.3	11.9	10.8
Korea	19.6	19.6	26.7	20.8	15.9	18.2	a	m	m	m
Luxembourg[2]	m	12.8	11.3	x(6)	x(6)	9.0	m	m	m	m
Mexico	28.1	28.1	28.0	33.4	25.4	30.2	a	13.0	14.6	14.5
Netherlands	m	x(3)	15.3	x(6)	x(6)	15.8	x(6)	m	14.9	m
New Zealand	9.8	9.8	17.7	16.6	12.7	14.6	15.8	15.3	17.1	16.7
Norway[2]	m	m	10.9	10.2	9.7	9.9	x(5)	x(10)	x(10)	10.5
Poland	m	18.0	11.5	12.6	12.8	12.7	11.1	12.5	17.4	17.3
Portugal	m	15.0	10.6	8.3	7.5	7.9	x(5)	x(10)	x(10)	12.7
Slovak Republic	13.4	13.5	18.6	13.7	14.2	13.9	10.6	9.7	12.4	12.4
Spain	m	14.0	14.2	12.5	7.8	10.5	a	6.9	12.2	10.8
Sweden	11.2	11.4	12.1	11.4	13.8	12.6	11.9	x(10)	x(10)	9.0
Switzerland[1,2]	m	18.1	15.1	12.3	10.5	11.9	m	m	m	m
Turkey	m	26.3	26.7	a	15.8	15.8	a	57.1	12.5	16.8
United Kingdom[1]	19.4	19.8	19.8	16.7	11.6	13.7	x(5)	x(10)	x(10)	16.4
United States	11.3	13.8	14.6	14.7	15.7	15.2	21.9	x(10)	x(10)	15.1
OECD average	*13.9*	*15.1*	*16.2*	*13.3*	*12.6*	*13.2*	*13.2*	*16.0*	*16.0*	*15.3*
EU19 average	*13.0*	*14.0*	*14.5*	*11.7*	*11.5*	*11.9*	*11.8*	*13.0*	*16.7*	*16.0*
Partner countries										
Brazil	m	18.2	22.5	17.6	17.0	17.3	a	x(10)	x(10)	15.6
Chile	18.8	20.1	25.5	25.5	26.3	26.0	a	m	m	m
Estonia	5.7	8.3	14.1	12.3	13.3	12.7	m	m	m	m
Israel	13.8	27.7	17.2	14.1	13.2	13.5	m	m	m	m
Russian Federation[4]	m	m	m	x(6)	x(6)	9.9	x(6)	10.9	13.9	13.1
Slovenia	9.4	9.4	14.9	10.2	14.0	12.9	x(5)	x(10)	x(10)	21.7

1. Includes only general programmes in upper secondary education.
2. Public institutions only (for Australia, at tertiary-type A and advanced research programmes only; for Ireland, at secondary level only).
3. Excludes independent private institutions.
4. Excludes general programmes in upper secondary education.
Source: OECD. See Annex 3 for notes (*www.oecd.org/edu/eag2008*).
Please refer to the Reader's Guide for information concerning the symbols replacing missing data.
StatLink ⬛⬛ http://dx.doi.org/10.1787/402267680060

Table D2.3.
Ratio of students to teaching staff by type of institution (2006)
By level of education, calculations based on full-time equivalents

D2

	Lower secondary education				Upper secondary education				All secondary education			
		Private				Private				Private		
	Public	Total private institutions	Government-dependent private institutions	Independent private institutions	Public	Total private institutions	Government-dependent private institutions	Independent private institutions	Public	Total private institutions	Government-dependent private institutions	Independent private institutions
	(1)	(2)	(3)	(4)	(5)	(6)	(7)	(8)	(9)	(10)	(11)	(12)
OECD countries												
Australia[1]	x(9)	x(10)	x(11)	a	x(9)	x(10)	x(11)	a	12.4	11.8	11.8	a
Austria	10.3	11.4	x(2)	x(2)	11.3	11.5	x(6)	x(6)	10.7	11.4	x(10)	x(10)
Belgium[2]	9.2	m	9.5	m	10.5	m	10.0	m	10.0	m	9.8	m
Canada	m	m	m	m	m	m	m	m	m	m	m	m
Czech Republic	12.4	9.3	9.3	a	11.7	12.9	12.9	a	12.1	12.2	12.2	a
Denmark[3]	11.5	10.8	10.8	a	m	m	m	a	m	m	m	a
Finland[4,5]	9.7	10.3	10.3	a	15.2	20.9	20.9	a	12.5	18.3	18.3	a
France	14.1	m	14.2	m	9.5	m	10.9	m	11.8	m	12.7	m
Germany	15.5	15.1	15.1	x(3)	14.4	13.8	13.8	x(7)	15.2	14.6	14.6	x(11)
Greece	8.1	7.6	a	7.6	8.4	6.9	a	6.9	8.2	7.2	a	7.2
Hungary	10.2	9.7	9.7	a	12.4	11.5	11.5	a	11.2	10.8	10.8	a
Iceland[3,4]	10.7	9.7	9.7	n	10.8	11.3	11.3	n	10.7	10.8	10.8	n
Ireland[2]	x(9)	m	a	m	x(9)	m	a	m	14.6	m	a	m
Italy	10.4	7.5	a	7.5	11.9	4.3	a	4.3	11.3	5.1	a	5.1
Japan[4]	15.1	13.2	a	13.2	12.0	14.6	a	14.6	13.5	14.3	a	14.3
Korea	20.8	20.9	20.9	a	15.3	16.6	16.6	a	18.5	17.7	17.7	a
Luxembourg	x(9)	m	m	m	x(9)	m	m	m	9.0	m	m	m
Mexico	36.0	22.1	a	22.1	29.8	16.0	a	16.0	33.7	18.8	a	18.8
Netherlands	m	m	m	a	m	m	m	a	m	m	m	a
New Zealand	16.8	15.7	16.6	14.0	12.9	12.2	13.5	9.4	14.9	13.6	14.6	11.3
Norway	10.2	m	m	m	9.7	m	m	m	9.9	m	m	m
Poland	12.7	10.0	12.7	9.2	13.0	9.9	15.9	9.3	12.8	9.9	14.3	9.3
Portugal	8.1	10.6	11.3	9.8	7.8	6.3	9.5	5.6	8.0	7.6	10.5	6.4
Slovak Republic	13.8	13.0	13.0	n	14.4	12.7	12.7	n	14.0	12.8	12.8	n
Spain	11.2	16.1	16.2	15.1	7.1	10.8	10.9	10.8	9.4	14.3	15.0	12.0
Sweden	11.4	11.3	11.3	n	13.8	14.4	14.4	n	12.6	13.0	13.0	n
Switzerland[6]	12.3	m	m	m	10.5	m	m	m	11.9	m	m	m
Turkey	a	a	a	a	16.7	5.3	a	5.3	16.7	5.3	a	5.3
United Kingdom[1]	18.5	6.6	18.1	6.0	12.2	8.0	4.7	8.2	14.9	7.0	2.7	7.2
United States	15.6	9.4	a	9.4	16.4	10.6	a	10.6	15.9	9.9	a	9.9
OECD average	*13.5*	*12.0*	*13.0*	*8.8*	*12.8*	*11.5*	*12.6*	*7.2*	*13.2*	*11.7*	*12.6*	*7.6*
EU19 average	*11.7*	*10.7*	*12.4*	*9.2*	*11.6*	*11.1*	*12.3*	*7.5*	*11.7*	*11.1*	*12.2*	*7.9*
Partner countries												
Brazil	18.7	11.1	a	11.1	19.4	10.0	a	10.0	19.0	10.5	a	10.5
Chile	26.0	25.0	26.7	17.4	26.7	25.9	29.5	14.0	26.4	25.6	28.6	15.0
Estonia	12.4	8.6	a	8.6	13.4	13.1	a	13.1	12.8	10.8	a	10.8
Israel	14.1	a	a	a	13.2	a	a	a	13.5	a	a	a
Russian Federation	m	m	a	m	m	m	a	m	m	m	a	m
Slovenia[2]	10.2	8.7	8.7	n	13.2	14.9	14.6	27.0	12.2	14.6	14.3	27.0

1. Includes only general programmes in lower and upper secondary education.
2. Upper secondary includes post-secondary non-tertiary education.
3. Lower secondary includes primary education.
4. Upper secondary education includes programmes from post-secondary education.
5. Upper secondary education includes tertiary-type B education.
6. Includes only general programmes in upper secondary education.
Source: OECD. See Annex 3 for notes (*www.oecd.org/edu/eag2008*).
Please refer to the Reader's Guide for information concerning the symbols replacing missing data.
StatLink ⌗ http://dx.doi.org/10.1787/402267680060

HOW MUCH ARE TEACHERS PAID?

This indicator shows the starting, mid-career and maximum statutory salaries of teachers in public primary and secondary education, and various additional payments and incentive schemes used to reward teachers. Together with teachers' working and teaching time (see Indicator D4), this indicator presents some key measures of teachers' working lives. Differences in teachers' salaries, along with other factors such as student-to-staff ratios (see Indicator D2), provide some explanation of the differences in expenditure per student (see Indicators B1 and B7).

Key results

Chart D3.1. **Teachers' salaries in lower secondary education (2006)**

Annual statutory teachers' salaries in public institutions in lower secondary education, in equivalent USD converted using PPPs, and the ratio of salary after 15 years of experience to GDP per capita

Salaries of teachers with at least 15 years' experience at the lower secondary level range from less than USD 15 000 in Hungary and in partner countries Chile and Estonia, to USD 51 000 or more in Germany, Korea and Switzerland, and exceed USD 90 000 in Luxembourg.

Equivalent USD converted using PPPs

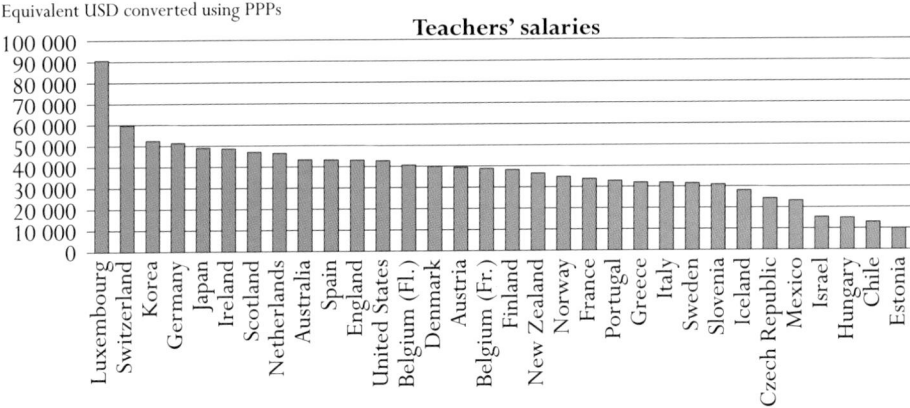

Salaries for teachers with at least 15 years' experience in lower secondary education are over twice the GDP per capita in Korea, whereas in Norway, and in partner countries Estonia and Israel, salaries are 75% or less than GDP per capita.

Countries are ranked in descending order of teachers' salaries in lower secondary education after 15 years of experience and minimum training.

Source: OECD. Table D3.1. See Annex 3 for notes (*www.oecd.org/edu/eag2008*).

StatLink ᐧᐧᐧ http://dx.doi.org/10.1787/402280862627

■ Teachers' salaries have risen in real terms between 1996 and 2006 in virtually all countries, with the largest increases in Finland, Hungary and Mexico (and in starting salaries in Australia) and in partner country Estonia. Salaries at the primary and upper secondary levels in Spain fell in real terms over the period, although they remain above the OECD average.

■ On average in OECD countries, upper secondary teachers' salaries per teaching hour exceed those of primary teachers by 44%; the difference is 5% or less in New Zealand, Scotland and the partner country Chile and is equal to or greater than 75% in Denmark and the Netherlands.

■ Salaries at the top of the scale are on average around 70% higher than starting salaries for both primary and secondary education, although this differential largely varies among countries in line with the number of years it takes to progress through the scale. Top-of-the-scale salaries in Korea are almost three times the starting salaries, but it takes 37 years to reach the top of the scale. In Portugal, while the ratio is similar to Korea's, teachers reach the top of the salary scale after 26 years of service. However, not all teachers reach the top of the salary scale. For example, in the Netherlands there are three different salary levels for teachers in secondary education. In 2006 only 14.8% of the teachers in secondary education were at the maximum salary level.

INDICATOR D3

D3

Policy context

Teachers' salaries are the largest single cost in school education. Compensation is therefore a critical consideration for policy makers seeking to maintain both the quality of teaching and a balanced education budget (see Indicator B6). The size of education budgets naturally reflects trade-offs among many related factors: teachers' salaries, ratio of students to teaching staff, instruction time planned for students and designated number of teaching hours.

Ensuring a sufficient number of skilled teachers is a key issue in all OECD countries. In a competitive labour market, the equilibrium rate of salaries paid to different types of teachers would reflect the supply of and demand for those teachers. This is often not the case in OECD countries, as salaries and other conditions are often set centrally for all teachers. Teachers' salaries and conditions are therefore policy malleable factors that can affect both the demand for and supply of teachers. In addition, salaries and working conditions can be important in attracting, developing and retaining skilled and effective teachers.

Comparing salary levels at different career points allows for some analysis of the structure of careers and the salary associated with advancement in the teaching profession. Theoretically, the salary structure can provide salary incentives and rewards so as to attract high-quality teachers and increase their job satisfaction and performance. Other important aspects of the career structure are probationary periods at the beginning of teachers' careers and the issue of tenure (see Indicator D3 in *Education at Glance 2007*). Salary increases can be concentrated at different points in the salary structure, for example, early in the career or for more experienced employees, or can have a more linear structure, with gradual salary increases throughout a career.

Evidence and explanations

Comparing teachers' salaries

This indicator compares the starting, mid-career and maximum statutory salaries of teachers with the minimum level of qualifications required for certification in public primary and secondary education. First, teachers' salaries are examined in absolute terms at three career points: starting, mid-career and top-of-the-scale. Next, levels of salaries are compared in relative terms. At last, changes in these salaries between 1996 and 2006 are presented.

International comparisons of salaries provide simplified illustrations of the compensation received by teachers for their work. They provide a snapshot of the systems of compensation and the welfare inferences that can be made. Large differences in taxation and social benefit systems in OECD countries as well as the use of financial incentives (including regional allowances for teaching in remote regions, family allowances, reduced rates on public transport, tax allowances on purchases of cultural goods, and other quasi-pecuniary entitlements that contribute to a teacher's basic income) make it important to exercise caution in interpreting comparisons of teachers' salaries.

Statutory salaries as reported here must be distinguished from actual expenditures on wages by governments and from teachers' average salaries, which are also influenced by factors such as the age structure of the teaching force and the prevalence of part-time work. Indicator B6 shows the total amounts paid in compensation to teachers. Furthermore, since teaching time, teachers' workloads and the proportion of teachers in part-time employment vary considerably among countries, these factors should be taken into account when using comparisons of statutory salaries to judge teachers' overall benefits in different countries (see Indicator D4).

Chart D3.2. Teachers' salaries (minimum, after 15 years of experience, and maximum) in lower secondary education (2006)

Annual statutory teachers' salaries in public institutions in lower secondary education, in equivalent USD converted using PPPs, and the ratio of salary after 15 years of experience to GDP per capita

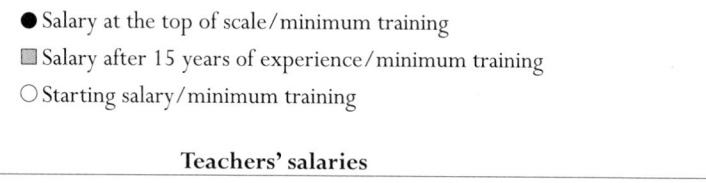

● Salary at the top of scale / minimum training
▨ Salary after 15 years of experience / minimum training
○ Starting salary / minimum training

D3

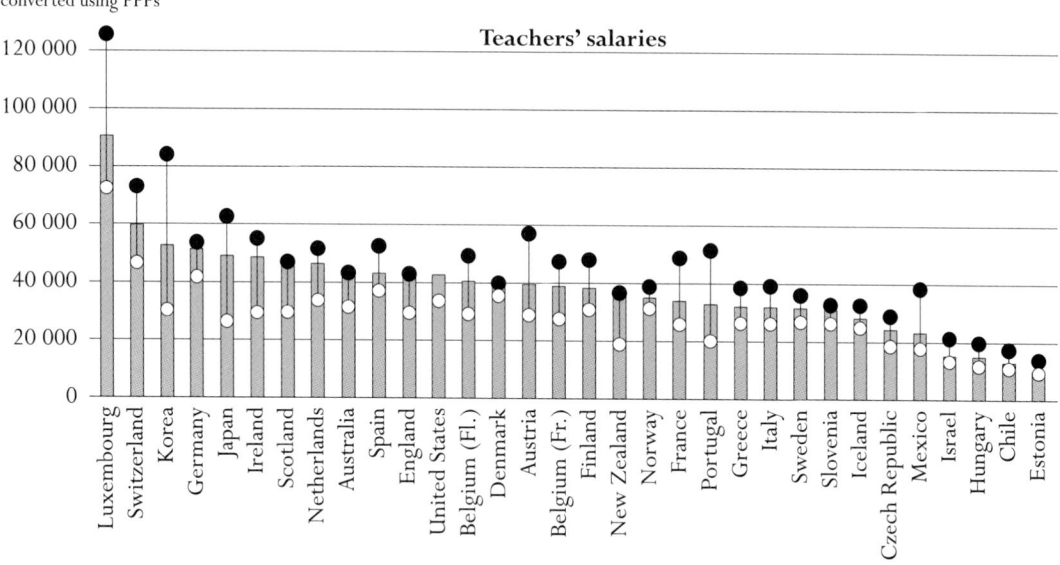

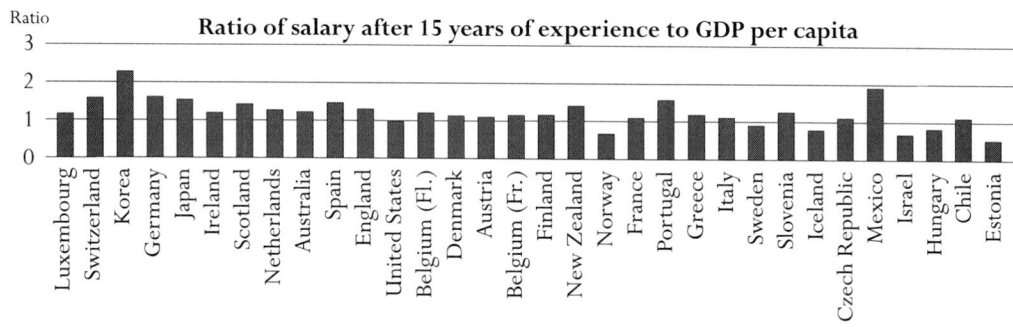

Countries are ranked in descending order of teachers' salaries in lower secondary education after 15 years of experience and minimum training.

Source: OECD. Table D3.1. See Annex 3 for notes (*www.oecd.org/edu/eag2008*).

StatLink ᐧᐧᐧ http://dx.doi.org/10.1787/402280862627

When considering the salary structure of teachers it is also important to recall that not all teachers reach the top of the salary scale. For example, in the Netherlands there are three different salary levels for teachers in secondary education. In 2006 only 14.8% of the teachers in secondary education were at the maximum salary level.

The annual statutory salaries of lower secondary teachers with 15 years of experience range from less than USD 15 000 in Hungary and in the partner countries Chile and Estonia to over USD 51 000 in Germany, Korea and Switzerland and exceed USD 90 000 in Luxembourg (Table D3.1).

D3

In most OECD countries, teachers' salaries increase with the level of education at which they teach. For example, in Belgium (Fl.), Belgium (Fr.), Luxembourg, the Netherlands and Switzerland, the salary of an upper secondary teacher with at least 15 years experience is at least 25% higher than that of a primary school teacher with the same experience. In contrast, in Australia, the Czech Republic, England, Greece, Ireland, Japan, Korea, New Zealand, Portugal, Scotland, Turkey and the United States, and in the partner countries Chile, Estonia, Israel and Slovenia, upper secondary and primary teachers' salaries are more comparable (a difference of less than 5%, see Table D3.1). The extent of the variation is influenced by the structure of teachers' salaries up to the mid-career point. In countries such as the United States, teachers' salaries are also influenced by the teachers' educational attainment. As this is not constant at all levels of teachers' careers, care should be taken in interpreting the differences in teachers' salaries at different levels of school education.

Comparatively large differences in teachers' salaries at different levels may influence how schools and school systems attract and retain teachers of different levels. It may also influence the extent to which teachers move among different educational levels and with that, the degree of segmentation in the labour market for teachers.

Statutory salaries relative to GDP per capita

Countries invest in teaching resources relative to their ability to fund educational expenditure, among other things. Comparing statutory salaries to GDP per capita is thus a way of assessing the relative value of teachers' salaries. Comparative data on salaries for comparable professions would provide a better benchmark, but since such data are not yet available, comparisons with GDP per capita provide some basis for standardised comparisons.

Relative to GDP per capita, salaries for teachers with at least 15 years of experience (in primary and lower secondary education) are relatively low in Hungary (0.82), Iceland (0.79), Norway (0.67), Sweden (0.88 in primary, 0.91 in lower secondary) and in the partner countries Estonia (0.52) and Israel (0.68). They are highest in Korea (2.29 in primary, 2.28 in lower secondary) and Mexico (1.91 in lower secondary). In upper secondary general education, the lowest ratios are found in Norway (0.72) and in the partner countries Estonia (0.52) and Israel (0.68). Relative to GDP per capita, mid-career salaries are highest in Korea (2.28) (Table D3.1).

Countries such as the Czech Republic, Hungary, Mexico and Turkey, as well as the partner countries Chile, Estonia and Israel, have both comparatively low GDP per capita and low teachers' salaries compared to OECD averages. Others, such as Korea, New Zealand, Portugal and Spain, have GDP per capita lower than the average but teachers' salaries that are comparable to those in countries with much higher GDP per capita. Germany, Luxembourg and Switzerland have a higher GDP per capita than the OECD average and high teachers' salaries (Chart D3.2 and Table D3.1), whereas Norway has higher GDP per capita than the OECD average but average mid-career salaries.

Statutory salaries per hour of net teaching time

An alternative measure of salaries that better illustrates the overall cost of classroom teaching time is the statutory salary for a full-time classroom teacher relative to the number of hours per year that a teacher is required to spend teaching students (see Indicator D4). Although this

D3

measure does not adjust salaries for the amount of time that teachers spend in other various teaching-related activities, it nonetheless provides an approximate estimate of the cost of the actual time teachers spend in the classroom.

The average statutory salary per teaching hour after 15 years of experience is USD 46 in primary, USD 58 in lower secondary, and USD 68 in upper secondary general education. In primary education, the Czech Republic, Hungary, Mexico and Turkey, and the partner countries Chile, Estonia and Israel, have the lowest salary costs per teaching hour (USD 30 or less). By contrast, salaries are relatively high in Denmark, Germany, Korea and Luxembourg (USD 60 or more). There is even more variation in salaries per teaching hour in general upper secondary education, ranging from about USD 25 or less in Turkey, and in the partner countries Chile, Estonia and Israel, to USD 80 or more in Belgium (Fl.), Belgium (Fr.), Denmark, Korea, Luxembourg and the Netherlands (Table D3.1).

As secondary teachers are required to teach fewer hours than primary teachers, their salaries per teaching hour are usually higher than those of teachers at lower levels, even in countries where statutory salaries are similar (see Indicator D4). On average among OECD countries, upper secondary teachers' salaries per teaching hour exceed those of primary teachers by around 44%. In New Zealand and Scotland and in the partner country Chile, this difference is 5% or less, but it is 60% or more in France and Hungary, over 80% in the Netherlands and more than 100% in Denmark (Table D3.1). However, the large difference between primary and upper secondary teachers' salaries per teaching hour does not necessarily exist when comparing salaries per hour of working time. In Portugal, for example, where there is a large difference in salaries per teaching hour between primary and upper secondary teachers, the difference between teaching time at the primary and upper secondary level is among the greatest in OECD countries, even though their statutory salaries and working time at school are the same (Table D4.1).

Teaching experience and qualifications influence teachers' salary scales

Salary structures illustrate the salary incentives available to teachers at different points in their careers. There is some evidence that a sizeable proportion of teachers and school administrators do not want to move to higher positions in the hierarchy in schools (*e.g.* to school principal) (OECD, 2005b). Presumably, this is because the negative aspects of a promotion outweigh positive aspects such as increased salaries, prestige and other rewards. If this is the case, then changes can make the promotion more attractive either through changing the duties and requirements of the position or by changing the salary amount and other rewards offered.

As Table D3.1 shows, OECD data on teachers' salaries are limited to information on statutory salaries at three points of the salary scale: starting salaries, salaries after 15 years of service and salaries at the top of the scale. These salaries are those of teachers with the minimum required training. They must be interpreted with caution as further qualifications can lead to additional wage increases in some OECD countries. Some inferences can be drawn from the data on the degree that salary structures for teachers provide salary increases with different levels of promotion and tenure.

Deferred compensation is a key incentive for workers in many industries. Organisations can design complex deferred compensation schemes to attract high-quality workers and then provide

D3

them with appropriate incentives throughout their careers. Deferred compensation rewards employees for staying in organisations or professions and for meeting established performance criteria. Pensions are an important form of deferred compensation. In most OECD countries, teachers receive some pension that accrues with their experience in the teaching profession. However, pension schemes are not considered here.

Deferred compensation exists in teachers' salary structure. In OECD countries, statutory salaries for primary, lower and upper secondary general teachers with 15 years of experience are, on average, 37, 37 and 41% higher, respectively, than starting salaries. The increases from starting salary to the top of the salary scale are, on average, 71, 71 and 72%. For lower secondary teachers, the average starting salary is USD 30 047. With minimum training, it rises to USD 40 682 after 15 years and to USD 49 778 at the top of the salary scale, which is reached, on average, after 24 years of experience. A similar increase is therefore evident between first, the starting salary and that at 15 years of experience and second, the salary at 15 years of experience and at the top of the salary scale (reached, on average, after 24 years of experience).

Salary structures differ widely. A number of countries have relatively flat structures with small increases. For example, teachers at the top of the salary scale in Denmark (except at the upper secondary level), Germany, Norway and Turkey, and in the partner country Slovenia, only earn up to 30% more than teachers at the bottom of the salary scale.

Salary increases between the points on a salary structure should be seen in terms of the number of years it takes for a teacher to advance through the salary scale, a factor which varies substantially across countries. In lower secondary education, teachers in Australia, Denmark, New Zealand and Scotland reach the highest step on the salary scale within five to nine years. Monetary incentives therefore disappear relatively quickly compared to other countries. If job satisfaction and performance are determined, at least in part, by prospects of salary increases difficulties may arise as teachers approach the peak in their age-earnings profiles.

In Austria, the Czech Republic, France, Greece, Hungary, Italy, Japan, Korea, Luxembourg and Spain, and in the partner country Israel, teachers in lower secondary education reach the top of the salary scale after 30 or more years of service (Table D3.1). It is difficult to categorise countries simply by steep or flat salary structures. A number of countries have both steep and flat portions that vary across teachers' tenure. For example, teachers in Germany and Luxembourg have the opportunity for similar salary increases in the first 15 years but then face very different growth rates: in Luxembourg salaries rise faster, while in Germany increases are relatively small. Policy makers in these countries face different issues for these more experienced teachers.

While the salary opportunities available to teachers are emphasised here, there may also be benefits to compression in pay scales. It is often argued that organisations in which employees have smaller salary differences have greater levels of trust and information flows and a higher degree of collegiality. These benefits need to be weighed against the benefits of salary incentives.

Teachers' salaries between 1996 and 2006

In comparing the index of change between 1996 and 2006 in teachers' salaries, it is evident that salaries have grown in real terms at both primary and secondary levels in virtually all countries. The biggest increases at all levels have taken place in Hungary, although salaries remain below the OECD average. In some countries, salaries fell in real terms between 1996 and 2006, most notably at the primary and upper secondary levels in Spain (Table D3.2 and Chart D3.3), although they remain above the OECD average.

Salary trends have also varied at different points on the salary scale. For instance, starting salaries have risen faster than mid-career or top-of-the-scale salaries for all education levels in Australia, Denmark, England and Scotland. By contrast, salaries of teachers with at least 15 years of experience have risen relatively more quickly than both starting and top-of-the-scale salaries in Japan, the Netherlands and Portugal. In Finland and Greece and in partner country Estonia, top-of-the-scale salaries have risen faster than starting and mid-career salaries. In New Zealand, the top-of-the-scale salary has risen faster than the starting salary and in the same proportion as the salary of teachers with at least 15 years of experience. However, with a relatively short salary scale (eight years to reach the top), recruitment is a key issue in New Zealand. This may be an issue in Australia as well, as starting salaries have risen considerably. A potential problem is the fact that if teachers are attracted by higher salaries in the early stages of their careers, they may expect salary increases to continue throughout their careers. Using resources to attract more early-career teachers to the profession needs to be weighed against potential implications in terms of retention and reduced satisfaction and motivation. Moreover, comparing changes in salaries at three points of the salary structure may not account for changes in other aspects of the structure of teachers' salaries.

Chart D3.3. **Changes in teachers' salaries in lower secondary education, by point in the salary scale (1996, 2006)**

Index of change between 1996 and 2006 (1996=100, 2006 price levels using GDP deflators)

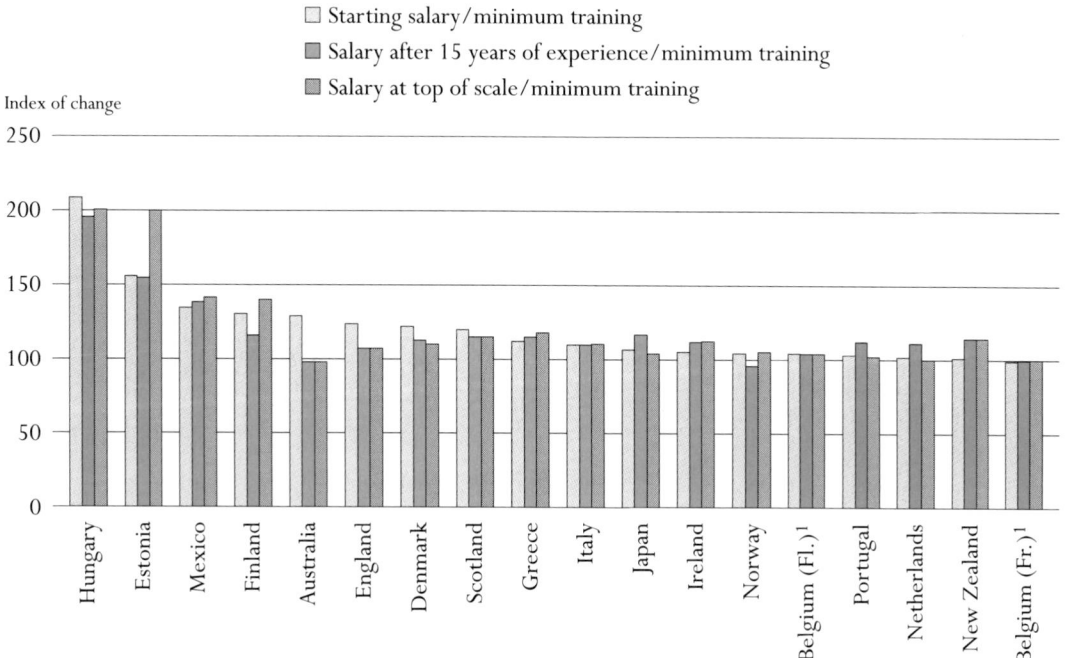

1. The 1996 data for Belgium are based on Belgium as a whole.
Countries are ranked in descending order of index of change between 1996 and 2006 in teachers' starting salaries.
Source: OECD. Table D3.2. See Annex 3 for notes (*www.oecd.org/edu/eag2008*).
StatLink http://dx.doi.org/10.1787/402280862627

D3

Additional payments: incentives and allowances

In addition to basic pay scales, many school systems have schemes that offer additional payments for teachers, which may take the form of financial remuneration and/or reduction in the number of teaching hours. Greece and Iceland, for example, use a reduction in required teaching hours to reward experience or long service, and in Portugal, teachers may receive a reduction of their teaching hours for carrying out special tasks or activities (*e.g.* leading a drama club, acting as a supervisor of student teachers, etc.). Together with the starting salary, such payments may affect a person's decision to enter or stay in the teaching profession. Early-career additional payments may include family allowances and bonuses for working in certain locations, and higher initial salaries for higher-than-minimum teaching certification or qualifications, such as qualifications in multiple subjects or certification to teach students with special educational needs.

Adjustments to the base salary may be awarded to teachers yearly or on an incidental basis in public schools either by the head teacher or school principal, or by the local, regional or national government. A distinction is made between an addition to teachers' base salary, a yearly payment and an incidental or "one-off" payment. As may be expected, additional payments based on years of experience are made in virtually all OECD countries through changes to teachers' base salary. Additional payments made for specific teaching conditions or responsibilities are more commonly made through yearly or incidental payments. The key exception is for teachers who assume management responsibilities with additional payments offered more frequently through changes to base salaries as well as yearly and incidental payments.

Types of additional payments

Data on additional payments fall into three broad areas:

- Those based on responsibilities assumed by teachers and on particular conditions (*e.g.* additional management responsibilities or teaching in high-need regions, disadvantaged schools).

- Those based on the demographic characteristics of teachers (*e.g.* age and/or family status).

- Those based on teachers' qualifications, training and performance (*e.g.* higher than the minimum qualifications and/or completing professional development activities).

Data have not been collected on payment amounts but on whether they are available and on the level at which the decision to award such payments is taken (see Table D3.3a and Tables D3.3b, D3.3c and D3.3d available on line, as well as Annex 3 at *www.oecd.org/edu/eag2008*).

Additional payments are most often awarded for particular responsibilities or working conditions, such as teaching in more disadvantaged schools, particularly those located in very poor neighbourhoods or with a large proportion of students whose language is not the language of instruction. Such teachers face demands that teachers elsewhere may not encounter. These schools often have difficulty attracting teachers and are often more likely to have less experienced teachers (OECD, 2005b). These additional payments are provided yearly in about two-thirds of OECD and partner countries. Ten countries also offer additional payments for teachers who teach in certain fields in which there are shortages of teachers and are made yearly in almost all of these countries.

Over half of OECD countries offer additional payments based on teachers' demographic characteristics and in most cases these are yearly payments. Additional payments based on teachers' qualifications, training and performance are also very common in OECD countries and partner countries. The most common types of payments based on teachers' initial education and qualifications are for an initial education qualification higher than the minimum requirement and/or a level of teacher certification and training higher than the minimum requirements. These are available in nearly half of OECD countries and partner countries with one-third offering both types; they are used in nearly all countries as criteria for base salary. Fifteen OECD countries and partner countries offer additional payments for the successful completion of professional development activities. In two-thirds of these, they are used as criteria for the base salary, but in Korea and Turkey they are only offered on an incidental basis.

Fifteen OECD countries and three partner countries offer an additional payment for outstanding performance in teaching. This is the only additional payment that may be classified as a performance incentive. In half of these countries they are incidental payments, and in the other half, they are mostly yearly additions to teachers' salaries. In 12 of the 18 countries that offer this incentive (Austria, the Czech Republic, Denmark, England, Finland, Hungary, Mexico, the Netherlands, New Zealand, Sweden and Turkey and the partner country Slovenia), the decision to award the additional payments can be made at the school level.

The method for identifying outstanding performance and the form of incentive varies. In Mexico, outstanding performance is calculated on the basis of students' achievements and criteria relating to teachers' experience, performance and qualification. In Portugal, it is based on the assessment of the head teacher and in Turkey on assessments by the provincial directorate of education and the Ministry of Education.

As may be expected, additional payments made due to the years of experience are, in virtually all OECD countries, made through changes to teachers' base salary. Additional payments made for specific teaching conditions or responsibilities are more commonly made through yearly or incidental payments. The key exception is when a teacher assumes management responsibilities with additional payments offered more frequently through changes to base salaries as well as yearly and incidental payments.

A mixture of all three types of additional payment are offered in relation to teachers' qualifications, training and performance. Given that an initial teacher qualification higher than the minimum requirement is often identified at the beginning of a teacher's career, it is not surprising that it is more often provided through changes to teachers' base salaries. Additional payments due to teacher demographics are mainly made through additional yearly payments in 11 of the 15 countries offering a form of additional payment in this category.

Definitions and methodologies

Data on statutory teachers' salaries and bonuses are derived from the 2007 OECD-INES Survey on Teachers and the Curriculum. Data refer to the school year 2005/06, and are reported in accordance with formal policies for public institutions.

Statutory salaries (Table D3.1) refer to scheduled salaries according to official pay scales. The salaries reported are gross (total sum paid by the employer) less the employer's contribution to social security and pension (according to existing salary scales). Salaries are "before tax" (*i.e.* before deductions for income taxes). In Table D3.1, salary per hour of net contact divides a teacher's annual statutory salary (Table D3.1) by the annual net teaching time in hours (Table D4.1).

Gross teachers' salaries were converted using GDP and purchasing power parities (PPPs) and exchange rate data from the OECD National Accounts database. The reference date for GDP per capita is the calendar year 2006, while the period of reference for teachers' salaries is 30 June 2005 to 30 June 2006. The reference date for PPPs is 2005/06. Data are adjusted for inflation with reference to January 2006. For countries with different financial years (*i.e.* Australia and New Zealand) and countries with slightly different salary periods (*e.g.* Hungary, Iceland, Norway and Spain) from the general OECD norm, a correction to the deflator is made only if this results in an adjustment of over 1%. Small adjustments have been discounted because even for salaries for 2004/05, the exact period to which they apply, is only slightly different. Reference statistics and reference years for teachers' salaries are provided in Annex 2.

For the calculation of changes in teachers' salaries (Table D3.2), the GDP deflator is used to convert 1996 salaries to 2006 prices.

Starting salaries refer to the average scheduled gross salary per year for a full-time teacher with the minimum training necessary to be fully qualified at the beginning of the teaching career.

Salaries after 15 years of experience refer to the scheduled annual salary of a full-time classroom teacher with the minimum training necessary to be fully qualified plus 15 years of experience. The maximum salaries reported refer to the scheduled maximum annual salary (top of the salary scale) of a full-time classroom teacher with the minimum training to be fully qualified for the job.

An adjustment to base salary is defined as any difference in salary between what a particular teacher actually receives for work performed at a school and the amount that he or she would expect to receive on the basis of experience (*i.e.* number of years in the teaching profession). Adjustments may be temporary or permanent, and they can effectively move a teacher off the scale and to a different salary scale or to a higher step on the same salary scale.

Further references

The following additional material relevant to this indicator is available on line at:

StatLink 🔗 http://dx.doi.org/10.1787/402280862627

- *Table D3.3b. Adjustments to base salary for teachers in public schools made by head teacher / school principal (2006)*

- *Table D3.3c. Adjustments to base salary for teachers in public schools made by local or regional authority (2006)*

- *Table D3.3d. Adjustments to base salary for teachers in public schools made by national authority (2006)*

See also: OECD (2005b), *Teachers Matter: Attracting, Developing and Retaining Effective Teachers*, OECD, Paris.

Specific notes on definitions and methodologies regarding this indicator for each country are given in Annex 3 at *www.oecd.org / edu / eag2008*.

In addition, a more comprehensive analysis of decision making is available in Indicator D6.

As a complement to Table D3.1, which presents teachers' salaries in equivalent USD converted using PPPs, a table with teachers' salaries in equivalent EUR converted using PPPs is included in Annex 2.

D3

Table D3.1.
Teachers' salaries (2006)
Annual statutory teachers' salaries in public institutions at starting salary, after 15 years of experience and at the top of the scale, by level of education, in equivalent USD converted using PPPs

D3

		Primary education				Lower secondary education				Upper secondary education			
		Starting salary/ minimum training	Salary after 15 years of experience/ minimum training	Salary at top of scale/ minimum training	Ratio of salary after 15 years of experience to GDP per capita	Starting salary/ minimum training	Salary after 15 years of experience/ minimum training	Salary at top of scale/ minimum training	Ratio of salary after 15 years of experience to GDP per capita	Starting salary/ minimum training	Salary after 15 years of experience/ minimum training	Salary at top of scale/ minimum training	Ratio of salary after 15 years of experience to GDP per capita
		(1)	(2)	(3)	(4)	(5)	(6)	(7)	(8)	(9)	(10)	(11)	(12)
OECD countries	Australia	31 171	42 688	42 688	1.20	31 346	43 289	43 289	1.22	31 346	43 289	43 289	1.22
	Austria	27 649	36 580	54 914	1.02	28 860	39 424	57 141	1.10	29 186	40 404	59 958	1.13
	Belgium (Fl.)	29 029	40 557	49 392	1.21	29 029	40 557	49 392	1.21	35 960	51 799	62 214	1.54
	Belgium (Fr.)	27 551	38 813	47 506	1.16	27 551	38 813	47 506	1.16	34 290	49 874	60 122	1.49
	Czech Republic	18 591	24 340	28 974	1.11	18 591	24 340	28 974	1.11	18 824	24 685	29 428	1.12
	Denmark	35 368	39 898	39 898	1.13	35 368	39 898	39 898	1.13	35 287	49 634	49 634	1.41
	England	29 460	43 058	43 058	1.31	29 460	43 058	43 058	1.31	29 460	43 058	43 058	1.31
	Finland	27 708	35 798	45 164	1.09	30 793	38 269	48 192	1.17	30 962	42 440	53 867	1.30
	France	23 317	31 366	46 280	1.01	25 798	33 846	48 882	1.09	26 045	34 095	49 155	1.10
	Germany	40 277	50 119	52 259	1.57	41 787	51 435	53 696	1.61	45 193	55 404	57 890	1.73
	Greece	26 262	32 030	38 525	1.18	26 262	32 030	38 525	1.18	26 262	32 030	38 525	1.18
	Hungary	11 788	14 976	19 839	0.82	11 788	14 976	19 839	0.82	13 114	17 921	24 240	0.99
	Iceland	24 951	28 097	32 705	0.79	24 951	28 097	32 705	0.79	27 863	34 127	36 264	0.95
	Ireland	29 370	48 653	55 132	1.19	29 370	48 653	55 132	1.19	29 370	48 653	55 132	1.19
	Italy	24 211	29 287	35 686	1.01	26 084	31 890	39 162	1.10	26 084	32 781	40 934	1.14
	Japan	26 256	49 097	62 645	1.54	26 256	49 097	62 645	1.54	26 256	49 097	64 499	1.54
	Korea	30 528	52 666	84 263	2.29	30 405	52 543	84 139	2.28	30 405	52 543	84 139	2.28
	Luxembourg	50 301	69 269	102 519	0.89	72 466	90 582	125 895	1.16	72 466	90 582	125 895	1.16
	Mexico	13 834	18 200	30 193	1.50	17 736	23 161	38 325	1.91	m	m	m	m
	Netherlands	32 494	42 199	47 125	1.15	33 685	46 417	51 705	1.27	34 017	62 073	68 446	1.70
	New Zealand	18 920	36 602	36 602	1.41	18 920	36 602	36 602	1.41	18 920	36 602	36 602	1.41
	Norway	31 256	34 917	38 887	0.67	31 256	34 917	38 887	0.67	33 453	37 626	40 785	0.72
	Poland	m	m	m	m	m	m	m	m	m	m	m	m
	Portugal	20 072	32 866	51 552	1.58	20 072	32 866	51 552	1.58	20 072	32 866	51 552	1.58
	Scotland	29 498	47 050	47 050	1.43	29 498	47 050	47 050	1.43	29 498	47 050	47 050	1.43
	Slovak Republic	m	m	m	m	m	m	m	m	m	m	m	m
	Spain	33 024	38 483	47 695	1.31	37 153	43 171	52 691	1.47	37 957	44 146	53 782	1.50
	Sweden	26 217	30 782	35 728	0.88	26 739	31 565	36 130	0.91	28 369	34 086	38 760	0.98
	Switzerland	40 338	52 191	64 057	1.38	46 550	59 781	72 993	1.58	54 042	70 346	82 954	1.86
	Turkey	12 670	14 138	15 780	1.61	a	a	a	a	12 670	14 138	15 780	1.61
	United States	34 895	42 404	m	0.97	33 546	42 775	m	0.98	33 695	42 727	m	0.98
	OECD average	*27 828*	*37 832*	*46 290*	*1.22*	*30 047*	*40 682*	*49 778*	*1.26*	*31 110*	*43 360*	*52 369*	*1.34*
	EU19 average	*28 536*	*38 217*	*46 752*	*1.16*	*30 545*	*40 465*	*49 180*	*1.21*	*31 706*	*43 873*	*53 139*	*1.31*
Partner countries	Brazil	m	m	m	m	m	m	m	m	m	m	m	m
	Chile	10 922	12 976	17 500	1.11	10 922	12 976	17 500	1.11	10 922	13 579	18 321	1.16
	Estonia	9 473	10 047	13 922	0.52	9 473	10 047	13 922	0.52	9 473	10 047	13 922	0.52
	Israel	13 257	15 311	21 389	0.68	13 257	15 311	21 389	0.68	13 257	15 311	21 389	0.68
	Russian Federation	m	m	m	m	m	m	m	m	m	m	m	m
	Slovenia	26 309	30 924	32 819	1.26	26 309	30 924	32 819	1.26	26 309	30 924	32 819	1.26

Source: OECD. See Annex 3 for notes (*www.oecd.org/edu/eag2008*).
Please refer to the Reader's Guide for information concerning the symbols replacing missing data.
StatLink ☞☞ http://dx.doi.org/10.1787/402280862627

D3

Table D3.1. *(continued)*
Teachers' salaries (2006)
Annual statutory teachers' salaries in public institutions at starting salary, after 15 years of experience and at the top of the scale,
by level of education, in equivalent USD converted using PPPs

		Ratio of salary at top of scale to starting salary			Years from starting to top salary (lower secondary education)	Salary per hour of net contact (teaching) time after 15 years of experience			Ratio of salary per teaching hour of upper secondary to primary teachers (after 15 years of experience)
		Primary education	Lower secondary education	Upper secondary education		Primary education	Lower secondary education	Upper secondary education	
		(1)	(2)	(3)	(4)	(5)	(6)	(7)	(8)
OECD countries	Australia	1.37	1.38	1.38	9	48	53	53	1.10
	Austria	1.99	1.98	2.05	34	47	65	69	1.45
	Belgium (Fl.)	1.70	1.70	1.73	27	51	59	81	1.59
	Belgium (Fr.)	1.72	1.72	1.75	27	54	59	83	1.54
	Czech Republic	1.56	1.56	1.56	32	29	38	40	1.42
	Denmark	1.13	1.13	1.41	8	62	62	136	2.21
	England	1.46	1.46	1.46	10	m	m	m	m
	Finland	1.63	1.57	1.74	16	53	65	78	1.46
	France	1.98	1.89	1.89	34	34	53	55	1.61
	Germany	1.30	1.28	1.28	28	62	68	78	1.25
	Greece	1.47	1.47	1.47	33	43	64	67	1.57
	Hungary	1.68	1.68	1.85	40	19	27	32	1.68
	Iceland	1.31	1.31	1.30	18	42	42	61	1.46
	Ireland	1.88	1.88	1.88	22	53	66	66	1.25
	Italy	1.47	1.50	1.57	35	40	53	55	1.37
	Japan	2.39	2.39	2.46	31	m	m	m	m
	Korea	2.76	2.77	2.77	37	66	96	95	1.45
	Luxembourg	2.04	1.74	1.74	30	89	141	141	1.58
	Mexico	2.18	2.16	m	14	23	22	m	m
	Netherlands	1.45	1.53	2.01	17	45	62	83	1.82
	New Zealand	1.93	1.93	1.93	8	37	38	39	1.04
	Norway	1.24	1.24	1.22	16	47	53	72	1.53
	Poland	m	m	m	m	m	m	m	m
	Portugal	2.57	2.57	2.57	26	38	43	48	1.25
	Scotland	1.60	1.60	1.60	6	53	53	53	1.00
	Slovak Republic	m	m	m	m	m	m	m	m
	Spain	1.44	1.42	1.42	38	44	61	64	1.46
	Sweden	m	m	m	a	m	m	m	m
	Switzerland	1.59	1.57	1.54	26	m	m	m	m
	Turkey	1.25	a	1.25	a	22	a	25	1.13
	United States	m	m	m	m	w	w	w	w
	OECD average	*1.71*	*1.71*	*1.72*	*24*	*46*	*58*	*68*	*1.44*
	EU19 average	*1.67*	*1.65*	*1.72*	*26*	*48*	*61*	*72*	*1.50*
Partner countries	Brazil	m	m	m	m	m	m	m	m
	Chile	1.60	1.60	1.68	m	15	15	16	1.05
	Estonia	1.47	1.47	1.47	m	16	16	17	1.09
	Israel	1.61	1.61	1.61	36	15	19	23	1.54
	Russian Federation	m	m	m	m	m	m	m	m
	Slovenia	1.25	1.25	1.25	13	44	44	48	1.09

Note: Ratio of salary at the top of the scale to starting salary has not been calculated for Sweden because the underlying salaries are estimates derived from actual rather than statutory salaries.

Source: OECD. See Annex 3 for notes (*www.oecd.org/edu/eag2008*).

Please refer to the Reader's Guide for information concerning the symbols replacing missing data.

StatLink http://dx.doi.org/10.1787/402280862627

Table D3.2.
Change in teachers' salaries (1996 and 2006)
Index of change[1] between 1996 and 2006 in teachers' salaries at starting salary, after 15 years of experience and at the top of the salary scale, by level of education, converted to 2006 price levels using GDP deflators (1996=100)

	Primary education			Lower secondary education			Upper secondary education, general programmes		
	Starting salary/ minimum training	Salary after 15 years of experience/ minimum training	Salary at top of scale/ minimum training	Starting salary/ minimum training	Salary after 15 years of experience/ minimum training	Salary at top of scale/ minimum training	Starting salary/ minimum training	Salary after 15 years of experience/ minimum training	Salary at top of scale/ minimum training
	(1)	(2)	(3)	(4)	(5)	(6)	(7)	(8)	(9)
OECD countries									
Australia	128	97	97	129	98	98	129	98	98
Austria	m	m	m	m	m	m	m	m	m
Belgium (Fl.)[2]	107	111	114	104	104	104	104	104	104
Belgium (Fr.)[2]	101	106	109	99	100	100	99	100	100
Czech Republic	w	w	w	w	w	w	w	w	w
Denmark	122	113	110	122	113	110	112	110	105
England	124	107	107	124	107	107	124	107	107
Finland	132	129	158	130	116	140	127	123	148
France	w	w	w	w	w	w	w	w	w
Germany	w	w	w	w	w	w	w	w	w
Greece	116	118	121	112	115	118	112	115	118
Hungary	209	196	201	209	196	201	182	189	204
Iceland	m	m	m	m	m	m	m	m	m
Ireland	111	118	113	105	112	112	105	112	112
Italy	111	111	111	110	110	110	110	110	110
Japan	107	117	104	107	117	104	107	117	104
Korea	w	w	w	w	w	w	w	w	w
Luxembourg	m	m	m	m	m	m	m	m	m
Mexico	134	133	134	135	138	142	m	m	m
Netherlands	103	110	100	102	111	100	102	107	99
New Zealand	101	115	115	101	115	115	101	115	115
Norway	104	96	105	104	96	105	103	100	101
Poland	m	m	m	m	m	m	m	m	m
Portugal	103	112	102	103	112	102	103	112	102
Scotland	120	115	115	120	115	115	120	115	115
Slovak Republic	m	m	m	m	m	m	m	m	m
Spain	95	95	92	m	m	m	94	94	91
Sweden	w	w	w	w	w	w	w	w	w
Switzerland	99	96	102	m	m	m	m	m	m
Turkey	w	w	w	a	a	a	w	w	w
United States	m	m	m	m	m	m	m	m	m
Partner countries									
Brazil	m	m	m	m	m	m	m	m	m
Chile	m	m	m	m	m	m	m	m	m
Estonia	156	155	200	156	155	200	156	155	200
Israel	m	m	m	m	m	m	m	m	m
Russian Federation	m	m	m	m	m	m	m	m	m
Slovenia	m	m	m	m	m	m	m	m	m

1. The index is calculated as teacher salary 2006 in national currency * 100/Teacher salary 1996 in national currency * GDP deflator 2006 (1996=100). See Annex 2 for statistics on GDP deflators and salaries in national currencies in 1996 and 2006.
2. The data for 1996 are based on Belgium as a whole.
Source: OECD. See Annex 3 for notes (*www.oecd.org/edu/eag2008*).
Please refer to the Reader's Guide for information concerning the symbols replacing missing data.
StatLink 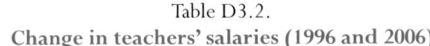 http://dx.doi.org/10.1787/402280862627

D3

Table D3.3a.

Decisions on payments for teachers in public institutions (2006)

Criteria for base salary and additional payments awarded to teachers in public institutions

	Experience	Criteria based on teaching conditions/responsibilities						
	Years of experience as a teacher	Management responsibilities in addition to teaching duties	Teaching more classes or hours than required by full-time contract	Special tasks (career guidance or counselling)	Teaching in a disadvantaged, remote or high cost area (location allowance)	Special activities (e.g. sports and drama clubs, homework clubs, summer school etc.)	Teaching students with special educational needs (in regular schools)	Teaching courses in a particular field
OECD countries								
Australia	−	−			▲		▲	
Austria	−	▲		▲	▲		△	
Belgium (Fl.)	−		△					
Belgium (Fr.)	−			▲				
Czech Republic	− ▲ △	− ▲ △	▲ △	▲ △		▲ △	− ▲ △	
Denmark	− ▲ △	− ▲ △	▲ △	▲ △	− ▲ △	▲ △	▲ △	▲ △
England	− ▲ △	− ▲ △			− ▲		▲	− ▲ △
Finland	▲	− ▲		▲ △	▲ △	▲ △	▲	− ▲ △
France	−	▲ △		▲ △	▲ △	− ▲	△	−
Germany	−	−		△				
Greece	−		△	△	▲			
Hungary	−	▲		▲	▲	▲	▲	△
Iceland	− ▲ △	− ▲ △	▲ △	▲ △		▲ △	− ▲ △	
Ireland	− ▲ △	− ▲			− ▲			
Italy	−		△	△	▲		△	
Japan	−	▲	▲		▲	▲	▲	
Korea	−	▲	△		△		▲	▲
Luxembourg	−		△		△			
Mexico	− ▲ △	− ▲	− ▲	− ▲	− ▲			− ▲
Netherlands	− ▲ △	− ▲ △	− ▲ △	− ▲ △	− ▲ △	− ▲ △	− ▲ △	− ▲ △
New Zealand	−	▲		▲	▲	▲	▲	▲
Norway	−	− ▲		△	▲	▲		−
Poland	m m m	m m m	m m m	m m m	m m m	m m m	m m m	m m m
Portugal	−	▲		△	▲		−	
Scotland	−				▲			
Slovak Republic	m m m	m m m	m m m	m m m	m m m	m m m	m m m	m m m
Spain	−	▲		▲	▲			
Sweden	−	−		△	−			−
Switzerland	−	−		△	△		△	−
Turkey	−		△	△	▲		△	
United States	−	▲			▲	▲		▲
Partner countries								
Brazil	m m m	m m m	m m m	m m m	m m m	m m m	m m m	m m m
Chile	−	▲			▲			
Estonia	m m m	m m m	m m m	m m m	m m m	m m m	m m m	m m m
Israel	−	−	−	−	−		−	
Slovenia	−	−		△	▲	△	▲	▲
Russian Federation	m m m	m m m	m m m	m m m	m m m	m m m	m m m	m m m

− : Base salary.
▲ : Additional yearly payment.
△ : Additional incidental payment.

Source: OECD. See Annex 3 for notes (*www.oecd.org/edu/eag2008*).

Please refer to the Reader's Guide for information concerning the symbols replacing missing data.

StatLink ᴍˢ⌐ http://dx.doi.org/10.1787/402280862627

D3

Table D3.3a. *(continued)*
Decisions on payments for teachers in public institutions (2006)
Criteria for base salary and additional payments awarded to teachers in public institutions

	Criteria related to teachers' qualifications, training and performance						Criteria based on demography		
	Holding an initial educational qualification higher than the minimum qualification required to enter the teaching profession	Holding a higher than minimum level of teacher certification or training obtained during professional life	Outstanding performance in teaching	Successful completion of professional development activities	Reaching high scores in the qualification examination	Holding an educational qualification in multiple subjects.	Family status (married, number of children)	Age (independent of years of teaching experience)	Other
OECD countries									
Australia	−	−					▲		
Austria			△				▲		▲
Belgium (Fl.)	−	▲							▲
Belgium (Fr.)									▲
Czech Republic			− ▲ △					− △	
Denmark	− ▲ △	− ▲ △	▲ △	▲ △		− ▲ △			
England	− ▲ △		− ▲ △						
Finland	− ▲		▲	▲		−			
France				−			▲		
Germany							−	−	
Greece	−	▲					▲		
Hungary	−		△ −			△			
Iceland	− ▲ △	− ▲ △	▲ △			△		− ▲	▲ △
Ireland	− ▲	− ▲							
Italy							−		
Japan							▲		▲
Korea			△	△			△	▲	
Luxembourg		−		−			▲	−	
Mexico	− ▲	− ▲	− ▲	− ▲	− ▲				
Netherlands	− ▲ △	− ▲ △	− ▲ △	− ▲ △	− ▲ △	− ▲ △			
New Zealand	−	−	▲						▲
Norway	−	−	△						
Poland	m m m	m m m	m m m m	m m m	m m m	m m m	m m m	m m m	m m m
Portugal	−	−	−	−	−		▲		
Scotland		−							
Slovak Republic	m m m	m m m	m m m m	m m m	m m m	m m m	m m m	m m m	m m m
Spain				−					
Sweden	−	−	−	−	−				
Switzerland							▲		▲
Turkey	−		−	△			▲		▲
United States	▲	▲	△						
Partner countries									
Brazil	m m m	m m m	m m m m	m m m	m m m	m m m	m m m	m m m	m m m
Chile			△						
Estonia	m m m	m m m	m m m m	m m m	m m m	m m m	m m m	m m m	m m m
Israel	−		△ −						
Slovenia	▲	−	△ −						▲
Russian Federation	m m m	m m m	m m m m	m m m	m m m	m m m	m m m	m m m	m m m

− : Base salary.
▲ : Additional yearly payment.
△ : Additional incidental payment.

Source: OECD. See Annex 3 for notes (*www.oecd.org/edu/eag2008*).
Please refer to the Reader's Guide for information concerning the symbols replacing missing data.
StatLink ᴴᴵˢᴸ http://dx.doi.org/10.1787/402280862627

INDICATOR D4

HOW MUCH TIME DO TEACHERS SPEND TEACHING?

This indicator focuses on the statutory working time and statutory teaching time of teachers at different levels of education. Although working time and teaching time only partly determine teachers' actual workload, they do give valuable insight into differences in what is demanded of teachers in different countries. Together with teachers' salaries (see Indicator D3) and average class size (see Indicator D2), this indicator presents some key measures of the working lives of teachers.

Key results

Chart D4.1. Number of teaching hours per year in lower secondary education (2006)

The number of teaching hours in public lower secondary schools averages 717 hours per year but ranges from 548 hours in Korea to over 1 000 in Mexico (1 047) and the United States (1 080).

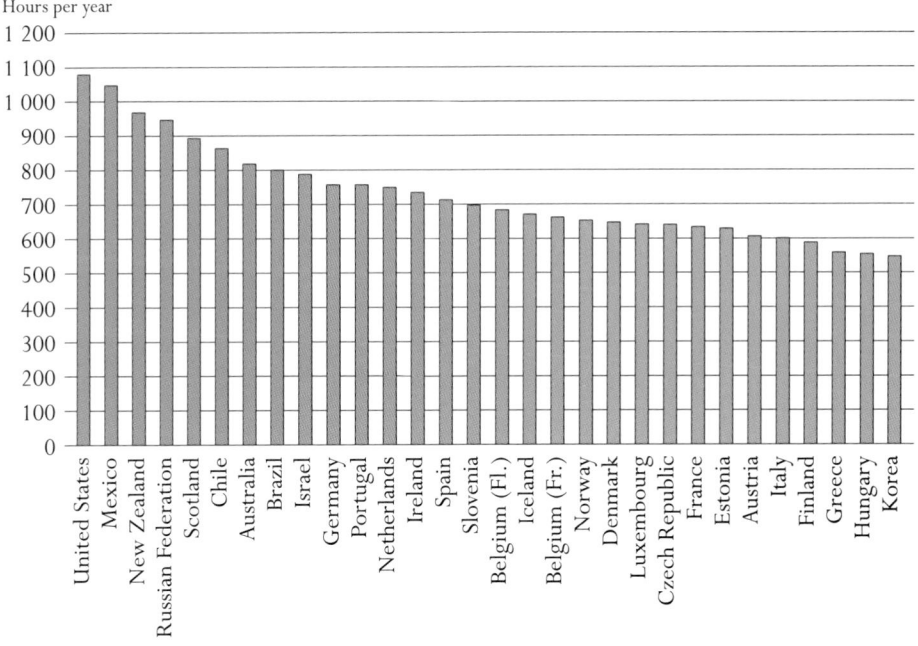

Countries are ranked in descending order of the number of teaching hours per year in lower secondary education.
Source: OECD. Table D4.1. See Annex 3 for notes (*www.oecd.org/edu/eag2008*).
StatLink ᵃᵃˢᴸ http://dx.doi.org/10.1787/402318043535

Other highlights of this indicator

▪ The number of teaching hours in public primary schools averages 812 per year (9 more than in 2005), but ranges from less than 650 in Denmark, Turkey and the partner country Estonia to 1 080 in the United States.

▪ The average number of teaching hours in upper secondary general education is 667, but ranges from 364 in Denmark to 1 080 in the United States.

▪ The composition of teachers' annual teaching time, in terms of days, weeks and hours per day, varies considerably. For instance, while teachers in Denmark teach for 42 weeks per year (in primary and secondary education) and teachers in Iceland for 35-36 weeks per year, teachers in Iceland have more total annual teaching time (in hours) than teachers in Denmark.

▪ Regulations concerning teachers' working time also vary. In most countries, teachers are formally required to work a specific number of hours; in some, teaching time is only specified as the number of lessons per week and assumptions may be made on the amount of non-teaching time required per lesson (at school or elsewhere). For example, in Belgium (Fr.), additional non-teaching hours at school are set at the school level; the government only defines the minimum and maximum number of teaching periods per week at each level of education.

INDICATOR D4

D4

Policy context

In addition to class size and the ratio of students to teaching staff (see Indicator D2), students' hours of instruction (see Indicator D1) and teachers' salaries (see Indicator D3), the amount of time teachers spend teaching affects the financial resources countries need to allocate to education (see Indicator B7). Teaching hours and the extent of non-teaching duties are also important elements of teachers' work and may be related to the attractiveness of the teaching profession.

The proportion of working time spent teaching provides information on the amount of time available for activities such as lesson preparation, correction, in-service training and staff meetings. A large proportion of working time spent teaching may indicate that less time is devoted to work such as student assessment and lesson preparation. However, such duties may be performed at the same level as for teachers with less teaching time but outside of regulatory working hours.

Evidence and explanations

Teaching time in primary education

In both primary and secondary education, countries vary in terms of the number of teaching hours per year required of the average public school teacher. There are usually more teaching hours in primary education than in secondary education.

Chart D4.2. Number of teaching hours per year, by level of education (2006)

Net contact time in hours per year in public institutions

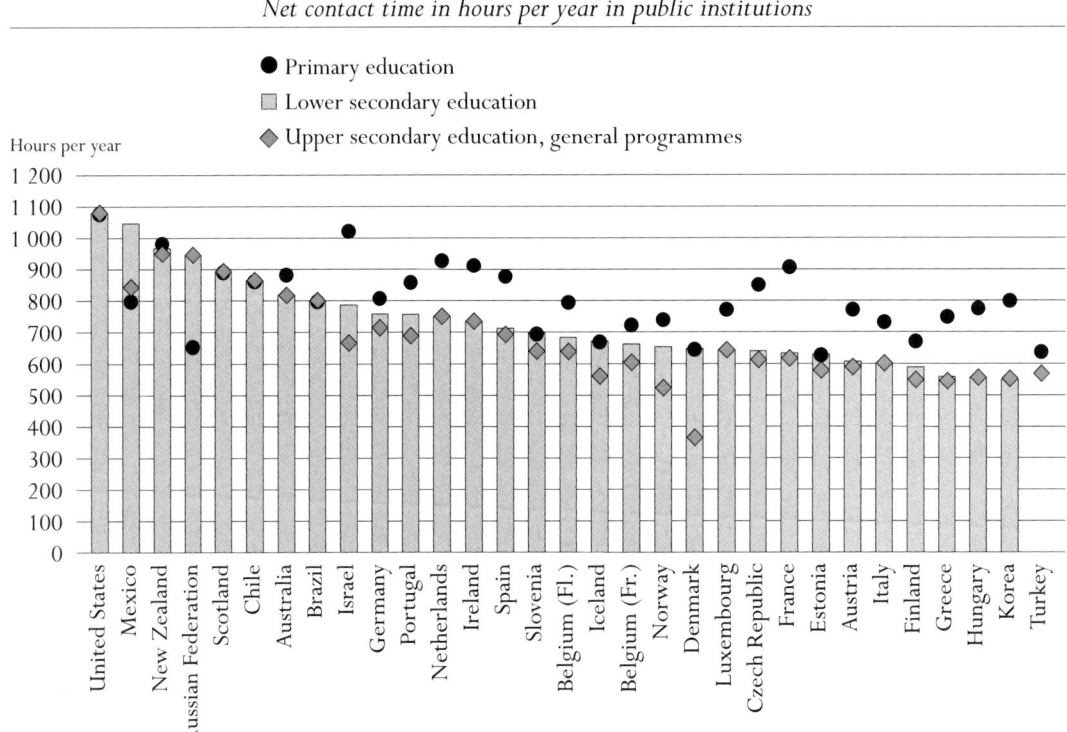

- ● Primary education
- ▢ Lower secondary education
- ◆ Upper secondary education, general programmes

Countries are ranked in descending order of the number of teaching hours per year in lower secondary education.
Source: OECD. Table D4.1. See Annex 3 for notes (*www.oecd.org/edu/eag2008*).
StatLink ᐃᔑᐳ http://dx.doi.org/10.1787/402318043535

D4

A primary school teacher teaches an average of 812 hours per year (9 more than the previous year), but this ranges from less than 650 hours in Denmark, Turkey and the partner country Estonia to 900 or more in France, Ireland, the Netherlands and New Zealand and over 1 000 in the United States and in partner country Israel (Chart D4.2 and Table D4.1).

Teaching time can be distributed quite differently throughout the year. Korea is the only country in which primary teachers teach for more than five days per week on average, yet their total annual teaching time is below the average because they teach, on average, fewer hours per day. Denmark and Iceland provide an interesting contrast in this respect. They have a similar annual net teaching time in hours (Chart D4.1). However, teachers in Denmark must complete 200 days of instruction in 42 weeks, and those in Iceland 180 days in 36 weeks. The number of hours taught per day of instruction explains the difference.

Primary teachers in Iceland complete 20 fewer days of instruction than teachers in Denmark, but each of these days would include, on average, 3.7 hours of teaching compared to 3.2 in Denmark. Iceland's teachers must provide just over half an hour more teaching time per day of instruction than Denmark's teachers, but this relatively small difference leads to a substantial difference in the number of days of instruction they must complete each year.

Teaching time in secondary education

Lower secondary education teachers teach an average of 717 hours per year. The teaching load ranges from less than 600 hours in Finland (589), Greece (559), Hungary (555) and Korea (548) to more than 1 000 hours in Mexico (1 047) and the United States (1 080) (Chart D4.1 and Table D4.1).

The upper secondary general education teaching load is usually lighter than in lower secondary education. A teacher of general subjects has an average statutory teaching load of 667 hours per year. Teaching loads range from fewer than 364 hours in Denmark to more than 800 in Australia (817), Mexico (843), Scotland (893) and the partner country Chile (864), over 900 in New Zealand (950) and the partner country the Russian Federation (946) and over 1 000 in the United States (1 080) (Chart D4.2 and Table D4.1).

As for primary teachers, the number of hours of teaching time and the number of days of instruction vary. As a consequence, the average hours per day that teachers teach vary widely, ranging at the lower secondary level from three or fewer per day in Hungary and Korea to five or more in Mexico and New Zealand and the partner country the Russian Federation, and six in the United States. Similarly, at the upper secondary general level, teachers in Denmark, Finland, Greece, Hungary, Korea and Norway teach for three hours (or less) per day on average, compared to five hours in New Zealand and the partner country the Russian Federation and six hours in the United States. Korea provides an interesting example of the differences in the organisation of teachers' work. Korea's teachers must complete the largest number of days of instruction (204) but have the lowest required number of hours of teaching time for lower secondary teachers and the fifth lowest for upper secondary teachers (Chart D4.3). The inclusion of breaks between classes in teaching time in some countries, but not others may explain some of these differences.

D4

Chart D4.3. Percentage of teachers working time spent teaching, by level of education (2006)

Net teaching time as a percentage of total statutory working time

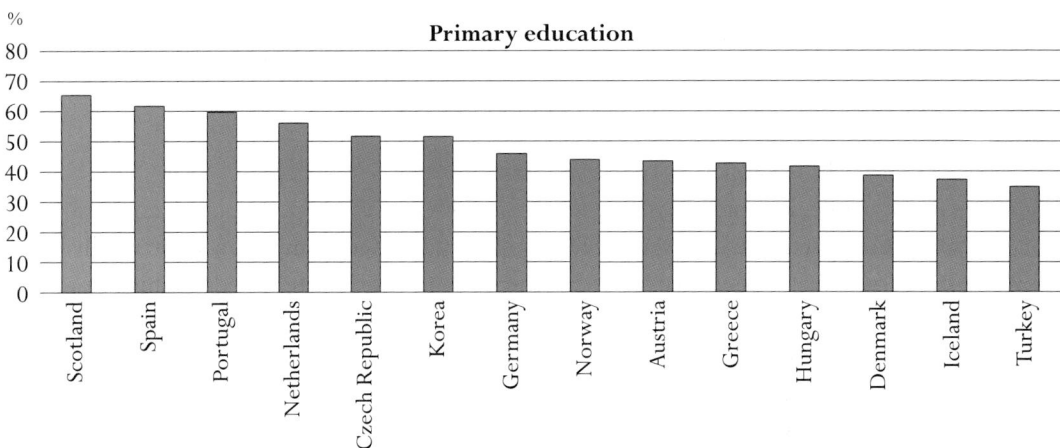

Primary education

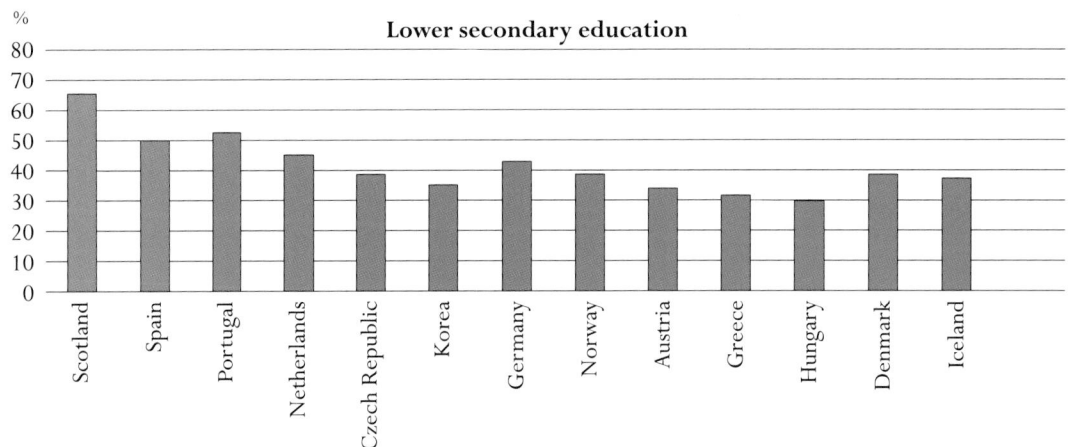

Lower secondary education

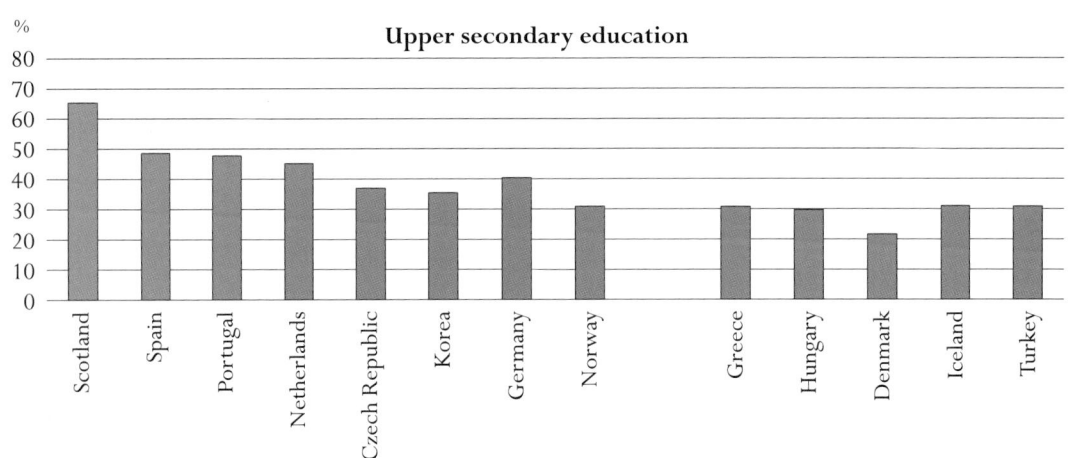

Upper secondary education

Countries are ranked in descending order of the percentage of teachers' working time spent teaching in primary education.
Source: OECD. Table D4.1. See Annex 3 for notes (*www.oecd.org/edu/eag2008*).
StatLink ⌐▥🖳 http://dx.doi.org/10.1787/402318043535

D4

Teaching time contrasts between levels

In France and Korea, and in the partner country Israel a primary teacher is required to teach over 220 hours more than a lower secondary teacher and 250 hours more than an upper secondary teacher (general programmes). In Hungary the large difference in teaching time between primary and lower secondary (222 hours) results mainly from taking into account at primary level short breaks for which teachers are responsible for the class. By contrast, there is less than 50 hours or no difference between the number of required instruction hours for primary and lower secondary teachers and sometimes also for primary and upper secondary teachers in Denmark, Iceland, New Zealand, Scotland and the United States, and the partner countries Brazil, Chile, Estonia and Slovenia. Mexico is the only OECD country and the Russian Federation the only partner country, in which secondary teachers complete a substantially larger number of hours of instruction than primary teachers. In Mexico, required teaching hours for lower secondary teachers are just over 30% more than for primary teachers. Upper secondary teachers in Mexico have a smaller number of teaching hours than lower secondary teachers but their required teaching hours are still 5% higher than for primary teachers (Chart D4.1). This is largely because of greater daily contact time.

In interpreting differences among countries in teaching hours, it should be noted that net contact time, as used for the purpose of this indicator, does not necessarily correspond to the teaching load. Contact time is a substantial component, but preparation for classes and the necessary follow-up (including correcting students' work) also need to be included in comparisons of teaching loads. Other relevant elements (such as the number of subjects taught, the number of students taught, and the number of years a teacher teaches the same students) should also be taken into account. These factors can often only be assessed at the school level.

Teachers' working time

The regulation of teachers' working time varies widely. While some countries formally regulate contact time only, others also establish working hours. In some countries, time is allocated for teaching and non-teaching activities within the formally established working time.

In most countries, teachers are formally required to work a specified number of hours per week to earn their full-time salary; this includes teaching and non-teaching time. Within this framework, however, countries differ in the allocation of time to teaching and non-teaching activities (Chart D4.3). Typically, the number of hours for teaching is specified (except in England and Sweden and in Switzerland where it is specified at the district level only), but some countries also regulate at the national level the time a teacher has to be present in the school.

Australia, Belgium (Fl. community for primary education), Denmark (primary and lower secondary education), England, Greece, Iceland, Ireland, Luxembourg, Mexico, New Zealand, Norway, Portugal, Spain, Sweden, Turkey (primary and upper secondary education) and the United States, and the partner countries Brazil, Chile, Estonia and Israel specify the time during which teachers are required to be available at school, for both teaching time and non-teaching time. Greece requires a reduction of teaching hours in line with years of service. Early-career teachers have 21 teaching hours per week. After six years, this drops to 19 and after 12 years to 18. After 20 years of service, teachers have 16 teaching hours a week, nearly three-quarters that of early career teachers. However, the remaining hours of teachers' working time must be spent at school.

In Austria (primary and lower secondary education), the Czech Republic, Germany, Hungary, Japan, Korea, the Netherlands and Scotland, teachers' total annual working time, at school or elsewhere, is specified (but the split between time spent at school and time spent elsewhere is not). In addition, in some countries the number of hours to be spent on non-teaching activities is also (partly) specified. However, it is not specified whether or not the teachers have to spend the non-teaching hours at school.

D4

Non-teaching time

In Belgium (Fr.), Finland, France, Italy and New Zealand and in partner country Slovenia, there are no formal requirements for how much time should be spent on non-teaching duties. However, this does not mean that teachers are given total freedom to carry out other tasks. In Austria, provisions concerning teaching time are based on the assumption that the teacher's duties (including preparing lessons and tests, marking and correcting papers, examinations, and administrative tasks) amount to total working time of 40 hours a week. In Belgium (Fr.), the additional non-teaching hours at school are set at the school level. There are no regulations regarding lesson preparation, correction of tests and marking students' papers, etc. The government defines only the minimum and maximum number of teaching periods a week (of 50 minutes each) at each level of education (Table D4.1).

Definitions and methodologies

Data are from the 2007 OECD-INES Survey on Teachers and the Curriculum and refer to the school year 2005/06.

Teaching time

Teaching time is defined as the number of hours per year that a full-time teacher teaches a group or class of students as set by policy. It is normally calculated as the number of teaching days per year multiplied by the number of hours a teacher teaches per day (excluding periods of time formally allowed for breaks between lessons or groups of lessons). Some countries, however, provide estimates of teaching time based on survey data.

At the primary level, short breaks between lessons are included if the classroom teacher is responsible for the class during these breaks.

Working time

Working time refers to the normal working hours of a full-time teacher. According to a country's formal policy, working time can refer to:

• The time directly associated with teaching (and other curricular activities for students, such as assignments and tests, but excluding annual examinations).

• The time directly associated with teaching and hours devoted to other activities related to teaching, such as lesson preparation, counselling students, correcting assignments and tests, professional development, meetings with parents, staff meetings, and general school tasks.

Working time does not include paid overtime.

D4

Working time in school

Working time in school refers to the time teachers are required to spend at work, including teaching and non-teaching time.

Number of teaching weeks and days

The number of teaching weeks refers to the number of weeks of instruction excluding holiday weeks. The number of teaching days is the number of teaching weeks multiplied by the number of days per week a teacher teaches, less the number of days on which the school is closed for holidays.

Further references

The following additional material relevant to this indicator is available on line at:

StatLink 🔗 http://dx.doi.org/10.1787/402318043535

- *Table D4.2. Number of teaching hours per year (1996, 2006)*

Specific notes on definitions and methodologies regarding this indicator for each country are given in Annex 3 (*www.oecd.org/edu/eag2008*).

D4

Table D4.1.
Organisation of teachers' working time (2006)
Number of teaching weeks, teaching days, net teaching hours and teachers' working time over the school year

	Number of weeks of instruction			Number of days of instruction			Net teaching time in hours			Working time required at school in hours			Total statutory working time in hours		
	Primary education	Lower secondary education	Upper secondary education, general programmes	Primary education	Lower secondary education	Upper secondary education, general programmes	Primary education	Lower secondary education	Upper secondary education, general programmes	Primary education	Lower secondary education	Upper secondary education, general programmes	Primary education	Lower secondary education	Upper secondary education, general programmes
	(1)	(2)	(3)	(4)	(5)	(6)	(7)	(8)	(9)	(10)	(11)	(12)	(13)	(14)	(15)
Australia	40	40	40	198	198	198	884	818	817	1211	1230	1230	a	a	a
Austria	38	38	38	180	180	180	774	607	589	a	a	a	1784	1784	a
Belgium (Fl.)	37	37	37	177	178	178	797	684	638	920	a	a	a	a	a
Belgium (Fr.)	37	37	37	181	181	181	724	662	603	a	a	a	a	a	a
Czech Republic	40	40	40	194	194	194	854	640	611	a	a	a	1652	1652	1652
Denmark	42	42	42	200	200	200	648	648	364	1306	1306	m	1680	1680	1680
England	38	38	38	190	190	190	a	a	a	1265	1265	1265	1265	1265	1265
Finland	38	38	38	187	187	187	673	589	547	a	a	a	a	a	a
France	35	35	35	m	m	m	910	634	616	a	a	a	a	a	a
Germany	40	40	40	193	193	193	810	758	714	a	a	a	1765	1765	1765
Greece	40	38	38	195	185	185	751	559	544	1500	1425	1425	1762	1762	1762
Hungary	37	37	37	185	185	185	777	555	555	a	a	a	1864	1864	1864
Iceland	36	36	35	180	180	175	671	671	560	1650	1650	1720	1800	1800	1800
Ireland	37	33	33	183	167	167	915	735	735	1036	735	735	a	a	a
Italy	38	38	38	167	167	167	735	601	601	a	a	a	a	a	a
Japan	35	35	35	m	m	m	m	m	m	a	a	a	1952	1952	1952
Korea	37	37	37	204	204	204	802	548	552	a	a	a	1554	1554	1554
Luxembourg	36	36	36	176	176	176	774	642	642	1022	890	890	a	a	a
Mexico	42	42	36	200	200	172	800	1047	843	800	1167	971	a	a	a
Netherlands	40	37	37	195	180	180	930	750	750	a	a	a	1659	1659	1659
New Zealand	39	39	38	197	194	190	985	968	950	985	968	950	a	a	a
Norway	38	38	38	190	190	190	741	654	523	1300	1225	1150	1688	1688	1688
Poland	m	m	m	m	m	m	m	m	m	m	m	m	m	m	m
Portugal	36	36	36	172	172	172	860	757	688	1260	1260	1260	1440	1440	1440
Scotland	38	38	38	190	190	190	893	893	893	a	a	a	1365	1365	1365
Slovak Republic	m	m	m	m	m	m	m	m	m	m	m	m	m	m	m
Spain	37	37	36	176	176	171	880	713	693	1140	1140	1140	1425	1425	1425
Sweden	a	a	a	a	a	a	a	a	a	1360	1360	1360	1767	1767	1767
Switzerland	m	m	m	m	m	m	m	m	m	m	m	m	m	m	m
Turkey	38	a	38	180	a	180	639	a	567	870	a	756	1832	a	1832
United States	36	36	36	180	180	180	1080	1080	1080	1332	1368	1368	a	a	a
OECD average	*38*	*38*	*37*	*187*	*185*	*183*	*812*	*717*	*667*	*1185*	*1214*	*1159*	*1662*	*1651*	*1654*
EU19 average	*38*	*37*	*37*	*185*	*182*	*182*	*806*	*672*	*634*	*1201*	*1173*	*1154*	*1619*	*1619*	*1604*
Brazil	40	40	40	200	200	200	800	800	800	800	800	800	800	800	800
Chile	40	40	40	192	192	192	864	864	864	1152	1152	1152	a	a	a
Estonia	39	39	39	175	175	175	630	630	578	1540	1540	1540	a	a	a
Israel	43	42	42	183	175	175	1025	788	665	1221	945	945	a	a	a
Russian Federation	34	35	35	164	169	169	656	946	946	m	m	m	m	m	m
Slovenia	40	40	40	192	192	192	697	697	639	a	a	a	a	a	a

Source: OECD. See Annex 3 for notes (*www.oecd.org/edu/eag2008*).

Please refer to the Reader's Guide for information concerning the symbols replacing missing data.

StatLink ⬛᠍ᒲ http://dx.doi.org/10.1787/402318043535

HOW ARE EVALUATIONS AND ASSESSMENTS USED IN EDUCATION SYSTEMS?

This indicator focuses on evaluation and accountability arrangements for lower secondary public schools. It examines the existence and use of student and school performance and evaluation information. It complements the quantitative information relating to teachers' salaries and working and teaching time (Indicators D3 and D4), instruction time of students (Indicator D1), and the relationship between numbers of students and of teachers (Indicator D2) by providing qualitative information on the type and use of particular school accountability and evaluation arrangements. It also complements the information relating to levels of decision making (Indicator D6). New information is provided about the criteria used for school evaluations and how various performance measures are used in different education systems.

Key results

- A total of 22 OECD and partner countries undertake student examinations and/or assessments and 17 require schools to be evaluated (either self-evaluations and/or inspections by an external body) at regular intervals. For student performance measures, student assessments (evaluations without civil effect for the student) are practised in 17 OECD and partner countries, whereas national examinations (with a civil effect for the student) are practised in 10 OECD and partner countries.

- School self-evaluations are required in 14 countries and are generally required on an annual basis, whereas school inspections are also required in 14 countries but tend to be required once every three years or so. Although school self-evaluations are held more often, evaluations by school inspectorates have, in general, appear to have more influence on schools and teachers in terms of the implications of the evaluation and the accountability structure.

- Both school evaluation and student performance measures are mainly used to provide performance feedback to schools. In general, they have relatively little influence on school financing and other financial implications such as changes to the school budget, provision of rewards or sanctions for schools, or remunerations and bonuses received by teachers.

- In a larger number of countries, the influence of school evaluations is greater than student examinations for the performance appraisals of schools (13 countries, compared to 7 for student examinations), for the appraisal of the performance of school management (9 countries, compared to 1 for student examinations) and the appraisal of the performance of individual teachers (4 countries, compared to 1 for student examinations).

D5

Policy context

School evaluation and accountability measures have received greater attention in recent years as the decentralisation of decision making in school education (see Indicator D6) and a greater focus on output rather than input measures in the public sector have increased the need for performance measures. Different kinds of performance measures can be used to create a system of school evaluation and accountability that can help improve schools (Box D5.1). They can focus on student performance and also on an evaluative framework for assessing the performance and operation of schools.

The impact of these performance measures depends on the objectives and context in which they are developed. As the context and scope of assessments may vary widely from one country to another, it is pertinent to look at the influence attributed to these measures of performance, such as the level of the influence of school self-evaluations on the appraisal of the performance of school management or on remuneration and bonuses received by teachers. This allows for a better understanding of the degree to which these measures are considered in the process of school evaluation and accountability.

Data were collected from countries to identify the existence of different types of information on student performance in 2006. Two categories of student information were identified: national examinations, which have a civil effect on students, and periodic national assessments, which do not. The latter assessments may have been implemented to compare student performance across schools or evaluate the performance of the system as a whole. Information was also collected on the subjects covered (mathematics, science, national language / language of instruction), whether assessments and examinations are compulsory, and at what year or grade level they take place.

For school evaluations, data were collected on the requirements for evaluations by school inspectorates (or equivalent institutions) and school self-evaluations, as well as on the criteria used to focus on different aspects of school performance and operations. Information was also collected on the influence of student performance and school evaluation measures on schools and teachers. Countries were asked whether these measures had a high, moderate, low or no influence upon each of five main areas: performance feedback to schools and teachers; financial implications for schools and teachers; assistance provided to teachers to improve their teaching skills; the likelihood of school closure; and the publication of school results.

Evidence and explanations

Student examinations and assessments and the frequency of school evaluations

In 2006, national student examinations existed in 9 OECD countries and 1 partner country among the 29 OECD and partner countries for which data are available and, except in Scotland and Turkey, were considered compulsory (Table D5.1). In terms of the subjects tested, these can change over years but for the 2006 reference year all countries that conducted national student examinations systematically assessed mathematics and national language or language of instruction. Science was not examined as frequently; this was also true for periodical national assessments of students. Only eight countries included science in their national examinations (seven OECD countries and one partner country). A number of countries included other subjects in their national examinations as well but data were not collected on the complete range of subjects offered across countries.

D5

National student assessments differ from national student examinations in that assessments do not have a civil effect for individual students. Nevertheless, national assessments were more widely conducted among OECD and partner countries (17 out of the 29 countries for which data are available) than national examinations (10 countries). Assessments were conducted in 12 OECD and partner countries which did not have national examinations (Tables D5.1 and D5.2). In terms of the subjects included, mathematics and national language are most common. As in the case of national examinations, science seemed to have less of a priority for national assessments. Only 7 countries conducted science assessments (5 OECD countries and 2 partner countries), whereas 15 countries include mathematics and national language (12 OECD countries and 3 partner countries for both). Whenever a country conducted a periodical national assessment, it covered these two subjects. The only exception is Belgium (Fl. community), where national assessments were exclusively undertaken in science in 2006 (but other assessment have been organised in other school years). Among the nine countries that conducted national assessments in mathematics and the national language, but not in science, only Luxembourg, Scotland and Sweden conducted them in other subjects. England, Korea and Turkey and the partner countries Israel and Slovenia conducted periodical assessments of mathematics, science and national language or language of instruction and other subjects.

National student assessments generally took place between grades 6 and 9, while national examinations generally took place between grades 8 and 10. Except for Italy and Turkey which carried out national examinations at grade 8, all the other countries do so between grades 9 and 10. National student assessments were carried out at grade 9 in England, Korea, Luxembourg, Mexico and Sweden and in the partner country Slovenia. Only Australia conducted national assessments at grade 7, and Belgium (Fl. Community), Scotland and the partner countries Brazil and Israel at grade 8. In Hungary and Turkey, national assessments were carried out at three different grades, from grade 6 to grade 10.

Whenever school self-evaluations are required, these are generally required annually, unlike evaluations by school inspectorates which tend to be required only every three years or so (Tables D5.5 and D5.6). In four countries the requirements for school evaluations are not applicable as there are no school evaluations in these countries. In Japan, there are no requirements for the frequency of school evaluations but these evaluations still take place in a substantial proportion of schools. Even though school self-evaluations are carried out more often than external evaluations, the latter appear to have a greater influence on schools and teachers in terms of the school evaluation and accountability framework and the results are more likely to be published.

Impact of student performance and school evaluation information

Information was collected to ascertain the influence of student examinations and assessments and school evaluations upon schools. For example, it was asked whether student assessments or examinations are used to provide financial incentives to schools and teachers. The information collected focused on: the appraisal and performance feedback to schools and teachers (performance feedback to the school, appraisal of the performance of school management and appraisal of the performance of individual teachers); financial implications (on the school budget, the provision of rewards or sanctions to schools, and remuneration of and bonuses for teachers); assistance provided to teachers to improve their teaching skills; the likelihood of school closure; and, the publication of results (whether or not results of evaluations are published) and if these are further used by governments for the creation of comparative tables of school performance.

D5

In regard to the impact of student performance results, student performance in national examinations appears to have more influence upon the performance feedback provided to schools and teachers than student results in national student assessments. Among the nine countries with data on the influence of national examinations, the results of these examinations were considered as having a high level of influence upon the performance feedback given to schools. This feedback includes: performance feedback to the school (high influence in Iceland, Ireland and Scotland and moderate influence in France and the partner country Estonia); appraisal of the performance of the school management (high influence in Scotland and moderate influence in Ireland); and appraisal of the performance of individual teachers (high influence in Ireland and moderate influence in the partner country Estonia) (Table D5.3). In Italy, Portugal and Turkey, results of national examinations were considered to have had little or no influence on the performance feedback provided to schools and teachers.

Student performance in national student examinations was considered to have had a moderate influence upon the assistance provided to teachers to improve their teaching skills in France, Ireland, Scotland and the partner country Estonia. In Ireland, national examinations were also considered to have had a moderate influence on the likelihood of school closure. The performance of students in national examinations was not considered to have an influence upon school budgets, the provision of financial rewards to schools and the remuneration or bonuses for teachers, except in Scotland, where it was considered to have had a low level of influence on school budgets and the provision of financial rewards or sanctions to schools and in the partner country Estonia, where it was considered to have had a low level of influence on the provision of financial rewards or sanctions.

All but one country with national student examinations published the results. Denmark, Iceland and the partner country Estonia published the results of national student examinations and also used them to compile comparative tables of school performance. Ireland is the only country that does not publish these student examination results.

Periodical national assessments of students were more widely performed than national student examinations (Tables D5.1 and D5.2) and were also considered to have had a large influence upon the performance feedback given to schools and teachers. Results of these assessments were considered to have had a high or moderate influence on the performance feedback provided to schools in Australia, England, Finland, France, Hungary and the partner country Israel. Results of national student assessments were also considered to have had a moderate level of influence on the appraisal of the performance of school management in Hungary. In Australia, England and France students' national assessment results were considered to have had a moderate influence on the assistance provided to teachers to improve their teaching skills. In England, they were also considered to have had a high degree of influence on the likelihood of school closure, in the context of other factors such as the results of school inspections (Table D5.4).

The results of student assessments were published in Australia, Belgium (Fl. community) (only synthetic report on school and system level), England, Italy, Korea, Scotland and Turkey and in partner country Slovenia. Only in England and Turkey were these results used by the government for the creation of comparative tables of school performance.

D5

The implications of school evaluations by an inspectorate or other external body were considered to have focused mainly upon the performance feedback provided to schools and, to a lesser extent, the appraisal of the performance of school management. In 10 OECD countries and one partner country, school evaluations by an inspectorate were considered to have had a high influence upon the performance feedback provided to schools. In seven OECD countries it was considered that there was a high influence upon the performance appraisal of the school management. School evaluations were considered to have had a high influence on the appraisal of the performance of teachers in the Czech Republic, Ireland and Turkey and in extreme cases on the likelihood of school closure in the Czech Republic and England. In Australia and Turkey, school evaluations were considered to have had a high degree of influence upon the assistance provided to teachers to improve their teaching skills. Only in Belgium (Fl. community), were school evaluations considered to have had a fairly (or rather) high influence on school budgets and the provision of financial rewards or sanctions. There was also considered to be a moderate influence on the assistance provided to teachers to improve their teaching skills in Belgium (Fl. community), the Czech Republic, England, Ireland, Portugal and Scotland. Evaluations by a school inspectorate were also considered to have had a moderate influence upon the performance feedback given to schools (Iceland), on appraisal of the performance of school management (Australia, Iceland and Ireland) and on appraisal of the performance of teachers (Australia and Iceland). Implications were also considered to have existed for the school budget (Australia and the Czech Republic), the remuneration and bonuses received by teachers (the Czech Republic and Turkey) and the likelihood of school closure (Belgium (Flemish community) and Ireland). In contrast, school evaluations were considered to have had little influence in Korea and in the partner country Estonia compared to other OECD and partner countries (Table D5.5).

Results of evaluations undertaken by school inspectorates were published by 12 out of 15 countries, but only in Iceland were they used by the government to publish comparisons of the performance of individual schools (Table D5.5). Belgium (Fl. community), the Czech Republic, England, Ireland, Korea, the Netherlands, New Zealand, Portugal, Scotland and Sweden and the partner country Estonia published the results of evaluations undertaken by school inspectorates (or an equivalent body) but did not use them for the creation of comparative tables of school performance. In Australia and Turkey and the partner country Israel results of school evaluations were not published.

School self-evaluations were considered to have had a high level of influence upon the performance feedback provided to schools (Australia, the Czech Republic, England, Luxembourg, Mexico, Scotland, Sweden and Turkey), on appraisal of the performance of school management (the Czech Republic, Mexico, Scotland, Turkey and the partner country Estonia), and on the appraisal of individual teachers (the Czech Republic and Mexico). In terms of the financial implications of school self-evaluations, only in Sweden were they considered to have a high degree of influence on school budget, and only in the Czech Republic were they considered to have a high degree of influence upon teachers' remuneration and bonuses. In the Czech Republic and Mexico, feedback from school self-evaluations has a high degree of influence on teachers and schools, on assistance to teachers to improve their teaching skills and on the remuneration and bonuses received by teachers (Table D5.6).

Results of self-evaluations were published in Hungary, Japan, Sweden, Turkey and the partner country Estonia, but they were only further used by the government for the creation of comparative tables of school performance in Sweden.

Comparing student examinations and assessments to school evaluations (by school inspectorates and self-assessments), a total of 22 countries undertake national student examinations or assessments and 17 require periodical school evaluations by inspectorates and/or self-evaluation.

D5

Box D5.1. Evaluation and accountability arrangements: Results from PISA 2006

Evaluation and accountability information was also collected in PISA 2006 and analysed to measure the impact upon student performance. System level information similar to that presented in this indicator was collected. Further information was also collected from School Principals to better analyse changes at the school and student-level. This information focused on the nature of school accountability and the ways in which the resulting information was used and made available to various stakeholders and the public at large.

In judging the impact upon student performance, it can be difficult to isolate the influence of single policies, practices or programmes as they tend to be related to each other and to other policies. Moreover, some of these practices are correlated with the demographic and socio-economic characteristics of students in schools. For example, students in countries with a standards-based external evaluation performed 36.1 score points higher on the PISA science scale, roughly equivalent to a school year's progress. However, this effect was not statistically significant once demographic and socio-economic background factors were taken into account.

The strongest impact upon student performance was found in regard to the publication of schools' student achievement data. This was found to have a statistically significant positive impact upon student performance even after accounting for all demographic and socio-economic background characteristics and other school institutional and policy or programme characteristics. Fifteen-year-old students in schools that published this student achievement data scored, on average, 3.5 score points higher on the PISA science scale than students in schools that did not publish achievement data, all other things being equal.

Source: OECD (2007) PISA 2006: Science Competencies for Tomorrow's World.

In general, school evaluations were considered to have had a greater influence upon the factors analysed in this indicator. In a majority of countries, feedback from school evaluations was considered to have had a greater influence upon the performance feedback provided to schools than the performance of students in national examinations and assessments (13 countries, compared to 7 countries for student examinations and assessments); on the appraisal of the performance of school management (9 countries, compared to 1 country for student examinations and assessments); and on the appraisal of the performance of individual teachers (4 countries, compared to 1 country for student examinations and assessments). Furthermore, school evaluations were considered to have had a high influence upon school financing in Belgium (Fl. community) and Sweden; the provision of financial rewards or sanctions to schools in Belgium (Fl. community); assistance provided to teachers to improve their teaching skills in Australia, the Czech Republic, England, Mexico and Turkey; the remuneration and bonuses received by teachers in the Czech Republic; and in extreme cases on the likelihood of school closure in Belgium (Fl. community), the Czech Republic and England. In contrast, the results of national student assessments and examinations were considered to only have had a high influence on the likelihood of school closure in England and a moderate influence in Ireland and this influence is pertinent only in the context of other information such as that obtained in school evaluations. The results of national student assessments and examinations were considered to have had a moderate influence on the assistance provided to teachers to improve their teaching skills in Australia, England, France, Ireland, Scotland and in the partner country Estonia and a low influence in Hungary and the partner country Israel.

Definitions and methodologies

Data are from the 2007 OECD-INES Survey on Teachers and the Curriculum and refer to the school year 2005/06.

Public institutions

An institution is classified as public if it is: controlled and managed directly by a public education authority or agency, or controlled and managed either by a government agency directly or by a governing body (a council, committee, etc.), most of whose members are either appointed by a public authority or elected by public franchise.

National examinations and assessments

National examinations are to be seen as assessments that have a formal civil effect for students. Countries were instructed to respond irrespective of the scope of the examinations in terms of the subject matter covered; the answer should be yes even if the examinations cover just one or two subject areas. Like examinations, national assessments are most frequently based on tests of student achievement; however, while examinations have a formal civil effect for students, this is not the case for national assessments.

School inspections and evaluations

Requirements for school inspections are the legal frameworks that may operate from the central administrative level or from lower administrative levels, such as regional offices or municipalities. A school inspection may be carried out by inspectors, visitation committees or review panels. School self-evaluation is internal evaluation of schools to improve their own practice and/or to inform parents and the local community.

School evaluation and accountability information

School evaluation and accountability information is defined as any kind of systematic descriptive information to which an evaluative interpretation is given; it may depend on test scores, inspection reports, audits, or statistical data.

Further references

Specific notes on definitions and methodologies regarding this indicator for each country are given in Annex 3 (*www.oecd.org/edu/eag2008*).

Table D5.1.

National examinations in general education programmes (lower secondary education, 2006)

	Do you have national examinations in your country?	Which subjects are assessed in these examinations?				Is it compulsory for schools to administer these examinations?	At what year/grade levels do these examinations take place?
		Mathematics	Science	National language or language of instruction	Other subjects		
	(1)	(2)	(3)	(4)	(5)	(6)	(7)
OECD countries							
Australia	No	a	a	a	a	a	a
Austria	No	a	a	a	a	a	a
Belgium (Fl.)	No	a	a	a	a	a	a
Belgium (Fr.)	m	m	m	m	m	m	m
Canada	m	m	m	m	m	m	m
Czech Republic	No	a	a	a	a	a	a
Denmark	Yes	Yes	Yes	Yes	Yes	Yes	9
England	No	a	a	a	a	a	a
Finland	No	a	a	a	a	a	a
France	Yes	Yes	No	Yes	Yes	Yes	9
Germany	m	m	m	m	m	m	m
Greece	m	m	m	m	m	m	m
Hungary	No	a	a	a	a	a	a
Iceland	Yes	Yes	Yes	Yes	Yes	Yes	10
Ireland	Yes	Yes	Yes	Yes	Yes	Yes	10
Italy	Yes	Yes	Yes	Yes	Yes	Yes	8
Japan	No	a	a	a	a	a	a
Korea	No	a	a	a	a	a	a
Luxembourg	No	a	a	a	a	a	a
Mexico	No	a	a	a	a	a	a
Netherlands	No	a	a	a	a	a	a
New Zealand	No	a	a	a	a	a	a
Norway	Yes	Yes	Yes	Yes	Yes	Yes	10
Poland	m	m	m	m	m	m	m
Portugal	Yes	Yes	No	Yes	No	Yes	9
Scotland[1]	Yes	Yes	Yes	Yes	Yes	No	10
Slovak Republic	m	m	m	m	m	m	m
Spain	No	a	a	a	a	a	a
Sweden	No	a	a	a	a	a	a
Switzerland	No	a	a	a	a	a	a
Turkey	Yes	Yes	Yes	Yes	Yes	No	8
United States	m	m	m	m	m	m	m
Partner countries							
Brazil	No	a	a	a	a	a	a
Chile	m	m	m	m	m	m	m
Estonia	Yes	Yes	Yes	Yes	Yes	Yes	9
Israel	No	a	a	a	a	a	a
Russian Federation	m	m	m	m	m	m	m
Slovenia	No	a	a	a	a	a	a

1. Year/Grade 10 refers to S4.

Source: OECD. See Annex 3 for notes (*www.oecd.org/edu/eag2008*).

Please refer to the Reader's Guide for information concerning the symbols replacing missing data.

StatLink 🖼🔗 http://dx.doi.org/10.1787/402323667230

D5

Table D5.2.
National periodical assessments in general education programmes (lower secondary education, 2006)

	Do you have national periodical assessments in your country?	Which subjects are assessed in these assessments?				Is it compulsory for schools to administer these assessments?	At what year/grade levels do these assessments take place?
		Mathematics	Science	National language or language of instruction	Other subjects		
	(1)	(2)	(3)	(4)	(5)	(6)	(7)
OECD countries							
Australia[1]	Yes	Yes	No	Yes	No	Yes	7
Austria	No	a	a	a	a	a	a
Belgium (Fl.)[2]	Yes	No	Yes	No	No	No	8
Belgium (Fr.)	m	m	m	m	m	m	m
Canada	m	m	m	m	m	m	m
Czech Republic	No	a	a	a	a	a	a
Denmark	No	a	a	a	a	a	a
England	Yes	Yes	Yes	Yes	Yes	Yes	9
Finland	Yes	Yes	No	Yes	No	Yes	3
France	Yes	Yes	No	Yes	No	Yes	6
Germany	m	m	m	m	m	m	m
Greece	m	m	m	m	m	m	m
Hungary	Yes	Yes	No	Yes	No	Yes	6, 8, 10
Iceland	No	a	a	a	a	a	a
Ireland	No	a	a	a	a	a	a
Italy	Yes	Yes	Yes	Yes	m	Yes	6
Japan	No	a	a	a	a	a	a
Korea	Yes	Yes	Yes	Yes	Yes	No	9
Luxembourg	Yes	Yes	No	Yes	Yes	Yes	9
Mexico	Yes	Yes	No	Yes	No	Yes	9
Netherlands	No	a	a	a	a	a	a
New Zealand	No	a	a	a	a	a	a
Norway	Yes	m	m	m	m	m	m
Poland	m	m	m	m	m	m	m
Portugal	No	a	a	a	a	a	a
Scotland[3]	Yes	Yes	No	Yes	Yes	No	8
Slovak Republic	m	m	m	m	m	m	m
Spain	No	a	a	a	a	a	a
Sweden	Yes	Yes	No	Yes	Yes	Yes	9
Switzerland	No	a	a	a	a	a	a
Turkey	Yes	Yes	Yes	Yes	Yes	Yes	6, 7, 8
United States	m	m	m	m	m	m	m
Partner countries							
Brazil	Yes	Yes	No	Yes	No	No	8
Chile	m	m	m	m	m	m	m
Estonia	No	a	a	a	a	a	a
Israel	Yes	Yes	Yes	Yes	Yes	Yes	8
Russian Federation	m	m	m	m	m	m	m
Slovenia	Yes	Yes	Yes	Yes	Yes	Yes	9

1. Assessments are administered at the state level.
2. Grade 7 refers to 2nd year A of 1st stage.
3. Year/Grade 8 refers to S2.
Source: OECD. See Annex 3 for notes (*www.oecd.org/edu/eag2008*).
Please refer to the Reader's Guide for information concerning the symbols replacing missing data.
StatLink 🔚🖘 http://dx.doi.org/10.1787/402323667230

D5

Table D5.3.
Possible influence of national examinations (lower secondary education, 2006)

	Performance feedback			Financial and other implications					Publication of results	
	The performance feedback to the school	The performance appraisal of the school management	The performance appraisal of individual teachers	The school budget	The provision of another financial reward or sanction	The assistance provided to teachers to improve their teaching skills	Remuneration and bonuses received by teachers	Likelihood of school closure	Are the results of evaluations published?	Published in tables that compare school performance?
	(1)	(2)	(3)	(4)	(5)	(6)	(7)	(8)	(9)	(10)
Australia	a	a	a	a	a	a	a	a	a	a
Austria	a	a	a	a	a	a	a	a	a	a
Belgium (Fl.)	a	a	a	a	a	a	a	a	a	a
Belgium (Fr.)	m	m	m	m	m	m	m	m	m	m
Canada	m	m	m	m	m	m	m	m	m	m
Czech Republic	a	a	a	a	a	a	a	a	a	a
Denmark	m	m	m	m	m	m	m	m	Yes	Yes
England	a	a	a	a	a	a	a	a	a	a
Finland	a	a	a	a	a	a	a	a	a	a
France	Moderate	None	None	None	None	Moderate	None	None	Yes	No
Germany	m	m	m	m	m	m	m	m	m	m
Greece	m	m	m	m	m	m	m	m	m	m
Hungary	a	a	a	a	a	a	a	a	a	a
Iceland	High	Low	Low	None	None	None	None	None	Yes	Yes
Ireland	High	Moderate	High	None	None	Moderate	None	Moderate	No	No
Italy	None	None	None	None	None	None	None	None	Yes	No
Japan	a	a	a	a	a	a	a	a	a	a
Korea	a	a	a	a	a	a	a	a	a	a
Luxembourg	a	a	a	a	a	a	a	a	a	a
Mexico	a	a	a	a	a	a	a	a	a	a
Netherlands	a	a	a	a	a	a	a	a	Yes	No
New Zealand	a	a	a	a	a	a	a	a	a	a
Norway	m	m	m	None	None	m	m	a	None	Yes	No
Poland	m	m	m	m	m	m	m	m	m	m
Portugal	None	None	None	None	None	None	None	None	Yes	No
Scotland	High	High	Low	Low	Low	Moderate	None	None	Yes	No
Slovak Republic	m	m	m	m	m	m	m	m	m	m
Spain	a	a	a	a	a	a	a	a	a	a
Sweden	a	a	a	a	a	a	a	a	a	a
Switzerland	a	a	a	a	a	a	a	a	a	a
Turkey	Low	None	None	None	None	None	None	None	Yes	No
United States	m	m	m	m	m	m	m	m	m	m
Brazil	a	a	a	a	a	a	a	a	a	a
Chile	m	m	m	m	m	m	m	m	m	m
Estonia	Moderate	None	Moderate	None	Low	Moderate	None	None	Yes	Yes
Israel	a	a	a	a	a	a	a	a	a	a
Russian Federation	m	m	m	m	m	m	m	m	m	m
Slovenia	a	a	a	a	a	a	a	a	a	a

None: No influence at all
Low: Low level of influence
Moderate: Moderate level of influence
High: High level of influence

Source: OECD. See Annex 3 for notes (*www.oecd.org/edu/eag2008*).
Please refer to the Reader's Guide for information concerning the symbols replacing missing data.
StatLink ᵃˢᴸ http://dx.doi.org/10.1787/402323667230

Table D5.4.
Possible influence of national periodical assessments (lower secondary education, 2006)

	Performance feedback			Financial and other implications					Publication of results	
	The performance feedback to the school	The performance appraisal of the school management	The performance appraisal of individual teachers	The school budget	The provision of another financial reward or sanction	The assistance provided to teachers to improve their teaching skills	Remuneration and bonuses received by teachers	Likelihood of school closure	Are the results of evaluations published?	Published in tables that compare school performance?
	(1)	(2)	(3)	(4)	(5)	(6)	(7)	(8)	(9)	(10)
Australia	High	Low	None	Low	None	Moderate	None	None	Yes	No
Austria	a	a	a	a	a	a	a	a	a	a
Belgium (Fl.)	m	m	m	None	None	m	None	None	Yes	No
Belgium (Fr.)	m	m	m	m	m	m	m	m	m	m
Canada	m	m	m	m	m	m	m	m	m	m
Czech Republic	a	a	a	a	a	a	a	a	a	a
Denmark	a	a	a	a	a	a	a	a	a	a
England	High	Low	None	None	None	Moderate	None	High	Yes	Yes
Finland	Moderate	a	a	m	m	m	m	a	No	No
France	Moderate	None	None	None	None	Moderate	None	None	No	No
Germany	m	m	m	m	m	m	m	m	m	m
Greece	m	m	m	m	m	m	m	m	m	m
Hungary	High	Moderate	Low	m	m	Low	Low	None	No	No
Iceland	a	a	a	a	a	a	a	a	a	a
Ireland	a	a	a	a	a	a	a	a	a	a
Italy	None	None	None	None	None	None	None	None	Yes	No
Japan	a	a	a	a	a	a	a	a	a	a
Korea	None	None	None	None	None	None	None	None	Yes	No
Luxembourg	None	None	None	None	None	None	None	None	No	No
Mexico	m	m	m	a	a	m	m	a	No	No
Netherlands	a	a	a	a	a	a	a	a	a	a
New Zealand	a	a	a	a	a	a	a	a	a	a
Norway	m	m	m	m	m	m	m	m	m	m
Poland	m	m	m	m	m	m	m	m	m	m
Portugal	a	a	a	a	a	a	a	a	a	a
Scotland	None	None	None	None	None	None	None	None	Yes	No
Slovak Republic	m	m	m	m	m	m	m	m	m	m
Spain	a	a	a	a	a	a	a	a	a	a
Sweden	m	m	m	m	m	m	m	m	m	m
Switzerland	a	a	a	a	a	a	a	a	a	a
Turkey	Low	None	None	None	None	None	None	None	Yes	Yes
United States	m	m	m	m	m	m	m	m	m	m
Brazil	m	m	m	m	m	m	m	m	m	m
Chile	m	m	m	m	m	m	m	m	m	m
Estonia	a	a	a	a	a	a	a	a	a	a
Israel	High	Low	Low	None	None	Low	None	None	No	No
Russian Federation	m	m	m	m	m	m	m	m	m	m
Slovenia	Low	Low	None	None	None	None	None	None	Yes	No

None: No influence at all
Low: Low level of influence
Moderate: Moderate level of influence
High: High level of influence

Source: OECD. See Annex 3 for notes (*www.oecd.org/edu/eag2008*).
Please refer to the Reader's Guide for information concerning the symbols replacing missing data.
StatLink ╤╧╘═ http://dx.doi.org/10.1787/402323667230

Table D5.5.
Possible influence of school evaluations by an inspectorate (lower secondary education, 2006)

D5

	Requirements for school evaluations[1]	Performance feedback[2]			Financial and other implications[2]					Publication of results	
		The performance feedback to the school	The performance appraisal of the school management	The performance appraisal of individual teachers	The school budget	The provision of another financial reward or sanction	The assistance provided to teachers to improve their teaching skills	Remuneration and bonuses received by teachers	Likelihood of school closure	Are the results of evaluations published?	Published in tables that compare school performance?
	(1)	(2)	(3)	(4)	(5)	(6)	(7)	(8)	(9)	(10)	(11)
OECD countries											
Australia	1 per 3y	High	Moderate	Moderate	Moderate	a	High	a	a	No	No
Austria	None	a	a	a	a	a	a	a	a	a	a
Belgium (Fl.)	1 per 3y+	High	High	Low	High	High	Moderate	a	Moderate	Yes	No
Belgium (Fr.)	m	m	m	m	m	m	m	m	m	m	m
Canada	m	m	m	m	m	m	m	m	m	m	m
Czech Republic	1 per 3y	High	High	High	Moderate	Low	Moderate	Moderate	High	Yes	No
Denmark	m	m	m	m	m	m	m	m	m	m	m
England	1 per 3y	High	Low	None	None	None	Moderate	None	High	Yes	No
Finland	a	a	a	a	a	a	a	a	a	a	a
France	m	m	m	m	m	m	m	m	m	m	m
Germany	m	m	m	m	m	m	m	m	m	m	m
Greece	m	m	m	m	m	m	m	m	m	m	m
Hungary	a	a	a	a	a	a	a	a	a	a	a
Iceland	1 per 3y	Moderate	Moderate	Moderate	a	a	a	a	a	Yes	Yes
Ireland	1 per 3y+	High	Moderate	High	None	None	Moderate	None	Moderate	Yes	No
Italy	None	a	a	a	a	a	a	a	a	a	a
Japan	m	a	a	a	a	a	a	a	a	a	a
Korea	1 per 3y	Low	Low	Low	None	Low	Low	None	None	Yes	No
Luxembourg	None	a	a	a	a	a	a	a	a	m	m
Mexico	m	m	m	m	m	m	m	m	m	m	m
Netherlands	1 per y	m	m	m	m	m	m	m	m	Yes	No
New Zealand	1 per 3y	High	High	Low	None	None	Low	None	Low	Yes	No
Norway	a	a	a	a	a	a	a	a	a	a	a
Poland	m	m	m	m	m	m	m	m	m	m	m
Portugal	1 per 3y+	High	High	a	a	a	Moderate	None	a	Yes	No
Scotland	1 per 3y+	High	High	Low	Low	Low	Moderate	None	None	Yes	No
Slovak Republic	m	m	m	m	m	m	m	m	m	m	m
Spain	None	a	a	a	a	a	a	a	a	a	a
Sweden	1 per 3y+	High	High	Low	Low	Low	None	Low	Low	Yes	m
Switzerland	m	m	m	m	m	m	m	m	m	m	m
Turkey	1+ per y	High	High	High	None	None	High	Moderate	Low	No	No
United States	m	m	m	m	m	m	m	m	m	m	m
Partner countries											
Brazil	None	a	a	a	a	a	a	a	a	a	a
Chile	m	m	m	m	m	m	m	m	m	m	m
Estonia	1 per y	None	None	None	None	None	None	None	None	Yes	No
Israel	m	High	m	m	None	None	None	None	None	No	No
Russian Federation	m	m	m	m	m	m	m	m	m	m	m
Slovenia	None	a	a	a	a	a	a	a	a	a	a

Note 1

None: There are no requirements for school evaluation
1+ per y: Greater than once per year
1 per y: Once per year
1 per 2y: Once every two years
1 per 3y: Once every three years
1 per 3y+: Once every three + years

Note 2

None: No influence at all
Low: Low level of influence
Moderate: Moderate level of influence
High: High level of influence

Source: OECD. See Annex 3 for notes (*www.oecd.org/edu/eag2008*).
Please refer to the Reader's Guide for information concerning the symbols replacing missing data.
StatLink ᵐᵖ http://dx.doi.org/10.1787/402323667230

D5

Table D5.6.
Possible influence of school self-evaluations (lower secondary education, 2006)

		Requirements for school self-evalautions[1]	Performance feedback[2]			Financial and other implications[2]					Publication of results	
			The performance feedback to the school	The performance appraisal of the school management	The performance appraisal of individual teachers	The school budget	The provision of another financial reward or sanction	The assistance provided to teachers to improve their teaching skills	Remuneration and bonuses received by teachers	Likelihood of school closure	Are the results of evaluations published?	Published in tables that compare school performance?
		(1)	(2)	(3)	(4)	(5)	(6)	(7)	(8)	(9)	(10)	(11)
OECD countries	Australia	1 per y	High	Moderate	Moderate	Moderate	a	High	a	a	No	No
	Austria	None	a	a	a	a	a	a	a	a	a	a
	Belgium (Fl.)	None	a	a	a	a	a	a	a	a	a	a
	Belgium (Fr.)	m	m	m	m	m	m	m	m	m	m	m
	Canada	m	m	m	m	m	m	m	m	m	m	m
	Czech Republic	1 per y	High	High	High	Moderate	Moderate	High	High	None	No	No
	Denmark	m	m	m	m	m	m	m	m	m	m	m
	England	1 per y	High	Low	Low	None	None	High	None	Moderate	No	No
	Finland	m	m	m	m	m	m	m	m	m	m	m
	France	m	m	m	m	m	m	m	m	m	m	
	Germany	m	m	m	m	m	m	m	m	m	m	m
	Greece	m	m	m	m	m	m	m	m	m	m	m
	Hungary	1 per 3y+	Low	Moderate	Low	Low	Low	Low	Low	None	Yes	No
	Iceland	1+ per y	Moderate	Moderate	Moderate	a	a	a	a	a	No	No
	Ireland	None	a	a	a	a	a	a	a	a	a	a
	Italy	None	a	a	a	a	a	a	a	a	a	a
	Japan	m	m	m	m	m	m	m	m	m	Yes	No
	Korea	1 per y	Low	None	None	None	None	Low	None	None	No	No
	Luxembourg	1 per y	High	Low	None	None	None	None	None	None	No	No
	Mexico	1+ per y	High	High	High	a	a	High	a	a	No	No
	Netherlands	m	m	m	m	m	m	m	m	m	m	m
	New Zealand	1 per 3y	m	m	m	m	m	m	m	m	No	No
	Norway	None	a	a	a	a	a	a	a	a	a	a
	Poland	m	m	m	m	m	m	m	m	m	m	m
	Portugal	1+ per y	None	None	None	None	None	None	None	None	No	No
	Scotland	1 per y	High	High	Low	Low	Low	Moderate	None	None	No	No
	Slovak Republic	m	m	m	m	m	m	m	m	m	m	m
	Spain	None	a	a	a	a	a	a	a	a	a	a
	Sweden	1 per y	High	Moderate	Low	High	Low	None	Low	None	Yes	Yes
	Switzerland	m	m	m	m	m	m	m	m	m	m	m
	Turkey	1 per y	High	High	None	None	Low	High	Low	None	Yes	No
	United States	m	m	m	m	m	m	m	m	m	m	m
Partner countries	Brazil	None	a	a	a	a	a	a	a	a	a	a
	Chile	m	m	m	m	m	m	m	m	m	m	m
	Estonia	1 per 3y	Moderate	High	Low	Moderate	Low	Moderate	None	None	Yes	No
	Israel	m	m	m	m	None	None	None	None	None	No	No
	Russian Federation	m	m	m	m	m	m	m	m	m	m	m
	Slovenia	None	a	a	a	a	a	a	a	a	a	a

Note 1
None: There are no requirements for school evaluation
1+ per y: Greater than once per year
1 per y: Once per year
1 per 2y: Once every two years
1 per 3y: Once every three years
1 per 3y+: Once every three + years

Note 2
None: No influence at all
Low: Low level of influence
Moderate: Moderate level of influence
High: High level of influence

Source: OECD. See Annex 3 for notes (*www.oecd.org/edu/eag2008*).
Please refer to the Reader's Guide for information concerning the symbols replacing missing data.
StatLink http://dx.doi.org/10.1787/402323667230

INDICATOR D6

WHAT IS THE LEVEL OF DECISION MAKING IN EDUCATION SYSTEMS?

This indicator shows where decisions are made in public institutions at the lower secondary level of education. The level of decision making (from central or state levels to school levels) is presented over all, as well as for different domains. The level of decision making for different aspects of the curriculum is also examined and complemented by the mode of decision making at school level, in general as well as in specific domains.

Highlights of this indicator

- Overall, in about one-quarter of OECD and partner countries, decisions are mostly highly centralised. The majority of decisions in Australia, Luxembourg, Mexico, Portugal and Spain and the largest share of decisions in Austria are taken at the central and/or state level of government.

- In more than one-half of OECD and partner countries, decisions are more often taken at the school level. In Belgium (Fl. community), the Czech Republic, Hungary and New Zealand and the partner countries Estonia and Slovenia, the majority of decisions are taken at the school level, as are nearly all decisions in England and the Netherlands.

- Decisions on the organisation of instruction are predominantly taken by schools in all OECD and partner countries. The scenario is more varied for other areas of decision making, but most decisions on personnel management and the use of resources are taken at local or school levels in the majority of countries. Decisions on planning and structures are mostly the domain of more centralised tiers of government.

- On average in OECD countries, just under half of the decisions taken by schools are taken in full autonomy, about the same proportion as those taken within a framework set by a higher authority. Yet, there are substantial differences between some countries. For example, decisions taken by schools in consultation with others levels are relatively rare, but constitute the majority of decisions at school level in Luxembourg.

- Schools are less likely to make autonomous decisions related to planning and structures than to other areas.

- Between 2003 and 2007, decision making continued to become more decentralised in about one-half of the countries, most notably in Australia and Iceland. The opposite trend was evident in Italy.

D6

Policy context

An important factor in educational policy is the division of responsibility among national, regional and local authorities, as well as schools. Placing more decision-making authority at lower levels of the educational system has been a key aim of educational restructuring and systemic reform in many countries since the early 1980s. Yet, simultaneously, there have been frequent examples of strengthening the influence of central authorities in setting standards, curriculum and assessments. For example, a freeing of "process" and financial regulations has often been accompanied by an increase in the control of output from the centre and by national curriculum frameworks.

There are many reasons for changes in patterns of responsibility and they vary from country to country. The most common goals are increased efficiency and improved financial control, reduction of bureaucracy, increased responsiveness to local communities, creative management of human resources, improved potential for innovation and the creation of conditions that provide better incentives for improving the quality of schooling. Among the more controversial policy-related issues are a heightened interest in measures of accountability. These sometimes provide the background for measures that are more "centralised", such as national assessment programmes and centrally established frameworks.

Various motives are attributed to the desire to increase the autonomy of schools, such as enhancing the quality, effectiveness and responsiveness of schooling. School autonomy is believed to foster responsiveness to local requirements but is also sometimes seen as involving mechanisms for choice that favour already advantaged groups in society. Setting centrally determined frameworks in which individual schools make decisions is a possible counterbalance against complete school autonomy.

This indicator presents results from data collected in 2007 on decision making at the lower secondary level of education and updates the previous survey, which took place in 2003. Responses were compiled in each country by a panel of experts representing different levels of the decision-making process at the lower secondary level. While the questionnaire was largely the same in both collections, the composition of the panel in each country may have somewhat changed.

Evidence and explanations

Level of decision making in public lower secondary education

In more than one-half of the OECD and partner countries for which data are available (15 out of 25) the largest share of the decisions that affect lower secondary education is taken by the school itself. In at least two-thirds of the OECD and partner countries, most decisions are taken at the local level or by schools. The school itself is by far the most important level of decision making in Belgium (Fl. community), the Czech Republic, England, Hungary, the Netherlands, and New Zealand, as well as in the partner countries Estonia and Slovenia, where well over half of decisions are taken at the school level. In England and the Netherlands, more than 90% of decisions are taken at the school level. Decision making at the local level as opposed to the school level is a feature of the lower secondary education system in Finland, where 70% of decisions are taken at that level, and to a lesser extent in Scotland, where 53% of decisions are taken at that level (Table D6.1).

D6

Central government dominates decision making in Luxembourg and to a lesser extent in Portugal, where around 50% or more of the decisions are taken by the central authority. By contrast, in Australia, Belgium (Fl. community), the Netherlands and Spain, the central government (Community for Flemish community of Belgium) often sets the framework for decision making, but does not take final decisions related to implementation. In the Czech Republic, England, Finland, Germany, Hungary, Korea, the Netherlands and Spain and the partner country Estonia, the central government takes less than 10% of decisions relating to public lower secondary education (Table D6.1).

In federal countries, as well as in countries with largely autonomous sub national entities, there is a tendency towards a greater role for the states or autonomous provinces as the most important centralised decision-making authority. This is particularly true in Australia, Mexico and Spain where 56%, 48% and 42%, respectively, of decisions are taken at the state level.

In Austria, France, Germany, Iceland and Norway, decision making is more evenly distributed among the central level, the intermediate level and the schools (Table D6.1). In Australia, Belgium (Fl. community), Luxembourg, the Netherlands, New Zealand and Portugal, only one level of government takes decisions regarding education beyond those made by schools.

Domains of decision making

Because a general assessment of the roles played in the decision-making process includes decisions made on different domains, an aggregate measure can hide differences in the degree of centralisation of decisions for those areas. For example, a country may centralise almost all decisions about the curriculum, whereas schools may have nearly complete control over decisions about teaching methods. The distribution of decisions taken by each administrative level across four domains of decision making (with respect to the organisation of instruction, personnel management, planning and structures, and resources – see "Definitions and methodologies") is an indicator of "functional decentralisation", which takes into account the fact that decision making may be decentralised in certain activities and centralised in others.

When decisions are differentiated according to domain, the data show that decisions about the organisation of instruction are predominantly taken by schools in all countries reporting data. Thus, decisions such as the choice of teaching methods and textbooks, criteria for grouping students within schools and day-to-day methods of student assessment are largely the responsibility of the school. They are the sole responsibility of the schools in England, Hungary and New Zealand (Table D6.2).

For personnel management, planning and structures, and resources, schools generally take fewer decisions and the patterns are more mixed. On average, schools are least likely to have decision-making responsibility in the area of planning and structures (ranging from decisions to open or close a school, through to programme design and credentialing). In 11 of the 25 OECD and partner countries for which data are available on decision making by domain, at least 50% of decisions in these areas are taken centrally; in Portugal, they are all taken centrally. In Australia, Germany and Spain, more than 70% of these decisions are taken at state level. Even in countries which tend to be more decentralised (less than 50% of decisions taken centrally), such as Austria, Iceland and Sweden, the central government has an important role in decision making concerning planning and structures of the education system (Tables D6.1 and D6.2b).

D6

For personnel management (including decisions on the hiring and dismissal of staff and on setting salary schedules and conditions of work), more than 50% of decisions are taken at school or local level in 14 out of the 25 OECD and partner countries. The majority of decisions are more often taken at school level in Belgium (Fl. community), the Czech Republic, England, Hungary, the Netherlands, New Zealand, Sweden and in the partner countries Estonia and Slovenia and at the local level in Finland, Iceland, Norway and Scotland. The majority of these decisions are taken centrally in France, Luxembourg and Portugal, and by the state or provincial government in Australia, Japan and Mexico (Table D6.2b).

Decision making at the central level is less frequent for the allocation and use of resources. Only Luxembourg and Portugal take 50% or more of the decisions on resources at the central level. The state level has most responsibility in Australia and even sole responsibility in Mexico. In Germany, where the *Länder* generally have a relatively high degree of responsibility for decisions, no decisions are taken by that tier of government on the allocation or use of resources; these are mainly in the hands of local government. At least 50% of decisions are in fact taken at the local level in about one-half of the OECD and partner countries, and at the school level in nearly one-quarter. In three countries, all decisions are taken at one level: at the school level in England and the Netherlands and at the local level in Finland (Tables D6.2a and D6.2b).

Modes of decision making

The degree of autonomy that schools have in their decision making is variable. On average in OECD countries, just under half of the decisions taken by schools are taken in full autonomy; about the same proportion as those taken within a framework set by a higher authority. Decisions taken after consultation with others in the education system or taken under other circumstances are relatively rare. Only in Luxembourg are most decisions taken at the school level taken in consultation with other levels.

Among the eight OECD and partner countries in which most decision making is in the hands of the schools, around 50% of these decisions are taken in full autonomy in Belgium (Fl. community), England, Hungary, the Netherlands and New Zealand or within a framework set by a higher authority in the Czech Republic and the partner countries Estonia and Slovenia. For the first five countries, the remainder of the decisions are mainly taken within a framework set by a higher authority, and for two of the last three, they are taken in full autonomy, while in Slovenia, they are taken after consultation with other bodies in the educational system. In Italy, Korea and Sweden, where the proportion of decisions taken by schools is also around the OECD average (46%), schools' decisions are also predominantly taken in full autonomy (Table D6.3).

Perhaps predictably, decisions taken by schools in countries which tend to have more centralised decision making are more likely to be subject to an overarching framework. This is the case in Australia, Austria, Portugal and Spain. However, in Mexico, where most decisions are taken centrally and only 20% by the school, schools have full autonomy for most of the decisions in their hands.

Whatever the proportion of decisions taken at school level, the majority of these decisions are taken in full autonomy in one-half of OECD and partner countries and are taken within a framework set by a higher authority in less than one-third.

D6

Modes of decision making by domain

Within the four broad domains of decision making, decisions taken by schools related to planning and structures are least likely to be taken in full autonomy and are most likely to be taken within a framework. This is well illustrated in the Netherlands, for instance, where school-level decisions are largely taken in full autonomy in all areas except planning and structures (where all decisions are taken within a framework). However, in Austria very few decisions on planning and structures are the responsibility of the school (only 10% of decisions), and all of these are taken after consultation with other bodies in the educational system. Belgium (Fl. community) also presents an unusual situation, as most decisions on planning and structures are made at the school level, mostly with full autonomy (Tables D6.4a and D6.4b).

For the organisation of instruction and personnel management, school decision making in most countries is a bit more likely to be taken in full autonomy than within a framework set by a higher authority. Generally, these are the only two modes of decision making used by schools in these domains. However the patterns vary among countries. In Korea and the Netherlands, for instance, all decisions taken by schools on the organisation of instruction are taken in full autonomy, whereas about 11% of such decisions are taken autonomously by schools in Austria, the Czech Republic, Portugal and Spain. However, for personnel management, decisions taken at other levels in consultation with schools are sometimes the main decision-making mode. This is particularly the case in Japan and Scotland where this is the only mode of decision used (but only 21% or less of decisions in this domain are made at school level).

Although, on average, schools are least likely to take decisions on the allocation and use of resources, they are most likely to be consulted on such decisions taken by others in the education system. In Austria, Denmark, Germany, Luxembourg, Scotland and Spain, more than 50% of decisions on resources are taken in consultation with schools. This is even the sole decision-making mode in Finland. However, when decisions are taken at school level in this domain, schools have full decision-making autonomy in Hungary, Italy, the Netherlands, Norway and Sweden (Table D6.4b).

Between 2003 and 2007, decision making in most countries has become more decentralised

Between 2003 and 2007, decision making continued to become more decentralised in nearly one-half of the countries examined. It is most noticeable in Australia and Iceland where at least 15% of decisions are now taken at a more decentralised level. However, the extent of the shift towards more decentralised decisions is generally less than 5 percentage points. It is less pronounced than between 1998 and 2003 when in 14 out of 19 countries decisions were taken at a more decentralised level over that five-year period and when the move towards decentralisation concerned 30% of decisions in the Czech Republic, Korea and Turkey (see Indicator D6 in *Education at a Glance 2004*). At the same time, there have been some small shifts towards more centralised decision making in some countries between 2003 and 2007. In Italy, the proportion of decisions taken at the central level increased from 23 to 31% between 2003 and 2007. Spain presents the particularity of a shift from fewer decisions at state level towards more decisions at central as well as local or school levels (Table D6.6).

Definitions and methodologies

Data are from the 2007 OECD-INES survey on decision making in education and refer to the school year 2006/07. This indicator shows the percentage of educational decisions taken at specific levels in public lower secondary education. Decentralisation is concerned with the division of power between levels of government. This concept has two dimensions: *i)* the locus of decision making, that is, the level of decision-making authority; and *ii)* the mode of decision making, which relates to the degree of autonomous or "shared" decision making.

D6

The questionnaire distinguished between six levels of decision making: central governments, state governments, provincial/regional authorities or governments, sub-regional or inter-municipal authorities or governments, local authorities or governments, schools or school boards or committees.

The questionnaire provided information on four domains:

• *Organisation of instruction*: student admissions; student careers; instruction time; choice of textbooks; grouping students; additional support for students; teaching methods; day-to-day student assessment.

• *Personnel management*: hiring and dismissal of teaching and non-teaching staff; duties and conditions of service of staff; salary scales of staff; influence over the careers of staff.

• *Planning and structures*: opening or closure of schools; creation or abolition of a grade level; design of programmes of study; selection of programmes of study taught in a particular school; choice of subjects taught in a particular school; definition of course content; setting of qualifying examinations for a certificate or diploma; credentialing (examination content, marking and administration).

• *Resources*: allocation and use of resources for teaching staff, non-teaching staff, capital and operating expenditure.

The questionnaire also sought information on how autonomously decisions are taken. The most important factor in determining the mode is "who decides". The following categories are provided: full autonomy, after consultation with bodies located at another level within the education system, independently but within a framework set by a higher authority, other mode.

More detailed information on specific countries (*e.g.* decentralisation in Denmark; a shifting four-layer administrative organisation in France; main objectives of Greek education policy; recruitment, selection and allocation of teachers in Norway) is available in the 2004 edition of *Education at a Glance* available at: *www.oecd.org/edu/eag2004*.

The indicators were calculated to give equal importance to each of the four domains. Each domain contributes 25% to the results. As the number of items is not the same in each domain, each item is weighted by the inverse of the number of items in its domain.

Table D6.1.
Percentage of decisions taken at each level of government in public lower secondary education (2007)

		Central	State	Provincial/ regional	Sub-regional	Local	School	Total
		(1)	(2)	(3)	(4)	(5)	(6)	(7)
OECD countries	**Australia**	n	56	n	n	n	44	**100**
	Austria	27	22	n	n	22	30	**100**
	Belgium (Fl.)	n	29	n	n	n	71	**100**
	Belgium (Fr.)	m	m	m	m	m	m	**m**
	Canada	m	m	m	m	m	m	**m**
	Czech Republic	6	n	n	n	33	61	**100**
	Denmark	19	n	n	n	40	41	**100**
	England	4	n	n	n	5	91	**100**
	Finland	2	n	n	n	76	22	**100**
	France	27	n	6	28	n	39	**100**
	Germany	4	31	17	n	18	30	**100**
	Greece	m	m	m	m	m	m	**m**
	Hungary	4	n	n	n	27	69	**100**
	Iceland	23	n	n	n	37	40	**100**
	Ireland	m	m	m	m	m	m	**m**
	Italy	31	n	16	n	6	47	**100**
	Japan	13	n	21	n	45	21	**100**
	Korea	7	n	36	n	8	49	**100**
	Luxembourg	68	n	n	n	n	32	**100**
	Mexico	30	48	2	n	n	20	**100**
	Netherlands	6	n	n	n	n	94	**100**
	New Zealand	24	n	n	n	n	76	**100**
	Norway	25	n	n	n	40	35	**100**
	Poland	m	m	m	m	m	m	**m**
	Portugal	57	n	n	n	n	43	**100**
	Scotland	17	n	n	n	53	30	**100**
	Spain	9	42	10	n	3	36	**100**
	Sweden	18	n	n	n	35	47	**100**
	Switzerland	m	m	m	m	m	m	**m**
	Turkey	m	m	m	m	m	m	**m**
	United States	m	m	m	m	m	m	**m**
Partner countries	**Brazil**	m	m	m	m	m	m	**m**
	Chile	m	m	m	m	m	m	**m**
	Estonia	4	n	n	n	30	66	**100**
	Israel	m	m	m	m	m	m	**m**
	Russian Federation	m	m	m	m	m	m	**m**
	Slovenia	38	n	n	n	4	58	**100**

Source: OECD. See Annex 3 for notes (*www.oecd.org/edu/eag2008*).
Please refer to the Reader's Guide for information concerning the symbols replacing missing data.
StatLink http://dx.doi.org/10.1787/402350028873

Table D6.2a.
Percentage of decisions taken at each level of government in public lower secondary education,
by domain (2007)

	Organisation of instruction							Personnel management						
	Central	State	Provincial/regional	Sub-regional	Local	School	Total	Central	State	Provincial/regional	Sub-regional	Local	School	Total
	(1)	(2)	(3)	(4)	(5)	(6)	(7)	(8)	(9)	(10)	(11)	(12)	(13)	(14)
OECD countries														
Australia	n	11	n	n	n	89	**100**	n	58	n	n	n	42	**100**
Austria	11	n	n	n	n	89	**100**	25	38	n	n	33	4	**100**
Belgium (Fl.)	n	11	n	n	n	89	**100**	n	25	n	n	n	75	**100**
Belgium (Fr.)	m	m	m	m	m	m	**m**	m	m	m	m	m	m	**m**
Canada	m	m	m	m	m	m	**m**	m	m	m	m	m	m	**m**
Czech Republic	11	n	n	n	n	89	**100**	4	n	n	n	21	75	**100**
Denmark	n	n	n	n	11	89	**100**	25	n	n	n	33	42	**100**
England	n	n	n	n	n	100	**100**	17	n	n	n	n	83	**100**
Finland	n	n	n	n	33	67	**100**	8	n	n	n	71	21	**100**
France	11	n	n	11	n	78	**100**	63	n	25	n	n	13	**100**
Germany	n	13	n	n	n	88	**100**	17	38	38	n	n	8	**100**
Greece	m	m	m	m	m	m	**m**	m	m	m	m	m	m	**m**
Hungary	n	n	n	n	n	100	**100**	17	n	n	n	25	58	**100**
Iceland	11	n	n	n	11	78	**100**	n	n	n	n	67	33	**100**
Ireland	m	m	m	m	m	m	**m**	m	m	m	m	m	m	**m**
Italy	11	n	n	n	n	89	**100**	42	n	25	n	n	33	**100**
Japan	n	n	n	n	44	56	**100**	n	n	54	n	46	n	**100**
Korea	11	n	n	n	11	78	**100**	17	n	33	n	8	42	**100**
Luxembourg	44	n	n	n	n	56	**100**	88	n	n	n	n	13	**100**
Mexico	33	n	n	n	n	67	**100**	29	63	8	n	n	n	**100**
Netherlands	11	n	n	n	n	89	**100**	13	n	n	n	n	88	**100**
New Zealand	n	n	n	n	n	100	**100**	17	n	n	n	n	83	**100**
Norway	13	n	n	n	25	63	**100**	n	n	n	n	54	46	**100**
Poland	m	m	m	m	m	m	**m**	m	m	m	m	m	m	**m**
Portugal	11	n	n	n	n	89	**100**	67	n	n	n	n	33	**100**
Scotland	n	n	n	n	11	89	**100**	25	n	n	n	75	n	**100**
Spain	n	11	n	n	n	89	**100**	25	38	n	n	n	38	**100**
Sweden	n	n	n	n	11	89	**100**	n	n	n	n	33	67	**100**
Switzerland	m	m	m	m	m	m	**m**	m	m	m	m	m	m	**m**
Turkey	m	m	m	m	m	m	**m**	m	m	m	m	m	m	**m**
United States	m	m	m	m	m	m	**m**	m	m	m	m	m	m	**m**
Partner countries														
Brazil	m	m	m	m	m	m	**m**	m	m	m	m	m	m	**m**
Chile	m	m	m	m	m	m	**m**	m	m	m	m	m	m	**m**
Estonia	n	n	n	n	11	89	**100**	n	n	n	n	25	75	**100**
Israel	m	m	m	m	m	m	**m**	m	m	m	m	m	m	**m**
Russian Federation	m	m	m	m	m	m	**m**	m	m	m	m	m	m	**m**
Slovenia	11	n	n	n	n	89	**100**	33	n	n	n	n	67	**100**

Source: OECD. See Annex 3 for notes (*www.oecd.org/edu/eag2008*).
Please refer to the Reader's Guide for information concerning the symbols replacing missing data.
StatLink ᐧᐧᐧᐧᐧ http://dx.doi.org/10.1787/402350028873

D6

Table D6.2b.
Percentage of decisions taken at each level of government in public lower secondary education, by domain (2007)

	Planning and structures							Resources						
	Central	State	Provincial/ regional	Sub-regional	Local	School	Total	Central	State	Provincial/ regional	Sub-regional	Local	School	Total
	(1)	(2)	(3)	(4)	(5)	(6)	(7)	(8)	(9)	(10)	(11)	(12)	(13)	(14)
Australia	n	71	n	n	n	29	100	n	83	n	n	n	17	100
Austria	70	20	n	n	n	10	100	n	29	n	n	54	17	100
Belgium (Fl.)	n	29	n	n	n	71	100	n	50	n	n	n	50	100
Belgium (Fr.)	m	m	m	m	m	m	m	m	m	m	m	m	m	m
Canada	m	m	m	m	m	m	m	m	m	m	m	m	m	m
Czech Republic	10	n	n	n	40	50	100	n	n	n	n	71	29	100
Denmark	50	n	n	n	50	n	100	n	n	n	n	67	33	100
England	n	n	n	n	20	80	100	n	n	n	n	n	100	100
Finland	n	n	n	n	100	n	100	n	n	n	n	100	n	100
France	33	n	n	33	n	33	100	n	n	n	67	n	33	100
Germany	n	71	n	n	14	14	100	n	n	29	n	54	17	100
Greece	m	m	m	m	m	m	m	m	m	m	m	m	m	m
Hungary	n	n	n	n	17	83	100	n	n	n	n	67	33	100
Iceland	85	n	n	n	15	n	100	n	n	n	n	54	46	100
Ireland	m	m	m	m	m	m	m	m	m	m	m	m	m	m
Italy	71	n	14	n	n	14	100	n	n	25	n	25	50	100
Japan	50	n	n	n	20	30	100	n	n	29	n	71	n	100
Korea	n	n	75	n	n	25	100	n	n	38	n	13	50	100
Luxembourg	71	n	n	n	n	29	100	67	n	n	n	n	33	100
Mexico	57	29	n	n	n	14	100	n	100	n	n	n	n	100
Netherlands	n	n	n	n	n	100	100	n	n	n	n	n	100	100
New Zealand	40	n	n	n	n	60	100	38	n	n	n	n	63	100
Norway	86	n	n	n	14	n	100	n	n	n	n	67	33	100
Poland	m	m	m	m	m	m	m	m	m	m	m	m	m	m
Portugal	100	n	n	n	n	n	100	50	n	n	n	n	50	100
Scotland	43	n	n	n	43	14	100	n	n	n	n	83	17	100
Spain	10	90	n	n	n	n	100	n	29	42	n	13	17	100
Sweden	70	n	n	n	30	n	100	n	n	n	n	67	33	100
Switzerland	m	m	m	m	m	m	m	m	m	m	m	m	m	m
Turkey	m	m	m	m	m	m	m	m	m	m	m	m	m	m
United States	m	m	m	m	m	m	m	m	m	m	m	m	m	m
Brazil	m	m	m	m	m	m	m	m	m	m	m	m	m	m
Chile	m	m	m	m	m	m	m	m	m	m	m	m	m	m
Estonia	14	n	n	n	36	50	100	n	n	n	n	50	50	100
Israel	m	m	m	m	m	m	m	m	m	m	m	m	m	m
Russian Federation	m	m	m	m	m	m	m	m	m	m	m	m	m	m
Slovenia	83	n	n	n	17	n	100	25	n	n	n	n	75	100

OECD countries (Australia–United States); *Partner countries* (Brazil–Slovenia)

Source: OECD. See Annex 3 for notes (*www.oecd.org/edu/eag2008*).
Please refer to the Reader's Guide for information concerning the symbols replacing missing data.
StatLink ᛗ᠍ᐤ http://dx.doi.org/10.1787/402350028873

Table D6.3.
Percentage of decisions taken at the school level in public lower secondary education,
by mode of decision making (2007)

D6

	In full autonomy	After consultation with other bodies in the educational system	Within framework set by a higher authority	Other	Total, excluding "in consultation"	Decisions taken at other levels in consultation with schools[1]	Total, including "in consultation"
	(1)	(2)	(3)	(4)	(5)	(6)	(7)
OECD countries							
Australia	11	n	33	n	44	3	47
Austria	3	7	20	n	30	4	34
Belgium (Fl.)	49	n	22	n	71	n	71
Belgium (Fr.)	m	m	m	m	m	m	m
Canada	m	m	m	m	m	m	m
Czech Republic	6	n	55	n	61	n	61
Denmark	19	4	18	n	41	19	60
England	48	4	39	n	91	n	91
Finland	18	n	4	n	22	17	39
France	27	6	6	n	39	8	48
Germany	8	n	22	n	30	17	47
Greece	m	m	m	m	m	m	m
Hungary	38	4	24	3	69	1	70
Iceland	22	12	3	3	40	n	40
Ireland	m	m	m	m	m	m	m
Italy	35	n	11	n	47	n	47
Japan	8	n	n	13	21	5	27
Korea	30	n	19	n	49	n	49
Luxembourg	n	8	25	n	32	36	68
Mexico	11	9	n	n	20	n	20
Netherlands	63	n	25	6	94	n	94
New Zealand	46	4	27	n	76	10	86
Norway	29	n	6	n	35	n	35
Poland	m	m	m	m	m	m	m
Portugal	7	n	36	n	43	n	43
Scotland	11	13	6	n	30	20	50
Spain	3	6	27	n	36	8	44
Sweden	42	n	5	n	47	n	47
Switzerland	m	m	m	m	m	m	m
Turkey	m	m	m	m	m	m	m
United States	m	m	m	m	m	m	m
Partner countries							
Brazil	m	m	m	m	m	m	m
Chile	m	m	m	m	m	m	m
Estonia	20	n	46	n	66	n	66
Israel	m	m	m	m	m	m	m
Russian Federation	m	m	m	m	m	m	m
Slovenia	9	16	33	n	58	n	58

1. The number of decisions taken at other levels but in consultation with schools as a percentage of all decisions.
Source: OECD. See Annex 3 for notes (*www.oecd.org/edu/eag2008*).
Please refer to the Reader's Guide for information concerning the symbols replacing missing data.
StatLink ⌨ http://dx.doi.org/10.1787/402350028873

D6

Table D6.4a.
Percentage of decisions taken at the school level in public lower secondary education,
by mode of decision making and domain (2007)

	Organisation of instruction							Personnel management						
	In full autonomy	After consultation with other bodies in the educational system	Within framework set by a higher authority	Other	Total, excluding "in consultation"	Decisions taken at other levels in consultation with schools	Total, including "in consultation"	In full autonomy	After consultation with other bodies in the educational system	Within framework set by a higher authority	Other	Total, excluding "in consultation"	Decisions taken at other levels in consultation with schools	Total, including "in consultation"
	(1)	(2)	(3)	(4)	(5)	(6)	(7)	(8)	(9)	(10)	(11)	(12)	(13)	(14)
OECD countries														
Australia	44	n	44	n	**89**	n	**89**	n	n	42	n	**42**	n	**42**
Austria	11	n	78	n	**89**	n	**89**	n	n	4	n	**4**	n	**4**
Belgium (Fl.)	78	n	11	n	**89**	n	**89**	42	n	33	n	**75**	n	**75**
Belgium (Fr.)	m	m	m	m	**m**	m	**m**	m	m	m	m	**m**	m	**m**
Canada	m	m	m	m	**m**	m	**m**	m	m	m	m	**m**	m	**m**
Czech Republic	11	n	78	n	**89**	n	**89**	n	n	75	n	**75**	n	**75**
Denmark	33	n	56	n	**89**	n	**89**	42	n	n	n	**42**	8	**50**
England	78	11	11	n	**100**	n	**100**	63	4	17	n	**83**	n	**83**
Finland	56		11	n	**67**	n	**67**	17		4	n	**21**	8	**29**
France	67	11	n	n	**78**	n	**78**	8	4	n	n	**13**	n	**13**
Germany	13	n	75	n	**88**	n	**88**	4	n	4	n	**8**	21	**29**
Greece	m	m	m	m	**m**	m	**m**	m	m	m	m	**m**	m	**m**
Hungary	56	n	33	11	**100**	n	**100**	46	n	13	n	**58**	4	**63**
Iceland	44	11	11	11	**78**	n	**78**	25	8	n	n	**33**	n	**33**
Ireland	m	m	m	m	**m**	m	**m**	m	m	m	m	**m**	m	**m**
Italy	67	n	22	n	**89**	n	**89**	25	n	8	n	**33**	n	**33**
Japan	33	n	n	22	**56**	n	**56**	n	n	n	n	**n**	21	**21**
Korea	78	n	n	n	**78**	n	**78**	25	n	17	n	**42**	n	**42**
Luxembourg	n	22	33	n	**56**	n	**56**	n	8	4	n	**13**	33	**46**
Mexico	44	22	n	n	**67**	n	**67**	n	n	n	n	**n**	n	**n**
Netherlands	89	n	n	n	**89**	n	**89**	63	n	n	25	**88**	n	**88**
New Zealand	89	n	11	n	**100**	n	**100**	38	n	46	n	**83**	n	**83**
Norway	38	n	25	n	**63**	n	**63**	46	n	n	n	**46**	n	**46**
Poland	m	m	m	m	**m**	m	**m**	m	m	m	m	**m**	m	**m**
Portugal	11	n	78	n	**89**	n	**89**	n	n	33	n	**33**	n	**33**
Scotland	44	33	11	n	**89**	n	**89**	n	n	n	n	**n**	13	**13**
Spain	11	n	78	n	**89**	n	**89**	n	25	13	n	**38**	n	**38**
Sweden	78	n	11	n	**89**	n	**89**	58	n	8	n	**67**	n	**67**
Switzerland	m	m	m	m	**m**	m	**m**	m	m	m	m	**m**	m	**m**
Turkey	m	m	m	m	**m**	m	**m**	m	m	m	m	**m**	m	**m**
United States	m	m	m	m	**m**	m	**m**	m	m	m	m	**m**	m	**m**
Partner countries														
Brazil	m	m	m	m	**m**	m	**m**	m	m	m	m	**m**	m	**m**
Chile	m	m	m	m	**m**	m	**m**	m	m	m	m	**m**	m	**m**
Estonia	22	n	67	n	**89**	n	**89**	25	n	50	n	**75**	n	**75**
Israel	m	m	m	m	**m**	m	**m**	m	m	m	m	**m**	m	**m**
Russian Federation	m	m	m	m	**m**	m	**m**	m	m	m	m	**m**	m	**m**
Slovenia	33	n	56	n	**89**	n	**89**	4	4	58	n	**67**	n	**67**

Source: OECD. See Annex 3 for notes (*www.oecd.org/edu/eag2008*).
Please refer to the Reader's Guide for information concerning the symbols replacing missing data.
StatLink ⣫ᵢᵢˢ⡇ http://dx.doi.org/10.1787/402350028873

Table D6.4b.
Percentage of decisions taken at the school level in public lower secondary education, by mode of decision making and domain (2007)

D6

	Planning and structures							Resources						
	In full autonomy	After consultation with other bodies in the educational system	Within framework set by a higher authority	Other	Total, excluding "in consultation"	Decisions taken at other levels in consultation with schools	Total, including "in consultation"	In full autonomy	After consultation with other bodies in the educational system	Within framework set by a higher authority	Other	Total, excluding "in consultation"	Decisions taken at other levels in consultation with schools	Total, including "in consultation"
	(1)	(2)	(3)	(4)	(5)	(6)	(7)	(8)	(9)	(10)	(11)	(12)	(13)	(14)
OECD countries														
Australia	n	n	29	n	29	n	29	n	n	17	n	17	13	29
Austria	n	10	n	n	10	n	10	n	17	n	n	17	17	33
Belgium (Fl.)	43	n	29	n	71	n	71	33	n	17	n	50	n	50
Belgium (Fr.)	m	m	m	m	m	m	m	m	m	m	m	m	m	m
Canada	m	m	m	m	m	m	m	m	m	m	m	m	m	m
Czech Republic	n	n	50	n	50	n	50	13	n	17	n	29	n	29
Denmark	n	n	n	n	n	14	14	n	17	17	n	33	54	88
England	20	n	60	n	80	n	80	33	n	67	n	100	n	100
Finland	n	n	n	n	n	n	n	n	n	n	n	n	58	58
France	n	8	25	n	33	17	50	33	n	n	n	33	17	50
Germany	n	n	14	n	14	n	14	17	n	n	n	17	46	63
Greece	m	m	m	m	m	m	m	m	m	m	m	m	m	m
Hungary	17	17	50	n	83	n	83	33	n	n	n	33	n	33
Iceland	n	n	n	n	n	n	n	n	17	29	n	46	n	46
Ireland	m	m	m	m	m	m	m	m	m	m	m	m	m	m
Italy	n	n	14	n	14	n	14	50	n	n	n	50	n	50
Japan	n	n	n	30	30	n	30	n	n	n	n	n	n	n
Korea	n	n	25	n	25	n	25	17	n	33	n	50	n	50
Luxembourg	n	n	29	n	29	43	71	n	n	33	n	33	67	100
Mexico	n	14	n		14	n	14	n	n	n	n	n	n	n
Netherlands	n	n	100	n	100	n	100	100	n	n	n	100	n	100
New Zealand	40	n	20	n	60	40	100	17	17	29	n	63	n	63
Norway	n	n	n	n	n	n	n	33	n	n	n	33	n	33
Poland	m	m	m	m	m	m	m	m	m	m	m	m	m	m
Portugal	n	n	n	n	n	n	n	17	n	33	n	50	n	50
Scotland	n	n	14	n	14	43	57	n	17	n	n	17	25	42
Spain	n	n	n	n	n	n	n	n	n	17	n	17	33	50
Sweden	n	n	n	n	n	n	n	33	n	n	n	33	n	33
Switzerland	m	m	m	m	m	m	m	m	m	m	m	m	m	m
Turkey	m	m	m	m	m	m	m	m	m	m	m	m	m	m
United States	m	m	m	m	m	m	m	m	m	m	m	m	m	m
Partner countries														
Brazil	m	m	m	m	m	m	m	m	m	m	m	m	m	m
Chile	m	m	m	m	m	m	m	m	m	m	m	m	m	m
Estonia	n	n	50	n	50	n	50	33	n	17	n	50	n	50
Israel	m	m	m	m	m	m	m	m	m	m	m	m	m	m
Russian Federation	m	m	m	m	m	m	m	m	m	m	m	m	m	m
Slovenia	n	n	n	n	n	n	n	n	58	17	n	75	n	75

Source: OECD. See Annex 3 for notes (*www.oecd.org/edu/eag2008*).
Please refer to the Reader's Guide for information concerning the symbols replacing missing data.
StatLink ᵐˢˡ http://dx.doi.org/10.1787/402350028873

Table D6.5.
**Level of government at which different types of decisions about curriculum are taken
in public lower secondary education (2007)**

	Choice of textbooks	Design of programmes	Selection of programmes offered	Range of subjects taught	Definition of course content
Australia	**School** Autonomous	**School** Framework at State level	**School** Framework at State level	**School** Framework at State level	**State** Autonomous
Austria	**School** Framework at Central level	**Central** Consultation with State level	**School** Consultation with State level	**Central** Consultation with State level	**Central** Consultation with State level
Belgium (Fl.)	**School** Autonomous	**State** Autonomous	**School** Framework at State level	**School** Framework at State level	**School** Framework at State level
Belgium (Fr.)	m	m	m	m	m
Canada	m	m	m	m	m
Czech Republic	**School** Framework at Central level	**School** Framework at Central level	**School** Framework at Central level	**Central** Autonomous	**School** Framework at Central level
Denmark	**School** Autonomous	**Central** Autonomous	**Local** Framework at Central level	**Central** Autonomous	**Local** Consultation with School
England	**School** Autonomous	**School** Framework at Central level	**School** Framework at Central level	**School** Framework at Central level	**School** Framework at Central level
Finland	**Local** Autonomous	**Local** Framework at Central level	**Local** Framework at Central level	**Local** Framework at Central level	**Local** Framework at Central level
France	**School** Autonomous	**Central** Consultation with School	**School** Consultation with sub-regional level	**School** Framework at regional level	**School** Framework at Central level
Germany	**School** Framework at State level	**State** Autonomous	**State** Autonomous	**State** Autonomous	**State** Autonomous
Greece	m	m	m	m	m
Hungary	**School** Framework at Central level	**School** Framework at Central level	**School** Autonomous	**School** Autonomous	**School** Framework at Central level
Iceland	**School** Other	**Central** Autonomous	**School** Other	**Central** Autonomous	**Central** Autonomous
Ireland	m	m	m	m	m
Italy	**School** Framework at Central level	**Central** Autonomous	**Central** Autonomous	**Central** Autonomous	**Central** Autonomous
Japan	**Local** Other	**Central** Autonomous	**Central** Autonomous	**School** Other	**School** Other
Korea	**School** Autonomous	**Regional** Framework at Central level	**Regional** Framework at regional level	**Regional** Framework at Central level	**School** Framework at regional level
Luxembourg	**Central** Autonomous	**Central** Consultation with School	**Central** Consultation with School	**Central** Consultation with School	**School** Framework at Central level
Mexico	**Central** Autonomous	**State** Framework at Central level	**Central** Consultation with State level	**Central** Autonomous	**Central** Autonomous
Netherlands	**School** Autonomous	**School** Framework at **Central** level	**School** Framework at **Central** level	**School** Framework at **Central** level	**School** Framework at **Central** level
New Zealand	**School** Autonomous	**School** Framework at Central level	**School** Autonomous	**School** Autonomous	**School** Autonomous

Source: OECD. See Annex 3 for notes (*www.oecd.org/edu/eag2008*).
Please refer to the Reader's Guide for information concerning the symbols replacing missing data.
StatLink ⌐⌐⌐ http://dx.doi.org/10.1787/402350028873

Table D6.5. *(continued)*
Level of government at which different types of decisions about curriculum are taken in public lower secondary education (2007)

	Choice of textbooks	Design of programmes	Selection of programmes offered	Range of subjects taught	Definition of course content
Norway	School	Central	Central	Central	Central
	Autonomous	Autonomous	Autonomous	Autonomous	Autonomous
Poland	m	m	m	m	m
Portugal	School	Central	Central	Central	Central
	Framework at central level	Autonomous	Autonomous	Autonomous	Autonomous
Scotland	School	Local	School	School	Central
	Autonomous	Framework at central level	Framework at central level	Framework at central level	Consultation with school
Slovak Republic	m	m	m	m	m
Spain	School	State	Central	State	State
	Framework at state level	Framework at central level	Autonomous	Framework at central level	Consultation with central level
Sweden	School	Central	Local	Central	Central
	Autonomous	Autonomous	Autonomous	Autonomous	Autonomous
Poland	m	m	m	m	m
Switzerland	m	m	m	m	m
Turkey	m	m	m	m	m
United States	m	m	m	m	m
Brazil	m	m	m	m	m
Chile	m	m	m	m	m
Estonia	School	Local	Local	School	School
	Framework at central level	Framework at central level	Framework at central level	Framework at central level	Framework at central level
Israel	m	m	m	m	m
Russian Federation	m	m	m	m	m
Slovenia	School	Central	Central	Central	Central
	Framework at central level	Autonomous	Autonomous	Autonomous	Autonomous

(left margin: Partner countries)

Source: OECD. See Annex 3 for notes (*www.oecd.org/edu/eag2008*).

Please refer to the Reader's Guide for information concerning the symbols replacing missing data.

StatLink ᛗᛁᛋᒪ http://dx.doi.org/10.1787/402350028873

Table D6.6.
Percentage of decisions taken at each level of government in public lower secondary education (2007, 2003 and difference)

	2007							2003							Difference 2007 with 2003					
	Central	State	Provincial/regional	Sub-regional	Local	School	Total	Central	State	Provincial/regional	Sub-regional	Local	School	Total	Central	State	Provincial/regional	Sub-regional	Local	School
	(1)	(2)	(3)	(4)	(5)	(6)	(7)	(8)	(9)	(10)	(11)	(12)	(13)	(14)	(15)	(16)	(17)	(18)	(19)	(20)
OECD countries																				
Australia	n	56	n	n	n	44	100	n	76	n	n	n	24	100	n	-20	n	n	n	20
Austria	27	22	n	n	22	30	100	27	22	n	n	23	29	100	n	n	n	n	-1	1
Belgium (Fl.)	n	29	n	n	n	71	100	m	m	m	m	m	m	m	m	m	m	m	m	m
Belgium (Fr.)	m	m	m	m	m	m	m	m	m	m	m	m	m	m	m	m	m	m	m	m
Canada	m	m	m	m	m	m	m	m	m	m	m	m	m	m	m	m	m	m	m	m
Czech Republic	6	n	n	n	33	61	100	7	n	1	n	32	60	100	n	n	-1	n	1	n
Denmark	19	n	n	n	40	41	100	19	n	n	n	38	44	100	n	n	n	n	3	-3
England	4	n	n	n	5	91	100	11	n	n	n	4	85	100	-7	n	n	n	1	6
Finland	2	n	n	n	76	22	100	2	n	n	n	71	27	100	n	n	n	n	5	-5
France	27	n	6	28	n	39	100	24	n	10	35	n	31	100	3	n	-4	-7	n	8
Germany	4	31	17	n	18	30	100	4	30	17		17	32	100	n	1	n	n	n	-2
Greece	m	m	m	m	m	m	m	m	m	m	m	m	m	m	m	m	m	m	m	m
Hungary	4	n	n	n	27	69	100	4	n	n	n	29	68	100	1	n	n	n	-1	1
Iceland	23	n	n	n	37	40	100	25	n	n	n	50	25	100	-2	n	n	n	-13	15
Ireland	m	m	m	m	m	m	m	m	m	m	m	m	m	m	m	m	m	m	m	m
Italy	31	n	16	n	6	47	100	23	n	16	n	15	46	100	8	n	n	n	-8	n
Japan	13	n	21	n	45	21	100	13	n	21	n	44	23	100	n	n	n	n	2	-2
Korea	7	n	36	n	8	49	100	9	n	34	n	8	48	100	-2	n	2	n	n	1
Luxembourg	68	n	n	n	n	32	100	66	n	n	n	n	34	100	2	n	n	n	n	-2
Mexico	30	48	2	n	n	20	100	30	45	2	n	n	22	100	n	3	n	n	n	-2
Netherlands	6	n	n	n	n	94	100	4	n	n	n	n	96	100	2	n	n	n	n	-2
New Zealand	24	n	n	n	n	76	100	25	n	n	n	n	75	100	-1	n	n	n	n	1
Norway	25	n	n	n	40	35	100	32	n	n	n	32	37	100	-7	n	n	n	8	-1
Poland	m	m	m	m	m	m	m	m	m	m	m	m	m	m	m	m	m	m	m	m
Portugal	57	n	n	n	n	43	100	50	n	8	n	n	41	100	6	n	-8	n	n	2
Scotland	17	n	n	n	53	30	100	m	m	m	m	m	m	m	m	m	m	m	m	m
Spain	9	42	10	n	3	36	100	n	57	15	n	n	28	100	9	-15	-4	n	3	8
Sweden	18	n	n	n	35	47	100	18	n	n	n	36	47	100	m	m	m	m	m	m
Switzerland	m	m	m	m	m	m	m	m	m	m	m	m	m	m	m	m	m	m	m	m
Turkey	m	m	m	m	m	m	m	m	m	m	m	m	m	m	m	m	m	m	m	m
United States	m	m	m	m	m	m	m	m	m	m	m	m	m	m	m	m	m	m	m	m
Partner countries																				
Brazil	m	m	m	m	m	m	m	m	m	m	m	m	m	m	m	m	m	m	m	m
Chile	m	m	m	m	m	m	m	m	m	m	m	m	m	m	m	m	m	m	m	m
Estonia	4	n	n	n	30	66	100	m	m	m	m	m	m	m	m	m	m	m	m	m
Israel	m	m	m	m	m	m	m	m	m	m	m	m	m	m	m	m	m	m	m	m
Russian Federation	m	m	m	m	m	m	m	m	m	m	m	m	m	m	m	m	m	m	m	m
Slovenia	38	n	n	n	4	58	100	m	m	m	m	m	m	m	m	m	m	m	m	m

Source: OECD. See Annex 3 for notes (*www.oecd.org/edu/eag2008*).
Please refer to the Reader's Guide for information concerning the symbols replacing missing data.
StatLink ⬛ http://dx.doi.org/10.1787/402350028873

Annex

CHARACTERISTICS OF EDUCATIONAL SYSTEMS

The typical graduation age is the age at the end of the last school/academic year of the corresponding level and programme when the degree is obtained. The age normally corresponds to the age of graduation. (Note that at some levels of education the term "graduation age" may not translate literally and is used here purely as a convention.)

Annex 1

Table X1.1a.
Typical age of graduation in upper secondary education (2006)

	Programme orientation		Educational/labour market destination			
	General programmes	Pre-vocational or vocational programmes	ISCED 3A programmes	ISCED 3B programmes	ISCED 3C short programmes[1]	ISCED 3C long programmes[1]
OECD countries						
Australia	17	17	17	m	m	17
Austria	18	17-18	18	17-18	15-16	17
Belgium	18	18	18	a	17	18
Canada	17-18	17-18	17-18	17-18	17-18	17-18
Czech Republic	19	18	19	19	a	18
Denmark	19	20	19	a	23	20
Finland	19	19	19	a	a	a
France	18-19	17-21	18-19	19-21	a	17-19
Germany	19-20	19-20	19-20	19-20	19-20	a
Greece	17	18-19	18	a	17	18
Hungary	19	19	19	a	m	19
Iceland	20	18	20	21	18	23
Ireland	18	19	18	a	19	18
Italy	19	18	19	18	17	a
Japan	18	18	18	18	16	18
Korea	17	17	17	a	a	17
Luxembourg	18	17-20	18-19	19-20	17-18	18-19
Mexico	18	18	18	a	a	18
Netherlands	17-18	18-20	17-20	a	18	18-19
New Zealand	17-18	17-18	18	17	17	17
Norway	18	19-20	18	a	m	19-20
Poland	19	20	19	a	a	19
Portugal	17	18	17	m	m	m
Slovak Republic	19-20	19-20	19-20	a	18	18-19
Spain	17	17	17	a	17	17
Sweden	19	19	19	a	a	19
Switzerland	18-20	18-20	18-20	18-20	17-19	18-20
Turkey	16	16	16	a	a	a
United Kingdom	16-18	m	18	18	16	16
United States	18	m	18	m	m	m
Partner countries						
Brazil	18	20	18	20	a	a
Chile	18	18	18	a	a	a
Estonia	19	19	19	a	19	a
Israel	17	17	17	a	a	17
Russian Federation	17	17	17	17	16	17
Slovenia	19	18-19	19	19	18	a

1. Duration of ISCED 3C short programme: at least one year less than ISCED 3A/3B programme; duration of ISCED 3C long programme: similar to ISCED 3A or 3B programmes.
Source: OECD.
Please refer to the Reader's Guide for information concerning the symbols replacing missing data.

Table X1.1b.
Typical age of graduation in post-secondary non-tertiary education (2006)

	Educational/labour market destination		
	ISCED 4A programmes	ISCED 4B programmes	ISCED 4C programmes
OECD countries			
Australia	a	a	18
Austria	19	19	20
Belgium	18-19	19-21	19-21
Canada	30-34	30-34	30-34
Czech Republic	21	a	21
Denmark	22	a	a
Finland	a	a	35-39
France	18-21	a	19-21
Germany	22	22	a
Greece	a	a	20-22
Hungary	a	a	20
Iceland	a	a	22
Ireland	a	a	18-19
Italy	a	a	20
Japan	19	19	19
Korea	a	a	a
Luxembourg	a	a	22-24
Mexico	a	a	a
Netherlands	a	a	20-21
New Zealand	18-19	18-19	18-19
Norway	20-21	a	21-22
Poland	a	a	21
Portugal	m	m	m
Slovak Republic	21-22	a	a
Spain	a	a	a
Sweden	a	a	20-23
Switzerland	21-23	21-23	a
Turkey	a	a	a
United Kingdom	m	m	m
United States	m	m	m
Partner countries			
Brazil	a	a	a
Chile	a	a	a
Estonia	a	21	a
Israel	m	a	a
Russian Federation	a	a	19
Slovenia	20-21	20-21	a

Source: OECD.
Please refer to the Reader's Guide for information concerning the symbols replacing missing data.

Table X1.1c.
Typical age of graduation in tertiary education (2006)

| | Tertiary-type B (ISCED 5B) | Tertiary-type A (ISCED 5A) | | | Advanced research programmes (ISCED 6) |
		3 to less than 5 years	5 to 6 years	More than 6 years	
Australia	19-22	20-22	22-24	24-25	25-26
Austria	20-21	22-24	24-26	a	25
Belgium	21-22	22	23-24	24	26-29
Canada	21-25	22	23-24	25	27-29
Czech Republic	22-23	23	25	a	28
Denmark	23-25	24	26	27	30-34
Finland	30-34	24	26	35-39	30-34
France	20-24	20-23	22-25	28-29	26
Germany	21-23	24-26	25-27	a	28-29
Greece	22-24	22-24	m	m	25-29
Hungary	21	23	24	a	30-34
Iceland	30-34	24	26	28	30-34
Ireland	20-21	21	23	25	27
Italy	22-23	22	23-25	30-34	27-29
Japan	20	22	24	a	27
Korea	19	21	23	a	30-34
Luxembourg	m	m	m	m	m
Mexico	20	23	m	m	24-28
Netherlands	a	21-23	21-24	a	28-29
New Zealand	20-23	21-22	23	25	30-34
Norway	21-22	22-23	24-25	26-27	28-29
Poland	22	23	25	a	25-29
Portugal	21-23	22	23-24	a	30-34
Slovak Republic	21-22	23	24	a	28-29
Spain	19	20	22	27-28	25-27
Sweden	22-23	25	25	a	30-34
Switzerland	23-29	24-26	25-27	25-27	30-34
Turkey	20-22	22-24	25-27	30-34	30-34
United Kingdom	19-24	20-22	22-24	23-25	25-29
United States	20	22	24	a	27
Brazil	21-24	21-24	m	m	25-29
Chile	20-22	22	24	25	29
Estonia	22	22	24	a	30-34
Israel	m	26	a	a	30-34
Russian Federation	20	19-24	19-25	a	24-26
Slovenia	23-26	25-26	25-26	a	29

Note: Where tertiary-type A data are available by duration of programme, the graduation rate for all programmes is the sum of the graduation rates by duration of programme.
Source: OECD.
Please refer to the Reader's Guide for information concerning the symbols replacing missing data.

Table X1.2a.
School year and financial year used for the calculation of indicators, OECD countries

Annex 1

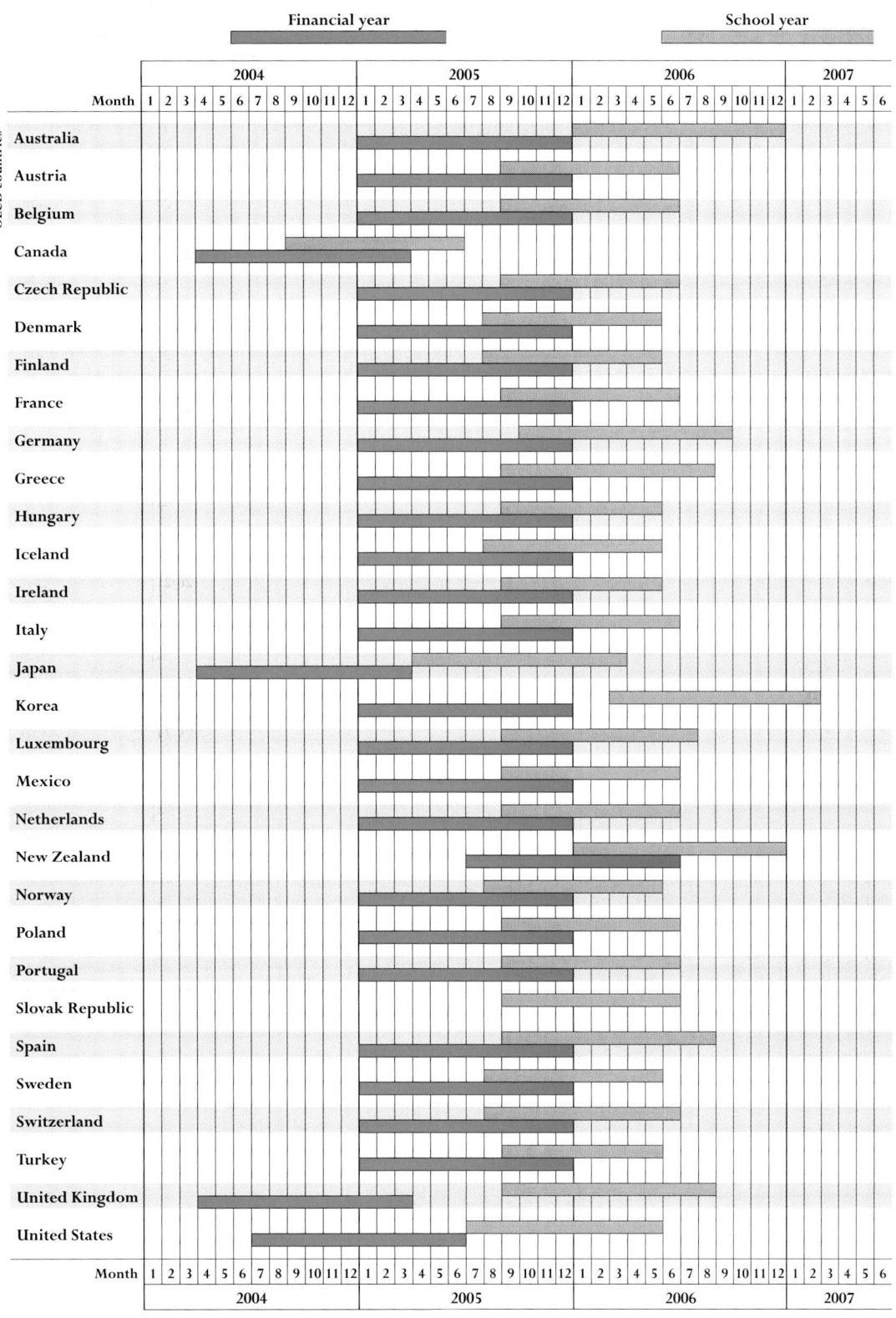

Source: OECD.

Table X1.2b.
School year and financial year used for the calculation of indicators, partner countries

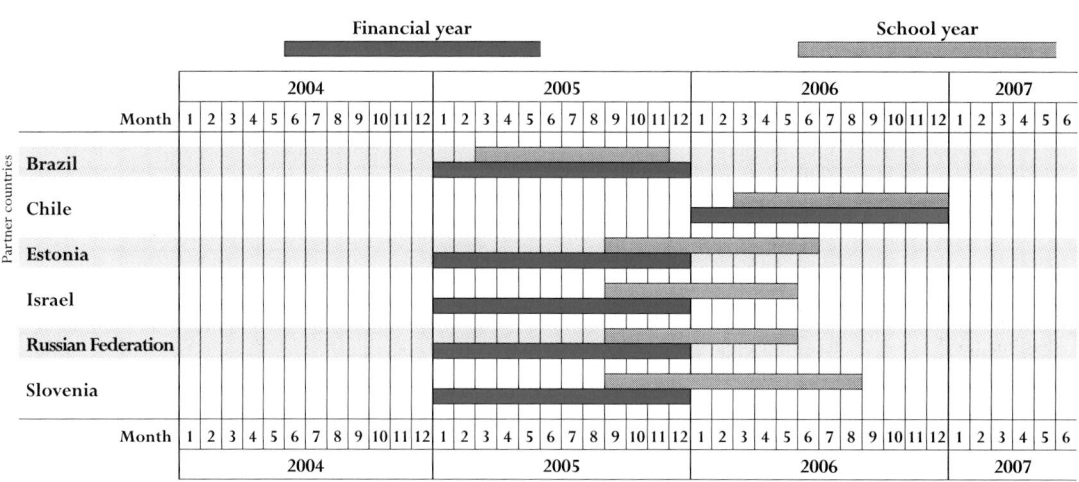

Source: OECD.

Table X1.3.
Summary of completion requirements for upper secondary programmes

	ISCED 3A programmes				ISCED 3B programmes				ISCED 3C programmes			
	Final examination	Series of examinations during programme	Specified number of course hours AND examination	Specified number of course hours only	Final examination	Series of examinations during programme	Specified number of course hours AND examination	Specified number of course hours only	Final examination	Series of examinations during programme	Specified number of course hours AND examination	Specified number of course hours only
Australia[1,2]	N/Y	Y	Y	N	N	Y	N	N	N	Y	N	N
Austria	Y	Y	Y	N	Y	Y	Y	N	N	Y	Y	N
Belgium (Fl.)[3]	Y	Y	N	N	a	a	a	a	Y	Y	N	N
Belgium (Fr.)	Y	Y	N	N	a	a	a	a	Y	Y	N	N
Canada (Québec)[1]	N	Y	Y	N					N	Y	Y	N
Czech Republic[1]	Y	Y	Y	N	N	Y	Y	N	Y	Y	Y	N
Denmark[1]	Y	Y	Y		a	a	a	a	Y	Y	Y	
Finland	Y/N	Y	Y	N								
France	Y	N	Y	N	a	a	a	a	Y/N	Y	N	
Germany	Y	Y	N	N	Y	Y	N	N	a	a	a	a
Greece[1]	N	Y	N	N					N	Y	N	N
Hungary	Y	N	Y	N	Y	N	Y	N	Y	N	Y	N
Iceland[1]	Y/N	Y	N	N	Y	Y	N	N	Y/N	Y	N	N
Ireland[1]	Y	N	N	N	a	a	a	a	Y	Y	Y	N
Italy	Y	N	Y/N	N	Y	Y/N	Y/N	N	Y	Y	Y/N	N
Japan	N	N	Y	N	N	N	Y	N	N	N	Y	N
Korea	N	N	N	Y					N	N	N	Y
Luxembourg	Y	Y	Y	N	Y	Y	Y	N	Y	Y	Y	N
Mexico	N	Y	Y	N					Y/N	Y	Y	N
Netherlands[1]	Y	Y	Y	N	a	a	a	a	Y	Y	Y	N
New Zealand	Y	N	N	N								
Norway	N	Y	Y	N	a	a	a	a	N	Y	Y	N.
Poland	Y/N	N	N	N	a	a	a	a	Y	N	N	N
Portugal	m	m	m	m	m	m	m	m	m	m	m	m
Slovak Republic[1]	Y	N	Y	N					Y	N	Y	N
Spain	N	Y	Y	N					Y/N	Y/N	Y/N	N
Sweden	Y/N	Y/N	N	Y/N								
Switzerland	Y	Y	Y		Y	Y	Y		Y		Y	
Turkey[1]	N	N	Y	N	N	N	Y	N	N	N	Y	N
United Kingdom[1]	N[4]	Y	N	N	a	a	a	a		Y	N	N
United States[1]	20Y/30N	SS	SS	Y[5]	a	a	a	a	a	a	a	a
Israel[1]	Y/N	Y	Y	N	a	a	a	a	Y/N	Y	Y	

Note: Y = Yes; N = No; SS = Some states

1. See Annex 3 for additional notes on completion requirements (*www.oecd.org/edu/eag2008*).

2. Completion requirements for ISCED 3A vary by state and territory. The information provided represents a generalisation of diverse requirements.

3. Covers general education only.

4. There is usually no final examination, though some ISCED 3A programmes can be completed this way.

5. Almost all states specify levels of Carnegie credits (*i.e.* acquired through completion of a two-semester course in specific subjects, which vary by state).

Source: OECD.

Please refer to the Reader's Guide for information concerning the symbols replacing missing data.

Annex

2

REFERENCE STATISTICS

Annex 2

Table X2.1.
Overview of the economic context using basic variables
(reference period: calendar year 2005, 2005 current prices)

	Total public expenditure as a percentage of GDP	GDP per capita (in equivalent USD converted using PPPs)	GDP deflator (1995 =100)	GDP deflator (2000 =100)	Number of full-time equivalents students enrolled in educational institutions as a percentage of total population
OECD countries					
Australia	m	33 983	131.0	119.2	22.3
Austria	49.9	34 107	112.5	108.5	19.0
Belgium	49.3	32 077	117.6	110.9	25.2
Canada[1]	39.9	35 078	122.2	112.7	14.4
Czech Republic	43.8	20 280	157.4	113.5	20.9
Denmark	53.1	33 626	123.7	112.2	25.5
Finland	50.5	30 468	114.5	104.8	24.8
France	53.7	29 644	115.5	109.9	23.6
Germany	46.9	30 496	106.8	105.8	20.2
Greece	m	25 472	151.2	117.7	19.6
Hungary	49.9	17 014	254.4	132.0	19.1
Iceland	42.4	35 571	144.0	121.8	30.3
Ireland	34.0	38 061	148.0	118.1	24.5
Italy	48.0	27 750	132.1	115.4	19.0
Japan	37.1	30 290	90.7	93.5	16.3
Korea	28.9	21 342	131.3	112.1	24.1
Luxembourg	41.8	69 984	123.0	113.7	m
Mexico	23.7	11 299	319.1	139.2	30.8
Netherlands	45.2	34 724	128.7	114.7	22.0
New Zealand	31.9	24 882	124.7	114.1	26.2
Norway	m	47 620	154.2	117.7	25.2
Poland	43.2	13 573	192.5	113.5	21.4
Portugal	47.2	19 967	137.4	116.9	19.8
Slovak Republic	19.9	15 881	169.4	124.9	22.1
Spain	38.1	27 270	141.5	122.7	18.9
Sweden	55.2	32 770	113.0	107.2	24.6
Switzerland	m	35 500	105.4	103.2	18.1
Turkey	m	7 786	4 186.4	316.5	m
United Kingdom	45.7	31 580	129.0	114.0	25.1
United States	37.2	41 674	122.7	113.0	22.7
Partner countries					
Brazil	31.2	9 255	224.7	170.7	26.7
Chile[2]	20.0	12 655	143.2	149.1	26.6
Estonia	32.7	16 660	188.0	123.6	23.6
Israel	46.3	22 810	148.7	108.6	30.1
Russian Federation	31.6	10 846	868.0	217.8	14.1
Slovenia	46.0	23 043	184.8	111.8	19.9

1. Year of reference 2004.
2. Year of reference 2006.
Source : OECD.
Please refer to the Reader's Guide for information concerning the symbols replacing missing data.

Table X2.2.
Basic reference statistics
(reference period: calendar year 2005, 2005 current prices)[1]

	Gross Domestic Product (in millions of local currency)[2]	Gross Domestic Product (adjusted to financial year)[3]	Total public expenditure (in millions of local currency)	Total population in thousand (mid-year estimates)	Purchasing Power Parity for GDP (PPP) (USD = 1)	Purchasing Power Parity for GDP (PPP) (Euro Zone = 1)	Purchasing Power Parity for private consumption (PPP) (US = 1)
Australia	965 969	911 867.000	m	20 474	1.38835579	1.6032	1.4641
Austria	245 330		122 415	8 233	0.87364077	1.0088	0.8905
Belgium	301 966		149 013	10 474	0.8987871	1.0379	0.9261
Canada[4]	1 375 080	1 290 829	515 468	32 299	1.21364403	1.4014	1.26
Czech Republic	2 987 722		1 308 565	10 234	14.39506056	16.6225	15.197
Denmark	1 551 967		824 841	5 419	8.51699624	9.8349	9.0881
Finland	157 162		79 338	5 245	0.98343625	1.1356	1.0765
France	1 717 921		921 800	62 818	0.92252574	1.0653	0.9381
Germany	2 244 600		1 052 590	82 464	0.89256209	1.0307	0.9054
Greece	198 609		m	11 104	0.70219694	0.8109	0.7718
Hungary	22 055 093		11 011 561	10 087	128.5082936	148.3929	137.5175
Iceland	1 021 510		433 346	296	97.06372403	112.0828	104.064
Ireland	161 498		54 979	4 149	1.02277774	1.1810	1.09
Italy	1 423 048		683 737	58 607	0.87500781	1.0104	0.908
Japan[5]	501 402 600	499 096 950	185 069 300	127 773	129.5519548	149.5981	142.9363
Korea	810 515 900		234 014 700	48 138	788.9201348	910.9932	879.3655
Luxembourg	30 032		12 545	465	0.9224559	1.0652	0.8968
Mexico	8 361 107		1 979 808	103 831	7.12686171	8.2296	7.6483
Netherlands	508 964		229 905	16 317	0.89828305	1.0373	0.9126
New Zealand	156 630		49 900	4 101	1.53500049	1.7725	1.5986
Norway	1 945 716		m	4 622	8.84008973	10.2080	9.7966
Poland	983 302		425 108	38 161	1.89842574	2.1922	2.1549
Portugal	149 010		70 343	10 549	0.7074053	0.8169	0.7448
Slovak Republic	1 471 131		292 580	5 387	17.19598047	19.8568	18.8277
Spain	908 450		346 297	43 398	0.76761043	0.8864	0.8032
Sweden	2 735 218		1 509 540	9 030	9.24328648	10.6735	9.5615
Switzerland	463 673		208 505	7 501	1.74121812	2.0106	1.865
Turkey	487 202		m	72 065	0.8683379	1.0027	1.0014
United Kingdom	1 233 976	1 196 716	546 872	60 218	0.64887707	0.7493	0.6584
United States	12 376 100	12 189 800	4 537 690	296 972	1	1.1547	1
Euro Zone					*0.866*	*1.0000*	
Brazil	2 147 944		670 514	184 184	1.2601	1.4551	
Chile[6]	77 337 698		15 482 148	16 452	371.4535	428.9301	
Estonia	175 392		57 382	1 348	7.812830425	9.0217	
Israel	588 970		272 497	6 930	3.726	4.3025	
Russian Federation	21 620 100		6 833 983	143 114	13.9282	16.0834	
Slovenia	6 768 266		3 111 246	1 998	147.0358503	169.7874	

Left margin labels: **OECD countries** (Australia–United States), **Partner countries** (Brazil–Slovenia)

1. Data on GDP, PPPs and total public expenditure in countries in the Euro zone are provided in EUR.
2. GDP calculated for the fiscal year in Australia and GDP and total public expenditure calculated for the fiscal year in New Zealand.
3. For countries where GDP is not reported for the same reference period as data on educational finance, GDP is estimated as: wt-1 (GDPt - 1) + wt (GDPt), where wt and wt-1 are the weights for the respective portions of the two reference periods for GDP which fall within the educational financial year. Adjustments were made in Chapter B for Australia, Canada, Japan, the United Kingdom and the United States.
4. Year of reference 2004.
5. Total public expenditure adjusted to financial year.
6. Year of reference 2006.
Source: OECD.
Please refer to the Reader's Guide for information concerning the symbols replacing missing data.

Table X2.3a.
Reference statistics used in the calculation of teachers' salaries, by level of education (1996, 2006)

		Teachers' salaries in national currency (1996)[1]								
		Primary education			Lower secondary education			Upper secondary education, general programmes		
		Starting salary/ minimum training	Salary after 15 years of experience/minimum training	Salary at top of scale/ minimum training	Starting salary/ minimum training	Salary after 15 years of experience/ minimum training	Salary at top of scale/ minimum training	Starting salary/ minimum training	Salary after 15 years of experience/ minimum training	Salary at top of scale/ minimum training
OECD countries	Australia	25 693	46 781	46 781	25 693	46 781	46 781	25 693	46 781	46 781
	Austria	19 911	25 522	40 136	20 598	26 791	42 910	21 891	29 334	48 204
	Belgium (Fl.)[2]	20 479	27 542	32 721	20 950	29 346	35 781	25 998	37 534	45 119
	Belgium (Fr.)[2]	20 479	27 542	32 721	20 950	29 346	35 781	25 998	37 534	45 119
	Czech Republic	w	w	w	w	w	w	w	w	w
	Denmark	200 000	244 000	250 000	200 000	244 000	250 000	218 000	310 000	325 000
	England	12 113	20 423	20 423	12 113	20 423	20 423	12 113	20 423	20 423
	Finland	17 660	23 378	24 051	19 846	27 751	28 928	20 519	28 928	30 610
	France	w	w	w	w	w	w	w	w	w
	Germany	w	w	w	w	w	w	w	w	w
	Greece	10 772	12 854	15 148	11 141	13 223	15 518	11 141	13 223	15 518
	Hungary	341 289	462 618	597 402	341 289	462 618	597 402	435 279	574 067	717 756
	Iceland	m	m	m	m	m	m	m	m	m
	Ireland	18 235	28 189	33 362	19 141	29 872	33 679	19 141	29 872	33 679
	Italy	14 939	18 030	21 864	16 213	19 796	24 233	16 213	20 412	25 442
	Japan	3 462 000	5 917 000	8 475 000	3 462 000	5 917 000	8 475 000	3 462 000	5 917 000	8 733 000
	Korea	w	w	w	w	w	w	w	w	w
	Luxembourg	m	m	m	m	m	m	m	m	m
	Mexico	29 105	38 606	63 264	37 092	47 174	76 196	m	m	m
	Netherlands	21 772	26 537	32 627	22 925	28 847	35 840	23 120	40 273	47 756
	New Zealand	23 000	39 220	39 220	23 000	39 220	39 220	23 000	39 220	39 220
	Norway	165 228	201 446	204 211	165 228	201 446	204 211	178 752	207 309	222 078
	Poland	m	m	m	m	m	m	m	m	m
	Portugal	9 970	15 001	25 902	9 970	15 001	25 902	9 970	15 001	25 902
	Scotland	12 510	20 796	20 796	12 510	20 796	20 796	12 510	20 796	20 796
	Slovak Republic	m	m	m	m	m	m	m	m	m
	Spain	18 609	21 823	27 940	m	m	m	21 582	25 327	31 780
	Sweden	w	w	w	w	w	w	w	w	w
	Switzerland	65 504	87 585	100 847	m	m	m	m	m	m
	Turkey	w	w	w	a	a	a	w	w	w
	United States	m	m	m	m	m	m	m	m	m
Partner countries	Brazil	m	m	m	m	m	m	m	m	m
	Chile	m	m	m	m	m	m	m	m	m
	Estonia	25 380	27 120	29 040	25 380	27 120	29 040	25 380	27 120	29 040
	Israel	m	m	m	m	m	m	m	m	m
	Russian Federation	m	m	m	m	m	m	m	m	m
	Slovenia	m	m	m	m	m	m	m	m	m

1. Data on salaries for countries now in the Euro zone are shown in EUR.
2. Data on teachers' salaries for 1996 refer to Belgium.
Source: OECD.
Please refer to the Reader's Guide for information concerning the symbols replacing missing data.

Table X2.3a. *(continued)*
Reference statistics used in the calculation of teachers' salaries by level of education (1996, 2006)[1]

	Teachers' salaries in national currency (2006)[2]									
	Primary education			Lower secondary education			Upper secondary education, general programmes			
	Starting salary/minimum training	Salary after 15 years of experience/minimum training	Salary at top of scale/minimum training	Starting salary/minimum training	Salary after 15 years of experience/minimum training	Salary at top of scale/minimum training	Starting salary/minimum training	Salary after 15 years of experience/minimum training	Salary at top of scale/minimum training	GDP deflator 2006 (1996 = 100)

OECD countries

Australia	44 719	61 243	61 243	44 971	62 106	62 106	44 971	62 106	62 106	136
Austria	24 138	31 935	47 941	25 195	34 418	49 885	25 480	35 273	52 344	113
Belgium (Fl.)	26 046	36 390	44 318	26 046	36 390	44 318	32 266	46 477	55 822	119
Belgium (Fr.)	24 720	34 825	42 625	24 720	34 825	42 625	30 767	44 750	53 945	119
Czech Republic	266 751	349 242	415 731	266 751	349 242	415 731	270 101	354 193	422 244	145
Denmark	302 287	341 001	341 001	302 287	341 001	341 001	301 595	424 212	424 212	124
England	19 161	28 005	28 005	19 161	28 005	28 005	19 161	28 005	28 005	128
Finland	27 050	34 947	44 091	30 061	37 360	47 047	30 226	41 432	52 587	116
France	21 403	28 791	42 481	23 680	31 068	44 869	23 907	31 296	45 120	116
Germany	35 746	44 481	46 380	37 086	45 648	47 655	40 108	49 171	51 377	107
Greece	18 169	22 159	26 653	18 169	22 159	26 653	18 169	22 159	26 653	146
Hungary	1 551 204	1 970 676	2 610 660	1 551 204	1 970 676	2 610 660	1 725 672	2 358 240	3 189 744	218
Iceland	2 520 168	2 837 950	3 303 336	2 520 168	2 837 950	3 303 336	2 814 280	3 446 964	3 662 796	153
Ireland	29 834	49 421	56 003	29 834	49 421	56 003	29 834	49 421	56 003	148
Italy	21 104	25 528	31 106	22 736	27 797	34 136	22 736	28 574	35 681	128
Japan	3 334 674	6 235 725	7 956 407	3 334 674	6 235 725	7 956 407	3 334 674	6 235 725	8 191 853	90
Korea	23 673 840	40 841 220	65 343 300	23 577 840	40 745 220	65 247 300	23 577 840	40 745 220	65 247 300	124
Luxembourg	46 251	63 692	94 265	66 632	83 289	115 759	66 632	83 289	115 759	127
Mexico	99 214	130 526	216 535	127 195	166 107	274 858	m	m	m	255
Netherlands	29 130	37 830	42 246	30 198	41 612	46 352	30 495	55 647	61 360	130
New Zealand	29 272	56 628	56 628	29 272	56 628	56 628	29 272	56 628	56 628	126
Norway	277 032	309 480	344 664	277 032	309 480	344 664	296 508	333 492	361 488	161
Poland	m	m	m	m	m	m	m	m	m	165
Portugal	14 160	23 186	36 368	14 160	23 186	36 368	14 160	23 186	36 368	138
Scotland	19 186	30 602	30 602	19 186	30 602	30 602	19 186	30 602	30 602	128
Slovak Republic	m	m	m	m	m	m	m	m	m	166
Spain	25 184	29 347	36 372	28 333	32 922	40 182	28 946	33 666	41 014	142
Sweden	241 200	283 200	328 700	246 000	290 400	332 400	261 000	313 600	356 600	114
Switzerland	69 492	89 909	110 352	80 193	102 985	125 747	93 098	121 187	142 907	107
Turkey	11 835	13 206	14 740	a	a	a	11 835	13 206	14 740	2 623
United States	34 895	42 404	m	33 546	42 775	m	33 695	42 727	m	124

Partner countries

Brazil	m	m	m	m	m	m	m	m	m	214
Chile	3 629 556	4 430 124	5 978 280	3 629 556	4 430 124	5 978 280	3 629 556	4 638 231	6 258 360	m
Estonia	79 200	84 000	116 400	79 200	84 000	116 400	79 200	84 000	116 400	200
Israel	49 396	57 050	79 695	49 396	57 050	79 695	49 396	57 050	79 695	m
Russian Federation	m	m	m	m	m	m	m	m	m	m
Slovenia	16 186	19 025	20 191	16 186	19 025	20 191	16 186	19 025	20 191	m

1. For the computation of teachers' salaries in equivalent USD shown in Indicator D3, teachers' salaries are converted from national currencies to USD using January 2005 PPPs for GDP and adjusted for inflation where necessary. Teachers' salaries in equivalent USD based on January 2005 PPPs for final consumption are shown in table X2.3c of Annex 2.

2. Data on salaries for countries now in the Euro zone are shown in Euros.

Source: OECD.

Please refer to the Reader's Guide for information concerning the symbols replacing missing data.

Table X2.3b.
Reference statistics used in the calculation of teachers' salaries (1996, 2006)

	Purchasing power parity for GDP (PPP) (2005)[1]	Purchasing Power Parity for GDP (PPP) (2006)[1]	Purchasing Power Parity for GDP (PPP) (Jan. 2006)[1]	Gross domestic product (in millions of local currency, calendar year 2006)[1]	Total population in thousands (calendar year 2006)	GDP per capita (in equivalent USD, calendar year 2006)[2]	Reference year for 2006 salary data	Adjustments for inflation (2006)
OECD countries								
Australia	1.39	1.41	1.40	1 038 652	20 741	35 453	2006	0.98
Austria	0.87	0.87	0.87	257 897	8 282	35 695	2005/2006	1.00
Belgium (Fl.)[3]	0.90	0.90	0.90	316 622	10 543	33 527	Jan. 2006	1.00
Belgium (Fr.)[3]	0.90	0.90	0.90	316 622	10 543	33 527	2004/2005	1.00
Czech Republic	14.40	14.30	14.35	3 231 576	10 267	22 009	2005/2006	1.00
Denmark	8.52	8.58	8.55	1 642 215	5 437	35 217	2005/2006	1.00
England[4]	0.65	0.65	0.65	1 301 914	60 533	32 990	2005/2006	1.00
Finland	0.98	0.97	0.98	167 062	5 266	32 736	01 oct. 2005	1.00
France	0.92	0.91	0.92	1 791 953	63 195	31 048	2005/2006	1.00
Germany	0.89	0.88	0.89	2 322 200	82 366	31 950	2005/2006	1.00
Greece	0.70	0.70	0.70	213 985	11 149	27 233	2005	1.02
Hungary	128.51	129.94	129.22	23 757 230	10 071	18 154	28 juin 1905	0.98
Iceland	97.06	104.94	101.00	1 141 747	304	35 749	2005/2006	1.00
Ireland	1.02	1.01	1.02	174 705	4 253	40 716	2005/2006	1.00
Italy	0.88	0.87	0.87	1 475 401	58 863	28 866	2005/2006	1.00
Japan	129.55	124.46	127.01	507 545 700	127 755	31 919	2005/2006	1.00
Korea	788.92	762.02	775.47	847 876 400	48 297	23 038	2006	1.00
Luxembourg	0.92	0.92	0.92	33 852	473	78 137	2005/2006	1.00
Mexico	7.13	7.22	7.17	9 149 911	104 748	12 104	2005/2006	1.00
Netherlands	0.90	0.89	0.90	534 324	16 341	36 548	2005/2006	1.00
New Zealand	1.54	1.52	1.53	163 416	4 142	25 910	2006	0.99
Norway	8.84	8.89	8.86	2 155 780	4 661	52 047	2004/2005	1.00
Poland	1.90	1.89	1.90	1 057 855	38 132	14 641	2003/2004	1.00
Portugal	0.71	0.70	0.71	155 167	10 584	20 839	2005/2006	1.00
Scotland[4]	0.65	0.65	0.65	1 301 914	60 533	32 990	2005/2006	1.00
Slovak Republic	17.20	17.26	17.23	1 636 263	5 391	17 585	2002/2003	1.00
Spain	0.77	0.76	0.76	980 954	44 068	29 382	2005/2006	1.00
Sweden	9.24	9.16	9.20	2 899 653	9 081	34 870	2005	1.00
Switzerland	1.74	1.70	1.72	486 178	7 558	37 747	2005/2006	1.00
Turkey	0.87	0.90	0.88	576 322	72 974	8 766	2006	0.95
United States	1.00	1.00	1.00	13 132 900	299 833	43 801	2005/2006	1.00
Partner countries								
Brazil	1.34	1.36	1.35	1 937 598	188 694	7 553	m	m
Chile	342.30	371.45	356.88	66 598 992	16 452	10 898	2006	0.96
Estonia	7.81	8.05	7.93	207 061	1 345	19 139	2006	0.95
Israel	3.73	3.73	3.73	585 821	6 938	22 661	2005/2006	1.00
Russian Federation	m	m	m	m	m	m	m	m
Slovenia	0.61	0.62	0.62	30 448	2 003	24 638	2005/2006	1.00

1. Data on PPPs and GDP for countries now in the Euro zone are shown in EUR.
2. GDP per capita in national currencies (2006) has been calculated from total population (2006) and total GDP (2006), and has been converted to USD using PPPs for GDP (2006). These data are available in this table.
3. Data on gross domestic product and total population refer to Belgium.
4. Data on gross domestic product and total population refer to the United Kingdom.
Adjustments for inflation are used if the reference year deviates from 2004/2005 and the inflation between the actual reference year and 2004/2005 would deviate more than 1 per cent.
Source: OECD.
Please refer to the Reader's Guide for information concerning the symbols replacing missing data.

Table X2.3c.
Teachers' salaries (2006)
Annual statutory teachers' salaries in public institutions at starting salary, after 15 years of experience and at the top of the scale by level of education, in equivalent EUR converted using PPPs

	Primary education				Lower secondary education				Upper secondary education			
	Starting salary / minimum training	Salary after 15 years of experience / minimum training	Salary at top of scale / minimum training	Ratio of salary after 15 years of experience to GDP per capita	Starting salary / minimum training	Salary after 15 years of experience / minimum training	Salary at top of scale / minimum training	Ratio of salary after 15 years of experience to GDP per capita	Starting salary / minimum training	Salary after 15 years of experience / minimum training	Salary at top of scale / minimum training	Ratio of salary after 15 years of experience to GDP per capita
	(1)	(2)	(3)	(4)	(5)	(6)	(7)	(8)	(9)	(10)	(11)	(12)
OECD countries												
Australia	27 368	37 480	37 480	1.20	27 522	38 008	38 008	1.22	27 522	38 008	38 008	1.22
Austria	24 276	32 117	48 215	1.02	25 339	34 615	50 170	1.10	25 626	35 475	52 643	1.13
Belgium (Fl.)	25 487	35 609	43 366	1.21	25 487	35 609	43 366	1.21	31 573	45 479	54 624	1.54
Belgium (Fr.)	24 190	34 078	41 710	1.16	24 190	34 078	41 710	1.16	30 107	43 790	52 787	1.49
Czech Republic	16 323	21 371	25 439	1.11	16 323	21 371	25 439	1.11	16 528	21 674	25 838	1.12
Denmark	31 053	35 030	35 030	1.13	31 053	35 030	35 030	1.13	30 982	43 578	43 578	1.41
England	25 866	37 805	37 805	1.31	25 866	37 805	37 805	1.31	25 866	37 805	37 805	1.31
Finland	24 328	31 430	39 654	1.09	27 036	33 600	42 313	1.17	27 184	37 263	47 295	1.30
France	20 472	27 539	40 634	1.01	22 650	29 717	42 918	1.09	22 868	29 935	43 158	1.10
Germany	35 363	44 005	45 883	1.57	36 689	45 160	47 145	1.61	39 679	48 645	50 827	1.73
Greece	23 058	28 122	33 825	1.18	23 058	28 122	33 825	1.18	23 058	28 122	33 825	1.18
Hungary	10 350	13 149	17 419	0.82	10 350	13 149	17 419	0.82	11 514	15 735	21 283	0.99
Iceland	21 907	24 669	28 715	0.79	21 907	24 669	28 715	0.79	24 464	29 963	31 840	0.95
Ireland	25 787	42 717	48 406	1.19	25 787	42 717	48 406	1.19	25 787	42 717	48 406	1.19
Italy	21 257	25 714	31 332	1.01	22 902	27 999	34 384	1.10	22 902	28 782	35 940	1.14
Japan	23 052	43 107	55 002	1.54	23 052	43 107	55 002	1.54	23 052	43 107	56 630	1.54
Korea	26 804	46 241	73 983	2.29	26 695	46 132	73 874	2.28	26 695	46 132	73 874	2.28
Luxembourg	44 164	60 818	90 012	0.89	63 626	79 531	110 536	1.16	63 626	79 531	110 536	1.16
Mexico	12 146	15 980	26 509	1.50	15 572	20 336	33 649	1.91	m	m	m	m
Netherlands	28 530	37 050	41 375	1.15	29 576	40 754	45 397	1.27	29 867	54 500	60 095	1.70
New Zealand	16 612	32 137	32 137	1.41	16 612	32 137	32 137	1.41	16 612	32 137	32 137	1.41
Norway	27 443	30 657	34 143	0.67	27 443	30 657	34 143	0.67	29 372	33 036	35 809	0.72
Poland	m	m	m	m	m	m	m	m	m	m	m	m
Portugal	17 624	28 857	45 263	1.58	17 624	28 857	45 263	1.58	17 624	28 857	45 263	1.58
Scotland	25 900	41 310	41 310	1.43	25 900	41 310	41 310	1.43	25 900	41 310	41 310	1.43
Slovak Republic	m	m	m	m	m	m	m	m	m	m	m	m
Spain	28 995	33 788	41 876	1.31	32 620	37 904	46 262	1.47	33 326	38 760	47 220	1.50
Sweden	23 018	27 027	31 369	0.88	23 476	27 714	31 722	0.91	24 908	29 928	34 031	0.98
Switzerland	35 417	45 823	56 242	1.38	40 871	52 487	64 088	1.58	47 449	61 764	72 834	1.86
Turkey	11 124	12 413	13 855	1.61	a	a	a	a	11 124	12 413	13 855	1.61
United States	30 638	37 230	m	0.97	29 454	37 556	m	0.98	29 584	37 514	m	0.98
OECD average	*24 433*	*33 216*	*40 643*	*1.22*	*26 381*	*35 719*	*43 705*	*1.26*	*27 314*	*38 070*	*45 980*	*1.34*
EU 19 average	*25 055*	*33 555*	*41 049*	*1.16*	*26 819*	*35 529*	*43 180*	*1.21*	*27 838*	*38 520*	*46 656*	*1.31*
Partner countries												
Brazil	m	m	m	m	m	m	m	m	m	m	m	m
Chile	9 589	11 393	15 365	1.11	9 589	11 393	15 365	1.11	9 589	11 922	16 086	1.16
Estonia	8 317	8 821	12 223	0.52	8 317	8 821	12 223	0.52	8 317	8 821	12 223	0.52
Israel	11 640	13 443	18 779	0.68	11 640	13 443	18 779	0.68	11 640	13 443	18 779	0.68
Russian Federation	m	m	m	m	m	m	m	m	m	m	m	m
Slovenia	23 100	27 151	28 815	1.26	23 100	27 151	28 815	1.26	23 100	27 151	28 815	1.26

Source: OECD. See Annex 3 for notes (*www.oecd.org/edu/eag2008*).
Please refer to the Reader's Guide for information concerning the symbols replacing missing data.

General notes

Definitions

Gross domestic product (GDP) refers to the producers' value of the gross outputs of resident producers, including distributive trades and transport, less the value of purchasers' intermediate consumption plus import duties. GDP is expressed in local money (in millions). For countries which provide this information for a reference year that is different from the calendar year (such as Australia and New Zealand), adjustments are made by linearly weighting their GDP between two adjacent national reference years to match the calendar year.

The **GDP deflator** is obtained by dividing the GDP expressed at current prices by the GDP expressed at constant prices. This provides an indication of the relative price level in a country. Data are based on the year 2000.

GDP per capita is the gross domestic product (in equivalent USD converted using PPPs) divided by the population.

Purchasing power parity exchange rates (PPP) are the currency exchange rates that equalise the purchasing power of different currencies. This means that a given sum of money when converted into different currencies at the PPP rates will buy the same basket of goods and services in all countries. In other words, PPPs are the rates of currency conversion which eliminate the differences in price levels among countries. Thus, when expenditure on GDP for different countries is converted into a common currency by means of PPPs, it is, in effect, expressed at the same set of international prices so that comparisons between countries reflect only differences in the volume of goods and services purchased.

Total public expenditure as used for the calculation of the education indicators, corresponds to the non-repayable current and capital expenditure of all levels of government. Current expenditure includes final consumption expenditure (*e.g.* compensation of employees, consumption intermediate goods and services, consumption of fixed capital, and military expenditure), property income paid, subsidies, and other current transfers paid (*e.g.* social security, social assistance, pensions and other welfare benefits). Capital expenditure is spending to acquire and/or improve fixed capital assets, land, intangible assets, government stocks, and non-military, non-financial assets, and spending to finance net capital transfers.

Sources

The 2008 edition of the *National Accounts of OECD Countries: Main Aggregates, Volume I.*

The theoretical framework underpinning national accounts has been provided for many years by the United Nations' publication *A System of National Accounts*, which was released in 1968. An updated version was released in 1993 (commonly referred to as SNA93).

OECD Analytical Data Base, January 2008.

Annex 2

Annex

Sources, Methods and Technical Notes

Annex 3 on sources and methods is available
in electronic form only. It can be found at:
www.oecd.org/edu/eag2008

References

HEIS (HIS) (2005), *Eurostudent Report 2005: Social and Economic Conditions of Student Life in Europe 2005,* Higher Education Information System, Hannover, *http://www.his.de/Eurostudent/report2005.pdf*

ILO (1982), *Resolution concerning statistics of the economically active population, employment, unemployment and underemployment*, adopted by the Thirteenth International Conference of Labor Statisticians.

Kelo, M., U. Teichler and **B. Wächter** (eds.) (2005), *EURODATA: Student Mobility in European Higher Education*, Verlags and Mediengesellschaft, Bonn.

Krueger, A.B. 2002. "Economic Considerations and Class Size." *National Bureau of Economic Research Working Paper: 8875.*

Mincer, J. (1974), "Schooling, experience, and earnings", National Bureau of Economic Research (NBER), New York.

OECD (2001), *Knowledge and Skills for Life: First Results from PISA 2000,* OECD, Paris.

OECD (2004a), *Internationalisation and Trade in Higher Education: Opportunities and Challenges,* OECD, Paris.

OECD (2004b), *Education at a Glance: OECD Indicators – 2004 Edition*, OECD, Paris.

OECD (2004c), *OECD Employment Outlook – 2004 Edition,* OECD, Paris.

OECD (2005a), *Education at a Glance: OECD Indicators – 2005 Edition*, OECD, Paris.

OECD (2005b), *Teachers Matter: Attracting, Developing and Retaining Effective Teachers*, OECD, Paris.

OECD (2006), *OECD Revenue Statistics 1965-2005,* OECD, Paris.

OECD (2007a), *Education at a Glance: OECD Indicators – 2007 Edition*, OECD, Paris.

OECD (2007b), "Effects of Tertiary Expansion: Crowding-out effects and labour market matches for higher education", OECD Education Working Paper Series, No. 10, OECD, Paris. (On line at: *www.oecd.org/edu/workingpapers*).

OECD (2007c), *PISA 2006: Science Competencies for Tomorrow's World*, OECD, Paris.

OECD (2008a), *Tertiary Education for the Knowledge Society: Thematic Review of Tertiary Education,* OECD, Paris.

OECD (2008b), *PISA 2006 Technical Report,* OECD, Paris.

OECD (2008c), *Main OECD Science and Technology Indicators/Principaux indicateurs de la science et de la technologie,* OECD, Paris.

OECD (2008d), "Job-Related Training and Benefits for Individuals: A review of evidence and explanations", OECD Education Working Paper Series, No. 19, OECD, Paris.

St. John, E.P. (2003), *Refinancing the College Dream: Access, Equal Opportunity and Justice for Taxpayers*, Baltimore: Johns Hopkins University Press.

Usher, A. (2006), "Grants for Students: What They Do, Why They Work", *Canadian Education Report Series*, Educational Policy Institute; Toronto, Ontario.

CONTRIBUTORS TO THIS PUBLICATION

Many people have contributed to the development of this publication. The following lists the names of the country representatives, researchers and experts who have actively taken part in the preparatory work leading to the publication of *Education at a Glance – OECD Indicators 2008*. The OECD wishes to thank them all for their valuable efforts.

INES National Co-ordinators[1]

Mr. Paul BALNAVES (Australia)
Mr. Mark NEMET (Austria)
Mr. Dominique BARTHÉLÉMY (Belgium)
Ms. Maddy BOLLEN (Belgium)
Ms. Maria das Graças MOREIRA COSTA (Brazil)
Ms. Amanda HODGKINSON (Canada)
Mr. Mauricio FARÍAS ARENAS (Chile)
Mr. Lubomír MARTINEC (Czech Republic)
Mr. Jakob Birklund ANDERSEN (Denmark)
Mr. Lars Bo JAKOBSEN (European Commission)
Ms. Silja KIMMEL (Estonia)
Ms. Kristi PLOOM (Estonia)
Mr. Matti KYRÖ (Finland)
Mr. Claude SAUVAGEOT (France)
Ms. Barbara MEYER-WYK (Germany)
Ms. Evelyn OBELE (Germany)
Ms. Melina PAPADAKI (Greece)
Ms. Judit KÁDÁR-FÜLÖP (Hungary)
Mr. Gunnar ARNASON (Iceland)
Mr. Pat MAC SITRIC (Ireland)
Ms. Rachel PERKIN (Ireland)
Mr. Yosef GIDANIAN (Israel)

Ms. Fiorella FARINELLI (Italy)
Mr. Kenji SAKUMA (Japan)
Mr. Sun-Ho KIM (Korea)
Mr. Jérôme LEVY (Luxembourg)
Mr. Rafael FREYRE MARTÍNEZ (Mexico)
Mr. Marcel SMITS VAN WAESBERGHE (Netherlands)
Mr. David LAMBIE (New Zealand)
Ms. Hege FORBORD (Norway)
Mr. Morten ROSENKVIST (Norway)
Mr. Jerzy WISNIEWSKI (Poland)
Mr. Nuno Miguel RODRIGUES (Portugal)
Mr. João Trocado MATA (Portugal)
Mr. Mark AGRANOVITCH (Russian Federation)
Mr. Vladimir POKOJNY (Slovak Republic)
Ms. Helga KOCEVAR (Slovenia)
Mr. Enrique ROCA COBO (Spain)
Mr. Dan ANDERSSON (Sweden)
Mr. Emanuel VON ERLACH (Switzerland)
Mr. Kamil YILDIRIM (Turkey)
Mr. Stephen LEMAN (United Kingdom)
Ms. Janice ROSS (United Kingdom)
Ms. Valena WHITE PLISKO (United States)

INES Working Party

Mr. Paul BALNAVES (Australia)
Ms. Oon Ying CHIN (Australia)
Mr. Mark NEMET (Austria)
Mr. Wolfgang PAULI (Austria)
Ms. Nathalie JAUNIAUX (Belgium)
Ms. Ann Van DRIESSCHE (Belgium)
Ms. Ana Carolina SILVA CIROTTO (Brazil)
Ms. Carmilva SOUZA FLORES (Brazil)
Mr. Jean-Claude BOUSQUET (Canada)
Mr. Patrice DE BROUCKER (Canada)
Mr. Albert MOTIVANS (UNESCO)
Mr. Cesar MUÑOZ HERNÁNDEZ (Chile)
Mr. Cristian Pablo YAÑEZ NAVARRO (Chile)
Ms. Michaela KLENHOVA (Czech Republic)
Mr. Felix KOSCHIN (Czech Republic)

Mr. Lubomir MARTINEC (Czech Republic)
Ms. Julie GRUNNET HANSEN (Denmark)
Mr. Leo ELMBIRK JENSEN (Denmark)
Ms. Signe PHILIP (Denmark)
Mrs. Kristi PLOOM (Estonia)
Mr. Anders HINGEL (European Commission)
Mr. Jean-Louis MERCY (European Commission)
Mr. Ville HEINONEN (Finland)
Mr. Matti KYRÖ (Finland)
Mr. Mika TUONONEN (Finland)
Mr. Matti VÄISÄNEN (Finland)
Ms. Michele JACQUOT (France)
Ms. Fabienne ROSENWALD (France)
Mr. Claude SAUVAGEOT (France)
Mr. Heinz-Werner HETMEIER (Germany)

---

1. The roles and functions of the INES National Coordinators and the INES Technical Group were subsumed within the new INES Working Party on 1 January 2008.

Ms. Evelyn OBELE (Germany)
Mr. Martin SCHULZE (Germany)
Ms. Melina PAPADAKI (Greece)
Ms. Judit KÁDÁR-FÜLÖP (Hungary)
Ms. Judit KOZMA-LUKÁCS (Hungary)
Mr. László LIMBACHER (Hungary)
Mr. Tamás MÓRÉ (Hungary)
Mr. Gunnar ARNASON (Iceland)
Ms. Asta URBANCIC (Iceland)
Ms. Gillian GOLDEN (Ireland)
Mr. Nicola TICKNER (Ireland)
Mr. Pat MAC SITRIC (Ireland)
Mr. Yosef GIDANIAN (Israel)
Ms. Hava KLEIN (Israel)
Mr. Yedidia SEGEV (Israel)
Ms. Maria Gemma DE SANCTIS (Italy)
Ms. Maria Teresa MORANA (Italy)
Ms. Claudia PIZZELLA (Italy)
Mr. Paolo TURCHETTI (Italy)
Ms. Ayaki KOBAYASHI (Japan)
Mr. Tokuo OGATA (Japan)
Mr. Kinichi TSUCHIYAMA (Japan)
Mr. Chang-Hwan KIM (Korea)
Ms. Jong-Hyo PARK (Korea)
Mr. Robert KERGER (Luxembourg)
Mr. Jérôme LEVY (Luxembourg)
Ms. Manon UNSEN (Luxembourg)
Mr. Gerardo FRANCO (Mexico)
Mr. Rafael FREYRE MARTÍNEZ (Mexico)
Ms. Daphne DE WIT (Netherlands)
Mr. Marcel SMITS VAN WAESBERGHE (Netherlands)
Mr. Dick TAKKENBERG (Netherlands)
Mr. Jit CHEUNG (New Zealand)

Mr. Paul GINI (New Zealand)
Ms. Birgitta BØHN (Norway)
Mr. Terje RISBERG (Norway)
Mr. Are TURMO (Norway)
Ms. Malgorzata CHOJNICKA (Poland)
Ms. Anna NOWOZYNSKA (Poland)
Mr. Wojciech SADOWNIK (Poland)
Ms. Elisa GONZALES (Portugal)
Mrs. Maria João VALENTE ROSA (Portugal)
Mr. Mark AGRANOVITCH (Russian Federation)
Ms. Alzbeta FERENCICOVA (Slovak Republic)
Ms. Zuzana JAKUBCOVA (Slovak Republic)
Ms. Elena REBROSOVA (Slovak Republic)
Ms. Helga KOCEVAR (Slovenia)
Mrs. Tatjana SKRBEC (Slovenia)
Ms. Rosa HUERTAS MORA (Spain)
Mr. Jesús IBAÑEZ MILLA (Spain)
Mr. Enrique ROCA COBO (Spain)
Ms. Carmen UREÑA UREÑA (Spain)
Mr. Dan ANDERSSON (Sweden)
Ms. Helena BJELVENIUS (Sweden)
Mr. Kenny PETERSSON (Sweden)
Ms. Katrin HOLENSTEIN (Switzerland)
Mr. Emanuel VON ERLACH (Switzerland)
Ms. Nilgün DURAN (Turkey)
Mr. Said OULD AHMEDOU VOFFAL (UNESCO)
Mr. Steve HEWITT (United Kingdom)
Mr. Stephen LEMAN (United Kingdom)
Ms. Rachel DINKES (United States)
Ms. Mary Ann FOX (United States)
Ms. Laurin GILBERTSON (United States)
Ms. Valena White PLISKO (United States)
Mr. Thomas SNYDER (United States)

Network A on Educational Outcomes

Lead Country: United States
Network Leader: Mr. Jay MOSKOWITZ

Mr. Tony ZANDERIGO (Australia)
Mrs. Helene BABEL (Austria)
Mr. Jürgen HORSCHINEGG (Austria)
Mrs. Christiane BLONDIN (Belgium)
Ms. Liselotte VAN DE PERRE (Belgium)
Ms. Tamara KNIGHTON (Canada)
Mr. Grant CLARKE (Canada)
Mr. Lubomir MARTINEC (Czech Republic)
Ms. Pavla ZIELENIECOVA (Czech Republic)
Mr. Joern SKOVSGAARD (Denmark)
Mr. Aki TORNBERG (Finland)
Mr. Thierry ROCHER (France)
Mr. Botho PRIEBE (Germany)
Mr. Panyotis KAZANTZIS (Greece)
Ms. Zsuzsa HAMORI-VACZY (Hungary)
Mr. Julius K. BJORNSSON (Iceland)
Mr. Gerry SHIEL (Ireland)
Mr. Raimondo BOLLETA (ITALY)
Mr. Ryo WATANABE (Japan)
Ms. Mee-Kyeong LEE (Korea)

Ms. Iris BLANKE (Luxembourg)
Mr. Felipe MARTÍNEZ RIZO (Mexico)
Mr. Renze PORTENGEN (Netherlands)
Ms. Lynne WHITNEY (New Zealand)
Ms. Anne-Berit KAVLI (Norway)
Mr. Carlos PINTO FERREIRA (Portugal)
Mr. Vladislav ROSA (Slovak Republic)
Ms. Lis CERCADILLO PÉREZ (Spain)
Ms. Anita WESTER (Sweden)
Mr. Erich RAMSEIER (Switzerland)
Ms. Meral ALKAN (Turkey)
Ms. Lorna BERTRAND (United Kingdom)
Mr. Eugene OWEN (United States)
Ms. Elois SCOTT (United States)
Ms. Maria STEPHENS (United States)
Ms. Micheline SCHEYS (Belgium)
Ms. Jude COSGROVE (Ireland)
Mr. Whan-sik KIM (Korea)
Mr. Myung-ho NAM (Korea)
Mr. Rafael FREYRE MARTÍNEZ (Mexico)
Mr. Anthony CLARKE (United Kingdom)

Network B on Education and Socio-economic Outcomes

Lead country: Sweden
Network Leader: Mr. Dan ANDERSSON

Mr. Paul BALNAVES (Australia)
Ms. Oon Ying CHIN (Australia)
Mr. Brendan O'REILLY (Australia)
Mr. Mark NÉMET (Austria)
Ms. Isabelle ERAUW (Belgium)
Ms. Geneviève HINDRYCKX (Belgium)
Ms. Maria das Graças MOREIRA COSTA (Brazil)
Mr. Patrice DE BROUCKER (Canada)
Ms. Shannon DELBRIDGE (Canada)
Ms. Sárka HONSOVÁ (Czech Republic)
Ms. Julie GRUNNET HANSEN (Denmark)
Ms. Irja BLOMQVIST (Finland)
Ms. Aila REPO (Finland)
Ms. Pascale POULET-COULIBANDO (France)
Ms. Christiane KRÜGER-HEMMER (Germany)
Mr. Nikolaos BILALIS (Greece)
Mr. Angelos KARAGIANNIS (Greece)
Ms. Éva TÓT (Hungary)
Mr. Philip O'CONNELL (Ireland)
Ms. Francesca BRAIT (Italy)
Ms. Paola UNGARO (Italy)
Ms. Johee CHOI (Korea)
Mr. Jos NOESEN (Luxembourg)
Mr. Héctor V. ROBLES VÁSQUEZ (Mexico)

Mr. Roy TJOA (Netherlands)
Mr. Marcel Smits VAN WAESBERGHE (Netherlands)
Mr. Cyril MAKO (New Zealand)
Ms. Cheryl REMINGTON (New Zealand)
Mr. Lars NERDRUM (Norway)
Mr. Terje RISBERG (Norway)
Ms. Barbara ANTOSIEWICZ (Poland)
Ms. Malgorzata CHOJNICKA (Poland)
Mr. José Luis ALBUQUERQUE (Portugal)
Ms. Rute GUERRA (Portugal)
Ms. Isabel FARIA VAZ (Portugal)
Mr. Mark AGRANOVITCH (Russia)
Ms. Slavica CERNOSA (Slovenia)
Ms. L'ubomíra SRNÁNKOVÁ (Slovak Republic)
Ms. Raquel ÁLVAREZ-ESTEBAN (Spain)
Mr. Dan ANDERSSON (Sweden)
Ms. Anna JÖNSSON (Sweden)
Mr. Kenny PETERSSON (Sweden)
Mr. Russell SCHMIEDER (Sweden)
Mr. Emanuel VON ERLACH (Switzerland)
Mr. Ali PANAL (Turkey)
Mr. David MCPHEE (United Kingdom)
Mr. Stephen LEMAN (United Kingdom)
Mr. Abe GEORGE (United States)
Ms. Lisa HUDSON (United States)
Mr. Dan SHERMAN (United States)

Network C on School Features and Processes

Lead Country: Netherlands
Network Leader: Mr. Jaap SCHEERENS

Mr. Paul CMIEL (Australia)
Mr. Christian KRENTHALLER (Austria)
Mr. François-Gérard STOLZ (Belgium)
Ms. Ann VAN DRIESSCHE (Belgium)
Mr. Raymond VAN DE SIJPE (Belgium)
Ms. Ana Carolina SILVA CIROTTO (Brazil)
Ms. Carmilva SOUZA FLORES (Brazil)
Mr. Raynald LORTIE (Canada)
Mr. Cesar MUÑOZ HERNÁNDEZ (Chile)
Ms. Pavlina STASTNOVA (Czech Republic)
Mr. Jørgen BALLING RASMUSSEN (Denmark)
Ms. Kristi PLOOM (Estonia)
Mr. Lars Bo JAKOBSEN (European Commission)
Mr. Hannu-Pekka LAPPALAINEN (Finland)
Ms. Clotilde LIXI (France)
Mr. Gerd MÖLLER (Germany)
Mr. Vassilios CHARISMIADIS (Greece)
Ms. Anna IMRE (Hungary)
Mr. Gunnar ARNASON (Iceland)
Mr. Pat MAC SITRIC (Ireland)
Mr. Yosef GIDANIAN (Israel)
Ms. Gianna BARBIERI (Italy)

Mr. Tokuo OGATA (Japan)
Ms. Jeongwon HWANG (Korea)
Ms. Jong-Hyo PARK (Korea)
Ms. Astrid SCHORN (Luxembourg)
Mr. Rafael FREYRE MARTÍNEZ (Mexico)
Ms. Maria HENDRIKS (Netherlands)
Mr. Hans RUESINK (Netherlands)
Mr. Marcel SMITS VAN WAESBERGHE (Netherlands)
Ms. Robyn SMITS (New Zealand)
Ms. Bodhild BAASLAND (Norway)
Mr. Jerzy CHODNICKI (Poland)
Mr. Nuno Miguel RODRIGUES (Portugal)
Mr. Mitja SARDOC (Slovenia)
Ms. Rosa HUERTAS (Spain)
Ms. Madeleine NYMAN (Sweden)
Mr. Eugen STOCKER (Switzerland)
Ms. Nilgün DURAN (Turkey)
Mr. Albert MOTIVANS (UNESCO)
Mr. Anthony CLARKE (United Kingdom)
Mr. Steve HEWITT (United Kingdom)
Mr. Stephen LEMAN (United Kingdom)
Mr. Mal COOKE (United Kingdom – Scotland)
Ms. Kerry GRUBER (United States)
Ms. Laura SALGANIK (United States)

Others contributors to this publication

Ms. Doranne LECERCLE (Editing)
Ms. Fung-Kwan TAM (Layout)

RELATED OECD PUBLICATIONS

Tertiary Education for the Knowledge Society: Thematic Review of Tertiary Education (2008)
ISBN 92-64-04652-6

PISA 2006: Science Competencies for Tomorrow's World: Volume 1 Analysis (2007)
ISBN 92-64-04000-5

Where Immigrant Students Succeed: A Comparative Review of Performance and Engagement in PISA 2003 (2006)
ISBN 92-64-02360-7

Are Students Ready for a Technology-Rich World: What PISA Studies Tell Us (2005)
ISBN 92-64-03608-3

Learning for Tomorrow's World – First Results from PISA 2003 (2004)
ISBN 92-64-00724-5

Problem Solving for Tomorrow's World – First Measures of Cross-Curricular Competencies from PISA 2003 (2004)
ISBN 92-64-00642-7

From Education to Work: A Difficult Transition for Young Adults with Low Levels of Education (2005)
ISBN 92-64-00918-3

Education Policy Analysis 2005-2006 (2006)
ISBN 92-64-02269-4

OECD Handbook for Internationally Comparative Education Statistics: Concepts, Standards, Definitions and Classifications (2004)
ISBN 92-64-10410-0

Completing the Foundation for Lifelong Learning: An OECD Survey of Upper Secondary Schools (2004)
ISBN 92-64-10372-4

OECD Survey of Upper Secondary Schools: Technical Report (2004)
ISBN 92-64-10572-7

Internationalisation and Trade in Higher Education: Opportunities and Challenges (2004)
ISBN 96-64-01504-3

Classifying Educational Programmes: Manual for ISCED-97 Implementation in OECD Countries (1999)
ISBN 92-64-17037-5

....

OECD publications can be browsed or purchased at the OECD Online Bookshop (*www.oecdbookshop.org*).

This book has...

StatLinks

A service that delivers Excel® files from the printed page!

Look for the *StatLinks* at the bottom right-hand corner of the tables or graphs in this book. To download the matching Excel® spreadsheet, just type the link into your Internet browser, starting with the *http://dx.doi.org* prefix.

If you're reading the PDF e-book edition, and your PC is connected to the Internet, simply click on the link.

You'll find *StatLinks* appearing in more OECD books.

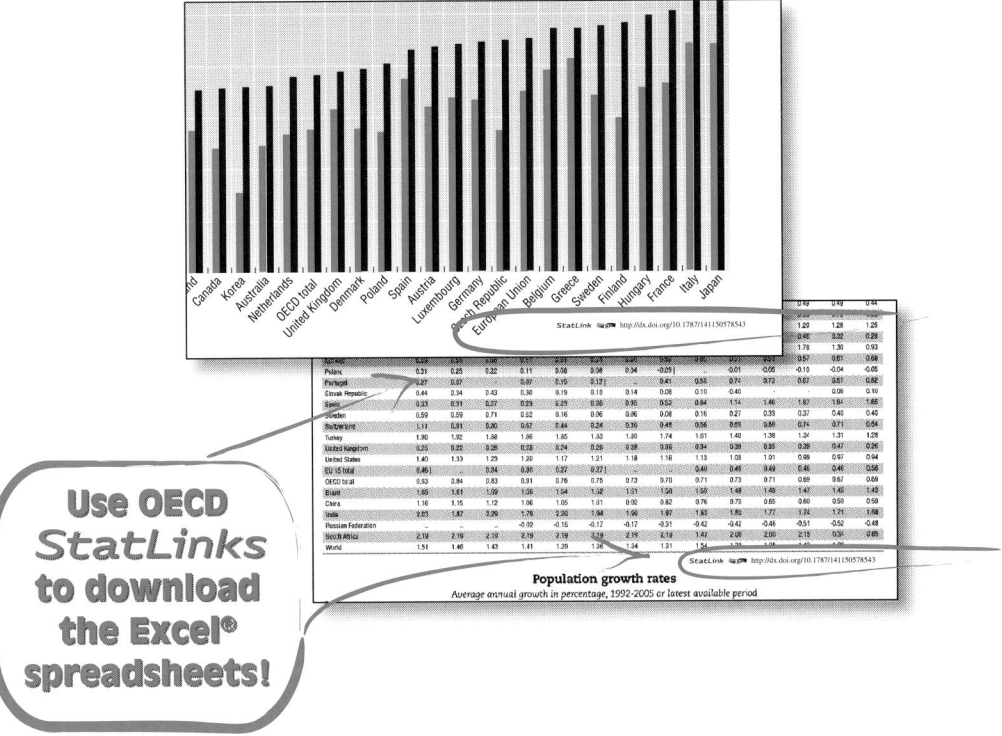

Use OECD StatLinks to download the Excel® spreadsheets!

StatLinks : another innovation from OECD Publishing.

Learn more at *www.oecd.org/statistics/statlink*

We'd like to hear what you think about our publications and services like *StatLinks*: e-mail us at oecd.publishing@oecd.org

OECD PUBLICATIONS, 2, rue André-Pascal, 75775 PARIS CEDEX 16
PRINTED IN FRANCE
(96 2008 04 1 P) ISBN 978-92-64-04628-3 – No. 56333 2008